The Royal Ancestry and Descendants of

George Blackiston

of

Durham, England and Kent Co., Maryland

(Including Royal Ancestors, Magna Carta Barons,
and Other Landed Gentry)

Written by

Guy E. Almony, Jr. and
Christos Christou, Jr.

HERITAGE BOOKS
2026

HERITAGE BOOKS

AN IMPRINT OF HERITAGE BOOKS, INC.

Books, CDs, and more—Worldwide

For our listing of thousands of titles see our website
at
www.HeritageBooks.com

Published 2026 by
HERITAGE BOOKS, INC.
Publishing Division
5810 Ruatan Street
Berwyn Heights, MD 20740

Heritage Books by the Authors:

*The Royal Ancestry and Descendants of George Blackiston of Durham, England
and Kent Co., Maryland (Including Royal Ancestors, Magna Carta Barons,
and Other Landed Gentry)*

Heritage Books by Christos Christou, Jr.:

Abstracts of Kent County, Maryland Wills, Volume 1: 1777–1816
Christos Christou, Jr. and John Anthony Barnhouser

Abstracts of Kent County, Maryland Wills, Volume 2: 1816–1867
Christos Christou, Jr. and John Anthony Barnhouser

Colonial Families of the Eastern Shore of Maryland, Volume 4
Christos Christou, Jr. and F. Edward Wright

Maryland Casualties in the War of 1812
Christos Christou, Jr. and Henry C. Peden, Jr.

International Standard Book Number
Paperbound: 978-0-7884-5408-0

At St. Paul's Church in Kent County Maryland, the Coat of Arms of the Blackiston family is prominently displayed along with other Founding families.

Table of Contents

"If you would not be forgotten, as soon as you are dead and rotten, either write things worth reading, or do things worth writing."
Benjamin Franklin, *Poor Richard's Almanack*

Acknowledgements

As with any publication, many people have helped in various ways from research of original records and secondary sources, providing and sharing their discoveries, and obtaining copies from distant places, etc. We also live off the backs of those historians and writers who have gone before us.

There have been several books that now include the royal ancestor of Marmaduke Blackiston by different authors over the decades, each picking up from the other and adding onto the prior work, including:

- *Royal Ancestry* by Douglas Richardson Vols. 1-5 copy. 2013 with George's lineage starting in Vol. 1 p 383. This is the best work yet in a series of publications documenting Royal ancestry.
- *Plantagenet Ancestry of 17th Century Colonists* by David Faris second edition 1999 includes ancestry of Marmaduke back to King Edward III.
- *Ancestral Roots* 7th Edition by Frederick L. Weis 1993 includes many of the European royal ancestors as well.
- *The Magna Carta Sureties 1215* 4th Edition by Frederick L. Weis 1993 also includes royal ancestors of the Blackiston family.
- *The Royal Descents of 500 Immigrants* by Gary B. Roberts 1993 includes the ancestry of George Blackiston to King Edward III p. 139
- *History of Durham* by Robert Surtee's The Blackiston pedigree is contained in Vol. 3 pp 159-166, p 402. This record discusses the Blackiston family back to the 1300s but does not mention the royal descent.
- *Maryland Genealogies* by Christopher Johnston. The Blackistone Family is contained in Vol. 2 pp 48-68, and includes descendants from Rev. Marmaduke Blackiston down to his descendants in the 1800s and refers to the Surtee's history for earlier generations.
- *Colonial Genealogist* by Mrs. Clarence Cummins 1970. "Blackiston of Maryland and Delaware" in Vol. III:2 discusses one line of the Blackiston family but has very interesting source material.

Some of these publications are referenced throughout this work in addition to primary records used.

Introduction

The objective of this work is to identify some prominent descendants and ancestors of George Blackiston who arrived in America in 1668-1669 after his family was persecuted by the returning King Charles II of England since the Blackiston family were involved in the execution of his father King Charles I. George's Uncle John Blackiston was one of the judges who signed the execution warrant of King Charles I.

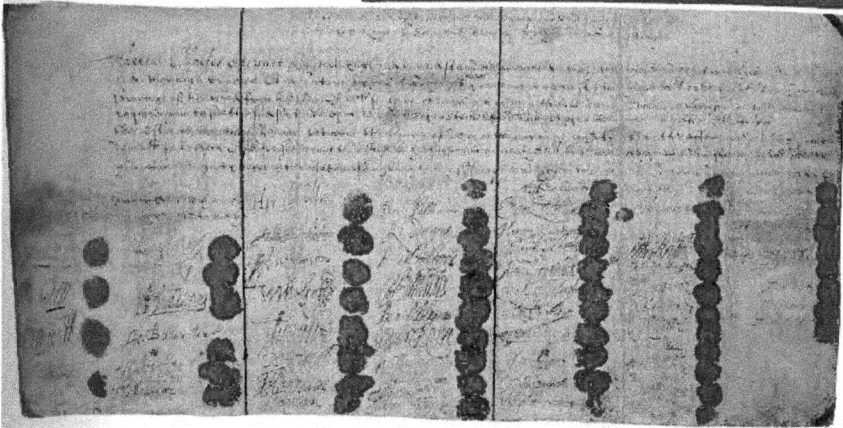

The original death warrant with Judge John Blackiston's signature.

Ironically several of George's descendants also became judges in Maryland. George Blackiston had descendants of many other professions too – governors, sheriffs, shoemakers, farmers, construction workers, entrepreneurs, businessmen, military men, etc. It is a proud legacy of this noble family.

For 300 years (1669-1962), Blackiston Island was so named. In 1962, it was changed to St. Clement's Island to honor Maryland's founding. It was owned by the Blackistone family until 1831 and only when the Federal Government purchased it in 1962 did the name change.

Due to the various spellings of the surname, but to make it easier for readers to use the index, we decided use one spelling of the name as Blackiston even though some variously used Blackistone, Blakiston, Blaxton, etc. over the many centuries. However to assist the reader, where various spellings were used, it was noted with the source records abstracted.

Some abbreviations used include:

AR for *Ancestral Roots* by Weis

The Descendants in Maryland
First Generation

1. **Rev. Marmaduke Blackiston,** son of John Blackiston and Elizabeth Bowes, born about 1563 in England. He died about 1 Sep 1639 at the age of 76 in Durham, England. He was buried in Saint Margarets Catholic Church, Crossgate, Durham, England. He was 16 when he entered Trinity College Oxford in April 1579. Vicar of Woodhorne, Rector of Redmarshall 1585, Rector of 1599, and Prebendary of the 7th Stall, Archdeacon of the East Riding of York, Prebendary of Wistow. He was Prebendary of York and Durham Cathedral which still stands today in Durham and is 900+ years old.

This Durham cathedral has been featured in numerous films including the first two Harry Potter movies - *Philosopher's Stone* and *The Chamber of Secrets* as part of Hogwarts School of Witchcraft and Wizardry. The cathedral cloisters also appeared in scenes as one of the school's courtyards. Interior views of the cathedral can be seen in the Marvel movie *Avengers: Endgame*, as the indoor location of Asgard.

The Royal Ancestry and Descendants of George Blackiston

Rev. Marmaduke was Archdeacon of Cleveland (which he resigned to his son-in-law John Cosin) and Marmaduke of Newton-Hall, County of Palatine and Old Malton, Yorkshire. His family was from Norton Parish, Durham County.

Newton Hall became the estate of Thomas Blakiston, esq; who conveyed it to Marmaduke Blakiston, clerk, one of the prebendaries of Durham, in the seventh year of bishop James (1613); and he sold it to the family of Liddell. The History & Antiquities of the County Palatine of Durham by William Hutchinson Vol. II Durham printed 1823. William James was appointed dean, on the 5th of June 1596, and was installed by Clement Comore, his proxy. p 153

Marmaduke Blakiston, A.M. was the son of J. Blakiston, of Blackiston, Esq. was installed in 1601, and was vicar of Woodhorne, and treasurer of this church, in 1606: on the 14th of October 1585, was collated to Redmarshall; and in July, 1599, to Sedgefield: On the 25th of November, 1615, was collated to the archdeaconry of the East Riding of Yorkshire; and the 5th of March, 1617, was installed prebendary of Willow in York Cathedral. IN 1623, he resigned his stall at York in favor of his son, Thomas Blakiston; in 1625, he did the same touching his archdeaconry, in favor, of J. Cosin, afterwards bishop, who married his daughter and in 1631, he resigned this prebend and Sedgefield, in favor of his son, Robert Blackiston. He died at Newton, near Durham, the family seat, and was interred in St. Margaret's Church, Crossgate, the 3rd December 1639. p 186-197 The History & Antiquities of the County Palatine of Durham by William Hutchinson Vol. II Newcastle printed 1787

The Blakistons were mainly Catholic. It was only after 1570, following the Rebellion of the Northern Earls, when the Pope took a more positive stand against Elizabeth, and when the intrigues of the Mary Stuart faction began, that a more definite anti-Catholic policy was adopted. The Rebellion of the Northern Earls was the first serious threat to the position of Elizabeth, and members of the Blakiston family joined it. The Rebellion was led by the Earls of Northumberland, and Westmoreland. It began on November 14, 1569, with the destruction of Protestant devices in Durham cathedral, and the celebration of the mass there. On November 16, a proclamation was issued at Darlington, pledging their loyalty to the "Queen" and blaming diverse news, set up nobles around her for destroying the true faith. In spite of their public pronouncements, however, the rebels supported Mary Stuart, and wished to see her wed to England's leading Catholic, the Duke of Norfolk. The Rebellion lasted just over a month before collapsing in total failure. The Earl of Sussex and Sir George Bowes, Martial of the Army, were commissioned to deal with the rebels, and in the returns which they sent to London, the names of several Blakistons did appear. Marmaduke Blakiston actually composed some of the manifestos, but fled to Brussels with the Earl of Westmoreland and was later pardoned. It is also known that Marmaduke Blakiston, the brother of John, was involved in the Rebellion and the subsequent papal bull, excommunicating Elizabeth, the government began to tighten its legislation against recusants (or practicing Catholics).

The Royal Ancestry and Descendants of George Blackiston

In 1578, John Blakiston had to do homage for his manor, and take the oath of Supremacy: "I, John Blakiston, do utterly testify and declare by my conscience, that the Queen's Highness, is the only supreme governor of this realm, as well as in all spiritual, or ecclesiastical things, or causes as temporal, and therefore, I do utterly renounce and forsake all foreign jurisdictions, powers, and authorities."

MARRIAGE: Marmaduke married at St. Mary le Less, South Baily Durham (now St. Mary Le Bow) on Jun 30 1595. Margareta James Marriage Date: 30 Jun 1595 Marriage Place: St. Mary-Le-Bow, Durham, Durham, England Spouse: Marmaducus Blaxton FHL Film Number: 2082460 Reference ID: 39

BURIED: St. Margaret's, Crossgate, 3 Sept. 1639 (Crossgate Parish Register).

Other members of the family suffered ill treatment as Catholics. Marmaduke was arraigned in Durham Cathedral for Romish practices. Two of Marmaduke's sons, Thomas Rev of Northallerton and Ralph Rev. of Ryton, were expelled from their benefices both for their Royalism and Catholic views in the 1640's. Ironic that their brother John was one of the trial judges of Charles I. (1 & 2). A Henry Blakiston is mentioned in a petition of 1648 as 'one of the bishop's gentlemen and now a papist living beyond the seas'."

Rev. Marmaduke Blackiston and Margaret James were married on 30 Jun 1595 in Saint Mary le Less, Durham, England. **Margaret James**, daughter of Richard James and Margaret Caldwell, born about 1580. She died about 8 Mar 1636 at the age of 56 in Durham, England. She was buried on 10 Mar 1636 in Saint Margaret's, Crossgate, Durham, England.

Marmaduke Blackiston and Margaret James had the following children:

+2   i. **Tobye Blackiston**, born about 1597, Durham County, England; married Frances Briggs, 3 Oct 1611, Sedgefield, Durham County, England; died Abt Dec 1646, Durham County, England.

3   ii. **Marmaduke Blackiston** born about 1599. He was christened in 1599. He died about Jun 1659 at the age of 60. He was at Queens College Oxford from 1615. He is likely the son of Marmaduke per Paul Garside descendant living in Durham England. Rev Marmaduke Blakiston had another son not mentioned in the Surtees pedigree other than a brief description, under Blakiston of Newton Hall. Marmaduke Blakiston of Monk Fryston, Gent, was born 1599, baptized 13 May 1599, at Redmarshall, the son of Rev Marmaduke Blakiston, he attended Oxford 1615 and was later married to Marie Birkbie at St Michaels, Spurrier Gate, York, Aug 5th 1619. Among his children was Mary born 1625, baptized 19 June 1625 at Monk Fryston York. Altogether eight children born and baptized at Monk Fryston between 1623 and 1636 to Marmaduke Blakiston. One other Alice, was baptized 12 years after

the 1836 entry, being baptized 13 Nov 1652. I have received a copy of the will of Marmaduke Blakiston of Monk Fryston from London dated 17/10/1657, but it makes no mention of Mary, or several other children. I will have to obtain further wills to prove/confirm the connections.

4   iii.   **Thomas Blackiston** born about 1599 in Durham County, England. He died after 1640 at the age of 41. Reverend, Vicar of North Allerton 1628, Prebendary of Wistow, ejected during the Civil Wars 1640-1. He was married and had at least two children Elizabeth baptized 1632 and Peter baptized 1638.

+5   iv.   **Henry Blackiston**, born abt 1601, Durham County, England; married Mary Mauleverer; died abt Jun 1666, Yorkshire County, England.

+6   v.   **Judge John Blackiston**, born abt 21 Aug 1603, Sedgefield, Durham County, England; married Susan Harrison, 9 Nov 1626, Newcastle, Northumberland, England; died abt Mar 1651, England.

+7   vi.   **Frances Blackiston**, born abt 2 Feb 1605–2 Feb 1606; married John Cosin Lord, 13 Aug 1626, Crossgate, Durham County, England.

+8   vii.   **Robert Blackiston**, born abt 7 Jan 1607, Durham County, England; married Elizabeth Howson; died abt 19 Jan 1635, Durham, England.

9   viii.   **Ralph Blackiston** born about 24 Jun 1608 in Durham, England. He was christened on 24 Jun 1608 in Sedgefield, Durham County, England. He died about 28 Jan 1677 at the age of 68 in Ryton, Durham County, England. Ralph was buried on 30 Jan 1677 in Ryton, Durham County, England. Reverend, A.M. Rector of Ryton in Palatine Co.

+10   ix.   **Margaret Blackiston**, born abt 1610; married Thomas Shadforth, 28 Nov 1631, Crossgate, Durham County, England.

+11   x.   **George Blackiston**, born abt Mar 1611, Crossgate, Durham County, England; married Barbara Lawson, 15 Oct 1638, Newcastle, Northumberland, England; died abt Sep 1669, Saint Mary's County, Maryland.

+12   xi.   **Mary Blackiston**, born abt 30 Jun 1613, Durham County, England; married Ralph Allenson, 9 Sep 1629, Brancepath, Durham County, England.

+13   xii.   **Peter Blackiston**, born abt 23 Oct 1614, Durham County, England; married Elizabeth Mauleverer.

Second Generation

2. **Tobye Blackiston** (Marmaduke-1) born about 1597 in Durham County, England. He died about Dec 1646 at the age of 49 in Durham County, England. He was buried in Newton Hall, Durham County, England. Eldest son and heir of Newton-Hall, near Durham, Gentleman. WILL: dated Apr 2 1642 and proved by brother John Blackiston, Esq. Dec 24 1646. Tobye Blackiston and Frances Briggs were married on 3 Oct 1611 in Sedgefield,

Durham County, England. **Frances Briggs** born about 1597 in England. She was living in 1642.

5. **Henry Blackiston** (Marmaduke-1) born about 1601 in Durham County, England. He died about Jun 1666 at the age of 65 in Yorkshire County, England. Henry of Old Malton, County York, Gentleman of Ingleby under Airncliff, 1655. WILL: dated June 13 1666 proved at York. Henry Blackiston and Mary Mauleverer were married. **Mary Mauleverer** born about 1615.

6. **Judge John Blackiston** (Marmaduke-1) born about 21 Aug 1603 in Sedgefield, Durham County, England. He was christened on 21 Aug 1603. He died about Mar 1651 at the age of 47 in England. He was a judge and one of the judges who signed the death warrant of King Charles I in 1649. It was because of this act that his family and his brother George's family moved to America. He was a Member of Parliament. His descendants are discussed in Maryland Genealogies.

NOTES: Surtees p. 402 John Blakiston's signature with his seals of arms is appended to the original warrant for the execution of King Charles. Act of Parliament April 16 1646. Ordered, a letter to be sent to the Hon. William Lenthall, Speaker etc. in vindication of Mr. Io. Blakiston from those unjust and false aspersions cast upon him by George Lilburne. Act of Parliament Aug 24 1649. Ordered that 200l be given to Mrs. Blakiston, that the expenses and disbursement which Mr. Io. Blakiston, lately a Burgess in Parliament for this Corporation, and did many good services to this town. John Blakiston, Mayor of Newcastle, 1645. A sketch of his life is in Dictionary of National Biography. MARRIAGE: at All Saints, Newcastle, Nov 9 1626

WILL: dated Jun 1 1649 and proved Mar 24 1650/1 in London by Susan his widow. John Blakiston of Newtown, Co Palatine, Gentleman, Jun 1 1649, wife Susanna and son Mr. John Blackiston, executors. To his son Neamiah Blakiston; daughter Rebecca, wife of Mr. James Lance, her two children; **to Mr. Lawrence, father-in-law of his brother George Blakiston; and whereas his said brother George hath suffered much with him the testator in public concerns, he gives to the six children of the same George, viz. Robert, Sarah, John, Esther, Hannah, and Justice, 50l each;** to his cousin Mr. Robert Young's wife and children; cousin Margaret Lyons.

Judge John Blackiston and Susan Harrison were married on 9 Nov 1626 in Newcastle, Northumberland, England. **Susan Harrison** born about 1603 in England. She died after 1661 at the age of 58. Her effects seized by the sheriff of Durham as widow of a Regicide, May 31 1661. When she married John Blackiston, she was Susan Chambers, but per Christopher Atkinson, she was the widow of Roger Chambers, whom she had married in 1616 at Whitburn.

John Blackiston and Susan Harrison had the following children:

+14	i.	**Rebecca Blackiston**, born abt 1627; married James Lance, 1649.
15	ii.	**Elizabeth Blackiston** was christened on 29 Sep 1629. She was buried on 30 Nov 1629.
16	iii.	**John Blackiston** was christened on 6 Jan 1630 in Durham County, England. He was buried on 13 Apr 1632 in Durham County, England.
+17	iv.	**John Blackiston**, married Phoebe Johnson; died abt 10 Mar 1701–10 Mar 1702.
18	v.	**Joseph Blackiston** born about Oct 1635. He was christened on 22 Oct 1635. He was buried on 28 Aug 1637.
+19	vi.	**Nehemiah Blackiston**, born abt 1639, Lancashire, England; married Elizabeth Gerard, 6 May 1669, Saint Mary's County, Maryland; died abt Nov 1693, Maryland.

7. **Frances Blackiston** (Marmaduke-1) born about 2 Feb 1605–2 Feb 1606. She was christened on 2 Feb 1605 or 2 Feb 1606.

Frances Blackiston and John Cosin Lord were married on 13 Aug 1626 in Crossgate, Durham County, England. **John Cosin Lord** born about 1605. Lord Bishop of Durham.

8. **Robert Blackiston** (Marmaduke-1) born about 7 Jan 1607 in Durham County, England. He was christened on 7 Jan 1607 in Durham, England. He died about 19 Jan 1635 at the age of 28 in Durham, England. Robert was buried in Durham Abbey, Durham County, England. Reverend, Rector of Sedgefield and Prebendary of Durham on the resignation of his father in 1631.

BURIED: Jan 19 1634 in Durham Abbey. ob.s.p.

Robert Blackiston and Elizabeth Howson were married. **Elizabeth Howson** born about 1607. She died about 18 Oct 1634 at the age of 27 in Durham County, England. She was buried in Durham Abbey, Durham County, England.

10. **Margaret Blackiston** (Marmaduke-1) born about 1610. Margaret Blackiston and Thomas Shadforth were married on 28 Nov 1631 in Crossgate, Durham County, England. **Thomas Shadforth** born about 1610.

11. **George Blackiston** (Marmaduke-1) born about Mar 1611 in Crossgate, Durham County, England. He was christened on 1 Mar 1611 or 1 Mar 1612 in Saint Margaret's, Crossgate, Durham County, England. He died about Sep 1669 at the age of 58 in Saint Mary's County, Maryland. He was a Mercer, Councillor 1644, Alderman 1655, Sheriff of Newcastle in 1656. At the restoration 1660 all property of the two brothers John and George were confiscated, although the Corporation of Newcastle voted 200l to John's widow and 500l to George because "he did many good services for this town." He emigrated to America between May 1668 (marriage of his son in England) and Sept 1669 (admin. of estate) (and possibly pre-May 1669 when Nehemiah was married and supposedly came

with George). Burke's American Families lists on p. 2565 the descent of John Blakiston through George the emigrant to Maryland and his son John. His descendants are listed in the MD Genealogies Vol. 1.

EMIGRATION: John Blakiston applied for proof of right to 800 acres on Jan 4 1670 in MD. Testamentary Proceedings Vol 3 p 272-3. He transplanted George, Barbara, John, Sarah, Robert, Hannah, and Justice Blackiston and others. (MD Land Office Vol 16 p 70)

Nehemiah came to Maryland before May 1669 when he married in MD. Nehemiah was Maryland's Attorney General and held many offices immediately upon his arrival to MD, showing the status of his family in England. They say Nehemiah arrived in 1668 as a free adult. The Settlers of MD says Nehemiah immigrated 1674 which does not mean when he transported only when he moved and settled into the area. He was involved in the revolution of 1689 which overthrew Lord Baltimore.

George Blackiston came to MD between May 1668 (marriage of his son in England) and Sept 1669 (admin. of his estate in MD). A Jan. 1670 application for land by his son John stated all the family that had been transported previously and included George, Barbara, John, Sarah, Robert, Hannah, and Justice Blackiston and others of different surnames. So I can safely say they both arrived in 1668 or 1669 and if they came together then it was between May 1668 and May 1669. No boat record has been found with their names so this may be the closest we can get to their arrival in America. He was Sheriff of Durham in 1656 before emigrating with his family to MD in 1668/9, taking up land in St. Mary's county.

Will of his brother John in Durham England states "to Mr. Lawrence, father-in-law of his brother George Blakiston; and whereas his said brother George hath suffered much with him the testator in public concerns, he gives to the six children of the same George, viz. Robert, Sarah, John, Esther, Hannah, and Justice, 50l each". The names of the children in the will in Durham England and the names of the people in the Emigration in MD show that this is the same family.

DEATH: administration of the estate of George Blakiston, late of St. Mary's County deceased, committed to his son John Blakiston. 20,000 lbs. tobacco on Sep 30 1669 Test. Proc. Vol 3 p 272. Inventory filed Oct 12 1669 p 273 included a silver dram cup, 2 fire lock guns, one old Cutles and Raipier staff, 3 pairs of spectacles, one thumb ring and 9 lbs. of sterling money.

John A. Barnhouser Sr. was accepted in the prestigious Order of the Crown of Charlemagne based on his descent from **George Blackiston** the immigrant back to Emperor Charlemagne - 43 generations and 1,200 years proven!! Member #2051 approved February 21, 2003. This application thus proved for all George Blackiston descendants they are also descendants of Emperor Charlemagne and many other Royal Houses of Europe.

The Royal Ancestry and Descendants of George Blackiston

George Blackiston and Barbara Lawson were married on 15 Oct 1638 at Saint Andrews in Newcastle, Northumberland, England. **Barbara Lawson**, daughter of Henry Lawson and Katheren Warmouth, born about 1620. She died before 1669 at the age of 49.

George Blackiston and Barbara Lawson had the following children:

+20   i.   **John Blackiston**, born abt 19 Sep 1639, Newcastle, Northumberland, England; married Sarah Prideaux, 28 May 1668, Newcastle, Northumberland, England; died 1679, Kent, Md, Kent County, Maryland.

21   ii.   **Robert Blackiston** born about 19 Sep 1639. He was christened on 19 Sep 1639 in Durham, England. He died after 1668 at the age of 29 in Maryland. BIRTH: baptized Robert, son of George and Barbary Blakiston, bapt. Sep 19 1639, St. Nicholas.

22   iii.   **Hannah Blackiston** born about 1640.

23   iv.   **Esther Blackiston** born about 1643.

24   v.   **Sarah Blackiston** born about 1645.

25   vi.   **Joseph Blackiston** born about 1646. He died about 14 Oct 1646 in Durham, England. DEATH: Mr. George Blackiston his son Joseph, buried in the church 14 Oct 1646.

26   vii.   **Samuel Blackiston** born about 1647 in Durham County, England. He died about 8 Oct 1647 in Durham County, England. He was buried in Durham County, England. DEATH: Samuel, son of Mr. George buried Oct 8 1647. All Saints.

+27   viii.   **Captain Ebenezer Blackiston**, born abt 1650, New Castle, Northumberland, England; married Elizabeth James, abt 1672, Maryland; married Rose Tucker, abt 1678, Maryland; died abt 23 Oct 1709, Saint Paul's Parish, Kent County, Maryland.

28   ix.   **Justice Blackiston** born about 1652 in England.

12. **Mary Blackiston** (Marmaduke-1) born about 30 Jun 1613 in Durham County, England. She was christened on 30 Jun 1613 in Sedgefield, Durham County, England. Mary Blackiston and Ralph Allenson were married on 9 Sep 1629 in Brancepath, Durham County, England.

13. **Peter Blackiston** (Marmaduke-1) born about 23 Oct 1614 in Durham County, England. He was christened on 23 Oct 1614 in Crossgate, Durham County, England. sometime of Old Malton Peter Blackiston and Elizabeth Mauleverer were married. **Elizabeth Mauleverer** born about 1614 in England.

Third Generation

14. Rebecca Blackiston (John-2, Marmaduke-1) born about 1627. She was christened on 29 Aug 1627. Rebecca Blackiston and James Lance were married in 1649. **James Lance.** His royal ancestry is given in Plantagenet Ancestry p. 161 by David Faris.

17. John Blackiston (John-2, Marmaduke-1) was christened on 18 Apr 1633. He died about 10 Mar 1701–10 Mar 1702. He was buried on 12 Mar 1701 or 12 Mar 1702 in Newcastle, England. He was admitted to Gray's Inn March 20 1649 and was an attorney. John Blackiston and Phoebe Johnson were married. **Phoebe Johnson.** dau. of William Johnson of Kibblesworth Durham England.

John Blackiston and Phoebe Johnson had the following children:

29	i.	**William Blackiston** was christened on 14 Aug 1665 in England. He was buried on 17 Sep 1665 in England.
+30	ii.	**Nathaniel Blackiston,** born abt 1663, England; married Thomasine Legard; married Mary ; died 1722, England.
31	iii.	**Jane Blackiston** was christened on 4 Jan 1668 in England. She was buried on 30 May 1671 in England.
32	iv.	**Robert Blackiston** born about 1673. He was christened on 3 Aug 1673 in England. He died before 1701 at the age of 28.
33	v.	**Sarah Blackiston** was christened on 12 Apr 1678 in England. She was buried on 26 Jan 1680 in England.
+34	vi.	**Margaret Blackiston,** married Edward Nott Major; died aft 1701.

19. Col. Nehemiah Blackiston (John-2, Marmaduke-1) born about 1639 in Lancashire, England. He died about Nov 1693 at the age of 54 in Maryland. He was a Colonel. He came to America in 1668 as a free adult. In March 1678/9 he sued because of a false arrest. He stated he married May 6 1669 to Elizabeth, dau. of Thomas Gerard Esq. with the consent of her father. He was an attorney of the Provincial Court.

He was commissioned Capt. of a troop of horse in St. Mary's Co Militia. On April 21 1691 he was appointed Chief Justice of the Provincial Court of Maryland and in the same year Speaker of the Assembly. He was commissioned as Colonel abt. April 9 1692 as he was on Apr. 8 a Capt. and thereafter a Col.

Nehemiah Blakiston was Governor of the Maryland colony from 1691 to 1692. He became Governor as the 2nd Leader of the Protestant Associators, succeeding John Coode, who has taken control of the colony, following the 1688 Glorious Revolution, in England. Blakiston was succeeded by the first Governor with an official royal appointment, Lionel Copley. He was living Aug 25 1693 but deceased by Dec. 11, 1693.

Madame Elizabeth Blackiston was cited to administer on the estate of her late husband Col. Nehemiah Blackiston. She married second Ralph Rymer about 1696 and third Joshua Guibert of St. Mary's Co. Her will dated Dec. 15 1715 was proved Oct. 2, 1716.

His ancestry is given in British Roots of MD Families by Robert Barnes. This author provided this information to Bob for inclusion. His biography is listed in the Biographies of the MD Legislature. With John Coode and Kenelm Cheseldine he was a prominent leader in the revolution of 1689 which overthrew Lord Baltimore's government. He became head of the interim government in 1690. Lengthy controversy over the settlement of his estate.

Nehemiah came to Maryland before May 1669 when he married in MD. Nehemiah was Maryland's Attorney General and held many offices immediately upon his arrival to MD, showing the status of his family in England. He was involved in the revolution of 1689 which overthrew Lord Baltimore. They say Nehemiah arrived in 1668 as a free adult. The Settlers of MD says Nehemiah immigrated 1674 which does not mean when he transported only when he moved and settled into the area.

Nehemiah Blackiston and Elizabeth Gerard were married on 6 May 1669 in Saint Mary's County, Maryland. **Elizabeth Gerard**, daughter of Thomas Gerard and Susanna Snow, born about 1650. She died about Sep 1716 at the age of 66 in Saint Mary's County, Maryland.

WILL: Elizabeth Guibert St. Mary's Co dated Dec. 19 1715 proved Sep 17, 1716 to son John Blackiston and male heirs being Protestants dwelling plantation Langworth Point on Potomac River in St. Clement's Hundred except 150 acres. dau. Mary Mason and heirs being Protestant 150 acres being part of tract of waste land bought of Michael Curtis of St. Clement's Hund. daus. Susanah Attoway, Rebecka Walters, Mary Mason and Ann Blackiston, granddau. Elizabeth Blackiston and Nehemiah Blackiston. to son John 1/2 personal estate, other ½ to equally be divided between daus. Witness John Coode, Wm Gibson, James Brian, Katherine Gibson. WB 14 p. 224.

Nehemiah Blackiston and Elizabeth Gerard had the following children:

+35   i. **John Blackiston**, born abt 1670, Saint Mary's County, Maryland; married Anne Guibert, bef 1695; died abt 1724.

+36   ii. **Susanna Blackiston**, born 1674; married Thomas Hatton; married John Attaway, abt 1703; died aft 1715.

+37   iii. **Rebecca Blackiston**, born abt 1677; married Gerard Newton, bef 1696; married Thomas Walters.

+38   iv. **Mary Blackiston**, born abt 1689; married Matthew Mason Jr.

20. **John Blackiston** (George-2, Marmaduke-1) born about 19 Sep 1639 at Durham in Newcastle, Northumberland, England. He was christened on 19 Sep 1639 in Saint

Nicholas, Newcastle, Northumberland, England. He died in 1679 at the age of 40 in Kent, Md, Kent County, Maryland. He came from England with his father in 1669 and other family members. settled in St. Mary's Co then about 1675-1678 moved to Kent Co, MD.

MARRIAGE: May 28 1668 to Sarah Prideaux at St. Andrew's Church, Newcastle Northumberland, England. Colonial Genealogist III:2.

MARRIAGE: John Blakiston Marriage Date: 28 May 1668 at Saint Andrew, Newcastle Upon Tyne, Northumberland, England Spouse: Sarah Pridicks FHL Film Number: 847927, 95010, 95011, 95012, 95013

DEED: John Blakiston purchased from Richard Foster Sr. of St. Mary's Co 100 acres in St. Clement's Manor on Mar 18 1668/9 (Prov. Court Vol. FF p 784).

He was a witness with brother Ebenezer to will of Robert Slye on 13 Mar 1670.

He was on the Jury held by Sir Thomas Gerard on Sep 8 1670 and Oct 28 1672 in St. Mary's.

He moved between Apr 1675 and Sep 1678 to "Boxley" on Swan Creek, Baltimore County (later Kent Co). He was the owner of pew 25 in St. Paul's Anglican Church.

DEED: John Blakiston of Kent Co and Sarah his wife bought of his brother Ebenezer of Cecil Co Gentleman and Elizabeth his wife a tract of 300 acres called Boxley near Swan Creek. (Kent Co Vol. A p 441)

DEATH: On Apr 3 1683, Ebenezer Blakiston of Cecil Co showed that Jno Blakiston of Kent Co died intestate in 1679 that Sarah his widow did not administer on his estate and is since also deceased giving by word and leaving when she died what belonged to ye orphan of ye said deceased to other persons and therefore the said Ebenezer prayed that he may administer on ye said Sarah her estate that he may secure ye estate to ye said orphan to whom in right it belonged which was granted. The court appointed him guardian of their only child John, still a minor. Test. Proc. Vol 3 p 272, Vol 13 p 23. Will book Vol 12 p 23.

He proved transportation of himself, Sarah, George, Barbara, Robert, Hannah, and Justice Blakiston and others and received 800 acres Dec 27 1670. John Blakiston of St. Mary's Co received 150 acres for transplanting 3 people. April 9 1675.

John Blackiston and Sarah Prideaux were married on 28 May 1668 at Saint Andrews Ch in Newcastle, Northumberland, England. **Sarah Prideaux**, daughter of Richard Prideaux and Phaire, born about 3 Jun 1647 in Newcastle Upon Tyne, Northumberland, England. She was baptized on 3 Jun 1647 in Newcastle Upon Tyne, Durham, England. She died before Apr 1683 at the age of 35 in Kent, Maryland. Colonial Families of America copied from the Colonial Genealogist III: 2 1970.

BAPTISM: Sarah Pruddiox Baptism Date: 3 Jun 1647 at All Saints, Newcastle Upon Tyne, Northumberland, England, Father: Richard Pruddiox FHL Film Number: 0095005-0095007 (misspelled Penddiox in index)

John Blackiston and Sarah Prideaux had the following child:

+39   i.   **John Blackiston**, born 1669, Saint Mary's County, Maryland; married Hannah Blackiston; died Dec 1733, Kent County.

27. Ebenezer Blackiston Capt. (George-2, Marmaduke-1) born about 1650 in New Castle, Northumberland, England. He died about 23 Oct 1709 at the age of 59 in Saint Paul's Parish, Kent County, Maryland. He was buried on 25 Oct 1709 in Saint Paul's Cemetery, Kent County, Maryland. He qualifies descendants to join the Colonial Wars and Order of the First Families of Maryland societies because of his service to the State of Maryland in the Maryland Assembly.

MARRIAGE: He is known to have married twice. His first wife Elizabeth James is named in her mother's will of 1677 and the second wife is named in a divorce request in 1681 from Wm Fitzhugh, her brother in law. The actual marriage records have not been found.

NOTES: Capt. Ebenezer Blakiston of Cecil County gives his age as 47 years in 1697 (Maryland Archives Vol 23 p 177). He was commissioned a Capt. of a foot company in Worton and South Sassafras Hundred, Kent Co (Maryland Archives Vol 13 p 244. Also was a justice of the county in 1697-8 and 1702 (Md Archives vol 23 p 129, 401, vol 25 p 125)

EMIGRATION: Ebenezer Blakiston of Baltimore County proved his right to 50 acres of land for transporting himself into the Province (Land Office, Vol 16 p 341). He transplanted himself several years before his parents and brothers bef Jan. 1673. Colonial Genealogist III:2.

DEED: According to the book "A Glossary of Place Names in Baltimore County" by John W. McGrain (former County Historian) present day Ebenezer Road was derived from Ebenezer Blackston's (or Blankenstein) tract of 200 acres in 1672 called "Ebenezer Park". The 1790 Bird River Chapel was renamed Ebenezer Chapel in 1806. Blankenstein received a Patent for the land in 1684, Liber SD No. A, folio 516.

DEED: Henry Eldersley, planter of Baltimore Co and Pennell his wife to Ebenezer Blackiston of the same co on Jan 1 1672/3 sold 100 acres on the Sassafras River. DB G p. 110

DEED: Ebenezer bought from Lawrence Symonds and William Davis 300 acres called Boxley Aug 25 1674. Vol A p 318. This land was sold to his brother John in 1678. Ebenezer obtained by virtue of several assignments Oct 17 1681, a certificate for a tract of 500 acres called St. Taunton's (Land Office Vol 21 p 347).

DEED: Abraham Ambrose age about 50 made a deposition regarding the bounds of a tract called Arcadia, he stated that the branch that comes on the east side of St. Paul's Church and runs to the Old Plantation of Capt. Ebenezer Blackstone where his father lived has ever been called the north branch of Langfords Bay. JS#10:39.

BIO: He was age 47 in 1697 in Cecil Co. He administered on the estate of his brother John and raised his son John. He probably arrived in America with his father according to A Biographical Dictionary of the Maryland Legislature 1635-1789 Vol. 1 p 134-5 by Edward Papenfuse et al. regarding his sons Ebenezer p. 134 and William. He was sheriff of Cecil Co and Justice of Cecil Co 1691, 1697-1698, militia captain in 1689.

DEEDS: Land Owner Ebenezer Blankenstein Settlers of Maryland 1679-1700 by Peter Wilson Colham p 15
Cecil Co St. Tanton's 500 acres 17 Oct 1681 24p 347, 32 p. 100
Cecil Co Hopeful Unity 150 acres 12 May 1682 24p454, 29 p 517
Baltimore Ebenezer's Park 200 acres 8 Apr 1684 25p33, 31 p. 516
Baltimore Ebenezer's Lot 200 acres 13 Jul 1684 25p109, 32p 102

DEATH: He was buried Oct 25 1709 per St. Paul's Parish register so likely died a day or two prior.

ESTATE: intestate, inventory of Mr. Ebenezer Blakiston late of Kent Co deceased appraised by Wm Ringgold and Edward Scott Dec 8 1709 (Annapolis, Inv. and Accts. Vol 31 p 193) Additional inventory by William Blakistone "contains an item of 2588 lbs. tobacco made on my father's plantation". Dec 14 1710 (Inventory Vol 1 p 71-2). Additional account of Wm Blackiston administrator of Capt. Ebenezer Blakiston late of Kent Co deceased, contained an item of a silver cup appraised to the estate but belonging to Ebenezer Blackiston son of the deceased (Annapolis Inv. and Accts. Vol 32B p 242)

A Biographical Dictionary of the Maryland Legislature 1635-1789 Vol. 1 p 134-5 by Edward Papenfuse et al. has son William's biography which includes parents and siblings info, sourced.

Colonial Families of the Eastern Shore by Barnes and Wright Vol. 1 p 35-46 names full family from Marmaduke down to MD descendants, sourced.

Colonial Genealogist III p 2 names direct line through William and immigration to MD, sourced.

MD Land Office Vol 16 p 341 (Immigration record)
MD Archives vol 23 p 129, 177, 401, vol 25 p 125 (Estate of Capt.)

MD Inventory Vol 1 p 71-2 (estate of Capt.)
MD Inv. and Accts. Vol 31 p 193, Vol 32B p 242 (estate of Capt. names both sons)
Kent Co DB Z p 84 (Ebenezer Jr sells land from his father Ebenezer)
MWB 5 p 202, 10 p 31 (stepfather to first wife name Ebenezer and Elizabeth and mother to first wife names granddau and son in law and unnamed dau)

Capt. Ebenezer Blackiston and Elizabeth James were married about 1672 in Maryland. **Elizabeth James**, daughter of Anna James, born about 1650. She died about 1679 at the age of 29. She must have died after 1678 when she and her husband qualified for the administrators of her mother's estate but by 1681 a 2nd wife Rose was claiming that she was abandoned by Ebenezer so she must have died shortly after 1678 and he remarried by 1679 to have 2 children by the 2nd wife.

WILL: John James dated Nov 26 1665 probate Jun 26 1666 mentions sisters Elizabeth and Ann and father in law (stepfather) William Toulson who is to be executor and manage the estates of sisters till they are of age or married. Bequests to Elizabeth wife of Thomas Hunt and Ann Pereman servant to Samuel Withers and to testators servants Edward Thomas and Morris Lloyd. Sister Eliza to have "Jame's Hill".

She is mentioned in the will of John James of 1665 as his sister. William Toulson was called father in law (stepfather). Ann Tolson names son Thomas Francis also, so her maiden name or a married name may also be Francis.

Ebenezer Blackiston and Elizabeth James had the following child:

+40   i. **Hannah Blackiston**, born abt 1673; married John Blackiston; died 7 Aug 1740, Kent County, Maryland.

Capt. Ebenezer Blackiston and Rose Tucker were married about 1678 in Maryland. They were divorced. **Rose Tucker**, daughter of John Tucker and Rose Sturman, born about 1660. She died after 1700 at the age of 40. BIRTH: Estimated to be before 1660 based on age of 18 at marriage. She was daughter of John Tucker and Rose (likely Sturman). She was under 18 in 1672 based on gift of Thomas Gerard.

DEED: 1/28/1672-73: Deed of gift from Thomas Gerard, Esq. of Westmoreland Co., VA to John Tucker, Gerard Tucker, Sarah Tucker, and Rose Tucker "children of the deceased Mr. John Tucker in the county afsd. begotten by him on my now loving wife, Mrs. Rose Gerard" to be delivered to them at the age of 18 (Colonial Virginians and Their Maryland Relatives, Tucker).

MARRIAGE: Ebenezer Blackiston of Cecil Co, Married Widow and admtrx of William Pike, A.A. Co. 1679. Liber VI p. 474 (not sure if this is Rose Tucker) MHM Vol. XVI NO 3 p. 290

MARRIAGE: Rose Tucker married Ebenezer Blackistone after 1677 and before 1681 to Ebenezer since Ebenezer's first wife was named in her mother's Ann Tolsons 1677 will and the 1681 Letter to the Attorney General of MD asking for a divorce for Rose from Ebenezer. This is extremely unusual in this period of early American history.

DIVORCE: This was a letter requesting a divorce for Rose from Ebenezer. Dated 6/8/1681: Letter to Kenelm Cheseldine, Attorney General of MD, from William Fitzhugh. "Sir. The cruelty of Mr. Blackston towards my sister-in-law is grown so notorious and cruel that there is no possibility of keeping it any longer private with the preservation of her life, his cruelty already having occasioned her to make two or three attempts to destroy herself, which is not timely prevented will inevitably follow, therefore Sr. in relation of my affinity to her, as also at the instance and request of Mr. Newton, to propose some remedy. I think there's some means to be used for a separation, because of his continued cruelty, which in England is practical, here in Virginia it is a rare case, of which nature I have known but one which was between Mrs. Brent and her husband, Mr. Giles Brent; the case thus managed; she petitions the Governor and Council, setting forth his inhumane usage, upon which Petition, the Court orders her to live separate from him and he to allow her a maintenance, according to his quality and estate and to make his appearance at the next General Court, before which Court he died and so no further proceedings therein. Mr. Newton can given you a full account of his cruelty and barbarity toward her and has evidences ready to prove, therefore I advised him to consult you for the manner of proceeding therein, and earnestly request you will assist him in it. It cannot properly be called a divorce, but a separation rather, for I find in Cooke on Littleton folio 235, several sorts of Divorces a Vinvulo Matromonii, but Divorces propter Saevitiam and cause Adulterii are more properly separations, because no Dissolutions a Vinculo Matromonii but only a Mensa et thoro, and the Coverture continues and consequently a maintenance allowed her and dower after his deceased, as is plentifully set forth by those that treat thereof. You may find one precedent in Cooke Car. Fol. 461-462 between Porter and his wife, whereupon prosecution it was decreed, Quod propter Sevitiam of her said husband and c. I question not but you are furnished with precedents of like nature, therefore your assistance and advice in this affair is desired by----Sir, Your W. ff.

DEATH: She likely died in Westmoreland VA where her family was from when she left her husband Ebenezer and she remarried Edward Bathhurst.

Ebenezer Blackiston and Rose Tucker had the following children:

+41   i.   **William Blackiston Sr.**, born abt 1679, Maryland; married Ann Park, bef 1711, Kent County, Maryland; married Ann Moore, bef 1729; died abt May 1737, Kent County, Maryland.

+42   ii. **Ebenezer Blackiston Major**, born abt 1681; married Sarah Joyce, bef Feb 1712, Kent County, Maryland; died Nov 1746, Kent County, Maryland.

Fourth Generation

30. **Governor Nathaniel Blackiston** (John-3, John-2, Marmaduke-1) born about 1663 in England. He died in 1722 at the age of 59 in England. He was Governor of Maryland on Jan. 2 1698/9. He resigned on June 1701 because of ill health. His biography is listed in the Biographies of the MD Legislature.

King James named Blackistone to take over the murdered Christopher Rousby's duties as the King's Tax Collector, presumably until a replacement could be found. However this did not sit well with Lord Baltimore who wanted his son in laws appointed. On April 20, 1685, Blackistone felt compelled to write a letter of complaint against Lord Baltimore's officers. His letter states:

"I hope my letter of the 10th of November last sent via Virginia and my duplicate of the same in another ship is come safe to your hands since which I met with divers testimonies and experience of the truth of what intelligence I therein gave to your Honors. The most horrid murder of His Majesty's Collector here hath been and is daily seconded with very apparent tokens of approvement both from Talbot, the bloody malefactor, and all his adherents who are busy in extenuating his crime and have conspired and procured his escape from prison in Virginia and from thence transported him to Maryland where he remains publicly known at his own house. There is little hope of his being brought to justice that he may receive condign punishment, there being a literal intercourse and correspondence between him and some principal magistrates of this Province, and no effectual course taken for apprehending him which I humbly conceive may be a strong argument and signal taken to your Honors of the ill and wicked carriage of things here."

Lord Baltimore responded the same day with his response:

"It plainly appears, by a letter from the Governor of Virginia to the Deputies of Maryland that the escape made by George Talbot out of prison, was occasioned by the corruption of the guard, and not procured by any persons of Maryland as is falsely suggested in the letter of the said Blackistone, and that as soon as the Governor of Virginia had given notice to the Deputies of Maryland of the said Talbot's escape, special care was taken immediately by them for his apprehension as appears by the hue and cry sent out into all parts of the Province, besides what other ways and means could be used for the speedy beginning (apprehension) of the said Talbot, who never was publicly seen at his own plantation (though the contrary is affirmed by the said Blackistone, but always kept himself out in the mountains to the northward, until at last he resolved to surrender himself to the Deputies of Maryland where now he is under a strong guard to be disposed of as His Majesty shall think fit.

His Lordship is very confident Mr. Blackistone has no just cause to compla of his being discountenanced in the execution of his place, for that he (Baltimore) very well knows his officers dare not presume to offer any contempt nor show the least disrespect either to his person or commission nor would they presume to dissuade masters of vessels from presenting themselves and their certificates to His Majesty's Officers, his Lordship having long since ordered that they should apply themselves to the King's Collector as well as to his own and such was the practice while Mr. Christopher Rousby was living and the truth of this may be easily known from several masters of ships and others now in town, after Mr. Christopher Rousby was so unfortunately killed by George Talbot....

Therefore his Lordship humbly begs that the said Blackiston may be required to prosecute his great charge contained in his said letter that in case Col. Diggs and the rest of the officers in Maryland be found guilty they may suffer, but if innocent as his Lordship hopes and believes they are, that then they may be cleared."

Rousby's successor John Payne was also murdered. King James was not pleased with Lord Baltimore and ultimately reduced some of his land charter carving out much of Maryland then to Delaware and Virginia today.

Colonel Nathaniel Blakiston was appointed the 8th Royal Governor of Maryland from 1698 to 1702 by King William III and Queen Mary. He succeeded Francis Nicholson and was succeeded by Thomas Tench. Nathaniel Blakiston was grandson of John Blakiston, a Judge in the execution of King Charles I of England. Blakiston joined the British Army and served in the West Indies. As a soldier, Blakiston attained the lieutenant-governor rank of Montserrat island, as acting colonel. In 1698, Nathaniel Blakiston was appointed governor of the British colony of Maryland. During that time he was charged with rooting out piracy in the colonies, for example accusing slaver Henry Munday of collaborating with Pennsylvanian pirate Henry King. However, his government only lasted three years, because he had to retire for health problems, in 1701. The court of delegates chose him to serve, as their colonial agent, in London in appreciation for his services, in Monserrat. Later, from 1706 onwards, Blakiston was agent, for the Virginia Colony, in London. Then, in 1715, he was returned as the member of parliament for Mitchell. He was a loyal Whig who consistently voted with the administration during this period. Nathaniel Blakiston died at the end of February 1722.

Nathaniel Blackiston and Thomasine Legard were married. **Thomasine Legard** died in 1697.

Nathaniel Blackiston and Mary were married.

34. **Margaret Blackiston** (John-3, John-2, Marmaduke-1) died after 1701. Margaret Blackiston and Edward Nott Major were married. **Edward Nott Major**. Major of Kingston, Surrey, England, the deputy governor of VA from 1705 to 1706.

35. **John Blackiston** (Nehemiah-3, John-2, Marmaduke-1) born about 1670 in Saint Mary's County, Maryland. He died about 1724 at the age of 54.

ESTATE: Mr. John Blackiston 10.292 SM £633.7.8 Jan 18 1724 Feb 5 1724
Appraisers: Mr. Gerrard Slye, John Haskins , Creditors: Thomas Flower, Raphael Neale.
Next of kin: Roswell Neale, Robert Mason. Executrix: Anne Blackiston

ESTATE: John Blackistone 7.185 A SM £633.7.8 £64.6.0 Nov 2 1725 Received from: William Jameston, Thomas Guibert. Payments to: Mr. Gerrard Slye, Capt. Richard Hopewell, William Snowden, Mr. John Donaldson, Thomas Glover, Mr. John Attaway, Phill. Key, Rev. Mr. John Donaldson. Administratrix: Anne Blackistone (also Anne Blackiston).

ESTATE: Mr. John Blackiston 8.292 A SM £4.17.4 Aug 2 1727 Received from: Daniell Kelley, Lewes More, Matthew Mason, Repall Neale, Thomas Guybert. Payments to: Capt. Richard Hopewell, Capt. Michael Jenifer, Mr. Phil. Key, Mr. William Cummings. Administratrix: Mrs. Anne Blackiston (also Anne Blackistone).

John Blackiston and Anne Guibert were married before 1695, daughter of Joshua Guibert and Elizabeth Barber.

John Blackiston and Anne Guibert had the following children:

43	i.	**Thomas Blackiston** born about 1695. He died about Nov 1742 at the age of 47. WILL: Names sister Elizabeth Neale, brother Roswell Neale and their children James, Bennett, and Raphael. his sister Susanna Mason and the child she is big with, Matthew Mason's 3 children, Matthew, Nehemiah Rodham and Dorcas Mason. and his three brothers John Blakistone, Roswell Neale, and Robert Mason. Dated Nov 10 1742 proved Dec 8 1742
+44	ii.	**Elizabeth Blackiston**, born abt 1695; married Roswell Neale.
+45	iii.	**John Blackiston**, born bef 1724; married Eleanor Dent; died 18 Jan 1756, Saint Mary's County, Maryland.

36. **Susanna Blackiston** (Nehemiah-3, John-2, Marmaduke-1) was born in 1674. She died after 1715 at the age of 41. Susanna Blackiston and Thomas Hatton were married. **Thomas Hatton** died in Aug 1701. Susanna Blackiston and John Attaway were married about 1703.

WILL: Thomas Hatton St. Mary's Co dated Aug. 11 1701 probate not stated. To brother in law John Blackston personalty. to dau. Eliza. 250 acres on Hunting Creek. to unborn child 500 acres being a grant of land not yet laid out. Wife Susanna exec. 1/2 tract during life and whole during minority of possible unborn child. In event of death to said child then to dau. Eliza. Witness Clement Hill Sr, Robert Carss, Wm Gibson, John Realey. By codicil date Aug. 22 1701 ratifies all bequests in his will and arranges for an exchange of 1000 acres in Chaptico Manor due him as heir of Thomas Hatton late Secretary of the Province for Rich Neck in Beaver Dam Manor and devises to unborn child. WB 11 p. 120.

37. **Rebecca Blackiston** (Nehemiah-3, John-2, Marmaduke-1) born about 1677. Rebecca Blackiston and Gerard Newton were married before 1696. **Gerard Newton**, son of John Newton and Rose Sturman, was born in 1677. Rebecca Blackiston and Thomas Walters were married.

38. **Mary Blackiston** (Nehemiah-3, John-2, Marmaduke-1) born about 1689. Mary Blackiston and Matthew Mason Jr. were married. **Matthew Mason Jr.** was born in 1689. He died in 1729 at the age of 40.

39. **John Blackiston** (John-3, George-2, Marmaduke-1) was born in 1669 in Saint Mary's County, Maryland. He died in Dec 1733 at the age of 64 in Kent County, Maryland. When his father died, he was raised by his uncle. He ended up marrying his first cousin. First of the family to be born in Maryland. He was 57 years old in 1726 and had lived "in these parts" (in Kent Co) 50 years (Deed IS 10 44). He and Ebenezer owned pew No. 25 in St. Paul's Church. He received Boxley from his father and in the Rent roll of 1707 was recorded as possessing it and he left it to his children in his will.

WILL: dated Dec 2 1733 proved Jan 2 1733/4 John Blackiston whole estate real and personal to his wife Hannah during her widowhood. to his sons Vincent and Ebenezer my now dwelling plantation 100a equally. to son Prideaux the plantation whereon said son now dwells. to his sons Thomas, William and Michael 150 acres part of Boxley; to his son John, with the remainder to the testator's son Benjamin 50 acres called Tolley's Chance; to his daughters Mary Covington and Sarah Blakiston, two seats in St. Paul's Church, with 2000 lbs. tobacco to Sarah at her mother's decease. Hannah abides by the will.

John Blackiston and Hannah Blackiston were married. **Hannah Blackiston**, daughter of Ebenezer Blackiston and Elizabeth James, born about 1673. She died on 7 Aug 1740 at the age of 67 in Kent County, Maryland. A granddaughter Anna Blackiston was named in the will of Anna Tolson as dau. of her son in law Ebenezer Blackiston and dau. and I believe this Anna is Hannah Blackiston. Family tradition says Hannah wife of John Blackiston was a Blackiston too and that her husband was raised in her father's house and that is when they fell in love. John named one of his children Ebenezer which lends credence to this story.

DEATH: land record Kent Co IS #23 p 45

John Blackiston and Hannah Blackiston had the following children:

+46   i. **Prideaux Blackiston Sr**, born 1696, Maryland; married Mary Slayfoot; married Martha Miller, 27 Jul 1729, Saint Paul's Parish, Kent County, Maryland; died bef 1775.

47   ii. **John Blackiston** born about 1698 in Maryland. He died about Aug 1720 at the age of 22 in Kent County, Maryland. He died unmarried. His brother administered on the estate on Aug 6 1720.

+48   iii. **Thomas Blackiston**, born abt 4 May 1701; married Margaret Hynson; died abt Sep 1753, Kent County, Maryland.

+49   iv. **Vincent Blackiston**, born abt 6 Feb 1703–6 Feb 1704; married Mary ; married Susanna , abt 1740–1742, Kent County, Maryland; died abt Mar 1769, Kent County.

50   v. **Hannah Blackiston** born about 24 Feb 1703–24 Feb 1704. She was christened on 24 Feb 1703 or 24 Feb 1704 in Kent County, Maryland.

+51   vi. **Ebenezer Blackiston**, born abt 1705; married Mary Maxwell, 14 Apr 1737, Kent County, Maryland; married Hannahretta Mahon, aft 1755; died abt Apr 1772, Kent County, Maryland.

+52   vii. **Mary Blackiston**, born abt 1708; married Henry Covington, 1712, Queen Annes County, Maryland.

+53   viii. **Benjamin Blackiston**, born abt 1710; married Sarah Strong, 27 Feb 1732, Kent County, Maryland; died abt Dec 1760, Kent County, Maryland.

+54   ix. **Michael Blackiston**, born abt 2 Dec 1711; married Ann Bradshaw, 8 Dec, Saint Paul's Parish, Kent County, Maryland; died abt Mar 1758, Kent County, Maryland.

+55   x. **William Blackiston**, born abt 1713; married Ann Glenn, 5 Feb 1736, Saint Paul's Parish, Kent, Maryland, British America; married Mary Courtney, abt 1755, Kent County, Delaware; died 1758, Kent County, Delaware.

56   xi. **Sarah Blackiston** born about 1715.

40. Hannah Blackiston (Ebenezer-3, George-2, Marmaduke-1) born about 1673. She died on 7 Aug 1740 at the age of 67 in Kent County, Maryland. A granddaughter Anna Blackiston was named in the will of Anna Tolson as dau. of her son in law Ebenezer Blackiston and dau. and I believe this Anna is Hannah Blackiston. Family tradition says Hannah wife of John Blackiston was a Blackiston too and that her husband was raised in her father's house and that is when they fell in love. John named one of his children Ebenezer which lends credence to this story.

DEATH: land record Kent Co IS #23 p 45

Hannah Blackiston and John Blackiston were married. **John Blackiston**, son of John Blackiston and Sarah Prideaux, was born in 1669 in Saint Mary's County, Maryland. He died in Dec 1733 at the age of 64 in Kent County, Maryland. When his father died, he was raised by his uncle. He ended up marrying his first cousin. First of the family to be born in Maryland. He was 57 years old in 1726 and had lived "in these parts" (in Kent Co) 50 years (Deed IS 10 44). He and Ebenezer owned pew No. 25 in St. Paul's Church. He received Boxley from his father and in the Rent roll of 1707 was recorded as possessing it and he left it to his children in his will.

WILL: dated Dec 2 1733 proved Jan 2 1733/4 John Blackiston whole estate real and personal to his wife Hannah during her widowhood. to his sons Vincent and Ebenezer my now dwelling plantation 100a equally. to son Prideaux the plantation whereon said son now dwells. to his sons Thomas, William and Michael 150 acres part of Boxley; to his son John, with the remainder to the testator's son Benjamin 50 acres called Tolley's Chance; to his daughters Mary Covington and Sarah Blakiston, two seats in St. Paul's Church, with 2000 lbs. tobacco to Sarah at her mother's decease. Hannah abides by the will.

41. **William Blackiston Sr.** (Ebenezer-3, George-2, Marmaduke-1) born about 1679 in Maryland. He died about May 1737 at the age of 58 in Kent County, Maryland. BIO: His full biography is in the Biographies of the Maryland Legislature p 135 William served in Lower House 1722-1724, bought 100 acres with inventory of 333 lbs. including 12 slaves and 1 servant. He administered his father's estates in 1709. He represented Kent Co in the Maryland Assembly 1722-4 (House Journals). He was of age by 1712.

BIRTH: His estimated birth year is 1679 which means his mother is the second wife not first wife.

MARRIAGE: He appears to have married twice to two Anns due to the wide range in his children's ages. His wife Ann Park could not have had children for so many years (37 years between oldest and youngest). It is my conclusion that the first wife was Ann Park and the second wife was Ann Moore.

WILL: William Blackiston Sr dated Mar 16 1736/7 pro May 10 1737. To wife Ann and to pay certain personalty to William Moore, daus. Mary, Ann Miller, Hanna and Rose, son William and unborn child. son Ebenezer. residue of personal estate divided among four youngest child and wife. WB 21-791. wife Ann abides by will. witness James Ringgold, Sarah Blackiston, Jonathan Whitworth.

His descendants are eligible to join the Order of the First Families of Maryland because of his service to the State of Maryland in the Maryland Assembly. His descendants John A. Barnhouser Jr. and Anna Christina Waterfield-Copeland are members.

William Blackiston Sr. and Ann Park were married before 1711 in Kent County, Maryland. **Ann Park**, daughter of Robert Park and Mary Hatcheson, born about 1683. She died before 1724 at the age of 41. Her parents names are given on p 135 of the Biographies of MD Legislature.

It appears that the wife Ann Park is not the mother of all the children. She is said to have married before 1711. She would have been too old to be the mother of the younger children and there is a large gap in ages of the children, especially with William's will saying she is currently pregnant. Could he have married Ann Moore too?

Mary Park Dunn's inventory in 1738 is signed by Mary Blackiston and explains why Hannah Blackiston was listed as next of kin. (She is Mary's granddau.)

William Blackiston and Ann Park had the following children:

+57   i. **William Blackiston Jr.**, born abt 1703; married Martha Jarvis.

+58   ii. **Ann Blackiston**, born abt 1704; married Arthur Miller, bef 1737; died aft 1737.

59   iii. **Mary Blackiston** was born on 9 Mar 1711/2 in Saint Paul's Parish, Kent County, Maryland.

60   iv. **Hannah Blackiston** born about 1715. Hannah signed as next of kin to Mary Dunn in inventory of 1739 (her grandmother)

+61   v. **Ebenezer Blackiston**, born abt 1720; married Mary Medford; died abt 1777, Kent County, Maryland.

William Blackiston Sr. and Ann Moore were married before 1729. **Ann Moore**, daughter of John Moore and Elizabeth Dowland, was born on 10 Aug 1708 in Saint Paul's Parish, Kent County, Maryland. She died after 1737 at the age of 29. The reference in the will of William Blackiston to a William Moore leads me to believe the 2nd wife Ann is actually Ann Moore. Also William Blackiston is named as next of kin in John Moore's estate in 1729. One record said Ann Moore married Hance Blackiston but due to chronology however, I believe she was his mother.

Jackson Griffith (d. 1755/61 Kent Co., MD) m. Ann Blackiston, whose marriage was recorded in Saint Paul's Parish, Kent Co., MD on 26 Jan 1738.
Martha Griffith dau of Jackson and Ann Griffith born Dec 25 1739. St. Paul's Parish.

There is a 1738 deed for James Moore (he married a Wilmer) and Lambert Wilmer and Jackson Griffith and William Harris to devise land from the Wilmers to Jackson Griffith son of Benjamin Griffith deceased as the land was not completed before his death. See again the Moore reference. It makes me think I am right that Jackson's wife Ann Blackiston was Ann Moore Blackiston.

William Blackiston and Ann Moore had the following children:

+62   i. **Rosamond Blackiston**, born abt 1730, Kent County, Maryland; married John Rasin, aft 1750, Kent County, Maryland; married Abraham Rasin, bef Jun 1763, Kent County, Maryland; died bef 1771.

+63   ii. **Hance Blackiston**, born 1737, Kent County, Maryland; married Ann , abt 1768; died abt Jan 1772, Kent County, Maryland.

42. **Major Ebenezer Blackiston** (Ebenezer-3, George-2, Marmaduke-1) born about 1681. He died in Nov 1746 at the age of 65 in Kent County, Maryland.

MARRIAGE: They were married before Feb 1712 when her father mentions his daughter Sarah Blackiston in his will.

DEED: Aug 15 1711 Kent Co DE deed Ebenezer Blackiston son and heir of Ebenezer Blackiston late of Cecil Co gent deceased sold to Mary Green spinster 500 acres of land being 1/2 part of a tract of land called Gravesend on the west side of the DE bay and on the south side of the NW Branch of Duck Creek. DB Z pg. 84

DEATH: His date of death was given in his daughter's bible record.

ESTATE: Accounts of John Garrett and Sarah his wife administratix of Ebenezer Blakiston late of Kent Co deceased. Jul 23 1748. Rosamond wife of William Wilmer is the daughter and sole representative of the deceased. (Accounts Bk 27 p 171).

NOTES: In Article in Maryland Genealogical Society Bulletin "Robert Jarman and Some Descendants" Vol 39 No. 2 p. 185 Robert Jarman sold part of Galloway Farm to Ebenezer Blackstone on Nov. 15, 1715. and another 80 acres on Aug. 16, 1721 and Thomas Gideons sold 95 acres to Ebenezer on Aug. 16, 1721 which Thomas had purchased of Robert Jarman.

BIO: His biography is listed in the Biographies of the Maryland Legislature. He arrived by 1712/3 Sarah Joyce dau of Thomas Joyce. Ebenezer served in the Lower House Kent Co 1724, 1727, 1728-1731, 1732-1734, served as justice of the Court of Oyer and Terminer and Gaol (Jail) Delivery 1733-1744, coroner, Kent Co 1740; captain 1724, major 1745. Served as guardian for his nephew Pascoa Joce from 1734-1742 at least. deceased by Jan. 19 1746/7. Large estate 1,013 lbs. including 11 slaves, books and plate. owned 775 acres.

Ebenezer Blackiston and Sarah Joyce were married before Feb 1712 in Kent County, Maryland. **Sarah Joyce**, daughter of Thomas Joce and Sarah , born about 1686. She died on 20 May 1761 at the age of 75. Her father's will dated Feb 27 1712 says dau. Sarah Blackiston. She later married John Garrett.

DEATH: Her date of death May 1761 was given in her daughter's bible. and May 20 1761 given in Chancery Vol. 10 p 241.

Deposition: Blackstone Wilmer, William Ringgold and Sarah his wife of Kent Co vs. John Garrett. complaint Jan 8, 1757 states that Sarah Blackstone on Jan. 26, 1747 was sole and unmarried and a made a deed of gift to Blackstone and Sarah Wilmer now Ringgold her grandchildren, the children of Rose Wilmer daughter of Sarah Blackstone. After said gift, Sarah Blackstone intermarried with John Garrett of Kent Co, mariner. Sarah Blackstone was the executrix of Ebenezer Blackiston, her former husband dec'd. Vol. 10 p 229. Jan. 6 1762 Rose Wilmer mother of plaintiffs in above case age 40 years that Sarah Garrett died May 20 1761 and no issue were born after her intermarriage with John Garrett. Rose Wilmer's husband was William Wilmer. Vol. 10 p. 237. Numerous other depositions in this case and a note that copy of will of Sarah Blackiston mentions 3 grandchildren Blackiston Wilmer, Sarah Wilmer, and Dorcas Wilmer Vol. 10 p. 246.

Ebenezer Blackiston and Sarah Joyce had the following child:

+64   i. **Rosamond Blackiston**, born 1712; married William Wilmer, 7 Feb 1733; died 30 Mar 1790.

Fifth Generation

44. Elizabeth Blackiston (John-4, Nehemiah-3, John-2, Marmaduke-1) born about 1695. Elizabeth Blackiston and Roswell Neale were married. **Roswell Neale**, son of Anthony Neale and Elizabeth Roswell, was born in 1685. He died about Apr 1751 at the age of 66 in Saint Mary's County, Maryland.

WILL: Roswell Neale, St. Mary's Co. To wife, Elizabeth Neale, for life, my dwelling house with 240a run from a br. of Tomachokin Crk. And at her death. to son James Neale, but if he d. s.p., to 3 sons, Raphael, Bennett, & Jeremiah. To son James Neale, the 30a he lives on, lately survd. by Basil Wheeler, adj. s land, & if he d. s. p., to s 3 sons. T s 4 sons, equ. div., my water mill & 6a. The rest of my lands to s 3 sons, Raphael, Bennett, & Jeremiah (Raphael to have the part he has built on), but if all s 4 sons d. s. p., to my 3 daus., Anne Gibson, Mary Wheeler, & Elizabeth Neale, & if they d. s. p., to 2 sons, William & Henry Neale. To my s wife, 2 negro women, Nell & Jenny, provided she not claim any more negroes than she has by her mar. settlement. To son James Neale I confirm his right to negroes Will & Lucy. If my wife takes back negroes Charles & Rose from my son Raphael, to him negroes Robin & Phillis. To son Bennett Neale, negroes Tom & Bridgett. To son Jeremiah, negroes Ned & Young Harry. To dau. Anne Gibson, wife of William Gibson, negroes Lucy & Tubtus. To dau. Wheeler, I confirm negroes Jack & Henry. To dau. Elizabeth Neale, negroes George & Nancy. The rest of my negroes to James Neale, Raphael Neale, Bennett Neale, Jeremiah Neale, Anne Gibson, Mary Wheeler, & Elizabeth Neale; of the residue of my p. e., 1/3 to s wife & 2/3 to s 7 children. Extrs: sons James, Raphael, Bennett, &Jeremiah Neale. Witn: John Somervell, John Daily, Abrm. Lovelace. To dau. Elizabeth Neale, negro Old Harry; to sons Wm. & Henry, each 1 sh. & lands & goods already given them. 7 May 1751, sworn to by all 3 witn., & the widow stood to the will. dated Mar. 24, 1751 proved May 1, 1751 Liber 28, folio 61

Roswell was the grandson of the famous Capt. James Neale.

Roswell Neale and Elizabeth Blackiston had the following children:

65   i. **James Neale** born about 1720. Died 14 Jan 1763
66   ii. **Bennett Neale** died 1771
67   iii. **Raphael Neale** born about 1724 die d6 Apr 1787

68	iv.	**Jeremiah Neale** died 19 Oct 1808
69	v.	**Anne Neale** Died 29 Nov 1789
70	vi.	**Mary Neale**
71	vii.	**Elizabeth Neale.**

45. John Blackiston (John-4, Nehemiah-3, John-2, Marmaduke-1) was born before 1724. He died on 18 Jan 1756 at the age of 32 in Saint Mary's County, Maryland. WILL: Made nuncupative will proven by oaths of John Coode, John Mason and Cyrus Simpson. He names his sons Nehemiah Herbert (eldest), George, and John Blackistone, his wife Eleanor Blakistone, and his sister Susanna Mason WB 30 p. 45

John Blackiston and Eleanor Dent were married. **Eleanor Dent.** dau. of George Dent of Charles Co, MD. She married second Alexander McFarlane, and 3rd Mr. Bayard.

John Blackiston and Eleanor Dent had the following child:

+72   i.   **Nehemiah Herbert Blackiston**, born bef 1755; married Mary Cheseldine, 30 Jan 1772; married Eleanor Gardiner Hebb, Aug 1801; died abt Jun 1816, Saint Mary's County.

46. Prideaux Blackiston Sr (John-4, John-3, George-2, Marmaduke-1) was born in 1696 in Maryland. He died before 1775 at the age of 79. He gives his age as 39 years in 1735. Administered on estate of his brother John Blakiston Jr. (Accts Vol 3 p 62). Priddox Blackston of St. Paul's Parish planter on July 10 1728 committed fornication with Mary Slayfoot and begat a bastard child.

MARRIAGE: Martha Miller Jul 27 1729 St. Paul's Parish, Kent County MD

A 1775 deed says that Prideaux Blackiston son of Prideaux inherited land of his grandfather John. The DAR says this Prideaux Jr. born about 1751 so if correct there is another child by Prideaux if Prideaux is not the child.

Prideaux Blackiston and Mary Slayfoot had the following child:

73   i.   **Blackiston** was born in 1728. It is not known what the name of this child he had out of wedlock with Mary Slayfoot is. The child could be named Blackiston or Slayfoot or another surname.

Prideaux Blackiston Sr and Martha Miller were married on 27 Jul 1729 in Saint Paul's Parish, Kent County, Maryland. **Martha Miller**, daughter of Michael Miller and Martha Wickes, was born on 16 Sep 1701. She died after 1761 at the age of 60. She was the widow of William Dunn when she married Prideaux as her second husband. She signed as next of kin to Samuel Miller in 1761 which would be her brother.

Prideaux Blackiston and Martha Miller had the following child:

+74   i. **Pvt Prideaux Blackiston (Jr)**, born bef 1751; married Bridget Shrader, bef Jan 1775; died 11 Feb 1778, Valley Forge, Chester County, Pennsylvania.

48. **Thomas Blackiston** (John-4, John-3, George-2, Marmaduke-1) born about 4 May 1701. He was christened on 4 May 1701 in Saint Paul's Parish, Kent County, Maryland. He died about Sep 1753 at the age of 52 in Kent County, Maryland.

DEED: Thomas Blakiston and Margaret his wife sell to Michael Blakiston 50 acres part of Boxley (Book IS no 23, p 240).

MARRIAGE: proved by deed (IS no 10 p 277) Margaret, dau of Col. Nathaniel Hynson and Mary (whom later married Joseph Young) Aug 26 1728. 100 acres part of Partnership.

WILL: dated Apr 17 1753 and proved Sep 7 1753 (Vol 28 p 526) Thomas Blackston names seven children: Elijah to get slave Phill, Thomas to get slave Prince, personal estate to all children except Hannah who gets a cow and calf and warming pan, children: Elijah, Thomas, John, Mary, Rebecca, and Lettice to get remainder split equally. Witn: C[ornelius] Comegys, J[ohn] Watson, Thos. Watson. 7 Sept. 1753, sworn to in presence of Margaret, widow.

Thomas Blackiston and Margaret Hynson were married. **Margaret Hynson**, daughter of Nathaniel Hynson and Hannah, was born on 22 Dec 1712 in Maryland. On 1 Feb 1738 Mrs. Catharine Kelley made oath that Margret Hynson dau of Col. Nathaniel Hynson deceased and now the wife of Mr. Thomas Blackston was 26 years old on 22 Dec. previous, she being present at her birth KEBI JS #18 p. 201.

DEED: Joseph Young of Kent and his wife Mary convey to Margaret Blackistone formerly Margaret Hynson and daughter of said Mary (stepdau.) and now the wife of Thomas Blackistone a tract which Col. Nathaniel Hynson deceased by his last will gave to said Mary 1,000 acres of a tract called Partnership containing 3,000. Aug 26, 1728.

Thomas Blackiston and Margaret Hynson had the following children:

75   i. **Elijah Blackiston** born about 1735.
76   ii. **Thomas Blackiston** born about 1737.
77   iii. **John Blackiston** born about 1739.
78   iv. **Rebecca Blackiston** born about 1743.
79   v. **Mary Blackiston** born about 1741.
80   vi. **Hannah Blackiston** born about 1745.
81 vii. **Lettice Blackiston** born about 1747.

49. Vincent Blackiston (John-4, John-3, George-2, Marmaduke-1) born about 6 Feb 1703–6 Feb 1704. He was christened on 6 Feb 1703 or 6 Feb 1704 in Kent County, Maryland. He died about Mar 1769 at the age of 66 in Kent County, Maryland.

WILL: dated Nov 11 1768 and proved March 20 1769 (Annapolis, Vol 37 p 561). whole estate to wife Susanna, during his widowhood. negro boy Tom to my wife's granddau. Rebecca Miller; negro boy Chester to James Blackiston, son of Ebenezer, bequest to my son in law Alexander Beck (stepson); remainder of land, 50 acres, to Alexander Beck and his children, if he has no children to above James son of Ebenezer.

His children mentioned in Maryland Genealogies p. 61

Vincent Blackiston and Mary were married. **Mary** born about 1701. Her maiden name may be Page since she named a son Page Blakiston and this son left everything to a Ralph Page. Three children were listed in the St. Paul's Parish records with Vincent and Mary.

Vincent Blackiston and Susanna were married about 1740–1742 in Kent County, Maryland. **Susanna** born about 1710. She was named in his will and must have been married previously as Vincent named "his wife's granddau. Rebecca Miller" in his own will in 1769. Susannah's first husband was Alexander Beck who had dau Elizabeth Miller who had dau Rebecca Miller. There is a Susanna Blackiston named in the 1765 will of Mary Yearly. She was married first to Richard Gibbs d. 1713 and second to William Yearly by 1715. She could be the dau of Richard or William depending on her birth year.

51. Ebenezer Blackiston (John-4, John-3, George-2, Marmaduke-1) born about 1705. He lived in 1733–1736. He died about Apr 1772 at the age of 67 in Kent County, Maryland.

DEED: Ebenezer Blackiston Jr. and his wife Mary of Kent Co sold to William Blakiston 50 acres part of Boxley on Swan Creek willed by his father John Blakiston deceased. Jul 29 1741 DB IS no 23 p 316. both signed marks E and M.

WILL: Ebenezer Blackiston dated Mar 15 1771 probated Apr 6 1772 Will Book 6 p 32. wife Henrietta, sons Stephen, Michael, James, Ebenezer, and Joseph.

Ebenezer Blackiston and Mary Maxwell were married on 14 Apr 1737 in Kent County, Maryland. **Mary Maxwell**, daughter of Robert Maxfield and Ann Park, born about Aug 1703 in Kent County, Maryland. She was christened on 15 Aug 1703 in Saint Paul's Parish, Kent County, Maryland.

DEED: JS 22 p 158 names Mary Blackiston as dau of Thomas and Ann and sister of Elizabeth Maxwell.

Ebenezer Blackiston and Mary Maxwell had the following children:

+82   i. **Ebenezer Blackiston**, born abt 1738.

+83   ii. **Stephen Blackiston**, born abt 1720; married Sarah Miller; died 20 Jul 1797, Kent County, Maryland.

+84   iii. **James Blackiston**, born 10 Jul 1744, Kent County, Maryland; married Catherine Kennard, 10 Jan 1769, Kent County, Maryland; married Catherine Baird, abt 1775; married Jemima Ford, 5 Dec 1807, Cecil County, Maryland; died 12 Sep 1816, Kent County, Maryland.

Ebenezer Blackiston and Hannahretta Mahon were married after 1755. **Hannahretta Mahon**, daughter of Thomas Mahon and Mary Moore, was born on 1 Oct 1725 in Saint Paul's Parish, Kent County, Maryland. She died after 1794 at the age of 69. She is called Hannah in her father's will. In his accounts she is said to have married Bartholomew Garnett Accts 21 p 165. In her husband's accounts she is called Hannahretta. She married 1st Bartholomew Garnett who died Jul 21 1755, 2nd to Ebenezer Blackiston, 3rd to Matthew Richardson.

DEED: DD p 159 Oct 21 1765 Ebenezer Blackistone and Hannahrietta and Nathaniel Ricketts and Ann, and Amelia Sophiah Charlotta Ricketts. whereas Thomas Mahon late of Kent Deceased by his last will and testament bearing date of Oct 3 1742 divided 200 acres called Queen Charlton 3 daus Henrietta, Ann and Amelia Sophia Charlotta. Amelia was a widow. divides land of their father, dau Mary relinquished her right to land for land called Quakers Neck. adj. Daniel Torrell's Land bought of James Wroth of the Queen Charlton all signed except Ebenezer.

DEED: Henrietta Richardson conveys 66 2/3 acres of Queen Charlton to her son Joseph Blackiston. BC #4 p 129 Oct 3 1794.Kent Co MD

Hannahretta moved to Charles Co MD Apr 6 1772 per Mrs. Mary Abel. Maryland Genealogies (Blackiston) p. 67-68 discusses her family and corrects genealogy of her husband and son.

Ebenezer Blackiston and Hannahretta Mahon had the following children:

+85   i. **Private Michael Blackiston**, born abt 1758; married Dorothy Wilcox; died 19 Dec 1806, Queen Anne County, Maryland.

+86   ii. **Corporal Joseph Blackiston**, born 17 Feb 1760, Saint Paul's Parish, Kent County, Maryland; married Mary Stephens, abt 1780; died aft 1797, New Castle County, Delaware.

52. **Mary Blackiston** (John-4, John-3, George-2, Marmaduke-1) born about 1708. Mary Blackiston and Henry Covington were married in 1712 in Queen Annes County, Maryland. **Henry Covington** was born in 1693. He died in 1744 at the age of 51.

53. Benjamin Blackiston (John-4, John-3, George-2, Marmaduke-1) born about 1710. He died about Dec 1760 at the age of 50 in Kent County, Maryland.

WILL: Benjamin Blackiston date May 3 1758 and proved Dec 23 1760. bequeaths large landed estate lying in Kent and Queen Anne Co. and mentions wife Sarah and sons John, William, and George (minor), his daughters Sarah Comegys, Ann Spearman and Priscilla Blackiston and grandchildren Benjamin, Richard, and Ebenezer sons of his son John. wife and son William executors.

His descendants are mentioned in Maryland Genealogies pp 63f and in Colonial Families III:2. He inherited land of his father and received 2,255 acres in Queen Annes Co on Jun 14 1733 from Lord Baltimore and called the whole "Deer Park". Here the Blackiston Cross Road's village and Blackiston's Chapel were built (now Delaware).

Benjamin Blackiston and Sarah Strong were married on 27 Feb 1732 in Kent County, Maryland. **Sarah Strong** born about 1710. She died in Jan 1764 at the age of 54 in Kent County, Maryland.

WILL: Sarah Blackiston date Jan 8 and proved Jan 21 1764. mentions son George, her granddau. Sarah Comegys, her grandson, John Thormond and granddau. Ann Worrell.

Her maiden name was given as Joyce which comes from Hodges lists of marriages from other sources. However she could not be the daughter Sarah Blackiston of Thomas Joyce's will who died 1712. Her maiden name of Strong also comes from a Wroth document written in 1908

Benjamin Blackiston and Sarah Strong had the following children:

+87   i.   **Ebenezer Blackiston**, born 21 Sep 1728, Shrewsbury, Kent County, Maryland; married Ann Wild, bef 1779.

+88   ii.   **William Blackiston**, born abt 1733; married Ann Spencer; died abt Jan 1775, Kent County, Maryland.

+89   iii.   **John Blackiston**, born abt 1735; married Frances Stewart; died 21 Dec 1774, Kent County, Maryland.

+90   iv.   **Sarah Blackiston**, born abt 1737; married Bartus Comegys, bef 1760; died Jan 1764.

+91   v.   **Ann Blackiston**, born abt 1739; married William Spearman, bef 1760.

+92   vi.   **Priscilla Blackiston**, born 24 Oct 1741, Kent County, Maryland; married Simon Worrell, abt 1760; married Kinvin Wroth, 23 Sep 1773, Kent County, Maryland; died 10 Apr 1812, Kent County, Maryland.

+93   vii.   **George Blackiston**, born 30 Apr 1744, Deer Park, Queen Annes County, Maryland; married Martha Redgrave, abt 1765; died 31 Aug 1778, Duck Creek, Kent County, Delaware.

54. Michael Blackiston (John-4, John-3, George-2, Marmaduke-1) born about 2 Dec 1711. He was christened on 2 Dec 1711 in Kent County, Maryland. He died about Mar 1758 at the age of 46 in Kent County, Maryland. He was listed in the Maryland Genealogies as the son of John. His children mentioned in Maryland Genealogies p. 63 He owned Boxley.

MARRIAGE: date of Dec 8 17--, date partly obliterated.

DEED: IS 23 p 45 Thomas, William, and Michael Blackiston 150 acres called Boxley divided equally according to their deceased's father (John's) will. Sep 17 1740.

WILL: Michael Blackiston date Oct 24 1757 and probated Mar 2 1758. names wife Ann sons William, Michael, and John, and dau. Sarah, and provides that the residue of his personal estate be divided among all my children at majority.

Historical House of Boxley Near Rock Hall c. 1758 Boxley, a 300 acre parcel of land, was acquired by Ebenezer Blackiston, a planter from Cecil County in 1674. It had previously been owned by Laurence Symonds and William Davis. The Blackiston family retained ownership for over a hundred years, as it passed from one family member to another. In the mid 18th Century, Michael Blackiston (grandson of Ebenezer) commenced the construction of his brick dwelling house. Although a typical 1-1/2 story, hall-parlor plan, Boxley possesses a few features which make it different from others. It lacks a basement and is built relatively close to the ground, like Marrowbone (K-179). Its south facade is laid in Flemish bond with glazed headers and the two windows and door have segmental arches above. Common bond exists on the other three walls, but on the west gable a little lower than the cornice level, there are two glazed diamonds flanking the chimney. There is a tiny window to light a closet and sloped weatherings at roof level. Michael Blackiston left his mark on the building, as he scratched his cypher in a brick on the facade. When Michael Blackiston wrote his will, a year before his death in 1758, he left the 200 acre farm to his wife for her lifetime and then it was to go to William, his son (his namesake, Michael, received half of Lot 13 in Chestertown).

Michael Blackiston and Ann Bradshaw were married on 8 Dec in Saint Paul's Parish, Kent County, Maryland. **Ann Bradshaw** born about 1711. She died about Dec 1771 at the age of 60 in Kent County, Maryland.

WILL: Ann Blakiston date Sep 29 1771 and proved Dec 7 1771. dau. Sarah and Ann, son John, grandchildren Richard and Ann Blackiston and leaves the residue among all my children.

Michael Blackiston and Ann Bradshaw had the following children:

94   i. **William Blackiston** was born on 27 Oct 1737 in Kent County, Maryland, USA. He died in 1763 at the age of 26.

+95   ii. **Michael Blackiston**, born 24 Sep 1738, Saint Pauls Parish, Kent, Maryland, British America; married Rachel ; died bef 1771.

96   iii. **Sarah Blackiston** was born on 22 Jul 1741 in Saint Pauls Parish, Kent County, Maryland. She died about Sep 1797 at the age of 56 in Kent County, Maryland. WILL: Sarah Blackiston date Oct. 13, 1794 proved Sep 19, 1797 WB 7 p. 578 names niece Sarah Blackiston dau of my brother James, my niece Ann Brice when she is 16, 2 nephews Benjamin and James Brice. remainder to niece Sarah Brice.

97   iv. **John Blackiston** was born on 14 May 1743 in Saint Pauls Parish, Kent County, Maryland. He died before 1777 at the age of 34 in Kent County Md. Estate of John Blackiston names George Blackiston as administrator. Kindred listed are Ann Brice and Sarah Blackiston. Creditors John Bradsha. March 19, 1777. Debtors included James Blackiston 68 lbs. 2 0 (out of total 86lbs) signed George Blakiston. Inv 399

+98   v. **James Blackiston**, born 28 Nov 1746, Saint Pauls Parish, Kent County, Maryland; married Priscilla Bradshaw; died 16 Nov 1822, Fayette County, Pennsylvania.

99   vi. **George Blackiston** was born on 2 Jan 1749 in Saint Pauls Parish, Kent, Maryland. He died about Apr 1787 at the age of 38 in Kent County, Maryland. WILL: George Blackiston of Kent Co to my two sisters Sarah Blackiston and Ann Brice all my estate. date June 13, 1778, proved Apr 13, 1787. WB 7 p 189

+100   vii. **Judith Ann Blackiston**, born 28 Mar 1750, Saint Pauls Parish, Kent County, Maryland; married William Brice; died bef Dec 1795, Kent County, Maryland.

101   viii. **Richard Blackiston** was born on 4 Mar 1757 in Saint Pauls Parish, Kent County, Maryland. DEED: Richard Blackiston of Kent Co sold for 150 Lbs. on Oct 13, 1797 to Nathan Hatcheson of the county and State aforesaid, Farmer of the other part a tract of Land called Providence lying bounded from the beginning of a tract of land called Hope's Choice and running with that tract South-East thirty perches then North twenty-seven degrees east twenty-six perches to a tract of land called Chance then with that tract North 55 perches to a bounded stone marked T.V. it being a corner stone of the Tract of land called Pages Farm then with that tract West 43 ½ perches to a stone then south 63 perches to the aforesaid Tract called Hicks Choice then with that tract to the beginning. containing twenty acres more Witness Phil Reed. Richard Blackiston Recorded October 16 1797

55. William Blackiston (John-4, John-3, George-2, Marmaduke-1) born about 1713. He died in 1758 at the age of 45 in Kent County, Delaware. He received 50 acres Boxley from his father and bought 50 acres from his brother Ebenezer. He sold these 100 acres to his brother Michael in 1742. His children mentioned in Maryland Genealogies p. 62 His lineage is given in the American Families by Burke p. 2565.

DEED: William Blackiston and Ann his wife convey to Michael of the same county 100 acres of Boxley, near Swan Creek, in Kent Co (Book IS no 24 p 71).

DEED: William Blackiston of Kent Co on Delaware, bought a tract of 200 acres on Longford's Bay call New Key from John Hanmer Dec 12 1745 (Vol IS no 25 p 352),

DEED: William Blackiston of Kent Co, upon Delaware and Ann his wife sold to John Ringgold of Kent Co 200 acres called New Key purchased of John Hanmer Dec 12 1745 (DB IS no 26 p 71).

DEED: John Scott, late of Kent Co, DE but now of Orange Co, VA sold to William Blakiston of Kent Co, DE part of a tract called Chester on Duck Creek.

ESTATE: 1758 committed to John Pleasanton since his widow Mary having renounced her right to administer. (Dover Lib. K, p 180).

William Blackiston and Ann Glenn were married on 5 Feb 1736 in Saint Paul's Parish, Kent, Maryland, British America. **Ann Glenn**, daughter of Jacob Alexander Glen and Anna Hanson, was born on 4 Oct 1714 in Saint Paul's Parish, Kent County, Maryland. She died in 1750 or 1755 at the age of 36 in Delaware. She is the dau of Jacob Glenn. She was living on Feb 28 1750 when she signed deed (Dover Lib O p 83) but.

William Blackiston and Ann Glenn had the following child:

+102   i. **Presley Blackiston**, born 1741; married Sarah Warnock; died 4 Apr 1819, Philadelphia, Pennsylvania.

William Blackiston and Mary Courtney were married about 1755 in Kent County, Delaware. **Mary Courtney** born about 1720. She was the widow of Thomas Williams when she married William Blackiston as his second wife. They married between Aug 1755 and May 1756 (Dover Records).

57. **William Blackiston Jr.** (William-4, Ebenezer-3, George-2, Marmaduke-1) born about 1703. There is a William Blackiston Jr. of St. Paul's Parish who committed fornication with Martha Jarvis and begat a bastard child. Found guilty on Nov 10 1726. A William Jr was of age by 1721.

William Blackiston and Martha Jarvis had the following child:

103   i. **Blackiston** born about 1726. Bastard child per Court record. Name and sex not given.

58. Ann Blackiston (William-4, Ebenezer-3, George-2, Marmaduke-1) born about 1704. She died after 1737 at the age of 33. Her father's will of 1737 calls her Ann Miller. She may have first married a Mr. Lewis as Thomas Lewis says his mother is the wife of Old Arthur Miller.

Ann Blackiston and Arthur Miller were married before 1737. **Arthur Miller**, son of Michael Miller and Martha Wickes, born about 1700. He died about Dec 1739 at the age of 39 in Kent County, Maryland.

WILL: Arthur Miller will dated Sep 5 1739 and proved Dec. 15 1739 to son Arthur tracts called Crawfords and Coopers Freehold in Kent Island. Exec brother Michael Miller witnesses Prideaux Blackiston, Mary Blackiston, Thomas Hynson WB 22 p. 127. estate record Apr 15 1740 next of kin noted Nathaniel Miller, Samuel Miller, admin. Michell Miller. Inv. 25 p. 84. [Prideaux Blackiston was his brother in law and Mary Blackiston was her sister.]

Maryland Genealogies on the Blackistons said he died 1739 and had son Arthur Miller (named in grandfather's will.) A Arthur Miller was mentioned in the will of John Moore 1724 (he purchased land of Arthur)

Arthur Miller and Ann Blackiston had the following children:

104	i.	**Arthur Miller Jr.** born about 1726. He died after 1773 at the age of 47. There is an Arthur Miller who was age 47 in 1773 in a dep. Kent Co xxiii p. 253.
+105	ii.	**Martha Miller**, born abt 1740; married Nathaniel Hatcheson, abt 1759, Saint Paul's Parish, Kent County, Maryland.

61. Ebenezer Blackiston (William-4, Ebenezer-3, George-2, Marmaduke-1) born about 1720. He died about 1777 at the age of 57 in Kent County, Maryland. MARRIAGE: married before Oct 1761 when the will of her father was probated and she is called "daughter Mary, wife of Ebenezer Blackiston".

ESTATE: Ebenezer Blackiston sureties on estate Thomas Medford and Marmaduke Medford. Nov 14 1777 Mary Blackiston widow gave bond in L1000 sterling (Adm. Bond Vol 6 p 32)

Ebenezer Blackiston and Mary Medford were married. **Mary Medford**, daughter of George Medford and Jane Tilden, was born on 4 Dec 1737 in Shrewsbury, Kent County, Maryland. She died about May 1780 at the age of 42 in Kent County, Maryland.

WILL: Mary Blackiston probated Nov 12 1780. dau Mary sons George and Ebenezer and her brother Marmaduke Medford. Account 2368 in 1791 Addl Account recorded.

Marmaduke Medford executor of estate of Mary Blackiston late of Kent Co. names John Gale who married Mary Blackiston of the decd daughters and George W. Blackiston one of the decd children.

Ebenezer Blackiston and Mary Medford had the following children:

106	i.	**Ebenezer Blackiston** born about 1759 in Kent County, Maryland.
107	ii.	**George W Blackiston** born about 1760.
+108	iii.	**Mary Blackiston**, born 29 Apr 1763, Saint Paul's Parish, Kent County, Maryland; married John Gale, bef 1791.

62. **Rosamond Blackiston** (William-4, Ebenezer-3, George-2, Marmaduke-1) born about 1730 in Kent County, Maryland. She died before 1771 at the age of 41.

BIRTH: Estimated but believed to by dau of 2nd wife Ann Moore not 1st wife Ann Park.

She was first married to John Rasin and then 2nd to Abraham Rasin. She was the second wife of John Rasin by 1753 but the first wife of Abraham Rasin by Jun 1763 having children by both men.

ESTATE: John Rasin Adm. Accts Vol 6 p 277-9 John Rasin, dec'd, Rosa Rasin admin. July 17 1762, Vol 6 p 377-8 Abraham and Rosa Rasin his wife admin. of John Rasin estate, Abraham called a Quaker and took affirmation, Rosa sworn in. Adm. Bond Vol 5 p 282 Rosa Rasin, Rasin Gale, McCaul Medford bond for 3000 pds March 17 1761.

Rosamond Blackiston and John Rasin were married after 1750 in Kent County, Maryland. **John Rasin**, son of Philip Rasin and Elizabeth Thackston, was born on 30 Jul 1713 in Kent County, Maryland. He died about Mar 1761 at the age of 47 in Kent County, Maryland.

BIRTH: Cecil Quaker Meeting, John son of Philip and Elizabeth was born 30th 7th mo. 1713.

MARRIAGE: 1st Margaret Spalden ca 1734
MARRIAGE: 2nd Rosamond Blackiston ca 1753

DEPOSITION: John Rasin age 39 in 1753 DB 7 p 296 100 acres Intermixt

He is mentioned in the will of his aunt Mary (widow of Thomas Rasin) dated Dec 17 1759.

ESTATE: Rosa Rasin, Rasin Gale, McCaul Medford bond for 3000 pds March 17 1761. (Admin. Bonds Vol 5 p 282) John Rasin inventory dated May 21 1761 totals 915 pds, nearest kin listed as Joseph Rasin, Philip Rasin. admin. May 27 1762. (Inv. Accts. Vol 5 p 136-8) Acct Distr. Vol 6 p 277-9 John Rasin, dec'd, Rosa Rasin admin. July 17 1762 total estate 915 pds, lists debts and credits, cash due to William Rasin 27 pds. Acct Distr. Vol 6 p 377-8 Abraham and Rosa Rasin his wife admin. of John Rasin estate, Abraham called a Quaker and took affirmation, Rosa sworn in. MD G.R.C. 1940 S1 vol. 67 was given in the DAR library.

John Rasin and Rosamond Blackiston had the following children:

109   i. **Mary Rasin** born about 1755. She died about Dec 1805 at the age of 50 in Kent County, Maryland. WILL: Mary Rasin date Oct 6 1798 prob. Dec 3 1805 WB 8 p 283. sisters' children Elizabeth and Ann Wroth and Martha Willis (minors), brother William B Rasin's dau Ann, cousin Joseph Rasin Jr., brother Warner Rasin dau Eliz., sister-in-law Araminta Rasin, brother's son Thomas Jr., sister Ann Willis, mother in law Jane Gale (stepmother), sister Ann Rasin, nephew John Rasin, cousin Samuel Rasin, witness Thomas Rasin 3rd, Mary Field, Ann Rasin. She is not the dau Mary born 1772 to Abraham and Jane since she calls Jane Gale her mother in law (stepmother).

+110   ii. **Ann Rasin**, born abt 1757; married John R. Willis.

+111   iii. **Captain William Blackiston Rasin**, born abt 1760, Kent County, Maryland; married Martha Wroth, 1787, Kent County, Maryland; died abt Aug 1810, Worton, Kent County, Maryland.

Rosamond Blackiston and Abraham Rasin were married before Jun 1763 in Kent County, Maryland. **Abraham Rasin**, son of Thomas Rasin and Mary Warner, was born on 21 Jan 1725 in Kent County, Maryland. He died on 26 Sep 1777 at the age of 52 in Kent County, Maryland.

BIRTH: Cecil Monthly Meeting. Abraham Rasin son of Thomas Rasin and Mary his wife was born the 21st day of the 11th month in the year 1725.

Batchelor's List in Shrewsbury Parish July 1758: 25 years and older includes William Blaxton and Abraham Rasin among others.

MARRIAGE: Cecil Quaker Meeting Minutes p 234 states Abraham Rasin made public confession June 1763 for marrying outside the church. "Dear Friends, whereon I was amongst the people called Quaker and am convinced of that doctrine by the said people maintained according to faither but not keeping close to those principles I have brought a reproach in truth by taking a wife not educated amongst friends and by going to the hireling priest therefore I take the whole reproach to myself and clear friends and hope for the future my life and conduct through divine assistance may be such as may recommend me to the Society of friends. Abraham Rasin" (Rosa Rasin named as wife and admin. of John Rasin on July 17 1762, but by Aug 2 1764 was referred to as Rosa administratix of John Rasin and wife of Abraham Rasin)

DEATH: Cecil Monthly Meeting. Abraham Rasin departed this life the 26th day of the 6th month 1777. He was a member of Cisel (Cecil) meeting.

WILL: Abraham Rasin will date May 4 1777 prob. Nov 14 1777 WB 6 p 38 Abraham Rasin wife Jane, dau Mary and Sarah Rasin, sons Thomas and Warner Rasin (minors), in care of Joshua Lamb, Thomas Bowers, Samuel Wallis and George Lamb, they to give a yearly account to Cecil Meeting. Warner under 21 to have land Standley's Hope, Pool, Howard's Lott, Friendship, Thomas to receive Fair Promise, Cammel's Farm, 50 acres bought of John Crow, Mary to have Fish Hall exec. wife Jane Rasin, witness Joseph Rasin, Thomas Corse, Daniel Lamb.

Abraham Rasin and Rosamond Blackiston had the following child:

+112   i.   **Warner Rasin**, born 2 Sep 1763, Kent County, Maryland; married Ann Miflin; married Margaret Wilkerson; died 4 Nov 1804, Kent County, Maryland.

63. **Hance Blackiston** (William-4, Ebenezer-3, George-2, Marmaduke-1) was born in 1737 in Kent County, Maryland. He died about Jan 1772 at the age of 35 in Kent County, Maryland.

WILL: Hance Blackiston will date Dec 24 1771 proved Jan 22 1772 WB 38 p 169 whole estate to wife Ann, witnesses John Moore, Augustine Moore.

It appears that Hance is the unborn child named in William's will. Note the reference to the Moore family in William's will and in Hance's will. Others have said Ann Moore married Hance Blackistone. However I believe Ann is his mother, based on chronology she was too old to be his wife and other records insinuate this mother connection. Hance did marry an Ann but not same one.

Hance Blackiston and Ann were married about 1768. **Ann** born about 1737. She died after 1767 at the age of 30. From Mrs. Mary Abel, Hans Blackistone m. Ann Christfield, widow of Arthur Christfield March 18 1769 MD Balance of Distribution Bk 5 p 175.

64. **Rosamond Blackiston** (Ebenezer-4, Ebenezer-3, George-2, Marmaduke-1) was born in 1712. She died on 30 Mar 1790 at the age of 78. Mrs. Rose Wilmer of Kent Co age 40 years in 1762 Chancery DD No. J p. 238. She married in 1733 so the age given here of 40 must be wrong.

WILL: Rose Wilmer of Kent Co To my son Lambert Wilmer all that tenement which is erected a tan yard, which land is bounded as follows beginning at the gate standing in the line dividing the land between land of Mr. Joseph Wickes and myself and running with the said line to the land of the late Mr. Ebenezer Blackiston then with the line of Mr. Blackiston to the land of Mr. Beal Bordleys then with Mr. Bordley's line until it intersects the main road called the Farley road, then with the road to the gate where it meets the road going from my house to Saint Pauls Parish Church then with said road to the beginning. To my son William Wilmer two seats in a pew in the new part of St. Pauls Parish Church and my part of the stills. To my dau. Mary Wilmer my negro man Sam and a feather bed. To my dau. Margaret Wilmer my negro man Hark and negro girl Hannah and a feather bed. To my dau. Frances Wilmer a negro woman Hen and her increase, my negro boy Sam and a feather bed. My negro woman Jane I give to my 2 daughters Margaret Wilmer and Frances Wilmer. To my 3 daughters Mary, Margaret and Frances my clock and all my silver spoons. I give my wearing apparel to my 4 daughters Mary, Margaret, Frances, and Martha. Remainder of estate to my daughters Mary Wilmer, Margaret Wilmer, Frances Wilmer and Martha Bond. My estate be taken into possession immediately after my death without administration. My sons in law William Ringgold, James Frisby, and Richard Miller to see that my will is fulfilled. Exec. Not Given. Witnesses James Williamson, William Ringgold son of William Jr., Ann Williamson. Written Oct. 19, 1785 Proved May 14, 1790 p. 280

Rosamond Blackiston and William Wilmer were married on 7 Feb 1733. **William Wilmer**, son of Simon Wilmer and Dorcas Hynson, born about 1712. He died in 1770 at the age of 58.

William Wilmer and Rosamond Blackiston had the following children:

+113	i.	**Blackiston Wilmer**, born 18 Sep 1742, Kent County, Maryland; married Sarah Williamson, 19 Feb 1778; died 31 Dec 1813, Kent County, Maryland.
+114	ii.	**Sarah Wilmer**, born abt 1743; married William Ringgold.
115	iii.	**Dorcas Wilmer** born about 1745.
+116	iv.	**Mary Wilmer**, born abt 1730; married William Ringgold.

Sixth Generation

72. **Nehemiah Herbert Blackiston** (John-5, John-4, Nehemiah-3, John-2, Marmaduke-1) was born before 1755. He died about Jun 1816 at the age of 61 in Saint Mary's County, Maryland.

Nehemiah Herbert Blackiston and Mary Cheseldine were married on 30 Jan 1772. **Mary Cheseldine** was born before 1755. She died before 1800 at the age of 45. dau of Kenelm and Chloe Cheseldine. He was made a prisoner and suffered losses by depredation; Took Oath of Allegiance sourced from Chronicles of St Mary's per Archives of Maryland V 47, 1781, PP 295-296

Nehemiah Herbert Blackiston and Mary Cheseldine had the following children:

+117   i. **George Blackiston**, born 28 Nov 1780; married Rebecca Goldsmith, abt 18 Jan 1813, Saint Mary's County, Maryland; died 7 Nov 1842, Saint Mary's County, Maryland.

118   ii. **John Blackiston** was born in 1806. He died on 14 Feb 1863 at the age of 57. He was buried in All Saints Episcopal Church Cemetery, St. Mary's, Maryland.

Nehemiah Herbert Blackiston and Eleanor Gardiner Hebb were married in Aug 1801. **Eleanor Gardiner Hebb** born about 1780. Colonel Nehemiah Herbert Blackistone lived on Blackistone Island (today it is called St. Clement's Island, the name it was called in 1634) During the Rev. War he was a private, St. Mary's County Militia, 1777. He took the Oath of Allegiance in 1778. He was elected to a General Committee in St. Mary's County in accordance with the resolves of the Continental Congress in 1775. He served on the Committee of Safety in 1774. He was captured by the British and his home was burned on 16 Jun 1781 because of his rebellious sympathies. When he returned home he put in a claim for 281 lbs. as property lost to him by the British. It is family history that John Colton came to live in the neighborhood and liked to play cards. Col. Nehemiah Herbert Blackistone sat in front of a large mantel mirror and John kept reading his cards. Col. Nehemiah Herbert Blackistone lost all personal property, horses, land and house. All hands had to scatter and live where they could find a roof. The affair was considered a great tragic event.

The famous Blackistone Lighthouse burned in 1956 but a replica was rebuilt in 2008.

74. **Pvt Prideaux Blackiston (Jr)** (Prideaux-5, John-4, John-3, George-2, Marmaduke-1) was born before 1751. He died on 11 Feb 1778 at the age of 27 in Valley Forge, Chester County, Pennsylvania. He is proven to be the son of Prideaux and grandson of John by 1775 deed, but who is his mother and what is birth year. The DAR states he was born ca 1751 and died 1778 at Valley Forge during the horrible winter encampment of Washington's troops.

DEED: Prideaux Blakiston of Kent Co conveys to John Page of the same county 44 acres part of Boxley, devised by my grandfather John Blackiston to my father Prideaux Blackiston Jan 25 1775 Wife Bridgett acknowledged her consent. Deed DD no. 5 p. 17 Kent Co Deeds.

SERVICE: Predox Blackiston Private signed for duration of war. served in Capt. Benjamin Harrison's Co 13th Virginia Regiment of Foot, commanded by Col. William Russell. NARA Compiled Service Records. Pridux Blackiston payroll 1778. Predox Blackiston muster roll Sep 6 1777 for August 1777, Oct 10 for Sep 1777, Dec 25 1777 for 9 months 6 days time of service pay of 6 2/3 dollars per month. Other pays Oct, Nov. etc., spelled as Predox Blaxston in Jan 1778, Predox Blockston in Jan 1778 pay receipt. March 1778 receipt says he died Feb. 11 1778. Total Pay as of 1783 for Pridox Blackson sol inf. for Virginia Continental Line by whom received George Rice Sep 12 1783 16 pds 13.4

BOUNTY LAND: Bounty land application by George Shilling for his parents George and Bridget who had first married Priticks Blackston and was the widow who then married second husband George Shilling who also served (Col. Morgan's Rifle comp) Widow is Biddy Shilling. Son George Shilling says his father George died March 1798, and Biddy died Feb 10, 1845. His mother was married to Prideaux who died during war and she married his father 1780. In 1846 Samuel Blackston of Mercer gave oath that he was 71 years old and Priticks Blackston ad Biddy Shilling were married before the Rev War and he died in 1776 at Philadelphia and Biddy married George Shilling in 1780 and he was a first sergeant and died in 1798 and left only son George as heir #R9508

The List of those killed at Valley Forge include his name: Prideaux Blackiston. Private 13th Virginia, Brigade: 1st Virginia, Division: 5th, Company: Capt. Benjamin Harrison, DEC 1777: Sick Present, Died February 11, 1778 ID: VA25736 Remarks: He born about 1751 in Yohogania Co., VA. Prideaux (his Mother's surname) was married to married to Bridget "Biddy" Shrader. After Prideaux Blackiston died at Valley Forge she married another Rev. War soldier, George Shilling in 1780 & he died March 1798. Pvt Prideaux Blackiston (Jr) and Bridget "Biddy" Shrader were married before Jan 1775. **Bridget "Biddy" Shrader** born about 1756. She died on 10 Feb 1845 at the age of 89. George Shilling decd $200 bond date Aug 28 1798 to Bridget Shillling, James1 Blackburn and Samuel Glasgow. bk 73 p 58 Biddy Shilling of South Huntingdon, Westmoreland PA was listed as 26-44y so 1756-1774 birth.

Prideaux Blackiston and Bridget Shrader had the following child:

> 119   i.   **Samuel Blackiston** was born on 19 Oct 1775 in Yohogania, Virginia, British America. He died on 3 Jan 1849 at the age of 73 in Lackawannock, Mercer, Pennsylvania. **WILL: Samuel Blackston** Mercer Will Date 4 Jun 1844 Probate Date Jan 29 1849 Probate Place Mercer, Pennsylvania, USA Item Description Will Books, Vol 1-3

p216-217 1804-1853 names wife Ann Blackston, daughter Nancy Smith, granddau Martha Ann Blackston, four sons James, George, John and Jones. George Hamilton and son James Blackston executors. Proved Jan 29 1849

82. Ebenezer Blackiston (Ebenezer-5, John-4, John-3, George-2, Marmaduke-1) born about 1738.

Ebenezer Blackeston – Males: 1-10y-15y, 1-26-44y, 1-45+; Females: 1-16-25y, 1-45+ 1800; Census Place: Duck Creek Hundred, Kent, Delaware; Series: M32; Roll: 4; Page: 15; Image: 15; Family History Library Film: 6413

83. Stephen Blackiston (Ebenezer-5, John-4, John-3, George-2, Marmaduke-1) born about 1740. He died on 20 Jul 1797 at the age of 37 in Kent County, Maryland. His lands called "Hinchenham" containing 116 acres "which my father died possessed of" per son Daniels 1802 will. He served in Revolution, per SAR Patriot Index. He had children. Rebecca m. John Glanville, John, Daniel Blackston m. Elizabeth Smith Nov. 3 1796, Milcah, Editha, Samuel, Benjamin, Hester, Richard, Anna, and Caroline, and Sarah. Stephen Blackiston witnessed will of John Bradshaw written 1788 who named a dau. Priscilla Blackiston and a granddau. Priscilla Miller.

Stephen Blackiston and Sarah Miller were married. **Sarah Miller** born about 1745. She died about Nov 1807 at the age of 62 in Kent County, Maryland.

WILL: Sary Blackiston dated Oct. 6 1805 proved Nov. 16 1807 to dau. Adah, upon settlement of husband's estate to son Richard, dau. Anna, dau. Milcah, dau. Hessy. exec. dau. Milcah (John Crouch brought will forward). She was awarded guardianship of Samuel, Hester, Richard, Anna, and Caroline.

Stephen Blackiston and Sarah Miller had the following children:

+120	i.	**Daniel Blackiston**, born abt 1775; married Elizabeth Smith, 3 Nov 1796; died abt Apr 1807, Kent County, Maryland.
121	ii.	**Samuel Blackiston**.
122	iii.	**John Blackiston**.
123	iv.	**Richard Blackiston** born about 1780.
+124	v.	**Sarah Blackiston**, born abt 1780; married John Ashley, 24 Dec 1798, Kent County, Maryland.
125	vi.	**Adah Blackiston** born about 1784.
+126	vii.	**Milcah Blackiston**, born abt 1785; married Ebenezer Blackiston, abt 1805; died 18 Jan 1840.
127	viii.	**Hester Blackiston** born about 1786.
128	ix.	**Caroline Blackiston**.
129	x.	**Benjamin Blackiston**.

84. James Blackiston (Ebenezer-5, John-4, John-3, George-2, Marmaduke-1) was born on 10 Jul 1744 in Kent County, Maryland. He died on 12 Sep 1816 at the age of 72 in Kent County, Maryland. He was buried in Shrewsbury Ch., Kent County, Maryland. The DAR has marked his grave. He was married three times.

WILL: date Feb 20 1815 pro Sep 18 1816 James Blackiston wife Jemima 1/3 estate children Kennard $100, Ebenezer $500, children of my son James lately dec'd $100 Ann Elizabeth, William Henry and any child born after me 1/3 when they arrive at age. To Ann Elizabeth, William Henry and child all residue of my personal estate. If either of my children Ann E. or William H. die, then to survivor of the surviving children born to me by my wife Jemima. If all my children by my said wife die then to my grandchildren: James, Thomas, Mary, David, Catherine. (It appears that James and Thomas are sons by Kennard and Mary, David and Catherine are children by James.)

Hanson Old Kent p. 166. Chancery Court papers 2834.

TOMBSTONE: James Blackiston died Sep 12 1816 age 72y 2 months 2 days.

James Blackiston and Catherine Kennard were married on 10 Jan 1769 in Kent County, Maryland. **Catherine Kennard**, daughter of Nathaniel Kennard and Hannah , born about 1744 in Centreville, Kent County, Maryland. She died on 9 Oct 1773 at the age of 29 in Kent County, Maryland. She is the dau of Nathaniel Kennard. She died in childbirth. The first and second wife have often been confused and called Catherine Baird Kennard.

James Blackiston and Catherine Kennard had the following children:

+130	i.	**Kennard Blackiston**, born 24 Nov 1769, Kent County, Maryland; married Elizabeth Medford, 18 Jun 1799, Kent County, Maryland; died bef 1816.
131	ii.	**Mary Blackiston** was born on 3 Jan 1771 in Kent County, Maryland. her name is not in father's will.
+132	iii.	**Ebenezer Blackiston**, born 1 Jun 1772, Kent County, Maryland; married E. Lattice Combs, 2 Jul 1798, Lincoln County, Kentucky; died likely Kentucky.
+133	iv.	**James Blackiston Jr.**, born 9 Oct 1773, Kent County, Maryland; married Mary Crane, 25 Feb 1806, Kent County, Maryland; died 6 Feb 1814, Kent County, Maryland.

James Blackiston and Catherine Baird were married about 1775. **Catherine Baird** born about 1745. She died before Apr 1796 at the age of 51. She is the dau of Alexander Baird and Elizabeth Ellis. James had no children by her.

WILL: Alexander Baird died Apr 1792. administration mentions dau. Catherine Blackiston, who married James Blackiston.

Deed BC 3 p 499 shows her father was Alexander Baird and she had no issue by James Blackiston Jul 31 1793. she died before Apr 25 1796.

James Blackiston and Jemima Ford were married on 5 Dec 1807 in Cecil County, Maryland. **Jemima Ford** born about 1785. She died about Nov 1858 at the age of 73.

1820 MD Kent Co p 124 index p. 124
Jemima Blackiston 100000-10020-07 widow of James Sr. two females age 26-45y, 1 male under 10y, 1 female under 10y.

MARRIAGE: she remarried 2nd Frederick G. Briscoe Nov 26 1821 and 3rd John A. Naudan.

WILL: Jemima Nauda of Middletown, New Castle Co, DE Widow of John A. Naudain late of Cecil Co, deceased. I give to my son William Henry Blackiston of Kent Co for his natural life and no longer my real estate in Kent Co, all my tract of land known by the name of "Davis' Industry", and "The Forest Farm", and all the tract of wood land called "The Sixty Acre lot", or by whatsoever name may be known. The said William keeping all the premises in good order and repair and after his death to his lawful children (except his dau. Josephine Blackiston) to be equally divided and to their children per stirpes if any child is deceased with issue. Josephine excepted because provision made for her in item fourth. To my nephew Alfred C. Nowland of Cecil Co land in Cecil Co known by the name of "Worsell Manor" in trust for the benefit of my grandchildren of my deceased dau. Ann Elizabeth Naudain, late the wife of Doctor James S. Nauda of St. Georges Hundred, in New Castle Co aforesaid namely: Mary Louisa Naudain, James Blackiston Naudain, Alice Schee Naudain, Lydia Eddowes Naudain, and Mary Jemima Naudain. Alfred to collect and manage rents for benefit of grandchildren. At 21 each grandchild receives his or her full share. At the age of 21 of the youngest grandchild a deed for them as tenants in common to be executed. To Alfred C. Nowland all that certain brick messuage and lot of land situate in the village of Middletown, New Castle Co which John M. Smith and Hannah his wife by date Dec. 24, 1842 and recorded at New Castle Book L. Vol. 5 p. 265 deeded to me in fee simple, in trust for benefit during her minority of granddau. Anne Matilda Naudain, a child of my said deceased dau. Ann Elizabeth Naudain, late the wife of the said Doctor James S. Naudain. After Anne is 21, duly executed deed to be issued, if she die under 21 then held in trust for her brother and sisters. To Alfred C. Nowland all the dwelling house and lot of land in Middletown the remainder or reversion whereof in fee simple was granted to me by Maria Moody, by deed of date June 7, 1842 recorded at New Castle Book J. Vol. 5, p 384 in trust for my granddau. Josephine Blackiston aforesaid dau. of my son William. At 21 to be issued a deed, if she die without heirs then to children of William H. Blackiston. To Alfred C. Nowland in trust for my two granddaughters Anne Jemima Blackiston and Emma Blackiston, children of my said son William, all sums of money my said son

William owes me. To Alfred C. Nowland in trust of my granddau. Mary Jemima Naudain all sums of money which Doctor James S. Naudain owes me for rent and for money lent him. If she die under 21 then to her two sisters Anne Matilda Naudain and Lydia Eddowes Naudain. Neither my son William or Doctor James Naudain or any person related to the said doctor by consanguinity be appointed trustee or administrator. For any person attempting hindrance to this will, all provisions for that person are revoked. Exec. Alfred C. Nowland (revoked by 3rd codicil and replaced by David C. Blackiston). Witnesses Robert A. Cochrane, David McKee, William Wood. Written Apr. 3, 1844 Proved Nov. 11, 1858 p. 126 Kent Co Wills

1st Codicil Doctor James S. Naudain has reduced his debt to me by disposing of some furniture to me which I have attached a schedule. Nephew Alfred C. Naudain (should be Nowland) of Cecil Co named in will as trustee shall have every piece of furniture in trust for my grandchildren. Written Apr. 6, 1844. Witnesses Robert A. Cochrane, David McKee, William Wood
Schedule A pair linen sheets, one pair linen pillow cases, a Bolster case for Maria Louisa Naudain. A mahogany pier table with marble top, a pier looking glass and two mahogany pedal dining table now at William Henry Blackiston for James Blackiston Naudain. A pair mantel lamps, a pair mantel ornaments, a mantel looking glass at Ann McIntires, one pair plated candlesticks snuffers and tray, one tea set French china, now at Ann McIntires, two linen pillow cases, one pair linen sheets, one Bolster case and one pair venetian blinds for Ann Matilda Naudain. One mahogany toilet table, one mahogany wash stand, with marble top, now at Ann McIntires, two pair linen pillow cases, one pair linen sheets, one Bolster case, one calico bed quilt for Alice Schee Naudain. One Boston rocking chair, 8 Rush bottom chairs now at William Henry Blackiston, one set granite tea ware now at Ann McIntires, one maple bedstead and feather bed, one pair venetian blinds, one pair linen sheets, two pair pillow cases, one linen Bolster case for Lydia Eddowes Naudain. One Marseilles quilt, two damask table clothes, 6 damask napkins, 6 table napkins and cake cover, one pair linen sheets, two pair pillow cases, one linen Bolster case for Mary Jemima Naudain

Second Codicil Whereas the real estate belonging to my deceased dau. Ann Elizabeth Naudain (formerly Ann Elizabeth Blackiston) the same lying in New Castle appears to have been encumbered with debts due to John Richardson and William Richardson at the time of her death, therefore I have signed over a mortgage of James S. Naudain to John Richardson for the sum of $1,500 and to William Richardson a judgement bond to Jonathan Catlin and Catherine Justice for $1,000. John Richardson's bond against James S. Naudain and wife transferred to Alfred C. Nowland in trust recorded at New Castle in Mortgage Record E Vol 1 p. 406 Nov 20 1846 and a judgement bond from Jonathan Catlin and Catherine Justice for $1,000 given to me on Nov. 29, 1848 for the children of my deceased dau. (all named again). Two shares held by me in the Cantwells Bridge Navigation and Steam Boat Cos to Alfred in trust for my granddau. Mary Jemima Naudain. Written Dec. 9, 1848. Witnesses Robert A. Cochrane, David McKee, William Wood

Third Codicil Since the execution of my will my son William Henry Blackiston hath died leaving a widow Hannah Maria Blackiston and nine children, I therefore revoke the two farms for life called "Davis' Industry" and "The Forest Farm" and "The Sixty Acre Lot" and my executor shall sell the land and ½ of "The Sixty Acre Wood Lot" shall pay the debts due from my late son William and to save the home or mansion farm of my son in the Upper part of Kent then I authorize the sale of my said farms. Any surplus money to the said H. Maria Blackiston the widow and the following children of my said son William Henry Blackiston, Samuel Hepburn, Henry Curtis, Anna Jemima, Emma Hepburn, Slater Clay, Clara Leite, Lizzie and Mary Euginia Blackiston. I have omitted my granddau. Joseph(ine) Blackiston from the foregoing since I have made other provision for her in my will. An addition of woodland remaining about 30 acres I have to my H. Maria Blackiston and my grandchildren Samuel H., Henry Curtis, Josephine, Anna Jemima, Emma Hepburn, Slater Clay, Clara Leite, Lizzie, Mary Euginia Blackiston as tenants in common. I revoke the appointment of my nephew Alfred C. Nowland as trustee or executor and appoint my friend David C. Blackiston of Kent Co trustee and executor. Written July 16, 1853. Witnesses Charles Tatman Jr., Edward T. Wroth, Joshua F. Biddle

James Blackiston and Jemima Ford had the following children:

+134   i. **Ann Elizabeth Blackiston**, born abt 1810, Maryland; married James Schee Naudain, 3 Sep 1832, Cecil County, Maryland; died 20 Apr 1843, New Castle County, Delaware.

+135   ii. **William Henry Blackiston**, born abt 1814, Maryland; married Hannah Maria Hepburn; died 13 Sep 1853, Middletown, Delaware.

85. Private Michael Blackiston (Ebenezer-5, John-4, John-3, George-2, Marmaduke-1) was born before 1755. He died on 19 Dec 1806 at the age of 48 in Queen Anne County, Maryland. Chancery Record 4935 for Michael's Administration.

Chancery Record 4935 for Michael's Administration.

Michael Blackston Home in 1800 (City, County, State): Queen Anne's, Maryland
1 Male 45+, 2 males under 10y, 1 Female 26-44y, 2 females 10-15y 2 females under 10y
1800; Census Place: Queen Anne's, Maryland; Series: M32; Roll: 11; Page: 322; Image: 217; Family History Library Film: 193664

Dolly Blackison Home in 1810 (City, County, State): Queen Anne's, Maryland
1 Female 26-44y, 1 male 10-15y, 2 males under 10y, 2 female 10-15y, 1 female under 10y.
1810; Census Place: Queen Anne's, Maryland; Roll: 16; Page: 120; Image: 00067; Family History Library Film: 0193669

Private Michael Blackiston and Dorothy Wilcox were married. **Dorothy Wilcox** born about 1760. Dorothy Wilcox may not be the mother of the children.

Michael Blackiston and Dorothy Wilcox had the following children:

136   i.   **Michael Blackiston Jr** was born in 1782 in Maryland. He died after 1810 at the age of 28. He is not mentioned in the MD Genealogies as a son of Michael but he is listed as Jr. and living near him in 1800. Michael Blackston Jr Home in 1800: Queen Anne's, Maryland with 2 males 16-25y, 1 m 10-15y, 1 female 16-25y in 1800; Census Place: Queen Anne's, Maryland; Series: M32; Roll: 11; Page: 322; Image: 217; Family History Library Film: 193664

                 Michl Blackiston (Michael Jr) Home in 1810 Kent, Maryland 1 Male 26-44y, 1 male 16-25y, 1 male 10-15y; 1 Female 16-25y, in 1810; Census Place: Kent, Maryland; Roll: 14; Page: 876; Image: 00180; Family History Library Film: 0193667

+137   ii.   **Ebenezer Blackiston**, born 4 Jul 1784; married Milcah Blackiston, abt 1805; married Rachel Kearnes, 18 Feb 1841, Kent County, Maryland; died 30 Sep 1846, Kent County, Maryland.

+138   iii.   **James Blackiston**, born abt 1785; died bef 1846.

139   iv.   **Jabez Blackiston** born about 1792. He died after 1820 at the age of 28. Jabez Blackston Company: 35 Regt (Brown's) MD Militia. Rank Private Roll Box: 18 Microfilm Publication: M602

+140   v.   **Ann Blackiston**, born abt 1794; married Barbage; died bef 1850.

+141   vi.   **Harriet Blackiston**, born abt 1798; married Thomas Miller, 3 Sep 1818, Queen Annes County, Maryland; died bef 1850. Married 2nd **Joseph Blackiston**

+142   vii.   **Mary Blackiston**, born abt 1800; married Aaron Davis, 21 Feb 1820, Kent County, Maryland.

86. Corporal Joseph Blackiston (Ebenezer-5, John-4, John-3, George-2, Marmaduke-1) was born on 17 Feb 1760 in Saint Paul's Parish, Kent County, Maryland. He died after 1797 at the age of 37 in New Castle County, Delaware. All children of Joseph are not documented.

BIRTH: From the St. Paul's Parish Records, Joseph Blackston son of Ebenr and Hennaritta Blackston born Feb 17 1760.

SOLDIER: Amer. Rev. Patriot - In the Jun 1775 militia list he is listed under the First Co. of 13th Battalion commanded by Richard Graves. In the SAR records 4 people have joined under Crpl. Joseph Blackiston (and his wife Mary Stevens) who is said to have been a crpl in the MD Militia through son James.

MARRIAGE: ca 1780, can't find record.

TAX: 1783 Tax List. Joseph Blackston. Queen Charlton, pt, 66 1/2 acres. KE 1st District, p. 1. MSA S 1161-7-1 1/4/5/50

Joseph Blackston Home in 1790 (City, County, State): Kent, Maryland
4 males under 16, 1 male over 16y, 3 females.
1790; Census Place: Kent, Maryland; Series: M637; Roll: 3; Page: 332; Image: 563; Family History Library Film: 0568143

DEED: He sold the land in BC #4 p. 315

DEED: 1796. Joseph Blackiston and his wife Mary of New Castle Co, DE sold Queen Charlton to George Hanson. Jan 5 1796 Kent Co MD Deed BC 4 p 566.

DEED: Joseph Blackiston and wife Mary bought land in Appoquinimink Hundred, New Castle Co, DE in 1796. F3 p 249.

CENSUS: 1800 Joseph Blackiston is listed in Appoquinimink Hundred, New Castle Co DE.

DEED: 1808. Lewis Allfree for 195 pounds sold to Joseph Blackiston on Dec 23 1797 100 acres of land on the west side of the messuage or tract of land that the said Joseph now lives on, 168 pounds paid at the sealing of this deed and the remaining 27 pounds to be paid on the Jan 23 next. signed Lewis Allfree, witnesses James Blackiston, Jacob Allfree. We each assign over rite title interest claim to the within mentioned land all and everything thereunto belonging to Jared Rothwell. Oct 16 1797 signed Joseph Blackiston, witness Abraham Rothwell, James H. Caulk. Date Oct. 16 1799 Joseph's wife Mary made her mark. proved by witness James Blackiston in New Castle Court of Common Pleas May 1807, recorded May 24 1808. New Castle Co DE deed.

Other deed references given by Mrs. Mary Abel for this family are:
DEED: Robert Maxwell and his wife Anne and Thomas Ayres and his wife Elizabeth dau of aforesaid Robert and Anne 170 acres called Hintongin in Kent Co at the mouth of Tavern Creek and running with Swan Creek Date Aug 15 1738 JS #22 p 156,
DEED: Ebenezer and wife Mary Blackiston sell to William Blackiston 50 acres "Boxley" land belonging to his deceased father John Blackiston. Dated July 29 1741 JS #23 p 316f
DEED: George Garnett and wife Mary sell to William Apsley sell 230 acres "Hermitage" Dated Apr 4 1749 JS #26 p 195f
DEED: Ebenezer Blackiston and Hannarietta, Nathaniel Rickets and Ann, Amelia Sophiah Charlotte Ricketts, whereas Thomas Mahon late of Kent deceased in his last well dated Oct 3 1742 did devise 200 acreas of land called Queen Charlton equally between his daughters Henrietta, Ann and Amelia Sophia Charlotta, on condition that his daughter Mary if she made a choice of a parcel lying in Quaker Neck that the Mary would relinquish her rights which she did, the remaining three divided the land into 3. Dated Oct 21 1764 recorded Oct 21 1765 DD #2 p 159

DEED: Matthew Richardson and wife Henrietta sell 66 acres of Queen Charlton to Joseph Blackiston Date Oct 3 1794 BC #4 p 129
BC #4 p 315,
(This land was sold to Joseph by his mother in 1794)

DEATH: SAR application says he died 1808.

NOTE: From a letter of Zelle Henry Blackstone in 1935 at the MD Hist. Soc. states Joseph son of Ebenezer is said to have married Mary Stevens, a daughter of Jacob Stevens. Joseph son of Ebenezer lived in Kent County MD and inherited from or was given some little bit of land by his mother who married Mr. Richardson after the death of Ebenezer. Joseph sold the land and moved to Delaware. He had a son Joseph who has descendants in Denton, MD, and another son James who came to Pennsylvania after the War of 1812. A widower with lots of kids he married Elizabeth West in Westmoreland County, PA. per notes sent by Mrs. Mary Abel. Letter from Franklin Blackiston (husband of Zelle) dated 1930, Director of PA and member of Sons of American Revolution says after death of Joseph Blackiston his widow nee Mary Stevens lived with her brother Topham (Toppin) Stevens near Rock Hall. Children of Joseph and Mary Blackiston were Ebenezer, Stephen, Mary (Mother of Mrs. Maye Harbec), James, Joseph.

PARENTS: Joseph and his wife Mary of DE sold the same land in 1796 that Joseph received from his mother in 1794 in Kent Co proving connection between Joseph and Henrietta from DE to MD.

Corporal Joseph Blackiston and Mary Stephens were married about 1780. **Mary Stephens**, daughter of Jacob Stephens, born about 1760. She died after 1810 at the age of 50 in New Castle County, Delaware. After death of Joseph Blackiston his widow nee Mary Stevens lived with her brother Topham (Toppin) Stevens near Rock Hall.

CENSUS: 1810 New Castle Co DE shows Mary Blackiston age over 45, one female age 16-26, one female 10-16, one female 1-10. Mary Blackston Township: St Georges Hundred County: New Castle State: Delaware
1810; Census Place: St Georges Hundred, New Castle, Delaware; Roll: 4; Page: 297; Image: 157.00.

DEATH: SAR application says she died 1819.

A letter from Zella Henry Allison Blackiston in 1935 said Mary Blackiston was the sister of Tophan Stevens whom she went to live with after the death of her husband.

Joseph Blackiston and Mary Stephens had the following children:

+143   i. **James Blackiston**, born abt 1780; married Elizabeth West, 1819, Westmoreland, Pennsylvania; died 1840, Delaware.

+144   ii. **4th Sgt. Joseph Blackiston**, born 1787, MD; married Henrietta , abt 1805; married Ann E. Wiggins, 20 Jan 1836, Queen Annes County, Maryland; died 20 Jan 1850, Rock Hall, Kent County, Maryland.

87. **Ebenezer Blackiston** (Benjamin-5, John-4, John-3, George-2, Marmaduke-1) was born on 21 Sep 1728 in Shrewsbury, Kent County, Maryland.

BIRTH: Shrewsbury church records show Ebenezer, son of Benjamin and Sarah Blackiston Birth: 21 Sep 1728 at Shrewsbury Parish, Kent, Maryland

His parents were married after his birth record unless Benjamin had a prior wife also named Sarah.

Ebenezer Blackiston and Ann Wild were married before 1779. **Ann Wild**. Her fathers will Robert Wilds of Appoquinimink dated Jun 2 1779 probated Mar 18 1789.

88. **William Blackiston** (Benjamin-5, John-4, John-3, George-2, Marmaduke-1) born about 1733. He died about Jan 1775 at the age of 42 in Kent County, Maryland. WILL: date Apr 3 1772 proved Jan 27 1775. William Blackiston of Kent County in MD farmer being sick and weak of body, To my wife Ann the dwelling plantation with the use of moveable estate during her widowhood and after marriage her former dowery of one third of my estate. To my foresaid wife Ann a horse and carriage. To my son Benjamin my dwelling house with the lands adjoining from the head of Chester Branch to the main road and to son Benjamin a tract of land called Benjamins Part and three other small tracts brought of Thomas? Burroughs in consideration of the legacies the said Benjamin hereby firmly bound to brother Samuel 400 pounds common money in 8 years after the said Samuel is of age and that is to say fifty pounds yearly. If he dies before of age to my daughter Betty. To my son William 400 acres lying on the north side of the road which I purchased of my brother George Blackiston. And in case of Williams death before of age I give to his sister Bettsy. To my dau Elizabeth 200 pounds money of Maryland and a negro girl Judah and the rest of my lands to my sons William to be reserved util he shall come of age to inherit then to be equally divided by my son Samuel and dau. Betsey and the residue to all my children each of my rights to a part of a land part of the Heny Manner which land I purchased in half of my brother George which said land I give to the said George provided always that he said George Blackiston clear the land of any encumbrances whatever and keep my heirs clear of the same so that they be not damaged. I nominated my wife Ann my whole executrix. Signed David Angers, William Hazlet, John Colgan. Jan 27 1775 proven

His children are given in Maryland Genealogies p 65.

William Blackiston and Ann Spencer were married. **Ann Spencer** born about 1735. She died after 1775 at the age of 40. dau. of Jarvis.

William Blackiston and Ann Spencer had the following children:

145   i. **Benjamin Blackiston** born about 1750. He died in 1801 at the age of 51. Information on his children comes from Maryland Genealogies p. 65 He had Ann, William and James Blackiston. DEED: Benjamin Blackiston of Kent Co DE sold to Samuel Blackiston of Kent co a 400 acre tract of land part of a larger tract of land called Deer Park adj to the old Chappel path, Simon Worrell and Priscilla his wife being the same tract of land which was sold by George Blackiston to William Blackiston father of the said Benjamin and Samuel on 24 Sep 1773 per DD N4 p 220 in Delaware Land Records Z pg p 110 dated May 29 1787.

+146   ii. **Samuel Spencer Blackiston**, born abt 1752; married Frances Blackiston, 27 May 1790, Delaware; died 21 Sep 1796, Kent County, Delaware.

+147   iii. **William Blackiston**, born abt 1754; married Mary Ann Hazel, bef 1831.

148   iv. **Elizabeth Blackiston** born about 1755.

89. John Blackiston (Benjamin-5, John-4, John-3, George-2, Marmaduke-1) born about 1735. He died on 21 Dec 1774 at the age of 39 in Kent County, Maryland.

His children are given in Maryland Genealogies p 65. He was given Ellis Industry by his father. This land was part of the land divided in 1819.
See also Scharf's History of Delaware Vol 2 p 1123.

WILL: John Blackiston will dated Apr 3 1772 proved Jan 27 1775.

John Blackiston and Frances Stewart were married.

John Blackiston and Frances Stewart had the following children:

+149   i. **Benjamin Blackiston**, born abt 1753; married Hannah Smith, bef 15 Jan 1770; died bef May 1785, Kent County, Delaware.

+150   ii. **Ebenezer Blackiston**, born abt 1755; married Sara Sela; died abt May 1785, Kent County, Maryland.

+151   iii. **John Blackiston**, born abt 1760; married Priscilla Blackiston, 13 May 1794, Kent County, Delaware; died bef 1800.

+152   iv. **Lewis Blackiston**, born abt 1763; married Massy, bef 1789; married Rebecca Meads; died abt May 1821, Queen Annes County, Maryland.

153   v. **Richard Blackiston** born about 1764. He died before 1774 at the age of 10.

90. Sarah Blackiston (Benjamin-5, John-4, John-3, George-2, Marmaduke-1) born about 1737. She died in Jan 1764 at the age of 27. Sarah Blackiston and Bartus Comegys were married before 1760. **Bartus Comegys**, son of Cornelius Comegys, born about 1735. He died about Jan 1775 at the age of 40 in Kent County, Maryland.

WILL: Bartus Comegys date Dec 10 1772 probate Jan 31 1775 WB 5 p 179 eldest son John, 2nd Cornelius, 3rd Benjamin and 4th William; daus. eldest Sarah, youngest Ann and Honour Milke. wife not named. witness Samuel Wilson, Pearce Bowers, John Williamson. see Accounts no 6 p 136.

91. **Ann Blackiston** (Benjamin-5, John-4, John-3, George-2, Marmaduke-1) born about 1739. Ann Blackiston and William Spearman were married before 1760. **William Spearman** born about 1735.

92. **Priscilla Blackiston** (Benjamin-5, John-4, John-3, George-2, Marmaduke-1) was born on 24 Oct 1741 in Kent County, Maryland. She died on 10 Apr 1812 at the age of 70 in Kent County, Maryland. She was the widow of Simon Worrell and had 7 children by him per Wroth Genealogy written in 1905.

WILL: Priscilla Wroth of Kent Co To son John Wroth £40 except as administrator of Kinvin Wroth, deceased, in trust for his son John Kinvin Worrell Wroth. To my son Benjamin B. Wroth £200 in trust for his son William B. Wroth. To my son Peregrine Wroth my negro boy Samuel to serve him until Jan. 1, 1826 and my negro child Benjamin to Jan. 1, 1839. To my dau. Elizabeth Maslin £75. To my dau. Martha Wroth £125. I give £75 to my son John Wroth in trust for William Peregrine Smith and Mary Smith son and dau. of my dau. Priscilla Comegys. My negro man Joseph and my negro woman Aimey to be free at the end of the year. My son Peregrine Wroth shall not be chargeable with interest on any money he may owe. All the residue of my estate to my daughters Elizabeth Maslin and Martha Wroth, my son Peregrine Wroth, my grandson John K.W. Wroth. Execs. my son John Wroth and Benjamin B. Wroth. Witnesses William Wroth, James Smith, Isaac Smith. Written Nov. 21, 1811 Proved May 21, 1812 p. 174
bl
Priscilla Blackiston and Simon Worrell were married about 1760. **Simon Worrell**, son of Edward Worrell and Mary Wilmer, born about 1735. He died about 1772 at the age of 37.

Simon Worrell and Priscilla Blackiston had the following children:

154	i.	**Simon Worrell** was born on 14 Feb 1761.
155	ii.	**Anne Worrell** was born on 2 Aug 1762.
156	iii.	**Edward Worrell** died in 1763. He was born on 23 Oct 1763.
157	iv.	**William Worrell** was born on 19 Apr 1767.
158	v.	**Edward Worrell** was born on 29 Jan 1769. He died in 1830 at the age of 61 in New Castle County, Delaware.
159	vi.	**Mary Worrell** was born on 15 Jul 1770.
160	vii.	**Sarah Worrell** was born on 2 May 1772. She died about Sep 1807 at the age of 35 in Kent County, Maryland. WILL: Sarah Worrell dated

Jan. 22, 1807 probated Sep 21, 1807 WB 8 p. 355 niece Mary Smith (under 16), Sarah Elizabeth Hartshorn (under 16) who lives in PA, half sister Elizabeth Maslin, half brothers Benjamin B. and Peregrine Wroth, nephews William P. Smith, and George W. Worrell, execs. half brother Peregrine Wroth, witnesses John Wroth, Joseph Maslin, Martha Wroth.

Priscilla Blackiston and Kinvin Wroth were married on 23 Sep 1773 in Kent County, Maryland. **Kinvin Wroth**, son of John Wroth and Priscilla Covington, was born on 3 Apr 1754 in Kent County, Maryland. He died on 9 Nov 1804 at the age of 50 in Kent County, Maryland. Information regarding his family comes from Old Kent by Hanson p. 200. His children's names and dates of birth are given in Hanson.

He served as executor on estate of James Wroth, per Republican Star July 5, 1803 (his first cousin). Orphan's Court Proceedings Feb 14 1804. His son Peregrine is named in the will of James Wroth.

Kinvin Wroth and Priscilla Blackiston had the following children:

+161	i.	**Priscilla Wroth**, born 10 Sep 1774; married William Smith; married Jesse Comegys.
+162	ii.	**Elizabeth Wroth**, born 1 Mar 1777; married Thomas Maslin, 2 Sep 1802, Kent County, Maryland; died 27 May 1823.
+163	iii.	**Martha Wroth**, born 17 Oct 1778; married Levi Wroth, 18 Oct 1808, Kent County, Maryland.
+164	iv.	**John Wroth**, born 26 Aug 1781, Kent County, Maryland; married Sarah Worrell, 11 Jun 1805, Kent County, Maryland; married Mary Granger; died Jul 1827, Kent County, Maryland.
+165	v.	**Benjamin Blackiston Wroth Sr.**, born 30 Sep 1783; married Martha Ann Gleaves, 2 Feb 1808, Kent County, Maryland; married Mary Groome, abt 1815; died abt Apr 1825, Kent County, Maryland.
+166	vi.	**Dr. Peregrine Wroth**, born 7 Apr 1786, Kent County, Maryland; married Anna Granger, 19 Jun 1806, Kent County, Maryland; married Martha Page, 27 Aug 1807, Kent County, Maryland; married Martha Smyth Nicols, 19 Jun 1827; married Catherine Hanson, 3 Oct 1839, Kent County, Maryland; married Louisa Tilden, bef 1866; died 13 Jun 1879, Baltimore City, Maryland.

93. George Blackiston (Benjamin-5, John-4, John-3, George-2, Marmaduke-1) was born on 30 Apr 1744 in Deer Park, Queen Annes County, Maryland. He died on 31 Aug 1778 at the age of 34 in Duck Creek, Kent County, Delaware. His children are mentioned in Maryland Genealogies p. 65.

WILL: George Blakiston, farmer, of Duck Creek Hundred. DE. Heirs were wife Martha, sons Ebenezer and John, daughters Frances, Sarah, Prisilah. Exec is wife Martha. Witness Samuel West, James Cheffins, Abraham Parsons. date Aug 9 1778 proved Oct 1 1778 recorded at Dover Delaware. Arch. vol A 4 p 129-131. Liber L p 205-6 Arch Vol A4 p 130 says Martha Blackiston married James Berry.

Guardianship records state George Blackiston died seized of lands in the Duck Creek Hundred in Kent Co, farmer deceased petitioned by James Berry and Martha his wife, late the widow of the said George Blackiston. Martha the widow since intermarried to James Berry and issue viz. Frances, Ebenezer above the age of 14 years, Sarah, Priscilla, John and George. (Sarah, Priscilla, John, and George under the age of 14) Nov 20 1783

Per Kent County Hist Society record, a Redgraves Bible record from Dover DE (Bible was owned by Dr. C. R. Cummins of Dover DE in 1946) says:
Sarah Blackiston died 2/7/1800 age 28,
John Blackiston was born 10/20/1776,
George Blackiston my father was born 4/30/1744 and died 8/31/1778 age 34, [He is buried at Duck Creek, Kent Co, DE]
Ebenezer Blackiston son of George and Martha was born 2/14/1767.

George Blackiston and Martha Redgrave were married about 1765. **Martha Redgrave** born about 1747. She died on 6 Jun 1790 at the age of 43. I believe that Martha is a Redgrave because she is listed in the Redgrave family bible. She was listed as died 6/6/1790 age 43 Martha Redgraves Berry. I think she was first also married to George Blackiston because there is an entry in the same bible that says George and Martha Blackiston had a son born named Ebenezer born 2/14/1767.

George Blackiston and Martha Redgrave had the following children:

+167 i. **Ebenezer Blackiston**, born 14 Feb 1767; married Susannah Holliday, 1792, Kent County, Delaware; died 11 Dec 1829, Smyrna, Kent, Delaware.

+168 ii. **Frances Blackiston**, born 25 May 1769, Deer Park, Queen Annes County, Maryland; married Samuel Spencer Blackiston, 27 May 1790, Delaware; married Rev Joseph Whitby, 12 Jun 1798; died 1 Oct 1813, New Castle County, Delaware.

169 iii. **George Blackiston** was born after 1770. He is mentioned in sister Sarah Blackiston's will but not his father's.

170 iv. **Sarah Blackiston** born about 1772. She died on 7 Feb 1800 at the age of 28 in Kent County, Delaware. WILL:

+171 v. **Priscilla Blackiston**, born 30 Aug 1774, Kent Co, Delaware, British America; married John Lockwood, 13 May 1798, Kent County, Delaware; died 13 Aug 1858, Kent Co, Delaware.

172 vi. **John Blackiston** was born on 20 Oct 1776.

95. Michael Blackiston (Michael-5, John-4, John-3, George-2, Marmaduke-1) was born on 24 Sep 1738 in Saint Pauls Parish, Kent, Maryland, British America. He died before 1771 at the age of 33. BIRTH: Michael Blackston Male Birth Date: 24 Sep 1738 Birth Place: Saint Pauls Parish, Kent, Maryland Father's name: Michl Blackston Mother's name: Ann FHL Film Number: 14206

Michael Blackiston and Rachel were married. **Rachel** born about 1740.

Michael Blackiston and Rachel had the following children:

173   i. **Richard Blackiston** was born on 27 Apr 1768 in Saint Paul's Parish, Kent County, Maryland. BIRTH: Richard Blackston son of Michael and Rachel born Apr 27 1768. He is named in will of his grandmother Ann.

174   ii. **Ann Blackiston** was born on 7 Jul 1769 in Saint Paul's Parish, Kent County, Maryland. BIRTH: Ann Blackston dau of Michael and Rachel born Jul 7 1769. She is named in will of her grandmother Ann.

98. James Blackiston (Michael-5, John-4, John-3, George-2, Marmaduke-1) was born on 28 Nov 1746 in Saint Pauls Parish, Kent County, Maryland. He died on 16 Nov 1822 at the age of 75 in Fayette County, Pennsylvania. The Colonial and Revolutionary Lineages of America Vol 11 p 368-440. Traces back his ancestry to Royalty.

James Blackiston, younger son of Michael and Ann (Bradshaw) Blackiston, was born November 28, 1746, according to the records of St. Paul's Parish, Kent County, Maryland. Deprived of his father at a tender age, he was given his share of the estate in money, and in 1773 he was made sole executor of his mother's will. Sometime before 1780 James left Kent County, MD and moved to Fayette Co, PA, taking his wife, his children and some slaves, these last being according to a new law at that time, registered by him. He settled on land known as "Summit Point Farm" in Tyrone Twp. He was a prominent citizen, serving as appraiser of damages for Fayette County in 1784, and was appointed, April 18, 1798, justice of the peace. Died Nov. 16, 1822. He left to his children and grandchildren extensive possessions, including money, bank stocks, and hundreds of acres of PA lands, which subsequently became exceedingly valuable. Married Priscilla Bradshaw, who was born in 1746 died Mar 1 1796. Issue: James Blackiston married Rogers, Sarah Blackiston on whom further. When the Boxley farm was sold to William Crane in 1805, the grantors included the heirs of Richard Blackiston and James Blackiston of Fayette County, Pennsylvania.4 Crane's son, William Bowers Crane, owned the farm in 1852, but it was tenanted by Gary H. Leaverton. The buildings were listed as "in bad repair." In an 1858 equity case, the farm was sold to Richard Hinson, the Chestertown lawyer who was to build his residence next to River House in 1870. Boxley remained in the Hynson family until the 1940's. In the 1970's the house was rehabilitated and again occupied by its owners.

WILL: James Blackiston dated Sep 4 1819 probated Nov 19 1822. names grandchildren Priscilla, Robert and James Taylor, the children of deceased daughter Frances, who intermarried with Joseph Taylor, to son in law James Hurst, to his granddaughter Elizabeth, to dau. Sarah intermarried James Hurst, to second dau. Mary intermarried with Rev. Boyd Mercer, to 3rd dau. Ann intermarried with Thomas Hurst, all residue to 3 surviving daughters equally.

James Blackiston and Priscilla Bradshaw were married. **Priscilla Bradshaw**, daughter of John Bradshaw and Ann , born about 1746. She died on 1 Mar 1796 at the age of 50 in Fayette County, Pennsylvania. There is a Priscilla Bradshaw in St. Pauls Parish born Mar 30 1785 dau of James and Rachel Bradshaw, but a deed of 1818 says she was daughter of John Bradshaw. John Bradshaw's will of 1789 says to my dau. Priscilla Blackiston and my granddau
. Priscilla Miller.

James Blackiston and Priscilla Bradshaw had the following children:

+175   i.   **Sarah Blackiston**, born abt 1790; married James Hurtt.
+176   ii. **Mary Blackiston**, born abt 1792; married Boyd Mercer.
+177   iii. **Ann Blackiston**, born abt 1794; married Thomas Hurtt.
+178   iv. **Frances Blackiston**, born abt 1795; married Joseph Taylor; died bef 1819.

100. **Judith Ann Blackiston** (Michael-5, John-4, John-3, George-2, Marmaduke-1) was born on 28 Mar 1750 in Saint Pauls Parish, Kent County, Maryland. She died before Dec 1795 at the age of 45 in Kent County, Maryland. Ann Blackiston dau of Michael and Ann born March 1750 St. Pauls.

This family needs more research to sort out all of the children. In the will of Judith Brice of 1795 she names her children as James, Joseph, Mary Harrigan, Sarah Brice, Ann Brice, and Susanna Brice, but Susanna in her will names her another sister Elizabeth Airs and a brother John. Benjamin Brice, James Brice, Sarah Brice who were named as niece and nephews of Sarah Blackiston in her will of 1797.

WILL: Judith Brice of Kent Co To my sons James and Joseph Brice all that tract that I bought of Rebecca and Joseph Copper called "Wedge's Recovery" containing 54 3/4 acres. If one dies, then to the survivor. If both die then to my 3 daughters Mary Harragan, Sarah Brice and Ann Brice. For those of my children that has not had their part of their father's estate, that it be paid to them by my executor. I give to my 4 daughters Susannah Brice, Mary Harragan, Sarah Brice and Ann Brice all the rest of my estate. Exec. Not Given (William Brice eldest son of Judith Brice presented will to court). Witnesses Hezekiah Dunn, Thomas Urie, Michael Miller, Edward Worrell. Written Feb. 15, 1790 Proved Dec. 3, 1795 WB 7 p. 503

Judith Ann Blackiston and William Brice were married. **William Brice**, son of Richard Brice and Judah Grant, was born on 13 Aug 1744 in Saint Paul's Parish, Kent County, Maryland. William Brice served in 7th Comp, 13th Batt 1775/78

William Brice and Judith Ann Blackiston had the following children:

179	i.	**William Brice** born about 1769.
+180	ii.	**James Brice**, born abt 1770; married Elizabeth ; died 1798.
181	iii.	**Joseph Brice** born about 1771. He died after 1820 at the age of 49.
+182	iv.	**Mary Brice**, born abt 1772; married Harrigan.
183	v.	**Sarah Brice** born about 1773. She died about Mar 1835 at the age of 62 in Kent County, Maryland. WILL: Sarah Brice of Kent Co dated Feb. 22, 1832 proved Mar. 17, 1835 WB 12 p 1. to Mary Henrietta and Martha Louisa Stevens all my real estate but if they die then to Sarah Ann Brice dau of Henrietta Stevens. To Henrietta Stevens all the remainder of my personal estae with negroes. Codicil To Martha Brice my brother's dau. all my part of the undivided land lying in Skinner's Neck date Apr 28, 1832.
184	vi.	**Elizabeth Brice** born about 1774.
185	vii.	**Susannah Brice** born about 1776. She died about Nov 1821 at the age of 45 in Kent County, Maryland. WILL: Susanna Brice of Kent Co date Oct. 21, 1815 proved Nov. 28, 1821 WB 10 p 251. to Mary Aris dau of my sister Elizabeth Airs 1/5 part then to her son Richard Thomas Airs. to my 2 nieces Sarah and Ann Harrigan daus of my sister Mary Harrigan 1/5 part, to my 2 nieces Mary and Martha Brice daus of my brother John Brice 1/5 part. to my niece Henrietta Brice dau. of my sister Ann Brice 1/5 part. to the 3 daus. of my nephew Richard Airs 1/5 part. to my 2 sisters Ann and Sarah Brice one spice mortar and then to Sarah Harrigan for it to be continued in the family forever.
186	viii.	**Benjamin Brice** born about 1778.
+187	ix.	**Ann Brice**, born abt 1780; died abt Mar 1832, Kent County, Maryland.
+188	x.	**John Brice**, born abt 1782; married Martha Hatcheson.
189	xi.	**Richard Brice** died in 1824 in Kent County, Maryland. Richard Brice of Kent Co To my wife Rebecca Brice all my plantation I purchased of John Wallis also my houses and lots in Chestertown during her life and after her death to my niece Martha Brice but if she dies then to my niece Mary Brice but if she dies then to my nephew Joseph W. Brice (son of Joseph Brice). To my wife Rebecca Brice all my personal property during her life and after to my niece Martha Brice. My negroes all free at 40. If the land descends to Joseph W. Brice at age 21, I then appoint Philip Brooks as the guardian and Philip Brooks and Unit Corse to have oversight of my executrix. Execs. my wife Rebecca Brice and my niece Martha Brice. Witnesses Edward Nicholson, Unit

Corse, Philip Brooks. Written Dec. 18, 1824 Proved Dec. 28, 1824 p. 371

102. **Presley Blackiston** (William-5, John-4, John-3, George-2, Marmaduke-1) was born in 1741. He died on 4 Apr 1819 at the age of 78 in Philadelphia, Pennsylvania. He was buried in Saint Peter's Episcopal Churchyard, Philadelphia, Pennsylvania. His grandson Kenneth MacKenzie Blakiston was President of P. Blackiston, Son and Co, publishers in Philadelphia. Burke's American Families names Presley as a descendant of Rev. Marmaduke Blackiston p. 2565 and gives their ancestry back to Hugo de Blackiston in 1341. Also names Bowes ancestry.

Presley Blackiston and Sarah Warnock were married. **Sarah Warnock** born about 1749. She died in 1789 at the age of 40.

105. **Martha Miller** (Ann Blackiston-5, William-4, Ebenezer-3, George-2, Marmaduke-1) born about 1740. She is possibly dau. of Arthur Miller. She signed as next of kin to Samuel Miller in 1761. which would be her uncle if she was the dau. of Arthur Miller.

Martha Miller and Nathaniel Hatcheson were married about 1759 in Saint Paul's Parish, Kent County, Maryland. **Nathaniel Hatcheson**, son of Vincent Hatcheson and Rachel Workman, was born on 13 Apr 1732 in Kent County, Maryland. He died about Mar 1793 at the age of 60 in Kent County, Maryland. He was christened in Saint Paul's Parish, Kent County, Maryland. BIRTH: Nathaniel Hatcheson son of Vincent and Rachel Hatcheson born April 13, 1732 St. Pauls.

MARRIAGE: Nathan Hatcheson m. Martha Miller date not readable between 1758-1763 marriages. in St. Paul's Register.

WILL: Nathan Hatcheson of Kent Co, My dwelling plantation where I now live on called "Standaway" containing 130 acres to my son Nathan Hatcheson. To my son Samuel Hatcheson £20. To my 2 granddaughters Martha Brice and Mary Brice daughters of John Brice and my dau. Martha his wife £10 and no more when they are 16. Residue to my son Nathan and my daughters Sarah, Mary and Ann Hatcheson. Exec. my son Nathan Hatcheson. Witnesses Morgan Hurtt, Daniel Groome, Ringgold Hynson. Written Jan. 26, 1793 Proved Mar. 19, 1793 p. 386

Nathan Hatcheson age 43 in 1775 Kent Co xxiv p.83. Per Col. Families of the Eastern Shore Vol. 1 they had 12 children.

Nathaniel Hatcheson and Martha Miller had the following children:

+190   i. **Sarah Hatcheson**, born 15 Oct 1760, Kent County, Maryland; married Nathaniel Miller Sr., 13 Feb 1797; died abt Jan 1827, Kent County, Maryland.

+191   ii. **Martha Hatcheson**, born 8 May 1762; married John Brice.

192   iii. **Rachel Hatcheson** was born on 20 Mar 1764 in Kent County, Maryland. She died before 1772 at the age of 8. BIRTH: Rachel Hatcheson dau. of Nathan and Martha Hatcheson born Mar 20, 1764. She must have died young as another dau. of the same name was born 1772

+193   iv. **Rebecca Hatcheson**, born 3 Mar 1766, Kent County, Maryland; married Bartus Piner; married John Burgin; died aft 1796.

+194   v. **James Hatcheson**, born 26 Jan 1768, Kent County, Maryland; died aft 1821.

+195   vi. **Nathan Hatcheson**, born 27 Jan 1770, Kent County, Maryland; married Ann Nicholson, 29 Sep 1817; married bef 1800; died 22 Oct 1843, Kent County, Maryland.

196   vii. **Rachel Hatcheson** was born on 23 Jan 1772 in Kent County, Maryland. She died about Sep 1824 at the age of 52 in Kent County, Maryland. BIRTH: Rachel Hatcheson dau. of Nathan and Martha Hatcheson born Jan. 23, 1772 WILL: Rachel Hatcheson of Kent Co My negroes Mosses, Jenny and Suck shall be free from slavery. To my sister Ann Hatcheson during her life the whole of my estate. Then to my nephew Vincent Hatchison and my niece Mary Hatcheson. Exec. Not Given. Witnesses James Tennant, John Wallis, Sarah Hackett. Written Sep. 23, 1817 Proved Sep. 3, 1824 p. 349

197   viii. **Samuel Hatcheson** was born on 3 Dec 1775 in Kent County, Maryland.

198   ix. **Mary Hatcheson**.

199   x. **Ann Hatcheson** died about Sep 1824 in Kent County, Maryland. WILL: Ann Hatcheson of Kent Co To my sister Rachel Hatcheson during her life the ½ of the tract we now reside and also the personal estate. After the death of my sister Rachel Hatcheson the above land called "Killingsworth More" to be divided between my nephew Vincent Hatcheson and my niece Mary Hatcheson. Exec. Not Given. Witnesses James Tennant, John Wallis, Sarah Hackett. Written Sep. 23, 1817 Proved Sep. 3, 1824 p. 350

200   xi. **Vincent Hatcheson** died in May 1821 in Kent County, Maryland. WILL: Vincent Hatcheson of Kent Co, To my nephew Vincent Hatcheson son of my brother James Hatcheson my old negro man Sam for 3 years. To my nephew Vincent Hatcheson my negro girl Millicent during her life, my duck gun, my saddle and bridle and the balance still due me from my father's estate. My brother James Hatcheson shall have the use of said property until my nephew is at age, except old Sam who is to be free at 3 years. To my sister Mary Hatcheson my negro boy Abe a slave for life but if she dies without issue then to my nephew Vincent Hatcheson. All my wearing apparel to my brother James

Hatcheson. Exec. Not Given. Witnesses Samuel M. Sutton. Written May 1, 1821 Proved May 18, 1821 p. 229

DEED: Kent County Land Records W.S. 1/373 March 1817 names Nancy Hatcheson, Rachel Hatcheson, Mary Hackett, formerly Mary Hatcheson and James Hatcheson and Mary Hatcheson, all of Kent County by William Barroll their attorney to the Judges of Kent County Court their petition on the following words to wit: To the Honorable, the Judge of Kent County Court the petition of Nancy Hatcheson, Rachel Hatcheson, Mary Hackett, formerly Mary Hatcheson, and James Hatcheson and Mary Hatcheson all of Kent County humbly showeth that Vincent Hatcheson formerly of Kent County died seized of lands lying and being in Kent County and intestate and without issue which hath descended to your petitioners who are all of age and to Rebecca Piner married to Bartus Piner, Vincent Hatcheson and William Hatcheson (this must be the William James mentioned later)under age of twenty-one years that in consequence of the infancy of the above named persons our petitioners

108. Mary Blackiston (Ebenezer-5, William-4, Ebenezer-3, George-2, Marmaduke-1) was born on 29 Apr 1763 in Saint Paul's Parish, Kent County, Maryland. Mary Blackiston and John Gale were married before 1791. **John Gale** died after 1791.

110. Ann Rasin (Rosamond Blackiston-5, William-4, Ebenezer-3, George-2, Marmaduke-1) born about 1757. Ann Rasin and John R. Willis were married. **John R. Willis**, son of Richard Willis, born about 1755. He died about 1823 at the age of 68 in Kent County, Maryland. John Willis Home in 1790 (City, County, State): Kent, Maryland
1792 - Feb. 9: John Willis son of Richard Willis deceased, sells to Benjamin Chambers, for 234 pounds, c.m., part of tract of land which was devised to him by his father, Richard Willis, being that part of the dwelling plantation where his father lived, called Conney Warren, adjoining land of Richard Graves, Mary Vandyke and others and supposed to contain 73 ¼ acres. Ann Willis, wife of John Willis examined separately.
John Wallis Home in 1820 (City, County, State): Chestertown, Kent, Maryland
Enumeration Date: August 7, 1820
Admin Papers of John R. Willis 1823 list Ann Willis as his widow who relinquishes right to administer estate - Nov. 4, 1823

John R. Willis and Ann Rasin had the following child:

+201   i. **Martha Willis**, born abt 1780; married William Apsley Jr., aft 1798.

111. Captain William Blackiston Rasin (Rosamond Blackiston-5, William-4, Ebenezer-3, George-2, Marmaduke-1) born about 1760 in Kent County, Maryland. He died about Aug 1810 at the age of 50 in Worton, Kent County, Maryland. He was buried in Kent

County, Maryland. An article in the Maryland Genealogical Society bulletin Vol 36 No. 2 Spring 1995 by Christos Christou, Jr. provides a history of Capt. William Blackiston Rasin and proofs of this line and corrects mistakes in older histories, with full details of primary records most of which were found by Carolyn E. Cooper. Ms. Cooper provided the original information from her privately printed book called Genealogy and History of William Blackiston Rasin for an application to the Children of the American Revolution for John Barnhouser in 1995. She had researched for 20 years on the Rasins and found the primary and family records that prove the descendants of William Blackiston Rasin and she provided the information that was used in the MGS Bulletin article to prove the difference between the Capt. William Blackiston Rasin and the William Ras of Georgetown which have often been confused (including an incorrect DAR application).

NOTES: Will of Philip Rasin mentions his brother William Rasin (dated 1771), Will of Mary Rasin mentions her brother William B Rasin and his daughter Ann (dated 1798).

SOLDIER: Amer. Rev. Raisin, William (Md). Sergeant 5th Maryland, 12th February, 1779; 2d Lieutenant, 26th January, 1780; transferred to 1st Maryland, 1st January, 1781, and served to April, 1783. Heitman, Francis B. Historical Register of Officers of the Continental Army During the War of the Revolution. Rev. ed. Washington, D.C.: The Rare Book Shop Pub. Co., 1914.

SOLDIER: Percey Skirven Notes from MHS states William B. Rasin 17 years old, enlisted as a private without the knowledge of his father (stepfather), a wealthy farmer of Kent Co. He was promoted to Lt. at Camden. Later was elected Capt. for Chester Hundred Light Infantry. His oldest brother was the father of Philip F. Rasin. William B. Rasin's only surviving son (at the time this was written) was Cyrus Rasin. He fought at Camden, Eutaw and Cowpens.

SOLDIER: He was an Ensign at Battle of Camden SC Aug 10 1780. He was a Capt. of the Light Infantry.

William B. Rasin was appointed guardian of William Apsley (son of his wife Martha by her first husband).

SOLDIER: List of MD Officers and soldiers entitled to lots westward of Ft. Cumberland. In April 1787, in lots of 50 acres each: Lt. William Raison lots 2405, 2406, 2407, 2408. Also Federal Bounty Land Grant Lt. William Raisin 200 acres date of issue Oct 4 1800 warrant number 1,844.

SOLDIER: The Maryland Line in the Rev. War by Rieman Steuart 1969 p 121 William Raisin Enlisted Jan. 10 1777 corpl, sergeant 5th regt. Feb 12 1779, 2nd lieut. 5th regt. Jan 26 1780, transferred to 1st regt. Jan 1 1781, retired Apr 12 1783.

ORPHAN BOND: William Blackiston Rasin to Ann Bayley. Ann Bayley is an orphan age 12 on Feb. 12 last. The court is giving her to William Blackiston Rasin after the manner of apprentice to dwell until she is 16. He is to teach her to read well in the Bible, to knit, spin and sew. Date July 2, 1793 Bk BC 3 p. 200-1.

SOLDIER: Index 49 at Annapolis Archives Box 3 folder 21 Lt. Wm Rasin Oct 11 1781 pay receipt. Box 3 folder 18 Lt. Wm Rasin paid 1st Regt. troops Oct 24 1781. Index 50 at AA 1794 Capt. of Kent Co Militia. Index 51 Capt. Wm Rasin Jun 18 1794 Capt. of Kent Co Militia. Militia Appointments no 1 p 52, no 2 p 29.
Aug 5 -7 1783 Lt. Wm Raisin Intendent's Ledger A no 9 p 30,44 no 15 p 24, A no 10 p 8, 62.

MARRIAGE: ca 1787/1788 to Martha Wroth Apsley

DEED: Chattel Records William Blackiston Rasin sells to Philip Brooks for 4pds, 14 sh and 8p one negro George about the age of 18 years. Feb. 21, 1788. witness James Strong. (This same George was given to Martha Apsley in the will of her father Kinvin Wroth, the administration calls him Capt. Rasin. Another proof that Capt. Rasin and William Blackiston Rasin were the same person.) AB1 p 1-2

DEED: William B. Rasin selling the following slaves to James Wroth for 250 pounds, negro Richard, negro George and negro woman called Beck. JW 1 p. 211 Date Mar 1800. Chattel Records.

PENSION: William B. Ras of Kent Co, late a lieutenant in the revolutionary war, or his order, a sum of money equal to half pay as a lieutenant, annually in quarterly payments, during his life, as a further reward to those meritorious services which he rendered his country in establishing her liberty and independence. Nov 1804 Session of Laws of MD Resolutions Vol 7.

DEATH: A list of the Tracts and lots of land in Kent county charged for the payment of taxes, includes in Second District: persons charged Rasin, William Capt's heirs, names of tracts and number of lots "Part of Hermitage and Towns Relief, amount due $1.36. (Republican Star Oct 15 1811). (also published in the Baltimore Whig). [Town Relief was land that belonged to the Wroth family since their earliest days in Kent County. The land of Hermitage and Town Relief is located on Porter Grove Road near the intersection of Route 297.]

DEED: Petition of Elie Ridgely for patent June 13 1832 recorded in Liber GGB No 2 p 308, agreeable to an act of the General Assembly of MD passed at November session 1788, that a certain William Raisin, a Lieutenant of the Maryland line, was entitled to the following lots viz No. 2405, 2406, 2407, 2408 lying continuous to each other, to the westward of fort Cumberland, in Allegany County and containing fifty acres each, making in all two hundred acres of land, that two of said lots No 2405 and 2406 were on the 28th day of August 1826, exposed to public sale to the highest bidder by William McMahon, collector of the county charges, as the property of said William Raisin for payment of the county charges, when your petitioner became the purchaser and fully paid the purchase money for the same, that William McMahon, collector aforesaid, has since by his deed bearing date the 3rd day of January 1827, conveyed said land to your petitioner. Jun 1 1832 ordered that a patent issue.

SOLDIER: Worton Gleanings by Carolyn E. Cooper 1983 says served in Revolution in teens.

DEED: Heirs of William Rasin sell 200 acres of land that William Rasin received from commission agreeable to the act of assembly passed at November session 1788 designated as lot numbers 2405, 2406, 2407, 2408 land was west of Fort Cumberland and this land descended to his 4 children upon his decease: Philip Rasin, Cyrus Rasin, Rachel Rasin now Rachel Duyer and Ann Rasin now Ann Denning. Philip Rasin and Sarah his wife, Cyrus Rasin and Wilamina Rasin his wife, Philip Duyer and Rachel his wife, and Daniel Denning and Ann his wife signed. (Allegany Co MD DB AB No. W p 184-7 dated May 10 1838 recorded May 29, 1838) (This deed of 1838 shows William B Rasin heirs selling four lots 200 acres in Alleghany Co which their father received in 1788 for his service in the Rev. Philip, Cyrus, Rachel Dyer and Anna Denning.)

CAR: The Children of the American Revolution have approved members descended from William B. Rasin through son Philip R. Rasin namely John Barnhouser Sr. (#142106 approved on May 1995), John A. Barnhouser, Jr. (#144465 approved on Jan. 6, 1998), Guy Edward Almony, Jr. (#145958 approved on Nov. 15, 1999), Samantha Rose Barnhouser (#147969 approved Dec. 17, 2001), and Sarah Nicole Barnhouser (CAR #148965 approved Nov 2002).

SAR: The Sons of the American Revolution have approved members descended from William B. Rasin through son Philip R. Rasin namely John Barnhouser Sr. (#148242 approved May 1997) and Guy E. Almony Jr. (#160713 approved July 2003).

Captain William Blackiston Rasin and Martha Wroth were married in 1787 in Kent County, Maryland. **Martha Wroth**, daughter of Kinvin Wroth and Frances Beck, born about 1760 in Kent County, Maryland. She died after 1827 at the age of 67 in Kent County, Maryland. She was buried in Kent County, Maryland.

Martha was 1st to William Apsley

MARRIAGE: 2nd to William Rasin. After Oct 16 1786 [date of her father's will when she is called Martha Apsley] and before Jun 1 1788 [administrative bond of Martha Rasin for her deceased husband's estate].

ADMIN BOND: Martha Apsley Admin. (also called Absoley), Edward (x) Apsley, Kinvin Wroth, James Wroth appointed executors for 2,000 pds bond, for will of William Apsley. dated Jan 22, 1785. (Kent Co MD Admin. Bond Vol. 6 p. 301)

ADMIN BOND: William Wroth, Kinvin Wroth Jr., Robert Meeks and Edward Apsley sureties for 3,000 pds on the testament of Capt. William Rasin and Martha his wife executors of the testament of Wm Apsley late of Kent Co. MD dated Jun 1, 1788 (Kent Co Admin. Bond Vol. 6 p. 400)

ESTATE: The account of Capt. William Rasin and Martha his wife executrix of William Apsley of Kent County dec'd. mentions distribution to his son George Apsley and Daniel Kennard who married a dau of William Apsley (Kent Co Admin. Accts Vol 10 p 202-204 dated April 12, 1799)

NEWS: Martha Rasin owns Part of Town's Relief and Hermitage 93 acres taxes owed 1824-1828, (May 23, 1828 Article Telegraph)

The 1833 Conference Report of the Methodist Church for Kent on p. 3 of Worton Chapel lists Martha Reason as exp. (expelled or expired member).

William Blackiston Rasin and Martha Wroth had the following children:

+202   i.   **Corporal Philip Reed Rasin**, born abt 1793, Kent County, Maryland; married Sarah Bennett, 22 Mar 1811, Kent County, Maryland; died 1 Apr 1841, Kent County, Maryland.

+203   ii.   **Cyrus B. Rasin**, born abt 1794, Kent County, Maryland; married Wilhelmina Steen, 2 Mar 1819, Kent County, Maryland; married Henrietta M. Beck, 1 Aug 1840, Kent County, Maryland; married Sarah Smith, 31 Jan 1850, Kent County, Maryland; married Mary , 15 Dec 1856, Kent County, Maryland; died 13 Mar 1865, Chestertown, Kent County, Maryland.

+204   iii. **Rachel Rasin**, born abt 1795; married John Clark, 24 Apr 1819; married Phillip Duyer, 16 May 1826, Kent County, Maryland; died Nov 1857, Kent County, Maryland.

+205   iv.   **Nancy Ann Rasin**, born abt 1797, Maryland; married John Willis; married Daniel Denning, 6 Jan 1828, Kent County, Maryland; died 30 Sep 1881, Kent County, Maryland.

112. **Warner Rasin** (Rosamond Blackiston-5, William-4, Ebenezer-3, George-2, Marmaduke-1) was born on 2 Sep 1763 in Kent County, Maryland. He died on 4 Nov 1804 at the age of 41 in Kent County, Maryland.

BIRTH: Cecil Monthly Meeting Quaker. Warner Rasin, son of Abraham Rasin and Rosamond his wife was born the 23rd day of the 9th month 1763. (Nov)

DEATH: Cecil Monthly Meeting Quaker. Warner Rasin, son of Abraham & Rosamond Rasin departed this life the fourth day of the eleventh month 1804. Transcribed notes in the MD GRC 1940 S1 vol 67 says Thomas Rasin son of Abraham and Rosamond Rasin died 4th day 11 month 1804.

Chancery Record 1806/09/23 4961: Edward Simms vs. Warner Rasin, Margaret Black, Frederick Wilson, Thomas Wilson, Mary Perkins Stuart, Rebecca Rasin Stuart, Ann Maria Stuart, Elizabeth Rasin, and Abraham Rasin. KE. Estate of Alexander Stuart - Taylors Place, Rigby, Providence, Camelsworthmore. Recorded (Chancery Record) 113, p. 182. Accession No.: 17,898-4961-1/4 MSA S512-6- 5108 Location: 1/37/1/

Warner Rasin and Ann Miflin were married. **Ann Miflin** born about 1763. She died on 19 Dec 1799 at the age of 36 in Kent County, Maryland.
DEATH: Ann Rasin wife Warner departed this life 19th day of the 12 month 1799. She was a member of Cecil meeting aged 26.

Warner Rasin and Ann Miflin had the following children:

206   i.   **Elizabeth Rasin** was born on 30 Jan 1791 in Kent County, Maryland.
207   ii.   **Abraham Rasin** was born on 24 Nov 1799 in Kent County, Maryland.

Warner Rasin and Margaret Wilkerson were married. **Margaret Wilkerson** born about 1765.

113. **Blackiston Wilmer** (Rosamond Blackiston-5, Ebenezer-4, Ebenezer-3, George-2, Marmaduke-1) was born on 18 Sep 1742 in Kent County, Maryland. He died on 31 Dec 1813 at the age of 71 in Kent County, Maryland. He was buried in Saint Paul's Cemetery, Kent County, Maryland. 6 Sep 1763 Blackstone Wilmer, William Ringgold and Sarah his wife of Kent Co vs. John Garrett. The bill of complaint dated 8 Jan 1757 states that Sarah Blackstone on 26 Jan 1747 was sole and unmarried and made a deed of gift to Blackstone Wilmer and Sarah Wilmer (now Ringgold), her grandchildren, the children of Rose Wilmer, daughter of Sarah Blackstone. After said gift, Sarah Blackstone intermarried with John Garrett of Kent Co, mariner. Sarah Blackstone was the executrix of Ebenezer Blackiston, her former husband deceased. MSA Vol. 10 p. 229.

His family is listed in Old Kent by Hanson p. 326

TOMBSTONE: In Memory of Blackiston Wilmer Died Dec. 31, 1813 in the 72d year of his age.

Blackiston Wilmer and Sarah Williamson were married on 19 Feb 1778. **Sarah Williamson** born about 1758. She died on 14 Jun 1823 at the age of 65 in Kent County. She was buried in Saint Paul's Cemetery, Kent County.

WILL: Sarah Wilmer of Kent Co, widow of the late Blackistone Wilmer To be decently buried at the discretion of my son William B. Wilmer in a plain manner in a walnut coffin and I give money to pay my funeral charges different from a larger claim of $3,400 due me and in my son's hands which is to remain a part of my estate. To my 2 executrixes the interest for 2 years of all my money in lieu of administration fees and all my debts. To my dau. Mary Tate $600 paid before Jan. 1, 1827, one negro boy James to serve until Dec. 25, 1847, one pair of large looking glasses which are now in her parlor in her house in Chestertown. To my 2 daughters Sarah Rebecca Wilmer and Harriett Wilmer each $800 paid before Jan. 1, 1827 and they shall share my pew in the church in Chestertown. To my son John Wilmer and William B. Wilmer $100 each to be paid by Jan. 1, 1827. To my granddau. Sarah Maria Tate $600 to be paid by Jan. 1, 1827 and to my grandson William B. Tate $400 to be paid by Jan. 1, 1827 but if either or both die, then to survivor then to issue or back to my heirs. If my estate is not sufficient to pay my debts and legacies (which I do not presume to be the case), their share to be reduced in proportion. Execs. my 2 daughters Sarah Rebecca Wilmer and Harriett Wilmer. Witnesses James E. Barroll, Josiah Gears. Written July 13, 1822 Proved July 2, 1823 p. 301

Codicil Whereas I gave $800 to my 2 daughters, if they marry before they receive their legacy then $100 each come out to my sons John and William B. Wilmer. Whereas I gave to my 2 grandchildren Sarah Maria Tate $600 and William B. Tate $400, if they die without issue $100 to each of my sons John and William B. Wilmer. Written July 26, 1822. Witnesses James E. Barroll, John H. Holt

Blackiston Wilmer and Sarah Williamson had the following children:

+208   i.   **Maria Wilmer**, born 22 Dec 1780; married Robert Tate; died abt May 1843, Kent County, Maryland.

+209   ii.   **William Blackiston Wilmer II**, born 27 Apr 1790; married Mary Ann Taylor, 16 Apr 1816; died 20 Jan 1853.

114. **Sarah Wilmer** (Rosamond Blackiston-5, Ebenezer-4, Ebenezer-3, George-2, Marmaduke-1) born about 1743. Sarah Wilmer and William Ringgold were married. **William Ringgold**.

116. **Mary Wilmer** (Rosamond Blackiston-5, Ebenezer-4, Ebenezer-3, George-2, Marmaduke-1) born about 1730. Mary Wilmer and William Ringgold were married. **William Ringgold**, son of Thomas Ringgold and Rebecca Wilmer, was born on 23 Feb 1723. He died about Dec 1789 at the age of 66 in Kent County, Maryland. William is named as son in law of Rosemond Wilmer.

Seventh Generation

117. George Blackiston (Nehemiah Herbert-6, John-5, John-4, Nehemiah-3, John-2, Marmaduke-1) was born on 28 Nov 1780. He died on 7 Nov 1842 at the age of 61 in Saint Mary's County, Maryland. He was buried at All Saints Episcopal Church Cem in Oakley, Saint Mary's County, Maryland.

WILL: George Blakistone of St. Marys Co to my wife Rebecca Blakistone the plantation on which I reside called Water loo except so as otherwise dispose of and after her death to my son Zacharias Deminu Blakistone forever. And my three daughters Lucinda Blakistone, Ann Rebecca Blakistone, and Priscilla Hebb Blakistone shall have a home at my mansion house and a support during their single lives. To my son George W. Blakistone my family commonly called "Dick Harts" and he paying each of his sister Lelias D. Dent, Lucinda Blakistone, Ann Rebecca Blakistone, and Priscilla Hebb Blakistone $150 in six equal annual installments, a small portion of said farm I design for my son Richard Pinkney Blakistone, which is contained in the following devise. To my son Richard Pinkney Blakistone the farm where Edward Arnold now lives all the land formerly occupied by Mrs. Watson outside of the fence on the side of the road leading to my house up to the gate that leads to my mill until it comes to 30 years of the mill with an angle of 20 yards and then to the nearest line of water. to my son Richard Pinkney the following woodlands of Dick Harts beginning at the outer gate at Edward Arnolds and running on the line between Peregrine Shanks and myself 100 yards east parallel to Edward Arnolds fence and he to pay his four sisters Lelias D. Dent, Lucinda Blakistone, Ann Rebecca Blakistone and Priscilla Hebb Blakistone $50 in six equal annual installments. to my son James T. Blakistone negro boy John and negro girl Jane. To my dau Lelia D. Dent negro woman Sarah, negro boy James Aaron and Negro girl Mary Ellen. To my son George W. Blakistone negro boy Robert. to my son Zachariah Deminu Blakistone negro man Little Harry. to my son Richard Pinkney Blakistone negro boy William. To my dau Lucinda Blakistone negro woman Chloe, negro boy Marcellus, and negro girl Eleanor. To my dau Ann Rebecca Blackistone, negro man big Harry, negro boys Joseph and cousin and negro woman Sylvia. to my dau Priscilla Hebb Blakistone negro woman Patience, negro boy Hillary and negro girl Cassandria. To my wife Rebecca Blakistone negro man Leonard, negro boy Frederick, negro woman Kitty and her child Margarett, and negro girl Betsey. to my wife all of my personal estate and she is to pay all my debts and afterwards all to be divided amongst my children. I appoint my wife Rebecca and my son Zachariah Deminu Blakistone joint executors. Dated Nov 7 1842. Witnesses Thomas Matthews, John H. T. Tarlton, Wm J. Blakistone. Proven Jan 17 1843. James Thomas Blakistone and Zachariah D. Blackiston two of the sons of & next of k of the said deceased appeared. WB 2 p. 70-73

TOMBSTONE: George Blackiston son of N & Mary C. Blackiston born Dec. 18 1780 Died Nov. 15 1842

George Blackiston and Rebecca Goldsmith were married about 18 Jan 1813 in Saint Mary's County, Maryland. **Rebecca Goldsmith** was born in 1781. She died on 18 Dec 1851 at the age of 70 in Saint Mary's County, Maryland. She was buried at All Saints Episcopal Church Cem in Oakley, Saint Mary's County, Maryland.

George Blackiston and Rebecca Goldsmith had the following children:

+210   i.   **Zachariah Demeneau Blackiston**, married Harriet Ann Shanks, 10 Jan 1860, Saint Mary's County, Maryland.

+211   ii. **Ann Rebecca Blackiston**, born 1828; married Biscoe Cheseldyne, 25 Nov 1856; died 10 Jul 1908, Saint Mary's County, Maryland.

120. **Daniel Blackiston** (Stephen-6, Ebenezer-5, John-4, John-3, George-2, Marmaduke-1) born about 1775. He died about Apr 1807 at the age of 32 in Kent County, Maryland. Will of Simon Smith date Oct 3, 1805 pro. Feb. 18, 1806 WV 8 p. 287. names son in law Daniel Blackiston.

WILL: Daniel Blackiston of Kent Co Whereas Ebenezer Blackiston and I have an agreement for the exchange of my right to the mill lands and houses where I now live which I purchased of William Pearce for a tract which Ebenezer holds called "Hinchenham" adjoining lands of mine and whereas Ebenezer is not yet of age to make a conveyance which I believe he will. Executors to have power to convey a deed to Ebenezer if he conveys the said land to my son Daniel Blackiston. If Daniel dies, then to my 2 daughters Emily and Martha. I give to my son Daniel my lands called "Hinchenham" containing 116 acres which my father died possessed of, also the land Ebenezer shall convey to my son. My personal estate to be sold and pay my debts, then to my daughters Emily and Martha. To my dau. Emily £200 and to my dau. Martha £200 to be paid by their brother Daniel. My guardian to cloth and supporting Daniel, Emily and Martha until Daniel is 21 then the guardian to give lands to Daniel and personal estate to Emily and Martha. He is to pay Emily £50 at 21, Martha £50 at 23, and so on until full payment. If Daniel dies, then to my daughters. If Ebenezer does not convey said land "Hinchenham" and the mill land I purchased of William Pearce to be sold on credit of 6 years. If land is sold, then money to my 3 children. My brother John to be guardian of my 3 children. Execs. my brother John Blackiston and brother in law Samuel W. Smith. Witnesses John Maxwell, William Pearce, Lambert Beck. Written Mar. 23, 1807 Proved Apr. 24, 1807 p. 335

A Stephen Blackstone owned Hinchingham in 1783.

Daniel Blackiston and Elizabeth Smith were married on 3 Nov 1796. **Elizabeth Smith**, daughter of Simon Smith and Ann H., born about 1750.

Daniel Blackiston and Elizabeth Smith had the following children:

212   i.   **Daniel Blackiston** was born in 1798.
213   ii. **Emily Blackiston** born about 1800.
214   iii. **Martha Blackiston** born about 1802.

124. Sarah Blackiston (Stephen-6, Ebenezer-5, John-4, John-3, George-2, Marmaduke-1) born about 1780. MARRIAGE: Sarah Blackiston m. John Ashley per licenses in Kent Co Dec. 24 1798 per Chesapeake Cousins p. 10. Sarah Blackiston and John Ashley were married on 24 Dec 1798 in Kent County, Maryland. **John Ashley**, son of David Ashley and Ann Emerich, born about 1780.

126. Milcah Blackiston (Stephen-6, Ebenezer-5, John-4, John-3, George-2, Marmaduke-1) born about 1785. She died on 18 Jan 1840 at the age of 55. Milcah Blackiston and Ebenezer Blackiston were married about 1805. **Ebenezer Blackiston**, son of Michael Blackiston and Dorothy Wilcox, was born on 4 Jul 1784. He died on 30 Sep 1846 at the age of 62 in Kent County, Maryland. He was buried in Still Pond Cem, Kent County, Maryland. He owned a shoe store. In estate of Sarah Blackiston in 1808 he is listed as Ebenezer Blackston of Queen Annes Co

Ebenezer Blackston Home in 1810 (City, County, State): Queen Anne's, Maryland. 1 Male 26-44y, 3 males 16-25y, 2 females 26-44y.
1810; Census Place: Queen Anne's, Maryland; Roll: 16; Page: 142; Image: 00078; Family History Library Film: 0193669

MARRIAGE: Ebenezer Blackiston m. Rachel Kernes (Q.A.) Feb 18 1841 by Offley.

WILL: Ebenezer Blackiston dec'd intestate, granted to Rachel Blackiston and Henry Blackiston 1846. Estate Acct 731 Oct 21 1846 appeared Rachel Blackiston and Henry Blackiston, heirs include Rachel his wife 1/2 of estate and no children, To Mary Davis wife of Aaron Davis and sister 1/5. to children of James a brother, 1/7 of 1/5 to wit John, Mary, Benjamin, Elizabeth Grace wife of James H. Grace, James Blackiston, Ebenezer, Lewis, John, son of Jabez Blackiston a brother of intestate, John Burbage a son of Ann Burbage formerly Blackiston and a sister of intestate, John T. Miller only child of a decd sister of intestate, Harriet Miller. settled Jan 29 1850

TOMBSTONE: Ebenezer Blackiston d. Sep 30 1846 age 62y

Ebenezer Blackiston and Milcah Blackiston had the following children:

215	i.	**Ezekial Cooper Blackiston** was born on 21 Jun 1811. He died on 27 Sep 1830 at the age of 19 in Kent County, Maryland. He was buried in Still Pond Cem, Kent County, Maryland. TOMBSTONE: Ezekial C. Blackiston son of Ebenezer & Milkey his wife June 21, 1811--Sep 27, 1830 age 19y.
216	ii.	**Wesley Blackiston** was born on 19 Oct 1821. He died on 6 Jun 1843 at the age of 21 in Kent County, Maryland. He was buried in Still Pond Cem, Kent County, Maryland. TOMBSTONE: Wesley Blackiston died Jun 6 1843 age 22y

130. Kennard Blackiston (James-6, Ebenezer-5, John-4, John-3, George-2, Marmaduke-1) was born on 24 Nov 1769 in Kent County, Maryland. He died before 1816 at the age of 47. His full name may be James Kennard Blackiston because a deed of 1834 for his sons says James Blackiston.

Kennard Blackiston and Elizabeth Medford were married on 18 Jun 1799 in Kent County, Maryland. **Elizabeth Medford**, daughter of Marmaduke Medford and Hannah , born about 1779. DEED TW 2 p 437 names heirs of George Medford.

Kennard Blackiston and Elizabeth Medford had the following children:

+217   i. **James Kennard Blackiston**, born bef 1795; married Mary Ann Hatcheson, 3 Dec 1822, Queen Annes County, Maryland; died bef Nov 1835.

+218   ii. **Thomas Medford Blackiston**, born abt 1801, Kent County, Maryland; married Louisa Ann Elliott, 25 Aug 1828, Kent County, Maryland; married Mary Malvina Blackiston, 4 Apr 1836, Kent County, Maryland; married Maria ; died abt Jan 1859, Kent County, Maryland.

132. Ebenezer Blackiston (James-6, Ebenezer-5, John-4, John-3, George-2, Marmaduke-1) was born on 1 Jun 1772 in Kent County, Maryland. He died in likely Kentucky. MARRIAGE: 2 Jul 1798 in Lincoln County, Kentucky. Bondsman Wm Warren and witnesses Wm Warren & Thomas Patton. Consent by Wm Combs

Ebenezer Blackiston and E. Lattice Combs were married on 2 Jul 1798 in Lincoln County, Kentucky. **E. Lattice Combs** born about 1775.

133. James Blackiston Jr. (James-6, Ebenezer-5, John-4, John-3, George-2, Marmaduke-1) was born on 9 Oct 1773 in Kent County, Maryland. He died on 6 Feb 1814 at the age of 40 in Kent County, Maryland. He was buried in Shrewsbury Ch., Kent County, Maryland. BIRTH: His tombstone says born Apr 10 1780. Wife born 1776. His birth record says Oct. 9 1773. He is mentioned in grandfather Nathanial Kennard's will in 1794.

MARRIAGE: The Star Mar 4 1806 says married on Tues 25th ult.

In Kent Co, 9 Jul 1812 James Blackiston Jr. private listed in return of quota for 33rd Regt of MD by Lt. Col. William Spencer. by Capt. Charles Kankey and James Blackiston 8 days August 1813 under Capt. Ephraim Vansant MD Militia in War of 1812 Ed Wright Vol 1 p2, 30

TOMBSTONE: J. Blackiston Jr. Born April 10 1780 Died Feb 6 1814.

James Blackiston Jr. and Mary Crane were married on 25 Feb 1806 in Kent County, Maryland. **Mary Crane**, daughter of David Crane and Mary Reed, was born on 19 Oct 1776 in Kent County, Maryland. She died on 17 Jan 1859 at the age of 82 in Kent County, Maryland. She was buried in Shrewsbury Ch., Kent County, Maryland.

CENSUS: 1850 Mary Megennis 74 MD living with son David and his family

MARRIAGE: Mary Blackiston to Casparis Meginess Sep 12 1816

Her parents were Capt. David Crane and Mary Reed. Her grandfather David Crane was the original owner of the site of Elizabethtown, NJ.

TOMBSTONE: Mrs. Mary Maginnis 19 Oct 1776-17 Jan 1859. Church records says Mrs. Mary Maginnis 83y buried in Shrewsbury Churchyard. Mar 17 1859. She was of North Kent Parish.

Crane Genealogy says they had a son Jonathan that died in infancy.
James Blackiston and Mary Crane had the following children:

219   i.   **Catherine Amanda Blackiston** born about 1807. She died on 13 Apr 1827 at the age of 20 in Kent County, Maryland. WILL: Catharine Amanda Blackiston, dau. of late James Blackiston of Kent, All my real estate left to me by my late father and in Kent Co along with 3 negroes Tilly Ann, Persey Hemsley and Jim to my brothers David Crane Blackiston in trust for my mother now the wife of Casperis Meginniss during her life and after her death to my brother David Crane Blackiston and my sister Mary Malvina Blackiston. All my estate not named to David Crane Blackiston in trust for my mother Mary during her life and after her death to my sister and brother above named. Exec. James Blackiston residing near Masseys Creek Cross Roads. Witnesses Adam Waldic, David Crane, Joseph H. Sawyer. Written Mar. 9, 1827 at Philadelphia Proved Apr. 13, 1827 (before Joseph Watson Esq and Mayor of Philadelphia, PA the 3 witnesses confirmed will) p. 25

+220   ii.   **David Crane Blackiston**, born 19 Feb 1809, Brighthelmstone, Kent County, Maryland; married Rachel Motte Hooten, 4 Apr 1837, Philadelphia, Pennsylvania; died 24 Dec 1888, Glenndale, Prince Georges, Maryland.

+221   iii.   **Mary Malvina Blackiston**, born abt 1810; married Thomas Medford Blackiston, 4 Apr 1836, Kent County, Maryland; died 10 Apr 1845, Kent County, Maryland.

134. Ann Elizabeth Blackiston (James-6, Ebenezer-5, John-4, John-3, George-2, Marmaduke-1) born about 1810 in Maryland. She died on 20 Apr 1843 at the age of 33 in New Castle County, Delaware. She was buried in Old Drawyers Church Cemetery, New

Castle County, Delaware. Ann Elizabeth Blackiston and James Schee Naudain were married on 3 Sep 1832 in Cecil County, Maryland. **Dr. James Schee Naudain** was born on 24 Sep 1811 in Harrisburgh, Pennsylvania. He died on 23 May 1844 at the age of 32 in Wilmington, Delaware. He was buried in Drawyer's Church Cemetery, New Castle County, Delaware. He was a doctor. His wife's mother married John Naudain, his cousin, both grandsons of Arnold. DEED: Oct 17, 1854 A. Snow Nauda of the City of Philadelphia PA, Mary Pennell Naudai, James B. Naudain, Alice Schee Naudain, Annie M. Naudain, Lydia E. Naudain and Mary J. Naudain, minor children and heris at law of James S. Naudain deceased, late of St. Georges Hundred in New Castel Co, DE to Rober tT. Cochran of Hundred of St. Georges Co New Castele DE. Whereas Dr. Arndold Naudain then of Wilmington DE and Mary his wife hd indentrua Nov 24, 1834 converyed said plantation and track of land to bounded by lands of Arnold S. Naudain, John Ginn and Noxontown, Mill Poin, where eDr. Arnold Naudain lately resided contained 365 acres o fland to James. S. Naudain in trust of said Andrew S. Naudain and Mary Pennell Naudain his wife during their lives, whichever survivor of the couple in Book V Vol. 4 p 85, wherease the said A. Snow Naudain and Mary Pennnell Naudain by an agreement converyed to Robert T. Cochran, the legal title could not be conveyed by reason of the infancy of the said trustees, Recorded Oct 23 1854 New Castle Co DE p221-225

TOMBSTONE: In memory of Ann Eliabeth Naudain wife of Docr James S. Naudain who departed this life April 20th 1845 aged 31 years at Old Drawyers Church Cemetery, Odessa, New Castle Co DE.

CENSUS: A S Naudain 37 Tanner, M B Naudain 36, M C Naudain 15 f, James B Naudain 15 m, C J Naudain 12 f, M J Naudain 7 m Group Number: *29*; Series Number: *M432*; Residence Date: *1850*; Home in 1850: *Spring Garden Ward 3 Precinct 1, Philadelphia, Pennsylvania*; Roll: *818*; Page: *511a*

Her mother's will says to "my deceased dau. Ann Elizabeth Naudain, late the wife of Doctor James S. Nauda of St. Georges Hundred, in New Castle Co aforesaid namely: Mary Louisa Naudain, James Blackiston Naudain, Alice Schee Naudain, Lydia Eddowes Naudain, and Mary Jemima Naudain and in trust for benefit during her minority of granddau. Anne Matilda Naudain, a child of my said deceased dau. Ann Elizabeth Naudain, late the wife of the said Doctor James S. Naudain."

James Schee Naudain and Ann Elizabeth Blackiston had the following children:

222   i.   **Mary Louisa Naudain** born about 1831 died 28 Apr 1853. TOMBSTONE: Marie Louise daughter of Dr. James S. and Ann E. Naudain, Died April 28th 1853 in the 20th year of her age.at Old Drawyers Church Cemetery.

223   ii.   **James Blackiston Naudain** was born 2 May 1835 died 8 Jul 190 Marinette, Wisconsin. TOMBSTONE: James B. Naudain, son of Dr. James .S. and Anna E. Naudain Born May 2nd 1835 died July 8th 1890. Grant him O Lord eternal rest at Old Drawyers Church Cemetery.

224   iii. **Anna Matilda Naudain** was born 4 Nov 1837 died 8 Jul 1922. TOMBSTONE: Annie M. Naudain wife of William R. Cochran Nov 4 1837 July 8. 1922 at Forest Presbyerian Church Cemetery.

225   iv.   **Alice Schee Naudain** was born 8 Sep 1839 died 29 Oct 1900. TOMBSTONE: Alice Naudain wife of Myers Clarke Conwell Sep 8, 1839-Oct. 28, 1907 at Lakeside Cemetery, Dover, DE.

226   v.   **Lydia Eddowes Naudain** was born 2 Jul 1841 died 5 Oct 1910 . TOMBSTONE: Lydia E. Naudain wife of Robert A. Cochran July 2, 1841 Oct 5 1910 at Forest Presbyterian Church Cemetery, Middletown, New Castle Co DE.

227   vi.   **Mary Jemima Naudain** was born 1 Apr 1843 died 6 Jun 1925. TOMBSTONE: Mary J. Naudain wife of Edward Reynolds April 1 1843 June 6 1925 at Forest Presbyterian Church Cemetery.

135. William Henry Blackiston (James-6, Ebenezer-5, John-4, John-3, George-2, Marmaduke-1) born about 1814 in Maryland. He died on 13 Sep 1853 at the age of 39 in Middletown, Delaware. Wm. H. Blackiston, Sheriff of Kent Co 1843.

CENSUS: 1850 Kent Co, MD
William H Blackeston 36 MD farmer, Hanna M Blackeston 35 PA, Heppun Blackeston 13, Henny Blackeston 12, Josephine Blackeston 10, Anna Blackeston 9, Emah Blackeston 7, Slater C Blackeston 5, Clara Blackeston 2, Liza Blackeston 8/12, Sarah R Beck 35, Stephen Harding 27 black, Group Number: 29; Series Number: M432; Residence Date: 1850; Home in 1850: District 3, Kent, Maryland; Roll: 294; Page: 281b Next door is David C. Blackiston and family.

OBITUARY: William H. Blackiston on Monday last at Middletown DE former sheriff of Kent Co Mar 19 1853 Kent Co News.

William Henry Blackiston and Hannah Maria Hepburn were married. **Hannah Maria Hepburn** was born 25 Dec 1812 to Samuel Hepburn and Ann Clay of Milton PA. They married Jun 8, 1835 Per Swedish Holsteins in America from 1644 to 1892 p 123. She died before 1879 at the age of 64. ESTATE: Estate 462 Hannah Maria Blackiston. Kent Co MD. Slater C. Blackiston minister of the Gospel, now of Spokane Washington one of the children and heirs of law of Hannah M. Blackiston, late of Kent Co received of Josephine Blackiston, administratrix. dated April 4 1879. List of heirs include Josephine, Slater, Hepbron, Emma, Clara, Elizabeth, Mary dated 1918. R. Thomas Cochran and wife on May 26 1875 executed a mortgage to my mother H. Maria Blackiston and letters of admin. to Josephine Blackiston her daughter who has since died and I Slater C. Blackiston, the only surviving child of the said H. Maria Blackiston. dated Jun 18 1818.

William Henry Blackiston and Hannah Maria Hepburn had the following children:

+227   i.   **Samuel Hepburn Blackiston**, born 1836, Maryland; married Sarah Turner Rasin, 12 Sep 1868, Kent County, Maryland; married Josephine ; died 1885.

+228   ii. **Henry Curtis Blackiston**, born abt 1838, Maryland; married Kate ; died 3 Sep 1864, Bunker Hill, Virginia.

229   iii. **Josephine Blackiston** born about 1840.

230   iv. **Anna Jemima Blackiston** was born 6 Feb 1841 died 14 Aug 1870. TOMBSTONE: Annie Blackiston Born Feb. 6, 1841 Died Aug. 14, 1870 "I am the resurection and the life. He that believeth in me though he were dead yet shall he live. So he giveth his beloved sleep" Cemetery records show middle name as Jemima

231   v.   **Emma Hepburn Blackiston** born about 1843 in Maryland. Died 3 Jan 1918. WILL: Emma H. Blackiston of the town of Middletown, New Castle County, Delaware to my niece Mary Nowland Shallcross $1500, my grandfather's clock, mahogany center table, gilt frame mirror and mahogany sewing table now in her possession. To the children of my deceased sister, Mary Blackiston Patton, $500 in consideration of my sister's kindness to me during her lifetime, residue of estate to my brother Slater C. Blackiston or if he should die before me, 1/4 part to his children in equal shares, 1/4 part to children Samuel Hepburn Blackiston, 1/4 part to children of my sister Mary Blackiston Patton in equal shares, and 1/4 part to deceased sister Elizabeth Howland. Sep 28, 1917. TOMBSTONE: Emma Hepburn Blackiston Jan. 3 1918 The Lord is my Shepherd.

232   vi. **Rev. Slater Clay Blackiston Sr.** was born 13 Jan 1846 Maryland died 21 Mar 1927 Portland, Oregon. DEATH: Rv. Slater Clay Blakiston died Mar. 21, 1927 of senility, male white married wife Margaret born Jan. 13, 1835 clergyman born Baltimore, MD. Parents unknown. Info. Mrs. S.F. Blackiston. Buried Mt. Moriah Cem. TOMBSTONE: Reverend Slator Clay Blackiston 1846-1927 at Mt. Moriah Cemetery, Butte, Montana. He married Margeret Monroe born 23 May 1848 in Mississippi and died 2 Nov 1929 in Portland Oregon.

233   vii. **Clara Leete Blackiston** was born 1848 in Kent County, Maryland. Died 22 Nov 1907 TOMBSTONE: Clara Leete Blakciston Nov. 22, 1907 at Old Saint Anne's Church Cemetery, Middletown.

234   viii. **Lizzie Blackiston** was born 18 Oct 1849 in Kent County, Maryland. Died 1 Dec 1883 TOMBSTONE: Lizzie Blakiston beloved wife of Henry A. Nowland 1843-1883 at Old Saint Anne's Church Cemetery, Middletown, New Castle Co, DE.

235   ix. **Mary Euginia Blackiston** born about 14 Mar 1852 died 4 Jan 1909. DEATH: Mary B Patton Gender: Female Race: White Age: 56 Birth Date: 14 Mar 1852 Birth Place: Maryland Death Date: 4 Jan 1909 Death Place: Philadelphia, Pennsylvania, USA Father: Wm H Blackiston Mother: Hannah M Hepburn Certificate Number: 7158

Buried Laurel Hill Cemetery, Philadelphia, PA. Her husband John W. Patton was a Professor of Law at the University of Pennsylvania. He studied at Harvard Law School.

137. **Ebenezer Blackiston** (Michael-6, Ebenezer-5, John-4, John-3, George-2, Marmaduke-1) was born on 4 Jul 1784. He died on 30 Sep 1846 at the age of 62 in Kent County, Maryland. He was buried in Still Pond Cem, Kent County, Maryland. He owned a shoe store.

CENSUS: 1820 Kent Co, MD
Ebenezer Blackiston Enumeration Date 7 Aug 1820
Male: 1 26-44y, 3 16-25y, 2 under 10y; Female: 1 26-44y, 1 16-25y, 1 10-15y.
Home in 1820 (City, County, State) Election District 1, Kent, Maryland, USA

MARRIAGE: Ebenezer Blackiston m. Rachel Kernes (Q.A.) Feb 18 1841 by Offley.

WILL: Ebenezer Blackiston dec'd intestate, granted to Rachel Blackiston and Henry Blackiston 1846. Estate Acct 731 Oct 21 1846 appeared Rachel Blackiston and Henry Blackiston, heirs include Rachel his wife 1/2 of estate and no children, To Mary Davis wife of Aaron Davis and sister 1/5. to children of James a brother, 1/7 of 1/5 to wit John, Mary, Benjamin, Elizabeth Grace wife of James H. Grace, James Blackiston, Ebenezer, Lewis, John, son of Jabez Blackiston a brother of intestate, John Burbage a son of Ann Burbage formerly Blackiston and a sister of intestate, John T. Miller only child of a decd sister of intestate, Harriet Miller. settled Jan 29 1850

TOMBSTONE: Ebenezer Blackiston d. Sep 30 1846 age 62y

Ebenezer Blackiston and Milcah Blackiston were married about 1805. **Milcah Blackiston**, daughter of Stephen Blackiston and Sarah Miller, born about 1785. She died on 18 Jan 1840 at the age of 55.

Ebenezer Blackiston and Milcah Blackiston had the following children:

215   i. **Ezekial Cooper Blackiston**, born 21 Jun 1811; died 27 Sep 1830, Kent County, Maryland.
216   ii. **Wesley Blackiston**, born 19 Oct 1821; died 6 Jun 1843, Kent County, Maryland.

Ebenezer Blackiston and Rachel Kearnes were married on 18 Feb 1841 in Kent County, Maryland. **Rachel Kearnes** born about 1820.

138. **James Blackiston** (Michael-6, Ebenezer-5, John-4, John-3, George-2, Marmaduke-1) born about 1785. He died before 1846 at the age of 61. died before brother Ebenezer 1846. James' children received distribution of Ebenezer's estate of $52.60 4/7 cent.

Voucher Book 6 p 248-9 Mary and James received their shared of estate of Ebenezer date Jan 29 1850 as children of James brother of Ebenezer Blackiston. James Blackiston was married.

James Blackiston had the following children:

+236   i.   **John B. Blackiston**, born abt 1802; married Catherine ; died aft 1880.

237   ii.   **Mary Blackiston** born about 1804. Vouchers Kent Co Book 6 p 248,249. Feb 1 1850 Mr. Henry Blackiston, one of the administrators for Ebenezer Blackiston, dec'd, paid $52.60 to Mary Blackiston and James Blackiston for their distributive share of James Blackiston of the personal estate of Ebenezer as struck by the Orphans Court on Jan 29 1850 the said Mary and James being children of James Blackiston who was a brother of Ebenezer.

238   iii.   **Benjamin Blackiston** born about 1806.

239   iv.   **Elizabeth Blackiston** born about 1808.

240   v.   **James Blackiston** born about 1810. Vouchers Book 6 p 253. I, James Blackiston, son of James Blackiston and a nephew of Ebenezer Blackiston received $52.60 Feb 1850. personally appeared James of Queen Anne Co.

241   vi.   **Ebenezer Blackiston** born about 1812.

242   vii.   **Lewis Blackiston** born about 1814. He died 7 Apr 1880 at the age of 56 in Washington Dc. Vouchers Kent Co. Book 6 p 249. I, Lewis Blackiston, of Georgetown, District of Columbia for $52.60 received from Henry Blackiston and Rachel Blackiston, administrators of Ebenezer Blackiston deceased's estate, release from all claim. Mar 26 1850. Recorded Baltimore City. He married on 30 Nov 1844 in DC to Mary Caroline Dashield. According to an obit. in the Washington Post of 8 Apr 1880, Lewis Blackiston, aged 60, died 7 Apr 1880 of paralysis. Another DC paper: "BLACKISTON--On Thursday, December 30, 1909, at 4 p.m. MARY CAROLINE, wife of the late Lewis Blackiston. Funeral from her residence 911 Westminster street, Saturday, January 1, at 2 p. m."

140. **Ann Blackiston** (Michael-6, Ebenezer-5, John-4, John-3, George-2, Marmaduke-1) born about 1794. She died before 1850 at the age of 56. Vouchers shows she died before 1850 and had one son John Burbage. Ann Blackiston and Barbage were married. **Barbage**.

141. **Harriet Blackiston** (Michael-6, Ebenezer-5, John-4, John-3, George-2, Marmaduke-1) born about 1798. She died before 1850 at the age of 52. Vouchers She had one son John T. Miller. She died before 1850. Harriet Blackiston and Thomas Miller were married on 3 Sep 1818 in Queen Annes County, Maryland. **Thomas Miller** born about 1798. He died 1819 and she married **Joseph Blackiston.**
MARRIAGE: Thomas Miller m. Harriett Blackiston Sep 3 1818 Queen Anne's Co MD

MARRIAGE: Joseph Blackiston m. Harriett Miller Feb 11 1819 Kent Co MD
CENSUS: 1850 Kent Co, MD
John Miller 30 Carpenter, Julia 28. next door is Thomas M. Blackiston and family.
Census; Record Group Number: 29; Series Number: M432; Residence Date: 1850; Home in 1850: District 2, Kent, Maryland; Roll: 294; Page: 229b

142. **Mary Blackiston** (Michael-6, Ebenezer-5, John-4, John-3, George-2, Marmaduke-1) born about 1800. Mary Blackiston and Aaron Davis were married on 21 Feb 1820 in Kent County, Maryland. **Aaron Davis** born about 1794. DEATH: Mary Davis Birth Date abt 1792 Birth Place Philadelphia, Pennsylvania Death Date 7 Dec 1863 Death Place Camden, New Jersey Age at Death 71 Burial Date 10 Dec 1863 Gender Female Street Address 413 Hamilton St Residence Philadelphia, Pennsylvania Cemetery American Mechanics FHL Film Number 1986420. BURIAL: Div B Lot 26 shows gr 1 Aaron Davis buried Mar. 11, 1861 age 67y and Mary Davis buried Dec 10 1863 age 71y. Grave 3 Catherine Taylor buried Dec 19 1916 age 90y, gr 4 Emily Davis buried Sep 26 1849, 11 mos, and John Davis buried Jan 16 1856 age 5yrs 5mos.

143. **James Blackiston** (Joseph-6, Ebenezer-5, John-4, John-3, George-2, Marmaduke-1) born about 1780. He died in 1840 at the age of 60 in Delaware. CENSUS: New Castle Co DE 1810 Appoquinimink Hundred. James Blackiston age 16-26, female 16-26, one male 1-10, one female 1-10. He is said to have had a lot of children and moved to Pennsylvania after the War of 1812 per 1935 letter of Zelle Henry Blackiston wife of Franklin Blackiston born 1874 (member of PA SAR) at M.H.S.

James Blackiston and Elizabeth West were married in 1819 in Westmoreland, Pennsylvania. **Elizabeth West**, daughter of Martin West, born about 1800. She died in Jun 1863 at the age of 63.

James Blackiston and Elizabeth West had the following children:

+243   i. **Robert West Blackiston**, born 24 Mar 1823; married Jane Barren, 25 Jun 1847; died 4 Oct 1881.

244   i. **Blackiston** born about 1806. Statements by the family indicate there were more children. Their names are not known.

245   ii. **Blackiston** born about 1808.

144. **4th Sgt. Joseph Blackiston** (Joseph-6, Ebenezer-5, John-4, John-3, George-2, Marmaduke-1) was born in 1787 in MD. He died on 20 Jan 1850 at the age of 63 in Rock Hall, Kent County, Maryland. He owned "Yearly's Beginning" and "Prevention of Inconvenience"

BIRTH: His age in his obituary is 68 (c1782) but the 1850 mortality schedule says 63 (c1787). His son Henry's 1880 census says father born MD (and he administered his estate) but younger son John's 1880 census says his father was born DE. The 1850 mortality Schedule says he was born in MD.

MARRIAGE: ca 1806 since son James born 1808. Have not the marriage record in MD to Henrietta (who I believe her maiden name was Eagle since her son's name was James Eagle Blackiston and they had a neighbor James Eagle).

NEWS: July 10 1804 RSM Joseph Blackiston Jr. has a letter remaining at PO Chestertown Per MD Eastern Shore Newspaper Abstracts 1790-1805 Vol 1 by F. Edward Wright (This is likely the same Joseph since if the father was still living he would be called Joseph Jr.)

CENSUS: 1810
Two J Blackiston's listed for father and son, one owns slaves and over 45.
J Blackiston 45+
Home in 1810 (City, County, State): Kent, Maryland
Number of Household Members: 5
1810; Census Place: Kent, Maryland; Roll: 14; Page: 891; Image: 00188; Family History Library Film: 0193667

J Blackiston
Home in 1810 (City, County, State): Kent, Maryland
Number of Household Members: 14
1810; Census Place: Kent, Maryland; Roll: 14; Page: 894; Image: 00189; Family History Library Film: 0193667

SERVICE: 1812. Maryland Militia War of 1812 Vol. Eastern Shore by F Edward Wright page 29: Aug 14-25 1813/ Head of Chester Company, ordered on service as mounted rifle corps and stationed at Comegys Point / Joseph/James Blackston 9 days served. Also mentioned others. on page 32: Sept. 12-23 1814/ Joseph Blackson, 4th Sgt. 13 days served.

DEED: 1819. James Eagle sold Joseph Blackiston "Yearly's Beginning" and "Prevention of Inconvenience" west side of main road leading to Eastern neck. Oct 11, 1819 WS #3 p 83.

DEED: 1819. Joseph Blackiston and Henrietta his wife sold Yearly's Beginning to John Yearly 12 acres Dec. 15, 1819 WS #3 p. 162, 174.

CENSUS: 1820
Joseph Blackiston 000110-20100-00 M 26-45y
Count likely includes Henrietta F 16-26, with a M 16-18y, two F 1-10y
1820; ED 1, Kent, MD; P.87; Roll: M33 44; I:80

MARRIAGE: Joseph Blackiston m. Ann E. Wiggins Jan 20 1836 Queen Annes Co, MD

CENSUS: 1840
Joseph Blackiston
Total Free White Persons: 2
1840; Census Place: District 4, Queen Anne's, Maryland; Roll: 169; Page: 124; Family History Library Film: 0013186

DEED: 1843. Joseph Blackiston and Anna his wife to Sarah Jane Ashley 4 3/4 acres of "Yearly's Beginning" May 29, 1843. (his will says she is his daughter)

WILL: Joseph Blackiston of Kent Co To my son Henry Blackiston all my lands with all my personal property forever excepting my negro girl Eliza Ann under the condition that he pay each of my sons and daughters James E. Blackiston, John T. Blackiston, William C. Blackiston and Henrietta B. Count $300 at $30 annually. If any die without heirs then to be retained by Henry. To my wife Ann Blackiston over and above her right of dower in my estate the above mentioned negro Eliza Ann during her life and after the death of my wife to be free. [Freedom pass granted to Eliza Ann June 24, 1856, written in margin]. As I have already deeded a part of my farm and given some personal property to my dau. Sarah J. Ashley I consider that she has her full portion of my estate. If there shall be brought against my children or accounts then it is to be deducted from legacies of $300 each. Exec. my son Henry Blackiston. Witnesses Thomas D. Burgess, James H. Edes, Thomas A. Strong. Written Nov. 6, 1849 Proved Jan. 29, 1850 JFB #1 p. 295. Administration bond Mar 4 1850 Henry Blackiston, Joseph Harris, and Jacob Stevens.

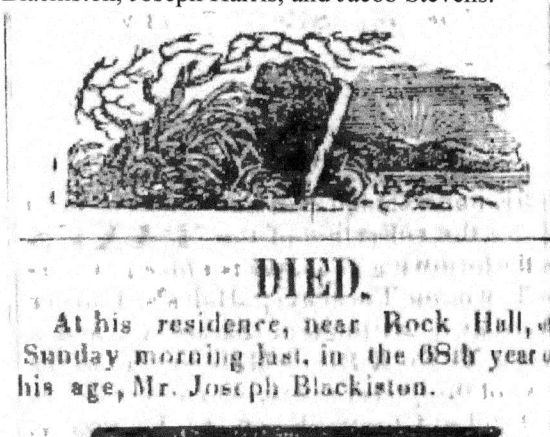

DIED.

At his residence, near Rock Hall, on Sunday morning last, in the 68th year of his age, Mr. Joseph Blackiston.

OBITUARY: Died. At his residence, near Rock Hall, on Sunday morning last, in the 68th year of his age, Mr. Joseph Blackiston. Kent Co News Jan. 26 1850.

CENSUS: 1850 Mortality Schedule
Joseph Blackiston June 1850 Kent county, Kent, Maryland, Age: 63 Marital Status: Married Birth Year (Estimated): 1787 Birthplace: Maryland Death Date: May (1850) died of pneumonia. Long illness. Schedule Type: 1850 Mortality (May 1850 is incorrect)

CENSUS: 1850 Kent Co, MD
Henry Blackiston 56, Sarah C Blackiston 19, Anna Blackiston 40 (the step mother), Samuel J Nicks 35, Ann E Nicks 27, Mary E Benton 15
1850; Census Place: District 1, Kent, Maryland; Roll: M432 294; Page: 264B; Image: 535

Joseph Blackiston and Henrietta were married about 1805. **Henrietta** born about 1784 in Maryland. She died after Dec 1819 at the age of 35. Her maiden name may be Eagle due to deed transactions and her son's middle name. She was living in 1819. It is believed that her father is James Eagle. She named her oldest son James Eagle Blackiston.

DEATH: Between 1819-1836. She signed a deed in Dec 1819 and her husband was remarried by 1836 so she died somewhere in between.

Joseph Blackiston and Henrietta had the following children:

+246 i. **James Eagle Blackiston Sr.**, born 1808, Kent County, Maryland; married Rebecca T. Ashley, 30 May 1830, Kent County, Maryland; married Mary Emily Stephens, 19 Oct 1843, Kent County, Maryland; died 30 Mar 1869, Rock Hall, Kent County, Maryland.

+247 ii. **Mary Ann Blackiston**, born abt 1810; married John D. Lewis, 17 Feb 1836, Queen Annes County, Maryland; died 20 Mar 1845, Kent County, Maryland.

+248 iii. **Henrietta Blackiston**, born 2 May 1811, Hagerstown, Washington County, Maryland; married Count.

+249 iv. **Henry Blackiston**, born 2 Mar 1813, Maryland; married Marietta Durding, 13 Nov 1841, Kent County, Maryland; married Sarah Catherine Shaw, 30 Apr 1849, Baltimore, Maryland; died 12 May 1891, Kent County, Maryland.

+250 v. **William C. Blackiston**, born abt 1815; married Elizabeth Tomlinson, 16 Jan 1838, Cecil County, Maryland; died 21 Jan 1890, Baltimore City, Maryland.

+251 vi. **John Thomas Blackiston**, born 16 Mar 1819; married Marie Antoinette Copper, 3 Jan 1845, Kent County, Maryland; died 17 Jul 1893, Westernport, Allegany County, Maryland.

+252 vii. **Sarah Jane Blackiston**, born abt 1820, Maryland; married Lemuel Washington Ashley, 1842, Kent County, Maryland; died bef 1876.

4th Sgt. Joseph Blackiston and Ann E. Wiggins were married on 20 Jan 1836 in Queen Annes County, Maryland. **Ann E. Wiggins** born about 1810. She died before Jun 1856 at the age of 46.

CENSUS: 1850 Kent Co 840-840
Anna Blackiston age 40 living with Henry and Sarah Blackiston. (her stepson)

1850; Census Place: District 1, Kent, Maryland; Roll: M432 294; Page: 264; Image: 531.

She died before June 24 1856 because slave Eliza Ann in her husband's will was only to be granted freedom after wife's death and Eliza Ann was granted her freedom on June 24 1856.

146. Samuel Spencer Blackiston (William-6, Benjamin-5, John-4, John-3, George-2, Marmaduke-1) born about 1752. He died on 21 Sep 1796 at the age of 44 in Kent County, Delaware. Letters of Administration granted to Frances Blackiston widow and Benjamin Blackiston who at the same time give bond with Ebenezer Blackiston their surety. Oct 21 1796. Delaware WB N p 153

Samuel Spencer Blackiston and Frances Blackiston were married on 27 May 1790 in Delaware. **Frances Blackiston**, daughter of George Blackiston and Martha Redgrave, was born on 25 May 1769 in Deer Park, Queen Annes County, Maryland. She died on 1 Oct 1813 at the age of 44 in New Castle County, Delaware.

Samuel Spencer Blackiston and Frances Blackiston had the following children:

253   i.   **William Blackiston** was born in 1791. He died in 1794 at the age of 3.

254   ii.   **Martha Blackiston** was born in 1794. She died in 1796 at the age of 2.

147. William Blackiston (William-6, Benjamin-5, John-4, John-3, George-2, Marmaduke-1) born about 1754. He may be William who married Mary Ann Hazel dau. of George Hazel who names him in his will but it would be a later wife.

William Blackiston and Mary Ann Hazel were married before 1831. **Mary Ann Hazel**. Her father's will says to my dau. Mary Ann Blackiston wife of William Blackiston of Kent Co, DE $50 and to dau. Susan Hazel all that tract called "Blackiston's Fancy Farm" lying on the N side of farm on which I now live containing about 460 acres it being the land formerly belonging to Lewis Blackiston. will dated Feb. 27 1831 and proved March 7 1831.

WILL: George Hazel of Kent Co, To my dau. Mary Ann Blackiston wife of William Blackiston of Kent Co DE $50. To my dau. Elizabeth Spear wife of James Spear of Kent Co DE jointly with my dau. Susan Hazel all that tract called "Blackiston's Fancy Farm" lying on the N side of the farm on which I now live containing about 460 acres it being the land formerly belonging to Lewis Blackiston equally to my 2 daughters Elizabeth and Susan and to them all my personal estate in MD. To my eldest son William A. Hazel my farm situated in Kent Co DE but part is in MD in Queen Anns Co and Kent Co, MD but are adjoining said farm and on which he now resides and to him all my personal property in DE. Whereas all my slaves are free except for George being lately bought of Jesse Knock out of Newman's estate, he is to be free on Jan. 1, 1846. Whereas my sons James Hazel and

Benjamin Hazel have been provided for by their grandfather William Anderson I give to each $1. Execs. my son William A. Hazel and my son in law James Spear. Witnesses Eli S. Pardee, John Whittington, John Hurlock. Written Feb. 27, 1831 Proved Mar. 7, 1831 p. 206

149. **Benjamin Blackiston** (John-6, Benjamin-5, John-4, John-3, George-2, Marmaduke-1) born about 1753. He died before May 1785 at the age of 32 in Kent County, Delaware. ESTATE: Benjamin Blackiston administration to Hannah Blackiston. May 25 1785 Arch. vol A 4 p 117-120. Liber M p 55. Arch Vol A4 p 120 mentions heirs John, Benjamin, Sarah, Ann, Francis, and Nicholas Blackiston. P. 117 says administrators are Barnet Everson and wife Hannah.

Benjamin Blackiston and Hannah Smith were married before 15 Jan 1770. **Hannah Smith**, daughter of Nicholas Smith and Ann Vansant, was born on 25 Aug 1753 in Shrewsbury, Kent County, Maryland. BAPTISM: Hannah Smith dau of Nicholas and Ann Smith b Aug 25 1753. Shrewsbury.

She is mentioned in her father's will of 1770 as Hannah Blackiston.

Benjamin Blackiston and Hannah Smith had the following children:

255	i.	**John Blackiston** was born before 1776. He died before 1796 at the age of 20.
256	ii.	**Benjamin Blackiston**.
+257	iii.	**Sarah Blackiston**, married Oliver Smith, bef 1796.
+258	iv.	**Ann Blackiston**, married William Spearman.
259	v.	**Frances Blackiston**.
260	vi.	**Nicholas Blackiston**.

150. **Ebenezer Blackiston** (John-6, Benjamin-5, John-4, John-3, George-2, Marmaduke-1) born about 1755. He died about May 1785 at the age of 30 in Kent County, Maryland.

WILL: Ebenezer Blackiston of Kent Co To my eldest son Richard Blackiston £3 gold and silver currency when he arrives at 21. To my dau. Elizabeth Blackiston £100 gold and silver currency to be paid when she arrives at 16. To my son John Blackiston a tract of land containing 100 acres adjoining lands of John Ward Penington called "Jones' Neglect" which I lately purchased of James Lowman; also a tract of 50 acres which was formerly the property of John Tucker and sold by him to Risdon Bishop of Kent Co, DE who sold it to me; and 8 acres adjoining the E end of the last mentioned tract with its improvements to son John. To my wife Sarah Blackiston my riding carriage. To my brother Benjamin Blackiston the following negroes David, Priss, Isaac, and Margaret after they serve my wife Sarah Blackiston until the following ages: negro David until he is age 31, negro Priss until she is age 21, negro Isaac until he is 25, negro Margaret until she is 20. My brother Benjamin is to manumit each of them at the designated ages that they are to serve my wife.

The residue of my estate to be divided between my 3 children Richard, John, and Elizabeth Blackiston. Exec. my wife Sarah Blackiston. Witnesses George Jackson, William Walls, John Blackiston. Written Mar. 17, 1785 Proved May 20, 1785 p. 102

Ebenezer Blackiston and Sara Sela were married. **Sara Sela** born about 1755. She died about Jun 1796 at the age of 41 in Kent County, Maryland.

WILL: Sarah Turner, wife of Ebenezer of Kent Co To my son Richard Blackiston all that tract of land which fell to me by the death of my brother John Sela containing 190 acres, 140 acres of "Chesterfield" and 50 acres "Tucker's Neglect" lying adjoining the road leading from head of Chester to Duck Creek. If he dies then the land to my two sons I had by Ebenezer Turner: Daniel and William Exec. Not Given. Witnesses James H. Graves, John Rogers, Isabel Rogers. Written Apr. 1796 Proved June 14, 1796 p. 533

ESTATE: Kent Co Administration Liber 10 p. 433 says 3rd Additional Account of Ebenezer Turner and Sarah his wife executors of Ebenezer Blackiston late of Kent Co deceased. $146.10.7 minus $98.1.9 equals $48.8.10 December Term 1801. (This Sarah died in 1796, not sure how papers were filled in her name in 1801.)

Ebenezer Blackiston and Sara Sela had the following children:

261	i.	**Richard Blackiston** born about 1777.
262	ii.	**Elizabeth Blackiston** born about 1780. MARRIAGE: Stephen Adkinson m. Elizabeth Blackiston Marriage Date: 15 Oct 1799 in Kent County MD
263	iii.	**John Blackiston** born about 1782.

151. **John Blackiston** (John-6, Benjamin-5, John-4, John-3, George-2, Marmaduke-1) born about 1760. He died before 1800 at the age of 40. MARRIAGE: John Blackiston Date: 13 May 1794 in Kent Co Delaware to Priccilla Blackiston Vol 15 p 241 Kent Co DE.

Administration in Queen Annes Co Oct 10 1795 #4911 bond signed by Lambert Vansant of Kent Co, Nathan Peacock, and William L. Newcomb.

DEED: Kent Co WS #3 p 465 Jun 21 1819. Benjamin and Mary Ann Blackiston, Joseph and Harriett Blackiston, Samuel and Rebecca Blackiston, William Blackiston, John Maslin and Eliza his wife, Daniel Chance and Sarah his wife of Queen Annes of one part to William Thomas of Kent Co sold land Ellis Industry, Bordley's Gift, Outrange, Part of Bordley's Gift traded by Naylor Bouchell for part of Ellis Industry in 1789 with John Blackiston. The above are heirs of John Blackiston, deceased. except for the family burying ground of John Blackiston with free ingress. Ellis' Industry is 114 acres.

DEED: Kent Co WS 3 p 479 date Aug 2 1819 recorded Jun 21 1819. same names as above to John Turner, John Turner Jr. and Samuel R. Turner of Balto. 27 1/4 acres "Bordley's Gift" by exchange and $.25 "Ellis Industry". all signed except Daniel who gave his mark.

John Blackiston and Priscilla Blackiston were married on 13 May 1794 in Kent County, Delaware. **Priscilla Blackiston** born about 1774 in Kent County, Delaware,. She died after 1808 at the age of 34. She was buried in Odd Fellows Cemetery, Kent, Delaware. She was probably his second wife.

CENSUS: 1800 Kent Co Priscilla Blackiston. 2 males under 10, 3 males 10-16, 1 male 16-26, 2 females under 10, 1 female 16-26, 1 female 26-45.

GUARDIAN ACCTS: Book 4 p 359, 650 Kent Co MD Jun 8 1802. Priscilla Blackiston, guardian to Benjamin, Samuel, William, Joseph, John Blackiston. Book 2 Jun 1803 Kent Co, Samuel Lewis Blackiston, Henrietta, Eliza, Joseph, William, Benjamin, and John Blackiston. Book 3 Priscilla Denning, guardian to Eliza Blackiston, William, Samuel, Joseph, and Benjamin Blackiston. p 39 Aug 14 1805 Priscilla Blackiston guardian, John, Joseph, William, Samuel, Benjamin, and Eliza Blackiston. p. 163 Mar 5 1808 Priscilla Denning, administratix of James Denning.

ESTATE: James Denning 16 Jan 1807 by Priscilla Denning Administratix Liber 12 p 88. Priscilla Denning Mar 5 1808 Book 12 p 26 allowance for 2/3 of the balance of John Blackiston's estate which came into the deceased's hands by virtue of his intermarriage with this accountant and which belongs to the heirs of John Blackiston.

John Blackiston and Priscilla Blackiston had the following children:

+264   i. **Benjamin Blackiston**, born abt 1795; married Mary Ann Brown, 17 Jan 1819, Queen Annes County, Maryland.

+265   ii. **Joseph Blackiston**, born abt 1796; married Harriet Miller, 11 Feb 1819, Kent County, Maryland.

+266   iii. **Samuel Lewis Blackiston**, born abt 1797; married Rebecca Mead, 1814.

+267   iv. **William Blackiston**, born abt 1798; married Rebecca C. Brown, 18 Dec 1824, Kent County, Maryland.

+268   v. **Eliza Blackiston**, born abt 1799; married John A. Maslin, 6 Feb 1819, Kent County, Maryland.

152. **Lewis Blackiston** (John-6, Benjamin-5, John-4, John-3, George-2, Marmaduke-1) born about 1763. He died about May 1821 at the age of 58 in Queen Annes County, Maryland.

WILL: Lewis Blackiston of QA Co MD to my daughter Hannah Susannah Thomas my plantation whereon I now dwell and purchased of William Wallace Esq known by the name

Boothsbys Fortune containing 500 acres. To Mrs. Tabitha Wright $50 for her kindness during my present illness. My grandson William Blackiston Thomas my silver watch which I wear. My negroes to be freed (requirement to not hire out slaves farther than 10 miles or they are free, children born of the mother to be born free, etc.) Son in law William Thomas sole executor. witness Samuel G. Osborn, Isaac Jackson, Edward Eubanks. TCE 1 p 151

March 19, 1798: Proceedings of the Second Judicial District of the State of Maryland William Massey, Ebenezer Palmer & his wife Sarah, Lewis Blackiston & Milcah Massey Blackiston, by her guardian Lewis Blackiston, petition the court that they, together with Daniel Massey, Mary Massey, and Araminta Massey are entitled as heirs to Ebenezer Massey, who died intestate, to the following tracts of land in Kent County: Massey's Venture Resurveyed, Exchange and part of Partnership. Daniel Massey, Mary Massey, and Araminta Massey are infants, under the age of twenty one years, the lands were sold at public auction to Lewis Blackiston for £7 15/- 8p per acre, thereby amounting to a total price of £2,076 4/- 1p. The proceeds were allotted as follows: Lewis Blackiston produced two deeds, one dated May 25, 1795 and the other dated April 14, 1796 which conveyed to him the interests of William Massey and Daniel Massey; Lewis Blackiston is further entitled to one sixth of the land by virtue of his guardianship of his daughter Milcah Massey Blackiston; one half of the purchase money goes to Lewis Blackiston to be retained in his own hands; Ebenezer Palmer gets £346 8p; Mary Massey is allotted £346 8p; and Araminta Massey gets £346 8p. Signed by all of the aforesaid commissioners; Thomas Worrell is Kent County clerk.

Lewis Blackiston and Miss Massy were married before 1789, a daughter of Ebenezer Massy and Milcah Massey. Milcah Massy whose will dated Nov. 25 1789 and proved Jan. 18 1790 named her son in law Lewis Blackiston as guardian to her young son William Massy.

Lewis Blackiston and Miss Massy had the following child:

269   i.   **Milcah Massey Blackiston**.

Lewis Blackiston and Rebecca Meads were married. **Rebecca Meads**.

Lewis Blackiston and Rebecca Meads had the following child:

+270   i.   **Hannah Susannah Blackiston**, born abt 1800; married William Thomas, 17 Jan 1818.

161. **Priscilla Wroth** (Priscilla Blackiston-6, Benjamin-5, John-4, John-3, George-2, Marmaduke-1) was born on 10 Sep 1774. Priscilla Wroth and William Smith were married. **William Smith** born about 1774. Priscilla Wroth and Jesse Comegys were married. **Jesse Comegys,** son of William Comegys and Ann Cosden, was born on 30 Oct 1749. A Revolutionary Soldier

162. Elizabeth Wroth (Priscilla Blackiston-6, Benjamin-5, John-4, John-3, George-2, Marmaduke-1) was born on 1 Mar 1777. She died on 27 May 1823 at the age of 46. Elizabeth Wroth and Thomas Maslin were married on 2 Sep 1802 in Kent County, Maryland. **Thomas Maslin**, son of Thomas Maslin and Martha Glenn, was born on 12 Sep 1768. He died on 4 Oct 1818 at the age of 50.

Thomas Maslin and Elizabeth Wroth had the following child:

+271   i.   **Martha Priscilla Maslin**, born 11 Oct 1813; married Sewell Hepbron, 12 Mar 1832, Kent County, Maryland; died 15 May 1882.

163. Martha Wroth (Priscilla Blackiston-6, Benjamin-5, John-4, John-3, George-2, Marmaduke-1) was born on 17 Oct 1778. She witnessed will of her half aunt Sarah Worrell 1807.

Martha Wroth and Levi Wroth were married on 18 Oct 1808 in Kent County, Maryland. **Levi Wroth**, son of Kinvin Wroth and Araminta , born about 1774. MARRIAGE: They were 2nd cousins.

There was a Levi Wroth, Justice of Kent Co. 1843. He served in the War of 1812 from Kent Co.

Levi Wroth and Martha Wroth had the following child:

272   i.   **Elizabeth Wroth** born about 1810. Her ancestry is given in Hanson's Old Kent p. 199-201

164. John Wroth (Priscilla Blackiston-6, Benjamin-5, John-4, John-3, George-2, Marmaduke-1) was born on 26 Aug 1781 in Kent County, Maryland. He died in Jul 1827 at the age of 45 in Kent County, Maryland.

WILL: John Wroth of Kent Co My negro man Charles to be free at the end of the year and to pay him $20 per year if he shall conduct himself properly. My negro woman Rachel to be free at end of year but if she cannot support herself then to be supported out of my estate. My servant Charlotte be free end of the present year, Emmeline my servant to be free in 1833. My boy William to be free at 1830. My boy Moses to be free in 1839. My servant girl Ann to be free in 1841. My girl Sarah to be free in 1841. My boy George to be free in 1845. My Harriet to be free in 1845. If my personal estate in $1,600 all my land to be divided between my sons to be agreed upon by them when of age. I give my 2 sons the land on condition that my son Thomas pay to my dau. Margaret $500 within 5 years and my son Edward pay to dau. Louisa within 5 years. If $1,600 or more of personal estate then divided between my daughters. If not more, then my sons to make up difference in 7 years. My estate to the maintenance of all my children during their minority. My executor and my brother Peregrine to guard their morals. A tenant selected to rent my land and continue the improvement and my brother Peregrine to assist in selecting the tenant and if he dies then Levi Wroth should take his place. My friend Peregrine Granger of Centreville in Queen Anns Co executor and guardian. Exec. Peregrine Granger of Centreville. Witnesses George Watts, William Wroth, Samuel Elbert. Written July 11, 1827 Proved July 31, 1827 p. 33

He served in the War of 1812 from Kent Co.

John Wroth and Sarah Worrell were married on 11 Jun 1805 in Kent County, Maryland. **Sarah Worrell**, daughter of William Worrell, born about 1780.

John Wroth and Mary Granger were married. **Mary Granger**, daughter of Thomas Granger and Margaret Hanson, born about 1780. She died on 20 Sep 1826 at the age of 46 in Kent County, Maryland.

OBITUARY: Mary Wroth died near Chestertown on Wed. 20 inst. Mrs. Mary Wroth consort of John Wroth Fed. Gaz. Sep 30 1826.

John Wroth and Mary Granger had the following children:

+273	i.	**Edward Theodore Wroth**, born abt 1812; married Eugenia Maria Wroth; married Margret T. Perkins; died aft 1860.
+274	ii.	**Thomas Granger Wroth**, born abt 1814, Kent County, Maryland; married Mary Elizabeth Wroth; died 11 Jun 1888.
275	iii.	**Benjamin Wroth** born about 1814.
276	iv.	**Margaret Wroth** born about 1816.
277	v.	**Louisa Wroth** born about 1818.

165. Benjamin Blackiston Wroth Sr. (Priscilla Blackiston-6, Benjamin-5, John-4, John-3, George-2, Marmaduke-1) was born on 30 Sep 1783. He died about Apr 1825 at the age of 41 in Kent County, Maryland. Benjamin married Editha Gleaves according to Revolutionary Patriots by Henry Peden, however wife was Martha Gleaves and daughter was Editha Gleaves Wroth. He is mentioned in the will of his half-sister Sarah Worrell 1807. His family is given in Old Kent p. 200 by Hanson. He served in the War of 1812.

WILL: Benjamin B. Wroth dated Mar 12, 1825 probated April 4, 1825 WB 10 p 395, daughter Editha G. Wroth, sons Benjamin B. and William Wroth, brother Peregrine Wroth's wife Mary Wroth, trust estate of Hannah Burneston, deceased, dated Jan. 26, 1821, land bought of Edward and Henry Tilghman, land bought of Levi Wroth. exec. wife Mary Wroth. witness Elizabeth Maslin, Mary A. Rinngold, Josias Ringgold, codicil. March 12 1825. grandmother Hannah Burneston, and children mentioned in will. witness Elizabeth Maslin, Mary A. Ringgold, and Josias Ringgold.

Benjamin Blackiston Wroth Sr. and Martha Ann Gleaves were married on 2 Feb 1808 in Kent County, Maryland. **Martha Ann Gleaves**, daughter of John Gleaves and Hannah Freeman, born about 1784. She died before 1814 at the age of 30. She was a widow of William Granger. She and Benjamin had one daughter Editha Gleaves Wroth.

Benjamin Blackiston Wroth and Martha Ann Gleaves had the following child:

+278   i. **Editha Gleaves Wroth**, born abt 1810; married Francis Asbury Ruth, 30 Mar 1837.

Benjamin Blackiston Wroth Sr. and Mary Groome were married about 1815. **Mary Groome** was born on 2 Mar 1785. She died about Apr 1860 at the age of 75 in Kent County, Maryland.

WILL: Mary G. Wroth of Kent Co To my son Benjamin B. Wroth my negro man Perry, my negro woman Melvina, my girl Maria and my negro man Ben and the young child Charlotte that is now at the breast of her mother (Melvina) all of which negroes I leave to my son Benjamin for life, also my stock of horses, cattle, sheep and hogs and all my farming utensils of every description and also all of my household and kitchen furniture of every description excepting such parts thereof as is herein after otherwise disposed. To my son Josias Ringgold I leave one bed quilt. To my dau. in law Mary Wroth wife of my son William G. Wroth of Baltimore I will my negro girl Hannah and my negro girl Margaret to serve during life, and also a set of silver table spoons. To my dau. Mary Fisher all my wearing apparel and a bed quilt with the figure of birds in it. To my granddau. Mary Matilda Frisby I bequeath a bed quilt with a wreath on it. To my granddau. Mary Groome Ringgold I will a bed quilt and to my grandson Joseph Rasin I also give a bed quilt. Exec. Not Given. Witnesses Levi Wroth, Octavius H. Jones. Written Feb. 9, 1857 Proved Apr. 17, 1860 p. 175

She was a widow of Josias Ringgold. She had two children by him Benjamin and William Groome Wroth.

Benjamin Blackiston Wroth and Mary Groome had the following children:

+279   i. **Benjamin Blackiston Wroth**, born 1 Mar 1824; married Anne Caroline Clayton, 16 Nov 1848; died 18 Jan 1899.
+280   ii. **William Groome Wroth**, born abt 1820; married Mary Poits.

166. **Dr. Peregrine Wroth** (Priscilla Blackiston-6, Benjamin-5, John-4, John-3, George-2, Marmaduke-1) was born on 7 Apr 1786 in Kent County, Maryland. He died on 13 Jun 1879 at the age of 93 in Baltimore City, Maryland.

BIO: Peregrine Wroth, 1803 (Apr. 7, 1786 – June 13, 1879) Baptized as an infant by Washington College founder Dr. William Smith, Peregrine Wroth, class of 1803, never

lost his loyalty to and love for the school in Chestertown. At age eight, Wroth entered the college's preparatory school. After graduation, he studied medicine at the University of Pennsylvania before returning to Kent County where he practiced for nearly fifty years. During his years as "one of the ablest and most learned physicians on the Eastern Shore," Wroth wrote a well-known paper on the history and treatment of Endemic Bilious Fever, or malaria, which was prevalent on the Eastern Shore. His advocacy for the establishment of a school for training pharmacists, led to the formation of the Maryland College of Pharmacy. From 1846-1854, Wroth was a lecturer and professor of chemistry at his alma mater. He served on the Board of Visitors and Governors at the college, and was the president of that body for several years, until he moved to Baltimore. He was married and widowed four times. His first wife, Martha Page, the daughter of Milcah and John Page, who served on the founding Board, bore him nine children, of whom three, including his favorite daughter, Eugenia Maria (Feb. 26, 1817- Sept. 30, 1861), survived to maturity. Upon Martha's death, he married on June 19, 1827 Margaret S. Nicols, who had five more children. He was also a close friend and correspondent of Mrs. Robert E. Lee. Throughout his life, Wroth's "active mind continued to keep him in the forefront of chemical thought." He also remained dedicated to Washington College. In a letter to a friend in 1874, five years before his death at age 93, Wroth wrote: "I still feel and, forever shall while I live, a deep interest in my dear old College – with which so many delightful memories are associated." Sources: J. M. Miller, "Vignette of medical history: Peregrine Wroth, MD (Hon.) and his Maryland descendants." Maryland Medical Journal, 43 (9) (1994): 807-09., Gina Ralston '04: "Dr. Peregrine Wroth, George Alfred Townsend, and the Literary Life of 19th-Century Chestertown." WC senior English thesis, McLain, Joseph H. "Dr. Peregrine Wroth (1786-1879) and Chemistry at Washington College 1846-1854." Maryland Historical Magazine 75 (1980): 233-237, Dr. Peregrine Wroth letter to Wm. J. Rivers, Esq.,. 25 July 1874.
Lower photo courtesy of William Jones '88.

He was buried in Chestertown, Kent, Maryland. He was mentioned as still living in 1876 in Hanson's Old Kent. He was then 91 years old. He is mentioned in the will of his half-sister Sarah Worrell in 1807. He is mentioned as Peregrine, son of Kenvin Wroth, in the will of James Wroth in 1803 who is assumed to be his uncle. Information on his children comes from information provided to me by Rennie Stavely from Manuscript written 1905 by James H. Wroth.

MARRIAGE: Dr. Peregrine Wroth to Mrs. Anna Granger both of Chestertown June 19 1806 Thurs. Easton Star Jul 1 1806. She must have died shortly afterwards because he remarried the following year.

MARRIAGE: Dr. Peregrine of Chestertown m. Thur. Evening Aug 27 1807 by Rev. Dr. Kewley to Miss Martha Page of Kent. Sep 2, 1807 Federal Gazette.

MARRIAGE: Peregrin Wroth of Chestertown m. Martha Page on Aug 27 1807 by Rowley Balto. Amer. Sep 3 1807

DEATH: Peregrine Wroth died Jun 13 1879 Baltimore City, #32678, male 93y 2m 5d, white male widower, physician, born Kent Co, MD, lived in Baltimore City 10 years and 6 months, died at #26 Pleasant St, Baltimore, of old age, general decay, buried Kent Co, MD Jun 18 1879 by John H. Weaver of 22 Fayette St., Dr. John Johnson of #379 N. Gilmore Baltimore City. Transit #1433

OBITUARY: Dr. Peregrine Wroth died June 13 1879 age 94y burial at Chestertown. Sun Jun 17 1879.

CENSUS: 1850 1st Elect. Dist. Kent Co, MD Peregrine Wroth 64 doctor, Catherine H. 58, Margaret P. 16, Louisa Hausen 50.

CENSUS: 1860 Kent Co 1211-1295 Pere Wroth 74 physician, Louisa T. 48, Martha P. 13 (granddau.), William H. Meteir 37 DE.

"The Yule Log": Remembering Christmas in 18th-Century Kent County By Peregrine Wroth (Washington College Class of 1803) Dr. Peregrine Wroth (1786-1879) was born on his father's plantation, Town's Relief, just outside Chestertown, and lived in Kent County throughout his long life. An early graduate of Washington College, he became a noted physician, served as professor of chemistry at his alma mater, and published poems and essays on various subjects. Wroth composed the following essay shortly before the Civil War as a private reminiscence for his children. In it, he remembers the Christmas holiday as it was celebrated during his boyhood in Kent County at the end of the 18th century – not only by Wroth's family and their neighbors, but also by their African-American slaves. Especially fascinating is Wroth's description of customs and musical traditions that had been brought from Africa and melded with the European traditions of the season. And the latter part of his essay proves that complaints about the crassness and commercialism of "modern" Christmas are hardly unique to our own time. "The Yule Log" is included in one of several handwritten volumes of Wroth's reminiscences that were discovered by Professor Davy McCall and donated to the Washington College Archives by Wroth's descendants. It was transcribed from the original manuscript by Peter W. Knox '06. The footnotes to the essay are Wroth's own.

From an article in the December 1927-January 1928 edition of the Washington College Bulletin:

From the earliest days of the Republic Washington College has given to the state and nation men who have been outstanding in the various fields of human endeavor. An examination of the list of alumni discloses many notable physicians, and foremost among them stands **Peregrine Wroth,** who lived both long and usefully.

The Wroth family in America began with James Wroth, who emigrated from England in or about 1660. Peregrine Wroth, of the fifth generation after James, was a native of Chestertown, Maryland, where he was born on the 7th day of April, 1786. In a letter written 91 years later he notes with an evident touch of pride that he was baptized when only a few days old by Doctor William Smith, the first principal of Washington College, and this fact seems to have inspired an interest in the College which continued unabated throughout his long life.

He records that he "was not entered at Washington College until 1794" (when he was 8 years old), and that he graduated there in 1803 under Dr. Colin Ferguson, the second principal. Before he left college he had been adopted by his father's cousin and was intended as a student of law under Hon. James A. Bayard, of Delaware, but as the cousin died before the father, he was persuaded to take up the study of medicine. In this connection, Dr. Morgan Browne, an eminent physician of Chestertown and an earlier graduate of Washington College in 1788, is spoken of as his preceptor. After graduating from the medical school of the University of Pennsylvania in 1807, Dr. Wroth began a practice in Chestertown which continued for fifty years, lacking two months. During the War of 1812 he offered his services to the cause and was enrolled as a surgeon's mate in the 8th Regimental Cavalry, which included Cecil and Kent Counties.

He was a member of the Medical and Chirurgical Faculty of Maryland, and was once its President. While occupying this position he urged the establishment of a pharmaceutical college for the training of druggists and was the author of a memorial to the Legislature on the subject. A law was passed in response to this memorial, establishing the Maryland College of Pharmacy.

From 1846 to 1854 he held the position of professor of chemistry in Washington College, and upon the death of Judge E. F. Chambers in 1867 he became chairman of the Board of Visitors and Governors. In the second volume of the Life of Rev. William Smith will be found some interesting letters from Dr. Wroth regarding the history of the endowment of Washington and St. John's Colleges.

Dr. Wroth was a voluminous writer and correspondent, the author of several medical books, and left many unpublished works in manuscript on different subjects. He is described as having been a man of fine physique and possessed of such an excellent constitution that he retained his physical and mental faculties to a remarkable degree until within a short time of his death.

At the age of 70 years he relinquished his practice and retired from public life, and in 1868 removed to Baltimore, where he died on June 13, 1879, in his 94th year. On June 17th his funeral services were held in Emmanuel P. E. Church in Chestertown, of which he had been a devoted member and communicant for 70 years, and he was laid to rest in the family burial ground on the Morris farm about 2½ miles from Chestertown. [Pages 8-9]

Dr. Peregrine Wroth and Anna Granger were married on 19 Jun 1806 in Kent County, Maryland. **Anna Granger**, daughter of Thomas Granger and Margaret Hanson, born about 1775. She was Mrs. Anna Granger at time of marriage to Dr. Peregrine.

Dr. Peregrine Wroth and Martha Page were married on 27 Aug 1807 in Kent County, Maryland. **Martha Page** was born on 5 Aug 1779. She died on 23 Sep 1826 at the age of 47 in Chestertown, Kent County, Maryland. OBITUARY: Martha Wroth died in Chestertown Sat. Even. last 23 Sept. consort of Dr. Peregrine. Federal Gazette Sep 30 1826.

Peregrine Wroth and Martha Page had the following children:

281	i.	**Mary Cecilia Wroth** was born on 10 Jul 1808. She died on 30 Jul 1808.
282	ii.	**Martha Cecilia Wroth** was born on 23 Oct 1809. She died on 23 Aug 1820 at the age of 10.
283	iii.	**Peregrine Wroth** was born on 26 Nov 1810. He died on 26 Apr 1812 at the age of 1.
284	iv.	**Peregrine Wroth** was born on 13 May 1813. He died on 16 Sep 1816 at the age of 3.
285	v.	**James Page Wroth** was born on 15 May 1815. He died on 3 Sep 1820 at the age of 5.
+286	vi.	**Eugenia Maria Wroth**, born 26 Feb 1817, Kent County, Maryland; married Edward Theodore Wroth; died 30 Sep 1861, Kent County, Maryland.
287	vii.	**Edward Worrell Wroth** was born on 8 Nov 1818 in Maryland. He died on 18 Feb 1877 at the age of 58 in Baltimore City, Maryland. He was buried in Greenmount Cemetery, Baltimore City, Md. DEATH: Edward W. Wroth Feb 18 1877 Cert. #15735 Baltimore City, male 58y, 3m, 10d, married, druggist, born MD, resided in Baltimore City 34 years, died at 139 W. Biddle St., malignant carbunile and ensifelas, 6 days, buried Greenmount Cem. Feb 20 1877, undertaker John H. Weaver, #22 W. Fayette St., Dr. G.K. Taneyhill of 129 W. Biddle St.

+288   viii.   **Mary Elizabeth Wroth**, born 6 Jul 1820, Kent County, Maryland; married Thomas Granger Wroth; died 1887.

289   ix.   **Henry Page Wroth** was born on 31 Jul 1822.

Dr. Peregrine Wroth and Martha Smyth Nicols were married on 19 Jun 1827. **Martha Smyth Nicols** was born on 31 Mar 1802. She died in 1836 at the age of 34. See will of Mary S. Nicols which says to Editha G. Wroth my bead reticula. To Mary E. Wroth my large white cashmere shawl and my guards. All the remainder of my clothes to Eugenia M. and Mary E. Wroth under the direction of my sister Margaret. To my friends Dr. P. Wroth a handsome Bible to be lettered in gilt on the back. My beds and bedding to my brother James Nicols and $100. To Edward W. Wroth a handsome vest with a handsome pen knife and ivory pocket comb with his name on each. To my nephew William Jackson Wroth a handsome suit of black cloth and small red chair. All the rest of my estate to my sister Margaret S. Wroth. Exec. my friend Dr. P. Wroth. Witnesses Mary Ann Ringgold, George S. Hollyday. Written Nov. 29, 1833 Proved Dec. 17, 1833 p. 288

See will of James Nicols. James Nicols of Kent Co To my nephew William J. Wroth $100. To Edward W. Wroth my silver watch. To Eugenia M. Wroth my gold breast pin set in jet. To Mrs. Tamacina Glenn "Clarks Commentary on the New Testament" also my pitchers, wash basin and tumblers. Also one dress. Mary E. Wroth $50 when she is 16. All my wearing apparel to William Meginniss. All the rest of my estate to my niece Margaret Priscilla Wroth when she is 16. Exec. my friend Dr. Peregrine Wroth. Witnesses Joseph Osborne Jr., Joseph Osborne Sr. Written Aug. 21, 1834 Proved Sep. 2, 1834 p. 317. Memo J. Nicols directs his executor to his kind friend Miss Martha Brice his "History of Methodism", Hymn book, and pocket testament.

Peregrine Wroth and Martha Smyth Nicols had the following children:

290   i.   **Kinvin Wroth** was born on 3 Aug 1828.

291   ii.   **William Jackson Wroth** was born on 13 Mar 1830. He died in 7 Apr 1907 at the age of 77. OBITUARY: DR. WILLIAM J. WROTH. Dr. William J. Wroth, formerly a practicing physician in this city, died yesterday at his home, 18 Pennhurst avenue, West Arlington, after a short illness. He had suffered from rheumatism all winter, which prevented him attending to outside business. Sunday night he was taken ill suddenly of Intestinal trouble and he grew steadily worse until the end. Dr. Wroth was 77 years old: He leaves a widow, who was a Miss Nichols, and a married daughter, who lives in New York. He moved to West Arlington nearly two years ago, having formerly lived at Chestertown, Md.

292   iii.   **Margaret Priscilla Wroth** was born on 27 Jul 1834.

The Royal Ancestry and Descendants of George Blackiston

Dr. Peregrine Wroth and Catherine Hanson were married on 3 Oct 1839 in Kent County, Maryland. **Catherine Hanson** born about 1800. She died about Jan 1855 at the age of 55 in Kent County, Maryland.

WILL: Catharine H. Wroth of Kent Co My dear husband Doctor Peregrine Wroth my farm whereon Edward T. Wroth now resides during his life, then to my nephew George A. Hanson, son of my beloved brother Alexander B. Hanson and to Peregrine $1,000. My cousin Susan Anderson, wife of Dr. Alexanders Anderson of Chestertown $100. All other cash and bonds to my said brother Alexander B. Hanson until my nephew Edward A. Hanson is 25. My servants Maria, Ellen, Thomas Wright, Thomas Worrell, Emory and Harry to be set free at the end of the year in which I may depart this life. I give to Richard Worrell, the husband of my servant Ellen, my servant girls Jane, Emily, Alice Alfred and Louis Jerome, until they arrive at 21 then to be set free. My husband to have all furniture except those articles I held jointly with my late sister Lavinia which things I give to my cousins Ann Elizabeth and Susan Anderson. All remaining estate to my nephew Edward A. Hanson. Exec. my brother Alexander B. Hanson. Witnesses Thomas B. Hynson, Margaret S. Wroth, R.A. Starn. Written Dec. 27, 1854 Proved Jan. 18, 1855

See will of Lavinia Hanson of Kent Co To my sister Catharine Wroth my negro man Levi for his unexpired term of service. My negroes Ezekal, Daniel, Mary, Harriet, William, Allen, Emily and Louis to be free. To my brother Alexander B. Hanson during his life and after his death to his children all monies due me except $200 to my said brother in trust if he pays the annual sum of $125 to my sister Catharine Wroth during her life, not subject to her husband. If my nephew Perry W. Hanson and my niece Catharine R. Hanson children of my late brother George W. Hanson die without leaving children I give my reversionary interest in the claim of due me from their late father and existing as a lien on the Ratcliff Farm to my nephew Edward Alexander Hanson on condition that he pay my sister Catharine Wroth $50. I give my watch and chain to my niece Catharine R. Hanson when she is 18 and until then to be held by my sister Catharine Wroth. To my sister Catharine Wroth all my household furniture and after her death to my relatives Susan R. Frisby and Elizabeth Anderson wife of John B.H. Anderson. I give my house and lot in Queen Street in Chestertown to my former servant Rachel Sampson during her life and after her death to my servants Harriett and Emily. To my brother Alexander B. Hanson $200 mentioned in the first part to erect a good and substantial enclosure around the family burial ground. Exec. my brother Alexander B. Hanson. Witnesses J.B. Ricaud, J.F. Gordon, Joseph N. Gordon. Written Apr. 5, 1845 Proved Nov. 11, 1851 p. 343 Codicil To my sister Catharine Wroth 3 shares of stock in the Cotton Factory at Harpers Ferry, separate from her husband. My servant boy Lewis son of Harriet shall be free. Written May 22, 1849. Witnesses J. B. Ricaud, J. F. Gordon

Dr. Peregrine Wroth and Louisa Tilden were married before 1866. **Louisa Tilden**, daughter of Tilden, born about 1800. She died on 13 Dec 1875 at the age of 75 in Baltimore City, Maryland. She was buried in Queen Annes County, Maryland. widow of a Mr. Ringgold

See WILL of Charles Tilden of Kent Co To my wife Amelia Octavia Tilden all my real estate during her life. My wife to pay $50 annually to my sister the wife of Dr. Peregrine Wroth. To Julius Perkins son of Henry Perkins $1,000 when 21. After her death ½ to Charles T. Ireland and his youngest son James Ireland and the other ½ to Mary Cecelia World and Catharine World. To my cousin Charles T. Ireland 3 notes totaling $700. All the rest of my personal estate I give ½ to my wife Amelia Octavia Tilden and the other ½ to my sister, the wife of Dr. Peregrine Wroth. Exec. Dr. Thomas G. Wroth. Witnesses George Gale, William M. S. Maxwell, P.C.A. Clements. Written Nov. 15, 1866 Proved Nov. 27, 1866 p. 343

DEATH: Louisa Wroth died Dec 13, 1875 Baltimore City, MD #06981 died age 74 white female widow, born Queen Annes Co, MD lived in Baltimore City 7 years, died at 85 E. Fayette St., of constriction of mitral and tricughs valve, cardiac dropsey, last sickness lasted 5 weeks, buried Queen Annes Co, MD Dec 16 1875 Wm. K. Hickman of 234 N. Gay St., Dr. D. Caldwell Ireland of 178 Aisquith St. transit #294

167. Ebenezer Blackiston (George-6, Benjamin-5, John-4, John-3, George-2, Marmaduke-1) was born on 14 Feb 1767. He died on 11 Dec 1829 at the age of 62 in Smyrna, Kent, Delaware. Listed as Ebenezer Blackiston Jr in Samuel Holliday's 1794 will. There are several deeds in Delaware that name Ebenezer and wife Susannah selling land to William Blackiston and his daughter Elizabeth Blackiston, mentioning Susannah inherited the land as dau of Richard Holliday late of Duck Creek Hundred, Kent Co, DE – 104 acres based on division of his land Nov 28 1788 to William for $1 then Williams sells it back to Ebenezer for $1 for his lifetime and then after to Elizabeth Blackiston, dau of Ebenezer, Oct 23 1807 P 155- 158

Ebenezer Blackiston and Susannah Holliday were married in 1792 in Kent County, Delaware. **Susannah Holliday**, daughter of Richard Holliday and Ann Johns, was born on 7 Nov 1770. She died on 24 Oct 1841 at the age of 70. They and their two sons are buried at Duck Creek Friends Burial Ground, Smyrna, Kent, DE and was restored in 2002 by a Boy Scout Eagle Project of Michael Desmond, Jr.

Ebenezer Blackiston and Susannah Holliday had the following children:

293   i. **Richard H Blackiston** was born in 1800. He died on 7 Apr 1853 at the age of 53. He was buried in Quaker Cem., Smyrna, Kent, Delaware. DEED: John M. Clayton and Sally of Camden, Kent, DE to Richard H. Blackiston of Smyrna, sold land of Dr. James Fisher of Camden in Duck Creek Hundred 43 acres who willed it to his dau Sally Ann who intermarried to John M. Clayton. Dated Jan 1 1823. CENSUS: 1850 Kent, DE. Richard H Blackiston 50 $18000 RE, Martha A Shannon 45 $1000 RE, George W Blackiston 39 $8,000 RE. Census; Record Group Number: 29; Series Number: M432; Residence Date: 1850; Home in 1850: Duck Creek Hundred, Kent, Delaware; Roll: 52; Page: 23a

294   ii. **George W Blackiston** was born on 26 Dec 1809. He died on 9 Mar 1867 at the age of 57. He was buried in Quaker Cem., Smyrna, Kent, Delaware. in Duck Creek DEATH: George W Blackiston Birth Date abt 1812 Birth Place Delaware, Death Date 10 Mar 1867, Philadelphia, Pennsylvania Age at Death 55 Burial Date 21 Mar 1867 Burial Place Philadelphia, Pennsylvania Male White Merchant Street Address Penn Hospital for Insane, 24 Ward, Residence Philadelphia, Pennsylvania, Cemetery Woodland, Marital Status Single, FHL Film Number 1993314

168. Frances Blackiston (George-6, Benjamin-5, John-4, John-3, George-2, Marmaduke-1) was born on 25 May 1769 in Deer Park, Queen Annes County, Maryland. She died on 1 Oct 1813 at the age of 44 in New Castle County, Delaware.

Frances Blackiston and Samuel Spencer Blackiston were married on 27 May 1790 in Delaware. **Samuel Spencer Blackiston**, son of William Blackiston and Ann Spencer, born about 1752. He died on 21 Sep 1796 at the age of 44 in Kent County, Delaware. Letters of Administration granted to Frances Blackiston widow and Benjamin Blackiston who at the same time give bond with Ebenezer Blackiston their surety. Oct 21 1796. Delaware WB N p 153

Samuel Spencer Blackiston and Frances Blackiston had the following children:

253   i. **William Blackiston**, born 1791; died 1794.
254   ii. **Martha Blackiston**, born 1794; died 1796.

Frances Blackiston and Rev Joseph Whitby were married on 12 Jun 1798. **Rev Joseph Whitby** was born in 1763 in Caroline County, Maryland. He died in 1820 at the age of 57.

171. Priscilla Blackiston (George-6, Benjamin-5, John-4, John-3, George-2, Marmaduke-1) was born on 30 Aug 1774 in Kent Co, Delaware, British America. She died on 13 Aug 1858 at the age of 83 in Kent Co, Delaware. She was buried in Odd Fellows Cemetery, Kent, Delaware. Priscilla Blackiston and John Lockwood were married on 13 May 1798 in Kent County, Delaware. **John Lockwood** was born on 15 Oct 1759 in Kent County, Maryland, British America. He died on 8 Oct 1811 at the age of 51. He was buried in Odd Fellows Cemetery, Kent, Delaware.

175. Sarah Blackiston (James-6, Michael-5, John-4, John-3, George-2, Marmaduke-1) was born 13 Nov 1776 Died 11 Apr 1855 buried Middle Presbyterian Cemetery, Mount Pleasant, Westmoreland County, PA. Sarah Blackiston and James Hurtt were married. **James Hurst** was born 13 May 1775 died 21 Mar 1850. Buried Middle Presbyterian Cemetery, Mount Pleasant, Westmoreland, PA.

176. Mary Blackiston (James-6, Michael-5, John-4, John-3, George-2, Marmaduke-1) born about 1792. Died 25 Feb 1829. Washington, PA. Mary Blackiston and Boyd Mercer were married. **Boyd Mercer**.

177. Ann Blackiston (James-6, Michael-5, John-4, John-3, George-2, Marmaduke-1) born about 1794. Ann Blackiston and Thomas Hurtt were married. **Thomas Hurst** born about 1794. Died 1861. Buried Middle Presbyterian Cemetery, Mount Pleasant, Westmoreland, PA.

178. Frances Blackiston (James-6, Michael-5, John-4, John-3, George-2, Marmaduke-1) born about 1795. She died before 1819 at the age of 24. Frances Blackiston and Joseph Taylor were married.

180. James Brice (Judith Ann Blackiston-6, Michael-5, John-4, John-3, George-2, Marmaduke-1) born about 1770. He died in 1798 at the age of 28.

WILL: James Brice of Chestertown, Kent Co, To my wife Elizabeth Brice my negro man Alec or Alexander and my negro woman Peg, my bureau, 2 small sealskin trunks, my walnut bedstead and bed on which I generally sleep and an umbrella. To my son Joseph W. Brice all my plate consisting of a soup spoon, 6 table spoons, 12 tea spoons and a pair of sugar tongs, and a bedstead with a bed, a large seal skin trunk, and my French silver watch. My negro woman Suke and her child Charlotte shall be sold. My wife to have 1/3 and my son to have 2/3. If my son dies then to my brother Joseph Brice whom I appoint guardian to my son. Exec. my brother Joseph Brice. Witnesses James Houston Esq., John Hyland. Written Aug. 1, 1798 Proved Oct. 18, 1798 p. 606

James Brice and Elizabeth were married.

James Brice and Elizabeth had the following child:

+295   i.   **Joseph W. Brice**, born bef 1798, Maryland; married Anna Maria Tilden, 1 Feb 1814, Kent County, Maryland.

182. Mary Brice (Judith Ann Blackiston-6, Michael-5, John-4, John-3, George-2, Marmaduke-1) born about 1772.

Mary Brice and Harrigan were married. **Harrigan** born about 1775.

Harrigan and Mary Brice had the following children:

296   i.   **Ann Harragan** born about 1800.
297   ii.   **Sarah Harragan** born about 1800. She died on 2 Apr 1820 at the age of 20 in Kent County, Maryland.

WILL: Sarah Harragan (Nunc) After my debts paid and those of my sisters then I leave my property to Martha Brice, Mary Brice, Tamasina Glenn, and Ann Brice dau of Henrietta Brice. Thomas Hynson to take charge of Ann Brice's part. My aunts Susanna, Sarah and Ann Brice all my mother's clothes. date not given, proved. Apr. 19, 1820 by George W. Thomas who said that on Mar. 13 last he went to her room in the house of Richard Brice of Chestertown where she had been confined and gave her a draft of the will and intending to make a formal will later but she died on Apr 2.

187. Ann Brice (Judith Ann Blackiston-6, Michael-5, John-4, John-3, George-2, Marmaduke-1) born about 1780. She died about Mar 1832 at the age of 52 in Kent County, Maryland. under 16 in 1794 per will of her aunt.

WILL: Ann Brice of Kent Co, To my dau. Henrietta Stevens all that part of land which I now live called "Wedge's Recovery" which I purchased of my nephew Joseph W. Brice containing 10 acres during her life, this tract is described in a deed dated Dec. 1, 1814 from Joseph W. Brice. To my dau. Henrietta Stevens my negro boy Peregrine Lewis aged 15 years in June last to serve until age 35 years and the residue to her also consisting of 2 cows, 8 hogs, 6 windsor chairs, 3 beds, 2 tables, 2 desks and a cupboard. To my granddau. Sarah Ann Brice after the decease of her mother Henrietta Stevens the 10 acres. If she dies without heirs then to my grandchildren James Brice Stevens, John Brice Stevens, Mary Henrietta Stevens, and Martha Louisa Stevens, children of Henrietta Stevens and Jacob Stevens her husband late of Kent Co. Exec. my dau. Henrietta Stevens. Witnesses Benjamin Crabbin, William Vannort, Sarah Brice, Philip M. Reed. Written Aug. 19, 1830 Proved Mar. 27, 1832 p. 242

Ann Brice had the following child:

+298   i.   **Henrietta Brice**, born abt 1800; married Jacob Stevens, 11 Nov 1823, Kent County, Maryland; died aft 1832.

188. John Brice (Judith Ann Blackiston-6, Michael-5, John-4, John-3, George-2, Marmaduke-1) born about 1782. John Brice and Martha Hatcheson were married. **Martha Hatcheson**, daughter of Nathaniel Hatcheson and Martha Miller, was born on 8 May 1762. BIRTH: Martha Hatcheson dau. of Nathan and Martha Hatcheson born May 8 1762. Her father names her daus. Martha Brice and Mary Brice daus. of John Brice and my dau. Martha to get 10 pds when they turn 16 in his will dated Jan. 1793.

John Brice and Martha Hatcheson had the following children:

299   i.   **Martha Brice** born about 1785. She died about Oct 1860 at the age of 75 in Kent County, Maryland.

WILL: Martha Brice of Chestertown, Kent Co To George Henry Brice (son of William A. Brice) of Kent Co $100, To Perry Price Howard, son of Asbury Howard and Mary his wife of Kent $100, To Perry Price Howard, William Penn Howard, Frank Houstin Howard, sons of Asbury and Mary Howard of Kent Co all my estate. Exec. Not Given. Witnesses Benjamin F. Houston, Samuel Franklin Smith, William S. Lapell. Written Jan. 12, 1859 Proved Oct. 16, 1860 p. 179 Codicil Whereas I sold my farm in Kent Co which was devised to me by Richard Brice my uncle unto William A. Brice and whereas Joseph Brice supposes he has some interest in said farm, now if the said Joseph Brice and his wife shall grant and release unto said William A. Brice in fee simple a deed to be executed by them within 12 months from the date hereof and delivered to said William A. Brice all and every supposed interest in said farm as they may think themselves possessed of then I hereby give and devise unto the children of said Joseph Brice and Mary Jane his wife $1,000. If they fail to execute such deed then I give the $1,000 to William to defend any suit that they may institute against him. I hereby give William A. Brice $500. Written Jan. 13, 1859. Witnesses Tamasina Glenn, John W. Usilton, and William S. Lapell

300	ii.	**Mary Brice** born about 1789.
+301	iii.	**Tamasina Brice**, born abt 1793; married Glenn; died aft 1859.

190. **Sarah Hatcheson** (Martha Miller-6, Ann Blackiston-5, William-4, Ebenezer-3, George-2, Marmaduke-1) was born on 15 Oct 1760 in Kent County, Maryland. She died about Jan 1827 at the age of 66 in Kent County, Maryland. BIRTH: St. Paul's Parish says Sarah Hatcheson dau of Nathan and Martha Hatcheson b. Oct. 15 1760

WILL: Sarah Miller of Kent Co being old and infirm. Frees several slaves, to Thomas James Blackiston son of James and Mary Ann Blackiston my negro Perry age 6 months but if he dies without issue then to my niece Mary Ann Blacksiton.
Niece Mary Ann Blackiston to have all residue of my estate. exec. James Blackiston husband of my niece Mary Ann Blackiston, witnesses Nathaniel Meginniss, Mary Ann Meginniss written Dec 7 1826 and proved Jan 24 1827 p. 464.

Sarah Hatcheson and Nathaniel Miller Sr. were married on 13 Feb 1797. **Nathaniel Miller Sr.**, son of Nathaniel Miller and Elizabeth Davis, born about 1729. He died about Jun 1802 at the age of 73 in Kent County, Maryland.

1790 census shows him with 2 males over 16, 22 slaves.

WILL: Nathaniel Miller of Kent Co date May 10, 1802 proved June 14, 1802 WB 8 p. 149. To my son John Miller, eldest son Nathaniel Miller, dau. Susannah Miller, after debts to divide among my children exclusive of the legacy to my dau. Susannah. exec. wife Sarah Miller and sons Nathaniel and John Miller. land named Miller's Delight

Original bond for Nathaniel Miller, the elder, was given by Nathaniel Miller, John Miller, Samuel Griffith and Michael Miller on Jun 15 1802. Bond No 8 p 316 Bond No. 9 p. 382 shows William Strong, Joseph W. Gordon, and George Thomas gave bond Feb 8 1812 for $20,000. William Strong adm. de bonis non of Nathaniel I suspect that this Nathaniel who died in 1802 was the son of Nathaniel
Miller (the elder) with a copy of his will. Inventory filed July 18, 18-- in Inventories No. 11, p 333 to 337 included 26 slaves. Kin were Elizabeth Walker, Alexander Miller. distribution in Accounts No. 13 p. 1-5. p. 3 Sarah Miller, to her part of her husbands estate. p.411 This accountant on account of his wife's distributive share of her father's estate (William Strong).

191. **Martha Hatcheson** (Martha Miller-6, Ann Blackiston-5, William-4, Ebenezer-3, George-2, Marmaduke-1) was born on 8 May 1762. BIRTH: Martha Hatcheson dau. of Nathan and Martha Hatcheson born May 8 1762. Her father names her daus. Martha Brice and Mary Brice daus. of John Brice and my dau. Martha to get 10 pds when they turn 16 in his will dated Jan. 1793. Martha Hatcheson and John Brice were married. **John Brice**, son of William Brice and Judith Ann Blackiston, born about 1782.

John Brice and Martha Hatcheson had the following children:

299	i.	**Martha Brice**, born abt 1785; died abt Oct 1860, Kent County, Maryland.
300	ii.	**Mary Brice**, born abt 1789.
+301	iii.	**Tamasina Brice**, born abt 1793; married Glenn; died aft 1859.

193. **Rebecca Hatcheson** (Martha Miller-6, Ann Blackiston-5, William-4, Ebenezer-3, George-2, Marmaduke-1) was born on 3 Mar 1766 in Kent County, Maryland. She died after 1796 at the age of 30. BIRTH: Rebecca Hatcheson dau. of Nathan and Martha Hatcheson born Mar 3, 176

Rebecca Hatcheson and Bartus Piner were married. **Bartus Piner**. Bartus Piner served in House of Delegates from Kent Co MD in 1830.

Rebecca Hatcheson and John Burgin were married. **John Burgin** died about Apr 1796 in Kent County, Maryland.

WILL: John Burg of Kent Co After my wife's 1/3 and my debts paid, my heirs, if I have any to have all my estate if not to my wife Rebecca Burgin during her life, and after her decease to her four children: Edward, Martha, Bartus, and Rebecca Piner. Exec. my wife Rebecca. Witnesses Thomas H. Mannix, William Turner, Joseph Newman. Written Feb. 15, 1796 Proved Apr. 2, 1796 p. 526

194. James Hatcheson (Martha Miller-6, Ann Blackiston-5, William-4, Ebenezer-3, George-2, Marmaduke-1) was born on 26 Jan 1768 in Kent County, Maryland. He died after 1821 at the age of 53. BIRTH: James Hatcheson son of Nathan and Martha Hatcheson born Jan. 26 176-

1790 Census p.82 James Hatcheson 2 Males 16 & over, 1 male 0-15, 1 Female.

He is named in the will of his brother to be responsible for property given to James' son Vincent during his minority.

MARYLAND EASTERN SHORE ABSTRACTS VOL 3 page 24 item 115 Republican Star December 6 1814 Sale at Samuel Chaplin Tavern in Centerville of 1 boy the property of Bartes Piner, admin James Hatcheson taken at the suit of Mary Cann use of Bartes Trew exec of William Wilkins.

James Hatcheson was married.

James Hatcheson had the following child:

+302   i. **Vincent Hatcheson**, born aft 1804; died 1840.

195. Nathan Hatcheson (Martha Miller-6, Ann Blackiston-5, William-4, Ebenezer-3, George-2, Marmaduke-1) was born on 27 Jan 1770 in Kent County, Maryland. He died on 22 Oct 1843 at the age of 73 in Kent County, Maryland. BIRTH: Nathan Hatcheson son of Nathan and Martha Hatcheson born Jan. 27 1770

One of the sons of Nathan Sr is the father of Mary Ann Hatcheson as her aunt Sarah Miller names her as her niece. This son must have had Henrietta N., Caroline, Mary Ann m. Mr. Blackiston, Ann M. m. Mr. Joseph Brown, Micha m. Simon Wicks, Jr. as there is a chancery record in 1845 to sell Stanway, Providence, Green Branch, Perkins Adventure, Chance, Bounty. Chancery Record 167, p. 505. The wife Ann was also named.

If Ann and Nathan were married in 1817, then Mary Ann must be by a different wife and the other children appear to be after 1817 so they are likely by the second wife.

Nathan Hatcheson and Ann Nicholson were married on 29 Sep 1817. **Ann Nicholson** died on 12 Aug 1845.

Nathan Hatcheson and Ann Nicholson had the following children:

303   i. **Henrietta N. Hatcheson** born about 1818 in Maryland. CENSUS: 1850 Kent Co H.N. Hatcheson age 32 female living in St. Michaels Talbot Co MD living with Gustavus Skinner farmer and family.

+304	ii.	**Micha Hatcheson**, born abt 1825; married Simon Wickes Jr, bef 1845.
+305	iii.	**Ann M. Hatcheson**, born abt 1825; married Joseph Brown, bef 1845.
306	iv.	**Caroline Hatcheson** born about 1831 in Maryland.

Nathan Hatcheson was married before 1800.

Nathan Hatcheson had the following child:

| +307 | i. | **Mary Ann Hatcheson**, born abt 1805; married James Kennard Blackiston, 3 Dec 1822, Queen Annes County, Maryland; married Daniel Ford, abt 1838; died 18 Apr 1872. |

201. **Martha Willis** (Ann Rasin-6, Rosamond Blackiston-5, William-4, Ebenezer-3, George-2, Marmaduke-1) born about 1780. She is mentioned as the niece of Mary Rasin in her will of 1798 probated 1805 as Martha Willis daughter of her sister. Martha Willis and William Apsley Jr. were married after 1798. **William Apsley Jr.**, son of William Apsley and Martha Wroth, born about 1782. He died on 13 Feb 1846 at the age of 64 in Kent County, Maryland. He was a minor in 1786. Of age in Apr 10, 1804. His father's will says he is under 21 in 1784. Also his father says if "both my children" die. He was a ward of William B. Rasin guardian accts 2 p24. Then in 1804 guardian was James Sappington. In Guardian accts #2 p 375 accounting by William B. Rasin began on p. 24 and on p. 97 taken over by Sappington.

202. **Corporal Philip Reed Rasin** (William Blackiston-6, Rosamond Blackiston-5, William-4, Ebenezer-3, George-2, Marmaduke-1) born about 1793 in Kent County, Maryland. He died on 1 Apr 1841 at the age of 48 in Kent County, Maryland. He rented farm in Worton Hundred, probably on Porter Grove Road. Information regarding Philip comes from Carolyn E. Cooper. He was born on a farm on Chinquapin Road, "Town Relief", land which belonged to the Wroth family for generations. Philip Reed Rasin was named after Col. Philip Reed, a friend of William B. Rasin per elder family members. Their first two children were named for his father and mother and 3rd and 4th child was named for her father and mother.

BIRTH: His birth year is estimated based on wife's age and parents marriage. Census says 30-39 and 40-49 so born 1790-1799. Marriage in 1811 would have to be 18 so before 1793. Narrows birth to 1790/93.

MARRIAGE: Bounty Land Application for widow Sarah 55-120-16554 No 12715 Warrant 4731 gives date of death and marriage date.

SOLDIER: War of 1812
Apr-Sep 1813 Capt. Matthew Tilghman, 33rd Regt (LTC. William Spencer)
Jul-Sep 1814 Capt. Aquila M. Uselton, 21st Regt (LTC. Philip Reed)

He served in 33rd Regt, 6th Brigade Kent Co MD Mil
Apr 1813-Sept 1813 Philip and Cyrus Rasin private served Apr 19-May 11 1813 and Aug 12-Aug 25 1813 33rd Regiment under Capt. Matthew Tilghman. Kent Co Jul 11-Jul 13 1814 Philip Rasin, Cyrus Rasin, privates. Capt. Aquila Usilton's Comp. 21st Regt. Aug 20 -Sep 6, 1814 Philip Rasin 4th Corporal, Cyrus Rasin privates. They were all in the battle at Caulk's field Aug 31 1814.

Philip Rasin Jr Company: 21 REG'T (REED'S) MARYLAND MILITIA. Rank - Induction: CORPORAL Rank - Discharge: CORPORAL Roll Box: 171 Microfilm Publication: M602

Republican Star issue of Oct 4 1814 "list of men who were in the action at Caulk's Field on the night of the 31st of Aug. Bounty Land Warrant 55-120-16554 and Maryland Militia in the War of 1812 by Ed Wright Vol 1 p 22, 27 29. The British Invasion of Maryland, 1812-1815 By William Matthew Marine p 124, 411 (Rasin, Raisin)

A LIST OF THE OFFICERS AND MEN, WHO WERE IN THE ACTION AT CAULK'S FIELD, ON THE NIGHT OF THE THIRTILTH OF AUGUST LAST, UNDER COL REED

Artillery Company

Aquilla M. Ussleton,	John Dugan
Captain	Joseph Gidley
John Reed,	Lieut Siras Rasin
Morgan Brou,	Lieut Benedict Pennington
Edward Nicholson	Ezekiel Forman
Henry H Stewart	Wm. Weaver
Wm Apsley, jr	James Usilton
Matthew Wickes	Philip Rasin, jr.
Philip Carroll	Edward Canpen
Charles Letherbury	James Harcutout
Dulany Apsley	Wm T Ussleton.

NEWSPAPER: Republican Star issue of Oct 4 1814 "list of men who were in the action at Caulk's Field on the night of the 31th of August last under Col. Reed. in Capt. Aquilla M. Usilton's Artillery Co. includes Lieut. Siras Rasin" (Cyrus) and Philip Rasin Jr.

Philip Rasin descendant Guy E. Almony Jr. at the memorial when young 2001.

1914   2014

A monument is erected at the site "The British commanded by Sir Peter Parker Baronet and the Americans commanded by Col. Philip Reed met in engagement on this field Aug. 31st 1814. The British were defeated and Sir Peter Parker killed. Erected A. D. 1902 by Marylanders to commemorate the patriotism and fortitude of the victor and vanquished."

CENSUS: 1830 Kent Co Philip Rasin Middle District.
Philip Rosen Home in 1830 (City, County, State): District 2, Kent, Maryland Free White Persons - Males - Under 5: 1 Free White Persons - Males - 10 thru 14: 1 Free White Persons - Males - 15 thru 19: 1 Free White Persons - Males - 30 thru 39: 1 Free White Persons - Females - Under 5: 2 Free White Persons - Females - 5 thru 9: 1 Free White Persons - Females - 10 thru 14: 1 Free White Persons - Females - 15 thru 19: 1 Free White Persons - Females - 30 thru 39: 1 Free White Persons - Under 20: 8 Free White Persons - 20 thru 49: 2 Total Free White Persons: 10 Total - All Persons (Free White, Slaves, Free Colored): 10

1830 U S Census; Census Place: District 2, Kent, Maryland; Page: 433; NARA Series: M19; Roll Number: 57; Family History Film: 0013180.

CENSUS: 1840 not listed because he died in Apr but Dulaney has older man living with him age 40-49 that may be him and female age 40-49 that could be his mother Sarah who is buried and marked on same stone as his.

DEATH: Date of death given in widow's bounty land warrant application.

OBITUARY: Kent Co News Dec 18 1841 issue mentioned the auction of the estate of Philip Rasin

TOMBSTONE: He is probably buried in Union Cemetery near his wife but no stone was found.

ESTATE: Sarah Rasin, adm of Philip Rasin gives inventory p. 161 Dec 7 1841. Kent Co News Dec 28 1841 issue notice of auction of estate of Philip Rasin, deceased by Sarah Rasin admin. sale Thur 30th July at the residence of the late Philip Rasin in Worton. In the minutes of Orphans Court Bk #4 p. 159 Nov 30 1841 letters granted on personal estate of Philip Rasin to Sarah Rasin and that William J. Skirven and Thomas Hynson appraise the same. On Dec. 7, 1841 Sarah Rasin presented the personal estate of Philip Rasin and it was ordered to sell the same and was to advertise same.

Rasin, Philip AB pg60 image 45 Sarah Rasin, Robert Usilton, William B Rasin. $5,000. 30 Nov 1841 (administration bonds KE 1837-50)

Family Notes: Old Family notes found and copied by Carolyn E. Cooper. state Philip Rasin married Sallie Bennett and had Wilhelmina married John William Crouch, Sarah married John Apsley, Mary Ann married Squire James A. Graves, Martha died not married, Ann Elizabeth married William J. Elliott, Richard married Elizabeth Jones, Samuel died when small, hung himself while playing, William married Elizabeth Crouch, sister of John William Crouch. These family bible pages are reprinted in the MGSB Vol. 40 No. 4 Fall 1999 p. 494 contributed by Christos Christou, Jr.

Corporal Philip Reed Rasin and Sarah Bennett were married on 22 Mar 1811 in Kent County, Maryland. **Sarah Bennett**, daughter of Samuel Bennett and Mary Willis, born about 1793 in Kent County, Maryland. She died after Apr 1855 at the age of 62 in Kent County, Maryland. She was buried at Union Meth. Epis in Worton, Kent County, Maryland.

BIRTH: Her son's death certificate says she was born in Kent Co, MD. Her bounty land application says she was 56 in Nov. 1850 (1794) and 63 in Mar. 1855 (1792). 1850 census says age 50 but would be 56.

CENSUS: 1850 Sarah Rasin age 50 living with son Dulaney in 1850 census. She would be about 58 by then.

DEATH: Caroline Cooper said she died Mar. 22 1856 and tombstone says she was 62y when she died. She died after 1855 when she applied for Bounty land

TOMBSTONE: Sarah B. Rasin Aged 62 yrs. (on son Dulany's Obelisk).

PENSION: BOUNTY LAND 40 acres bounty land for War of 1812 date Nov 25 1850 Mrs. Sarah Rasin age 56 was the widow of Philip Rasin deceased, a private in Capt. Usilton's Co. in the 21st Regt. of Infantry of Maryland Militia commanded by Col. Reed. She married Philip Rasin Mar 22 1811 by Rev. John Smith and was formerly Sarah Bennett. Phillip died Apr 1 1841. witnesses Cyrus Rasin and Mrs. Rachel (X) Duyer. 120 acres bounty land for War of 1812 date June 11 1855. Mar 19 1855 age 63y Mrs. Sarah Rasin received 40 acres. Mar 23 1855 given 120 acres on Jun 11 1855.

Samuel Bennett had an administration record that names daughter Sarah and son Samuel. Philip and Sarah named their son Samuel which is not a common Rasin name in his family.

Philip Reed Rasin and Sarah Bennett had the following children:

+308   i. **William Blackiston Rasin**, born abt 1813, Kent County, Maryland; married Sarah Elizabeth Crouch, 10 May 1836, Kent County, Maryland; died bef 4 May 1855, Kent County, Maryland.

309   ii. **Martha Rasin** born about 1814 in Kent County, Maryland. She died after 1830 at the age of 16. Old family record said she did not marry, per Carolyn E. Cooper.

+310   iii. **Dulany Rasin**, born 21 Jan 1816, Kent County, Maryland; married Mary Jane Beck, 15 Jan 1845, Kent County, Maryland; died 21 Jan 1890, Kent County, Maryland.

311   iv. **Samuel Rasin** born about 1818 in Kent County, Maryland. He died about 19 Dec 1828 at the age of 10 in Kent County, Maryland. He died young. He hung himself accidentally while playing. Article in the Princess Ann Village Herald states Samuel Rasin, son of Philip Rasin accidentally hung himself in his father's garret. Dec. 19th 1828 issue per Caroline Cooper. OBITUARY: A lad, son of Philip Rasin, hanged himself in his father's garret on 12th inst., by accident. VHL 30 Dec 1828

+312   v. **Mary Ann Rasin**, born abt 1819, Kent County, Maryland; married James A. Graves, 12 Jul 1841, Kent County, Maryland; died 19 Feb 1905, Wilmington, Delaware.

+313   vi. **Sarah Matilda Rasin**, born abt 1820; married John Wroth Apsley, 1 Aug 1837, Kent County, Maryland; died abt Aug 1887.

+314   vii.   **Richard L. Rasin**, born Jun 1825, Kent County, Maryland; married Isabel E. Jones, 2 Jan 1855, Kent County, Maryland; died 24 Jan 1905, Kent County, Maryland.

315   viii.   **Private James Clinton Rasin** born about 1828 in Kent County, Maryland. He died on 16 Apr 1862 at the age of 34 in Baltimore, Maryland. He was buried at Union Meth. Epis. in Worton, Kent County, Maryland. OBITUARY: James C. Rasin Co B 2nd Regt E.S. (Eastern Shore) Volunteers at camp hospital, Baltimore died on Wednesday brought home for burial. Apr 19 1862 Kent Co News. Private James Rasin entered served Oct 2 1861 Company B 2nd Eastern Shore Vol. Inf. Died of Stroke apoplexy on April 16 1862. His body was returned to Chestertown for Burial. Kent News April 19 1862. ESTATE: Admin. Nov 17 1863 James C. Rasin dec. money from sale of real estate of the late Wm B Rasin trustee Richard Hynson, money due from the U.S. Army. p. 197 paid Sarah E Rasin, Wm Blakely, James Beck of John, Dulaney Rasin (dug grave), and other creditors. SOLDIER: Union soldier in the Civil War. Served MD. Enlisted B Co 2nd ES Inf. Reg. MD died of disease on April 16, 1862 private, per MD Vol. War of 1861-1865 James C. Rasin. James T. Rasin served in the Civil War and died on April 16 1862 of disease. per MD Vol, Civil War 1861-1865. The Roll Call by Walter J. Kirby lists James C. Rasin private entered service 10-2-1861 Company B, 2nd Eastern Shore Volunteer Infantry. Died of stroke of apoplexy 4-16-1862 and body returned to Chestertown for burial.

+316   ix.   **Willamina Rasin**, born 18 May 1830, Worton, Kent County, Maryland; married James Lynch, 19 Feb 1849, Kent County, Maryland; married John Wesley Crouch, 13 Aug 1856, Kent County, Maryland; died 8 Aug 1907, Chestertown, Kent County, Maryland.

+317   x.   **Emily Bertha Rasin**, born 30 May 1833, Kent County, Maryland; married Samuel S. Usilton, 22 Dec 1853, Kent County, Maryland; died 7 Oct 1903, Kent County, Maryland.

+318   xi.   **Ann Elizabeth Rasin**, born 26 Jul 1839, Kent County, Maryland; married William John Elliott, 19 Dec 1855, Kent County, Maryland; died 15 Oct 1913, Chestertown, Kent County, Maryland.

203. **Cyrus B. Rasin** (William Blackiston-6, Rosamond Blackiston-5, William-4, Ebenezer-3, George-2, Marmaduke-1) born about 1794 in Kent County, Maryland. He died on 13 Mar 1865 at the age of 71 in Chestertown, Kent County, Maryland. Family Notes found by Carolyn E. Cooper in family bible of Cyrus Rasin states "Grandmother's father Cyrus Rasin and his brothers and sisters Philip Rasin, Rachel Rasin married Phil Duyer and Nancy Rasin married a Willis and had two children John K. and Philmelia Willis and then Nancy married second Daniel Denning.

SOLDIER: July 9 1812 6th Brigade Capt. Edward Comegys- Cyrus Rasin. April 19 1813-May 11 1813 33rd Regt. Philip Raisen 2 days and Cyrus Raisin 2 days. July 12 -August 25 1813 33rd Regt. Philip Raisin 11 days and Cyrus Raisin 17 days, Jul 11-13, 1814 Artillery Co Siras Rasin pvt 3 days. Aug 20-Sep 6 1814 Artillery Co Philip Rasin Jr 4th Cpl 12 days and Siras Rasin pvt 17 days. Sep 11-23 1814 Siras Rasin 13 days.

MARRIAGE: Cyrus Rasin and Wilhelmina Steen on Mar 2 1819 by McCoon both of Kent Co.

DEED: William Ashley Jr. sells to Cyrus Rasin $500 "Hermitage" 122 acres DB 4 p 246 April 12 1823.

DEED: Cyrus Ras of Kent and William Wroth sell $100 "Hermitage" 26 5/8 acres, signed Willamina wife of Cyrus. DB 4 p 237 April 12 1823 dated.

DEED: Cyrus Rasin and Willemina his wife formerly (Stein) to Richard Smith $68 formerly property of James Stien and part of said Steins purchase of William Hemsley called Fair Lee, 8 acres. DB 4 p 353 date Jan 15 1824.

MARRIAGE: Cyrus Rasin m. Henrietta M. Beck on Sep 1 1840 by Starks both of Kent Co.

MARRIAGE: Cyrus Rasin m. Sarah Smith on Jan 31 1850 by Townsend both of Kent Co.

MARRIAGE: Cyrus Rasin m. Mrs. Mary Crawford on Dec 15 1856 by Wilson both of Kent Co.

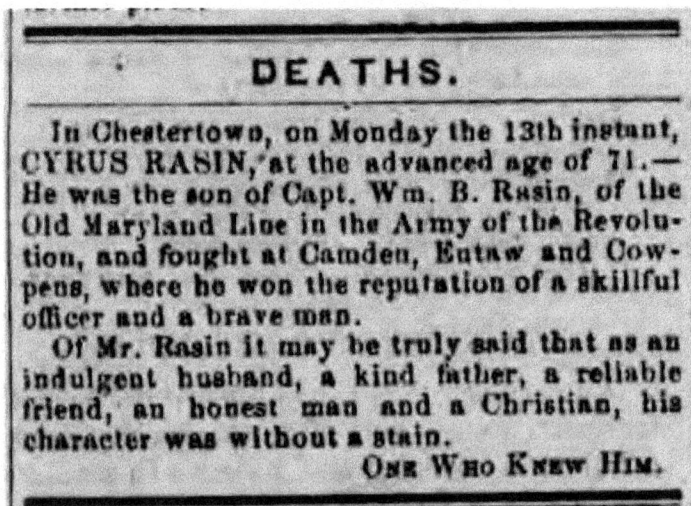

DEATHS.

In Chestertown, on Monday the 13th instant, CYRUS RASIN, at the advanced age of 71.— He was the son of Capt. Wm. B. Rasin, of the Old Maryland Line in the Army of the Revolution, and fought at Camden, Eutaw and Cowpens, where he won the reputation of a skillful officer and a brave man.

Of Mr. Rasin it may be truly said that as an indulgent husband, a kind father, a reliable friend, an honest man and a Christian, his character was without a stain.

ONE WHO KNEW HIM.

OBITUARY: In Chestertown, on Monday the 13th instant, Cyrus Rasin, at the advanced age of 71. He was the son of Capt. Wm. B. Rasin, of the Old Maryland Line in the Army of the Revolution, and fought at Camden, Eutaw and Cowpens, where he won the reputation of a skillful officer and a brave man. Of Mr. Rasin it may be truly said that as an indulgent husband, a kind father, a reliable friend, and honest man and a Christian, his character was without a stain. One Who Knew Him. Kent News March 18, 1865.

Cyrus B. Rasin and Wilhelmina Steen were married on 2 Mar 1819 in Kent County, Maryland. **Wilhelmina Steen**, daughter of James Steen and Rosamond Gale, born about 1801. She died on 1 Jun 1839 at the age of 38 in Kent County, Maryland.

OBITUARY: died on the 1st instant in Kent Co Wilhelmina Rasin, consort of Cyrus Rasin in the 28th years of her age, leaving a numerous circle of friends and seven children to deplore their untimely bereavement. Baltimore American on Jun 26 1839. p 3

Cyrus B. Rasin and Wilhelmina Steen had the following children:

+319	i.	**Rosetta M. Rasin**, born 7 Dec 1819; married John P. Beck, 30 Sep 1840, Kent County, Maryland; married Benjamin G. Howard, 3 Jun 1856, Kent County, Maryland.
320	ii.	**Rasin** born about 1820.
321	iii.	**Rasin** born about 1822.
+322	iv.	**Private Lewis H. B. Rasin**, born abt 1824; married Sarah J. Everitt, 4 Jun 1850, Kent County, Maryland; died 16 Aug 1865, Baltimore, Maryland.
+323	v.	**Joseph Orsburn Rasin**, born 1 Oct 1831; married Florence M. Rasin, 17 May 1854, Kent County, Maryland; died 10 Nov 1885.
+324	vi.	**John William Rasin**, born abt 1829, Kent County, Maryland; married Sarah Emma Jervis, 6 Oct 1873, New Castle County, Delaware; died 18 Dec 1896, Baltimore City, Md.
+325	vii.	**Cyrus C. Blackiston Rasin**, born 1835; married Laura C. Kelly, 18 Mar 1873, Kent County, Maryland; died 1895.

Cyrus B. Rasin and Henrietta M. Beck were married on 1 Aug 1840 in Kent County, Maryland. **Henrietta M. Beck** born about 1820.

Cyrus B. Rasin and Sarah Smith were married on 31 Jan 1850 in Kent County, Maryland. **Sarah Smith** born about 1825.

Cyrus B. Rasin and Mary were married on 15 Dec 1856 in Kent County, Maryland. **Mary** born about 1830. She died after 1860 at the age of 30. She was Mrs. Mary Crawford when she married Cyrus.

204. Rachel Rasin (William Blackiston-6, Rosamond Blackiston-5, William-4, Ebenezer-3, George-2, Marmaduke-1) born about 1795. She died in Nov 1857 at the age of 62 in Kent County, Maryland.

CENSUS: 1850 Kent Co, MD
Rachel Duyer 50, Rachel A 13, Philip 11, Mazel 8
1850; Census Place: District 2, Kent, Maryland; Roll M432_294; Page: 215; Image: 433.

OBITUARY: In this place on Tuesday last, of pneumonia, Mrs. Rachel Duyer, relict of the late Philip Duyer. Nov 14 1857 Kent News

Rachel Rasin and John Clark were married on 24 Apr 1819. **John Clark** born about 1795.

Rachel Rasin and Phillip Duyer were married on 16 May 1826 in Kent County, Maryland. **Phillip Duyer**, son of John Duyer and Mary Jane Gale, born about 1800. He died before 1860 at the age of 60.

Phillip Duyer and Rachel Rasin had the following child:

    326   i. **John W. Duyer** was born on 30 Dec 1832 in Kent County, Maryland. He died on 14 Feb 1915 at the age of 82 in Chestertown, Kent County, Maryland. He was buried in Chestertown, Kent County, Maryland. DEATH: Jno W. Duyer died Chestertown Kent Co male white married born Dec 30 1832 age 82y 1 m 13 days born Kent father Philip Duyer born Kent, mother Rachel Rasin born Kent. Info. Mary E. Duyer of Chestertown MD died Feb 14 1915 of Lobar Pneumonia, buried Chestertown MD by Chas L. Dodd of Chestertown.

205. Nancy Ann Rasin (William Blackiston-6, Rosamond Blackiston-5, William-4, Ebenezer-3, George-2, Marmaduke-1) born about 1797 in Maryland. She died on 30 Sep 1881 at the age of 84 in Kent County, Maryland. She was mentioned in the will of her aunt Mary Rasin (dated 1798) as Ann, daughter of William B. Rasin. She signed the sale of land as Ann Denning. The name Nancy appears on the 2nd marriage bond.

CENSUS: 1850 Baltimore Census 14th Ward
Ann Denning 53 MD Boarding house, Permilia Willis 28 MD, others
Census; Record Group Number: 29; Series Number: M432; Residence Date: 1850; Home in 1850: Baltimore Ward 14, Baltimore, Maryland; Roll: 285; Page: 408a

CENSUS: 1870 Kent Co, MD
John K. Willis 50 livery stable, Sarah M. 37, Mary A 12, Frank 10, Ruther A. 6, Ann Denning 73 born MD
Year: 1870; Census Place: Chestertown, Kent, Maryland; Roll: M593_590; Page: 174A

CENSUS: 1880 Kent Co, MD
Ann Denning 83 widowed homeworker at 355 High St.
Year: *1880*; Census Place: *Charlestown, Kent, Maryland*; Roll: *512*; Page: *131b*;
Enumeration District: *052*

OBITUARY: Nancy Denning died 9/30/1881 85 years old. She was the widow of late
Daniel Denning and mother of late John K. Willis. 10/1/1881 Kent News.

Nancy Ann Rasin and John Willis were married. **John Willis** born about 1790.

John Willis and Nancy Ann Rasin had the following children:

>   327   i. **Priscilla Willis** born about 1817. She died on 17 Sep 1882 at the age
>   of 65. 1880 Census living next to her mom.
>   +328   ii. **John K. Willis**, born abt 1819; married Sarah M. ; died 8 Aug 1876.

Nancy Ann Rasin and Daniel Denning were married on 6 Jan 1828 in Kent County,
Maryland. **Daniel Denning**, son of Denning and Mary Vansant, born about 1795.

208. **Maria Wilmer** (Blackiston-6, Rosamond Blackiston-5, Ebenezer-4, Ebenezer-3,
George-2, Marmaduke-1) was born on 22 Dec 1780. She died about May 1843 at the age
of 62 in Kent County, Maryland.

WILL: Maria Tate of Kent Co Whereas there are several transactions between my brother
William B. Wilmer and myself and is at this time indebted to me, I cancel all sums due me
from him. To my dau. in law Sarah Maria Gordon wife of James F. Gordon for her life all
my estate. My dau. in law to pay in 1850 to her half-brother Robert B. A. Tate $100
annually during his life. My negro woman Dolly to be free. My other negroes Jim to be
free on Jan. 1, 1846, my negro man Jacob to be free on Jan. 1, 1849, my negro Pere to be
free Jan. 1, 1852, Moses to be free Jan. 1, 1855, Julia and Ann to be free on Jan. 1, 1848,
and Henry to be free on Jan. 1, 1867. My executor to have head and foot stones on my
grave and on my deceased father and mother's grave, and a slab to be placed over my dau.
Louisa and my son Alexander and my friend James B. Ricaud to select, and if my relatives
shall desire to make repairs to the enclosure around the family burial ground my executor
to contribute my part of the same. To my sisters Sarah and Harriett Wilmer one pair of
white linen sheets marked number 3 and 4. As most of my estate goes to his wife and
children, no appraisement needed. [Freedom passes granted to Moses Apr. 28, 1855, Pere
Sep. 1, 1856, Jacob Oct. 4, 1864, written in margin] Exec. my friend and relative James F.
Gordon. Witnesses James B. Ricaud, Joseph N. Gordon Jr., Mary Gordon. Written Mar.
27, 1843 Proved May 13, 1843 p. 136

WILL: Alexander C.H. Tate of Port Deposit, Cecil Co, formerly of Kent Co, To my mother
Maria Tate all my estate. Exec. my mother. Witnesses William B. Wilmer, S. J. Wilmer,

Sarah A. Wilmer. Written June 16, 1835 Proved July 16, 1839 (July 23 came William) p. 58

Robert Tate Jr was married to Maria Wilmer, daughter of Blackiston Wilmer. KE Guardianship Files, Wilmer, Blackiston (2851) 7pgs 6 Jan 1814 Will pg2, 25 Jun 1812, daughters Maria Tate, Sarah Rebecca Wilmer, Harriett Wilmer. children of my daughter Elizabeth Tate decd ($88 being the amount bequeathed to them by their grandmother Elizabeth Williamson), grson William B Tate a Negro boy called Jam, 14yrs of age, living now with Mr Robert Tate Jr, dear wife, sons John & William; Wits: Bedingfield Hands, Joseph Forman, John B Eccleston, Proved 5 Jan 1814; bond pg6 John W Wilmer BA, William B Wilmer, Philip Taylor KE.$50,000. 6 Jan 1814

Maria Wilmer and Robert Tate were married.

209. **William Blackiston Wilmer II** (Blackiston-6, Rosamond Blackiston-5, Ebenezer-4, Ebenezer-3, George-2, Marmaduke-1) was born on 27 Apr 1790. He died on 20 Jan 1853 at the age of 62. He was buried in Saint Paul's Churchyard, Kent County, Maryland.

CENSUS: 1850 Kent Co, MD
Wm B Wilmer 60 farmer, Mary A Wilmer 50, Mary Wilmer 20, Ellen Wilmer 19, Nathaniel Wilmer 21
Census; Record Group Number: *29*; Series Number: *M432*; Residence Date: *1850*; Home in 1850: *District 2, Kent, Maryland*; Roll: *294*; Page: *235b*

William Blackiston Wilmer II and Mary Ann Taylor were married on 16 Apr 1816. **Mary Ann Taylor** was born on 22 Feb 1798. She died on 22 Jan 1860 at the age of 61. She was buried in Saint Paul's Churchyard, Kent County, Maryland. Daughter of Philip and Ann Taylor
WILL: Philip Taylor of Kent Co To my wife Ann Taylor a negro boy Isaac, a negro girl Cassa, my horse and carriage, my trunk and all my wearing apparel. The residue of my personal estate (my negroes excepted) to my wife Ann Taylor and my dau. Mary Ann Wilmer. To my wife Ann Taylor ½ of the profits of my estate during her life and the other ½ to my dau. Mary Ann Wilmer, and after my wife's death to have all during her life. After their deaths then to the children of my dau. Mary Ann Wilmer. If she has no heirs then to William B. Wilmer, James Frisby Brown, Thomas J. James and Richard J. Frisby's eldest son. My negroes to be free at age 31 and they may not be sold nor any hired out of the county except as they may select. Exec. William B. Wilmer. Witnesses Joseph Mitchell, Richard B. Page, James Wheeler. Written Feb. 21, 1818 Proved Feb. 28, 1818 p. 147
WILL: Ann Taylor of Kent Co To negress Minta Freeman her child Cassa to serve until 25. To my only child Mary Ann Wilmer I give all my property except my negro boy Isaac now 14 to serve until Dec. 31, 1833. Exec. William B. Wilmer my son in law. Witnesses Joseph T. Mitchell, Isabella Hynson. Written Sep. 14, 1821 Proved Aug. 7, 1822 p. 275

William Blackiston Wilmer and Mary Ann Taylor had the following child:

+330   i. **William Blackiston Wilmer III**, born 24 Jun 1818, Kent County,
       Maryland; married Mary Ann Brooks, 11 Oct 1852; died 9 Oct 1877,
       Kent County, Maryland.

Eighth Generation

210. **Zachariah Deminieu Blackiston** (George-7, Nehemiah Herbert-6, John-5, John-4, Nehemiah-3, John-2, Marmaduke-1). He was born 26 Jun 1821 in Montgomery County, MD and he died 23 Jan. 1888 in St. Mary's County, MD.
Zachariah Deminieu Blackiston and Harriet Ann Shanks were married on 10 Jan 1860 in Saint Mary's County, Maryland. **Harriet Ann Shanks**.

CENSUS: 1870 St. Mary's Co, MD
Zachariah Blackiston 30, Harriet A Blackiston 30, Elizabeth Blackiston 7 Gracy Blackiston 5 Francis Blackiston 3 Anney Blackiston 1
Year: *1870*; Census Place: *District 4, St Marys, Maryland*; Roll: *M593_594*; Page: *629A*

Zachariah Demeneau Blackiston and Harriet Ann Shanks had the following children:

+331   i. **Eleanor Grace Blackiston**, born 1 Jun 1865, Saint Mary's County,
       Maryland; married Walter Benjamin Dent, 19 Aug 1884, Saint Mary's
       County, Maryland; died 21 Mar 1959, Saint Mary's County, Maryland.
      ii. **Zachariah Deminieu "Zeddie Blackiston, Jr.** born Feb 16 1871 died
       18 Apr 1982 at 111 years old. Pioneering Washington florist. He
       served diplomats and politicians, statesmen and their ladies. During the
       Roosevelt administration, he was called almost daily by the White
       House to send flowers to Alice Roosevelt Longworth. At age 100, he
       was the guest of honor at a White House breakfast. At the age of 20 he
       left his family farm and headed for the nation's capital. "I have a
       distinct recollection of Benjamin Harrison's inauguration at about that
       time (1893). Every political big-wig would have his followers serenade
       him through the streets, maybe even more than they do today," he said.'
       'I can remember once when I was at work and I heard music coming
       from somewhere in the streets. Well, I followed it, as I've always loved
       music, and discovered it came from the old Normandy Hotel. And there
       I saw Sen. James G. Blaine from Maine standing on the second-floor
       balcony, waving to the crowds while the music played on. Old Senator
       Blaine was a hot political candidate at the time, but he never was
       elected President." He also had memories of "Uncle Joe" Cannon, the
       legendary Speaker of the House who gained a reputation for dictatorial
       leadership. "That fellow used to stop by every rooming to buy a
       carnation for his lapel, and he always had a big cigar in his mouth. For

however many years I saw him, day after day, there was that cigar sticking out of his mouth." Blackistone said his secret to longevity and success is "a good clean conscience. I think that's the key to a long and happy life. And also to live with God in my life. That's the secret, to live with God in your life." Information above taken from an article in the Pocono Record on February 17, 1975. His son III 1908-1992 became a Colonel in the US Army in Korea and Vietnam as is buried at Arlington National Cemetery.He was also a member of the Sons of the American Revolution through his ancestor Nehemiah H. Blackistone

211. Ann Rebecca Blackiston (George-7, Nehemiah Herbert-6, John-5, John-4, Nehemiah-3, John-2, Marmaduke-1) was born in 1828. She died on 10 Jul 1908 at the age of 80 in Saint Mary's County, Maryland. Ann Rebecca Blackiston and Biscoe Cheseldyne were married on 25 Nov 1856. **Biscoe Cheseldyne** was born in 1831. He died on 18 Apr 1871 at the age of 40 in Saint Mary's County, Maryland.

217. James Kennard Blackiston (Kennard-7, James-6, Ebenezer-5, John-4, John-3, George-2, Marmaduke-1) was born before 1795. He died before Nov 1835 at the age of 40. MARRIAGE: James K. Blackiston m. Mary A. Hatcheson Dec 3 1822

ESTATE: James K Blackiston adm. by Mary A Blackiston 1839. James K. Blackiston and Mary Ann Blackiston estate administered by Thomas Price Mar 19 1846.

James K. Blackiston heirs are Thomas J., Edwin H., Margaret and Ann Blackiston. These children were living with Thomas M. Blackiston as seen per 1850 census. (There is a Benjamin F living with Mary A. that is also likely a son)

James K. who had wife Mary Ann and Thomas M. Blackiston who had wife Louisa Ann Blackiston were sons of James Blackiston, per deed March 7 1834.

James Kennard Blackiston and Mary Ann Hatcheson were married on 3 Dec 1822 in Queen Annes County, Maryland. **Mary Ann Hatcheson**, daughter of Nathan Hatcheson, born about 1805. She died on 18 Apr 1872 at the age of 67. She was buried in Asbury Cem., Millington, Kent, Maryland. Her aunt Sarah Miller in her will dated Dec. 7, 1826 names Thomas James Blackiston, son of James and Mary Ann Blackiston, her niece. witnesses were Nathaniel and Mary Meginniss.

She inherited land from her father. Chancery Records Date: 1845/06/10 7888: Jacob Fisher vs. Ann Hatchison, Henrietta N. Hatchison, Caroline Hatchison, Mary Ann Blackiston, Joseph Brown, Ann M. Brown, Simon Wicks, Jr., and Micha Wicks. KE. Petition to sell Stanway, Providence, Green Branch, Perkins Adventure, Chance, Bounty. Plat. Recorded (Chancery Record) 167, p. 505. Accession No.: 17,898-7888-1/2 MSA S512-10-7886 Location: 1/38/3/

She must have remarried after James died to Daniel Ford.

CENSUS: 1850 Daniel Ford 50 DE, Mary Ann Ford 45 MD, Benjamin F Blackiston 20 student, Ann E Blackiston 15
1850; Census Place: Duck Creek Hundred, Kent, Delaware; Roll: M432 52; Page: 50; Image: 102.

TOMBSTONE: Mary A Ford Died April 18 1872 Age ? yres 8 Mos ? Days

James Kennard Blackiston and Mary Ann Hatcheson had the following children:

+332   i. **Thomas James Blackiston**, born 8 May 1826, Kent County, Maryland; married Bellerma Elinor Mead, 12 Dec 1851, Queen Annes County, Maryland; died 4 Aug 1891, Nebo, Oklahoma.

+333   ii. **Benjamin F. Blackiston**, born 9 Jun 1831, De; married Mary Raymond Denney; died 31 Jan 1903, Kent County, Delaware.

334   iii. **George W. Blackiston** was born on 16 Dec 1832 in De. He died on 9 May 1893 at the age of 60 in Millington, Kent, Maryland. He was buried in Asbury Cem., Millington, Kent, Marylan. His is born about 1832-33 per census but tombstone says 1831 when calculated but could not be born within 6 months of his brother. George W Blackiston 17 DE student at Del Academy of New Art. 1850; Census Place: Division 3, New Castle, Delaware; Roll: M432 53; Page: 400A; Image: 263

335   iv. **Ann E. Blackiston** born about 1834 in De. She died in 1923 at the age of 89. CENSUS: Anna E Blackiston 64 Head, Mary F Crouch 60 Sister Year: 1900; Census Place: Millington, Kent, Maryland; Roll: 625; Page: 2; Enumeration District: 0045

218. Thomas Medford Blackiston (Kennard-7, James-6, Ebenezer-5, John-4, John-3, George-2, Marmaduke-1) born about 1801 in Kent County, Maryland. He was christened on 30 Oct 1814 in Chester Parish, Kent County, Maryland. He died about Jan 1859 at the age of 58 in Kent County, Maryland.

BAPTISM: Thomas Medford Blackiston son of Kennard and Elizabeth Blackiston bapt. Oct. 30 1814.

MARRIAGE: Thomas M Blackiston m. Louise A. Elliott (Q.A.) 25 Aug 1828 Kent Co MD

DEED: WS 3 342 Mar 7 1834 James K Blackiston and his wife Mary Ann of Kent Co, Thomas M. Blackiston and Louisa Ann Blackiston his wife of Queen Anne Co TO Samuel Harlow $2,100. "His Lordships Gracious Crant cont. 177 1/4 acres from William Little to James Blackiston BC No 3 298-300 1790. also "Adventure" 24 acres John Little 1792 to

James Blackiston BC No 3 p 266-267. also "Spring Garden" south side fo the road of Massey's Cross Roads 20 3/4 acres from Joel Newman and Temperance to Kennard Blackiston LW #2 412-414 1803 descended from the said James Blackiston to James and Thomas his children.

MARRIAGE: Thomas M. Blackiston (Q.A.) m. Mary Blackiston 4 Apr 1836

WILL: Thomas M. Blackiston of Kent Co, all my estate to be sold and conveyed in fee to my dau. Mary Elizabeth Blackiston interest to be payed half yearly. To my wife in lieu of dower the sum of $3,000. To my dau. Mary $2,000. The balance to my son Thomas Medford Blackiston and my dau. Mary Elizabeth Blackiston. Various slaves given to both for Thomas' they are according to the manumission in Queen Annes Co. To my dear wife 3 slaves and household property she may desire. I appoint my relation David C. Blackiston guardian to my said dau. Mary. exec. my son Thomas M. Blackiston and my relation David C. Blackiston. written Jan. 31 1859

Thomas Medford Blackiston and Louisa Ann Elliott were married on 25 Aug 1828 in Kent County, Maryland. **Louisa Ann Elliott** born about 1808 in Queen Annes County, Maryland. She died in 1834 or 1836 at the age of 26 in Maryland.

Thomas Medford Blackiston and Louisa Ann Elliott had the following children:

336   i.   **Edwin H. Blackiston** born about 1829 in Kent County, Delaware. He died on 28 Jun 1854 at the age of 25 in Key West, Florida. OBITUARY: Edwin H. Blackiston at Key West Fl on Jun 28th in 25th years formerly of Kent Co Aug 26 1854 Kent News.

+337   ii.   **Thomas Medford Blackiston Jr.**, born abt 1831; married Sarah Henrietta Ringgold, 17 Dec 1856, Kent County, Maryland; died bef 1870.

338   iii.   **Margaret A. Blackiston** born about 1832 in Maryland.

Thomas Medford Blackiston and Mary Malvina Blackiston were married on 4 Apr 1836 in Kent County, Maryland. **Mary Malvina Blackiston**, daughter of James Blackiston and Mary Crane, born about 1810. She died on 10 Apr 1845 at the age of 35 in Kent County, Maryland. She was buried in Shrewsbury Ch., Kent County, Maryland.

TOMBSTONE: Mary M. Blackiston died April 10, 1845 age 36y

Thomas Medford Blackiston and Mary Malvina Blackiston had the following child:

+339   i.   **Mary Elizabeth Blackiston**, born 24 Mar 1843, De; married James Alfred Perkins; died 11 Jun 1903, Phladelphia, PA.

Thomas Medford Blackiston and Maria were married. **Maria** born about 1801 in Virginia. She died after 1859 at the age of 58.

220. David Crane Blackiston (James-7, James-6, Ebenezer-5, John-4, John-3, George-2, Marmaduke-1) was born on 19 Feb 1809 in Brighthelmstone, Kent County, Maryland. He died on 24 Dec 1888 at the age of 79 in Glenndale, Prince Georges, Maryland. He was buried in Shrewsbury Ch., Kent County, Maryland.

He was elected a State Senator in 1859. He owned Brighthelmstone. His story is given in the Biographical Cyclopedia p. 470. David Crane Blackiston son of James and Mary (Crane) Blackiston, was born, February 19, 1809, at his hereditary family estate Brighthelmstone. He was educated in Kent Co, MD, devoted himself to agricultural pursuits, and was appointed in 1850, by Gov. Enoch Louis Lowe, one of the Judges of the Orphan's Court of Kent Co. In 1859 he was elected to the Senate of Maryland, served five sessions, and was present at the critical meeting of that body in Frederick City in 1861. He was a member of the Constitutional Convention of 1864; was appointed in 1870, by Gov. Oden Bowie, Inspector General of grain; and in Nov. 1873, was elected Clerk of the Circuit Court for Kent Co, the position he now fills, with great satisfaction to the bench, the bar, and hte public. He married April 4, 1837, Rachel Mott Hooten, who was the dau. of Andrew and Mary (McKenzie) Hooten, and had the following children; Katharine Amanda, Mary Jane, Andrew Hooten, and David James, who married Jan. 26, 1870, Elizabeth Bruce, dau. of Col. Robert Bruce of Cumberland, MD. David Crane Blackiston is an Episcopalian, as all his ancestors, paternal and maternal, were before him, and in politics a Democrat.

OBITUARY: Kent Co News Dec 29 1888

David Crane Blackiston and Rachel Motte Hooten were married on 4 Apr 1837 in Philadelphia, Pennsylvania. **Rachel Motte Hooten** was born on 30 Sep 1809 in Pennsylvania. She died on 9 Feb 1884 at the age of 74 in Kent County, Maryland. She was buried in Shrewsbury Ch., Kent County, Maryland. The obituary of her father Andrew Hooten says he died at Bright Helmstone the residence of his son-in-law D.C. Blackiston on 12th inst. in 90th year May 16 1874 Kent Co. Biographical Cyclopedia p. 470 David Crane Blackiston m. Rachel Mott Hooten who was the daughter of Andrew and Mary (McKenzie) Hooten and had children: Katharine Amanda, Mary Jane, Andrew Hooten, and David James.

David Crane Blackiston and Rachel Motte Hooten had the following children:

340	i.	**Katharine Amanda Blackiston** was born Nov 28 1839 married Alfred Stille, MD June 14 1899 per Crane Genealogy and lived in Philadelphia.
341	ii.	**Mary Jane Blackiston** was born 12 Apr 1841 in Maryland. She died after 1900 at the age of 59. CENSUS: 1900 Kent Co MD M.J. Blackiston age 59 single born April 1841 MD MD PA

+342   iii. **Andrew Hooten Blackiston**, born 21 May 1844, Brighthelmstone, Kent County, Maryland; married Elizabeth Smith Pearre, 21 May 1874; died 30 Aug 1878, Cumberland, Maryland.

343   iv. **David James Blackiston** was born 23 Feb 1846 m. Elizabeth Bruce Jan. 26 1870. He was a lawyer by profession and elected Mayor of Cumberland MD several times. He died Jun 17 1915 Cumberland, Allegany, MD

    v. **Mary Hooton Blackiston** was born April 2, 1838 and died Aug 16 1939 per Crane Genealogy.

221. **Mary Malvina Blackiston** (James-7, James-6, Ebenezer-5, John-4, John-3, George-2, Marmaduke-1) born about 1810. She died on 10 Apr 1845 at the age of 35 in Kent County, Maryland. She was buried in Shrewsbury Ch., Kent County, Maryland.

TOMBSTONE: Mary M. Blackiston died April 10, 1845 age 36y

Mary Malvina Blackiston and Thomas Medford Blackiston were married on 4 Apr 1836 in Kent County, Maryland. **Thomas Medford Blackiston**, son of Kennard Blackiston and Elizabeth Medford, born about 1801 in Kent County, Maryland. He was christened on 30 Oct 1814 in Chester Parish, Kent County, Maryland. He died about Jan 1859 at the age of 58 in Kent County, Maryland. BAPTISM: Thomas Medford Blackiston son of Kennard and Elizabeth Blackiston bapt. Oct. 30 1814.

Thomas M Blackiston 49, Maria Blackiston 49 VA, Rebecca Satter 49, Margart A Blackiston 18, Thompson Baird 17 Student, Edwin Blackiston 21 DE Carriage maker, Mary E Blackiston 7 DE
Census; Record Group Number: *29*; Series Number: *M432*; Residence Date: *1850*; Home in 1850: *District 2, Kent, Maryland*; Roll: *294*; Page: *229b*

Military record for **Edwin H. Blackiston** Dec 1851 says age 22y joined Dec 1851 died Jun 23, 1854 at Key West Florida a Sergeant in US Army

WILL: Thomas M. Blackiston of Kent Co, all my estate to be sold and conveyed in fee to my dau. Mary Elizabeth Blackiston interest to be payed half yearly. To my wife in lieu of dower the sum of $3,000. To my dau. Mary $2,000. The balance to my son Thomas Medford Blackiston and my dau. Mary Elizabeth Blackiston. Various slaves given to both for Thomas' they are according to the manumission in Queen Annes Co. To my dear wife 3 slaves and household property she may desire. I appoint my relation David C. Blackiston guardian to my said dau. Mary. exec. my son Thomas M. Blackiston and my relation David C. Blackiston. written Jan. 31 1859

Genealogy of the Crane family Vol. II says they had 1 daughter Mary Elizabeth who married Dr. James Perkins and had 8 sons and 1 daughter. It says Mary M. died April 10 1845 aged 36 years 4 mos and 9 days.

Thomas Medford Blackiston and Mary Malvina Blackiston had the following child:

+339   i. **Mary Elizabeth Blackiston**, born 24 Mar 1843, De; married James Alfred Perkins; died 11 Jun 1903, Phladelphia, PA.

          ii. Thomas Medford Blackiston may have died after 1959

227. Samuel Hepburn Blackiston (William Henry-7, James-6, Ebenezer-5, John-4, John-3, George-2, Marmaduke-1) was born on 12 Jul 1836 in Maryland. He died in Oct 1885 at the age of 49. He was buried in Christ I.U. Church, Kent, Maryland.

MARRIAGE: S. Hepbron Blackiston m. Sallie T. Brooks on Sep 12, 1868 by Rev. Mr. Goodwin. She was a widow.

A Roll Call - The Civil War in Kent Co, MD by Walter J. Kirby lists Private Samuel Hepbron Blackiston, CSA. Served in Company B, 1st MD Cavalry. He was born in 1836, the first son of William H. Blackiston of Sassafras and older brother of Lt. H.C. Blackiston. He married Sarah Turner Brooks at I.U. church, Worton. It is believed he moved to VA with his wife and children, Henry Curtis, Helen, McCall, and Slater and died in 1888.

CENSUS: 1870 Kent Co, MD
S. H. Blackiston 34 Farmer $25000 RE, $3600 PE, Sarah T. 26, Helen Blackiston 1, Philip A.M. Brooks 9
Year: 1870; Census Place: District 2, Kent, Maryland; Roll: M593 590; Page: 89B

CENSUS: 1880 Kent Co, MD
S. Hepbron Blackiston 43 Self (Head) Dep. Clerk to State court, father born MD mother born PA, Sarah T. Blackiston 35 Wife, Harry C. Blackiston 8 Son, Josephene Blackiston 6 Daughter, McCall M. Blackiston 2 Son, Philip A.M. Brooks 18 Son-in-law
Year: 1880; Census Place: Charlestown, Kent, Maryland; Roll: 512; Page: 134c; Enumeration District: 052

Samuel Hepburn Blackiston and Sarah Turner Rasin were married on 12 Sep 1868 in Kent County, Maryland. **Sarah Turner Rasin**, daughter of Mccall Medford Rasin and Margaret Ann Boyer, was born on 1 Mar 1844. She died on 21 Jul 1917 at the age of 73. She was buried in Christ I.U. Church, Kent, Maryland.

OBITUARY: Mrs. Sarah Rasin Blackiston died at 2 o'clock yesterday morning at the home of her niece, Mrs. Percy G. Skirven, 3900 Cottage avenue, in her seventy-fourth year. Mrs. Blackiston suffered a stronke of paralysis 10 days ago. The funeral will take place at noon today at the old Christ I.U. church, in Kent County, of which Rev. Dr. Sewell S. Hepburn is rector. Mrs. Blackiston was a daughter of Macall Medford Rasin and Margaret Ann Boyer Rasin and was born at St. Martin's near Still Pond, Kent county. Her first husband was Medford Brooks and she is survived by one son by this marriage - P.A.M. Brooks, of

Chestertown. She later married Sewell Hepburn Blackiston, long Clerk of the Circuit Court of Kent, and had been a widow about 25 years. One of their sons is Harry C. Blackiston, of New York, the American representative of Furness, Withy & Co., the British steamship firm; another is Slater C. Blackiston, of the Bush Terminal Company, New York, and she is also survived by a daughter, Miss Helen Elizabeth Blackiston. Mrs. Blackiston was a sister of Capt. William I. Ras of the First Maryland Cavalry, a distinguished soldier of the Confederacy and long connected with the Baltimore Custom House, who died at Newport News a year ago. Lieut. Macall Medford Rasin, another brother, Longstreet's dispatch bearer at Gettysburg, died two years ago. Mrs. Blackiston was a sister of the late Mrs. James S. Gemmill, of Kent County, mother of Mrs. William R. Kay, Mrs. J.B. Carnett and Miss Sarah M. Gemmill of Philadelphia, and Mrs. Percy G. Skirven. The Baltimore Sun, Sat. July 31, 1917 p 11.

Per record of McCall M. Rasin he had neice Elizabeth Blackiston too.

Samuel Hepburn Blackiston and Sarah Turner Rasin had the following children:

+   344   i.   **Henry Curtis Blackiston** was born 15 Jan 1872 Chestertown MD. Died 23 Jan. 1951 at Hampton, VA. DEATH: Henry Curtis Blackiston died at Elize. City, Hampton, at home, 501 Bridge Ave. on Jan 23, 1951 age 79y male white married born Jan 15 1872 Chestertown, MD, retired shipping executive parents Hepburn Blackiston and Sarah Turner Rasin, wife Mary Marrow. Information Miss Helen Blackiston died of chronic arteriosclerotic nephritis, hypertension heart disease. burial St. Johns at Hampton VA. Buried St. John's Church Cemetery, Hampton, Virginia. OBITUARY: Mr. Blackiston Final Rites at 4pm today. Funeral Services for Henry Curtis Blackiston, 79, for many ears an internationally known shipping official, who died Tuesday at his home on Bridge St., will be held at 4 this afternoon at St. John's Episcopal Church, Hampton. (list of pallbearers and honorary pallbearers). Mr. Blackiston was born in Chestertown, Md., Jan. 15, 1872, the son of the late Hepburn Blackiston and Mrs. Sarah Turner Rasin Blackiston. Rose Rapidly. He attended Washington College and upon the death of his father went to work to support his mother, two younger brothers and sisters. At the age of 18, in 1899, he became a checking clerk in the office of Furness-Withy and Company, Ltd. world-wide British steamship operators and owners- a firm he remained with 45 years. He became manager of that office before his 25th birthday, and in 1914 was chosen by the company's directors to head the New York Office. In 1920 he became American director for the company with offices in New York City, and until his retirement April 30, 1935, directed the company operations in the United States and Canada. Mr. Blackiston during his service with Furness-Withy had a large part in its enormous expansion of its facilities and operations.

He was the first American to become a director of the company. Other Offices. Until his retirement in 1935, he was also a director of the Irving Trust Company and was formerly a member of Indian House, the Ardsley County Club, the Garden City Golf Club, the Lawrence Beach Club and the Mid-Ocean Club of Bermuda. It was after Mr. Blackiston took over as American director that the company acquired the old Quebec Steamship Company which operated the Bermuda line, and the Furner Bermuda Line was developed. Building of several hotels there, the Furness interests were responsible in large part for developing Bermuda's tourist trade. In addition to survivors listed in previous news accounts, Mr. Blackiston is survived by a sister, Miss Helen Blackiston of Montevallo, Ala. Daily Press Jan 25 1951 p 5

345   ii.   **Josephine Blackiston** born about 1874 died 3 Mar 1898 Buried Christ Church Cemetery, Worton, Kent County, MD.

+ 346   iii.   **McCall Medford Rasin Blackiston** born about 1880 died 26 Feb 1911 in Milwaukee, Wisconsin. Buried St. John's Church Cemetery, Hampton, Virginia. TOMBSTONE: McCall R. Blackiston 1880-1911

347   iv.   **Helen Blackiston** was born 10 Aug 1882 died 12 Jun 1962. Buried St. John's Church Cemetery, Hampton, Virginia.

+ 348   v.   **Slater Clay Blackiston** Sr. born about 1883 died 28 Dec 1947 Erie County, NY. Buried Christ Church Cemetery, Worton, Kent County, MD. Attended College of William and Mary Senior 1905 Williamsburg VA. Capta of Football Team, Class President, President of the German Club, Medal Winner in 220-yard dash, Diplomas in Pedagogy, American History and Politics.

DEATH: Slater Clay Blackiston Race White Gender Male Death Age 64 Birth Date 18 May 1883 Birth Place Chestertown, Maryland Death Date 23 Dec 1947 Death Place Erie, Erie, Pennsylvania, Pres. Union Storage Co. Father Samuel H Blackiston born Chestertown MD Mother Sally Rasin born Chestertown MD Spouse Eugenia Gaylor died of coronary occlusion Certificate Number 107646. His son Slator Clay Jr. was LcDr in US Navy in World War II and died 1994. His grandson Slater Clay Blackiston III was Lt Blackiston a Navy SEAL, Class 040. He was killed during a training jump in 1984 in France. The cause of death was drowning. His chute deployed, but he got tangled in the strings when he landed in the water because he was unconscious. Lt Blackiston was awarded 4 Bronze Star Medals (With Combat V) in Vietnam 1968-1971.

228. Henry Curtis Blackiston (William Henry-7, James-6, Ebenezer-5, John-4, John-3, George-2, Marmaduke-1) born about 1838 in Maryland. He died on 3 Sep 1864 at the age of 26 in Bunker Hill, Virginia. He was buried in Episcopal Chapel, Bunker Hill, West Virginia.

CENSUS: 1860 Henry C Blackiston 22, Stephen Harden 33 1860; Census Place: District 3, Kent, Maryland; Roll: M653 477; Page: 0; Image: 400.

Henry C. served as Lt. in Company B of the First Maryland Cavalry CSA. He saw fighting at several VA battles. A report from Capt. Frank Bond dated July 4 1863 states that Lt. Cook and Blackiston were sent foraging. The advance picket had been on duty but a short time when I was notified of the advance of a large body of Federal Cavalry and artillery from the direction of Emmitsburg. The firing brought up Lt. Blackiston with the rest of my troop. After fully an hour we heard the enemy advancing, this time with more caution and with dismounted skirmishers thrown out on each side of the road. Lying on the ground we reserved our fire until they were within ten or fifteen paces of us, when we gave them a volley which caused another precipitate retreat. Lt. Blackiston had charge of the horses and prisoners in the rear.

Roll Call the Civil War in Kent Co by Walter J. Kirby lists 2nd Lt. Henry Curtis Blackiston, CSA. He entered service Sep 10 1862, 3rd Lt Company B, 1st MD Cavalry. He was elected 2nd Lt in 1864. His military records show that he requested a 24-day leave of absence on Jan. 22 1864 for the purpose of attending to business requiring my personal attention. He was granted 15 days as of Jan. 23. His hospital records show that he was on the register of the CSA General Hospital, Charlottesville from Oct. 10-Nov 3, 1863. He was hospitalized from March 8 to April 17, 1864, at the General Hospital Nov. 4, Richmond VA for orchitis. Blackiston was wounded in the battle of Bunker Hill, VA Sep 3 1864. He was taken to the porch of a home owned by Judge Boyd, where he died after a short time. He was buried in the Episcopal Church Cem. in Bunker Hill. He was born Jun 9 1838, the second son of William H. Blackiston of Sassafras. His widow Kate died in Denton and was buried in the Chester Cem, Chestertown.

Marriage 47837 Blackiston Jr, Henry Curtis m. Nugent, Elizabeth Parker Vol. 5

TOMBSTONE: Lt. Henry C. Blackiston Co. B. 1st MD. Cav. C.S.A. Born in Kent County MD June 8 1838 Killed at Bunkers Hill, Virginia Sep 3, 1864. And God Shall wipe away all tears from their eyes and there shall be no more death.

Henry Curtis Blackiston and Kate were married. **Kate**.

236. **John B. Blackiston** (James-7, Michael-6, Ebenezer-5, John-4, John-3, George-2, Marmaduke-1) born about 1802. He died after 1880 at the age of 78. Vouchers Book 6 p 252 I, John B. Blackiston of the City of Baltimore and a son of James Blackiston who was a brother of Ebenezer have received of Rachel administratix and Henry administrator $52.60 as struck by the Orphans Court of Kent Co Jan 29 1850. Feb 13 1850. also has John T. Blackiston.

John B. Blackiston and Catherine Berry were married. **Catherine** was born in 1816 in MD. She died after 1880 at the age of 64.

John B. Blackiston and Catherine Berry had the following children:

+328   i. **Sarah Catherine Blackiston**, born 13 Sep 1832 Died 26 Jun 1906 married **John K. Willis**

+349   ii. **Thomas Jefferson Blackiston**, born 4 Aug 1853; married Mary Malinda Stevens; died 2 Nov 1912, Vanderbilt, Fayette, Pennsylvania.

243. **Robert West Blackiston** (James-7, Joseph-6, Ebenezer-5, John-4, John-3, George-2, Marmaduke-1) was born on 24 Mar 1823. He died on 4 Oct 1881 at the age of 58. Ancestor of 4 members of the SAR.

Col. Franklin Blackston born 1874 who married Zella Henry Alllison in 1925 was SAR member 16440. He lived and died in PA. His grandfather was Robert West Blackstone. He said Robert was the grandson of Joseph Blackiston and Mary Stevens. Franklin joined under Joseph Blackiston saying he was a corporal in the MD militia born 1760 and married to Mary Stevens.

CENSUS: 1850 Indiana Co, PA
Robert Blackson 27 laborer PA, Jane Blackson 38, Mary Sharp 13, Hannah Sharp 7, William Blackson 1
Census; Record Group Number: 29; Series Number: M432; Residence Date: 1850; Home in 1850: Wheatfield, Indiana, Pennsylvania; Roll: 785; Page: 120a

CENSUS: 1860 Alleghany Co, PA
Robert Blarson   38 PA, Jane Blarson 48, Isaack Sharp 25, Hiloniny Hana Sharp 16, William Blackson 12, Isibel Blackson 9, Hugh B Wear, Agnes Blackson 6
Census; Record Group Number: 29; Series Number: M653; Residence Date: 1860; Home in 1860: Pittsburgh Ward 9, Alleghany, Pennsylvania; Roll: M653_1060; Page: 505; Family History Library Film: 805060
CENSUS: 1880 Allegheny Co, PA
Jane Blackstone 66, William Blackstone 21, Isabell Blackstone 18, Agnes Blackstone 16, Thomas Doty 27, Hanna Doty 27, John Fanning, Jane Graham 4/12 (Robert was in Indiana Co PA census working.)
Year: *1870*; Census Place: *Pittsburgh   Ward   10,   Allegheny,   Pennsylvania*; Roll: *M593_1296*; Page: *332B*

CENSUS: 1880 Allegheny Co, PA
Jane Vaxon 77 Self (Head) widowed, Jennie Graham 10 Niece
Year: *1880*; Census Place: *Pittsburgh, Allegheny, Pennsylvania*; Roll: *1092*; Page: *559a*; Enumeration District: *124*

Robert West Blackiston and Jane Barren were married on 25 Jun 1847. **Jane Barren** was born on 17 Feb 1807. She died on 17 Feb 1890 at the age of 83.

246. **James Eagle Blackiston Sr.** (Joseph-7, Joseph-6, Ebenezer-5, John-4, John-3, George-2, Marmaduke-1) was born in 1808 in Kent County, Maryland. He died on 30 Mar 1869 at the age of 61 in Rock Hall, Kent County, Maryland.

MARRIAGE: James E. Blackiston m. Rebecca T. Ashley May 30 1830 by T. Smith, Kent Co.

CENUS: 1830 Kent Co, MD
James Blackestin [James Blackiston]
Home in 1830 (City, County, State) District 2, Kent, Maryland
Free White Persons - Males - 20 thru 29   1
Free White Persons - Females - 10 thru 14   1
Free White Persons - Females - 20 thru 29   1
Year: *1830*; Census Place: *District 2, Kent, Maryland*; Series: *M19*; Roll: *57*; Page: *418*; Family History Library Film: *0013180*

MARRIAGE: James E. Blackiston m. Mary Emily Stevens Oct 19 1843 by Rev. Kesley Kent Co.

CENSUS: 1850 Kent Co MD
HSE 367-367 James E Blackiston 42 shoemaker, Mary E 30, Henrietta 14, Mary R 12, John A 6, Wm H, 4, Anna 2. 2nd Elect. Dist. p. 232
Census; Record Group Number: *29*; Series Number: *M432*; Residence Date: *1850*; Home in 1850: *District 2, Kent, Maryland*; Roll: *294*; Page: *232a*

CENSUS: 1860 Kent Co MD
James E Blackiston 52 shoemaker, Mary E 35, John 14, William H 12, Caroline 10, Adaline 4, James L 1. 1st Elect. Dist. Rock Hall p 1064
Census; Record Group Number: *29*; Series Number: *M653*; Residence Date: *1860*; Home in 1860: *District 1, Kent, Maryland*; Roll: *M653_477*; Page: *1064*; Family History Library Film: *803477*

> On the 30th. March, of Paralysis, after a lingering illness, JAMES E. BLACKISTON, aged 60 years. He leaves a wife and several children to mourn his loss. By the bright evidence we witnessed on his dying bed, we are sure he has gone where there is no suffering, and where ne will forever join in singing praises to God.

OBITUARY: On the 30th March of paralysis, after a lingering illness, James E. Blackiston, aged 60y. He leaves a wife and several children to mourn his loss. By the bright evidence we witnessed on his dying bed, we are sure he has gone where there is no suffering, and where he will forever join in singing praises to God. Kent News April 10 1869.

ESTATE: Estate of father. Vouchers p 247 I James E Blackiston son and legatee of Joseph Blackiston late of Kent Co deceased, received $300 from Henry Blackiston executor. Feb 10 1851 witness Martin Allen.

James Eagle Blackiston Sr. and Rebecca T. Ashley were married on 30 May 1830 in Kent County, Maryland. **Rebecca T. Ashley** born about 1810. She died about 1840 at the age of 30.

James Eagle Blackiston and Rebecca T. Ashley had the following children:

+350	i.	**Anna Matilda Blackiston**, born abt 1832; married Jacob Stevens, 8 Mar 1852, Kent County, Maryland; married Abraham Taylor, bef 1860; died abt 1860.
351	ii.	**Henrietta Blackiston** born about 1836 in Maryland.
352	iii.	**Mary R. Blackiston** born about 1838 in Maryland.

James Eagle Blackiston Sr. and Mary Emily Stephens were married on 19 Oct 1843 in Kent County, Maryland. **Mary Emily Stephens**, daughter of John Topping Stevens and Anna Emily Brown, was born on 21 Jan 1825 in Kent County, Maryland. She died on 21 Feb 1902 at the age of 77 in Rock Hall, Kent County, Maryland. She was buried at Wesley Chapel in Rock Hall, Kent County, Maryland. She went by her middle name. She was left estate by Mary H. Stevens in her will of 1849.

DEATH: Mary Emily Leary widow died Feb 21 1902 Rock Hall. age 77y 1m born MD one child living. parents Toppings Stephens and Emilie Brown, bronch. pneumonia, heart failure, reported by T. B. Wilson.

WILL: Mary E. Leary dated Sep 1 1888 probate Mar 4 1902 JTD 1-451. son John J. Blackiston land purchased of late husband George Leary's estate sale, also $350 from my James E. Blackiston, grandson William C. Blackiston now in Caroline Co, son James E. Blackiston one acre at Rock Hall CrossRoads on north corner and the above $350, son James exec. signed by Mary. witness Samuel Burgess, Thomas Cousey, James L. Leary.

TOMBSTONE: M. Emily Leary 1825-1902.

OBITUARY: Mrs. Emily Leary., widow of the late Rev. George Leary, died at her home in Rock Hall, on Friday evening of last week, of pneumonia. The funeral services were conducted at Wesley Chapel M.P. church, on Monday afternoon, interment in the cemetery adjoining. The deceased was married twice, her first husband being James Blackiston, Mr.

John J. Blackiston, Esq., being a son. She was also the mother of James E. Blackiston who died about two years ago. The deceased was in her 77 years. The Chestertown Transcript March 1 1902.

DEED: Mary Emily Blackiston wife of James E. Blackiston bought of Jacob and Ann M. Stevens. Nov. 6 1855 JFG 3 p. 235 Kent Co MD

James Eagle Blackiston and Mary Emily Stephens had the following children:

+353   i.   **John Joseph Blackiston**, born 1 Mar 1846, Kent County, Maryland; married Julia Christina Leary, 15 Jun 1869, Kent County, Maryland; died 1 Feb 1913, Rock Hall, Kent County, Maryland.

354   ii.   **William H. Blackiston** born about 1848 in Kent County, Maryland. He died on 23 Nov 1872 at the age of 24 in Denton, Caroline County, Maryland. CENSUS: 1870 Living with his uncle Henry in Caroline Co. William H. Blackiston 22. OBITUARY: William J. Blackiston at Denton MD on 23rd inst. aged about 25 formerly Kent Co Nov 30 1872 Kent Co News.

+355   iii.   **Susan Caroline Blackiston**, born 25 Nov 1849, Kent County, Maryland; married John E. Beck, 8 Dec 1869, Kent County, Maryland; died 29 Oct 1874, Kent County, Maryland.

356   iv.   **Kate Adaline Blackiston** was born on 9 Oct 1855 in Kent County, Maryland. She died on 2 Feb 1867 at the age of 11 in Kent County, Maryland. OBITUARY: Kate Adaline Blackiston at Rock Hall on 2nd instant 11y 3m 24d dau of James E and Mary E Blackiston Feb 9 1867 Kent Co. MD

+357   v.   **James Eagle Blackiston Jr.**, born 7 Jul 1860, Kent County, Maryland; married Mary Henrietta Hudson, 2 Dec 1884, Kent County, Maryland; died 8 Jan 1900, Kent County, Maryland.

247. **Mary Ann Blackiston** (Joseph-7, Joseph-6, Ebenezer-5, John-4, John-3, George-2, Marmaduke-1) born about 1810. She died on 20 Mar 1845 at the age of 35 in Kent County, Maryland. MARRIAGE: Mary Ann Blackiston m. John D. Lewis on Feb. 17 1836. OBITUARY: Mary Ann Lewis died March 20 1845 2nd dau of Mr. Joseph Blackiston wife of John B. Lewis. Sentinel April 1845. Mary Ann Blackiston and John D. Lewis were married on 17 Feb 1836 in Queen Annes County, Maryland. **John D. Lewis** born about 1810.

248. **Henrietta Blackiston** (Joseph-7, Joseph-6, Ebenezer-5, John-4, John-3, George-2, Marmaduke-1) was born on 2 May 1811 in Hagerstown, Washington County, Maryland. She was christened on 3 Sep 1811 in Hagerstown, Washington County, Maryland. BIRTH: Joseph Blackiston and Henrietta his wife had dau Henrietta baptized Sep 3 1811 at Evangelical Lutheran Cong. born May 2 1811 at Hagerstown sponsor the mother. church records p 80

CENUSS: 1850 Providence, RI
Antonio L Crout 44 PA Exchange Broker, H B Crout 34 MD, Charles H Crout 4 RI, Virginia Crout 12 Maine, Henrietta Crout 3 RI, Jane Donnelly 20 Ireland, Anna W Blackstone 18 MD
Census; Record Group Number: 29; Series Number: M432; Residence Date: 1850; Home in 1850: Providence Ward 4, Providence, Rhode Island; Roll: 845; Page: 258b

CENSUS: 1860 Providence RI
Henrietta B. Crout 44y born MD, Henrietta A. Crout 17, Charles E. Crout 13.
Census; Record Group Number: 29; Series Number: M653; Residence Date: 1860; Home in 1860: Providence Ward 7, Providence, Rhode Island; Roll: M653 1209; Page: 433; Family History Library Film: 805209
DEATH: Henrietta Blackiston Crout Gender Female Race White Marital Status Widowed Age 73 Birth Date abt 1812 Birth Place Chestertown, MD. Death Date 3 Nov 1885 Death Place Rhode Island, USA Death Registration Place Providence Father John Blackiston Mother Mary Blackiston Spouse Antonio L. Crout. Index says Henrietta B Crout Relation wid Kin 1 Antonio L Crout Kin 2 Annie Croughan Death Date 03 Nov 1885 Age 73 Yrs

Henrietta Blackiston and Antonio L. Crout were married.

249. **Henry Blackiston** (Joseph-7, Joseph-6, Ebenezer-5, John-4, John-3, George-2, Marmaduke-1) was born on 2 Mar 1813 in Maryland. He died on 12 May 1891 at the age of 78 in Kent County, Maryland. He was buried in Chestertown Cemetery, Chestertown, Kent County, Maryland. He administered on estate of Ebenezer Blackiston (who m. Rachel Kearnes) in 1850 (who could be his father's first cousin)

MARRIAGE: Henry Blackiston married Marietta Durding on 13 Nov 1841 in Kent County, MD.

MARRIAGE: Henry Blackinston m. Sarah Catharine Shaw on 30 Apr 1849 Baltimore, Maryland

CENSUS: 1850 Kent Co
HSE 840-840 Henry Blackiston 36, Sarah C. 19, Anna 40, (this appears to be his stepmother), Samuel J. Wicks 35, Anne E. 27, Mary E. Benton 15.
1850; Census Place: District 1, Kent, Maryland; Roll: M432 294; Page: 264; Image: 531.

CENSUS: 1880
Henry Blackiston 67 born MD father born DE mother born MD, Sarah C. Blackiston 47, Wm. J. Blackiston 26, Chas. H. Blackiston 24, Florence M. Blackiston 20, William Shaw 18, Harriet Coleman 20
1880; Census Place: Denton, Caroline, Maryland; Roll: T9 506; Family History Film: 1254506; Page: 165.3000; Enumeration District: 3; Image: 0086.

Henry Blackiston and Marietta Durding were married on 13 Nov 1841 in Kent County, Maryland. **Marietta Durding**, daughter of John T. Durding, born about 1815.

Henry Blackiston and Sarah Catherine Shaw were married on 30 Apr 1849 in Baltimore, Maryland. **Sarah Catherine Shaw** was born on 9 Feb 1832 in Maryland. She died on 18 Feb 1904 at the age of 72 in Kent County, Maryland. She was buried in Chestertown Cemetery, Chestertown, Kent County, Maryland.

OBITUARY: Death of a Prominent Merchant. Mr. Henry Blackiston passes away at the age of seventy-eight. Death closed the long career of Mr. Henry Blackiston on Tuesday morning last, at nine o'clock. He was seventy-eight years of age, and was , perhaps the oldest merchant in Caroline county. Although he had lived somewhat retired for years past, he had attended to business matters until a short time before his death. By industry and constant attention to his business he built up a fine trade and amassed a considerable fortune. His was for many years one of the leading mercantile establishments of the county. Despite many losses attributed to a heavy credit business, his estate is estimated to be worth about twenty thousand dollars. Mr. Blackiston was born in Hagerstown, but when small child removed to Kent county. In early life he married Miss Durden, who only lived a few months after the union. Sometime thereafter, and when still a young man, he married Miss Kate Shaw, daughter of William Shaw, Esq. Also of Kent. Mrs. Blackiston, two sons – Messrs. Wiliam J. and Charles H. Blackiston, and one daughter – Miss Florence Blackiston – survive. The subject of this sketch began his long business career in Kent county, Maryland, being at a very early age – about fourteen – a business partner of a merchant in Chestertown – a Rev. Mr. Wiley. He subsequently learned the shoemaking business and conducted a large shop at Port Deposit, Md. In 1853 he moved to Denton, and with the exception of a interval of a few months conducted the mercantile business until succeeded by his son. His former business partners here were Mr. James A Dixon, now deceased, and Mr. James K. Saulsbury, of Ridgely. He was a member of a family of three brothers and two sister, only of whom, Mr. John T. Blackiston of Piedmont, West Va, now survives. The remains were on Thursday removed to Chestertown and interred. The following gentlemen acted as pallbearers: T.W. Eliason, Henry Bramble, H.M. Stuart, Dr. J. T. Twilley, Thomas France, ad Captain J. H. Thompson, Revs. G.W. Townsend and James H. Rich, of Denton, read the burial rites.

Sarah C Blackstene 69 Head, Wm J Blackstene 46 Son, Chas H Blackstene 44 Son Divorced, Florence M Blackstene 40 Daughter, Linwood Sparks 32 Nephew, Thos Dansen 46 Brother
Year: *1900*; Census Place: *Denton, Caroline, Maryland*; Roll: *619*; Page: *6*; Enumeration District: *0005*

Wm J Blackiston 65 Head single, Chas H Blackiston 63 Brother divorced, Florence M Blackiston 59 Sister single
Year: *1920*; Census Place: *Denton, Caroline, Maryland*; Roll: *T625_669*; Page: *10A*;

Enumeration District: *5*

Henry Blackiston and Sarah Catherine Shaw had the following children:

358   i.   **William James Blackiston** was born Dec 1853 Died 22 Mar. 1939 Denton, Caroline Co, MD. OBITUARY: William J. Blackiston dies at Denton, MD. Funeral services will be held tomorrow at 2pm for William J. Blackiston, 85, retired merchant who died Wednesday after a long period of failing health. Blackiston, a graduate of Dickinson Seminary, studied both law and medicine but gave them up to aid his father in the mercantile business The Daily Times, Salisbury, MD March 24, 1939 p 1 NEWS: Personal property of Wm. J. Blackiston, deceased, including a few valuable books, will be sold at 2pm today (Saturday) at his late home, near the yards of the Nuttle Lumber and Coal Company. Denton Journal April 1 1939. Buried Denton Cemetery, Denton, MD

359   ii. **Charles H. Blackiston** was born 3 Feb 1856 in Kent, Maryland. Died 9 Dec 1934 Denton, Caroline, MD OBITUARY: Charles H. Blackiston, 78, who once conducted a jewelry store here and later was in partnership with the late Dr. Charles Williamson in a drug business in this town, died at his home here this week. Mr. Blackiston retired from business several years ago and until recently lived on a farm near Denton. He died suddenly, although he had been failing in health for five years. A native of Denton, he was the son of the late Henry Blackiston, one of the leading merchants here, and Mrs. Sarah Catherine Shaw Blackiston, formerly of Kent county. He was educated at Dover Academy, Dover, De. He is survived by a brother, William J. Blackiston, with whom he lived. Funeral services were conducted at the Moore funeral home on Thursday afternoon at one o'clock and interment was made in the family lot in Chestertown, The Rev. M. Andrews, pastor Denton M.E. Church, officiated. Denton Journal Dec 15 1934 p 5 Buried in Chester Cem., Chestertown, MD

360   iii. **Florence M. Blackiston** was born 12 May 1860 and died Sep 13, 1933. OBITUARY: Miss Florence M. Blackiston, aged 73 years, died last Thursday at the Cambridge State Hospital where she was a patient. She had been an invalid for many years. Funeral services will be held tomorrow (Sunday) Afternoon at two o'clock at the home of Mrs. C.H. Stewart in Easter Denton and the burial will be in Denton Cemetery. Miss Blackiston was the daughter of the late Henry Blackiston and Sarah Shaw Blackiston. She was born in Denton and lived here practically all of her life. Two brothers, William J. and Charles H. Blackiston of Denton, survive. Denton Journal Sep. 16 1933 p 5. Buried Denton Cemetery, Denton, MD

250. William C. Blackiston (Joseph-7, Joseph-6, Ebenezer-5, John-4, John-3, George-2, Marmaduke-1) born about 1815. He died on 21 Jan 1890 at the age of 75 in Baltimore City, Maryland. He was buried in Loudon Park Cemetery, Baltimore City, Md. MARRIAGE: William C. Blackiston m. Eliz. Tomlinson on Jan 16 1838 in Cecil Co MD marriage records.

In 1842 he was selected Lumber Inspector for Cecil Co – William C. Blackiston. The Cecil Whig Mar. 12, 1842 p. 3

CENSUS: 1850 Cecil Co, MD
William C Blackiston 31 Apothecary, Elizabeth Blackiston 32, Albert Blackiston 5. Helen Blackiston 2, Susan Gibbs 19
Census; Record Group Number: *29*; Series Number: *M432*; Residence Date: *1850*; Home in 1850: *Port Deposit, Cecil, Maryland*; Roll: *290*; Page: *147a*

ESTATE: Vouchers Aug 10 1853 $230 of Henry Blackiston as full legacy left to me by my father Joseph Blackiston. W.C. Blackiston. witness John T. Blackiston.

CENSUS: 1860 Baltimore City, MD
Wm C Blackston 44 Lumber Inspector, Elizabeth Blackston 42, Albert Blackston 14, Helen Blackston 12, Laura Blackston 10, Kate Blackston 6, Ida Blackston 3, Harry Blackston 3/12, and others
Census; Record Group Number: *29*; Series Number: *M653*; Residence Date: *1860*; Home in 1860: *Baltimore Ward 15, Baltimore, Maryland*; Roll: *M653_464*; Page: *431*; Family History Library Film: *803464*

CENSUS: 1870 Baltimore City, MD
William Blackiston 53 Lumber inspector, Elizabeth Blackiston 50, Laura Blackiston 18, Kate Blackiston 16, Ida Blackiston 13
Year: *1870*; Census Place: *Baltimore Ward 15, Baltimore (Independent City), Maryland*; Roll: *M593_578*; Page: *84A*

CENSUS: 1880 Baltimore City, MD
William C. Blackstone 63 Self (Head) Lumber Inspector, Elizabeth Blackstone 61 Wife, Ida Blackstone 21 Daughter, James K. Hardesty 30 Son-in-law, Laura Hardesty 28 Daughter, Wallace Hardesty 4/12 Grandson
Year: *1880*; Census Place: *Baltimore, Baltimore (Independent City), Maryland*; Roll: *502*; Page: *516a*; Enumeration District: *138*

William C. Blackiston and Elizabeth Tomlinson were married on 16 Jan 1838 in Cecil County, Maryland. **Elizabeth Tomlinson** born about 1818. She died in Sep 1902 at the age of 84. She was buried in Loudon Park Cemetery, Baltimore City, Md. OBITUARY: Mrs. Elizabeth Blackiston, 84 years old, widow of Wiliam C. Blackiston, died on Tuesday of heart trouble at her home, 2804 Woodbrook avenue. Mrs. Blackiston had bene in failing health since January. She was born in Charlestown, Cecil county, and was the daughter of the late John Tomlinson. For many years she was a devoted member of Wesley Chapel Methodist Episcopal Church. Mrs. Blackiston is survived by five daughters – Mrs. Susan Beck, Mrs. Kate Barnes, Mrs. Milton White, Mrs. Helen M. perry and Mrs. Laura V. Hardesty – and one son, Mr. Albert C. Blackiston. The Baltimore Sun Sep 11, 1902 p 7

William C. Blackiston and Elizabeth Tomlinson had the following children:

361   i. **Harvey Rowland Blackiston** born about 1860 in Kent County, Maryland. He died on 28 Mar 1863 at the age of 3 in Baltimore, Maryland. OBITUARY: Harvey Rowland Blackiston in Baltimore 28th ult, 3yrs youngest son of William C and Elizabeth Blackiston Apr 4 1863 Kent News.

ii. **Albert C. Blackiston** was born 16 Feb 1845 Died 10 Mar 1916. Buried at Lorraine Park Cemetery, Woodlawn, Baltimore Co, MD

iii. **Helen May Blackiston** was born 7 May 1848 died 5 Aug 1919. Buried at Lorraine Park Cemetery, Woodlawn, Baltimore Co, MD. Married Israel J. Perry 1844-1906.

iv. **Laura V. Blackiston** was born Jun 1852. Died 20 Jun 1915. Married George Walter Hopwood. Buried at Lorraine Park Cemetery, Woodlawn, Baltimore Co, MD

v. **Kate Blackiston** was born 1854 died 27 Jun 1929. Buried at Lorraine Park Cemetery, Woodlawn, Baltimore Co, MD Married Colin R. Bierbower 1846-1894 and William E. Barnes.

vi. **Ida Belle Blackiston** was born 20 Jul 1857 Died 12 Jul 1923. Buried at Lorraine Park Cemetery, Woodlawn, Baltimore Co, MD. Married Milton White 1854-1930

251. John Thomas Blackiston (Joseph-7, Joseph-6, Ebenezer-5, John-4, John-3, George-2, Marmaduke-1) was born on 16 Mar 1819. He died on 17 Jul 1893 at the age of 74 in Westernport, Allegany County, Maryland. He was buried at Philos Cemetery in Westernport, Maryland.

MARRIAGE: John T. Blackiston (QA Co) m. Marie Antoinette Copper on Jan. 3, 1845. Kent Co, MD.

NOTE: Vouchers John T. Blackiston received $260 Aug 10 1853 of Henry Blackiston executor, full legacy left to me by my father Joseph Blackiston. witness W.C. Blackiston.

OBITUARY: Death and Burial of Mr. John T. Blackiston. In the demise of Mr. John T. Blackiston on Monday morning, July 17, 1893, at about seven o'clock, this community lost one of its oldest and most thoroughly respected citizens, a man whom every one looked up to as a gentlemen of the highest type of integrity and honor, and one whose life of more than forty years among these hills reflected continued credit upon his manhood and gentleness of character. Mr. Blackiston was one of those whom we often delight to call "A gentleman of the old school," He was always polite, always considerate of others, and always in practice and in preaching the happy counsellor of those in want of advice and sympathy. No one ever went to him for a favor, great or small, but what found him ready to extend a listening ear and a helping hand. His fellow citizens delighted to honor him, and for many years he was a valued member of the Board of Education, where his conservatism and good judgment were displayed to great advantage. Mr. Blackiston was a native of Kent county, Maryland, where he was born nearly seventy-five years ago. In early life, he went to Baltimore City, where he was apprenticed to the carpenter trade. He soon entered the employ of the Baltimore and Ohio railroad at Mr. Clare station and was not long in reaching the confidence of the officials of the road. When the system was extended west, Mr. Blackiston was dispatched to Cumberland where he had full charge of the company's interests in his line. From Cumberland, Mr. Blackiston came to Piedmond, in 1852, with the advance line of the company's people, and was again placed in charge of the important interests of the company in the carpenter shop at a station that was then the most important along the whole line. Since that time he has continued to reside here, always holding the esteem of his employee, and the full confidence of his employers. By reason of such long continued service in the company Mr. Blackiston was retired some four years ago in accordance with the rules and regulations of the Relief Association, and has been borne on the rolls in that capacity. In the quiet retirement of his home on Western-port Hill he has continued to reside, surrounded by loving relatives and kind friends. Mr. Blackiston was an exemplary Christian, being a consistent member of the Methodist Episcopal church, in which for a great many years he has held the position of trustee. He was always faithful to his calling and delighted more in the service of God's house than in possibly anything else. He leaves a widow well known and highly esteemed in the community, and in whose affection the sympathy of all friends and acquaintances finds expression. Three sons and two daughters also survive him - William J, John Ambrose, Thomas Copper, Rebecca Jane, and Emma Helen Christina Blackiston. All the children are well known here having been raised in the community. The funeral services took place on Wednesday afternoon at the Methodist Episcopal church, and were conducted by the pastor, Rev. Alex Dielacki. After procession entered the church the choir sang that beautiful selection of Montgomery's "Low in the Grave." Scripture readings followed by the pastor, and prayer was offered by the Rev. H.H. Kight. "Home at Last" was sung by the choir and Mr. Bielaski preached a most interesting sermon from the words of Paul: "The sting of death is sin." A very touching solo, "Christ is All," was rendered by Mr. Neal, and addresses were made by Messrs. William and Henry Kight. Both of these gentlemen had known the deceased intimately since he had first come to Piedmont, and naturally their intercourse had been of the most pleasant nature. They were both visibly affected, and their tributes of respect were touching and full of feeling. The burial of the body was in charge of the Masonic Fraternity, Mr. Blackiston having for many years been a member of Mt. Carbon Lodge No 28 of Piedmont. This lodge, together with a very large representation from the Davis Lodge, of Keyser, and Hiram Lodge, of Westernport, escorted the remains from the house to the church, and after the services there took immediate charge of the body, and proceeded to Philos Cemetery where the impressive rites of the fraternity were conducted. The master of Mr. Carbon lodge, of Piedmont, Robt. M. Williams, Esq. and Past Master O.H. Bruce, Esq. of Hiram Lodge, of Westernport performed the ceremony. Many floral tributes from relatives, friends, and societies, were laid upon his casket. The pall bearers were all taken from the Masonic lodges, and consisted of E.J. Fredlock, John Gardner, H.H. Mansbach, H.H. Kight, J.P. Williams, and W.T. Jamesson.

WILL: John T. Blackiston wife Maria A. farm in Kent about 3 or 4 miles from Rock Hall "Burge" or "Chesterview Farm" 150 acres bought of Alexander Harris, sons William T, John Ambrose Blackiston, dau Rebecca J. Bauty. dated Apr 20 1892 probate Aug 4 1893 WB CSH #1 p 276

TOMBSTONE: Grave Marker has 4 sides - one is for John T. and gives details the other 3 sides list children of J.T. and M.A Blackiston
One Stone
John T. Blackiston, died July 17, 1893, aged 74yrs, 4ms, and 11 dys.
Joseph H. died July 25, 1847 aged 1 yr and 6 mos.
Henry K. died Feb 8, 1851 aged 16 days
George E died Aug 27, 1854, aged 6yrs and 11 mos.
Mary A. died June 28, 1857, aged 4 mos and 11 days
Eliza M. died Oct. 26, 1861 aged 1 yr 6 m 5d
Alonza died June 21, 1862 aged 1 mo and 4 dys
Samuel H. died Aug. 28 1863 aged 7yrs, 3mos 28 ds.
Charles E.C. died Sep 18 1878 aged 11yrs
Children of J.T. and M.A. Blackiston

John Thomas Blackiston and Marie Antoinette Copper were married on 3 Jan 1845 in Kent County, Maryland. **Marie Antoinette Copper**, daughter of George Copper, born about 1825. She died after 1880 at the age of 55. She is named as the granddau. in the will of Jane Copper dated 1847. To my granddau. Antoinietta Blackiston one house and lot situated at the head of Rock Hall containing 12 acres.

John Thomas Blackiston and Marie Antoinette Copper had the following children:

362	i.	**Joseph H. Blackiston** was born on 25 Jan 1846. He died on 25 Jul 1847 at the age of 1. He was buried in Westernport, Allegany County, Maryland.
363	ii.	**George E. Blackiston** was born on 16 Aug 1848. He died on 27 Aug 1854 at the age of 6. He was buried in Westernport, Allegany County, Maryland.
364	iii.	**William Thomas Blackiston** born about 1849 in De. He died on 6 Mar 1915 at the age of 66 in Sun De Fuca, Island, Washington.
+365	iv.	**Rebecca J. Blackiston**, born abt 1850; married Beaty.
366	v.	**Henry K. Blackiston** was born on 23 Jan 1851. He died on 8 Feb 1851. He was buried in Westernport, Allegany County, Maryland.

+367	vi.	**John Ambrose Blackiston,** born abt 1853; married Martha F. ; died 28 Mar 1923, Washington, District of Columbia.
368	vii.	**Emma Helen Christina Blackiston** born about 1854. OBITUARY: From a descendant, Emily (Emma) Helen Christina Blackiston -- daughter of John T. Blackiston and M. A. Blackiston of Westernport MD her brothers and sisters of whom we are aware are: William J., John Ambrose, Thomas Copper, and Rebecca Jane per the obituary.
369	viii.	**Samuel H. Blackiston** was born on 30 Apr 1856 in Maryland. He died on 28 Aug 1863 at the age of 7. He was buried in Westernport, Allegany County, Maryland.
370	ix.	**Mary A. Blackiston** was born on 17 Feb 1857. She died on 28 Jun 1857. She was buried in Westernport, Allegany County, Maryland.
+371	x.	**Dr Thomas Copper Blackiston,** born abt 1858, West Virginia; married Sarah S Raleigh; married Elizabeth Lane, 20 Feb 1893, Washington, District of Columbia; died 28 Sep 1908, Los Angeles, California.
372	xi.	**Eliza M. Blackiston** was born on 21 Apr 1860. She died on 26 Oct 1861 at the age of 1.
373	xii.	**Alonza Blackiston** was born on 17 May 1862. He died on 21 Jun 1862. He was buried in Westernport, Allegany County, Maryland.
374	xiii.	**Charles E. C. Blackiston** born about 1868. He died on 18 Sep 1878 at the age of 10.

252. Sarah Jane Blackiston (Joseph-7, Joseph-6, Ebenezer-5, John-4, John-3, George-2, Marmaduke-1) born about 1820 in Maryland. She died before 1876 at the age of 56. MARRIAGE: Lemuel W. Ashley m. Sarah J. Blackiston on 23 Nov 1840 Baltimore Co, MD.

DEED: Joseph Blackiston & Anna (x) gave land to Sarah Jane Ashley 1842.

CENSUS: 1850 Kent co, MD
Lemuel W Ashley 30 laborer, June Ashley 30, Sarah Ashley 0, June Kindall 8
Census; Record Group Number: *29*; Series Number: *M432*; Residence Date: *1850*; Home in 1850: *District 1, Kent, Maryland*; Roll: *294*; Page: *264b*

CENSUS: 1860 Kent Co, MD
Lemuel W Ashley 39 Blackiston, Sarah J Ashley 38, Sarah G Ashley 10, Jacob Kendall 18, Benjamin F Ashley 20, Nathan Satterfield 18
Census; Record Group Number: *29*; Series Number: *M653*; Residence Date: *1860*; Home in 1860: *District 1, Kent, Maryland*; Roll: *M653_477*; Page: *1073*; Family History Library Film: *803477*

CENSUS: 1870 Kent Co, MD
Lemuel W Ashley 50, Sarah J Ashley 49

Year: *1870*; Census Place: *District 5, Kent, Maryland*; Roll: *M593_590*; Page: *214A*

Sarah Jane Blackiston and Lemuel Washington Ashley were married in 1842 in Kent County, Maryland. **Lemuel Washington Ashley,** son of Isaiah Ashley and Mary Dudley, was born in Mar 1821 in Rock Hall, Kent County, Maryland. He died on 12 Jan 1897 at the age of 75 in Centreville, Queen Annes County, Maryland. OBITUARY: Capt. Lemuel Washington Ashley at residence Centreville last Tuesday 75 years 10 months born Rock Hall, March 1821, son of Isaiah Ashley of Lower Kent Co. Married 3 times 1842, 1876, 1887 and leaves daughters Mrs. William J. Gardner and Miss Lillie W. Ashley. Jan. 16, 1897 Centreville Record.

OBITUARY: Captain Lemuel Washington Ashley died at his residence in Centreville last Tuesday age 75 years 10 months born Rock Hall in March 1821 son of Isaiah Ashley of Lower Kent Co. He was married three times in 1842, 1876, and 1887 and leaves daughters Mrs. William J. Gardner and Miss Lillie W. Ashley. Centreville Record January 16 1897 issue.

257. **Sarah Blackiston** (Benjamin-7, John-6, Benjamin-5, John-4, John-3, George-2, Marmaduke-1). Sarah Blackiston and Oliver Smith were married before 1796. **Oliver Smith**.

258. **Ann Blackiston** (Benjamin-7, John-6, Benjamin-5, John-4, John-3, George-2, Marmaduke-1). Ann Blackiston and William Spearman were married. **William Spearman**.

264. **Benjamin Blackiston** (John-7, John-6, Benjamin-5, John-4, John-3, George-2, Marmaduke-1) born about 1795. Benjamin Blackiston and Mary Ann Brown were married on 17 Jan 1819 in Queen Annes County, Maryland. **Mary Ann Brown** born about 1800. MARRIAGE: BLACKISTON, Benjamin m. BROWNE, Mary A on January 17,1819 Rev Spry Queen Annes Co Pg 23 #47.
CENSUS: 1850 New Castle Co, DE
Benjamin Blackston 52 letter carrier postal service, born MD, Mary A Blackston 48 born Germany, Louisa Blackston 3 born DE, Rebecca Blackston 16, Elizabeth Blackston 14, George Blackston 6, Polly Bennett 66, William Blackston 78 Salor/ or Labor? born DE
Group Number: *29*; Series Number: *M432*; Residence Date: *1850*; Home in 1850: *Wilmington, New Castle, Delaware*; Roll: *53*; Page: *73a*

265. **Joseph Blackiston** (John-7, John-6, Benjamin-5, John-4, John-3, George-2, Marmaduke-1) born about 1796. Joseph Blackiston and Harriet Miller were married on 11 Feb 1819 in Kent County, Maryland. **Harriet Miller** born about 1800. She died after 1826 at the age of 26.
MARRIAGE: Harriet Blakiston Marriage Date 3 Sep 1818 Marriage Place Queen Anne, Maryland, to Thomas Miller.

266. Samuel Lewis Blackiston (John-7, John-6, Benjamin-5, John-4, John-3, George-2, Marmaduke-1) born about 1797. Samuel Lewis Blackiston and Rebecca Mead were married in 1814. **Rebecca Mead** born about 1800.

Samuel Lewis Blackiston and Rebecca Mead had the following children:

+375	i.	**John W. Blackiston**, born 12 Oct 1815, Maryland; married Mary Ann Watson, 23 Feb 1848, Kent County DE; died 11 Jan 1889, Millington, Kent, Maryland.
+376	ii.	**Janetta F. D. Blackiston**, born 1816; married James Nichols; died 15 Dec 1862.
+377	iii.	**Samuel Lewis Blackiston**, born abt 1824; married Mary Elizabeth Stewart, 21 May 1852, Millington, Kent County, Maryland; died 4 Oct 1885, Millington, Kent, Maryland.

267. William Blackiston (John-7, John-6, Benjamin-5, John-4, John-3, George-2, Marmaduke-1) born about 1798. William Blackiston and Rebecca C. Brown were married on 18 Dec 1824 in Kent County, Maryland. **Rebecca C. Brown** born about 1800. He has a son named William DEATH: William L Blackiston Birth Date 1833 Birth Place Maryland Death Date 26 Sep 1911 Death Place Philadelphia, Philadelphia, Pennsylvania Age at Death 78 years 9 months 12 days Burial Date 29 Sep 1911 Gender Male Single Race White Occupation None Cemetery Greenwood K Of P Marital Status Married Father William L Blackiston Father's Birth Place Maryland Mother Rebecca Brown Mother's Birth Place Maryland FHL Film Number 1405448. OBITUARY: Willam L. Blackiston On Septembe 26, 1911, William l. Blackiston, in his 81st year, Funeral Friday at 2pm from his late residence. 2908 W. Gordon St., Interment private. The Philadelphia Inquirer, Thu, Sep 28, 1911 ·Page 7

268. Eliza Blackiston (John-7, John-6, Benjamin-5, John-4, John-3, George-2, Marmaduke-1) born about 1799. Eliza Blackiston and John A. Maslin were married on 6 Feb 1819 in Kent County, Maryland. **John A. Maslin** born about 1800.

270. Hannah Susannah Blackiston (Lewis-7, John-6, Benjamin-5, John-4, John-3, George-2, Marmaduke-1) born about 1800. Hannah Susannah Blackiston and William Thomas were married on 17 Jan 1818.

WILL: Ann Thomas of Kent Co To my nephew William Blackiston Thomas in fee all my real estate but if he dies under age, then to my brother William Thomas. My negro boy George to be free. To Ms. Tabitha Wright $100 as a friendly compliment. I give my bureau to Mary Thomas, my brother William's present wife. My forte piano to be sold to pay my burial expenses and the balance if any to my nephew. Exec. my brother William Thomas. Witnesses James H. Smith, Sophia Smith, Elizabeth Wheatley. Written June 9, 1831 Proved Mar. 13, 1832 p. 238

William Thomas and Hannah Susannah Blackiston had the following child:

378   i.   **William Blackiston Thomas** born about 1820. Ann Thomas of Kent Co. To my nephew William Blackiston Thomas in fee all my real estate but if he dies under age, then to my brother William Thomas. My negro boy George to be free. To Ms. Tabitha Wright $100 as a friendly compliment. I give my bureau to Mary Thomas, my brother William's present wife. My forte piano to be sold to pay my burial expenses and the balance if any to my nephew. Exec. my brother William Thomas. Witnesses James H. Smith, Sophia Smith, Elizabeth Wheatley. Written June 9, 1831 Proved Mar. 13, 1832 p. 238

271. Martha Priscilla Maslin (Elizabeth Wroth-7, Priscilla Blackiston-6, Benjamin-5, John-4, John-3, George-2, Marmaduke-1) was born on 11 Oct 1813. She died on 15 May 1882 at the age of 68. Martha Priscilla Maslin and Sewell Hepbron were married on 12 Mar 1832 in Kent County, Maryland. **Sewell Hepbron**, son of John Hepburn and Mary Redgrave Stavely, was born on 15 Dec 1806. He died on 7 Sep 1879 at the age of 72.

Sewell Hepbron and Martha Priscilla Maslin had the following children:

379   i.   **John Thomas Hepbron** was born on 14 Mar 1833. He died on 24 Sep 1854 at the age of 21.
+380   ii.   **Margaret Elizabeth Hepbron**, born 11 Jul 1834; married James Reyner Stavely, 27 Dec 1854; died 18 Jan 1891.
381   iii.   **Norval Wilson Hepbron** was born on 26 May 1836. He died on 11 Apr 1846 at the age of 9.
382   iv.   **Sewell Hepbron Jr.** was born on 17 Jul 1843. She died on 17 Jul 1843.
+383   v.   **Rev Sewell Stavely Hepbron Sr**, born 9 Jun 1845; married Selina Powell; died 4 Nov 1932, Kent County, Maryland.
384   vi.   **Edward Wroth Hepbron** was born on 8 Jan 1847. He died on 21 Jun 1919 at the age of 72. He was buried at Union Meth. Epis in Worton, Kent County, Maryland.

273. Edward Theodore Wroth (John-7, Priscilla Blackiston-6, Benjamin-5, John-4, John-3, George-2, Marmaduke-1) born about 1812. He died after 1860 at the age of 48. CENSUS: 1850 Kent Co 61-61 Edward T. Crouch 34, Eugenia M. 33

CENSUS: 1860 Kent Co, MD 1382-1406 E. Wroth 43 boarding house, Eugenia 43, and others including H. Blackiston 16 m, James Blackiston 14, G. Berry Blackiston 18, S. Bradley 17, R. Emerson 15, M. Emerson 14.

Edward Theodore Wroth and Eugenia Maria Wroth were married. **Eugenia Maria Wroth**, daughter of Peregrine Wroth and Martha Page, was born on 26 Feb 1817 in Kent County, Maryland. She died on 30 Sep 1861 at the age of 44 in Kent County, Maryland.

Edward Theodore Wroth and Margret T. Perkins were married. **Margret T. Perkins** was born in 1845 in Kent Co., MD.

274. **Thomas Granger Wroth** (John-7, Priscilla Blackiston-6, Benjamin-5, John-4, John-3, George-2, Marmaduke-1) born about 1814 in Kent County, Maryland. He died on 11 Jun 1888 at the age of 74.
CENSUS: 1860 Kent Co, MD 468-471 Thomas G. Wroth 46, Mary E. 40, Martha P. 13, Peregrine 11, Edward W. 8, Mary E. 5.

Thomas Granger Wroth and Mary Elizabeth Wroth were married. **Mary Elizabeth Wroth**, daughter of Peregrine Wroth and Martha Page, was born on 6 Jul 1820 in Kent County, Maryland. She died in 1887 at the age of 67. Her son Dr. Peregrine says she was born Jul 20 1820 and was the daughter of Peregrine Wroth.

Thomas Granger Wroth and Mary Elizabeth Wroth had the following children:

385   i.   **Martha Page Wroth** was born on 6 Aug 1846. She died on 28 Nov 1928 at the age of 82 in Westminster, Carroll County, Maryland. She was buried at Loudon Park Cemetery in Westminster, Carroll County, Maryland. OBITUARY: Miss Martha Page Wroth sister of the late Rev. Peregrine Wroth and Rev. Edward W. Wroth died at Westminster born Kent Co in Westminster since 1892. survived by sister Mel Wroth of Westminster. OBITUARY: Martha Page Wroth dau of Dr. Thomas G. Wroth aged 82 y died Nov 28 1928 interment at Loudon Park Cem. In 1860 she was living with her maternal grandfather.

+386   ii.   **Rev Dr Peregrine Wroth**, born 19 Jul 1848, Kent County, Maryland; married Mary Augusta Counselman, 13 Jun 1880, Kent County, Maryland; died 9 Dec 1927, Baltimore, Maryland.

387   iii.   **Mary Eugenia Lane Wroth** born about 1850.

+388   iv.   **Rev. Edward Worrell Wroth**, born 5 Oct 1851; married Margaret Gilpin Price, 30 May 1882; died Aug 1924, Harford County, Maryland.

278. **Editha Gleaves Wroth** (Benjamin Blackiston-7, Priscilla Blackiston-6, Benjamin-5, John-4, John-3, George-2, Marmaduke-1) born about 1810. Editha Gleaves Wroth and Francis Asbury Ruth were married on 30 Mar 1837. **Francis Asbury Ruth**, son of Christopher Ruth and Elizabeth Stavely, born about 1801 in Queen Annes County, Maryland. He died in May 1880 at the age of 79 in Queen Annes County, Maryland.

Francis Asbury Ruth and Editha Gleaves Wroth had the following child:

389   i.   **Enoch George Ruth**. ancestor of Wendy Cotter of Edgewater, MD

279. **Benjamin Blackiston Wroth** (Benjamin Blackiston-7, Priscilla Blackiston-6, Benjamin-5, John-4, John-3, George-2, Marmaduke-1) was born on 1 Mar 1824. He died on 18 Jan 1899 at the age of 74. He was buried in Christ Church Cem., Worton, Kent Co, MD.

CENSUS: 1850 Kent Co, MD 447-450 Benjamin B. Wroth 36, Anne C. 33, William F. 11, Walter C. 9, Henrietta E. 7, Charles G. 5, Thomas G. 2, Clinton W. 2/12.

TOMBSTONE: Benjamin B. Wroth 1827-1899. Ann C. his wife 1830-1875.
Birthdate on his stone is wrong as his father died in 1825.

Benjamin Blackiston Wroth and Anne Caroline Clayton were married on 16 Nov 1848. **Anne Caroline Clayton**, daughter of Walter Clayton, was born in 1830. She died on 5 Oct 1875 at the age of 45.

Benjamin Blackiston Wroth and Anne Caroline Clayton had the following children:

390	i.	**William Frisby Wroth** was born on 5 Sep 1849. He died on 3 Apr 1893 at the age of 43.
391	ii.	**Walter J. G. Wroth** was born in 1851. He died in 1864 at the age of 13.
392	iii.	**Henrietta E. Wroth** was born in 1852. She died in 1864 at the age of 12.
393	iv.	**Charles Groome Wroth** was born in 1855. He died in 1864 at the age of 9.
394	v.	**Thomas Granger Wroth** was born on 2 Mar 1858 in Chestertown, Kent County, Maryland.
395	vi.	**Clinton Wright Wroth** was born on 27 May 1860. He died in 1923 at the age of 63.
396	vii.	**Emory Sudler Wroth** was born on 17 Feb 1862.
397	viii.	**Levi Perkins Wroth** was born in 1863. He died in 1864 at the age of 1.
398	ix.	**Margaret Perkins Wroth** was born on 23 Nov 1865.
399	x.	**Peregrine Wroth** was born in 1871. He died in 1875 at the age of 4.

280. **William Groome Wroth** (Benjamin Blackiston-7, Priscilla Blackiston-6, Benjamin-5, John-4, John-3, George-2, Marmaduke-1) born about 1820.

William Groome Wroth and Mary Poits were married. **Mary Poits** born about 1820.

286. **Eugenia Maria Wroth** (Peregrine-7, Priscilla Blackiston-6, Benjamin-5, John-4, John-3, George-2, Marmaduke-1) was born on 26 Feb 1817 in Kent County, Maryland. She died on 30 Sep 1861 at the age of 44 in Kent County, Maryland.

Eugenia Maria Wroth and Edward Theodore Wroth were married. **Edward Theodore Wroth**, son of John Wroth and Mary Granger, born about 1812. He died after 1860 at the age of 48.
CENSUS: 1850 Kent Co 61-61 Edward T. Crouch 34, Eugenia M. 33

CENSUS: 1860 Kent Co, MD 1382-1406 E. Wroth 43 boarding house, Eugenia 43, and others including H. Blackiston 16 m, James Blackiston 14, G. Berry Blackiston 18, S. Bradley 17, R. Emerson 15, M. Emerson 14.

288. **Mary Elizabeth Wroth** (Peregrine-7, Priscilla Blackiston-6, Benjamin-5, John-4, John-3, George-2, Marmaduke-1) was born on 6 Jul 1820 in Kent County, Maryland. She died in 1887 at the age of 67. Her son Dr. Peregrine says she was born Jul 20 1820 and was the daughter of Peregrine Wroth.

Mary Elizabeth Wroth and Thomas Granger Wroth were married. **Thomas Granger Wroth**, son of John Wroth and Mary Granger, born about 1814 in Kent County, Maryland. He died on 11 Jun 1888 at the age of 74.

295. **Joseph W. Brice** (James-7, Judith Ann Blackiston-6, Michael-5, John-4, John-3, George-2, Marmaduke-1) was born before 1798 in Maryland. Anne Brice in will of 1832 says land which I purchased of my nephew Joseph W. Brice containing 10 acres during her life, this tract is described in a deed dated Dec. 1, 1814 from Joseph W. Brice

Jos W Brice Home in 1840 (City, County, State): Districts 1 and 2, Queen Anne's, Maryland Free White Persons - Males - 5 thru 9: 2 Free White Persons - Males - 10 thru 14: 1 Free White Persons - Males - 15 thru 19: 1 Free White Persons - Males - 40 thru 49: 1 Free White Persons - Females - Under 5: 2 Free White Persons - Females - 10 thru 14: 1 Free White Persons - Females - 15 thru 19: 2 Free White Persons - Females - 40 thru 49: 1 Slaves - Males - Under 10: 3 Slaves - Males - 24 thru 35: 1 Slaves - Females - Under 10: 1 Slaves - Females - 10 thru 23: 2 Persons Employed in Agriculture: 5 Free White Persons - Under 20: 9 Free White Persons - 20 thru 49: 2 Total Free White Persons: 11 Total Slaves: 7 Total All Persons - Free White, Free Colored, Slaves: 18
1840; Census Place: Districts 1 and 2, Queen Anne's, Maryland; Roll: 169; Page: 91; Image: 193; Family History Library Film: 0013186

Joseph W. Brice and Anna Maria Tilden were married on 1 Feb 1814 in Kent County, Maryland. **Anna Maria Tilden**, daughter of Marmaduke Tilden and Sarah Bowers, born about 1795 in Maryland. She died on 6 Jul 1846 at the age of 51.

WILL: Marmaduke Tilden To my dau. Mary H. Handy during her life my dwelling plantation and the land I purchased of Samuel and William H. Groome being part of "Worton Manor". To my granddau. Mary H. Handy after her death the two tracts and if she dies then to the eldest son of my dau. Mary that may be living after the death of my granddaughter. If my dau. dies before the marriage of my granddau. then my son in law

George D. S. Handy shall have the use of my lands until she is marriage allowing her a reasonable support. To my grandson Thomas B. Tilden my plantation part of which I bought of Thomas and William Ringgold it being part of a tract called "Great Oak Manor" and adjoins the lands of the late John Carville provided within 6 months of his being 21 that he conveys to my granddau. Ann Maria Brice all his part of the real estate which Thomas and Ann Maria are entitled to in right of their mother. If he does not then the plantation to my granddau. Ann Maria Brice. The interest of said land to both Thomas and Ann Maria, until Thomas makes above conveyance. To my granddau. Ester Ann and Susan L. Handy each $500 charged to land of granddau. Mary was given within 2 years after my granddau. Mary or my grandson Marmaduke shall come into position of said land. To my grandson Marmaduke P. Hardy $500 put to bank stock and held till he is 21. If he dies under age or comes into possession of land given to granddaughter Mary then the $500 to my granddaughters Ester Ann and Susan. To my dau. Mary F. Hardy my negro man Paul until Dec. 31, 1818, my negro woman Tene until Dec. 21, 1823, my negro boy Henry until Dec. 31, 1840, my negro boy Ewing until Dec. 31, 1840, my negro boy Jere until Dec. 31, 1842, my negro boy David until Dec. 31, 1844. To my granddau. Ann Maria Brice my negro man Perry and my negro girl Fanny until the Dec. 31, 1842, also my negro girl Hetty until Dec. 31, 1846. To my grandson Thomas B. Tilden my negro girl Caroline until Dec. 31, 1821, my negro girl Sarah until Dec. 31, 1823 and my negro boy Thomas until Dec. 31, 1840. After my debts, the remainder of my personal estate to my dau. Mary, my granddau. Ann Maria Briscoe (sic) and my grandson Thomas B. Tilden. My negro man Cuff and my negro woman Fanny free at my death and if unable to support themselves then my dau. Mary to take care of them. Exec. my son in law George D. S. Hardy. Witnesses Catharine Bordley, Mary Ann Bordley, Thomas Worrell. Written June 9, 1815 Proved Mar. 18, 1816 p. 23

Joseph W. Brice and Anna Maria Tilden had the following child:

+400   i.   **Thomas Bowers Tilden Brice**, born Mar 1832, Kent County, Maryland; married Araminta Bramble, 2 Nov 1855, Kent County, Maryland; died 21 Dec 1904, Kent County, Maryland.

298. **Henrietta Brice** (Ann Brice-7, Judith Ann Blackiston-6, Michael-5, John-4, John-3, George-2, Marmaduke-1) born about 1800. She died after 1832 at the age of 32. Henrietta was apparently illegitimate as her mother remained Ann Brice her whole life. Henrietta also apparently had an illegitimate child of her own before 1820 named Ann Brice. Her children are named in her mother's will.

Henrietta Brice and Jacob Stevens were married on 11 Nov 1823 in Kent County, Maryland. **Jacob Stevens**, son of John Topping Stevens and Sophia Woolihand, born about 1799 in Kent County, Maryland. He died about Nov 1856 at the age of 57 in Kent County, Maryland. Not sure if all these records apply to the same Jacob Stephens. Also not sure who his mother is as his father was married multiple times per his will.

DEED: James and Catherine Copper of Kent co sold to Jacob Stevens of Kent Co "William and Mary's Adventure" 25 acres date April 8 1800. DB TW #1 p. 439
DEED: James Copper of Kent Co sold to Jacob Stevens of Kent Co "Provident" 6 3/4 acres. date April 8 1800 DB TW #1 p. 441

DEED: Robert Norris Copper and Christina his wife of Kent Co sold to Jacob Stevens of Kent Co "William and Mary's Adventure" 30 1/2 acres and mentions "Providence". date March 11 1807 DB B#5 p. 19

CENSUS: 1820 Jacob Stevens 000001-00201 with 3 free blacks. This is one Male 45+, 2 females 17-26 and one 45+.
Township: Election District 1 County: Kent State: Maryland. 1820; Census Place: Election District 1, Kent, Maryland; Roll M33 44; Page: 86; Image: 79.

MARRIAGE: Jacob Stevens of Kent Co to Henrietta Brice of Kent Co Nov 11 1823 by Thomas Dodson.

DEED: Jacob Stevens and wife Henrietta sold to Horace Kendle $100 2 acres of "William and Mary's Adventure" and "Providence". dated Mar 18 1825. DB TW #4 p. 559.

CENSUS: 1830 Jacob Stephens 0100001-101111. Male 5-9, male 40-49, female 5, 10-14, 15-19,20-29,30-39
1830; Census Place: District 1, Cecil, Maryland; Roll 56; Page: 2.

MARRIAGE: Jacob Stevens to Mary Jane Smith Jan. 12 1847.

DEED: Deed of 1849 Jacob Stevens and wife Mary Jane Smith Stevens dau of Capt. John T. Smith deceased selling "Piney Grove".

CENSUS: 1850 can't find him but he was living until 1856.
Jacob Steven 32 married within the year
Henrietta Steven 18 married within the year
1850; Census Place: District 1, Kent, Maryland; Roll M432 294; Page: 266; Image: 534.
next door is Samuel Stevens and his wife Eliza

MARRIAGE: Jacob Stevens to Anna Matilda Blackiston Mar 8 1852. by Rev. Wm J. Dale

DEED: Mary Emily Blackiston wife of James E. Blackiston bought of Jacob and Ann M. Stevens. Nov. 6 1855 JFG 3 p. 235 Kent Co MD

WILL: Jacob Stevens of Kent Co. to my unborn child or children as the case may be which my wife is now pregnant with all my estate. If my wife Anna Matilda Stevens outlive the child or children she is now pregnant with, I give to my wife forever. date Oct. 9 1856 and proved Nov. 23 1856 BK 13 p. 72.

Jacob Stevens and Henrietta Brice had the following children:

+401   i.   **James Brice Stevens**, born abt 1824; married Mary A. Mosher, 11 Nov 1845, Kent County, Maryland.

+402   ii.   **Captain John Brice Stevens**, born 12 Feb 1826, Maryland; married Sarah Jane Jolly, 26 Jun 1861, Kent County, Maryland; married Susan Welsh, 30 Mar 1847, Talbot County, Maryland; died 9 Mar 1891.

+403   iii.   **Martha Louisa Stevens**, born abt 1827, Kent County, Maryland; married William Henry Stevens, 6 Aug 1849.

404   iv.   **Mary Henrietta Stevens** born about 1828 in Maryland. She died about Mar 1849 at the age of 21 in Kent County, Maryland.
WILL: Mary H. Stevens of Kent Co. To Mary Emily Blackiston all my right in that tract of land in Kent and adjoining Mrs. Jane Copper it being the same that was willed to myself and sister Miss Sarah Brice. To Emily Blackiston all my estate including my wearing apparel. My negro girl Jane shall be free at the end of her term with Mrs. Emily Stevens at which time she will be 18. [pass granted to Jane Apr. 28, 1843] Exec. Not Given. Witnesses Joseph Blackiston, Samuel A. J. Wickes, Samuel B. Stevens. Written Jan. 30, 1849 Proved Mar. 9, 1849 (Joseph Blackiston and Samuel A. J. Wickes came Mar. 10) WB 12 p. 278

Henrietta Brice had the following child:

405   i.   **Sarah Ann Brice** born about 1819. She is called Ann Brice in the will of her mother's cousin Sarah Harrigan. She is called Miss Sarah Brice in 1849 will of her sister Mary

301. **Tamasina Brice** (John-7, Judith Ann Blackiston-6, Michael-5, John-4, John-3, George-2, Marmaduke-1) born about 1793. She died after 1859 at the age of 66.

Tamasina Brice and Mr. Glenn were married and had the following child:

+406   i.   **Mary Rebecca Glenn**, born 2 Feb 1829, Kent County, Maryland; married Asbury Howard.

302. **Vincent Hatcheson** (James-7, Martha Miller-6, Ann Blackiston-5, William-4, Ebenezer-3, George-2, Marmaduke-1) was born after 1804. He died in 1840 at the age of 36. BIRTH: He was under age in 1821 will of his uncle Vincent who died 1821. He is named as Vincent son of James who is under age.

DEATH: He died by 1840 and had heirs George B. Usilton, Vincent Hatcherson, John Hatcherson, Bartus Piner Hatcherson, and James Hatcherson.

NOTE: Bartus P. had son George W. Hatcherson who died in 1909 and named cousin Robert R. Hatcherson and Henry Clay Usilton as cousins. Henry Clay was son of George B. Usilton and Sarah Hatcherson and Robert was son of Vincent Hatcherson.

Vincent Hatcheson had the following children:

+407   i. **Vincent Hatcheson**, born abt 1823; married Mary Lessenby, 29 Dec 1841, Kent County, Maryland; died Apr 1847, Belle Aire, Kent County, Maryland.

+408   ii. **Bartus Pinder Hatcheson**, born abt 1822; married Rachel ; died 1890.

+409   iii. **Sarah E. Hatcheson**, born abt 1825; married George B. Usilton.

304. **Micha Hatcheson** (Nathan-7, Martha Miller-6, Ann Blackiston-5, William-4, Ebenezer-3, George-2, Marmaduke-1) born about 1825. It looks like she was called Elizabeth in the 1850 census and must have died shortly after as Simon appears to have remarried before 1858.

Micha Hatcheson and Simon Wickes Jr were married before 1845. **Simon Wickes Jr**, son of Simon Wickes and Elizabeth Blake, born about 1818. He died in Sep 1870 at the age of 52 in Kent County, Maryland.

CENSUS: 1850 Kent Co. Simon Wickes age 31 druggist, Elizabeth 25, Mary 8, Thomas 2, Andrew Cruickshanks 23 clerk, Caroline Hatcherson 19.

CENSUS: 1860 Kent Co Simon Wickes 41 druggist, Elizabeth R. 22, Thomas W. 12, Emma H. 9, Annette 1, Polly 2/12, and 3 others.

CENSUS: 1870 Kent Co. Simon Wickes 51, Lizzie R. 30, Nellie 11.

OBITUARY: Simon Wickes died suddenly Wed last age 52 Kent New Sep 24 1870

305. **Ann M. Hatcheson** (Nathan-7, Martha Miller-6, Ann Blackiston-5, William-4, Ebenezer-3, George-2, Marmaduke-1) born about 1825. Ann M. Hatcheson and Joseph Brown were married before 1845. **Joseph Brown** died after 1845.

307. **Mary Ann Hatcheson** (Nathan-7, Martha Miller-6, Ann Blackiston-5, William-4, Ebenezer-3, George-2, Marmaduke-1) born about 1805. She died on 18 Apr 1872 at the age of 67. She was buried in Asbury Cem., Millington, Kent, Maryland. Her aunt Sarah Miller in her will dated Dec. 7, 1826 names Thomas James Blackiston, son of James and Mary Ann Blackiston, her niece. witnesses were Nathaniel and Mary Meginniss.

She inherited land from her father.

Chancery Records Date: 1845/06/10 7888: Jacob Fisher vs. Ann Hatchison, Henrietta N. Hatchison, Caroline Hatchison, Mary Ann Blackiston, Joseph Brown, Ann M. Brown, Simon Wicks, Jr., and Micha Wicks. KE. Petition to sell Stanway, Providence, Green Branch, Perkins Adventure, Chance, Bounty. Plat. Recorded (Chancery Record) 167, p. 505. Accession No.: 17,898-7888-1/2 MSA S512-10-7886 Location: 1/38/3/

She must have remarried after James died to Daniel Ford.

CENSUS: 1850
Daniel Ford 50 DE, Mary Ann Ford 45 MD, Mary F Ford 11 DE, James T Ford 9 DE, William H Ford 7, John H Ford 1, Benjamin F Blackiston 20 student, Ann E Blackiston 15 1850; Census Place: Duck Creek Hundred, Kent, Delaware; Roll: M432 52; Page: 50; Image: 102. Nathaniel Hutchinson 42 living next door with wife Ann 39y

Mary Ann Ford 64, Annie E Blackiston 33, Sally Ann Cook 45
Year: 1870; Census Place: Millington, Kent, Maryland; Roll: M593 590; Page: 48A

TOMBSTONE: Mary A Ford Died April 18 1872 Age ? yrs 8 Mos ? Days

Mary Ann Hatcheson and James Kennard Blackiston were married on 3 Dec 1822 in Queen Annes County, Maryland. **James Kennard Blackiston**, son of Kennard Blackiston and Elizabeth Medford, was born before 1795. He died before Nov 1835 at the age of 40. MARRIAGE: James K. Blackiston m. Mary A. Hatcheson Dec 3 1822.

ESTATE: James K Blackiston adm. by Mary A Blackiston 1839. James K. Blackiston and Mary Ann Blackiston estate administered by Thomas Price Mar 19 1846.

James K. Blackiston heirs are Thomas J., Edwin H., Margaret and Ann Blackiston. These children were living with Thomas M. Blackiston as seen per 1850 census. (There is a Benjamin F living with Mary A. that is also likely a son)

James K. who had wife Mary Ann and Thomas M. Blackiston who had wife Louisa Ann Blackiston were sons of James Blackiston, per deed March 7 1834.

James Kennard Blackiston and Mary Ann Hatcheson had the following children:

+332   i. **Thomas James Blackiston**, born 8 May 1826, Kent County, Maryland; married Bellerma Elinor Mead, 12 Dec 1851, Queen Annes County, Maryland; died 4 Aug 1891, Nebo, Oklahoma.
+333   ii. **Benjamin F. Blackiston**, born 9 Jun 1831, De; married Mary Raymond Denney; died 31 Jan 1903, Kent County, Delaware.
334   iii. **George W. Blackiston**, born 16 Dec 1832, De; died 9 May 1893, Millington, Kent, Maryland.
335   iv. **Ann E. Blackiston**, born abt 1834, De; died 1923.

Mary Ann Hatcheson and Daniel Ford were married about 1838. **Daniel Ford** was born in 1800. He died before 1855 at the age of 55. Benjamin F. Blackiston was the administrator of the estate of Daniel Ford, late of Kent Co deceased as of Dec 5 1854, per Smyrna Times Jan 17 1855.

Daniel Ford and Mary Ann Hatcheson had the following child:

+410   i.   **Mary Frances Ford**, born 6 Nov 1838, Maryland; married Edwin Crouch Jr, 22 Jan 1867, Kent County, Maryland; died 19 Oct 1919, Kent Co, Maryland.

308. **William Blackiston Rasin** (Philip Reed-7, William Blackiston-6, Rosamond Blackiston-5, William-4, Ebenezer-3, George-2, Marmaduke-1) born about 1813 in Kent County, Maryland. He died before 4 May 1855 at the age of 42 in Kent County, Maryland.

MARRIAGE: William B. Rasin m. Sarah E. Crouch May 10 1836 by Heritage.

CENSUS: 1850
William B Rasin 37 farmer, Sarah E Rasin 31,, Florence M Rasin 13, James 9, Sarah A 6,William B 2, Sarah A Crouch 58, (her mother), Ruth A Crouch 20, (her sister), James A Rasin 26 (James Clinton Rasin) (his brother)
1850; Census Place: District 2, Kent, Maryland; Roll: 294; Page: 227a

OBITUARY: William B. Rasin died at res. this co. May 5 1855 Kent Co News.

ESTATE: May 22 1855 Sarah E Rasin, Pere L Lynch and Dulany Rasin qualify as administrator. Estate Docket p. 36 June 26 $1521.46 inv., Mar 4, 1856 $771.37 sales, Sep 9, 1856 $1197.15.

He was named after his grandfather William B Rasin. His children's names comes from Carolyn E. Cooper's book. In the estate settlement of his father in law James Crouch in 1843, he stated that a grey mare included in the estate belonged to William Crouch.

William Blackiston Rasin and Sarah Elizabeth Crouch were married on 10 May 1836 in Kent County, Maryland. **Sarah Elizabeth Crouch**, daughter of James Crouch and Sarah Ann Freeman, was born on 12 Sep 1819 in Kent County, Maryland. She died after 1860 at the age of 41.

CENSUS: 1860 Kent Co, MD 1354-1378 S.E. Raisin 39 f, James 18, William 11, Perry 5, A. Benjamin 23 and blacks.

William Blackiston Rasin and Sarah Elizabeth Crouch had the following children:

+411	i.	**Florence M. Rasin**, born abt 1837; married Joseph Orsburn Rasin, 17 May 1854, Kent County, Maryland.
+412	ii.	**Sarah E. Rasin**, born abt 1840; married A. H. Ferdinand Crew, 21 Aug 1856, Kent Co, Maryland.
413	iii.	**James Rasin** born about 1841.
+414	iv.	**Sarah A. Rasin**, born abt 1846, Maryland; married Ambrose Carroll, 6 Jan 1861.
415	v.	**William Blackiston Rasin** was born in 1848. He died on 12 May 1877 at the age of 29 in Centreville, Queen Annes County, Maryland. OBITUARY: Died in Centreville May 12th after short illness, Wm. B. Rasin, aged 28 years and 3 months, son of the late Wm. B. Ras of Kent Co. May 17, 1877 Centreville Record.
416	vi.	**Perry L. Rasin** born about 1854. mentioned as pallbearer for Wilhelmina Rasin Crouch as her nephew. CENSUS: 1870 Queen Annes p. 280 Pere Lynch 48, Ruth 39.

310. **Dulany Rasin** (Philip Reed-7, William Blackiston-6, Rosamond Blackiston-5, William-4, Ebenezer-3, George-2, Marmaduke-1) was born on 21 Jan 1816 in Kent County, Maryland. He died on 21 Jan 1890 at the age of 74 in Kent County, Maryland. He was buried at Union Meth. Epis in Worton, Kent County, Maryland. Dulany Rasin his brother Richard L. Rasin and their mother, Sarah Bennett Rasin, are buried in Union, as well as many of their children. Worton Gleaning by Cooper 1983.

He was probably named for his father's uncle Daniel Dulaney who married Philip's mother Martha's sister. His children's names and information comes from Carolyn E. Cooper's work William Blackiston Rasin Family.

CENSUS: 1850 Kent Co Dulaney Rasin 35, Mary J. 28, Anaditha 5, Emily 1, Sarah 50, Richard 26, George Beck 26, Margaret 17 Black.

CENSUS: 1860 Kent Co, MD 456-459 Delany Raisin 44, Mary 39, Ann E. 14, Emma J. 11, Thomas 9, Mary 7, McCall M. 5, Roby 2, Perry 5/12, Berry Beck 35, George Beck 35.

CENSUS: 1870 Kent Co, MD
Dulany Rasin 54, Mary J Rasin 49, Emily J Rasin 21, Thomas Rasin 19, Mary Rasin 17, Medford Rasin 15, Roby Rasin 12, Perry Rasin 10, Blackiston Rasin 37
1870; Census Place: District 3, Kent, Maryland; Roll M593 590; Page: 122; Image: 244.

CENSUS: 1880 Kent Co, MD D. Rasin 64 Farming, Mary J. Rasin 59, Thomas Son 29 Work Farm, Perry Rasin Son 20 Work Farm
Source Information: Census Place Worton, Kent, Maryland NA Film NumberT9-0512 Page Number99B

OBITUARY: Death of Dulaney Rasin. Mr. Dulaney Rasin, one of the oldest citizens of Worton district, died at the residence of his son-in-law, Mr. Samuel F. Cooper, near Worton Station, on Tuesday last. He was in his 75th year. Mr. Rasin was one of the best known men in his district. He was for several years a constable and in 1883 was a candidate for sheriff on the Democratic ticket. He was generous to a fault and had many warm friends all over the county. Kent News Jan. 25, 1890.

OBITUARY: same issue Jan. 25, 1890 Died Near Worton Station, January 21, of pneumonia, Dulaney Rasin, aged 74 years.

OBITUARY: Dulaney Rasin departed this life Jan. 21, 1890, being his seventy-fourth birthday. The subject of these few lines was a kind husband. He and his companion had journeyed together forty-five years the 6th instant. He was an affectionate father and a much loved grandfather. Good neighbor, none were turned from his door whom he could help as far as his means permitted. He was ever cheerful and would entertain young people with incidents of by-gone days much to their enjoyment. We have been acquainted with him many years and always looked upon him as an inoffensive man forgiving in disposition with a desire to be at peace with all men. We visited him several times during his illness and he expressed himself entirely submissive to the will of his Heavenly Father, saying he was all right and not afraid of death. We have no doubt his family's loss is his eternal gain. A Friend. same issue Jan. 25, 1890 Kent News.

Dulany Rasin and Mary Jane Beck were married on 15 Jan 1845 in Kent County, Maryland. **Mary Jane Beck**, daughter of Peregrin Beck and Editha Phillips, was born in 1822. She died on 15 Oct 1896 at the age of 74. age 28 in 1850 and 39 in 1860. They had George Beck living with them in 1850

Dulany Rasin and Mary Jane Beck had the following children:

+417   i. **Ann Editha Rasin**, born 15 Oct 1845; married Samuel Ford Cooper, 21 Jan 1869, Kent County, Maryland; died 22 Jul 1918.

418   ii. **Philip C. Rasin** was born on 14 Feb 1847. He died on 13 Jul 1850 at the age of 3.

+419   iii. **Emily J. Rasin**, born 21 Aug 1849; married Amos Parsons, aft 1880; married Frank Rouse, 24 Nov 1886, Kent County, Maryland; died 30 Dec 1930.

+420   iv. **Thomas Franklin Rasin**, born 9 Apr 1851; married Alice R. Jewell, 5 Jan 1882, Kent County, Maryland; died 1893.

421   v. **Mary E. Rasin** was born on 18 May 1853. She died on 9 Sep 1881 at the age of 28.

+422   vi. **Medford Macall Rasin**, born 2 Feb 1855; married Alphonsia Parks, 11 Jan 1882, Kent County, Maryland; died 27 Jun 1906, Kent County, Maryland.

+423   vii. **Charles Roby Rasin**, born 2 Mar 1858; married Rose Anna Crew, 4 Mar 1885, Kent County, Maryland; died 1945.

+424   viii. **Perry Beck Rasin**, born 12 Feb 1860; married Henrietta Sewell, 2 Nov 1887, Kent County, Maryland; died 15 Oct 1931, Kent County, Maryland.

425   ix. **Rachel Rasin** was born on 14 Jul 1862. She died on 13 Aug 1862.

426   x. **William Blackiston Rasin** was born on 6 Jan 1865. He died on 23 Feb 1865. He was buried at Union Methodist Episcopal in Worton, Kent, Maryland. OBITUARY: On Thursday last, WILLIAM B., youngest child of Dulaney and Mary Rasin, aged 7 weeks. He is free from pain and care, Let him softly, sweetly, sleep; Earth's rude jars he'll never share, Nevermore will weep. Kent News Saturday Morning Feb 25, 1865 p. 2

312. Mary Ann Rasin (Philip Reed-7, William Blackiston-6, Rosamond Blackiston-5, William-4, Ebenezer-3, George-2, Marmaduke-1) born about 1819 in Kent County, Maryland. She died on 19 Feb 1905 at the age of 86 in Wilmington, Delaware. She was buried in Chester Cem, Kent, Maryland. Author has posted her photo on findagrave.

Living with Arthur J. Toulson 40 and family.
Mary A. Graves 61, Mary G. Graves 44
1880; Census Place: Wilmington, New Castle, Delaware; Roll T9 119; Family History Film: 1254119; Page: 323.1000; Enumeration District: 13; Image: 0126.

Living with Arthur J Toulson 60 and family
Mary A Graves 81
1900; Census Place: Wilmington Ward 5, New Castle, Delaware; Roll T623 154 Page: 1B; Enumeration District: 21.

OBITUARY: Mrs. Mary A. Graves died last Sunday, March 19th, at the home of her son-in-law, Mr. Arthur J. Toulson, in Wilmington, Del. Of the infirmities of old age. The deceased was the widow of the late James Graves, formerly a prominent citizen in Chestertown. She was 85years and 11 months of age and leaves four grandchildren, two sisters and a number of nieces and nephews. Mrs. Graves joined Christ M.P. Church, Chestertown, in 1863 under the pastorate of the late Dr. J.T. Murray, and has ever since retained her membership in this church... The remains were brought to Chestertown Wednesday and funeral services were held in Christ M.P. Church, conducted by Rev. J. M. Sheriden, in the absence of the pastor, Rev. D.L. Greenfield. The pallbearers were the following nephews of the deceased-Messrs. M.M. Rasin, P.B. Rasin, C.R. Rasin, George R. Rasin, J.W. Elliott and Wm. M. Lynch. Undertake John N. Dodd had charge of the funeral arrangements. Interment in Chester Cemetery. Chestertown Transcript, Chestertown, MD. March 25 1905

Mary Ann Rasin and James A. Graves were married on 12 Jul 1841 in Kent County, Maryland. **James A. Graves** born about 1819. He died before 1880 at the age of 61.

James A. Graves and Mary Ann Rasin had the following children:

+427	i.	**Sarah Graves**, born 1842; married Arthur Toulson, 7 May 1868, Kent County, Maryland; died 12 Feb 1877.
428	ii.	**Isabel Graves** born about 1850. She died young.
429	iii.	**Martha Graves** born about 1855.
430	iv.	**Mary Annie Graves** was born in 1859. She died on 24 Sep 1866 at the age of 7. She died young.

313. **Sarah Matilda Rasin** (Philip Reed-7, William Blackiston-6, Rosamond Blackiston-5, William-4, Ebenezer-3, George-2, Marmaduke-1) born about 1820. She died about Aug 1887 at the age of 67. Her children's names come from Carolyn E. Cooper's book. A DAR application for Edna Apsley Entler says her grandfather was Joseph R. Apsley 1818-1874 son of John W. Apsley and Sarah M. Rasin, son of George Apsley, son of William Apsley.

ESTATE: Aug 1887 Sarah Apsley, her bondsmen for her estate Wickes, Edes, Crosby and her son Philip 15-108, JCS1-262,268,540

Sarah Matilda Rasin and John Wroth Apsley were married on 1 Aug 1837 in Kent County, Maryland. **John Wroth Apsley**, son of George Apsley and Rachel Ford, born about 1809 in Delaware. He died after 1870 at the age of 61.

CENSUS: 1850 J W Apsley 41 DE, Sarah M 28, William 17, Philip 10, Eugene 7, Belmitta 5, Miriam 4, John W 2, Edward 1/12

CENSUS: 1870 J.W. Apsley 71, Sarah 58, Melinda 35, Belle 20, Walter 18, granddau. Minnie Benton 2.

John Wroth Apsley and Sarah Matilda Rasin had the following children:

+431	i.	**William Blackiston Apsley**, born 1838; married Mary Ann ; died 18 Jul 1864, Snickers Gap, Virginia.
+432	ii.	**Philip Rasin Apsley**, born 18 Jan 1840; married Rachel Elizabeth Woolyhand, 11 Aug 1875, Kent County, Maryland; died 3 Oct 1912, Edesville, Kent County, Maryland.
433	iii.	**John Wroth Apsley Jr.** born about 1845. He died on 7 Aug 1876 at the age of 31.
434	iv.	**Malinda Apsley** born about 1845. She died on 18 Feb 1896 at the age of 51.
435	v.	**Martha Apsley** born about 1846. She died in Sep 1846.

+436	vi.	**Edward Apsley**, born abt 1847; died abt Dec 1875, Piney Neck, Kent County, Maryland.
+437	vii.	**Mary Emiline Apsley**, born abt 1858; married Darius Bendon, 1 Nov 1874, Kent County, Maryland.
438	viii.	**Bell Apsley** born about 1860.
439	ix.	**Walter Apsley** born about 1862.
440	x.	**Eugene Apsley** born about 1843.

314. **Richard L. Rasin** (Philip Reed-7, William Blackiston-6, Rosamond Blackiston-5, William-4, Ebenezer-3, George-2, Marmaduke-1) was born in Jun 1825 in Kent County, Maryland. He died on 24 Jan 1905 at the age of 79 in Kent County, Maryland.

CENSUS: 1860 Kent Co Richard I. Rasin 35, Isabella E. 25, Mary 3, Effer 8/12 f, Daniel W. Lynch 10, William M. Lynch 8, 1st Elect. Dist. 187-187

CENSUS: 1880 Queen Anne p 197
Richard L. Rasin 45, William Lynch 18

His children's names comes from Carolyn E. Cooper's book.

DEATH: Richard L. Rasin died Jan 24 1905 near Kennedysville, age 79y7m15d, farmer, widowed, parents Philip Rasin and Sarah Bennett both born Kent Co, informant Mrs. Anna Elizabeth Elliott sister, cause of death arterial atheronia, heart failure, (Worton written on back).

OBITUARY: Mr. Richard Rasin, one of Kent's oldest and best known citizens died at the residence of his daughter, Mrs. Thomas Johns, near Kennedysville, on Tuesday, aged 79 years. He leaves three sisters, Mrs. Wm. J. Elliott and Mrs. Wilmina Crouch, of Chestertown, and Mrs. Mary Graves, of Wilmington, and the following children: Mrs. Thomas Jones, of near Kennedysville, Mrs. Q.L. Morrow, of Savannah, Georgia, Mrs. Robert Carter, of Wilmington, Mrs. William Carter, of Worton, Mrs. Thomas P. Vandyke, of Locust Grove, and one son Mr. Richard Rasin. He was also an uncle of County Commissioner Perry B. Rasin, Mr. M.M. Rasin, of Melitota, and Mrs. Frank Rouse, of Worton. Funeral services were held at the residence of his daughter, Mrs. Thomas Jones, near Kennedysville, yesterday morning at 11 o'clock, conducted by Rev. R.S. Rowe, pastor of Kennedysville M.P. Church. Interment in Union M.E. cemetery, Worton. Undertake Wm. H. Krusen had charge of funeral arrangements. The Chestertown Transcript, Chestertown, MD Jan 28 1905.

OBITUARY: Mr. Richard Rasin, of Still Pond died yesterday, aged about 70. Jan. 28, 1905 issue of Kent News. (Blizzard mentioned in this issue and massacre at St. Petersburg by czar's troops.)

OBITUARY: Death of Mr. Rasin. The News last week noted the death of Mr. Richard Rasin at the home of his daughter, Mrs. Thomas Jones, near Kennedyville, aged 79 years. He leaves three sisters, Mrs. Wm. J. Elliott and Mrs. Wilmina Crouch, of Chestertown, and Mrs. Mary Graves, of Wilmington, and the following children: Mrs. Thomas Jones, of near Kennedysville, Mrs. Q.L. Morrow, of Savanah, Georgia, Mrs. Robert Carter, of Wilmington, Mrs. Wm. Carter, of Worton, Mrs. Thomas P. Vandyke, of Locust Grove, and one son, Mr. Richard Rasin. He was also an uncle of County Commissioner Perry B. Rasin, Mr. M.M. Rasin, of Melitota, and Mrs. Frank Rouse, of Worton. Funeral Services were held at the residence of his daughter Mrs. Thomas Jones, near Kennedyville, conducted by Rev. R. S. Rowe, pastor of Kennedyville M.P. Church. Interment in Union M.E. Cemetery, Worton. Undertaker Wm. H. Krusen had charge of funeral arrangements. Kent News Feb. 4, 1905 issue.

OBITUARY: same issue Feb. 4. The funeral of the late Richard Rasin who died near Kennedyville, had to be postponed from Tuesday to Thursday of the following week because of the blizzard. Rev. R. S. officiated.

Richard L. Rasin and Isabel E. Jones were married on 2 Jan 1855 in Kent County, Maryland. **Isabel E. Jones** born about 1825.

Richard L. Rasin and Isabel E. Jones had the following children:

+441   i.   **Clara Rasin**, born abt 1856; married Robert Carter; married Dorney.

+442   ii.   **Mary E. Rasin**, born Jan 1857; married William David Carter, 9 Jan 1877; died 12 Jun 1905.

443   iii.   **Effie Rasin** was born on 19 Sep 1859 in Kent County, Maryland. She died on 9 Dec 1862 at the age of 3 in Kent County, Maryland. OBITUARY: Effie Rasin on 9th inst. 3y 2m 20 dau of Richard L and Isabel Rasin Dec 20, 1862 Kent Co News.

+444   iv.   **Nellie Rasin**, born abt 1862; married William T. Jones, 17 Apr 1878; died 1933.

445   v.   **Olivia Rasin** was born in 1864. She died on 9 Mar 1865 at the age of 1.

+446   vi.   **Regina Rasin**, born abt 1865; married Thomas Vandyke, abt 1885; died 16 Apr 1936.

+447   vii.   **George Richard Rasin**, born 8 Feb 1867; married Jane Hill, 24 Mar 1892; died 25 Aug 1958.

+448   viii.   **Gertrude Rasin**, born abt 1870; married Quincy Marrow, 24 Dec 1890.

316. **Willamina Rasin** (Philip Reed-7, William Blackiston-6, Rosamond Blackiston-5, William-4, Ebenezer-3, George-2, Marmaduke-1) was born on 18 May 1830 in Worton, Kent County, Maryland. She died on 8 Aug 1907 at the age of 77 in Chestertown, Kent

County, Maryland. She was buried at Union Meth. Epis in Worton, Kent County, Maryland.

MARRIAGE: 1st. James Lynch m. Willy Rasin on Feb 19 1849 by Williams both of Kent Co.

MARRIAGE: 2nd. John Crouch m. Wilhelmina Lynch near Chestertown on Aug 13 1856 next house to J. Merchants, family attended.

CENSUS: 1900 Kent Co Chestertown Dist. 4 ED 51 p 10 222-223 Wilimina Crouch May 1830 10 children 8 living. living with dau. Margaret and Joseph McIntyre.

DEATH: Willimina Crouch died at Chestertown Kent Co Aug 8 1907 age 76y retired, widow number of children living 8, wife of John W Crouch, father's name Rasin, acute indigestion and heart failure, reported by Harry L. Dodd, MD.

OBITUARY: Mrs. Wilhelmina Crouch, relict of John W. Crouch, died at the home of her daughter, Mrs. J. B. McIntyre, in Chestertown, Thursday morning, after a long illness aged 76y. The deceased was a good woman, a devoted mother, kind neighbor and beloved by a large circle of friends. She leaves the following children: Daniel Webster Lynch, of Marshalltown, NJ; Wm M. Lynch, Chestertown; Mrs. J.B. McIntyre; J.L. Crouch, Baltimore; Mrs. J.W. Barnes, Mrs. Ruth A. McIntyre, Mrs. Carrie A. Harkins, Wilmington; Charles W Crouch, Rock Hall. Mrs. J. W. Elliott is her sister. The funeral will take place this Saturday morning at 10:30o'clock from the home of her daughter on Kent Street, Rev. W.L. White officiating. The bearers will be her nephews, Robey, Perry B. and Richard Rasin. Wm. Elliott, Harry and Frank Ivens. The interment will be in Union Cem. Worton, J.E. Ferguson undertaker. Kent News Aug 10 1907.

TOMBSTONE: Willamina Crouch his wife May 18 1830 died Aug 8, 1907 Resting

Willamina Rasin and James Lynch were married on 19 Feb 1849 in Kent County, Maryland. **James Lynch** born about 1829. He died before 1856 at the age of 27.

James Lynch and Willamina Rasin had the following children:

449	i.	**Daniel Webster Lynch** born about 1851 in Kent County, Maryland. He died on 25 Jun 1933 at the age of 82 in Kent County, Maryland. He was buried in Silverbrook Cem and Memorial Park, Wilmington, New Castle Co, DE. Living with uncle Richard Rasin in 1860 census.
+450	ii.	**William Maxwell Lynch**, born 11 Oct 1852, Kent County, Maryland; married Sallie L. Reed; died 10 Sep 1931, Kent County, Maryland.
+451	iii.	**Margaret A. Lynch**, born Jan 1854, Kent County, Maryland; married Joshua B. McIntire, 1875, Kent County, Maryland; died 1933, Kent County, MD.

Willamina Rasin and John Wesley Crouch were married on 13 Aug 1856 in Kent County, Maryland. **John Wesley Crouch**, son of James Crouch and Sarah Ann Freeman, was born on 9 Dec 1823 in Kent County, Maryland. He died on 13 Dec 1897 at the age of 74 in Worton, Kent County, Maryland. He was buried at Union Meth. Epis in Worton, Kent County, Maryland.

BIRTH: bible record of his father and tombstone say Dec 9 1823.

CENSUS: 1850 Kent Co p. 298 John W Crouch 25.

MARRIAGE: Kent Co Circuit Methodist Episcopal Church Aug 13 1856 John Crouch and Wilhelmina Lynch near Chestertown next house to J. Merchants, by Quigley witnesses family.

CENSUS: 1860 Kent Co p. 895 John Crouch 35, Wilhelmenia 30, Sarah 3, Ruth 9/12, Margaret Lynch 7.

CENSUS: 1870 Chestertown p. 9 3rd Elec. Dist. 55-52 John W Crouch 45, Wilminia 40, Sallie B. 13, Ruth 10, Rachel 8, James 6, Caroline 4, male not named 4/12 (Feb).

CENSUS: 1880 Skinner's Neck near Rees' Corner ED 54 p. 21 5th Elec. Dist. 158-158 John W Crouch 55, Willmina 50, James R 16, Carrie 13, Charles 10.

DEATH: Dec 13, 1897 by obit (Mon.) and tombstone, but Dec 14, 1897 by Memoriam

OBITUARY: John W. Crouch, an aged and well known farmer died at his home near Worton Station on Monday, aged 73 years and 3 days. Mr. Crouch had for some time been a sufferer with consumption and the end was expected. He leaves a wife and five children namely: Sallie B. Barnes, Ruth McIntire, Carrie Shandley, James and Charles Crouch. Services were held at his late home on Tuesday afternoon at 3 o'clock; Dr. J.B. Merritt officiating; interment at Union. The bearers were: Webster Lynch, William Lynch, John W. Barnes, J.B. McIntyre, Charles Crouch and James Crouch. Chestertown Transcript Dec. 16, 1897 p 5

OBITUARY: John W. Crouch died at his home near Worton on Monday last, 73 years. Leaves a wife and five children: Mrs. John W. Barnes, Mrs. John W. McIntyre of Edesville, Mrs. Carrie Shandly of Wilmington, Messrs James Crouch of Kennedyville and Charles Crouch of Rock Hall. Services in the Home Dr. J.B. Merritt. Interment at Union Cemetery. Kent News Dec. 18, 1897.

OBITUARY: In memoriam: In loving memory of John W. Crouch, who died just one year ago, Dec. 14, 1897. Our father is dead. He passed. Chestertown Transcript 12/15/1898.

TOMBSTONE: John W. Crouch Dec 9 1823 died Dec 13 1895. (incorrect year of death. Should be 1897).

His family was given in notes written by Daisy Barnes and have been reprinted in the MGSB Vol. 40 no. 4 Fall 1999 p. 495 contributed by Christos Christou, Jr.

John Wesley Crouch and Willamina Rasin had the following children:

+452   i.   **Sarah Bennett Crouch**, born 10 Feb 1857, Kent County, Maryland; married John Wesley Barnes, 2 Jan 1878, Kent County, Maryland; died 5 Jun 1932, Chestertown, Kent County, Maryland.

+453   ii.   **Ruth A. Crouch**, born 19 Nov 1859, Kent County, Maryland; married John W. McIntire, 16 Apr 1879, Kent County, Maryland; died 13 May 1944, Kent County, Maryland.

454   iii.   **Rachel Rasin Crouch** born about 1862 in Kent County, Maryland. She died on 6 Apr 1877 at the age of 15 in Maryland. She died young. OBITUARY: On April 6, Rachael R., dau. of John W. and Wilmina Crouch, aged 15 years and 20 days. Centreville Record April 19, 1877.

+455   iv.   **James R. Lee Crouch**, born 19 Jul 1865, Kent County, Maryland; married Emma L. Noblett; died 24 Jul 1953, Brooklyn, Baltimore, Maryland.

+456   v.   **Caroline Allen Crouch**, born 1866, Kent County, Maryland; married T. Shanley, bef 1897; married Harry E. Harkins, bef 1900; died 27 Nov 1948, Wilmington, New Castle County, Delaware.

+457   vi.   **Charles Wesley Crouch**, born 21 Feb 1870, Kent County, Maryland; married Grace Florence Blackiston, 12 Jan 1891, Rock Hall, Kent County, Maryland; died 18 Jul 1944, Rock Hall, Kent County, Maryland.

317. **Emily Bertha Rasin** (Philip Reed-7, William Blackiston-6, Rosamond Blackiston-5, William-4, Ebenezer-3, George-2, Marmaduke-1) was born on 30 May 1833 in Kent County, Maryland. She died on 7 Oct 1903 at the age of 70 in Kent County, Maryland. She was buried at Union Meth. Epis in Worton, Kent County, Maryland. The children comes from her records. Some of the dates of the children are wrong or they are by a previous marriage of Samuel. 1880 census says E. Bertha but Carolyn's book says Emily Bennett.

Emily B Usilton died Chestertown Kent Co MD 1903 Oct 17 age 70y 4m female white born Kent co widowed housewife, father Philip Rasin born MD, mother Sarah Bennett born MD Info. John W. Elliott nephew, died of Tuberculosis 16y, asthenia 10 weeks.

Emily Bertha Rasin and Samuel S. Usilton were married on 22 Dec 1853 in Kent County, Maryland. **Samuel S. Usilton** born about 1830 in Maryland. He died after 1880 at the age of 50.

Samuel S. Usilton and Emily Bertha Rasin had the following children:

458	i.	**Rose E. Usilton** was born in 1850. She died in 1850.
459	ii.	**S. Franklin Usilton** born about 1853.
460	iii.	**Addison Usilton** born about 1853.
461	iv.	**M. Temperance Usilton** born about 1854. She died on 13 Jul 1857 at the age of 3 in Kent County, Maryland. OBITUARY: Temperance Usilton in Centreville 13th instant about 4 years old only child of Samuel S and Emily Usilton July 26 1857 Kent News
462	v.	**Sarah G. Usilton** born about 1856. She died in 1857 at the age of 1.
463	vi.	**Franklin R. Usilton** born about 1857. He died on 1 Jun 1866 at the age of 9.
464	vii.	**Henry A. Usilton** was born on 19 Jun 1860. He died in Mar 1876 at the age of 15.
465	viii.	**Usilton** born about 1864. She died about 1864.

318. **Ann Elizabeth Rasin** (Philip Reed-7, William Blackiston-6, Rosamond Blackiston-5, William-4, Ebenezer-3, George-2, Marmaduke-1) was born on 26 Jul 1839 in Kent County, Maryland. She died on 15 Oct 1913 at the age of 74 in Chestertown, Kent County, Maryland. She was buried in Chestertown Cemetery, Chestertown, Kent County, Maryland. She is mentioned in obituary of sister Wilhelmina.

MARRIAGE: Ann E. Ras of Kent Co m. William J. Elliott of Cecil Co by Quigley on Dec. 19, 1855.

OBITUARY: Mrs. Annie Elizabeth Elliott died at her home on High Street Wednesday after a short illness of pneumonia. She was the daughter of the late Philip Rasin and the wife of John W. Elliott, for a long term of years employed by the late J. K. Aldridge. The faithful companion whom she leaves here with the sympathy of a large circle of friends and is certainly blest in having a daughter and son who will minister to him a best they can. She leaves on son J.W. Elliott, and a daughter, Mrs. Sarah Ivens and husband, W.J. Elliott. The following are the bearers: Harry Ivens, Frank Ivens, Morris Ivens, Preston Ivens, Eli Elliott and Wm. P. Milby. The funeral will take place Saturday afternoon at 3pm Rev. W. R. Graham, officiating, C.L. Dodd undertaker. Kent News Oct 18, 1913.

She was living next door to her aunt Ann Rasin Willis Denning in the 1880 census.

DEATH: Annie Elizabeth Elliott female white married died Oct 15 1913 Chestertown, High Street, Kent Co born July 26 1839 age 74y 2m 19d housekeeper born Kent Co MD father Philip Rasin, birthplace Kent Co MD maiden name of mother Sarah Bennett, born Kent Co, MD, Info. Mrs. Sarah Ivens born Chestertown MD cardiac failure, burial Chestertown undertaker Chas L. Dodd

Ann Elizabeth Rasin and William John Elliott were married on 19 Dec 1855 in Kent County, Maryland. **William John Elliott**, son of Ann , was born on 15 Mar 1835 in Pa. He died on 12 Jul 1917 at the age of 82 in Kent County, Maryland. He was buried in Chestertown Cemetery, Chestertown, Kent County, Maryland. MARRIAGE: William J. Elliott of Cecil Co m. Ann E. Rasin on Dec 19 1855 by Quigley.

1880 Census MD
William J. Elliot Self M Male W 45 PA Tinner parents born P, Ann E. Elliot Wife M Female W 41 MD Keeps House parents born MD, Mary N. Elliot Dau S Female W 8 MD At School father born PA mother born MD
Census Place Charlestown, Kent, Maryland Family History Library Film 1254512 NA Film Number T9-0512 Page Number 131B

William John Elliott and Ann Elizabeth Rasin had the following children:

+466   i.   **Sarah Ann Elliott**, born 21 Mar 1857, Kent County, Maryland; married John Henry Ivens, 25 Feb 1880, Kent County, Maryland; died 20 Aug 1921, Chestertown, Kent County, Maryland.

467   ii.   **Harry Adolphus Elliott** was born on 19 Jun 1858 in Kent County, Maryland. He died on 28 Nov 1868 at the age of 10 in Chestertown, Kent County, Maryland. He was buried at Union Meth. Epis in Worton, Kent County, Maryland. OBITUARY: Harry A Elliott on 22nd at res. of James Graves Chestertown 10y 5m 3d son of William J and Annie E. Elliott Nov 28 1868 Betty said he died Nov. 23, 1867.

+468   iii.   **John William Elliott**, born 28 Oct 1862; married Amanda Lusby; died 1925.

469   iv.   **Allen Jackson Elliott** was born on 6 Mar 1863 in Kent County, Maryland. He died on 26 Jun 1864 at the age of 1 in Kent County, Maryland. He was buried at Union Meth. Epis. in Worton, Kent County, Maryland. OBITUARY: Allen Jackson Elliott on 26th ult. 1 yr 3m 20d son of A.E. and William J. Elliott Jul 2 1864 Kent News. Betty said he was born Mar. 6, 1862 and died Feb. 26, 1864.

470   v.   **Charles Lusby Elliott** was born on 20 Nov 1867. He died on 26 Jun 1871 at the age of 3 in Kent County, Maryland. He was buried at Union Meth. Epis in Worton, Kent County, Maryland. He died young. TOMBSTONE: Elliott, son of W.J. and Ann E. Elliott. Died June 26, 1871.

471   vi.   **Mary Nelson Elliott** was born on 5 Mar 1872. She died on 29 Jun 1909 at the age of 37.

319. Rosetta M. Rasin (Cyrus B.-7, William Blackiston-6, Rosamond Blackiston-5, William-4, Ebenezer-3, George-2, Marmaduke-1) was born on 7 Dec 1819.

Rosetta M. Rasin and John P. Beck were married on 30 Sep 1840 in Kent County, Maryland. **John P. Beck**, son of Peregrin Beck and Editha Phillips, was born on 6 Jun 1817. He died before 1855 at the age of 38 in Kent County, Maryland. MARRIAGE: John P. Beck of Kent Co m. Rosetta M. Ras of Kent Co. Sep 3, 1840 by Rev. Storks.

John P. Beck and Rosetta M. Rasin had the following children:

472	i.	**James T. Beck** was born on 3 Jun 1841. He died about 1906 at the age of 65. He had children Sophia born 1881, Alberta and Thomas H. Beck born 1885 per Carolyn Cooper.
473	ii.	**Willamina Editha Downey Beck** was born on 5 Dec 1850 in Kent County, Maryland. She died on 1 Mar 1867 at the age of 16 in Kent County, Maryland. OBITUARY: Willmina Editha Downey Beck on 1st inst. 16y,2m,24d, dau of John and Rosetta Beck Mar 16 1867 Kent Co News

Rosetta M. Rasin and Benjamin G. Howard were married on 3 Jun 1856 in Kent County, Maryland. **Benjamin G. Howard** born about 1820.

Benjamin G. Howard and Rosetta M. Rasin had the following child:

474	i.	**Cyrus G. Howard** was born on 10 Dec 1859.

322. Private Lewis H. B. Rasin (Cyrus B.-7, William Blackiston-6, Rosamond Blackiston-5, William-4, Ebenezer-3, George-2, Marmaduke-1) born about 1824. He died on 16 Aug 1865 at the age of 41 in Baltimore, Maryland. He was buried in Chester Cem, Chestertown, Kent, Maryland.

MARRIAGE: Lewis H. Rasin m. Sarah Jane Everitt Date 4 Jun 1850 in Kent County

CENSUS: 1860 Kent Co, MD 458-461
Louis H. Raisin 36, Sarah J. 27, Margaret J. 9, Rachael V. 7, Wilhelmina 3, Sarah J. 3/12.

SOLDIER: Lewis H. B. Rasin served in Civil War. Enlisted Oct. 9 1861 private served MD, transferred 1st ES Inf. Reg. MD. Mustered out on July 25 1865 per MD Vol. War of 1861-1865 published 1899. Approved Pension Application File for Sarah J Everitt Rasin, Widow of Lewis H B Rasin, Company H, 2nd Maryland Infantry Regiment (Application No. WC123831).

Private Lewis H. B. Rasin and Sarah J. Everitt were married on 4 Jun 1850 in Kent County, Maryland. **Sarah J. Everitt**, daughter of William Everitt, born about 1832. She died after 1870 at the age of 38. She has a William Everett age 61 living with her in 1870 census. He may be her father.

CENSUS: 1870 Sarah J. Rasin age 38 listed with children.
Sarah J Rasin 38, Mary Rasin 19 (Margaret), Virginia Rasin 16 (Rachel), Wileminia Rasin 12, John W Rasin 40 (brother of Louis), William Everett 61, Ann Dilihunt 20, Isaac Wilson 40
1870; Census Place: Chestertown, Kent, Maryland; Roll M593 590; Page: 170; Image: 341.

Lewis H. B. Rasin and Sarah J. Everitt had the following children:

+475 i. **Margaret Jane Rasin**, born 6 Sep 1851, Maryland; married James H. Sheets; died 1937.

+476 ii. **Rachael Virginia Rasin**, born 10 Dec 1853, Maryland; married Noble Benjamin Gears; died 5 Feb 1924, Chestertown, Kent, Maryland.

477 iii. **Wilhelmina Rasin** was born on 27 Jul 1856 in Maryland. Listed as Willie Ann in the Civil War pension application of her father by her mother.

478 iv. **Sarah Isabella Rasin** was born on 29 Mar 1860 in Maryland. She died in Apr 1869 at the age of 9 in Kent County, Maryland. OBITUARY: Isabella Rasin 9 yr 5 days youngest dau. of Louis C. and Sarah J. Rasin. Kent News 4/10/1869.

323. **Joseph Orsburn Rasin** (Cyrus B.-7, William Blackiston-6, Rosamond Blackiston-5, William-4, Ebenezer-3, George-2, Marmaduke-1) was born on 1 Oct 1831. He died on 10 Nov 1885 at the age of 54. He was buried in Chesterfield Cem., Centreville, Queen Anne's Co, MD.

CENSUS: 1850 Kent Co 101-101 Joseph O. Rasin p. 286 Kent Co 1850 census 3rd Dist. living with Alfred Christfield and Elizabeth.

Joseph Orsburn Rasin and Florence M. Rasin were married on 17 May 1854 in Kent County, Maryland. **Florence M. Rasin**, daughter of William Blackiston Rasin and Sarah Elizabeth Crouch, born about 1837.

324. **John William Rasin** (Cyrus B.-7, William Blackiston-6, Rosamond Blackiston-5, William-4, Ebenezer-3, George-2, Marmaduke-1) born about 1829 in Kent County, Maryland. He died on 18 Dec 1896 at the age of 67 in Baltimore City, Md. He was buried in Chester Cem, Chestertown, Kent, Maryland.

MARRIAGE: John W Rasin married Sarah E Jervis Date: 2 Jan 1873

CENSUS: 1850
Williams Greenwood 71, Rachael Greenwood 37, John Coffer 25, John W Ruser (Rasin) 22, Emeline Browning 20, Levis Browning 14
1850; Census Place: District 2, Kent, Maryland; Roll M432 294; Page: 244; Image: 491.

CENSUS: 1860 Chestertown John W Rasin 31 living with father

CENSUS: 1870 he is living with his brother Louis' widow as a caretaker.
John W Rasin 40 caretaker with Sarah J Rasin

CENSUS: 1880
J. William Rasin 51 livery stable, widower, Rosa S. Rasin 7 dau, Jas. W. Rasin 6 son, John Clough 22 hostler, Mary Eakman 54 housekeeper, John Jervis 12 son in law
1880; Census Place: Chestertown, Kent, Maryland; Roll T9 512; Family History Film: 1254512; Page: 130.3000; Enumeration District: 52; Image: 0259.

US National Home for Veterans John W Rasin Birth Year: abt 1829 Keyed Birth Location: Maryland Birth State: Maryland Admitted Year: 1891 Age at Admission: 62 State: Virginia City: Hampton Branch: Roseburg Branch

SOLDIER: He served in the Civil War enlisted Oct. 2, 1861 Sergeant in Union Army. Transferred K Co 11th Inf. Reg. MD Mustered out on My 27 1865. Per MD Vol. War of 1861-1865 published 1899. The Roll Call by Walter J. Kirby lists Sergeant John W. Rasin, entered service 10-2-1861, Company B, 2nd Eastern Shore Volunteer Infantry. Transferred to Company K, 11th Regt. Maryland Infantry (d.u.) Rasin returned to Kent Co in Aug 1862 to recruit additional volunteers. He was taken prisoner at the Battle of Winchester, VA July 28 1864 and confined to a prison in Danville, VA. He married Sarah E. Jervis 10-6-1873 in New Castle, DE, owned lots 89 and 90 in Chestertown on the west side of High street at the corner of Kent Circle) He wrote his will while in poor health and died 12-26-1896. He was survived by a dau. Rose Steen Rasin and a son John W. Rasin.

NEWS: Kent County News, March 11, 1865. "Sergt. John W. Rasin, of this town, has been exchanged, and reached home on Monday. He was taken prisoner last summer during the retreat from Winchester, and has been confined at Danville, Va. He is much reduced in flesh, and states that the rations served to the prisoners were barely sufficient to maintain life."

OBITUARY: John W. Rasin, formerly of Chestertown, died at his home in Baltimore yesterday, aged about 68. He had been in bad health for a long time and death came as a relief to his suffering. He leaves four children. His remains will be brought over on the Ford today and be buried in Chester cemetery in the family lot. Kent News, Chestertown, MD, Saturday, December 19, 1896.

John William Rasin and Sarah Emma Jervis were married on 6 Oct 1873 in New Castle County, Delaware. **Sarah Emma Jervis** was born on 14 Feb 1846 in Maryland. She died on 1 Jul 1877 at the age of 31 in Kent County, Maryland. She was buried in Chestertown Cemetery, Chestertown, Kent County, Maryland.

John William Rasin and Sarah Emma Jervis had the following children:

479   i. **Rose Steen Rasin.**
480   ii. **John William Rasin Jr.**

325. **Cyrus C. Blackiston Rasin** (Cyrus B.-7, William Blackiston-6, Rosamond Blackiston-5, William-4, Ebenezer-3, George-2, Marmaduke-1) was born in 1835. He died in 1895 at the age of 60. He was buried in Chester Cem, Chestertown, Kent County, Maryland. Went by the name Blackiston Rasin.

MARRIAGE: Cyrus B. Rasin m. Laura C. Kelly by Oct. 18 1873 by Rev. A. W. Milby (not to be published)

CENSUS: 1870 Kent Co MD
Blackiston Rasin 37 He is living with his cousin Dulaney.
1870; Census Place: District 3, Kent, Maryland; Roll M593 590; Page: 122; Image: 244.

CENSUS: Kent Co MD
C.C.B. Rasin 45, Laura C. Rasin 30, Anna E. Rasin 6, Laura E. Rasin 3, Albert Cooling 25, Saml. Maguire 25, Wm. Gudgeon 27, Henry Painter 24,
1880; Census Place: Chestertown, Kent, Maryland; Roll T9 512; Family History Film: 1254512; Page: 115.1000; Enumeration District: 52; Image: 0229.

TOMBSTONE: C.C. Blackiston Rasin 1835-1895

Cyrus C. Blackiston Rasin and Laura C. Kelly were married on 18 Mar 1873 in Kent County, Maryland. **Laura C. Kelly** was born in 1849. She died on 18 Jan 1890 at the age of 41 in Kent County, Maryland. She was buried in Chestertown Cemetery, Chestertown, Kent County, Maryland.

TOMBSTONE: Laura C. Rasin his wife 1849-1890

Cyrus C. Blackiston Rasin and Laura C. Kelly had the following children:

481   i. **Annie Elmer Rasin** was born in 1873 in Kent County, Maryland. She died on 2 Sep 1913 at the age of 40 in Kent County, Maryland. She was buried in Chestertown Cemetery, Chestertown, Kent County, Maryland. CENSUS: 1910 Kent Co MD William H McKee 43 born MD parents born Ireland, Laura E McKee 33 born MD parents born Maryland, Mary C McKee 13, William D McKee 10, Rose E McKee 8, Annie E Rasin 36 born MD parents born Maryland sister in law 1910; Census Place: Chestertown, Kent, Maryland; Roll T624 566; Page: 3A; Enumeration District: 55; Image: 210.

DEATH: Annie Elmer Rasin listed as a Millener born July 28 173 single age 40y 11m died Sep 2 1913 Kent Co white parents C.C.B. Rasin born MD, mother Laura C. Kelley, born MD died of pulmonary tuberculosis. Info. Estelle McKee of Chestertown. buried Chester Cemetery. TOMBSTONE: Elmer Rasin 1873-1913

482 ii. **Laura E. Rasin** born about 1877 in Maryland.

328. John K. Willis (Nancy Ann Rasin-7, William Blackiston-6, Rosamond Blackiston-5, William-4, Ebenezer-3, George-2, Marmaduke-1) born about 1819. He died on 8 Aug 1876 at the age of 57. John K. Willis and Sarah M. were married. **Sarah M. Blackiston** born about 13 September 1832 Died June 26, 1906 Brockton, MA. Buried Coleman. OBITUARY: Willis. At his residence in Chestertown, on Tuesday morning last, after a lingering and very painful illness, in the full triumps of ths Christian Faith, Mr. John K. Willis – in the 57th year o fhis age. [Centreville papers please copy.]
DEATH: Sarah C. Willis 22 Chester Ave Brockton MA died June 26 1906 age 73y 9m 13 day female white widowed, husband John K. Willis, born Baltimore MD, father John B. Blackiston born MD, Catherine Berry born MD, Informant Daughter, died of Myoma. buried Colebrook Cem. Whitman.

330. William Blackiston Wilmer III (William Blackiston-7, Blackiston-6, Rosamond Blackiston-5, Ebenezer-4, Ebenezer-3, George-2, Marmaduke-1) was born on 24 Jun 1818 in Kent County, Maryland. He died on 9 Oct 1877 at the age of 59 in Kent County, Maryland.

CENSUS: 1850 Kent Co MD
John McDaniel 65, Louisa McDaniel 40, Maria L McDaniel 23, John N McDaniel 21, Emma P McDaniel 15, Anna G McDaniel 6, William B Wilmer 28, Edward A Moore 22, Alfred M Russel 26, Louisa Russel 18, James Barnett 15, Hiram Bram 36, John Armstrong 49, John Armstrong 37
1850; Census Place: District 2, Kent, Maryland; Roll: M432 294; Page: 209B; Image: 426

CENSUS: 1860 Kent Co, MD
William B Wilmer 42 farmer, Mary A Wilmer 34, Alice Wilmer 7, Mary Wilmer 4, Philip Wilmer 1, William Wilmer 1, John Wilmer 2/12, Ann McCleary 20, Henry Robinson 22
Census; Record Group Number: 29; Series Number: M653; Residence Date: 1860; Home in 1860: District 2, Kent, Maryland; Roll: M653_477; Page: 887; Family History Library Film: 803477

CENSUS: 1870 Kent Co, MD
Wm B Wilmer 52 farmer, Mary A Wilmer 49, M B Wilmer 15, M A Wilmer 17, Philip G Wilmer 11, H T Wilmer 8, Wm B Wilmer 6
1870; Census Place: District 2, Kent, Maryland; Roll: M593 590; Page: 91B; Image: 186; Family History Library Film: 552089

William Blackiston Wilmer III and Mary Ann Brooks were married on 11 Oct 1852. **Mary Ann Brooks** was born on 8 Sep 1822. She died on 24 Jan 1896 at the age of 73.

CENSUS: 1880 Kent Co, MD
M. Ann Wilmer 58 Self (Head), Alice M. Wilmer 25 Daughter, Mary B. Wilmer 23 Daughter, Philip G. Wilmer 21 Son, Lina T. Wilmer 18 Daughter, Wm. B. Wilmer 16 Son.
Year: *1880*; Census Place: *Chestertown, Kent, Maryland*; Roll: *512*; Page: *121a*; Enumeration District: *052*

William Blackiston Wilmer and Mary Ann Brooks had the following child:

+483   i. **William Blackiston Wilmer IV**, born 21 Nov 1863, Kent County, Maryland; married Ada Lenora Jessop; died 23 Nov 1918, Kent County, Maryland.

Ninth Generation

331. **Eleanor Grace Blackiston** (Zachariah Demeneau-8, George-7, Nehemiah Herbert-6, John-5, John-4, Nehemiah-3, John-2, Marmaduke-1) was born on 1 Jun 1865 in Saint Mary's County, Maryland. She died on 21 Mar 1959 at the age of 93 in Saint Mary's County, Maryland.

Eleanor Grace Blackiston and Walter Benjamin Dent were married on 19 Aug 1884 in Saint Mary's County, Maryland. **Dr. Walter Benjamin Dent** was born on 20 Feb 1859 in Saint Mary's County, Maryland. He died on 7 Feb 1946 at the age of 86 in Saint Mary's County, Maryland.

CENSUS: 1860 St. Mary's Co MD
Walter L Dent 35, Mary T Dent 24, Walter B Dent 1
 1860; Census Place: District 4, St Marys, Maryland; Roll M653 479; Page: 132; Image: 433.

CENSUS: 1870 St. Mary's Co, MD
Walter L Dent 47, Mary T Dent 28, Walter B Dent 11, Richard Quade 19, Henry Somerwill 23, Laura Norris 23
1870; Census Place: District 4, St Marys, Maryland; Roll M593 594; Page: 613; Image: 259.
Couple doors away is John F. Dent 55y and Lillia (Blackiston) and they have a Martha Blackstone 16 living with them.

CENSUS: 1900 St. Mary's Co, MD

Walter B Dent 41 Doctor born Feb 1859, Ellenore G Dent 34 born June 1865 7 children 5 living, May L Dent 13 born July 1886, Harriet E Dent 9 born Sep 1890, John F Dent 7 born Nov 1892, Hellen M Dent 15 born Nov 1895, Richard D Dent 2 born Nov 1897
1900; Census Place: Milestown, Saint Marys, Maryland; Roll T623 627 Page: 24B; Enumeration District: 115.

Walter B Dent 51, Elenenar G Dent 44 9 children 7 living, Mary L Dent 24, Harriet E Dent 20, John F Dent 18, Helen M Dent 15, Richard D Dent 13, Benjamin B Dent 8, Theodore H Dent 4
1910; Census Place: Election District 7, St Mary's, Maryland; Roll T624 568; Page: 7A; Enumeration District: 87; Image: 307.

Walter B Dent 60, Grace B Dent 54, Benjiman B Dent 18, Theodore H Dent 14, Alice F Butler 21, James E Butler 7/12, Camelier Thomas 17
1920;Census Place: Milestown, St Marys, Maryland; Roll T625 677; Page: 12A; Enumeration District: 113; Image: 275. Next door is J. Marshall Dent age 75

Walter B Dent 71 Doctor, Eleanor G Dent 65, 1930; Census Place: Bay, St Mary's, Maryland; Roll 879; Page: 5B; Enumeration District: 11; Image: 252.0.

332. **Thomas James Blackiston** (James Kennard-8, Kennard-7, James-6, Ebenezer-5, John-4, John-3, George-2, Marmaduke-1) was born on 8 May 1826 in Kent County, Maryland. He died on 4 Aug 1891 at the age of 65 in Nebo, Oklahoma. Information on Thomas and his wife came from Tom Cooper of McKinney, TX. T.J. was reared by an uncle who owned slaves and T.J. had a slave who was voluntarily freed. T.J. wanted to join the union forces but his wife objected so he bought his way out. He was a Sunday School superintendent and possibly a preacher at some point in the Methodist church.

He was named in will of his great aunt as Thomas James Blackiston, son of James and Mary Ann Blackiston, her niece. Will was dated Dec 7, 1826, so much be born May 1826 not 1827.

MARRIAGE: Thomas M. Blackiston Jr. m. Ellenora M. Gould on Dec. 12 1851 Queen Annes Co, MD by Rev. Mr. Green.

CENSUS: 1860 Greensburgh Washington Twp Decatur Co, IN
Thomas J. Blackiston age 33 carriage maker born MD, Bellerma Blackiston 23 born OH, William B. Blackiston 4 MD, Emily Mead 27 teacher born OH.
p. 760 950-950

CENSUS: 1870 Owen Co, IN
Thomas J. Blackiston 42 MD, Balerma E. 33 OH, Annie D. 9 MD, Frank E. 3 MD, Mary L. 11/12 MD.

CENSUS: 1880 Cooke Co TX
Thomas James Blackiston age 52 MD, Bellerma Elinor Mead Blackiston 42 OH, Anna 19 IN, Frank 13 IN, Maime 10 IN, Maud 3 TX

Thomas James Blackiston and Bellerma Elinor Mead were married on 12 Dec 1851 in Queen Annes County, Maryland. **Bellerma Elinor Mead** was born on 22 Jan 1837 in Delaware, Ohio. She died on 2 May 1922 at the age of 85 in Roswell, New Mexico. She was listed as Bellerma Elinor Mead per Tom Cooper but marriage bond said Ellenora M. Gould. She must have been previously married. Tom Cooper's father said Bellerma was born Jan. 21, 1838 but his aunt said she was born Jan. 22, 1838 in Delaware OH. Her father was Daniel Mead from VT who moved to Delaware OH and then to Greensburgh, IN

Thomas James Blackiston and Bellerma Elinor Mead had the following child:

484   i.   **Frank Edward Blackiston** was born on 26 Feb 1867 in In. He died on 22 Apr 1944 at the age of 77 in Crosby County, Texas. DEATH: Frank Edward Blackiston Death Date: 22 Apr 1944 Crosbyton, Crosby, Texas Race: white Death Age: 77 years 1 month 22 days Birth Date: 26 Feb 1867 Birthplace: Indiana Marital Status: Married Father's Name: Thoms J. Blackiston Father's Birthplace: Indiana Mother's Name: Bell Mead Mother's Birthplace: Indiana Occupation: Farmer, Retired Place of Residence: Crosbyton, Crosby, Texas, Adams Funeral Home. Baptist Cemetery: Burial Place: Crosbyton, Texas Burial Date: 23 Apr 1944 Film Number: 2137735 Digital Film Number: 4029615 Image Number: 2761 Reference Number: cn 17365 Collection: Texas Deaths, 1890-1976

333. **Benjamin F. Blackiston** (James Kennard-8, Kennard-7, James-6, Ebenezer-5, John-4, John-3, George-2, Marmaduke-1) was born on 9 Jun 1831 in De. He died on 31 Jan 1903 at the age of 71 in Kent County, Delaware. He was buried in Glenwood Cem, Kent County, Delaware. He is living with Mary Ann Ford and likely his mother. Benjamin F. Blackiston and Mary Raymond Denney were married. **Mary Raymond Denney** was born in 1834 in Delaware. She died on 15 Oct 1918 at the age of 84. She was buried in Glenwood Cem, Kent County, Delaware.

337. **Thomas Medford Blackiston Jr.** (Thomas Medford-8, Kennard-7, James-6, Ebenezer-5, John-4, John-3, George-2, Marmaduke-1) born about 1831. He died before 1870 at the age of 39. Thomas M. Blackiston Jr. of DE m. Sarah Henrietta Ringgold per Ringgold Family History of 12-17-1856 had dau. Emma R. Blackiston baptized 9-23-1867 Christ Church, Chestertown; James Thomas, and Laura Blackiston. Per Old Kent p.40

CENSUS: 1860 Kent Co First Elect. Dist. 190-190
Thomas M. Blackiston 29 farmer, George T. Holliday 26.

Census; Record Group Number: *29*; Series Number: *M653*; Residence Date: *1860*; Home in 1860: *District 1, Kent, Maryl*

Thomas Medford Blackiston Jr. and Sarah Henrietta Ringgold were married on 17 Dec 1856 in Kent County, Maryland. **Sarah Henrietta Ringgold**, daughter of Josias Ringgold and Ann Elizabeth Cruickshank, was born on 9 Nov 1831. She died in 1887 at the age of 56. Children given in Book on Ringgold family quoting Old Kent.

MARRIAGE: Kent Co News Major Richard Smythe m. Mrs. S. Henrietta Blackiston on Tue. last at Chestertown. Nov. 23, 1872.

CENSUS: 1870 Kent Co MD
Josiah Ringgold 66, Anne E. 67, Kate 21, Hennie Blackiston 38, Emma 13, Laura 10, Thomas 8.

CENSUS: 1880 Kent Co MD:
Josias Ringgold 75 MD Retired Farmer, Catharine Ringgold Dau 32 MD, Emma Blackiston GDau S 22 MD, Laura E. BLACKISTON GDau S 20 MD, James Thomas Blackiston GSon S 17 MD, Sarah H. Smyth Dau 47 MD,
Source Information: Charlestown, Kent, Maryland NA Film Number T9-0512 Page Number 147A

Thomas Medford Blackiston and Sarah Henrietta Ringgold had the following children:

485	i.	**Emma Ringgold Blackiston** born about 1858 in Kent County, Maryland. She was christened on 23 Sep 1867 at Christ Church in Chestertown, Kent County, Maryland.
486	ii.	**Laura E. Blackiston** born about 1860.
+487	iii.	**James Thomas Blackiston**, born 10 Aug 1860, Kent County, Maryland; married Florence Adelaide Keyser, 14 Feb 1883; died 15 Sep 1928, Kent County, Maryland.

339. Mary Elizabeth Blackiston (Thomas Medford-8, Kennard-7, James-6, Ebenezer-5, John-4, John-3, George-2, Marmaduke-1) was born on 24 Mar 1843 in De. She died on 11 Jun 1903 at the age of 60 in Philadelphia, PA. She was buried in Chester Cem, Chestertown, Kent County, Maryland. She had children James Alfred Jr., Thomas Blackiston, Walter Wickes, David Blackiston, Benjamin, Francis, and Henry Norman Perkins.

Mary Elizabeth Blackiston and Dr. James Alfred Perkins were married.

342. Andrew Hooten Blackiston (David Crane-8, James-7, James-6, Ebenezer-5, John-4, John-3, George-2, Marmaduke-1) was born on 21 May 1844 in Brighthelmstone, Kent County, Maryland. He died on 30 Aug 1878 at the age of 34 in Cumberland, Maryland. His story is given in the Biographical Cyclopedia p. 100 by Jacob Tome. Mentioning his great grandfather James Blackiston born Jul 14 1744 and that he married Catharine Kennard and died Sep 12 1816 leaving a son James Jr. who marred Mary Crane. Andrew Hootoon Blackiston, was born May 21, 1844, at Brighthelmstone, the homestead of his father, David C. Blackiston, in Kent Co, MD. His great grandfather, James Blackiston, was born July 14, 1744. He married Catherine Kennard, of Centreville, MD and died September 12, 1816, leaving a son, James Blackiston, Jr. who married Mary Crane, dau. of Capt. David Crane, of the Revolution, son of David Crane, the originator of the site of Elizabethtown, NJ. Andrew Hooton Blackiston was educated and graduated at Washington College, near Chestertown, MD, taking the first honors of his class. While reading law he was Professor of Mathematics, for one year, in the MD Agricultural College. He then went to the University of Virginia and was graduated in the Law School, and continued his studies for six months in the office of Hon. E.G. Kilbourne, in Baltimore and was admitted to the bar by the Superior Court of Baltimore City. In Jan. 1867 he removed to Cumberland, MD, where he resided until his death. For a time his younger brother practiced with him, but after his marriage returned to Kent Co. Mr. Blackiston acquired an extensive and lucrative practice, and at the time of his death was regarded as one of the leading members of the bar of Cumberland. His integrity and business capacity were such that he was constantly employed in grave and complicated transactions, and was the trusted attorney of the Chesapeake and Ohio Canal Company, Adams Express Company, the First National Bank of Cumberland and other corporations. He was a devout member of the Episcopal Church from his earliest manhood, and never gave up the hope of becoming a useful minister of the Gospel. He was a firm Democrat, from intelligent conviction, but not what is called a politician. He was a bright and zealous Free Mason, and was a member of the Odd Fellows, Knights of Pythias, Red Men, and other beneficiary societies. He was shot and killed, August 30, 1878, in Cumberland, MD by a member of the Allegany bar. A brother lawyer said of him, that "he was courteous, gentle, frank and true. His force of character, his moral and social qualities were in keeping with the temple in which they were enshrined - a body the perfection of symmetry, a face and form a model of physical development and manly beauty." He was six feet tall, strictly temperate in his habits, a hard and thorough student and conscientious and unswerving from the strictest line of duty. He married, May 21, 1874, Elizabeth Smith Pearre, dau. of Judge George A. Pearre, of Cumberland, MD and had a son, Andrew Hooton Blackiston, born April 21, 1877.

OBITUARY: "The funeral of the late A.H. Blackiston took place from Emmanuel Episcopal Church of Cumberland on Sunday afternoon and was attended by a large number of people. The attendance showed the universal respect and esteem in which the deceased was held. The members of the bar attended the funeral in a body." Washington Post dated Sept.9,1878: In another item: Thomas Cook Hughey has been committed to the Cumberland jail, in default of $3,000 bail for the murder of A.H. Blackiston.

Andrew Hooten Blackiston and Elizabeth Smith Pearre were married on 21 May 1874. **Elizabeth Smith Pearre** born about 1850.

Andrew Hooten Blackiston and Elizabeth Smith Pearre had the following child:

488   i.   **Andrew Hooton Blackiston Jr.** was born on 21 Apr 1877.

346. **McCall Medford Rasin Blackiston** (Samuel Hepburn-8, William Henry-7, James-6, Ebenezer-5, John-4, John-3, George-2, Marmaduke-1) born about 1880 died 26 Feb 1911 in Milwaukee, Wisconsin. Buried St. John's Church Cemetery, Hampton, Virginia. He married Lenore Ashmore 1880-1923 buried at Mountain View Cemetery and Mausoleum.

OBITUARY: Will Bring Body Here. McCall Blackiston to be buried at Hampton. He dies in Milwaukee. Former well known resident of this city passes away suddenly in the Far West-Remains expected to arrive Thursday. Unless there is a change in the arrangements, the remains of McCall Blackiston, who died suddenly in Milwaukee, Wis., Sunday afternoon, will be brought to Hampton for burial in Old St. John's cemetery. It was expected that the body would be taken to Chestertown, Md., but a telegram received during the afternoon yesterday from Mrs. Blackiston said that the body would be brough here. The message came to Joseph C. Otten, father of Mrs. Blackston. It is expected that the remains, accompanied by Mrs. Blackiston, Harry Blackiston and Mrs. J.C. Outten will leave Milwaukee this afternoon and probably will reach Hampton Thursday. Mrs. Outten and Mr. Blackiston left Hampton for Milwaukee Sunday night and are scheduled to reach there this morning. The complete arrangements for the funeral services will not be announced until the house of the arrival of the body is known. The news of the death of Mr. Blackiston was received here at 4 o'clock Sunday afternoon and caused the greatest sorrow among the wide circle of friends of the young man. McCall Blackiston was known as a young man of highest integrity and during his residence here he was universally esteemed. His mother Mrs. T. T. Blackiston and his brother H.C. Blackiston, head of the Furness-Withy Company, reside in Hampton, while another brother Sclater Blackiston is principal of a school in Richmond. Mr. Blackiston was attacked with a paralytic stroke at 11 o'clock Sunday morning and gradually continued to sink until dissolution took place at 1:30 o'clock. He had been in the best of health and the news of his death was a severe shock to his aged mother, brothers and friends here. He went West about six years ago and about three years ago settled in Milwaukee. Mrs. Blackston, who spent the winter here with her parents, Mr. and Mrs. J.C. Outten, had returned to Milwaukee about three weeks ago and was with her husband when the end came. Miss Helen Blackiston, a sister of the deceased is now studying art in New York City. Mr. Blackiston was born in Chestertown, Md., about 36 years ago, but came to Hampton when quite a youth. He held a number of positions here and was always regarded as a trustworthy and faithful employee. He was a social favorite and had a way of making friends rapidly and keeping them by his true worth. Daily Press, [Newport News, Virginia], 28 Feb 1911, Tue, p.6.

TOMBSTONE: McCall R. Blackiston 1880-1911

McCall Blackiston married **Lenora "Nora" Ashmore Outten**. Her lengthy 1923 obituary says she died at the home of her parents. She was a woman of refinement and education, having attended the State Normal School in Virginia and also Randolph-Macon Women's college in that state. She was one of the 4 founders of Kappa Delta National Sorority. "Lenora, known to most as Nora, was a romantic. Idealistic and imaginative, she was drawn throughout her life to causes. She was the one to suggest forming a sorority. She went on to attend Randolph-Macon Woman's College". She was survived by her parents and one brother Edgar C. Outten.

348. **Slater Clay Blackiston** Sr. (Samuel Hepburn-8, William Henry-7, James-6, Ebenezer-5, John-4, John-3, George-2, Marmaduke-1) born about 1883 died 28 Dec 1947 Erie County, NY. Buried Christ Church Cemetery, Worton, Kent County, MD. Attended College of William and Mary Senior 1905 Williamsburg VA. He was Capta of Foot Ball Team, Class President, President of the German Club, Medal Winner in 220-yard dash, Diplomas in Pedagogy, American History and Politics.

DEATH: Slater Clay Blackiston Race White Gender Male Death Age 64 Birth Date 18 May 1883 Birth Place Chestertown, Maryland Death Date 23 Dec 1947 Death Place Erie, Erie, Pennsylvania, Pres. Union Storage Co. Father Samuel H Blackiston born Chestertown MD Mother Sally Rasin born Chestertown MD Spouse Eugenia Gaylor died of coronary occlusion Certificate Number 107646.

His son Slator Clay Jr. was LCDR in US Navy in World War II and died 1994. His grandson Slater Clay Blackiston III was Lt Blackiston a Navy SEAL, Class 040. He was killed during a training jump in 1984 in France. The cause of death was drowning. His chute deployed, but he got tangled in the strings when he landed in the water because he was unconscious. Lt Blackiston was awarded 4 Bronze Star Medals (With Combat V) in Vietnam 1968-1971.

349. **Thomas Jefferson Blackiston** (John B.-8, James-7, Michael-6, Ebenezer-5, John-4, John-3, George-2, Marmaduke-1) was born on 4 Aug 1853. He died on 2 Nov 1912 at the age of 59 in Vanderbilt, Fayette, Pennsylvania. He was buried in Liberty Cemetery, Liberty, Fayette County, Pennsylvania. Info. sent by Jackie Britton. Had children Millard Fillmore, Harry Blackistone, Grover Blackistone.

DEATH: Thomas J Blackiston Male White 59y Birth Date: 3 Aug 1853 Birth Place: Maryland Death Date: 2 Nov 1912 Death Place: Vanderbilt, Fayette, Pennsylvania, USA Father: Samuel Blackiston Buried Dickinson Run Union Cem., Info. Millard Blackiston

Thomas Jefferson Blackiston and Mary Malinda Stevens were married. **Mary Malinda Stevens** was born on 31 Aug 1858 in Baltimore, Maryland. She died on 12 Nov 1936 at the age of 78 in Lowellville, Ohio.

Thomas Jefferson Blackiston and Mary Malinda Stevens had the following children:

489   i. **Mary Rosella Blackiston** was born in 1875 in Baltimore, Maryland. She died on 24 Feb 1953 at the age of 78 in Youngstown, Mahoning, Ohio.

490   ii. **Millard Fillmore Blackiston** was born on 21 Apr 1884 in Kent County, Maryland. He died after 1930 at the age of 46 in Youngstown, Mahoning, Ohio.

350. **Anna Matilda Blackiston** (James Eagle-8, Joseph-7, Joseph-6, Ebenezer-5, John-4, John-3, George-2, Marmaduke-1) born about 1832. She died about 1860 at the age of 28. She could be dau of James Blackiston who lived next door in census records.

Anna Matilda Blackiston and Jacob Stevens were married on 8 Mar 1852 in Kent County, Maryland. **Jacob Stevens**, son of John Topping Stevens and Sophia Woolihand, born about 1799 in Kent County, Maryland. He died about Nov 1856 at the age of 57 in Kent County, Maryland. Not sure if all these records apply to the same Jacob Stephens. Also not sure who his mother is as his father was married multiple times per his will.

DEED: James and Catherine Copper of Kent co sold to Jacob Stevens of Kent Co "William and Mary's Adventure" 25 acres date April 8 1800. DB TW #1 p. 439
DEED: James Copper of Kent Co sold to Jacob Stevens of Kent Co "Provident" 6 3/4 acres. date April 8 1800 DB TW #1 p. 441
DEED: Robert Norris Copper and Christina his wife of Kent Co sold to Jacob Stevens of Kent Co "William and Mary's Adventure" 30 1/2 acres and mentions "Providence". date March 11 1807 DB B#5 p. 19

CENSUS: 1820 Jacob Stevens 000001-00201 with 3 free blacks. This is one Male 45+, 2 females 17-26 and one 45+.
Township: Election District 1 County: Kent State: Maryland. 1820; Census Place: Election District 1, Kent, Maryland; Roll M33 44; Page: 86; Image: 79.

MARRIAGE: Jacob Stevens of Kent Co to Henrietta Brice of Kent Co Nov 11 1823 by Thomas Dodson.

DEED: Jacob Stevens and wife Henrietta sold to Horace Kendle $100 2 acres of "William and Mary's Adventure" and "Providence". dated Mar 18 1825. DB TW #4 p. 559.

CENSUS: 1830 Jacob Stephens 0100001-101111. Male 5-9, male 40-49, female 5, 10-14, 15-19,20-29,30-39
1830; Census Place: District 1, Cecil, Maryland; Roll 56; Page: 2.

MARRIAGE: Jacob Stevens to Mary Jane Smith Jan. 12 1847.

DEED: 1849 Jacob Stevens and wife Mary Jane Smith Stevens dau of Capt. John T. Smith deceased selling "Piney Grove".

CENSUS: 1850 can't find him but he was living until 1856.
Jacob Steven 32 married within the year, Henrietta Steven 18 married within the year 1850; Census Place: District 1, Kent, Maryland; Roll M432 294; Page: 266; Image: 534. next door is Samuel Stevens and his wife Eliza

MARRIAGE: Jacob Stevens to Anna Matilda Blackiston Mar 8 1852. by Rev. Wm J. Dale

DEED: Mary Emily Blackiston wife of James E. Blackiston bought of Jacob and Ann M. Stevens. Nov. 6 1855 JFG 3 p. 235 Kent Co MD

WILL: Jacob Stevens of Kent Co. to my unborn child or children as the case may be which my wife is now pregnant with all my estate. If my wife Anna Matilda Stevens outlive the child or children she is now pregnant with, I give to my wife forever. date Oct. 9 1856 and proved Nov. 23 1856 BK 13 p. 72.

Jacob Stevens and Anna Matilda Blackiston had the following child:

491   i.   **Emily Stephens** born about 1857 in Kent County, Maryland.

Anna Matilda Blackiston and Abraham Taylor were married before 1860. **Abraham Taylor** born about 1816. He died after 1880 at the age of 64. Per descendants, Abraham was married three times 1st Sarah Smith, 2nd Mrs. Anna Stephens and 3rd Ann Blackiston. I have not found proof of the second marriage but there is a Stevens girl living in the 1860 and 1870 census with him and the 3rd wife is in the 1870 census.

MARRIAGE: George Abraham Taylor Gender: Male Marriage Date: 3 Aug 1841 Spouse: Sarah Rebecca Smith Spouse gender: Male State: Maryland County: Kent

CENSUS: 1850 Kent Co, MD
Abraham Taylor 45, Sarah 26, John 8, Samuel 2, Anna Smitty 18,
A few doors away is Jacob Stevens age 32 Henrietta 18.
1850; Census Place: District 1, Kent, Maryland; Roll M432 294; Page: 266A; Image: 538.

CENSUS: 1860 Kent Co, MD
Abraham Taylor 44, John Taylor 18, Medford Taylor 10, Anna Taylor 1, Emily Stevens 3
1860; Census Place: District 1, Kent, Maryland; Roll: M653 477; Page: 0; Image: 511. next door is James E. Blackiston 52 shoemaker and wife Mary E (Stevens) 35 and children

CENSUS: 1870 Kent Co, MD
Abram Taylor 55 oysterman born MD, Ann E Taylor 36, Emma Stevens 13, Ann E Taylor 11, Nora Taylor 4, Lily Taylor 1, 1870; Census Place: Chestertown District 5, Kent, Maryland; Roll: M593 590; Page: 215; Image: 430.
Next door is Mary E (Stevens) Blackiston 45 and son James Blackiston 10

CENSUS: 1880 Kent Co, MD
Abram Taylor 65 fisherman, Norah dau 14, Lillie 10 dau.
1880; Census Place: Swan Creek Neck, Kent, Maryland; Roll T9 512; Family History Film: 1254512; Page: 177.4000; Enumeration District: 55;.

353. **John Joseph Blackiston** (James Eagle-8, Joseph-7, Joseph-6, Ebenezer-5, John-4, John-3, George-2, Marmaduke-1) was born on 1 Mar 1846 in Kent County, Maryland. He was christened on 14 Jan 1880 in Rock Hall, Kent County, Maryland. He died on 1 Feb 1913 at the age of 66 in Rock Hall, Kent County, Maryland. John was buried at Wesley Chapel in Rock Hall, Kent County, Maryland.

BIRTH: Death cert says Mar 1 1847, baptism in 1880 says Mar 1 1846. Census ages match closer to 1846 birth.

BAPTISM: John Joseph Blackiston born Mar. 1, 1846 baptized Jan. 14 1880, parents James and Mary E. Blackiston by Rev. George Leary. Rock Hall.

CENSUS: 1850 Kent Co, MD
James E Blackiston 42 shoemaker married within the year, Mary E Blackiston 24
Henrietta Blackiston 14, Mary R Blackiston 12, John S Blackiston 6, Wm H Blackiston 4, Anna Blackiston 2
Census; Record Group Number: 29; Series Number: M432; Residence Date: 1850; Home in 1850: District 2, Kent, Maryland; Roll: 294; Page: 232a

CENSUS: 1860 Kent Co, MD
James E Blackiston 52 shoemaker $500 RE $200 PE, Mary E Blackiston 35, John Blackiston 14, William H Blackiston 12, Caroline Blackiston 10, Adaline Blackiston 4, James L Blackiston 1
Census; Record Group Number: 29; Series Number: M653; Residence Date: 1860; Home in 1860: District 1, Kent, Maryland; Roll: M653 477; Page: 1064; Family History Library Film: 803477

MARRIAGE: Licenses says John J. Blackiston to Julia C. Adkinson of Kent Co m. June 14, 1869 by Rev. D.C. Ridgeway.

MARRIAGE: Kent Co. Jno J. Blackiston 23 single shoemaker res. Kent Co m. Jun 15 1869 to Julia C. Adkinson 22 widow res. Kent Co. at Rees' Corner by Rev. D.C. Ridgeway.

MARRIAGE: Blackiston-Atkinson On Tue. (15th) last 8pm at the M.E. Parsonage, Rees' Corner by the Rev. D.C. Ridgeway, John Blackiston to Mrs. Julia Atkinson-- all of this county. Kent Co News June 19 1869

CENSUS: 1870 Kent Co, MD
John Blackiston 24, Carrie 22, Nancy 3/12 (Mar), Charlotte Adkinson 5.
Chestertown p. 201 5th Dist 279-275

CENSUS: 1880 Kent Co, MD
J.J. Blackiston 34 shoemaker, Julia C 34, Mary N 10, Grace F 4, Columbus 4, Edgar A
8/12 (Oct), Edna 8/12 (Oct) twins, E.L. Adkinson 16 dau.
HSE: 281-281, Rock Hall Swan Creek Neck, 5th Elec. Dist. ED 55 p 30

NEWS: John J. Blackiston selected as democratic supervisor of elections in Kent Co. The
following Supervisors were nominated for Kent county: J. Henry Hurtt, John J. Blackiston,
Wm. S. Walker. The Baltimore Sun, Baltimore, Maryland • Sat, Feb 8, 1896 Page 2

CENSUS: 1900 Kent Co, MD
John J Blackiston Mar 1847, Julia C. Dec 1846 8 children 2 living married 29y, owned
own home, merchant.

CENSUS: 1910 Kent Co, MD
242-259 John J. Blackiston 63 salesman m1 40y, Julia C 63 8 children 2 living, retail
merchant, m2
Coleman's Corner 57 ED p 16A lived next door to Charles and Grace (Blackiston) Crouch

DEATH: John Joseph Blackiston Rock Hall, Kent Co, married, born Mar 1 1847 age 65y
11m0d, born Kent Co parents James E. Blackiston born Kent Co and Mary E. Stevens born
Kent Co, info. Julia C. Blackiston of Rock Hall, heart disease, died Feb 1 1913 at 4pm,
always lived in Kent, merchant. Cert. 2094

OBITUARY: Rock Hall Notes Death of Mr. Blackiston, Mr. John J. Blackiston, long a
prominent citizen and businessman of this section, died very suddenly on Saturday
afternoon at his home. John was a fine neighbor, good citizen and a hustler in business. He
had been in poor health for several years during which time his going in and out among us
has been retarded, and everyone has missed him greatly. Besides his widow, two children,
Columbus Blackiston and Mrs. Charles Crouch survive. Funeral services conducted by
Elder Paap took place at S.D. at church on Tuesday afternoon in the presence of a large
assembly. Kent News February 8, 1913

ROCK HALL NOTES

Death of Mr. Blackiston—Rebekah Lodge Entertains—Other Items.

Mr. John J. Blackiston, long a prominent citizen and business man of this section, died very suddenly on Saturday afternoon at his home. John was a fine neighbor, good citizen and a hustler in business. He had been in poor health for several years during which time his going in and out among us has been retarded and everyone has missed him greatly. Besides his widow, two children, Columbus Blackiston and Mrs. Charles Crouch survive. Funeral services conducted by Elder Paap took place at S. D. A. church on Tuesday afternoon in the presence of a large assembly.

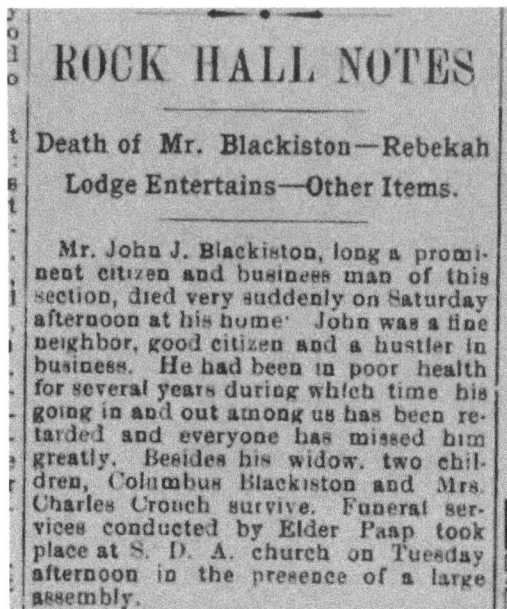

BIBLE: Bible record of Leonard Leary Rock Hall has The Cottage Bible published 1835 which says "George Leary Jr. and Mrs. Mary E. Blackiston were married Oct. 15, 1871, John Joseph Blackiston and Julia Christianna Leary Adkinson were m. June 15, 1869, William T. Adkinson and Julia C. Leary were m. Jan. 4, 1863, George Leary m. Mary Ann Sims were m. Nov. 15, 1832."

John Joseph Blackiston and Julia Christina Leary were married on 15 Jun 1869 in Kent County, Maryland. **Julia Christina Leary**, daughter of George B. Leary and Mary Ann Sims, was born on 25 Dec 1845 in Kent County, Maryland. She died on 30 Sep 1915 at the age of 69 in Rock Hall, Kent County, Maryland. She was buried at Wesley Chapel in Wesley Chapel, Rock Hall, Kent County, Maryland.

MARRIAGE: Her first marriage. Kent Co. William F. Atkinson Jr. Kent Co. m. Julia C. Leary Kent Co. Dec 31 1862 by Leary (her father George Leary - he records the marriage in his ministers book). Marriage records Kent Co says Dec. 31 1862 Julia C. Leary married William T. Atkinson Jr. by Leary. Family Bible record says William T. Adkinson m. Julia C. Leary Jan. 4, 1863.

DEATH: Julia Christana Blackiston Rock Hall, Kent Co, widowed born Dec 25 1845 age 67y9m5d born Kent Co parents George Leary MD and Mary Sims MD died Sep 30 1915 burial at Wesley Chapel. info. Columbus Blackiston of Rock Hall., died of Cancer of Rectum. fun. dir. Thomas H. Casey of Rock Hall. Cert. #1574

OBITUARY: Mrs. Julia C. Blackiston, widow of the late John Blackiston, died at the home of her daughter, Mrs. Charles Crouch, at Piney Neck, Oct. 1st, age 69 years. Mrs. Blackiston, since the death of her husband, had been conducting her store near Rock Hall, until failing health compelled her to take to her bed. Five weeks ago Mrs. Crouch moved her to her home where she could more tenderly administer to her sufferings. Mrs. Blackiston was the daughter of George and Mary Leary. She leaves one son Columbus A. and one daughter, Mrs. Charles Crouch; three brothers, Isaac L., James L. and Oregan P. Leary. Funeral services were held Saturday afternoon at the Rock Hall Adventis Church, of which the deceased had been a member. Services were conducted by Elder Shadel; Casey and Bro. undertakers. The bearers were: Isaac L., Jas. L. and Oregan P. Leary, brothers of the deceased; Jas. F., Elmer E. and Edward Leary, nephews. Mother, thou are sweetly sleeping. Free from pain and toil and care; Dearest mothers, how we miss thee! Miss thee in the house of prayer. Thou will sleep, but not forever; Jesus died, and rose again; Soon He'll come in clouds of glory- thou wilt rise with Him to reign. Mother, then we hope to meet thee; Then we'll take thee by the hand, Then we'll twine our arms around thee in that bright and happy land. Son and Daughter. The Transcript, Saturday October 9, 1915.

WILL: Julia C. Blackiston names dau Grace F Crouch, son Columbus A Blackiston, dau Naomi Davis decd, Jump grandchildren (children of Purnell Jump) named Bertha Jones, William Jump. the 3 grandchildren are already well provided for so only $1. JRC 1-141 date Jun 18 1913 probate Oct 5 1915

John Joseph Blackiston and Julia Christina Leary had the following children:

+493	i.	**Mary Naomi Young Blackiston**, born 5 Apr 1870, Kent County, Maryland; married Henry Landon Davies, abt 1890; died 1895.
494	ii.	**George Edward Blackiston** was born on 12 Jun 1873 in Kent County, Maryland. He was christened on 25 Dec 1873 in Rock Hall, Kent County, Maryland. He died before 1880 at the age of 7. BAPTISM: George Edward Blackiston born Jun 12, 1873 baptized Dec. 25 1873 parents John J. and Julia C. Blackiston by Rev. George Leary. Rock Hall.
+495	iii.	**Grace Florence Blackiston**, born 27 Jul 1875, Rock Hall, Kent County, Maryland; married Charles Wesley Crouch, 12 Jan 1891, Rock Hall, Kent County, Maryland; died 3 Feb 1948, Baltimore City, Maryland.
+496	iv.	**Columbus Augustus Blackiston**, born 6 Feb 1877, Kent County, Maryland; married Sarah Elizabeth Walbert, 29 Apr 1896; died 11 Oct 1928, Kent County, Maryland.
497	v.	**Edna Anna Blackiston** was born on 5 Oct 1879 in Kent County, Maryland. She was christened on 14 Jan 1880 in Rock Hall, Kent County, Maryland. She died before 1900 at the age of 21.
498	vi.	**Edgar Andrew Blackiston** was born on 5 Oct 1879 in Kent County, Maryland. He was christened on 14 Jan 1880 in Rock Hall, Kent County, Maryland. He died before 1900 at the age of 21. Died young.
499	vii.	**Blackiston** died before 1900. 1900 and 1910 census says she had 8 children and only 2 living so 6 died before 1900.
500	viii.	**Blackiston** died before 1900. 1900 and 1910 census says she had 8 children and only 2 living so 6 died before 1900.

355. Susan Caroline Blackiston (James Eagle-8, Joseph-7, Joseph-6, Ebenezer-5, John-4, John-3, George-2, Marmaduke-1) was born on 25 Nov 1849 in Kent County, Maryland. She died on 29 Oct 1874 at the age of 24 in Kent County, Maryland. She was christened at Wesley Chapel in Rock Hall, Kent County, Maryland. Susan was buried at Wesley Chapel in Rock Hall, Kent County, Maryland. In the 1850 Census she is listed as Anna age 2.

BIRTH: James E and Mary E Blackiston residence at Rock Hall baptized Susan Carrie born Nov 25 1869. Wesley Chapel.

MARRIAGE: Jno E. Beck 22 white Kent Co Md shoemaker m. Susan Blackiston 20 white Kent Co single on Dec 8 1869 at M.P. Parsonage bond Sep 15 1869 by J.W. Gray M.G.

CENSUS: 1870 Queen Annes Co, MD
Charlotte Meredith 64 Keeping House $1000 PP, Susan Beck 19 at home, Kate 16, Jane 12 domestic servant. Crumpton

TOMBSTONE: Susan Carrie wife of John Beck, dau of James E and Mary E Blackiston died Oct 29 1874 in her 25th year.

Susan Caroline Blackiston and John E. Beck were married on 8 Dec 1869 in Kent County, Maryland. **John E. Beck**, son of John A. Beck and Sarah Ann Webb, born about 1846. He died on 26 Nov 1869 at the age of 23 in Near Hanesville, Kent County, Maryland.

MARRIAGE: Licenses says John E. Beck to Susan Carey Blackiston on Sep 15 1869 by Rev. Mr. Gray.

OBITUARY: John Beck on the 26th ult in 24th year son of John A. Beck, at residence of William H. Watts near Hanesville. Kent News Dec 11 1869

357. **James Eagle Blackiston Jr.** (James Eagle-8, Joseph-7, Joseph-6, Ebenezer-5, John-4, John-3, George-2, Marmaduke-1) was born on 7 Jul 1860 in Kent County, Maryland. He was christened on 5 Apr 1868 in Rock Hall, Kent County, Maryland. He died on 8 Jan 1900 at the age of 39 in Kent County, Maryland. James was buried at Wesley Chapel in Rock Hall, Kent County, Maryland. He was an undertaker.

BAPTISM: James Eagle Blackiston baptized by Rev. George Leary. Parents James E. and Mary E. Blackiston. Born July 7 1860 baptized Apr 5 1868 Rock Hall.

MARRIAGE: Jas E. Blackiston 24 undertaker m. Mollie H. Hudson 24 white Kent Co single at Bride's residence Dec 2 1884 by Thomas O. Crouse M.G.

CENSUS: 1870 Kent Co MD
James Blackiston age 10 living with mother and stepfather.

CENSUS: 1880 Kent Co MD
James Blackiston age 19 living with mother and stepfather.

DEATH: James E Blackston, died Jan 8 1900 wife Mary Hudson, parents James E. Blackiston and Mary Stevens

TOMBSTONE: James E. Blackiston 1860-1900

James Eagle Blackiston Jr. and Mary Henrietta Hudson were married on 2 Dec 1884 in Kent County, Maryland. **Mary Henrietta Hudson** was born on 31 Jul 1860. She died on 3 Sep 1904 at the age of 44 in Rock Hall, Kent, Maryland.

CENSUS: 1900 Kent Co, MD
Mary E. Blackiston age 39y born April 1861, widow 4 children married 17y, 4 living, Edith dau. 16y, born May 1884, Carry E. age 14, born July 1886, William J. 11y, born Nov. 1889, James E. age 4 born Jan. 1896, Emily J. Leary Mother, widow age 67y born Feb. 1833 married 47y, William Leary 25y born Oct 1875 niece (sic should say nephew).

DEATH: Mary Henrietta Blackiston died at Rock Hall, Kent Co Sep 3 1904 age 44y 1 m 3 days female white born MD housewife, widow of James E Blackiston. father's name Thomas A Hudson born MD, mother's name Adeline L. Usilton born MD, Informant Ada V. Satterfield, cousin. died of consumptions 2 years, exhaustion 1 day

WILL: Mary H Blackiston names children Carrie, Edith, William and James Blackiston. William and James to attend school in Balto. witnesses Wm E Leary, Chas N Satterfield, T.B. Durding. will dated Jul 18 1904 pro Sep 6 1904 CSH 1-299

TOMBSTONE: Mary H. Blackiston 1860-1904

James Eagle Blackiston and Mary Henrietta Hudson had the following children:

+501   i.   **Edith Blackiston**, born May 1884, Maryland; married E. Frank Kerr; died 1975.

502   ii.   **Carrie Wells Blackiston** was born on 12 Aug 1887 in Maryland. She died on 19 Aug 1905 at the age of 18 in Kent County, Maryland. She was buried in Wesley Chapel, Kent County, Maryland. DEATH: Carrie Wells died August 19 1905 Kent Co age 18y 7d female white born Kent Co MD father James E Blackiston born Kent Co MD, mother Mary H. Hudson born Kent Co MD, Info. Edith H. Blackiston sister. died of tuberculosis Pulmonary exhaustion TOMBSTONE: Carrie W. Blackiston 1887-1905

503   iii.   **William Henry Blackiston** was born on 14 Dec 1889 in Maryland. He died on 23 Oct 1905 at the age of 15 in Kent County, Maryland. He was buried in Wesley Chapel, Kent County, Maryland. DEATH: William Henry Blackiston near Rock Hall, Kent Co died Oct 23 1905 age 15y 10 m 9 day male white MD single, father James E. Blackiston born MD, mother Mary H. Hudson born M. Info. Edith Blackiston sister. died of tuberculosis pulmonalis, 6 months. Exhaustion. TOMBSTONE: William H. Blackiston 1889-1905

504   iv.   **Addie E. Blackiston** was born in 1892. She died in 1895 at the age of 3. She was buried in Wesley Chapel, Kent County, Maryland.

505   v.   **James T. Blackiston** was born in 1894. He died in 1895 at the age of 1. He was buried in Wesley Chapel, Kent County, Maryland.

+506   vi.   **James Eagle Blackiston Sr**, born 25 Mar 1896; married Annabelle C Hornberger; died 6 Oct 1965, Baltimore City, Maryland.

365. Rebecca J. Blackiston (John Thomas-8, Joseph-7, Joseph-6, Ebenezer-5, John-4, John-3, George-2, Marmaduke-1) born about 1850. Rebecca J. Blackiston and Mr. Beaty were married.

367. John Ambrose Blackiston (John Thomas-8, Joseph-7, Joseph-6, Ebenezer-5, John-4, John-3, George-2, Marmaduke-1) born about 1853. He died on 28 Mar 1923 at the age of 70 in Washington, District of Columbia. John Ambrose Blackiston and Martha F. were married. **Martha F. Haughton** was born on 13 Sep 1856. She died on 11 Feb 1898 at the age of 41. TOMBSTONE: Martha F. wife of John A Blackiston Sep 13, 1856-Feb 11, 1898 John married 2nd **Mary Jane Sever** on Feb 27 1899 and moved to San de Fuca on Whidbey Island. TOMBSTONE: Mary Jane Blackiston Grasser 1870-1959.

371. **Dr Thomas Copper Blackiston** (John Thomas-8, Joseph-7, Joseph-6, Ebenezer-5, John-4, John-3, George-2, Marmaduke-1) born about 1858 in West Virginia. He died on 28 Sep 1908 at the age of 50 in Los Angeles, California.

OBITUARY: Dr. Thomas C. Blackiston died at his residence 621 Temple Street Monday Sep 28. Services will be held at the cemetery, Sixteenth and Grover Streets, at 10 o'clock am Thu. Oct 1. Grant R. Bennett Esq will deliver an address. Members of the Liberal club and all other friends are invited. Los Angeles Herald (Los Angeles, California) 30 Sep 1908, Wed Page 5

Dr Thomas Copper Blackiston and Sarah S Raleigh were married. **Sarah S Raleigh** was born on 23 Nov 1867. She died on 26 Jul 1889 at the age of 21. She was buried in Chester Cem, Chestertown, Kent, Maryland.

Dr Thomas Copper Blackiston and Elizabeth Lane were married on 20 Feb 1893 in Washington, District of Columbia. **Elizabeth Lane.**

375. **John W. Blackiston** (Samuel Lewis-8, John-7, John-6, Benjamin-5, John-4, John-3, George-2, Marmaduke-1) was born on 12 Oct 1815 in Maryland. He died on 11 Jan 1889 at the age of 73 in Millington, Kent, Maryland. He was buried in Asbury Cem., Millington, Kent, Maryland. He lived near the George W Blackiston and Samuel L. Blackiston families.

Information on this family came from the file at the MHS in Filing Case A by Frances Davis Cummins entitled George Blackiston emigrant to Maryland 1668.

MARRIAGE: John W Blackiston m Mary Ann Watson Marriage Date: 23 Feb 1848 Marriage Place: Kent Co DE

CENSUS: 1850 Kent Co MD
455-455 John Blackiston 36 born MD farmer, Mary A. 19, Samuel 2, John 2/12 born MD 1850; Census Place: District 3, Kent, Maryland; Roll: M432 294; Page: 310A; Image: 627

CENSUS: 1860 Kent Co, MD
904-920 John W Blackiston 44 farmer born DE, Mary Ann Blackiston 30 born DE, Samuel J Blackiston 12 born MD, John W Blackiston 10 born DE, William Blackiston 9 born DE, Laura J Blackiston 3 born MD

Year: 1860; Census Place: Galena, District 3, Kent, Maryland; Roll M653 477; Page: 0; Image: 402.

CENSUS: 1870 Kent Co, MD
John Blackiston 52 born MD laborer, Mary Ann 38 born MD, John B. 19 apprentice to shoemaker (John W?), William F. 16, Laura J. 12. In Millington

CENSUS: 1880 New Castle, DE
John W. Blackiston 56 Grocer born MD parents place not listed, Mary Ann Blackiston 50 born DE parents born DE, Laura Blackiston 19 born DE father born MD mother born DE. 1880; Census Place: Wilmington, New Castle, Delaware; Roll T9 119; Family History Film: 1254119; Page: 392.3000; Enumeration District: 15; Image: 0264 Living nearby is Samuel Blackiston 32 born DE Grocer with Josephine 30 wife, Mary V.E. born June and Emma Pierce 18 boarder, Tillie Warren 34 boarder, Pauline Hirzel 27 servant.

John W. Blackiston and Mary Ann Watson were married on 23 Feb 1848 in Kent County de. **Mary Ann Watson** was born on 15 Mar 1830 in De. She died on 22 Feb 1895 at the age of 64 in Millington, Kent, Maryland. She was buried in Asbury Cem., Millington, Kent, Maryland.

John W. Blackiston and Mary Ann Watson had the following children:

+507   i. **Samuel J. Blackiston**, born abt 1848, Maryland; married Josephine Elliott, 26 Nov 1877; married Lou Alridge, 14 Apr 1886.

+508   ii. **John Wesley Blackiston**, born 30 Jun 1850, Kent Co, Maryland; married Susan Ann Covington, 21 Apr 1880, Kent Co, Maryland; died 10 Jan 1894, Wilmington, New Castle, Delaware.

+509   iii. **William Holding Blackiston**, born 6 Jan 1852, Smyrna, Delaware; married Mary Elizabeth Roberts, 4 Dec 1877, Smyrna, Delaware; died 4 Oct 1948.

+510   iv. **Laura J. Blackiston**, born 5 Feb 1857, Maryland; married Haulsey Maston; died 26 Oct 1932, Wilmington, New Castle, Delaware.

376. **Janetta F. D. Blackiston** (Samuel Lewis-8, John-7, John-6, Benjamin-5, John-4, John-3, George-2, Marmaduke-1) was born in 1816. She died on 15 Dec 1862 at the age of 46. It is possible that Janetta is the dau. of Samuel. A researcher Bob Nichols thinks that Samuel Blackiston m. Benedicta Maddox and that she was the dau. of Basil and Margaret Fernandis Maddox which would explain why Janetta's first son was named Samuel Fernandis Nichols and her grandchild was named Alfred Fernandis Nichols Betton.

Janetta F. D. Blackiston and James Nichols were married. **James Nichols** died on 1 Oct 1859.

377. **Samuel Lewis Blackiston** (Samuel Lewis-8, John-7, John-6, Benjamin-5, John-4, John-3, George-2, Marmaduke-1) born about 1824. He died on 4 Oct 1885 at the age of 61 in Millington, Kent, Maryland. He was buried in Asbury Cem., Millington, Kent, Maryland. His daughter Mary Elizabeth was a member of the DAR 159973. names her father Samuel Lewis Blackiston d. 1885 and mother Mary Elizabeth Stewart 1823-1900, m 1852.

CENSUS: 1850 Kent Co, MD
William F Meeks 38, Mary E Meeks 25, William B Meeks 7, Samuel Meeks 9, John O Meeks 5, Mary R Meeks 2, Samuel Blackiston 25, Benjaman Dealey 20, William Dolen 16, Thomas Moffitt 15, James Dothard 25, Alexander Dothard 20, Margarett Wilson 50 1850; Census Place: District 3, Kent, Maryland; Roll: M432 294; Page: 312A; Image: 631

CENSUS: 1860 Kent Co, MD
Samuel S Blackiston 36 shoemaker, Mary E Blackiston 35, Steward Blackiston 1, Horace McSteward 32, George McSteward 26, Martha McSteward 23, John Meeks 14, Elizabeth Ford 10
1860; Census Place: Millington, Kent, Maryland; Roll: M653 477; Page: 1048; Family History Library Film: 803477 Fords also lived with G. W. Blackiston.

CENSUS: 1870 Kent Co, MD
Samuel L Blackiston 46 books/shoemaker, Mary E Blackiston 42, Mary E Blackiston 9 1870; Census Place: Millington, Kent, Maryland; Roll: M593 590; Page: 51A; Family History Library Film: 552089

CENSUS: 1880 Kent Co, MD
S.L. Blackiston 57, Mary E. 56, Mary E. 16
1880; Census Place: Millington, Kent, Maryland; Roll: 512; Page: 23B; Enumeration District: 048 nearby is G.W. Blackiston 54-56 Household.

Samuel Lewis Blackiston and Mary Elizabeth Stewart were married on 21 May 1852 in Millington, Kent County, Maryland. **Mary Elizabeth Stewart** was born in Nov 1823 in Maryland. She died on 29 Aug 1900 at the age of 76 in Kent County, Maryland.

OBITUARY: Mrs. Mary Blackiston resident of dau. Mrs. M.E.B. Mallalieu, Millington, on Wed. widow of Samuel Blackiston, 75 years, dau is only child. Centreville Record Aug 29, 1900.

Samuel Lewis Blackiston and Mary Elizabeth Stewart had the following children:

511   i. **Francis H. Blackiston** died about 1856. He was born on 28 Jul 1856. He was buried in Asbury Cem., Millington, Kent, Maryland.

512   ii. **Stewart Blackiston** born about 1859. He died about 1860 at the age of 1.

+513   iii. **Mary Elizabeth Blackiston**, born 30 Jun 1861; married James Mallolieui, 3 Feb 1887; married Frank Sloane Bottomley, abt 1901; died 9 Dec 1931.

380. **Margaret Elizabeth Hepbron** (Martha Priscilla Maslin-8, Elizabeth Wroth-7, Priscilla Blackiston-6, Benjamin-5, John-4, John-3, George-2, Marmaduke-1) was born on 11 Jul 1834. She died on 18 Jan 1891 at the age of 56.

Margaret Elizabeth Hepbron and James Reyner Stavely were married on 27 Dec 1854. **James Reyner Stavely**, son of Joseph Stavely and Rachel Cann, was born on 29 Oct 1829 in Kent County, Maryland. He died on 29 Nov 1895 at the age of 66 in Kent County, Maryland.

James Reyner Stavely and Margaret Elizabeth Hepbron had the following children:

+514   i. **Harry Maslin Stavely**, born 24 Nov 1863, Kent County, Maryland; married Florence Kelley Bowers, 17 Dec 1890; died 13 Jul 1947, Kent County, Maryland.

+515   ii. **Bayard Cann Stavely**, born 14 Jan 1870, Kent County, Maryland; married Ada Worrell, 22 Apr 1897, New Jersey; died 8 Jul 1944, Haddonfield, New Jersey.

383. **Rev Sewell Stavely Hepbron Sr** (Martha Priscilla Maslin-8, Elizabeth Wroth-7, Priscilla Blackiston-6, Benjamin-5, John-4, John-3, George-2, Marmaduke-1) was born on 9 Jun 1845. He died on 4 Nov 1932 at the age of 87 in Kent County, Maryland. He was buried at I. Upper Church Cemetery in Worton, Kent County, Maryland. Preacher at Christ I.U. Church. His granddaughter was the famous actress Katherine Hepburn and when she died conferred $10,000 on the Episcopal church where he had served as a clergyman.

Rev Sewell Stavely Hepbron Sr and Selina Powell were married. **Selina Powell** was born on 12 Dec 1842. She died on 5 Mar 1918 at the age of 75. She was buried at I. Upper Church Cemetery in Worton, Kent County, Maryland.

Sewell Stavely Hepbron and Selina Powell had the following children:

516   i. **Charles Levin Hepburn** was born on 4 Dec 1872. He died on 16 Apr 1915 at the age of 42.

517   ii. **Sewell S. Hepburn Dr.** was born on 4 Feb 1874. He died on 5 Apr 1921 at the age of 47.

518   iii. **Lloyd Powell Hepburn** was born on 20 May 1876. He died on 16 Jan 1961 at the age of 84.

519   iv. **Selina Lloyd Hepburn** was born on 9 Apr 1878. She died on 25 Feb 1970 at the age of 91.

+520   v. **Dr Thomas Norval Hepburn**, born 18 Dec 1879, Richmond, Virginia; married Katherine Matha Houghton; died 20 Nov 1962, Hartford County, Connecticut.

386. Rev Dr Peregrine Wroth (Thomas Granger-8, John-7, Priscilla Blackiston-6, Benjamin-5, John-4, John-3, George-2, Marmaduke-1) was born on 19 Jul 1848 in Kent County, Maryland. He died on 9 Dec 1927 at the age of 79 in Baltimore, Maryland. He was buried in Loudon Park Cem., Baltimore, Maryland. He was a Dr. of Divinity and submitted an application for membership in the Maryland Historical Society in 1908. He has personal papers in their archives. On his application is a chart with his Wroths back to James Wroth.

DEATH: Baltimore City. Cert 28282

OBITUARY: Rev. Peregrine Wroth DD age 79y husband of Mary A. died Dec 9 1927 Baltimore, laid in state at Church of the Messiah. Buried Loudon Park.

Rev Dr Peregrine Wroth and Mary Augusta Counselman were married on 13 Jun 1880 in Kent County, Maryland. **Mary Augusta Counselman** born about 1850. She died on 18 Dec 1930 at the age of 80 in Baltimore, Maryland. She was buried in Church of Messia, Hamilton, Baltimore, Maryland. OBITUARY: Mary Augusta died Dec 18 1930 wife of the late Rev. Peregrin Wroth DD
buried at Church of the Messiah on Harford and White Ave in Hamilton.

Peregrine Wroth and Mary Augusta Counselman had the following children:

+521   i. **Dr Peregrine Wroth Jr. MD**, born 17 Feb 1882, Kent County, Maryland; married Woe Townsend; died 25 Dec 1956, Hagerstown, Washington, Maryland.

522   ii. **Lawrence Counselman Wroth** was born on 14 Jan 1884.

523   iii. **Thomas Page Wroth** was born on 30 Oct 1887 in Baltimore, Maryland. He died on 12 Aug 1905 at the age of 17 in Westminster, Carroll, Maryland. drowned

388. Rev. Edward Worrell Wroth (Thomas Granger-8, John-7, Priscilla Blackiston-6, Benjamin-5, John-4, John-3, George-2, Marmaduke-1) was born on 5 Oct 1851. He died in Aug 1924 at the age of 72 in Harford County, Maryland. Rector of Episcopal churches in Harford Co, MD

Rev. Edward Worrell Wroth and Margaret Gilpin Price were married on 30 May 1882. **Margaret Gilpin Price**.

Edward Worrell Wroth and Margaret Gilpin Price had the following children:

524   i. **John Wroth** was born on 4 Mar 1883.

525   ii. **Edward Pinkney Wroth** was born on 11 Jan 1889.

526   iii. **Mary Parker Wroth** was born on 9 Dec 1890.

527   iv. **Margaret Price Wroth** was born on 23 Nov 1894.

400. Thomas Bowers Tilden Brice (Joseph W.-8, James-7, Judith Ann Blackiston-6, Michael-5, John-4, John-3, George-2, Marmaduke-1) was born in Mar 1832 in Kent County, Maryland. He died on 21 Dec 1904 at the age of 72 in Kent County, Maryland.

CENSUS: 1870 Kent Co, MD
Thos B T Brice 38, Araminta Brice 30, Horace Brice 14, Jas T Brice 10, Ellen Brice 8, Thos Brice 6, Samuel Brice 2
1870; Census Place: District 2, Kent, Maryland; Roll: M593 590; Page: 81B; Image: 166; Family History Library Film: 552089.

CENSUS: 1880 Kent Co, MD
Thomas Brice 47, Araminta Brice 40, James T. Brice 20, Thomas Brice 15, Samuel Brice 12, Lucile Brice 7, Mary E. Brice 4, Frank H. Brice 1m
1880; Census Place: Worton, Kent, Maryland; Roll: 512; Family History Film: 1254512; Page: 92C; Enumeration District: 003; Image: 0184.

CENSUS: 1900 Kent Co, MD
Thomas B T Brice 68, Araminta Brice 60, Harper Brice 20
1900; Census Place: Worton, Kent, Maryland; Roll: 625; Page: 21B; Enumeration District: 0049; FHL

DEATH: Thomas H. T. Brice died Betterton Kent Co MD Dec 21 1904 aged 72y 6m male white born MD, fisherman, widower, father Joseph Brice born MD, mother's maiden name Mariah Tilden born MD, Informant Horace Brice son, cardiac asthma Phys. Lewis P. Atwell MD of Still Pond MD.

Thomas Bowers Tilden Brice and Araminta Bramble were married on 2 Nov 1855 in Kent County, Maryland. **Araminta Bramble**.

401. James Brice Stevens (Henrietta Brice-8, Ann Brice-7, Judith Ann Blackiston-6, Michael-5, John-4, John-3, George-2, Marmaduke-1) born about 1824.

MARRIAGE: James B. Stevens m. Mary A. Mosher Nov. 11, 1845

James Brice Stevens and Mary A. Mosher were married on 11 Nov 1845 in Kent County, Maryland.

402. Captain John Brice Stevens (Henrietta Brice-8, Ann Brice-7, Judith Ann Blackiston-6, Michael-5, John-4, John-3, George-2, Marmaduke-1) was born on 12 Feb 1826 in

Maryland. He died on 9 Mar 1891 at the age of 65. He was buried at Wesley Chapel in Rock Hall, Kent County, Maryland. Copies of his family Bible was given to me by Erma Carchedi of Silver Spring, MD He was a Capt. on a boat and listed as Capt. in the baptismal records of Rev. George Leary.

CENSUS: 1850 Talbot Co, MD
John B Stevens 24, Susan Stevens 21, Charles Stevens 2
1850; Census Place: St Michaels, Talbot, Maryland; Roll: M432 297; Page: 85B; Image: 582.

CENSUS: 1860 Kent Co, MD
John B Stephens 37, Susan Stephens 37, Charles Stephens 13, Margaret Stephens 9, John Stephens 6, John Hynson 26, John Welch 40, Tempy Eischy 14
1860; Census Place: District 1, Kent, Maryland; Roll: M653 477; Page: 1073; Image: 519; Family History Library Film: 803477.

MARRIAGE: John Brice Stephens m. Sarah Jane Jolly by June 26, 1861 by Rev. W. W. Walton.

CENSUS: 1870
John B Stevens 33 oysterman born MD, Sarah Stevens 25, John T Stevens 15 farmhand, Mary F Stevens 6, James F Stevens 3, Harry B Stevens 1
1870; Census Place: District 5, Kent, Maryland; Roll: M593 590; Page: 214A; Image: 431; Family History Library Film: 552089.

CENSUS: 1880 Kent Co, MD Census
John B. Stevens 54 MD Fisherman, Sarah J. Stevens Wife 35 Keeps House, Florance Stevens Dau 16, James F. Stevens Son 13 Fisherman, Harry B. Stevens Son 11 Fisherman, Clarrie O. Stevens Dau 9, Fannie E. Stevens Dau 8, Jessie C. Stevens Son 5, Rutherford Stevens Son 3, Lillie A. Stevens Dau 1
Source Information: Census Place Edesville, Kent, Maryland Family History Library Film 1254512 NA Film Number T9-0512 Page Number 174A

TOMBSTONE: In Loving Remembrance of Capt. John B. Stevens Born Feb. 12, 1826-Died Mar. 9, 1891

Captain John Brice Stevens and Sarah Jane Jolly were married on 26 Jun 1861 in Kent County, Maryland. **Sarah Jane Jolly**, daughter of Mazy Jolly and Susan , was born on 16 Nov 1845 in Maryland. She died on 3 Jun 1923 at the age of 77.

CENSUS: 1850 Queen Anne's Co, MD
John N. Dodds 25, Sarah 22, Wm 6, Mary 2, Sarah Jolly 7
Maryland Gender: Male Home in 1850 District 5, Queen Anne's, Maryland Page: 251 Roll: M432 296

CENSUS: 1860 Baltimore, MD
Mary Jolly 37, Susan Jolly 34, Sarah Jolly 16, Indiana Jolly 8, Wilhelmina Jolly 3, Mary Jolly 1, Frances Ensley 44
1860; Census Place: Baltimore Ward 18, Baltimore (Independent City), Maryland; Roll: M653 465; Page: 760; Image: 760; Family History Library Film: 803465. (numbered p 714)

DEATH: Sarah Jane Jolly. She was born on Nov. 16,1845 and died on June 3rd,1923. mother Fairbanks.

John Brice Stevens and Sarah Jane Jolly had the following children:

528	i.	**Susie M. Stevens** was born on 8 Nov 1862 in Kent County, Maryland. She died in Apr 1863 in Kent County, Maryland.
+529	ii.	**Mary Florence Stevens**, born 21 Jun 1864, Kent County, Maryland; married Frank Waxter, 23 Aug 1884, Kent County, Maryland; married John Bockmen, 4 Sep 1907, Kent County, Maryland.
+530	iii.	**James Frank Stevens**, born 18 Jan 1867, Kent County, Maryland; married Cassie Kerr, May 1887.
+531	iv.	**Henry Brice Stevens**, born 24 Apr 1869, Kent County, Maryland; married Virgie B. Kendall, 16 Sep 1891, Kent County, Maryland; married Clara Hartlover, 13 Sep 1907, Kent County, Maryland.
+532	v.	**Clara O. Stevens**, born 2 Oct 1870, Kent County, Maryland; married William J. Downey, 12 Oct 1887, Kent County, Maryland.
+533	vi.	**Fannie E. Stevens**, born 23 Apr 1872, Kent County, Maryland; married James F. Brown, 23 Apr 1889, Kent County, Maryland.
+534	vii.	**Jesse Columbus Stevens**, born 20 Oct 1874, Kent County, Maryland; married Mable Stacy, 8 Feb 1899, Kent County, Maryland.
+535	viii.	**Elmer Rutherford Stevens**, born 22 Jun 1877, Kent County, Maryland; married Ada Brenner, 15 Nov 1899, Kent County, Maryland; died 27 Aug 1907, Washington County, Maryland.
+536	ix.	**Lily Elmira Stevens**, born 18 Nov 1878, Kent County, Maryland; married George R. Apsley, 15 Jan 1896, Kent County, Maryland; died 17 Jul 1936.

Captain John Brice Stevens and Susan Welsh were married on 30 Mar 1847 in Talbot County, Maryland. **Susan Welsh** died about 1860.

John Brice Stevens and Susan Welsh had the following child:

537	i.	**John T. Stevens** was born on 6 Apr 1855 in Maryland. He died on 20 Feb 1940 at the age of 84 in Kent County, Maryland. He was buried in Welsey Chapel, Kent County, Maryland.

403. **Martha Louisa Stevens** (Henrietta Brice-8, Ann Brice-7, Judith Ann Blackiston-6, Michael-5, John-4, John-3, George-2, Marmaduke-1) born about 1827 in Kent County, Maryland. OBITUARY: Mrs. Louisa A. Stevens in Queen Annes Co on 4th instant, widow of the late William Stevens. Easton Gazette Issue 5/12/1855.

Martha Louisa Stevens and William Henry Stevens were married on 6 Aug 1849. **William Henry Stevens** was born in 1826 in Kent County, Maryland. He died after 1850 at the age of 24. Was living in Baltimore City

CENSUS: 1850 Baltimore City, MD
William Stevens 24, Martha 20, Emily 1/12 living with John Finch 26, Elizabeth Finch 25, William Finch 23.

William Henry Stevens and Martha Louisa Stevens had the following children:

+538   i.   **Mary Emily Stevens**, born 26 May 1850; married James W. Tracy, 15 Sep 1867; died 28 Dec 1941.
539   ii.   **Sarah Henrietta Stevens** was born on 28 Sep 1855 in MD. She died on 6 May 1948 at the age of 92 in Chester, Delaware. She was buried in Wesley Chapel Cem., Rock Hall, Kent, Maryland.
540   iii.   **Ann Rebecca Stephens** was born on 3 Jan 1862 in Kent County, Maryland. She was christened on 9 Aug 1862 in Rock Hall, Kent County, Maryland.

406. **Mary Rebecca Glenn** (Tamasina Brice-8, John-7, Judith Ann Blackiston-6, Michael-5, John-4, John-3, George-2, Marmaduke-1) was born on 2 Feb 1829 in Kent County, Maryland. Mary Rebecca Glenn and Asbury Howard were married. **Asbury Howard** was born on 6 May 1823 in Kent County, Maryland. He died after 1850 at the age of 27. Will of Martha Brice of Chestertown, Kent Co names Perry Price Howard, son of Asbury Howard and Mary his wife of Kent $100, To Perry Price Howard, William Penn Howard, Frank Houstin Howard, sons of Asbury and Mary Howard of Kent Co all my estate.

407. **Vincent Hatcheson** (Vincent-8, James-7, Martha Miller-6, Ann Blackiston-5, William-4, Ebenezer-3, George-2, Marmaduke-1) born about 1823. He died in Apr 1847 at the age of 24 in Belle Aire, Kent County, Maryland. Son Robert Rogers Hatcheson died on Oct 30 1917. Death cert. lists his parents as Vincent Hatcherson and Mary Lessenbury. His brother James P. Hatcherson died April 1 1908 and his obituary names brother Robert R. and cousin George W. Hatcherson. The cousin George Hatcherson's will of 1909 names children of his deceased cousin Henry Clay Usilton and deceased cousin James P. Hatcherson's children and children of cousin Robert R. Hatcherson. George W. Hatcherson is the son of Bartus P. Hatcherson who died Aug 1 1890. Henry's parents were George B. Usilton and Sarah E. Hatcherson.

In 1857 property descended to Sarah E. Hatcherson Usilton, Bartus P. Hatcherson, Mary L. Piner Beaston, and Louisa H. Piner Price wife of Joseph Price. MARRIAGE: Ann M. Piner m. James M. Beaston Marriage Date: 24 Jan 1840 Kent County MD. MARRIAGE: Mary L Piner m. James L Beasten Marriage Date: 27 Aug 1846 Marriage Place: Wilmington, New Castle

MARRIAGE: Vincent Hatcheson m. Mary Lessenby Dec 29 1841 Kent Co.

OBITUARY: April 10 1847 Kent Co New Died near Belle Air, MD Wed. last Vincent Hatcherson.

Vincent Hatcheson and Mary Lessenby were married on 29 Dec 1841 in Kent County, Maryland. **Mary Lessenby** born about 1823.

CENSUS: 1850
Mary Hatcherson age 28, Tamara age 6, James age 5, William 8/12.

MARRIAGE: Married on July 27, by the Rev. J. Dale; Mr. Joseph Middleton to Mrs. Mary E. Hatcherson, all of this county. Kent News Saturday, August 9, 1851

CENSUS: 1870
Mary Middleton age 63 and Joseph Middleton age 59 in Kent Co. 1860 has a Joseph Middleton 47 and Susan 31.

Vincent Hatcheson and Mary Lessenby had the following child:

541   i.   **Robert Rogers Hatcheson** was born in 1846 in Maryland. He died on 30 Oct 1917 at the age of 71 in Kent County, Maryland. CENSUS: 1860 Robert 16 with William Legg. 1870 Robert 22 with uncle Bartus. DEATH: Robert Rogers Hatcherson died in Kent County near Chestertown, Maryland on October 30, 1917 at 4:45 P.M. being age 67 years, 7 months and 6 days

408. **Bartus Pinder Hatcheson** (Vincent-8, James-7, Martha Miller-6, Ann Blackiston-5, William-4, Ebenezer-3, George-2, Marmaduke-1) born about 1822. He died in 1890 at the age of 68.

CENSUS: 1850 Kent Co, MD
Bartas Hatchersen 32, Rachel Hatchersen 27, George W Hatchersen 4, Jackson Hatchersen 13, John Gerred 9, Samuel Gerred 8
1850; Census Place: District 2, Kent, Maryland; Roll: M432 294; Page: 235B; Image: 477.

CENSUS: 1860 Kent Co, MD
Bartus P Hutchison 38, Rachael Hutchison 35, George Hutchison 14, Henry Ward 50, John C Lambers 22, William Wye 21, John Goalding 17, Joseph Hynson 9, Ane Gale Hynson 8, Emily Worrell 14
1860; Census Place: District 2, Kent, Maryland; Roll: M653 477; Page: 886; Image: 332; Family History Library Film: 803477.

CENSUS: 1880 Kent Co, MD
B. P. Hatcherson 58, H. C. Usilton 36 nephew, Fannie Harris 30, Mag. Harris 6 Wm. Guli 12, A. Gleeves 14
1880; Census Place: Worton, Kent, Maryland; Roll: 512; Family History Film: 1254512; Page: 108C; Enumeration District: 003; Image: 0215.

Bartus Pinder Hatcheson and Rachel were married.

409. **Sarah E. Hatcheson** (Vincent-8, James-7, Martha Miller-6, Ann Blackiston-5, William-4, Ebenezer-3, George-2, Marmaduke-1) born about 1825.

CENSUS: 1850 Kent Co, MD
Sarah Usilton 37, Mickey Usilton 15, George Usilton 10, Clay Usilton 6, John Usilton 4, Mary Johnson 11
1850; Census Place: District 2, Kent, Maryland; Roll: M432 294; Page: 218B; Image: 4

CENSUS: 1860 Kent Co, MD
Sarah E Usilton 48, John Usilton 11, Clay Usilton 16, B Elliott 29, Milcka Elliott 27, Thomas W Elliott 4, L Hutchinson 17, E Johnson 14
1860; Census Place: Chestertown, Kent, Maryland; Roll: M653 477; Page: 1016; Image: 462; Family History Library Film: 803477.

Sarah E. Hatcheson and George B. Usilton were married.

410. **Mary Frances Ford** (Mary Ann Hatcheson-8, Nathan-7, Martha Miller-6, Ann Blackiston-5, William-4, Ebenezer-3, George-2, Marmaduke-1) was born on 6 Nov 1838 in Maryland. She died on 19 Oct 1919 at the age of 80 in Kent Co, Maryland. She was buried in Asbury Cem., Millington, Kent, Maryland.

CENSUS: 1860 Kent Co, MD
George W Blackiston 28 farmer 10000 RE 1000 PP born DE, Anna E Blackiston 25, Mary A Ford 54, Mary F Ford 21, William H Ford 17, John H Ford 11, John White 22, Jacob Jeffers 14
1860; Census Place: District 3, Kent, Maryland; Roll: M653 477; Page: 1030; Family History Library Film: 803477 Next door is Richard Holliday 58 and family born England. Fords also lived with S.L. Blackiston.

CENSUS: 1880 Kent Co, MD
G. W. Blackiston 46 born DE father born DE mother born MD single, Annie E. Blackiston 44 sister born DE father born DE mother born DE single, Mary F. Crouch 40 sister born DE father born DE mother born DE married, Mary E. Crouch 11 dau single
1880; Census Place: Millington, Kent, Maryland; Roll: 512; Page: 23B; Enumeration District: 048 nearby in 46-48 household is S.L. Blackiston.

DEATH: Mary Frances Crouch female widow died Oct 19, 1919 Kent Co parents Daniel Ford born MD and Mary A Hazel born Delaware. Info. Ethel C. Moffett of Millington, MD. burial at Millington.

Mary Frances Ford and Edwin Crouch Jr were married on 22 Jan 1867 in Kent County, Maryland. **Edwin Crouch Jr**, son of Edwin Crouch and Mary R. Keatting, born about 1838. He died after 1870 at the age of 32.

MARRIAGE: Edwin Crouch Jr m. Mary F. Ford on Jan. 22, 1867 by Rev. James Bryan.

CENSUS: 1870 Kent Co, MD
4-4 Edwin Crouch 28, Mary F Crouch 30 (Ford), Mary E Crouch 1, Charlotte Hall 40 cook.
5-5 Mary Ann Ford 64, Annie E Blackiston 33, Sally Ann Cook 45
Year: 1870; Census Place: Millington, Kent, Maryland; Roll: M593 590; Page: 48A

CENSUS: 1880 Kent Co, MD
G. W. Blackiston 46 Self (Head), Annie E. Blackiston 44 Sister single, Mary F. Crouch 40 Sister (maiden name Ford) married, Mary E. Crouch 11 Daughter
Year: 1880; Census Place: Millington, Kent, Maryland; Roll: 512; Page: 23B; Enumeration District: 048

CENSUS: 1900 Kent Co, MD
Anna E Blackiston 64 Head, Mary F Crouch 60 Sister, Mary E Crouch 31 Niece
Year: 1900; Census Place: Millington, Kent, Maryland; Roll: 625; Page: 2; Enumeration District: 0045

CENSUS: 1920 Kent Co, MD
Richard W Moffett 58 Head, Ethel C Moffett 50 Wife, Anna E Blackiston 84 Step Aunt, Lula Duckery 21 Servant
Year: 1920; Census Place: Masseys, Kent, Maryland; Roll: T625 673; Page: 16B; Enumeration District: 60

Edwin Crouch and Mary Frances Ford had the following child:

+542   i. **Mary Ethel Crouch**, born 1869; married Richard Wesley Moffett; died 3 Feb 1955.

411. Florence M. Rasin (William Blackiston-8, Philip Reed-7, William Blackiston-6, Rosamond Blackiston-5, William-4, Ebenezer-3, George-2, Marmaduke-1) born about 1837. Florence M. Rasin and Joseph Orsburn Rasin were married on 17 May 1854 in Kent County, Maryland. **Joseph Orsburn Rasin**, son of Cyrus B. Rasin and Wilhelmina Steen, was born on 1 Oct 1831. He died on 10 Nov 1885 at the age of 54. He was buried in Chesterfield Cem., Centreville, Queen Anne's Co, MD.

CENSUS: 1850 Kent Co 101-101 Joseph O. Rasin p. 286 Kent Co 1850 census 3rd Dist. living with Alfred Christfield and Elizabeth.

412. Sarah E. Rasin (William Blackiston-8, Philip Reed-7, William Blackiston-6, Rosamond Blackiston-5, William-4, Ebenezer-3, George-2, Marmaduke-1) born about 1840. Ms. Cooper said that Sarah E Rasin married Ferdinand Crew and had dau Ida Crew.

CENSUS: 1870 Kent Co, MD
A H Crew 38, Sarah E Crew 30, Walter W Crew 13, Daniel Crew 11, Adelia Brich 18, Ida Crew 7, Alfred Crew 3, Agnes Crew 7/12, Geo Washington 35, John Dorsey 15, Lorenzo Knock 30, John H Caster 28
1870; Census Place: District 2, Kent, Maryland; Roll M593 590; Page: 62; Image: 124.

Sarah E. Rasin and A. H. Ferdinand Crew were married on 21 Aug 1856 in Kent Co, Maryland. **A. H. Ferdinand Crew** born about 1840.

414. Sarah A. Rasin (William Blackiston-8, Philip Reed-7, William Blackiston-6, Rosamond Blackiston-5, William-4, Ebenezer-3, George-2, Marmaduke-1) born about 1846 in Maryland.

CENSUS: 1870 Kent Co, MD
Ambrose Carroll 34, Sarah A Carroll 24, Sarah A Carroll 9, William Carroll 5, Carroll 1/12
1870; Census Place: Chestertown, Kent, Maryland; Roll M593 590; Page: 169; Image: 338.

Sarah A. Rasin and Ambrose Carroll were married on 6 Jan 1861. **Ambrose Carroll** born about 1844.

417. Ann Editha Rasin (Dulany-8, Philip Reed-7, William Blackiston-6, Rosamond Blackiston-5, William-4, Ebenezer-3, George-2, Marmaduke-1) was born on 15 Oct 1845. She died on 22 Jul 1918 at the age of 72. She was buried in Chester Cem, Chestertown, Kent, Maryland. Ann Editha Rasin and Samuel Ford Cooper were married on 21 Jan 1869 in Kent County, Maryland. **Samuel Ford Cooper** was born on 6 Jul 1840. He died on 22 Jul 1922 at the age of 82. They are the Great grandparents of Carolyn Ethel Cooper 1942-2021 who wrote the William Blackiston Rasin family history and many Worton family histories. She ran the Worton Descendants Day events every year in May.

419. Emily J. Rasin (Dulany-8, Philip Reed-7, William Blackiston-6, Rosamond Blackiston-5, William-4, Ebenezer-3, George-2, Marmaduke-1) was born on 21 Aug 1849. She died on 30 Dec 1930 at the age of 81.

CENSUS: 1880 Kent Co, MD
C. R. Rasin 22, Emely J. Rasin 30 sister, C. G. Howard 20, M. C. Pearson 6
1880; Census Place: Worton, Kent, Maryland; Roll T9 512; Family History Film: 1254512; Page: 99.1000; Enumeration District: 51; Image: 0197.

CENSUS: 1900 Kent Co, MD
Franklin R Rouse 63 born Sep 1836 m 14y, Emily Rouse 50 born Aug 1849 m 14y 2 children 2 living, Thomas B Rouse 11 son, Robert F Rouse 30 son
1900; Census Place: Worton, Kent, Maryland; Roll T623 625 Page: 9B; Enumeration District: 49.

CENSUS: 1910 Kent Co, MD
Thomas R Rouse 21, Emily J Rouse 60 divorced mother
1910; Census Place: Worton, Kent, Maryland; Roll T624 566; Page: 19B; Enumeration District: 54; Image: 191.

CENSUS: 1920 Kent Co, MD
Norman P Massey 48, Anna B Massey 48, Dorothy Massey 18, Morris H Cooper 30 brother in law, Emily J Rause 70 widow aunt, Lester Bulter 33
1920; Census Place: Betterton, Kent, Maryland; Roll T625 674; Page: 5A; Enumeration District: 64; Image: 26.

CENSUS: 1930 Kent Co, MD
R Frank Rouse 61, Emily F Rouse 80 stepmother widow, Katherine Harris 56 stepsister widow, Edgar A Harris 18 step nephew
1930; Census Place: Worton, Kent, Maryland; Roll 876; Page: 6B; Enumeration District: 6; Image: 462.0.

Emily J. Rasin and Amos Parsons were married after 1880. **Amos Parsons** born about 1849 in Pa. He died on 29 Jul 1882 at the age of 33 in Kent County, Maryland.

CENSUS: 1880 Kent Co, MD
T. C. PARSONS 64 PA Farming, Elizabeth PARSONS Wife 64 PA Keeps House, Amos PARSONS Son 34 PA Works On Farm, Thomas A. PARSONS Son 31 PA Works On Farm, Annie PARSONS Dau 23 PA Assistant, Mary PARSONS Dau 21 PA Assistant
Census Place Worton, Kent, Maryland Family History Library Film 1254512 NA Film Number T9-0512 Page Number 105B

Emily J. Rasin and Frank Rouse were married on 24 Nov 1886 in Kent County, Maryland. **Frank Rouse** born about 1849.

420. Thomas Franklin Rasin (Dulany-8, Philip Reed-7, William Blackiston-6, Rosamond Blackiston-5, William-4, Ebenezer-3, George-2, Marmaduke-1) was born on 9 Apr 1851. He died in 1893 at the age of 42. He was buried at Union Meth. Epis in Worton, Kent County, Maryland. TOMBSTONE: Thomas F Rasin 1851-1893 (buried with parents) Thomas Franklin Rasin and Alice R. Jewell were married on 5 Jan 1882 in Kent County, Maryland. **Alice R. Jewell** born about 1851.

422. Medford Macall Rasin (Dulany-8, Philip Reed-7, William Blackiston-6, Rosamond Blackiston-5, William-4, Ebenezer-3, George-2, Marmaduke-1) was born on 2 Feb 1855. He died on 27 Jun 1906 at the age of 51 in Kent County, Maryland. He was buried in Chester Cem, Chestertown, Kent, Maryland. He appears to be named after a 3rd cousin McCall Medford Rasin. who was prominent in the community and served in the Legislature. Dulaney and McCall's family are buried in the same cemetery so they may have known each other and been close even though they were 3rd cousins.

DEATH: Medford M. Rasin June 27 1906 Kent Co white 52y filed under Rosin per the index.

OBITUARY: He fell overboard on boat. Kent News. Several obituaries including The Baltimore Sun Fri, Jun 29, 1906 ·Page 10

Medford Macall Rasin and Alphonsia Parks were married on 11 Jan 1882 in Kent County, Maryland. **Alphonsia Parks** born about Jun 1856 in Maryland. She died in 1933 at the age of 77.

CENSUS: 1880 Kent Co, MD
A. R. PARKS Self M 55 Farming, Annie E. PARKS Wife 60 Keeps House, Fosanie A. PARKS Dau Female W 22 MD Assistant Housekeeper, Etta PARKS Dau 21 Assistant Housekeeper
Source Information: Census Place Worton, Kent, Maryland NA Film NumberT9-0512 Page Number92D

Medford Macall Rasin and Alphonsia Parks had the following children:

+543   i.   **Merritt Gale Rasin**, born May 1884; married Luelle Hamilton Bangert; died 28 Apr 1932.

+544   ii. **Alexander Parks Rasin Sr.**, born 30 Sep 1886; married Katherine Adele Catlin; died 24 Feb 1952.

545   iii. **Mary E. Rasin** born about May 1889 in Maryland.

423. Charles Roby Rasin (Dulany-8, Philip Reed-7, William Blackiston-6, Rosamond Blackiston-5, William-4, Ebenezer-3, George-2, Marmaduke-1) was born on 2 Mar 1858. He died in 1945 at the age of 87. He was buried in Still Pond Cem, Kent County, Maryland.

mentioned in obituary of his aunt Wilhelmina as Roby one of the pallbearers who were her nephews.

CENSUS: 1880 Kent Co MD
C. R. Rasin Self 22 Farming, Emely J. Rasin Sister 30 Keeps House, C. G. HOWARD 20 Works On Farm Hand, M. C. PEARSON W 6
Source Information: Census Place Worton, Kent, Maryland Family History Library Film 1254512 NA Film Number T9-0512 Page Number 99A

Charles Roby Rasin and Rose Anna Crew were married on 4 Mar 1885 in Kent County, Maryland. **Rose Anna Crew** born about 1858. She died in 1930 at the age of 72.

424. **Perry Beck Rasin** (Dulany-8, Philip Reed-7, William Blackiston-6, Rosamond Blackiston-5, William-4, Ebenezer-3, George-2, Marmaduke-1) was born on 12 Feb 1860. He died on 15 Oct 1931 at the age of 71 in Kent County, Maryland. He was buried in Chestertown Cemetery, Chestertown, Kent County, Maryland. He was mentioned in obituary of his aunt Wilhelmina as one of the pallbearers who were her nephews. He was mentioned in the obituary of his uncle Richard Rasin as a County Commissioner and his nephew.

CENSUS: 1900 Kent Co, MD
Perry Rasin 40, Henretta Rasin 34, Henry S Rasin 8, George P Rasin 6, Joseph M Rasin 2, Aura M Bacon 61, Minnie C Jones 14, Thomas Holdson 24, Romie Holdson 22, Joseph Cottman 15
1900; Census Place: Worton, Kent, Maryland; Roll T623 625 Page: 5A; Enumeration District: 49.

CENSUS: 1910 Kent Co, MD
Percy B Rasin 50, Henrietta S Rasin 44 born MD 5ch 4 lvg, Henry S Rasin 19, George B Rasin 16, Medford M Rasin 12, Helen B Rasin 9
1910; Census Place: Worton, Kent, Maryland; Roll: T624 566; Page: 17A; Enumeration District: 0054; Image: 188; FHL microfilm: 1374579.

CENSUS: 1920 Kent Co, MD
Perry B Rasin 59, Henrietta Rasin 54 wife
1920; Census Place: Betterton, Kent, Maryland; Roll T625 674; Page: 2B; Enumeration District: 63; Image: 5.

CENSUS: 1930 Kent Co, MD
Perry Rasin 70, Henrietta Rasin 64, George B Rasin 36 son, George D Rasin 12 grandson
1930; Census Place: Worton, Kent, Maryland; Roll 876; Page: 7A; Enumeration District: 6; Image: 463.0.

Perry Beck Rasin and Henrietta Sewell were married on 2 Nov 1887 in Kent County, Maryland. **Henrietta Sewell** was born in 1866. She died in 1942 at the age of 76. She was buried in Chestertown Cemetery, Chestertown, Kent County, Maryland.

Perry Beck Rasin and Henrietta Sewell had the following children:

546	i.	**Henry Sewell Rasin** was born in 1891. He died in 1979 at the age of 88. He was buried in Chester Cem, Chestertown, Kent County, Maryland.
+547	ii.	**George Bacon Rasin Sr**, born 9 Nov 1893, Worton, Kent County, Maryland; married Hortence Liberman; died 11 Nov 1949, Kent County, Maryland.
548	iii.	**Joseph M. Rasin** born about 1898.
549	iv.	**Medford McCall Rasin** was born on 1 Apr 1898 in Kent County, Maryland. He died on 19 Oct 1988 at the age of 90 in Kent County, Maryland. He was buried in Chester Cem, Chestertown, Kent, Maryland.

427. Sarah Graves (Mary Ann Rasin-8, Philip Reed-7, William Blackiston-6, Rosamond Blackiston-5, William-4, Ebenezer-3, George-2, Marmaduke-1) was born in 1842. She died on 12 Feb 1877 at the age of 35. Sarah Graves and Arthur Toulson were married on 7 May 1868 in Kent County, Maryland. **Arthur Toulson** born about 1842.

431. William Blackiston Apsley (Sarah Matilda Rasin-8, Philip Reed-7, William Blackiston-6, Rosamond Blackiston-5, William-4, Ebenezer-3, George-2, Marmaduke-1) was born in 1838. He died on 18 Jul 1864 at the age of 26 in Snickers Gap, Virginia. He was buried in Winchester Nat., Virginia. William B. Apsley is killed at the Battle of Cool Spring, Snickers Gap on July 18 by a gunshot wound to the groin. He was buried at Reamers Farm, Berryville, Va but then later moved to Winchester National Cem. Grave #3990. Kent Co News issue Aug 6 1864 reported death. Enlisted Oct. 2 1861 in Company B, 2nd Eastern Shore MD Vol. Inf. as privates. William Blackiston Apsley and Mary Ann were married. **Mary Ann** born about 1838.

432. Philip Rasin Apsley (Sarah Matilda Rasin-8, Philip Reed-7, William Blackiston-6, Rosamond Blackiston-5, William-4, Ebenezer-3, George-2, Marmaduke-1) was born on 18 Jan 1840. He died on 3 Oct 1912 at the age of 72 in Edesville, Kent County, Maryland. Named for his grandfather Philip Rasin. Enlisted Oct. 2 1861 in Company B, 2nd Eastern Shore MD Vol. Inf. as privates.

CENSUS: 1880 Kent Co, MD
Philip APSLEY 29 Fisherman, Elizabeth APSLEY 25 Keeps House, Ruthie APSLEY 4, Mary E. APSLEY 9m,
Source Information: Census Place Piney Neck, Kent, Maryland NA Film Number T9-0512 Page Number 183D

Philip Rasin Apsley and Rachel Elizabeth Woolyhand were married on 11 Aug 1875 in Kent County, Maryland. **Rachel Elizabeth Woolyhand** was born on 9 Jan 1855 in Kent County, Maryland. She died on 12 Feb 1921 at the age of 66 in Newark, Delaware.

Philip Rasin Apsley and Rachel Elizabeth Woolyhand had the following child:

+550   i.   **Mary Emmaline Apsley**, born 10 Sep 1878; married Edward Milton Coleman, 1 Feb 1898, Kent County, Maryland; died 10 Aug 1950, Kent County, Maryland.

436. **Edward Apsley** (Sarah Matilda Rasin-8, Philip Reed-7, William Blackiston-6, Rosamond Blackiston-5, William-4, Ebenezer-3, George-2, Marmaduke-1) born about 1847. He died about Dec 1875 at the age of 28 in Piney Neck, Kent County, Maryland. OBITUARY: He died at his father's farm and was 25 in Kent Co News Dec. 18 1875 issue. Edward Apsley was married.

437. **Mary Emiline Apsley** (Sarah Matilda Rasin-8, Philip Reed-7, William Blackiston-6, Rosamond Blackiston-5, William-4, Ebenezer-3, George-2, Marmaduke-1) born about 1858. Mary Emiline Apsley and Darius Bendon were married on 1 Nov 1874 in Kent County, Maryland. **Darius Bendon** born about 1858.

441. **Clara Rasin** (Richard L.-8, Philip Reed-7, William Blackiston-6, Rosamond Blackiston-5, William-4, Ebenezer-3, George-2, Marmaduke-1) born about 1856. Clara Rasin and Robert Carter were married. **Robert Carter** born about 1856. Clara Rasin and Mr. Dorney were married.

442. **Mary E. Rasin** (Richard L.-8, Philip Reed-7, William Blackiston-6, Rosamond Blackiston-5, William-4, Ebenezer-3, George-2, Marmaduke-1) was born in Jan 1857. She died on 12 Jun 1905 at the age of 48. Mary E. Rasin and William David Carter were married on 9 Jan 1877. **William David Carter** born about 1857.

444. **Nellie Rasin** (Richard L.-8, Philip Reed-7, William Blackiston-6, Rosamond Blackiston-5, William-4, Ebenezer-3, George-2, Marmaduke-1) born about 1862. She died in 1933 at the age of 71. Nellie Rasin and William T. Jones were married on 17 Apr 1878. **William T. Jones** born about 1862.

446. **Regina Rasin** (Richard L.-8, Philip Reed-7, William Blackiston-6, Rosamond Blackiston-5, William-4, Ebenezer-3, George-2, Marmaduke-1) born about 1865. She died on 16 Apr 1936 at the age of 71. Regina Rasin and Thomas Vandyke were married about 1885. **Thomas Vandyke** born about 1865.

447. **George Richard Rasin** (Richard L.-8, Philip Reed-7, William Blackiston-6, Rosamond Blackiston-5, William-4, Ebenezer-3, George-2, Marmaduke-1) was born on 8

Feb 1867. He died on 25 Aug 1958 at the age of 91. He was buried in Still Pond Cem, Kent, Maryland. George Richard Rasin and Jane Hill were married on 24 Mar 1892. **Jane Hill** born about 1872. She died in 1956 at the age of 84. She was also known as Jennie Hill. Jane was buried in Still Pond Cem, Kent, Maryland.

448. **Gertrude Rasin** (Richard L.-8, Philip Reed-7, William Blackiston-6, Rosamond Blackiston-5, William-4, Ebenezer-3, George-2, Marmaduke-1) born about 1870. Gertrude Rasin and Quincy Marrow were married on 24 Dec 1890. **Quincy Marrow** born about 1870.

450. **William Maxwell Lynch** (Willamina Rasin-8, Philip Reed-7, William Blackiston-6, Rosamond Blackiston-5, William-4, Ebenezer-3, George-2, Marmaduke-1) was born on 11 Oct 1852 in Kent County, Maryland. He died on 10 Sep 1931 at the age of 78 in Kent County, Maryland. He was buried at Chester Cemetery in Chestertown, Kent County, Maryland.

CENSUS: 1860 Kent Co, MD In 1860 he was 8 living with his uncle Richard Rasin.

CENSUS: 1870 Kent Co, MD
In 1870 he was the William Lynch age 18 living with his uncle Richard L. Rasin 45.

William Maxwell Lynch and Sallie L. Reed were married. **Sallie L. Reed** was born on 3 Sep 1862. She died on 21 Apr 1924 at the age of 61.

William Maxwell Lynch and Sallie L. Reed had the following children:

551	i.	**Effie Lynch** was born in Jul 1883. She died in 1961 at the age of 78.
552	ii.	**Carl M. Lynch** was born in Aug 1885.
553	iii.	**Norris Lynch** was born in Oct 1886. He died on 15 Nov 1887 at the age of 1.
554	iv.	**William C. Lynch** was born on 10 Dec 1899. He died on 2 Oct 1988 at the age of 88.

451. **Margaret A. Lynch** (Willamina Rasin-8, Philip Reed-7, William Blackiston-6, Rosamond Blackiston-5, William-4, Ebenezer-3, George-2, Marmaduke-1) was born in Jan 1854 in Kent County, Maryland. She died in 1933 at the age of 79 in Kent County, MD. She was buried in Chester Cem, Chestertown, Kent, Maryland. CENSUS: Margaret Lynch age 5 living with John and Wilhelmina Crouch in 1860.

CENSUS: 1870 living with her aunt Mary Ann Graves

CENSUS: 1900 Margaret born Jan 1854 has mother Wilhelmina living with her.

Margaret A. Lynch and Joshua B. McIntire were married in 1875 in Kent County, Maryland. **Joshua B. McIntire**, son of Joshua G McIntire, was born in May 1853.

Joshua B. McIntire and Margaret A. Lynch had the following child:

> 555   i. **Joshua Webster McIntire** was born in 1878. He died in 1936 at the age of 58. He was buried in Chester Cem, Chestertown, Kent, Maryland.

452. Sarah Bennett Crouch (Willamina Rasin-8, Philip Reed-7, William Blackiston-6, Rosamond Blackiston-5, William-4, Ebenezer-3, George-2, Marmaduke-1) was born on 10 Feb 1857 in Kent County, Maryland. She died on 5 Jun 1932 at the age of 75 in Chestertown, Kent County, Maryland. She was buried in Chestertown Cemetery, Chestertown, Kent County, Maryland.

DEATH: Sarah Bennett Barnes of 531 High St. Cert. #06646 died Chestertown, Kent Co female white married husband John Barnes, born Feb. 10 1857 age 75y 3m 25d, housewife, born Maryland, parents John W. Crouch born Maryland and Wilhelmina Rasin born Maryland, infor. Miss Daisy Barnes 531 High St, burial Chester June 8, 1932 by R. Ellis Clark, 118 Front St. died June 5, 1932, seen by Dr. May 10 to June 5, died at 11am. cardiac arrest, cardiac disease, Dr. Frank B. Herne Chestertown.

OBITUARY: Mrs. Sarah Bennett Barnes, aged 75 years, died at her home on High Street, Chestertown, Sunay morning after a lingering illness. She was the daughter of the late John W. and Wilhelmina Crouch, of Rock Hall. She had been an invalid for a number of years and she became suddenly worse two weeks before her death. She has been a member of the Chestertown M. E. Church for more than fifty years. She is survived by her husband, Mr. John W. Barnes, Councilman of Chestertown from the fourth ward and former Mayor. Also six children, Mrs. Mamie Wilkinson, of Baltimore; Miss Daisy O. Barnes, at home; Messrs. Harry W. Barnes, of Philadelphia; Earnest Barnes, of Nebraska; Earl A. Barnes and John E. Barnes, of Chestertown. She is also survived by three sisters and three brothers, Mrs. J. B. McIntyre, of Chestertown; Mrs. John McIntyre, and Mrs. Harry Harkins, of Wilmington; Messrs. Daniel W. Lynch, of near Chestertown; James T. Crouch of Baltimore, and Charles W. Crouch, of Rock Hall. Funeral services will be held at the home Wed. afternoon at 3pm, Revs. Frank White, of Chestertown M.E. Church and J. Harry Wright of --- officiating. Interment was at Chester Cemetery. The bearers were her five grandchildren, John W. Wilkinson of Baltimore; Walter, Richard, Allan and William Barnes and her son-in-law Harry Wilkinson, of Baltimore. R. Ellis Clark, undertaker. Chestertown Transcript June 11, 1932 issue.

TOMBSTONE: Sarah B. Barnes 1857-1932

Sarah Bennett Crouch and John Wesley Barnes were married on 2 Jan 1878 in Kent County, Maryland. **John Wesley Barnes**, son of George Barnes and Mary Frances

Parsons, was born on 10 Jul 1856 in Baltimore, Maryland. He died on 30 Sep 1941 at the age of 85 in Chestertown, Kent County, Maryland. He was buried in Chestertown Cemetery, Chestertown, Kent County, Maryland. Mayor of Chestertown

CENSUS: 1880 Kent Co, MD
John Barnes 23, Sally B. 23, Mamy 1
15-52, 8-50 Chestertown, Cross St.

DEATH: John Wesley Barnes male white widowed 212-18-6043, residence 533 West High St, stay in this community life, born July 10, 1856 age 85y 2m 20d, born Baltimore, MD, occupation printer, newspaper, father George Barnes, Baltimore, MD, mother Mary Frances Parsons Kent Co, MD, infor. Miss Daisey O. Barnes (daughter) of Chestertown, MD burial Oct. 13, 1941 at Chester Cem. Chestertown, MD fun. dir. Marim V. Williams Chestertown, MD died Sep. 30 194 12:30a, seen by Dr. Aug. 4 to Sep. 30, 1941 artier insufficiency, due to arteriosclerosis. Dr. H. B. Simmons of Chestertown, Registrar Clara S. Barnes Oct. 2, 1941. Cert. #09095 (mother's maiden name hard to read).

OBITUARY: John W. Barnes died at age of 85 years, Was 68 years with the Transcript. John Wesley Barnes, of Chestertown, died at his home here early Tuesday morning following an illness of several weeks. he was eighty-five years of age. When a youth of sixteen years, in 1872, he started to work in the composing room of the Chestertown Transcript then owned by the late Eben Perkins. He continued an uninterrupted period of employment with this newspaper until his retirement in the spring of 1940, a period of 68 years. Since his retirement he has been in failing health. In addition to his profession as a printer, he took an active interest in lodge and town affairs. For a number of years he served as one of the three Town Commissioners a part of which time he was president of the Board. Following the change in the charter he was councilman from the Second Ward. He served as secretary of the lodge of Modern Woodman and was active in the Junior Order United American Mechanics. For a long period of years he has been a devout member of the Methodist Episcopal Church and a member of the Official Board of the Chestertown Church. Surviving him are two daughters, Mrs. Harry Wilkinson, of Baltimore, and Miss Daisy O. Barnes, at home; and three sons, Harry, of Philadelphia; Earle and John E., of Chestertown. Funeral services were held Friday afternoon, were conducted by the Rev. Paul E. Reynolds, assisted by Rev. Dr. W. P. Roberts. Interment was in Chester Cem. with Marvin V. Williams the funeral director in charge. Bearers were six grandsons, Richard, William, John E. Jr., Walter and Allen Barnes and John Wilkison. Chestertown Transcript. Oct. 4, 1941.

TOMBSTONE: John W. Barnes 1856-1941

John Wesley Barnes and Sarah Bennett Crouch had the following children:

| 556 | i. | **Mamie Barnes** was born in Nov 1879. |
| 557 | ii. | **H. W. Barnes** was born in Dec 1882. |

558   iii.   **Earl Allen Barnes** was born on 14 May 1883. He died on 17 Feb 1963 at the age of 79.

559   iv.   **Earnest Barnes** was born in Mar 1885.

560   v.   **John E. Barnes Sr.** was born in Aug 1886. He died in Dec 1954 at the age of 68.

561   vi.   **Daisy O. Barnes** was born in Dec 1888 in Kent County, Maryland. She died on 7 Jan 1957 at the age of 68 in Kent County, Maryland. She was buried in Chestertown Cemetery, Chestertown, Kent County, Maryland. She wrote notes on the family in the 1920s naming her grandparents as Wilhelmina Crouch and John W. Crouch. Wilhelmina daughter of Sallie and Philip Rasin born in Kent Co, MD. John W. son of James and Sallie Crouch. Maiden name of mother, Vanderford. First marriage name Freeman. TOMBSTONE: Daisy O. Barnes 1887-1957. OBITUARY: Newspaperwoman for more than 50 years, Daisy O. Barnes dies suddenly. (includes huge picture of Daisy).

453. **Ruth A. Crouch** (Willamina Rasin-8, Philip Reed-7, William Blackiston-6, Rosamond Blackiston-5, William-4, Ebenezer-3, George-2, Marmaduke-1) was born on 19 Nov 1859 in Kent County, Maryland. She died on 13 May 1944 at the age of 84 in Kent County, Maryland.

CENSUS: 1900 Kent Co, MD
John Mcintire 45 Head, Ruth B Mcintire 42 Wife, Lillie B Mcintire 16 Daughter
1900; Census Place: Edesville, Kent, Maryland; Roll: 625; Page: 15; Enumeration District: 0053; FHL microfilm: 1240625

CENSUS: 1910 Kent Co, MD
John W Mc Intire 50 Head, Ruth Mc Intire 46 Wife
1910; Census Place: Edesville, Kent, Maryland; Roll: T624 566; Page: 10B; Enumeration District: 0058; FHL microfilm: 1374579

CENSUS: 1920 Kent Co, MD
Clarence V Jones 27 Head, John W Mcintire 65 Servant born MD parents born Ireland, Ruth Mcintire 60 Servant
1920; Census Place: Edesville, Kent, Maryland; Roll: T625 674; Page: 12A; Enumeration District: 68

Ruth A. Crouch and John W. McIntire were married on 16 Apr 1879 in Kent County, Maryland. **John W. McIntire**, son of Joshua G McIntire, born about 1855. He died in 1924 at the age of 69. He was buried in Chester Cem, Chestertown, Kent, Maryland.

455. **James R. Lee Crouch** (Willamina Rasin-8, Philip Reed-7, William Blackiston-6, Rosamond Blackiston-5, William-4, Ebenezer-3, George-2, Marmaduke-1) was born on 19 Jul 1865 in Kent County, Maryland. He died on 24 Jul 1953 at the age of 88 in Brooklyn,

Baltimore, Maryland. He was buried at Union Meth. Epis in Worton, Kent County, Maryland. No date of death on the tombstone. Was living in Baltimore at time of death of his brother Charles.

James R. Lee Crouch and Emma L. Noblett were married. **Emma L. Noblett** was born on 12 Mar 1863 in Kent County, Maryland. She died on 2 Jul 1923 at the age of 60 in Baltimore, Maryland. She was buried at Union Meth. Epis in Worton, Kent County, Maryland.

OBITUARY: Emma L. Crouch Kent News Jul. 7, 1923 Mrs. Emma L. Crouch wife of James L. died at her late home in Baltimore after a long illness on Mon. morning. Funeral was held from her late residence Thur. at 1pm. Her remains were brought to the home of her brother where funeral services were conducted Wed. afternoon at 3pm. Interment in Union Cem. Worton.

456. **Caroline Allen Crouch** (Willamina Rasin-8, Philip Reed-7, William Blackiston-6, Rosamond Blackiston-5, William-4, Ebenezer-3, George-2, Marmaduke-1) was born in 1866 in Kent County, Maryland. She died on 27 Nov 1948 at the age of 82 in Wilmington, New Castle County, Delaware. She was buried in Lombardy Cem., Wilmington, New Castle Co, DE. She was living in Wilmington at time of death of her brother Charles W. Crouch.

CENSUS: 1880 Kent Co, MD
John W Crouch 55, Willmina 50, James R 16, Carrie 13, Charles 10.
Skinner's Neck near Rees' Corner ED 54 p. 21 5th Elec. Dist. 158-158

CENSUS: 1900 New Castle Co, DE
Harry E Harkins 32, Carrie A Harkins 29 (1871)
1900; Census Place: Wilmington Ward 3, New Castle, Delaware; Roll: T623 154; Page: 5A; Enumeration District: 9.

CENSUS: 1910 New Castle Co, DE
Harry E Hackins 45, Carrie A Hackins 38 (1872)
1910; Census Place: Wilmington Ward 3, New Castle, Delaware; Roll: T624 146; Page: 12A; Enumeration District: 0028; Image: 1206; FHL Number: 1374159.

CENSUS: 1920 New Castle Co, DE
Harry Harkins 50, Caroline Harkins 45 (1875)
1920; Census Place: Wilmington Ward 7, New Castle, Delaware; Roll: T625 203; Page: 6B; Enumeration District: 66; Image: 57.

Caroline Allen Crouch and T. Shanley were married before 1897. **T. Shanley** born about 1866.

Caroline Allen Crouch and Harry E. Harkins were married before 1900. **Harry E. Harkins** born about 1861. He died on 31 Jul 1938 at the age of 77 in Wilmington, New Castle County, Delaware. He was buried in Lombardy Cem., Wilmington, New Castle, Delaware.

457. **Charles Wesley Crouch** (Willamina Rasin-8, Philip Reed-7, William Blackiston-6, Rosamond Blackiston-5, William-4, Ebenezer-3, George-2, Marmaduke-1) was born on 21 Feb 1870 in Kent County, Maryland. He died on 18 Jul 1944 at the age of 74 in Rock Hall, Kent County, Maryland. He was buried at Wesley Chapel in Rock Hall, Kent County, Maryland.

BIRTH: Feb 1869 per death cert but 1870 census shows he was born Feb 1870. Birth certificates for MD Counties did not start until 1898.

CENSUS: 1870 Kent Co, MD
John W Crouch 46 farmer, Wilminia Crouch 40 keeping house, Sallie B Crouch 13, Ruth Crouch 10, Rachel Crouch 8, James Crouch 6, Caroline Crouch 4, Crouch 4/12 (Charles)
Year: 1870; Census Place: District 3, Kent, Maryland; Roll: M593 590; Page: 105A

CENSUS: 1880 Kent Co, MD
John W. Crouch 55 Self (Head) farmer born MD parents born MD, Wilimina Crouch 50 Wife, James R. Crouch 16 Son, Carrie Crouch 13 Daughter, Charles Crouch 10 Son ill bilious,
Year: 1880; Census Place: Edesville, Kent, Maryland; Roll: 512; Page: 163a; Enumeration District: 054

MARRIAGE: Charles W. Crouch Kent Co age 22 m. Grace F. Blackiston on Jan 12, 1891 Wesley Chapel by W.R. Stricklin rec. Jan 16. 1891.

CENSUS: 1900 Kent Co, MD
257-257-257 John J. Blackiston born Mar 1847 53y m. 29y Merchant, Julia C. wife Dec 1846 52 m. 29y 8 ch 2 lvg born MD
258-258-258 Columbis Blackiston born Feb 1876 24 m 4y born MD Oysterman
Sarah E. wife born Sept 1877 y22 m 4y 1 ch 1 lvg born MD, Edna N. dau born Aug 1897 2y;
259-259-259 Charles W Crouch b Oct 1870 age 29 m 8y oysterman , Grace F Jul 1875 age 24, m 8y 2 ch 2 lvg, Julia Nov 1891 age 8, Charles W Dec 1898 age 1.
Year: 1900; Census Place: Edesville, Kent, Maryland; Roll: 625; Page: 11; Enumeration District: 0053

CENSUS: 1910 Kent Co, MD
HSE 242-259 John J. Blackiston 63y m1 40y born MD Salesman Fert., Julia C. wife 63y m2 40y 8 ch 2 lvg
HSE 243-260 Charles W Crouch 39 m 20y born MD fisherman Gn water, Grace F 35 m1 20y, 2 ch 2 lvg, forelady factory work, Wilmer age 13. fisherman on the water.

244-261 Columbus A Blackiston 33 m 14y born MD fisherman Gn water, Sadie E. 33y m 14 4 ch 4 lvg, Edna N. 13, Noble A. 10, Ralph M. 8, Columbus W. 4.
Year: 1910; Census Place: Edesville, Kent, Maryland; Roll: T624 566; Page: 16a; Enumeration District: 0057; FHL microfilm: 1374579

CENSUS: 1920 Kent Co, MD
Charles W Crouch 51, waterman fishing born MD, Grace F 42, Bernice 6
Year: 1920; Census Place: Rock Hall, Kent, Maryland; Roll: T625 674; Page: 11B; Enumeration District: 67

CENSUS: 1930 Kent Co, MD
Charles W. Crouch owned home 1,000 age 60 m age 20 able to read/write born MD, parents born MD, waterman fishing, Grace F. wife age 54y married age 16 born MD, parents born MD, Bernice S. dau. age 16 born MD, parents born MD seamstress factory,
Year: 1930; Census Place: Edesville, Kent, Maryland; Page: 7B; Enumeration District: 0010; FHL microfilm: 2340611

CENSUS: 1940 Kent Co, MD
Charles W Crouch 71 Head waterman fishing, Grace F Crouch 64 Wife
Year: 1940; Census Place: Kent, Maryland; Roll: m-t0627-01552; Page: 20B; Enumeration District: 15-12

DEATH: Charles Wesley Crouch Rock Hall resided at Haven St 55y, wife Grace Crouch (age 69y) born Feb 21 1869 age 75y4m27d born Kent Co., MD veterinarian parents John Crouch and Wilhelmina Raison Kent Co, info. Grace Crouch, burial at Wesley Chapel, funeral director Marion Williams of Chestertown. died on Jul 18 1944 at 8:15pm #8574.

Charles W. Crouch

After an illness of less than a week Charles W. Crouch, age 76, died on Tuesday night at his late home in Rock Hall.

The deceased is survived by his widow, Mrs. Grace F. Crouch, two daughters, Mrs. Julia Bloom, two daughters, Mrs. John Bloom and Mrs. Bernice Cook, both of Baltimore, and one son, Wilmer Crouch, of Chestertown. Twelve grandchildren and fourteen great grandchildren also survive.

Funeral rites conducted by Dan S. Harris, were held at Adventist Church, Rock Hall, on Friday at 1 p. m., interment in Wesley Chapel Cemetery.

Mrs. Carrie Harkins, of Wilmington, is a sister and James L. Crouch, of Baltimore, is a brother. Marvin Williams was in charge of funeral.

OBITUARY: Charles W. Crouch. After an illness of less than a week Charles W. Crouch, age 76, died on Tuesday night at his late home in Rock Hall. The deceased is survived by his widow, Mrs. Grace F. Crouch, two daughters, Mrs. Julia Bloom and Mrs. Bernice Cook [Koch], both of Baltimore, and one son, Wilmer Crouch, of Chestertown. Twelve grandchildren and fourteen great grandchildren also survive. Funeral rites conducted by Dan. S. Harris, were held at Adventist Church, Rock Hall, on Friday at 1pm, interment in Wesley Chapel Cemetery. Mrs. Carrie Harkins, of Wilmington, is a sister and James L. Crouch, of Baltimore is a brother. Marvin Williams was in charge of funeral. Kent Co New July 20, 1944.

Charles W. Crouch

ROCK HALL, Md., July 21—(Special).—Elder Curtis Quackenbush conducted funeral services in the Seventh Day Adventist Church here at 1 o'clock this afternoon for Charles W. Crouch, 75 years old, prominent resident of this town, who died at his home here on Tuesday night, following an illness of less than a week. Interment was in Wesley Methodist Chapel Cemetery.

The deceased had been one of the leading watermen in this section of the county for many years. Besides his widow, Mrs. Grace F. Crouch, he leaves a son, Wilmer Crouch of Chestertown, and two daughters, Mrs. Julia Bloom and Mrs. Bernice Cook, both of Baltimore, also 12 grandchildren and 14 great grandchildren.

OBITUARY: The News Journal Fri, Jul 21, 1944 ·Page 9

TOMBSTONE: Charles W. Crouch 1869-1944

Charles Wesley Crouch and Grace Florence Blackiston were married on 12 Jan 1891 in Rock Hall, Kent County, Maryland. **Grace Florence Blackiston**, daughter of John Joseph Blackiston and Julia Christina Leary, was born on 27 Jul 1875 in Rock Hall, Kent County, Maryland. She was christened on 25 Dec 1875 in Rock Hall, Kent County, Maryland. She died on 3 Feb 1948 at the age of 72 in Baltimore City, Maryland. Grace was buried at Wesley Chapel in Rock Hall, Kent County, Maryland.

BAPTISM: George Florence Blackiston (sic) born July 27 1875 baptized Dec. 25, 1875 parents John J. and Julia C. Blackiston. by Rev. George Leary. Rock Hall.

CENSUS: 1880 Kent Co, MD
J.J. Blackiston 34 Self (Head) shoemaker, Julia C. Blackiston 34 Wife, Mary N. Blackiston 10 Daughter, Grace F. Blackiston 4 Daughter, Columbus Blackiston 3 Son, Edger A. Blackiston 8/12 Son (Oct), Edna A. Blackiston 8/12 Daughter (Oct), C.L. Adkinson 16 dau Year: 1880; Census Place: Rock Hall, Kent, Maryland; Roll: 512; Page: 184b; Enumeration District: 055

DEATH: Grace Crouch died Feb 3 1948 at 1:15am at 1200 Valley St Home for the Aged, age 72y6m7d born Rock Hall, MD born Jul 27 1875 parents John Blackistone Kent Co and Julia Leary Kent Co, burial at Wesley Chapel, Rock Hall, funeral director Marion Williams, cerebral hemorrhage, arteriosclerosis, E. Gill Hall MD. widow of Charles Crouch. Cert. #G59746

> **Mrs. Grace Crouch**
>
> Mrs. Grace Crouch, age 72 years, widow of the late Charles W. Crouch, of Rock Hall, died in Baltimore on Tuesday of this week. Funeral services were held at the Williams Funeral Home, Chestertown, Thursday afternoon with interment in Wesley Chapel Cemetery.

OBITUARY: Mrs. Grace Crouch age 72 years, widow of the late Charles W. Crouch, of Rock Hall, died in Baltimore on Tues. of this week. Funeral services were held at the Williams Funeral Home, Chestertown, Thurs. afternoon with interment in Wesley Chapel Cem. Feb 4 1948 Kent Co News,

TOMBSTONE: Grace Crouch 1875-1948

Charles Wesley Crouch and Grace Florence Blackiston had the following children:

+562   i. **Julia Mae Crouch**, born 7 Nov 1892, Kent County, Maryland; married Henry Harper, 1912; married Arthur Bloom, 23 Jun 1935, Wilmington, New Castle County, DE; died 12 Apr 1964, Baltimore, MD.

+563   ii. **Charles Wilmer Crouch**, born 18 Dec 1898, Kent County, Maryland; married Edith Lillian Downey; died 30 Jan 1956, Kent County, MD.

+564   iii. **Susie Bernice Crouch**, born 26 Jul 1913, Rock Hall, Kent County, Maryland; married Harry Thornton States, 27 Dec 1930, Chestertown, Kent County, Maryland; married Conrad Andrew Koch, May 1939, Baltimore City, Baltimore County Maryland USA; married Edward Smith, 5 Sep 1944, Baltimore, Maryland; died 25 Oct 1965, Baltimore City, Maryland.

466. Sarah Ann Elliott (Ann Elizabeth Rasin-8, Philip Reed-7, William Blackiston-6, Rosamond Blackiston-5, William-4, Ebenezer-3, George-2, Marmaduke-1) was born on 21 Mar 1857 in Kent County, Maryland. She died on 20 Aug 1921 at the age of 64 in Chestertown, Kent County, Maryland. She was buried in Chestertown Cemetery, Chestertown, Kent County, Maryland. Obituary of sister Wilhelmina mentions nephews Harry and Frank Ivens as pallbearers.

Harry Ivens and Morris Ivens of Philadelphia visited their mother S.A. Ivens Oct. 9 1915 Chestertown Telegraph.

Sarah Ann Elliott and John Henry Ivens were married on 25 Feb 1880 in Kent County, Maryland. **John Henry Ivens**, son of James William Ivens and Mary Ann Shakespeare, was born on 12 Oct 1856 in Pa. He died on 12 Apr 1901 at the age of 44 in Worton, Kent County, Maryland. Information on family comes from Betty Waterfield.

CENSUS: 1880 Kent Co, MD
J. H. IVENS Self 25 PA Farmer, Sarah A. IVENS Wife 23 PA Keeps House,
Mary IVENS Mother 64 ENGLAND
Census Place Worton, Kent, Maryland Family History Library Film 1254512 NA Film Number T9-0512 Page Number 105A

DEATH: John H. Ivens died at Worton, Kent Co, MD on April 15, 1901 age 45y 6m 3d native of Kent Co, MD farmer, male white married 6 children living, husband of Sarah Elliot, father Dr. James W. Ivens, mother's name Mary S. Ivens, cause of death primary abscess of the liver 11 weeks and immediate biliary poisoning, reported by John H. Hessey, MD, of Hanesville, MD

John Henry Ivens and Sarah Ann Elliott had the following children:

565	i.	**Mary Shakespeare Ivens** died in 1881. She was born on 17 Jul 1881. May have died in childbirth
566	ii.	**William Henry Ivens** was born in Apr 1883. He died in Aug 1947 at the age of 64. Called Harry mentioned in obituary of his great aunt Wilhelmina as one of her pallbearers and nephews Harry Ivens
567	iii.	**Allen Ivens** was born in Apr 1885. He died on 29 Apr 1885. twin with Frank
+568	iv.	**Frank Shakespeare Ivens**, born Apr 1885; married Grace Boyer Fogwell; died Apr 1947.
+569	v.	**Ann Elizabeth Ivens**, born 15 Sep 1886, Worton, Kent County, Maryland; married Harry Cook Coleman, bef 1917; died 30 Oct 1961, Cambridge, Dorchester County, Maryland.
+570	vi.	**Eliza Worthington Ivens**, born 10 Mar 1888; married William P. Milby; married William Henry Cole; died Feb 1971.

571   vii.   **Maurice Elliot Ivens** was born in Jan 1889. He died in 1965 at the age of 76. Called Pop-pop Bauldy by Kay Blinebury.

572   viii.   **Preston Rasin Ivens** was born on 15 Jul 1892. He died in Aug 1969 at the age of 77. Kay said he died Aug 1969 but Betty said he died Jun 1968

573   ix.   **Ida Louise Ivens** died in 1894. She was born on 18 Jan 1894. May have died in childbirth

468. John William Elliott (Ann Elizabeth Rasin-8, Philip Reed-7, William Blackiston-6, Rosamond Blackiston-5, William-4, Ebenezer-3, George-2, Marmaduke-1) was born on 28 Oct 1862. He died in 1925 at the age of 63. mentioned in obituary of his aunt Wilhelmina as one of her pallbearers. John William Elliott and Amanda Lusby were married. **Amanda Lusby** was born on 14 Feb 1864.

475. Margaret Jane Rasin (Lewis H. B.-8, Cyrus B.-7, William Blackiston-6, Rosamond Blackiston-5, William-4, Ebenezer-3, George-2, Marmaduke-1) was born on 6 Sep 1851 in Maryland. She died in 1937 at the age of 86. She was buried in Chester Cemetery, Chestertown, Kent, Maryland. She was Margaret J in 1860 census but Mary in 1870 census.

Margaret Jane Rasin and James H. Sheets were married.

476. Rachael Virginia Rasin (Lewis H. B.-8, Cyrus B.-7, William Blackiston-6, Rosamond Blackiston-5, William-4, Ebenezer-3, George-2, Marmaduke-1) was born on 10 Dec 1853 in Maryland. She died on 5 Feb 1924 at the age of 70 in Chestertown, Kent, Maryland. She was buried at Union Methodist Episcopal Cemetery in Worton, Kent, Maryland. Rachael Virginia Rasin and Noble Benjamin Gears were married. **Noble Benjamin Gears** was born on 28 Feb 1858 in Kent County, Maryland. He died on 4 Jan 1928 at the age of 69 in Worton, Kent, Maryland. He was buried in Worton Union Methodist Episcopal Church Cemetery, Worton, Kent, Maryland.

483. William Blackiston Wilmer IV (William Blackiston-8, William Blackiston-7, Blackiston-6, Rosamond Blackiston-5, Ebenezer-4, Ebenezer-3, George-2, Marmaduke-1) was born on 21 Nov 1863 in Kent County, Maryland. He died on 23 Nov 1918 at the age of 55 in Kent County, Maryland.

CENSUS: 1870 Kent Co, MD
Wm B Wilmer 52, Mary A Wilmer 49, M B Wilmer 15, M A Wilmer 17, Philip G Wilmer 11, H T Wilmer 8, Wm B Wilmer 6
1870; Census Place: District 2, Kent, Maryland; Roll: M593 590; Page: 91B; Image: 186; Family History Library Film: 552089

CENSUS: 1880 Kent Co, MD
M. Ann Wilmer 58, Alice M. Wilmer 25 dau, Mary B. Wilmer 23 dau, Philip G. Wilmer 21 son, Lina T. Wilmer 18 dau, Wm. B. Wilmer 16 son, R. Woodland servant 54

1880; Census Place: Chestertown, Kent, Maryland; Roll: 512; Family History Film: 1254512; Page: 121A; Enumeration District: 052; Image: 0241

CENSUS: 1900 Kent Co, MD
William B Wilmer 36 born Nov 1863 MD, Ada L Wilmer 33 wife born Dec 1866 5 ch 5 lvg, Leonore P Wilmer 11 born Jan 1888, Wm B Wilmer 9 born Mar 1891, Phillip G Wilmer 7 born Jan. 1893, Geraldine N Wilmer 5 born Nov 1895, Albert I Wilmer 4 born Aug 1896, Thomas Roberts 21 hand, B Willis Jones 23 hand, Emma Jones 20 hand 1900; Census Place: Kennedyville, Kent, Maryland; Roll: 625; Page: 3B; Enumeration District: 0048; FHL microfilm: 1240625

CENSUS: 1910 Chas A Jessops 36y, Wm B. Wilmer 46 widow
1910; Census Place: Pomona, Kent, Maryland; Roll: T624 566; Page: 19A; Enumeration District: 0060; FHL microfilm: 1374579

William Blackiston Wilmer IV and Ada Lenora Jessop were married.

William Blackiston Wilmer and Ada Lenora Jessop had the following child:

+574   i.   **William Blackiston Wilmer V**, born 18 Mar 1891, Kent County, Maryland; married Florence Conrath, 3 Mar 1927, Kent County, Maryland; died Feb 1966, Accomack, Virginia.

Tenth Generation

487. **James Thomas Blackiston** (Thomas Medford-9, Thomas Medford-8, Kennard-7, James-6, Ebenezer-5, John-4, John-3, George-2, Marmaduke-1) was born on 10 Aug 1860 in Kent County, Maryland. He died on 15 Sep 1928 at the age of 68 in Kent County, Maryland. He was buried in Saint Paul's Cemetery, Kent County, Maryland. DEATH: J. Thomas Blackiston near Sassafras parents Medford Blackiston and Henrietta Ringgold info. Mrs. Claude Blackiston & sister born August 10 1860 died Sep 15 1928 Kent Co, MD age 68y 1m 5d buried St. Paul's Cem. buried by Charles Dodd. James Thomas Blackiston and Florence Adelaide Keyser were married on 14 Feb 1883. **Florence Adelaide Keyser** was born on 16 Mar 1864. She died on 20 Oct 1920 at the age of 56 in Baltimore, Maryland.

493. **Mary Naomi Young Blackiston** (John Joseph-9, James Eagle-8, Joseph-7, Joseph-6, Ebenezer-5, John-4, John-3, George-2, Marmaduke-1) was born on 5 Apr 1870 in Kent County, Maryland. She was christened on 3 Sep 1870 in Rock Hall, Kent County, Maryland. She died in 1895 at the age of 25. Mary was buried in Chestertown Cemetery, Chestertown, Kent County, Maryland. 1870 census had her name as Nancy.

BAPTISM: Mary Naomi Young Blackiston born Apr 5 1870 baptized Sep 3 1870 parents John J. and Julia C. Blackiston by Rev. George Leary.

Mary Naomi Young Blackiston and Henry Landon Davies were married about 1890. **Henry Landon Davies** was born on 25 May 1858 in Gloucester County, Virginia. He died on 18 Jan 1922 at the age of 63 in Baltimore City, Maryland. He was buried in Chester Cemetery, Chestertown, Kent, Maryland. Henry Landon Davies married Mary Naomi Blackiston (~1872-1895) when she died of TB) and had one daughter, my grandmother, born in Kennedyville in 1893 - Mary Naomi Davies (died in 1961 and is buried in the Russell lot in Chestertown).

Henry Landon Davies and Mary Naomi Young Blackiston had the following child:

> +575   i. **Mary Naomi Davies**, born 22 Jan 1893; married John Waters Russell Sr; died 10 Jul 1961.

495. Grace Florence Blackiston (John Joseph-9, James Eagle-8, Joseph-7, Joseph-6, Ebenezer-5, John-4, John-3, George-2, Marmaduke-1) was born on 27 Jul 1875 in Rock Hall, Kent County, Maryland. She was christened on 25 Dec 1875 in Rock Hall, Kent County, Maryland. She died on 3 Feb 1948 at the age of 72 in Baltimore City, Maryland. Grace was buried at Wesley Chapel in Rock Hall, Kent County, Maryland.

Grace Florence Blackiston and Charles Wesley Crouch were married on 12 Jan 1891 in Rock Hall, Kent County, Maryland. **Charles Wesley Crouch**, son of John Wesley Crouch and Willamina Rasin, was born on 21 Feb 1870 in Kent County, Maryland. He died on 18 Jul 1944 at the age of 74 in Rock Hall, Kent County, Maryland. He was buried at Wesley Chapel in Rock Hall, Kent County, Maryland.

496. Columbus Augustus Blackiston (John Joseph-9, James Eagle-8, Joseph-7, Joseph-6, Ebenezer-5, John-4, John-3, George-2, Marmaduke-1) was born on 6 Feb 1877 in Kent County, Maryland. He was christened on 22 Jul 1877 in Rock Hall, Kent County, Maryland. He died on 11 Oct 1928 at the age of 51 in Kent County, Maryland. Columbus was buried in Wesley Chapel Cemetery, Kent County, Maryland.

BAPTISM: Columbus Augusta Blackiston born Feb. 6 1877 baptized July 22 1877. Parents John J. and Julia C. Blackiston baptized by Rev. George Leary.

DEATH: Columbus Augustus Blackiston died Oct. 11, 1928 born Feb 6 1877 male white age 51y 8 m 5 d born Kent Co, MD father John Joseph Blackiston born Kent co, mother Julia C. Leary born Kent Co. Information Sarah E. Blackiston. paralysis, val. heart trouble. buried Wesley Chapel Cem., by Thomas A. Casey undertaker

He had 3 sons Noble (who had all girls), Ralph (had no children) and Columbus (who had 3 girls)

Columbus Augustus Blackiston and Sarah Elizabeth Walbert were married on 29 Apr 1896. **Sarah Elizabeth Walbert** was born on 12 Aug 1877. She died on 4 Apr 1966 at the age of 88 in Crumpton, Queen Anne's, Maryland. She was buried in Wesley Chapel Cemetery, Kent County, Maryland.

Columbus Augustus Blackiston and Sarah Elizabeth Walbert had the following children:

576   i.   **Noble Abraham Blackiston** was born on 15 Sep 1900 in Rock Hall, Kent, Maryland. He died on 26 Jul 1964 at the age of 63 in Rock Hall, Maryland. Father of Jean Foreman

577   ii.   **John Harold Blackiston** was born on 1 Jul 1911 in Kent County, Maryland. He died on 20 Sep 1911 in Kent Co, Maryland. He was buried in Wesley Chapel Cem, Kent, Maryland.

501. Edith Blackiston (James Eagle-9, James Eagle-8, Joseph-7, Joseph-6, Ebenezer-5, John-4, John-3, George-2, Marmaduke-1) was born in May 1884 in Maryland. She died in 1975 at the age of 91. She was buried in Wesley Chapel, Kent County, Maryland. Edith Blackiston and E. Frank Kerr were married. **E. Frank Kerr** was born in 1880. He died in 1972 at the age of 92. He was buried in Wesley Chapel, Kent County, Maryland.

506. James Eagle Blackiston Sr (James Eagle-9, James Eagle-8, Joseph-7, Joseph-6, Ebenezer-5, John-4, John-3, George-2, Marmaduke-1) was born on 25 Mar 1896. He died on 6 Oct 1965 at the age of 69 in Baltimore City, Maryland. He was buried in Bel Air Mem. Gar, Harford, Maryland. He should be James Eagle Blackiston III but he went by the name James Eagle Blackiston Sr. James Eagle Blackiston Sr and Annabelle C Hornberger were married. **Annabelle C Hornberger** was born on 27 Aug 1890. She died in Sep 1980 at the age of 90. She was buried in Bel Air Mem. Gar, Harford, Maryland.

507. Samuel J. Blackiston (John W.-9, Samuel Lewis-8, John-7, John-6, Benjamin-5, John-4, John-3, George-2, Marmaduke-1) born about 1848 in Maryland. Samuel J. Blackiston and Josephine Elliott were married on 26 Nov 1877. **Josephine Elliott**. Samuel J. Blackiston and Lou Alridge were married on 14 Apr 1886. **Lou Alridge**.

508. John Wesley Blackiston (John W.-9, Samuel Lewis-8, John-7, John-6, Benjamin-5, John-4, John-3, George-2, Marmaduke-1) was born on 30 Jun 1850 in Kent Co, Maryland. He died on 10 Jan 1894 at the age of 43 in Wilmington, New Castle, Delaware. He was a Shoemaker.

CENSUS: 1880 New Castle Co, DE
William H. Blackiston 27 retail grocer DE parents born MD, Mary E 23 wife born DE, Elva R 1 daughter born DE, Louisa Walker 23 servant born PA, John W. Blackiston 29 brother shoemaker born DE parents born MD, Annie Blackiston 27 sister in law born MD parents born MD

1880; Census Place: Wilmington, New Castle, Delaware; Roll: 118; Page: 220C; Enumeration District: 009

John Wesley Blackiston and Susan Ann Covington were married on 21 Apr 1880 in Kent Co, Maryland. **Susan Ann Covington** was born on 26 Feb 1853 in Centreville, Queen Anne's, Maryland. She died on 25 Jan 1940 at the age of 86 in Wilmington, New Castle, Delaware.

CENSUS: 1900 New Castle Co, DE
Sarah A Blackiston 40 widowed born Feb 1860 MD 5 ch 2 lvg (should be Susan Anne), Howard C Blackiston 17 born DE father born MD mother born MD (he was born before marriage), Edna Blackiston 13 born DE father born DE mother born DE (error), Harry C Bendere 43 boarder born PA.
1900; Census Place: Wilmington Ward 3, New Castle, Delaware; Page: 4; Enumeration District: 0009; FHL microfilm: 1240154

CENSUS: 1920 New Castle Co, DE
Susan A Blackiston 59, Edna Blackiston 31
1920; Census Place: Wilmington Ward 9, New Castle, Delaware; Roll: T625 202; Page: 6A; Enumeration District: 113

Edna Blackiston Gender: Female Birth Date: 14 Mar 1887 Birth Place: New Castle, Delaware, USA Mother: Anna S Blackiston, Father: John W Blackiston

John Wesley Blackiston and Susan Ann Covington had the following children:

578	i.	**Howard Covington Blackiston** was born on 12 Sep 1882 in Wilmington, New Castle, Delaware. He died on 3 Nov 1903 at the age of 21 in Wilmington, New Castle, Delaware. He was buried in Lombardy Cem., Wilmington, New Castle, Delaware.
579	ii.	**John Leroy Blackiston** was born on 29 Sep 1884 in New Castle County, Delaware. He died on 20 Jun 1893 at the age of 8 in Wilmington, New Castle, Delaware. He was buried in Lombardy Cem., Wilmington, New Castle, Delaware. BIRTH: John LeRoy Blackiston born Sep 29 1884 Wilmington Co DE. Parents John W. Blackiston 34 born Kent Co MD, a Shoe dealer and Anna Covington age 31 born QA. Children to this family 2, 2 number by this mother.
+580	iii.	**Edna Blackiston**, born 14 Mar 1887, Wilmington, New Castle, Delaware; married Frederick William Kraiker, 1 Jun 1944, Wilmington, New Castle, Delaware; died 19 Dec 1966, Wilmington, New Castle, Delaware.
581	iv.	**Lillian Blackiston** was born on 9 Mar 1889 in Wilmington, New Castle, Delaware. She died before 1900 at the age of 11.

509. **William Holding Blackiston** (John W.-9, Samuel Lewis-8, John-7, John-6, Benjamin-5, John-4, John-3, George-2, Marmaduke-1) was born on 6 Jan 1852 in Smyrna, Delaware. He died on 4 Oct 1948 at the age of 96. He was buried in Glenwood Cem, Kent County, Delaware. His Family Bible is published in the Delaware Bible Records Vol 6 by Lu Hall. It lists marriages, births, and deaths.

BIRTH: His bible says he was christened as William Watson Blackiston. He was listed as William H. Blackiston and his middle name Holding he never used.

CENSUS: 1880 New Castle Co, DE
William H. Blackiston 27 born DE, Mary E. Blackiston 23, Elva R. Blackiston 1
1880; Census Place: Wilmington, New Castle, Delaware; Roll: 118; Page: 220C; Enumeration District: 009

CENSUS: 1900 New Castle Co, DE
William H Blackiston 47, Mary E Blackiston 42, Florence V Blackiston 17, William E Blackiston 15, James V R Blackiston 12, Helen J Blackiston 11, Mary E Blackiston 8, Anna J Blackiston 7, John W Blackiston 5
Delaware Wilmington Ward 7, New Castle, Delaware

William H. Blackiston born Jan 6 1852 - Died Oct 4, 1948 Wilmington

Daughter Elva' 1898 marriage record says parents Wm H. Blackiston and Mary E. Roberts.

William Holding Blackiston and Mary Elizabeth Roberts were married on 4 Dec 1877 in Smyrna, Delaware. **Mary Elizabeth Roberts** was born on 1 Feb 1858. She died on 10 Feb 1941 at the age of 83. She was buried in Glenwood Cem, Kent County, Delaware.

William Holding Blackiston and Mary Elizabeth Roberts had the following children:

+582   i.   **James Voshell Roberts Blackiston**, born 10 Jan 1887, Wilmington, Delaware; married Elsie May Webster, 4 Dec 1906, Wilmington, Delaware; died 1961.

+583   ii. **Elva Roberts Blackiston**, born 5 Jan 1879; married Paul Woolley Taylor, 25 Apr 1898, Wilmington, Delaware.

584   iii. **Bertha Watson Blackiston** was born on 9 Dec 1880 in Wilmington, Delaware. She died on 27 Dec 1880. She was buried on 1 Jan 1881 in Smyrna, Delaware.

+585   iv. **Florence Veshell Blackiston**, born 7 Nov 1882, Wilmington, Delaware; married Leon Wilde Crawford, 7 Nov 1911.

586   v.   **William Edgar Blackiston** was born on 3 Feb 1885 in Wilmington, Delaware.

+587   vi. **Helen Irene Blackiston**, born 25 Apr 1889, Wilmington, Delaware; married Arthur Green Webber.

588   vii.   **Albert Watson Blackiston** was born on 4 Jun 1890 in Wilmington, Delaware. He died on 27 Dec 1890.

589   viii.   **Mary Elizabeth Blackiston** was born on 20 Sep 1891 in Wilmington, Delaware. She died on 12 Jul 1911 at the age of 19.

590   ix.   **Herbert Keyler Blackiston** was born on 8 Dec 1892 in Wilmington, Delaware. He died on 5 Jul 1893.

591   x.   **O. Lee Blackiston** was born on 8 Dec 1892 in Wilmington, Delaware. He died on 12 Dec 1892.

+592   xi.   **Anna Jones Blackiston**, born 8 Dec 1892, Wilmington, Delaware; married Charles M. Poplos, 15 Apr 1922.

593   xii.   **John Wesley Blackiston** was born on 23 Jul 1894 in Wilmington, Delaware.

594   xiii.   **Gwendolyn Pyle Blackiston** was born on 18 Nov 1902 in Wilmington, Delaware. She died on 2 Jul 1905 at the age of 2.

510. **Laura J. Blackiston** (John W.-9, Samuel Lewis-8, John-7, John-6, Benjamin-5, John-4, John-3, George-2, Marmaduke-1) was born on 5 Feb 1857 in Maryland. She died on 26 Oct 1932 at the age of 75 in Wilmington, New Castle, Delaware. She was buried in Millington, Kent County, Maryland. Laura J. Blackiston and Haulsey Maston were married. **Haulsey Maston** was born in 1865. He died in 1948 at the age of 83. He was buried in Millington, Kent County, Maryland.

513. **Mary Elizabeth Blackiston** (Samuel Lewis-9, Samuel Lewis-8, John-7, John-6, Benjamin-5, John-4, John-3, George-2, Marmaduke-1) was born on 30 Jun 1861. She died on 9 Dec 1931 at the age of 70. Mary Elizabeth Blackiston and James Mallolieui were married on 3 Feb 1887. **James Mallolieui** was born on 21 Jan 1843. He died on 7 Aug 1887 at the age of 44. Mary Elizabeth Blackiston and Frank Sloane Bottomley were married about 1901. **Frank Sloane Bottomley** was born on 12 Sep 1858. He died on 19 Sep 1949 at the age of 91.

514. **Harry Maslin Stavely** (Margaret Elizabeth Hepbron-9, Martha Priscilla Maslin-8, Elizabeth Wroth-7, Priscilla Blackiston-6, Benjamin-5, John-4, John-3, George-2, Marmaduke-1) was born on 24 Nov 1863 in Kent County, Maryland. He died on 13 Jul 1947 at the age of 83 in Kent County, Maryland.

Harry Maslin Stavely and Florence Kelley Bowers were married on 17 Dec 1890. **Florence Kelley Bowers**, daughter of Thomas Lamb Bowers and Susan Amanda Kelley, was born on 12 Oct 1867 in Kent County, Maryland. She died on 10 Mar 1910 at the age of 42 in Kent County, Maryland.

Harry Maslin Stavely and Florence Kelley Bowers had the following child:

+595   i. **Susan Frances Stavely**, born 31 Jul 1901, Kent County, Maryland; married Joseph Glover Stavely, 31 Oct 1933, Emporia, Virginia; died 5 Mar 1996, Chestertown, Kent County, Maryland.

515. Bayard Cann Stavely (Margaret Elizabeth Hepbron-9, Martha Priscilla Maslin-8, Elizabeth Wroth-7, Priscilla Blackiston-6, Benjamin-5, John-4, John-3, George-2, Marmaduke-1) was born on 14 Jan 1870 in Kent County, Maryland. He died on 8 Jul 1944 at the age of 74 in Haddonfield, New Jersey.

Bayard Cann Stavely and Ada Worrell were married on 22 Apr 1897 in New Jersey. **Ada Worrell** was born on 20 Aug 1875 in Burlington County, New Jersey. She died on 20 Oct 1969 at the age of 94 in Camden County, New Jersey.

Bayard Cann Stavely and Ada Worrell had the following child:

+596   i. **Joseph Glover Stavely**, born 14 Mar 1904, Haddonfield, New Jersey; married Susan Frances Stavely, 31 Oct 1933, Emporia, Virginia; died 9 Apr 1973, Chestertown, Kent County, Maryland.

520. Dr Thomas Norval Hepburn (Sewell Stavely-9, Martha Priscilla Maslin-8, Elizabeth Wroth-7, Priscilla Blackiston-6, Benjamin-5, John-4, John-3, George-2, Marmaduke-1) was born on 18 Dec 1879 in Richmond, Virginia. He died on 20 Nov 1962 at the age of 82 in Hartford County, Connecticut.

Dr Thomas Norval Hepburn and Katherine Martha Houghton were married. **Katherine Martha Houghton** was born on 2 Feb 1878. She died on 17 Mar 1951 at the age of 73 in West Harford County, Connecticut. She was buried in Cedar Hill Cemetery, Hartford County, Connecticut.

Thomas Norval Hepburn and Katherine Matha Houghton had the following child:

597   i. **Katharine Houghton Hepburn** was born on 12 May 1907 in Hartford, Connecticut. She died on 29 Jun 2003 at the age of 96 in Old Saybrook, Connecticut. She was buried in Cedar Hill Cemetery, Hartford County, Connecticut. The Actress. Won 4 academy awards. Quote: *"The single most important thing anyone needs to know about me is that I am totally, completely the product of two damn fascinating individuals who happened to be my parents."* Hepburn broke the record receiving her 11th nomination, making her the most-nominated actress and the first female to receive three awards) 1974-75:

NEWS: Hartford Courant. Hepburn's Beneficiaries In Will: A Beach Saved, A Church Remembered July 29, 2003 By CLAUDIA VAN NES, Courant Staff Writer OLD SAYBROOK -- While most of Katharine Hepburn's estate will go to her family, the actress left money to the small Maryland church where her grandfather was a pastor and 4 pristine beachfront acres for "exclusively public purposes." Hepburn's will, written in 1992, was filed with the town's probate court Friday. She died at her waterfront home in the exclusive Fenwick section June 29. The will does not say how much her estate is worth. Her Connecticut home and New York townhouse were left to brother Robert Hepburn, sister Margaret Perry and to the families of her late brother, Richard, and late sister, Marion. The house and 13 acres with a pond in back and Long Island Sound in front should be put on the market soon, said estate co-executor Erik Hanson, Hepburn's accountant, financial consultant and friend. Hepburn also left $10,000 to Christ Church, I.U., a tiny brick church in eastern Maryland where her grandfather, Sewell Hepburn, served as a minister. For a church of only 30 parishioners, the gift is an uncommon windfall. Eleanor Noble, a cous of Hepburn's, says the money might be used to fund two projects the membership has discussed. Both ideas involve a 200-year-old white oak that used to stand in back of the 1860s Greek Revival church, listed on the National Register of Historic Places. Under one scenario, the tree would be carved into a free-standing clock tower. In another, its giant stump, still rooted in the ground, would be preserved and turned into a timeline. "You have limited funds and a limited membership," said Noble, 71, whose husband, Thomas, is the church treasurer. "You have to be careful about money." Hepburn visited Christ Church during her stays at Shepherd's Delight, her grandparents' 250-acre wheat, corn and soybean farm nearby. Over the years, she regularly sent a check for $100 or so. Hepburn hadn't been back for more than 20 years, but few were surprised she left the church money. "I would have been surprised if she didn't," said Noble. "Family was important to her." Funeral be held and she will be cremated with her ashes interred in the family plot at Cedar Hill Cemetery Association in Hartford.

521. **Dr Peregrine Wroth Jr. MD** (Peregrine-9, Thomas Granger-8, John-7, Priscilla Blackiston-6, Benjamin-5, John-4, John-3, George-2, Marmaduke-1) was born on 17 Feb 1882 in Kent County, Maryland. He died on 25 Dec 1956 at the age of 74 in Hagerstown, Washington, Maryland. He was buried at I. Upper Church Cemetery in Worton, Kent County, Maryland. He was a Medical Doctor.

TOMBSTONE: Peregrine Wroth husband of Woe Townsend born Feb 17, 1882-died Dec 25 1956

Dr Peregrine Wroth Jr. MD and Woe Townsend were married. **Woe Townsend** born about 1882.

Peregrine Wroth and Woe Townsend had the following child:

598   i.   **Peregrine Wroth III** was born on 8 Mar 1914 in Hagerstown, Washington, Maryland. He died on 24 Jan 1940 at the age of 25 in Montreal, Quebec, Canada. He was buried at I. Upper Church Cemetery in Worton, Kent County, Maryland. He died of gas asphyxiation at College in Montreal just before he was to graduate.

TOMBSTONE: Peregrine son of Peregrine and Woe. Mar 8 1914-Jan. 24 1940.

529. **Mary Florence Stevens** (John Brice-9, Henrietta Brice-8, Ann Brice-7, Judith Ann Blackiston-6, Michael-5, John-4, John-3, George-2, Marmaduke-1) was born on 21 Jun 1864 in Kent County, Maryland. Mary Florence Stevens and Frank Waxter were married on 23 Aug 1884 in Kent County, Maryland. **Frank Waxter**. Mary Florence Stevens and John Bockmen were married on 4 Sep 1907 in Kent County, Maryland. **John Bockmen**.

530. **James Frank Stevens** (John Brice-9, Henrietta Brice-8, Ann Brice-7, Judith Ann Blackiston-6, Michael-5, John-4, John-3, George-2, Marmaduke-1) was born on 18 Jan 1867 in Kent County, Maryland. James Frank Stevens and Cassie Kerr were married in May 1887. **Cassie Kerr**.

531. **Henry Brice Stevens** (John Brice-9, Henrietta Brice-8, Ann Brice-7, Judith Ann Blackiston-6, Michael-5, John-4, John-3, George-2, Marmaduke-1) was born on 24 Apr 1869 in Kent County, Maryland. He was christened on 26 May 1870 in Rock Hall, Kent County, Maryland. In the family Bible he is called Harry B. Stevens.

Henry Brice Stevens and Virgie B. Kendall were married on 16 Sep 1891 in Kent County, Maryland. **Virgie B. Kendall** died on 26 May 1907 in Kent County, Maryland. Henry Brice Stevens and Virgie B. Kendall had the following child:

599   i.   **Fannie E. Stevens** was born on 10 Oct 1897 in Kent County, Maryland.

Henry Brice Stevens and Clara Hartlover were married on 13 Sep 1907 in Kent County, Maryland. **Clara Hartlover**.

532. **Clara O. Stevens** (John Brice-9, Henrietta Brice-8, Ann Brice-7, Judith Ann Blackiston-6, Michael-5, John-4, John-3, George-2, Marmaduke-1) was born on 2 Oct 1870 in Kent County, Maryland. Clara O. Stevens and William J. Downey were married on 12 Oct 1887 in Kent County, Maryland. **William J. Downey**.

533. **Fannie E. Stevens** (John Brice-9, Henrietta Brice-8, Ann Brice-7, Judith Ann Blackiston-6, Michael-5, John-4, John-3, George-2, Marmaduke-1) was born on 23 Apr 1872 in Kent County, Maryland. Fannie E. Stevens and James F. Brown were married on 23 Apr 1889 in Kent County, Maryland. **James F. Brown** died on 16 Feb 1919.

534. **Jesse Columbus Stevens** (John Brice-9, Henrietta Brice-8, Ann Brice-7, Judith Ann Blackiston-6, Michael-5, John-4, John-3, George-2, Marmaduke-1) was born on 20 Oct 1874 in Kent County, Maryland. He was christened on 27 Apr 1880 in Rock Hall, Kent County, Maryland. Family Bible says he was born Oct. 1 1874 Jesse Columbus Stevens and Mable Stacy were married on 8 Feb 1899 in Kent County, Maryland. **Mable Stacy**.

535. **Elmer Rutherford Stevens** (John Brice-9, Henrietta Brice-8, Ann Brice-7, Judith Ann Blackiston-6, Michael-5, John-4, John-3, George-2, Marmaduke-1) was born on 22 Jun 1877 in Kent County, Maryland. He was christened on 27 Apr 1880 in Rock Hall, Kent County, Maryland. He died on 27 Aug 1907 at the age of 30 in Washington County, Maryland. He was baptized as Rutherford Ellsworth Stevens. His father's Bible record says Aug 26 1907.

DEATH: Elmer R. Stevens died age 30y on August 27 1907 Washington Co, MD

Elmer Rutherford Stevens and Ada Brenner were married on 15 Nov 1899 in Kent County, Maryland. **Ada Brenner**.

536. **Lily Elmira Stevens** (John Brice-9, Henrietta Brice-8, Ann Brice-7, Judith Ann Blackiston-6, Michael-5, John-4, John-3, George-2, Marmaduke-1) was born on 18 Nov 1878 in Kent County, Maryland. She was christened on 27 Apr 1880 in Rock Hall, Kent County, Maryland. She died on 17 Jul 1936 at the age of 57.

Lily Elmira Stevens and George R. Apsley were married on 15 Jan 1896 in Kent County, Maryland. **George R. Apsley**, son of Joseph R. Apsley and Mary Coleman, born about 1873. He died on 27 May 1931 at the age of 58.

CENSUS: 1910 Kent Co, MD
George R Apsley 36, Lillie Apsley 31, Nellie Apsley 12, Carroll Apsley 7, Mildred Apsley 4, Clara Downey 39

1910; Census Place: Edesville, Kent, Maryland; Roll: T624 566; Page: 2A; Enumeration District: 57; Image: 280.

CENSUS: 1920 Baltimore, MD
George R Atchley 46, Lily Apsley 41, Nellie Apsley 21, Carville Apsley 16, Mildred Apsley 14
1920;Census Place: Baltimore Ward 15, Baltimore (Independent City), Maryland; Roll: T625 664; Page: 20B; Enumeration District: 257; Image: 712.

CENSUS: 1930 Wicomico Co, MD
George R Apsley 58, Lillie Apsley 51
1930; Census Place: Salisbury, Wicomico, Maryland; Roll: 882; Page: 4B; Enumeration District: 8; Image: 60.0.

538. **Mary Emily Stevens** (Martha Louisa Stevens-9, Henrietta Brice-8, Ann Brice-7, Judith Ann Blackiston-6, Michael-5, John-4, John-3, George-2, Marmaduke-1) was born on 26 May 1850. She died on 28 Dec 1941 at the age of 91. She was buried at Loudon Park Cemetery in Catonsville, Baltimore County, Maryland.

Mary Emily Stevens and James W. Tracy were married on 15 Sep 1867. **James W. Tracy**, son of Gilson C. Tracy and Jane Wilson, was born in 1846. He died on 22 Nov 1892 at the age of 46. He was buried at Loudon Park Cemetery in Catonsville, Baltimore County, Maryland. Death Cert. says cause of death struck and run over by #214 locomotive and train on B&P RR tracks near Garrison Lane, Served as pvt in Union Army 11/12/1861 until 11/14/1864 and 2/10/1865-June 15, 1965, WIA/POW Front Royal, VA. Was a methodist and a stonemason 1867-92

542. **Mary Ethel Crouch** (Mary Frances Ford-9, Mary Ann Hatcheson-8, Nathan-7, Martha Miller-6, Ann Blackiston-5, William-4, Ebenezer-3, George-2, Marmaduke-1) was born in 1869. She died on 3 Feb 1955 at the age of 86. She was buried in Asbury Cem., Millington, Kent, Maryland.

Mary Ethel Crouch and Richard Wesley Moffett were married. **Richard Wesley Moffett**, son of Richard Frisby Moffett and Sarah Ann Melvin , was born on 1 Sep 1861. He died on 25 Feb 1925 at the age of 63. He was buried in Asbury Cem., Millington, Kent, Maryland.

CENSUS: 1870 Kent Co, MD
Richard F Moffett 43, Sarah A Moffett 39, Anna Moffett 11, Richard W Moffett 8, Samuel E Moffett 4, Walter M Moffett 2
Year: 1870; Census Place: District 1, Kent, Maryland; Roll: M593 590; Page: 12B

543. **Merritt Gale Rasin** (Medford Macall-9, Dulany-8, Philip Reed-7, William Blackiston-6, Rosamond Blackiston-5, William-4, Ebenezer-3, George-2, Marmaduke-1)

was born in May 1884. He died on 28 Apr 1932 at the age of 47. He was buried in Green Mount Cemetery, Baltimore City, Md. Middle name came from granddaughter. Merritt Ras of Baltimore visited his brother A. Parks Rasin per Oct. 2 1915 Chestertown Telegraph issue.

Merritt Gale Rasin and Luelle Hamilton Bangert were married. **Luelle Hamilton Bangert** was born on 5 Mar 1890. She died on 7 Nov 1921 at the age of 31. She was buried in Green Mount Cemetery, Baltimore City, Md. From descendant, wife was Luelle Hamilton Bangert, born March 5, 1890 in Baltimore City, Maryland and died November 7, 1921 at Enoch Pratt Hospital, Baltimore City, Maryland. She was the daughter of Daniel L Bangert and Fannie D. Hamilton.

Merritt Gale Rasin and Luelle Hamilton Bangert had the following child:

600   i. **Merritt Gale Rasin Jr.** was born on 20 Nov 1911. He died on 24 Mar 1974 at the age of 62. He was buried in Fort Lyon Nat. Cem., Bent County, Colorado. Master Sgt US Air Force Plot D Lot 16 J buried 3/27/1974.

544. Alexander Parks Rasin Sr. (Medford Macall-9, Dulany-8, Philip Reed-7, William Blackiston-6, Rosamond Blackiston-5, William-4, Ebenezer-3, George-2, Marmaduke-1) was born on 30 Sep 1886. He died on 24 Feb 1952 at the age of 65. He was buried in Chester Cem, Chestertown, Kent, Maryland.

Alexander Parks Rasin Sr. and Katherine Adele Catlin were married. **Katherine Adele Catlin** was born in 1885. She died in 1983 at the age of 98 in Ridgewood, Bergen Co, NJ. She was buried in Chester Cem, Chestertown, Kent, Maryland.

Alexander Parks Rasin and Katherine Adele Catlin had the following children:

601   i. **Margaret E. Rasin** was born 29 Jun 1910. Died 23 Jan 1978 NY.
+602   ii. **Alexander Parks Rasin Jr.**, born 9 Sep 1911; married Henrietta Bowen; died 29 Aug 1975.
603   iii. **Lucille Rasin** was born 27 Sep 1913. Died 27 Dec 1999 NJ. She married Peter Gray Meek.

547. George Bacon Rasin Sr (Perry Beck-9, Dulany-8, Philip Reed-7, William Blackiston-6, Rosamond Blackiston-5, William-4, Ebenezer-3, George-2, Marmaduke-1) was born on 9 Nov 1893 in Worton, Kent County, Maryland. He died on 11 Nov 1949 at the age of 56 in Kent County, Maryland. George B Rasin County: Kent State: Maryland Birthplace: Maryland; of America Birth Date: 9 Nov 1893 Race: Caucasian (White) FHL Roll Number: 1684374 DraftBoard: 0

CENSUS: 1920 Kent Co, MD
George B Rasin 26, Hortence Rasin 25, George B Rasin 2 9/12
1920; Census Place: Betterton, Kent, Maryland; Roll: T625 674; Page: 5B; Enumeration District: 64; Image: 31.

CENSUS: 1930 Kent Co, MD
Perry Rasin 70, Henrietta Rasin 64, George B Rasin 36 son widowed, George D Rasin 12 grandson
1930; Census Place: Worton, Kent, Maryland; Roll 876; Page: 7A; Enumeration District: 6; Image: 463.0.

George Bacon Rasin Sr and Hortence Liberman were married. **Hortence Liberman.**

George Bacon Rasin and Hortence Liberman had the following child:

+604   i.   **Judge George Bacon Rasin Jr**, born 28 May 1917; married Eleanor Brown; died 23 Dec 2011, Kent County, Maryland.

550. **Mary Emmaline Apsley** (Philip Rasin-9, Sarah Matilda Rasin-8, Philip Reed-7, William Blackiston-6, Rosamond Blackiston-5, William-4, Ebenezer-3, George-2, Marmaduke-1) was born on 10 Sep 1878. She died on 10 Aug 1950 at the age of 71 in Kent County, Maryland. She was buried in Wesley Chapel, Kent County, Maryland.

Mary Emmaline Apsley and Edward Milton Coleman were married on 1 Feb 1898 in Kent County, Maryland. **Edward Milton Coleman**, son of William Coleman and Jane Frances Benton, born about 1873.

Edward Milton Coleman and Mary Emmaline Apsley had the following child:

+605   i.   **Madison Rasin Coleman**, born 3 Dec 1899, Kent County, Maryland; married Helen Beatrice Bennett, 30 Dec 1920, Kent County, Maryland; died 31 May 1965, Kent County, Maryland.

562. **Julia Mae Crouch** (Charles Wesley-9, Willamina Rasin-8, Philip Reed-7, William Blackiston-6, Rosamond Blackiston-5, William-4, Ebenezer-3, George-2, Marmaduke-1) was born on 7 Nov 1892 in Kent County, Maryland. She died on 12 Apr 1964 at the age of 71 in Baltimore, MD. She was buried at Meadowridge Memorial Park, Baltimore, MD.

CENSUS: 1930 Baltimore City, MD
Henry N Harper 41 Head, Julia M Harper 36 Wife, Earl Harper 18 Son, Dolores Harper 15 Daughter, Doris Harper 14 Daughter, Eileen Harper 10 Daughter, Fern Harper 6 Daughter, Audrey Harper 5 Daughter, Gordon Harper 3 Son, Ida Adreon 15 Adopted Daughter, George Fields 8 Adopted Son, Alexander Roberts 19 Boarder

1930; Census Place: Baltimore, Baltimore City, Maryland; Page: 2B; Enumeration District: 0365; FHL microfilm: 2340600

CENSUS: 1940 Baltimore City, MD
Julia Bloom 47 Head, Author Bloom 34 Husband, Earl W Harper 27 Stepson (Step Son), Audrey Harper 15 Stepdaughter (Step Daughter), Elaine Hawey 25 Lodger, Gordom Hopper 13 Stepson (Step Son)
1940; Census Place: Baltimore, Baltimore City, Maryland; Roll: m-t0627-01535; Page: 8A; Enumeration District: 4-669

MARRIAGE: Julia M. Harper [Julia M. Crouch] Gender: Female Age: 42 Birth Date: abt 1893 widowed born MD Marriage Date: 23 Jun 1935 Marriage Place: Wilmington, New Castle, Delaware, USA Father: Charles Crouch Mother: Grace Crouch Spouse: Arthur Bloom age 29 born MD Saloon Keeper son of Adolph Bloom and Rose Bloom born Russia his first marriage, her second marriage Film Number: 002025106

SSA: Mrs Julia Harper [Mrs Julia Crouch] Gender: Female Race: White Birth Date: 7 Nov 1892 Birth Place: Rock Hall, Maryland Father: Charles Crouch Mother: Grace Blackiston SSN: 215244758

OBITUARY: Bloom. On April 12, 1964, Julia Mae (nee Crouch), of 4415 Washington Blvd, Halethorpe, beloved wife of Arthur Bloom, devoted mother of George W. Fields, Gordon Harper, Mrs. Doris Yates, Mrs. Eileen Marsh, Mrs. Audrey White, Mrs. Fern White and devoted sister of Mrs. Bernice Crouch [Chestertown (Md.) papers please copy] Services at her home, 4415 Washington Boulevard, on Thursday at 11 A.M. Interment in Meadowridge Memorial Park. The Evening Sun Thu, Apr 16, 1964 ·Page 83

Julia Mae Crouch and Henry Harper were married about 1912. **Henry Harper** was born on 23 Oct 1886. He died on 19 Nov 1944 at the age of 58.

Julia Mae Crouch and Arthur Bloom were married on 23 Jun 1935 in Wilmington, New Castle County, Delaware. **Arthur Bloom** was born on 19 Jun 1906. He died on 10 May 1974 at the age of 67.

563. **Charles Wilmer Crouch** (Charles Wesley-9, Willamina Rasin-8, Philip Reed-7, William Blackiston-6, Rosamond Blackiston-5, William-4, Ebenezer-3, George-2, Marmaduke-1) was born on 18 Dec 1898 in Kent County, Maryland. He died on 30 Jan 1956 at the age of 57 in Kent County, Maryland. He was buried at Wesley Chapel in Rock Hall, Kent County, Maryland. Charles had a son Charles who had no biological children.

CENSUS: 1930 Kent Co, MD
Charles W. Crouch age 31y male 21y born MD parents MD waterman fishing, Edith L. wife age 28 m18 born MD parents MD, Grace E. dau. age 9 9/12 born MD, Nellie M. dau. age 8 2/12, Mary L. dau. 6 7/12, Charles H. 1 7/12

172-173 Haven, Kent Co, MD Election District 5 Edesville, p7b

TOMBSTONE: Charles Wilmer Crouch Dec. 18, 1898-Jan. 30, 1956

Charles Wilmer Crouch and Edith Lillian Downey were married. **Edith Lillian Downey** was born on 5 Feb 1901 in Calvert Co, Maryland. She died on 28 May 1980 at the age of 79 in Baltimore City, Md.

Charles Wilmer Crouch and Edith Lillian Downey had the following child:

606   i. **Charles Harten Crouch** was born on 18 Dec 1928 in Rock Hall, Kent County, Maryland. He died on 5 Jan 2015 at the age of 86 in Kingwood, West Virginia. OBITUARY: KINGWOOD - Charles Harten Crouch, 86, of Kingwood, WV, passed away Monday, January 5, 2015 at Preston Memorial Hospital in Kingwood. Charles was born in Kent County, MD on December 18, 1928, a son of the late Edith and Charles Crouch. He was a veteran of WWII. He is survived by his wife Helen (Smith) Crouch; two sons, Jake Thornton of Bruceton Mills and Paul Cramer of Kingwood and many other loved ones. Friends may call at the Field Funeral Home in Masontown on Thursday, January 8 from 5 p.m. until the 8 p.m. service time with Pastor Lewis Beachy officiating. Private interment will follow at a later date. Condolences may be extended to the family online at www.fieldfuneralhome.com.

564. **Susie Bernice Crouch** (Charles Wesley-9, Willamina Rasin-8, Philip Reed-7, William Blackiston-6, Rosamond Blackiston-5, William-4, Ebenezer-3, George-2, Marmaduke-1) was born on 26 Jul 1913 in Rock Hall, Kent County, Maryland. She died on 25 Oct 1965 at the age of 52 in Baltimore City, Maryland. She was buried in Baltimore National Cem, Catonsville, Baltimore County, Maryland. She went by the name Bernice. She moved to Baltimore in 1943. She was called Bernice Cook in the obituary of her father. Her second husband was Conrad Koch but they used the English version of the name Cook too. During World War II she worked in the factories as a "Rosie the Riveter". She is buried in the Veterans Cemetery with her 3rd husband Ed Smith.

BIRTH: Susie Bernice Crouch born July 26, 1913 Rock Hall, Kent Co, white female, 3rd child parents Charles W Crouch waterman born MD age 43 and Grace F. Blackiston housewife born MD age 38. Dr. W.H. Schwatka MD of Rock Hall.

CENSUS: 1920 Kent Co, MD
Charles W Crouch 51 Head born MD parents born MD waterman fishing, Grace F Crouch 42 Wife, Bernice Crouch 6 Daughter
Year: 1920; Census Place: Rock Hall, Kent, Maryland; Roll: T625 674; Page: 11B; Enumeration District: 67

CENSUS: 1930 Kent Co, MD
Charles W Crouch 60 Head m 20y old, born MD parents born MD waterman fishing Owns home $1000, Grace F Crouch 54 Wife m 16y old born MD parents born MD, Bernice T Crouch 16 Daughter Seamstress in factory
Year: 1930; Census Place: Edesville, Kent, Maryland; Page: 7B; Enumeration District: 0010; FHL microfilm: 2340611

MARRIAGE: 1st Marriage likely in May 1939 in Baltimore City
MARRIAGE: News Article. Licenses Koch-States. Conrad 22; Bernice, 25, Brooklyn, MD. The Evening Sun Thu, May 18, 1939 ·Page 10

CENSUS: 1940 Anne Arundel Co, MD
Conrad A Koch 23 Head was at same place in 1935 sheet metal worker, Lyon and Conklin Comp., Bernice S Koch 26 Wife was in Baltimore in 1935, Lula G States 9 Stepdaughter (Step Daughter) was in Rock Hall Kent in 1935
live nearby Frank Tolodziecki 35 and family.
Year: 1940; Census Place: Glen Burnie, Anne Arundel, Maryland; Roll: m-t0627-01502; Page: 41B; Enumeration District: 2-29A

MARRIAGE: 2nd marriage to Edward Smith 28 born MD soldier single 18 W. Lee St. m. Bernice Crouch 31 born MD defense worker divorced on Sep. 5, 1944 by J.P. Dawson Jr. p. 519.

DEATH: Bernice Crouch Smith date of death Oct 25 1965 4am died at Balto City Hospital, resided at 914 S. Charles St. born 1914 waitress, father Charles Crouch and mother Grace O'Leary (wrong should be Blackiston) SSA 218-14-6329, carcinoma of cervix, I C III, urinary tract infection, staff physician William B. Cutts, MD burial at Baltimore National Cem. funeral director John F. Denny Inc. info. Bernard Barnhouser. Cert. #11001 (mother's name should be Grace Blackiston, Leary was her grandmother's maiden name.)

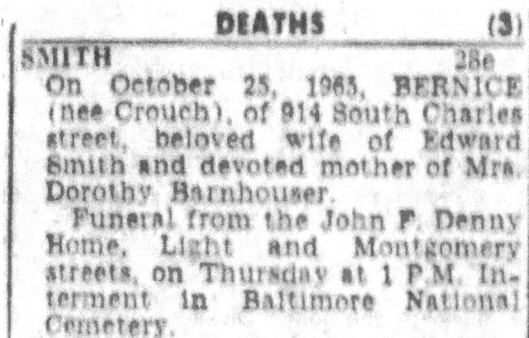

DEATHS (3)

SMITH 28e
On October 25, 1965, BERNICE (nee Crouch), of 914 South Charles street, beloved wife of Edward Smith and devoted mother of Mrs. Dorothy Barnhouser.
Funeral from the John F. Denny Home, Light and Montgomery streets, on Thursday at 1 P.M. Interment in Baltimore National Cemetery.

OBITUARY: On Oct, 25 1965 Bernice Smith (nee Crouch) at 914 S. Charles St, beloved wife of Edward Smith and devoted mother of Mrs. Dorothy Barnhouser. funeral from the

John F. Denny Home, Light and Montgomery street on Thurs at 1pm, interment in Baltimore National Cem. Oct. 27 1965 The Evening Sun,

TOMBSTONE: His wife Bernice Smith July 26, 1913-Oct. 25, 1965 Buried in Baltimore National cemetery with 2nd husband Edward Smith, Veteran, in Lot #H756.

Susie Bernice Crouch and Harry Thornton States were married on 27 Dec 1930 in Chestertown, Kent County, Maryland. They were divorced. **Harry Thornton States**, son of George Washington States and Lula Kirby, was born on 8 Jun 1910 in Queen Annes County, Maryland. He died on 27 Mar 1985 at the age of 74 in Chestertown, Kent County, Maryland. He was buried in Chestertown Cemetery, Chestertown, Kent County, Maryland.

BIRTH: Birth certificate of his daughter says he was born in Q.A. Co but SSA says Cambridge, MD.

MARRIAGE: 1st Harry T. States residence Kent Co age 21y single m. Bernice T. Crouch age 18y white single on Dec 27 1930 Chestertown, by E.A. Sexsmith recorded Dec 29.

MARRIAGE: 2nd Harry Thornton States 29 divorced resided Warwick MD married Myra Annabelle Parsons of Chestertown by W P Roberts on Feb 19 1940.

SSA: Harry States 217-30-8136 born Jun 8 1910 Cambridge and died Mar 1985 Kent Co

DEATH: Harry Thornton States died March 27, 1985 at 4:19a, male white born June 8, 1910 age 74 years, born Maryland, married, died in Chestertown, Kent Co at Kent & Queen Annes Hosp. farmer retired. resided at Worton, Kent Co address RR #1, Box 35 21678. father George W. States, mother Lula Kirby, SSA 217-36-8136. informant Annabelle States of RT #1 box 35, Worton, MD 21678. died of cardiac arrest, and arteriosclerotic heart disease, other factors invasive adenoma of prostate, diabetes mellitus. seen from 3/24 to 3/27. Dr. Kin Kue Wun of 216 High St. Chestertown. burial at Chester Cem. Chestertown. funeral director J. Willis Wells. Kent Co. Certificate #85-08742 (098172)

Harry T. States

Harry T. States of Worton died Wednesday, March 27, at Kent and Queen Anne's Hospital of natural causes. He was 74.

Mr. States retired from farming 10 years ago. He was the son of the late George W. and Lula Kirby States.

He is survived by his wife, Annabelle P. States; a brother, John States, Barclay; and three sisters, Emily Sanders, Baltimore; Lula Meekins and Clara Crew, both of Chestertown.

Funeral services were 1 p.m. Saturday at Willis Wells Funeral Home, Chestertown.

Bearers were Butch Crew, David Crew, Albert Parsons, Willie Parsons, Edwin Sanders and Richard Wheat.

Interment was in Chester Cemetery.

OBITUARY: Harry T. States of Worton died Wed. Mar. 27 at Kent and Queen Annes Hospital of natural causes. He was 74. Mr. States retired from farming 10 years ago. He was the son of the late George W and Lula Kirby States. He is survived by his wife, Annabell P. States, a brother John States, Barclay; and three sisters, Emily Sanders, Baltimore; Lula Meekings and Clara Crew, both of Chestertown. Funeral services were 1pm Sat. at Willis Wells Funeral Home, Chestertown. Bearers were Butch Crew, David Crew, Albert Parson, Willie Parson, Edwin Sanders and Richard Wheat. Interment was in Chester Cem. Apr 13 1985 Kent Co News.

TOMBSTONE: Harry T. States 1910-1985

Harry Thornton States and Susie Bernice Crouch had the following child:

+607   i. **Lula Grace "Dottie" States**, born 16 Apr 1931, Rock Hall, Kent County, Maryland; married Bernard Alfred Barnhouser Sr., 26 Jun 1948, Baltimore City, Maryland; died 11 Nov 1978, Baltimore City, Maryland.

Susie Bernice Crouch and Conrad Andrew Koch were married in May 1939 in Baltimore City, Baltimore County Maryland USA. They were divorced. **Conrad Andrew Koch** was born on 7 Feb 1916. He died on 14 Nov 1994 at the age of 78. He was also known as Conrad Andrew Cook. Conrad was buried in Glen Haven Cemetery, Glen Burnie, Anne Arundel, Maryland.

WWII Draft Card: Conrad Andrew Koch Race White Age 23 Relationship to Draftee Self (Head), Birth Date 7 Feb 1917 Birth Place Baltimore, Maryland, USA Residence Place Baltimore, Maryland, USA Registration Date 16 Oct 1940 Registration Place Baltimore, Maryland, USA Employer Rustless Iron and Steel Co Height 5 9 Weight 170 Complexion Light Hair Color Brown Eye Color Brown Next of Kin Bernice J Koch

Conrad Koch Gender Male Age 73 Birth Date abt 1917 Residence Place Brooklyn Park Marriage Date Abt 1990 Spouse Audrey Gibula

Susie Bernice Crouch and Edward Smith were married on 5 Sep 1944 in Baltimore, Maryland. **Edward Smith** was born on 22 Aug 1916. He died on 17 Jun 1970 at the age of 53 in Baltimore, Maryland. He was buried in Baltimore National Cem, Catonsville, Baltimore County, Maryland.

MARRIAGE: Edward Smith 28 born MD soldier single 18 W. Lee St. m. Bernice Crouch 31 born MD defense worker divorced on Sep. 5, 1944 by J.P. Dawson Jr. p. 519.

SSA: Social Security Edward Smith died June 1970 born 22 Aug 1916 SSA 217-14-7713.

OBITUARY: Smith. On June 17 1970, Edward, formerly of 914 South Charles street, beloved husband of the late Bernice Crouch Smith and devoted father of Mrs. Dottie L. Barnhauser and brother of Mrs. Frances Cougnet. Funeral from the John F. Denny Home, Light and Montgomery streets, on Friday at 1 P.M. Interment in Baltimore National Cemetery. The Evening Sun Fri, Jun 19, 1970 ·Page 45

TOMBSTONE: Edward Smith Maryland PFC 1386 Base Unit AAF World War II August 22, 1916-June 17, 1970.

His sister's SSA record names parents as John Smith and Frances Sliveck. SSA: Frances Sophie Grimm [Frances Sophie Cougnet] [Frances Cougnet] [Frances Sophie Smith] Gender Female Race White Birth Date 26 Aug 1912 Birth Place Baltimore, Maryland[Balto, Maryland] Death Date 10 May 1988 Father John Smith Mother Frances Sliveck SSN 215019732

568. **Frank Shakespeare Ivens** (Sarah Ann Elliott-9, Ann Elizabeth Rasin-8, Philip Reed-7, William Blackiston-6, Rosamond Blackiston-5, William-4, Ebenezer-3, George-2, Marmaduke-1) was born in Apr 1885. He died in Apr 1947 at the age of 62. mentioned in obituary of his great aunt Wilhelmina as one of her pallbearers and nephews. Frank Shakespeare Ivens and Grace Boyer Fogwell were married.

569. **Ann Elizabeth Ivens** (Sarah Ann Elliott-9, Ann Elizabeth Rasin-8, Philip Reed-7, William Blackiston-6, Rosamond Blackiston-5, William-4, Ebenezer-3, George-2, Marmaduke-1) was born on 15 Sep 1886 in Worton, Kent County, Maryland. She died on 30 Oct 1961 at the age of 75 in Cambridge, Dorchester County, Maryland. She was buried in Chester Cemetery, Chestertown, Kent County, Maryland. nickname Tom

Ann Elizabeth Ivens and Harry Cook Coleman were married before 1917. **Harry Cook Coleman**, son of William Bowers Coleman and Anna Macher Erdman, was born on 24 Sep 1885 in Kent County, Maryland. He died on 1 Sep 1970 at the age of 84 in Kent

County, Maryland. He was buried at Chester Cemetery in Chestertown, Kent County, Maryland.

Harry Cook Coleman and Ann Elizabeth Ivens had the following child:

+608   i. **Anna Cook Coleman**, born 21 Jul 1909, Kent County, Maryland; married William Barnaby Willis Jr., 22 Oct 1929, Kent Co, MD; died 9 Jan 1995, Kent County, Maryland.

570. **Eliza Worthington Ivens** (Sarah Ann Elliott-9, Ann Elizabeth Rasin-8, Philip Reed-7, William Blackiston-6, Rosamond Blackiston-5, William-4, Ebenezer-3, George-2, Marmaduke-1) was born on 10 Mar 1888. She died in Feb 1971 at the age of 82.

Eliza Worthington Ivens and William P. Milby were married. **William P. Milby** born about 1888. He died in 1915 at the age of 27.

Eliza Worthington Ivens and William Henry Cole were married. **William Henry Cole** born about 1888.

574. **William Blackiston Wilmer V** (William Blackiston-9, William Blackiston-8, William Blackiston-7, Blackiston-6, Rosamond Blackiston-5, Ebenezer-4, Ebenezer-3, George-2, Marmaduke-1) was born on 18 Mar 1891 in Kent County, Maryland. He died in Feb 1966 at the age of 74 in Accomack, Virginia.

CENSUS: 1900 Kent Co, MD
William B Wilmer 36 born Nov 1863 MD, Ada L Wilmer 33 wife born Dec 1866 5 ch 5 lvg, Leonore P Wilmer 11 born Jan 1888, Wm B Wilmer 9 born Mar 1891
 Phillip G Wilmer 7 born Jan. 1893, Geraldine N Wilmer 5 born Nov 1895, Albert I Wilmer 4 born Aug 1896, Thomas Roberts 21 hand, B Willis Jones 23 hand, Emma Jones 20 hand 1900; Census Place: Kennedyville, Kent, Maryland; Roll: 625; Page: 3B; Enumeration District: 0048; FHL microfilm: 1240625

CENSUS: 1930 Kent Co, MD
William B Wilmer 39, Florence Wilmer 31, William B Wilmer 2
1930; Census Place: Chestertown, Kent, Maryland; Roll: 876; Page: 22A; Enumeration District: 0007; Image: 525.0; FHL microfilm: 2340611

CENSUS: 1940 Baltimore City, MD
William Wilmer 49, Florence Wilmer 41, Page Wilmer 12, William Wilmer 7, Henrietta Bissell 67
1940; Census Place: Baltimore, Baltimore City, Maryland; Roll: T627 1541; Page: 9B; Enumeration District: 4-846

WWII: Draft Card William Blackiston Wilmer Birth Date: 18 Mar 1891 Birth Place: Kent, Maryland, USA Residence: Kent, Maryland, USA

William Wilmer SSN: 218-12-8544 Last Residence: 23367 Hallwood, Accomack, Virginia, USA BORN: 18 Mar 1891 Died: Feb 1966

William Blackiston Wilmer V and Florence Conrath were married on 3 Mar 1927 in Kent County, Maryland. **Florence Conrath**.

William Blackiston Wilmer and Florence Conrath had the following child:

+609   i. **William Blackiston Wilmer VI**, born 12 Mar 1928, Baltimore County, Maryland; died 28 Mar 2011, Park Springs, Georgia. William Blackiston Wilmer VI Birth Date: 12 Mar 1928 Birth Place: Baltimore, Baltimore County, Maryland, USA Death Date: 28 Mar 2011 Death Place: Georgia, USA Cemetery: Saint Pauls Kent Churchyard Burial Place: Chestertown, Kent County, Maryland, USA

Eleventh Generation

575. **Mary Naomi Davies** (Mary Naomi Young Blackiston-10, John Joseph-9, James Eagle-8, Joseph-7, Joseph-6, Ebenezer-5, John-4, John-3, George-2, Marmaduke-1) was born on 22 Jan 1893. She died on 10 Jul 1961 at the age of 68. MARRIAGE: Russell-Davies. Mr. J. Waters Russell of Chestertown, MD and Miss Mary Naomi Davies, daughter of Mr. and Mrs. H.L. Davies, were married yesterday afternoon at the home of the bride's parents, 618 N Fulton Ave. The ceremony was performed by the Rev. H.A. Griesemer, pastor of Franklin Square Baptist Church. Following a reception, Mr. and Mrs. Russell left for a Northern Trip. The Baltimore Sun Aug 25 1916. Mary Naomi Davies and John Waters Russell Sr were married. **John Waters Russell Sr** was born on 26 Mar 1879. He died on 3 Jun 1930 at the age of 51.

580. **Edna Blackiston** (John Wesley-10, John W.-9, Samuel Lewis-8, John-7, John-6, Benjamin-5, John-4, John-3, George-2, Marmaduke-1) was born on 14 Mar 1887 in Wilmington, New Castle, Delaware. She died on 19 Dec 1966 at the age of 79 in Wilmington, New Castle, Delaware. Edna Blackiston and Frederick William Kraiker were married on 1 Jun 1944 in Wilmington, New Castle, Delaware. **Frederick William Kraiker** was born on 11 Oct 1874 in Philadelphia, Pennsylvania.

582. **James Voshell Roberts Blackiston** (William Holding-10, John W.-9, Samuel Lewis-8, John-7, John-6, Benjamin-5, John-4, John-3, George-2, Marmaduke-1) was born on 10 Jan 1887 in Wilmington, Delaware. He died in 1961 at the age of 74. James Voshell Roberts Blackiston and Elsie May Webster were married on 4 Dec 1906 in Wilmington, Delaware. **Elsie May Webster** was born in 1888. She died in 1961 at the age of 73.

583. Elva Roberts Blackiston (William Holding-10, John W.-9, Samuel Lewis-8, John-7, John-6, Benjamin-5, John-4, John-3, George-2, Marmaduke-1) was born on 5 Jan 1879. Elva Roberts Blackiston and Paul Woolley Taylor were married on 25 Apr 1898 in Wilmington, Delaware.

585. Florence Veshell Blackiston (William Holding-10, John W.-9, Samuel Lewis-8, John-7, John-6, Benjamin-5, John-4, John-3, George-2, Marmaduke-1) was born on 7 Nov 1882 in Wilmington, Delaware. Florence Veshell Blackiston and Leon Wilde Crawford were married on 7 Nov 1911.

587. Helen Irene Blackiston (William Holding-10, John W.-9, Samuel Lewis-8, John-7, John-6, Benjamin-5, John-4, John-3, George-2, Marmaduke-1) was born on 25 Apr 1889 in Wilmington, Delaware. Helen Irene Blackiston and Arthur Green Webber were married. **Arthur Green Webber**.

592. Anna Jones Blackiston (William Holding-10, John W.-9, Samuel Lewis-8, John-7, John-6, Benjamin-5, John-4, John-3, George-2, Marmaduke-1) was born on 8 Dec 1892 in Wilmington, Delaware. Anna Jones Blackiston and Charles M. Poplos were married on 15 Apr 1922.

595. Susan Frances Stavely (Harry Maslin-10, Margaret Elizabeth Hepbron-9, Martha Priscilla Maslin-8, Elizabeth Wroth-7, Priscilla Blackiston-6, Benjamin-5, John-4, John-3, George-2, Marmaduke-1) was born on 31 Jul 1901 in Kent County, Maryland. She died on 5 Mar 1996 at the age of 94 in Chestertown, Kent County, Maryland.

Susan Frances Stavely and Joseph Glover Stavely were married on 31 Oct 1933 in Emporia, Virginia. **Joseph Glover Stavely**, son of Bayard Cann Stavely and Ada Worrell, was born on 14 Mar 1904 in Haddonfield, New Jersey. He died on 9 Apr 1973 at the age of 69 in Chestertown, Kent County, Maryland.

Joseph Glover Stavely and Susan Frances Stavely had the following child:

      610   i. **Joseph Rennie Stavely** was born on 28 May 1939 in Wilmington, Delaware. He died on 13 Oct 2019 at the age of 80 in Washington, District of Columbia. OBITUARY: Joseph Rennie Stavely of Silver Spring, MD died Sunday, Oct. 13, 2019 in Georgetown University Hospital. He was 80. J. Rennie Stavely was born May 28, 1939 in Wilmington, DE the son of the late Joseph Glover Stavely and Susan Frances Stavely. After graduating in 1957 from Newark High School, Mr. Stavely did his undergraduate program at the University of Delaware and then did his graduate program at the University of Wisconsin where he received his PHD in Plant Pathology in 1965. In August of the same year he married Nancy Carol Gall. In 1966 he

started working for the USDA and worked 34 years before retiring in 2000. He was a member of the Toast Masters Club in Beltsville, MD, a lifelong member of St. Philips Episcopal Church in Laurel, MD where he also served on the vestry for 2 terms. He was also a member of St. John's Episcopal Church in Ellicott City, Sons of American Revolution, and the American Phytopathological Society where he had over 400 publications. He was president of the Potomac division of the A.P.S. and president of I.U. Families Association. Over the years he received a number of awards including the George M. Worrilow Award, the American Phytopathological Society Distinguished Service Award for his research services by the National Dry Bean Council and the B.I.C. Meeting Service Award. His interests included genealogy and family research. He enjoyed traveling and gardening as well as many other interests. He is survived by his wife Nancy Carol Gall Stavely and his son Joseph Carl Stavely and daughter in law Sandi as well as nieces, nephews and cousins. A visitation will be held on Friday, Oct. 18, 2019 from 2-4pm at Fellows, Helfenbein and Newnam Funeral Home 130 Speer Rd Chestertown, MD. A memorial Eucharist will be held on Sat. Oct 19, 2019 at 11am at Christ Church I U in Worton, MD. Interment will be held at a later date. In lieu of flowers contributions can be sent to the American Diabetes Association of MD 3120 Tianus Lane, Suite 106 Baltimore, MD 21244 or the American Cancer Society 92 Read's Way, Suite 205 New Castle, DE 19720. The Kent County News on Oct. 17, 2019 He was a member of the Sons of the American Revolution.

596. Joseph Glover Stavely (Bayard Cann-10, Margaret Elizabeth Hepbron-9, Martha Priscilla Maslin-8, Elizabeth Wroth-7, Priscilla Blackiston-6, Benjamin-5, John-4, John-3, George-2, Marmaduke-1) was born on 14 Mar 1904 in Haddonfield, New Jersey. He died on 9 Apr 1973 at the age of 69 in Chestertown, Kent County, Maryland.

Joseph Glover Stavely and Susan Frances Stavely were married on 31 Oct 1933 in Emporia, Virginia. **Susan Frances Stavely**, daughter of Harry Maslin Stavely and Florence Kelley Bowers, was born on 31 Jul 1901 in Kent County, Maryland. She died on 5 Mar 1996 at the age of 94 in Chestertown, Kent County, Maryland.

Joseph Glover Stavely and Susan Frances Stavely had the following child:

> 610   i.   **Joseph Rennie Stavely**, born 28 May 1939, Wilmington, Delaware; died 13 Oct 2019, Washington, District of Columbia.

602. Alexander Parks Rasin Jr. (Alexander Parks-10, Medford Macall-9, Dulany-8, Philip Reed-7, William Blackiston-6, Rosamond Blackiston-5, William-4, Ebenezer-3, George-2, Marmaduke-1) was born on 9 Sep 1911. He died on 29 Aug 1975 at the age of

63. He was buried in Saint Pauls Kent Churchyard, Kent County, Maryland. He was an attorney

Alexander Parks Rasin Jr. and Henrietta Bowen were married. **Henrietta Bowen** was born on 17 Jun 1915. She died on 29 Aug 2007 at the age of 92. She was buried in St. Paul's Kent Churchyard, Chestertown, MD.

Alexander Parks Rasin and Henrietta Bowen had the following children:

611   i.   **Alexander Parks Rasin III** was born on 21 May 1943 in Chestertown, Maryland. He died in 2015 at the age of 72. He was buried in Saint Pauls Kent Churchyard, Kent County, Maryland. Attorney in Kent County. with the firm of Rasin, Wright and Wootton.

+612   ii.   **Judge Martha Frisby Rasin**, born 25 Jun 1947, Chestertown, Maryland; married Edward Blay Bryan.

604. **Judge George Bacon Rasin Jr** (George Bacon-10, Perry Beck-9, Dulany-8, Philip Reed-7, William Blackiston-6, Rosamond Blackiston-5, William-4, Ebenezer-3, George-2, Marmaduke-1) was born on 28 May 1917. He died on 23 Dec 2011 at the age of 94 in Kent County, Maryland.

OBITUARY: On December 23, 2011, George Bacon Rasin, Jr.; beloved husband of the late Eleanor Rasin (nee Brown); loving father of Gale Rasin, the late George Bacon Rasin, III. also survived by surrogate son John Nunn and his wife Nancy; dear grandfather of Christopher Rasin, Matthew Rasin, Alexander McCall Caplan, Claire Rasin Caplan, Jesse Nunn and Maggie Nunn. Graveside services private. Memorial service to be held at later date. www.ruckfuneralhomes.com Published in Baltimore Sun on December 26, 2011

OBITUARYL Judge George Bacon Rasin Jr., former Kent County Circuit Court judge who led a movement to modernize juvenile justice in Maryland, died of congestive heart failure Friday at the Edenwald Retirement Community in Towson. He was 94. "Judge Rasin was widely known and respected for his integrity, knowledge of the law and absolute fairness," said retired Baltimore County Circuit Court Judge John Fader, who was a friend. "He was a man who ran a very tight ship." Born in Worton in Kent County, he was a 1937 graduate of Washington College and earned his law degree from the University of Maryland School of Law. After enlisting in the Army in September 1941, he was assigned as a special agent to the Counter-Intelligence Corps in the Division of Military Intelligence. He left military service as a captain. According to a biography supplied by his family, he began his law practice in Baltimore in 1945 and returned to Kent County in 1946. In June 1950, he joined the U.S. foreign aid program and was a security officer in Paris. He resumed his law practice in Chestertown in 1952 and was elected state's attorney for Kent County in November 1954. In 1956, he was appointed to serve as Kent County's state senator. In 1958, he was elected to the same post.

As a local leader of the Democratic Party, he accompanied then-candidate John F. Kennedy to the Washington College gymnasium during his presidential campaign on May 11, 1960. "After John Kennedy gave a speech on disarmament, my father drove him in our black-and-white Dodge station wagon to the airstrip where he left," said his daughter, Gale Rasin, a Baltimore City Circuit Court judge. Judge George Rasin was a Kennedy delegate to the Democratic National Convention in Los Angeles that summer. Later that year, Gov. J. Millard Tawes appointed him as the Circuit Court judge for Kent County and he was elected in 1962 and 1978 15-year terms. His biography said that in May 1971 he became chief judge and administrative judge of the 2nd Circuit.

Judge Rasin was occasionally assigned to hear trials in Baltimore. In 1975, during the trial of a court clerk who had coerced employees to contribute to his re-election campaign, Judge Rasin said, "Other public officials need to know that if they violate their trust they shall pay the penalty." He said he hoped that the jury's guilty verdict "represented a return to puritanical standards of absolute truth, honesty and integrity" for elected officials. From 1975 to 1978, Judge Rasin was chairman of the Conference of Circuit Administrative Judges. He retired from the bench in 1987. In retirement he was a settlement judge for the 2nd Circuit from 1987 until 2006.

Family members said that during his time as a judge, he devoted himself to the improvement of the juvenile justice system in Maryland. When chairing the Legislative Council Committee on Juvenile Courts, he convinced the Maryland General Assembly that reform was needed in dealing with juvenile delinquency. In 1965, he became chairman of a special commission to study juvenile offender laws. Its findings, known as the Rasin Report, led to the creation of a state Department of Juvenile Services. Governor Tawes also named him chairman of a State Advisory Board for the Juvenile Services department. He served as chair of the Juvenile Justice Advisory Council for 14 years. Judge Rasin also held national juvenile justice posts and was a member of the National Council of Juvenile Court Judges' executive committee For two decades, Judge Rasin was a member of the Board of Visitors and Governors of Washington College. In 1987, the college awarded him an honorary degree of Doctor of Laws. His daughter said a 19th-century ancestor was Isaac Freeman Rasin, who was Clerk of Court for Baltimore City and, with Sen. Arthur Gorman, was head of the celebrated Gorman-Rasin political machine. A memorial service will be held at 3:30 p.m. Jan. 20 at the Kent County Court House in Chestertown. In addition to his daughter, survivors include six grandchildren. His wife of 43 years, the former Eleanor Brown, died in 1991. A son, George Bacon Rasin III, died in 1998.

Judge George Bacon Rasin Jr and Eleanor Brown were married. **Eleanor Brown** born about 1920. She died on 10 Jul 1991 at the age of 71. She was buried in Chester Cem, Chestertown, Kent, Maryland.

George Bacon Rasin and Eleanor Brown had the following children:

613   i. **Judge Gale E. Rasin** was born in 1952. GALE E. Rasin, Associate Judge, Baltimore City Circuit Court, 8th Judicial Circuit, September 3, 2004 to August 10, 2012. Retired August 10, 2012. Member, Mental Health, Alcoholism and Addiction Committee, Maryland Judicial Conference, 2002-11. Member, Specialty Courts and Dockets Committee, 2015, Retired and Recalled Judges Committee, 2015-17, and Senior Judges Committee, 2017-, Judicial Council. Presiding Judge, Mental Health Court, Baltimore City Circuit Court, 2014-. Associate Judge, District Court of Maryland, District 1, Baltimore City, April 16, 1992 to September 2, 2004. Member, Committee on Civil Procedures, 1999-2000, District Court of Maryland. Assistant State's Attorney, Anne Arundel County, 1976-77. Assistant U.S. Attorney for the District of Maryland, 1977-81. Assistant attorney general, Medicaid Fraud Unit, 1985-92 (chief, 1986-92). Member, Mayor's Anti-Animal Abuse Advisory Council, 2010-13. Born in Baltimore, Maryland, August 9, 1952. Attended Kent County public schools; National Cathedral School for Girls (valedictorian, 1970), Washington, DC; Duke University, B.A., magna cum laude, 1973; Georgetown University Law Center, J.D., 1976. Member, Phi Beta Kappa Society. Admitted to Maryland Bar, 1976. Associate, Piper & Marbury, 1981-85. Member, Maryland State Bar Association (criminal law & practice section; judicial administration section; secretary, judicial administration section, 2004-05; member, judicial administration council, 2006-08); Baltimore City Bar Association; Kent County Bar Association; Women's Bar Association of Maryland. Adjunct Professor (criminal law), University of Baltimore School of Law, 2000; Adjunct Professor (ethics), School of Professional Studies in Business and Education, The Johns Hopkins University, 2004-. Mediator, Creative Dispute Resolutions, LLC, 2012-.

614   ii. **George Bacon Rasin III** was born on 11 Jul 1949. He died on 10 Mar 1998 at the age of 48. He was buried in Chester Cem., Chestertown, Kent, Maryland.

605. Madison Rasin Coleman (Mary Emmaline Apsley-10, Philip Rasin-9, Sarah Matilda Rasin-8, Philip Reed-7, William Blackiston-6, Rosamond Blackiston-5, William-4, Ebenezer-3, George-2, Marmaduke-1) was born on 3 Dec 1899 in Kent County, Maryland. He died on 31 May 1965 at the age of 65 in Kent County, Maryland. He was buried in Wesley Chapel, Kent County, Maryland.

Madison Rasin Coleman and Helen Beatrice Bennett were married on 30 Dec 1920 in Kent County, Maryland. **Helen Beatrice Bennett**, daughter of Leonard Bennett and Bertha Hynson, was born on 16 May 1903 in Kent County, Maryland. She died on 30 Dec 1980 at the age of 77 in Kent County, Maryland. She was buried in Wesley Chapel, Kent County, Maryland.

Madison Rasin Coleman and Helen Beatrice Bennett had the following child:

+615   i.   **Mary Esther Louise Coleman**, born 3 Oct 1922; married Frederick Leroy Crouch, 11 Sep 1940; married William Easton; died 14 Jun 2001.

607. **Lula Grace "Dottie" States** (Susie Bernice Crouch-10, Charles Wesley-9, Willamina Rasin-8, Philip Reed-7, William Blackiston-6, Rosamond Blackiston-5, William-4, Ebenezer-3, George-2, Marmaduke-1) was born on 16 Apr 1931 in Rock Hall, Kent County, Maryland. She died on 11 Nov 1978 at the age of 47 in Baltimore City, Maryland. She was also known as Dottie States. Dottie was buried in Oak Lawn Cemetery, Baltimore County, Md. She went by the nickname Dottie as she did not like the name Lula. She was named for both of her grandmothers Lula States and Grace Crouch. Her sister in law Irene Barnhouser said she was quiet and easy-going. She was one of the few people who opened her home to her when she came from Germany. There was a lot of anti-German sentiment still around after WWII and the Barnhousers did not welcome Irene as she was German and had married in Germany. Her driver's license listed her name as Dottie L. Barnhouser born April 16 1931.

BIRTH: Lula Grace States born April 16 1931 at 8pm, full term, legitimate, fem at farm Morg. Neck. parents Harry States of Chestertown age 20 born Queen Annes Co MD farmer and Bernice Crouch of Chestertown age 17 born Kent Co housewife. H.P. Copeland of Chestertown delivered, recorded Apr 23 1931. Birth Cert #G6468

CENSUS: 1940
Conrad A Koch 23 Head was at same place in 1935 sheet metal worker, Lyon and Conklin Comp., Bernice S Koch 26 Wife was in Baltimore in 1935, Lula G States 9 Stepdaughter (Step Daughter) was in Rock Hall Kent in 1935, nearby Frank Tolodziecki 35 and family. Year: 1940; Census Place: Glen Burnie, Anne Arundel, Maryland; Roll: m-t0627-01502; Page: 41B; Enumeration District: 2-29A

DEATH: LulaGrace (Dottie) Barnhouser died Nov 10 1978 pronounced dead Nov 11 1978 at 5:10am born April 16 1931 age 47y born Maryland, married, place of death Baltimore City died at home 2009 Sparks Ct, parents Harry Stats and Bernice Smith, SSA #216-28-3338, infor. Bernard Barnhouser same address, arteriosclerotic cardiovascular disease. autopsy done, natural causes. Ann M. Dixon, MD assistant medical examiner. burial at Oaklawn Cem. funeral director John M. Weber and Sons. Death Cert. #27493. (Bernice Smith should be Bernice Crouch States Smith and States is spelled wrong).

SSN: Dottie Grace States[Dottie Grace Barnhouser][Dottie Barnhouser] Gender Female Race White Birth Date 16 Apr 1931 Birth Place Rock Hall, Maryland[Balto, Maryland] Death Date Nov 1978 Father Harry States Mother Bernice Crouch SSN 216283338 Notes Nov 1947: Name listed as DOTTIE GRACE STATES; Apr 1951: Name listed as DOTTIE

GRACE BARNHOUSER; Jan 1972: Name listed as DOTTIE LUL BARNHOUSER; 30 Dec 1987: Name listed as DOTTIE BARNHOUSER

Post drive, 21208.

BARNHOUSER 13e
On November 11, 1978.
DOTTIE (nee Stats), beloved
wife of Bernard A. Barnhous-
er, Sr. and devoted mother of
Bernard A. Barnhouser, Jr.
and the late David A. Barn-
houser. Also survived by three
grandchildren.
  Prayers at the John M.
Weber & Sons, Inc., Funeral
Home, 401 South Chester
street on Tuesday at 8:15
A.M. Mass of Christian Burial
in St. Patrick's Church at 9
A.M. Interment in Oaklawn
Cemetery. Friends may call 2
to 5 and 7 to 9 P.M.

OBITUARY: Barnhouser - On November 11, 1978, Dottie (nee States) beloved wife of Bernard A. Barnhouser, Sr. and devoted mother of Bernard A. Barnhouser Jr. and the late David A. Barnhouser. Also survived by three grandchildren [Laura, John, David]. Prayers at the John M. Weber & Sons, Inc. Funeral Home, 401 South Chester street on Tuesday at 8:15 A.M. Mass of Christian Burial in St. Patrick's Church at 9 A.M. Interment in Oaklawn Cemetery. Friends may call 2 to 5 and 7 to 9 P.M. Baltimore Sun Nov. 13, 1978.

TOMBSTONE: Dottie L. Barnhouser 1931-1978 Oakdale Sect. Lot #296 grave 2

Lula Grace "Dottie" States and Bernard Alfred Barnhouser Sr. were married on 26 Jun 1948 in Baltimore City, Maryland. **Bernard Alfred Barnhouser Sr.**, son of Joseph Sidney Francis Barnhouser and Agnes Catherine Tolodziecki, was born on 18 Oct 1928 in Baltimore City, Maryland. He died on 23 Sep 1996 at the age of 67 in Johns Hopkins H., Baltimore City, Maryland. He was buried on 26 Sep 1996 in Oak Lawn Cemetery, Baltimore County, Md. He worked hard his whole life. He invested in buying homes on his block and owned four by the time of his death. He became unwell as he got older and his son came back from TN to live with him to help. We would talk for hours about his life and I helped take care of him too.

BIRTH: Baby boy Barnhouser. parents Joseph and Agnes Barnhouser. Oct. 18, 1928 male born 10-18-1928 father Joseph Barnhouser, 3121 Remley St. white age 34 born Cumberland, MD, laborer. mother maiden name Agnes Tolodziecki white 27, born Baltimore, MD housework. number of children born to this mother 5, number living 5. Born at 11:40pm Baltimore City MD Birth Cert. #D42286

CENSUS: 1930 Baltimore City, MD 25th Ward
Bernard Barnhouser age 1 6/12 born MD living with his parents Joseph and Agnes Barnhouser.

CENSUS: 1940
Frank I Jollie 47 Head born Georgia shear cutter, car Foundry, Agnes Jollie 39 Wife, Joseph Barnhouser 19 Stepson (Step Son) grinder steel mill, George Barnhouser 18 Stepson (Step Son), Martin Barnhouser 16 Stepson (Step Son), Agnes Barnhouser 15 Stepdaughter (Step Daughter), Bernard Barnhouser 12 Stepson (Step Son), Daniel Barnhouser 9 Stepson (Step Son), Marylyn Barnhouser 4 Stepdaughter (Step Daughter), John Barnhouser 2 Stepson (Step Son) (this is John Walker), next door Joseph Tolodziecki 41 and family
Year: 1940; Census Place: Baltimore, Baltimore City, Maryland; Roll: m-t0627-01536; Page: 3A; Enumeration District: 4-707

WWII Draft Card: Bernard Alfred Barnhouser Race White Age 19 Relationship to Draftee Self (Head) Birth Date 18 Oct 1928 Birth Place Baltimore, Maryland, USA Residence Place Baltimore, Baltimore, Maryland, USA Registration Date 1947 Registration Place Baltimore, Baltimore, Maryland, USA Employer Davison Chemical Co Height 5 3 Weight 132 Complexion Ruddy Hair Color Blonde Eye Color Blue Next of Kin Agnes Jollie

MARRIAGE: Balto City: Bernard A Barnhouser age 19 MD carpenter's helper resided 4028 Pennington Ave m. Lula Grace States age 17 MD resided 29 W. West St. on Jun 26, 1948 by Alvin Thomas Perkins. recorded Jun 29 1948. Marriage Cert #57590 (Rev. Perkins was born in Kent Co. where Lula was.)

DEATH: Bernard A. Barnhouser, Sr. died Sept. 23, 1996 at 6:45p at The Johns Hopkins Hosp. in Baltimore City. SSAN 220-22-9805 age 67 born 10/18/1928 Maryland, resided at 2007 Spark Ct, Baltimore 21231 widowed white, 10th grade education, maintenance, grounds keeper, father Joseph F. Barnhouser and mother Agnes C. Tolodziecki (crossed out Lula Grace "Dottie") informant Bernard A. Barnhouser Jr. of same address. buried at Oak Lawn Cem. 9/26/96 fun. dir. David J. Weber Funeral Home, 401 S. Chester St. Baltimore, MD cerebral edema 48 hours, cerebral infarction 5 days, cerebral artery sterosis 5 days. tobacco probably contributed to death, no autopsy, natural death, phys. Steven Vath of Washington DC. Death Cert. #96-29454 [DIED: Bernard died at 6:45pm at Johns Hopkins Hosp. on Broadway. His son Bernard and his sister Agnes and her son Robert were there at the moment of his death. His grandson John visited him in the hospital and was up to an hour before he died.

SSN: Bernard Alfred Barnhouser[Bernard A Barnhouser] Gender Male Race White Birth Date 18 Oct 1927 (wrong should be 1928) Birth Place Fairfield MD, Maryland[Maryland][Baltimore] Death Date 23 Sep 1996 Father Joseph Barnhouser Mother Agnes Tolodziecki SSN 220229805 Notes Sep 1943: Name listed as BERNARD ALFRED BARNHOUSER;

ESTATE: #A-40474 Francis Dziennik, Esq. No will was ever found although it was thought he had one. Estate was handled as intestate case. Two homes he owned went to granddau. Laura Barnhouser Almony as she was named in the deed to receive them when he died. The other two homes were sold by the estate and the money divided between son Bernard Jr. and grandson David Barnhouser, Jr. (as part of his father's entitlement to half). I tracked down the grandson David whom the family had lost contact with so he could receive his inheritance.

Barnhouser Sr., Bernard On September 23, 1996 BERNARD A. BARNHOUSER SR., beloved husband of the late Lulu Grace "Dottie" Barnhouser, devoted father of Bernard A. Barnhouser Jr. and the late David Barnhouser, brother of Joseph F. Barnhouser Jr., Martin T. Barnhouser, John E. Walker, Agnes C. Poleski, Marilyn M. Deavers and the late George E. and Daniel R. Barnhouser. Grandfather of Lori, John, Dottie and David Barnhouser. Great-grandfather of Kayla Marie McDonald.

Friends may call at the David J. Weber Funeral Home, 401 S. Chester St, on Wednesday 2 to 5 and 7 to 9 P.M. A Christian Wake Service will be held at 7:30 P.M. Mass of Christian Burial at Holy Rosary Church, Thursday at 10 A.M. Interment Oak Lawn Cemetery. In Bernard's memory, contributions may be made to Our Daily Bread, 19 W. Franklin St, Balto. MD 21201.

OBITUARY: On Sep. 23, 1996, Bernard A. Barnhouser Sr. beloved husband of the late Lulu Grace "Dottie" Barnhouser, devoted father of Bernard A. Barnhouser, Jr. and the late David Barnhouser, brother of Joseph F. Barnhouser, Jr., Martin T. Barnhouser, John E. Walker, Agnes C. Poleski, Marilyn M. Deavers, and the late George E. and Daniel R. Barnhouser. Grandfather of Lori, John, Dottie, and David Barnhouser. Great grandfather of Kayla Marie McDonald. Friends may call at the David J. Weber Funeral Home, 401 S. Chester St. on Wed. 2 to 5 and 7 to 9 p.m. A Christian Wake Service will be held at 7:30pm. Mass of Christian Burial at Holy Rosary Church, Thu. at 10am. Interment Oak Lawn Cemetery. In Bernard's memory, contributions may be made to our Daily Bread 19 W. Franklin St, Baltimore, MD 21201. The Sun Sep. 25, 1996 p. 6B

Dundalk Eagle, Dundalk, Md. October 3, 1996 Page 45

Bernard A. Barnhouser Sr.

Bernard Alfred Barnhouser Sr., 67, died of a stroke September 23 at Johns Hopkins Hospital.

Born & raised in Baltimore, Mr. Barnhouser was a longtime resident of Fells Point before moving to Ballard Way two years ago.

He was a retired maintenance mechanic who worked at Suburban Country Club in Reisterstown for more than 20 years.

He is survived by his son, Bernard A. Barnhouser Jr., sister Agnes Catherine Poleski & brothers Martin Thomas & Joseph Barnhouser Jr. He also leaves behind half-brother John E. Walker Jr., half-sister Marilyn (Lawson) Deavers, four grandchildren & one great-granddaughter. His wife, the former Lula Grace "Dorothy" States, son David Barnhouser & two brothers preceded him in death.

A Mass of Christian Burial was held September 26 at Holy Rosary Church. Interment followed at Oak Lawn Cemetery.

OBITUARY: Bernard Alfred Barnhouser Sr., 67, died of a stroke Sep. 23 at Johns Hopkins Hospital. Born and raised in Baltimore, Mr. Barnhouser was a longtime resident of Fells Point before moving to Ballard Way two years ago. He was a retired maintenance mechanic who worked at Suburban Country Club in Reisterstown for more than 20 years. He is survived by his son, Bernard A. Barnhouser, Jr. sister Agnes Catherine Poleski and brothers Martin Thomas & Joseph Barnhouser Jr. He also leaves behind half-brother John E. Walker Jr., half-sister Marilyn (Lawson) Deavers, four grandchildren & one great granddaughter. His wife, the former Lula Grace "Dorothy" States, son David Barnhouser & two brothers preceded him in death. A Mass of Christian Burial was held September 26 at Holy Rosary Church. Interment followed at Oak Lawn Cemetery. Dundalk Eagle Sep. 25, 1996 p. 45

TOMBSTONE: Bernard A. Barnhouser, Sr. 1928 - 1996.

Bernard Alfred Barnhouser and Lula Grace States had the following children:

+616   i.   **Bernard Alfred Barnhouser Jr.**, born 10 Feb 1949, Univ. Hosp., Baltimore City, Maryland; married Charmaine May Guy, 16 Jul 1973, Baltimore City, Maryland; died 26 Mar 2010, Nashville, Davidson, Tennessee.

+617   ii.   **David Anthony Barnhouser Sr.**, born 12 Aug 1955, Baltimore City, Maryland; married Deborah Kerr, abt 1975; died 20 Aug 1977, Washington County, Maryland.

608. Anna Cook Coleman (Ann Elizabeth Ivens-10, Sarah Ann Elliott-9, Ann Elizabeth Rasin-8, Philip Reed-7, William Blackiston-6, Rosamond Blackiston-5, William-4, Ebenezer-3, George-2, Marmaduke-1) was born on 21 Jul 1909 in Kent County, Maryland. She died on 9 Jan 1995 at the age of 85 in Kent County, Maryland. She was buried in Chester Cem, Chestertown, Kent, Maryland.

Anna Cook Coleman and William Barnaby Willis Jr. were married on 22 Oct 1929 in Kent Co, MD. **William Barnaby Willis Jr.**, son of William Barnaby Willis and Lena Gale, was born on 7 Mar 1904 in Kent County, Maryland. He died on 21 Mar 1983 at the age of 79 in North Carolina. He was buried in Chester Cem, Chestertown, Kent, Maryland.

William Barnaby Willis and Anna Cook Coleman had the following child:

+618   i.   **Elizabeth Lena Willis**, born 13 Nov 1930, Chestertown, Kent County, Maryland; married Jack Donald Waterfield, 19 Oct 1951, College Park, Prince Georges County, Maryland. She has been a great supporter of our research on the family history.

609. William Blackiston Wilmer VI (William Blackiston-10, William Blackiston-9, William Blackiston-8, William Blackiston-7, Blackiston-6, Rosamond Blackiston-5, Ebenezer-4, Ebenezer-3, George-2, Marmaduke-1) was born on 12 Mar 1928 in Baltimore

County, Maryland. He died on 28 Mar 2011 at the age of 83 in Park Springs, Georgia. He was buried at Saint Paul's Churchyard in Chestertown, Kent County, Maryland.

CENSUS: 1930 Kent Co, MD
William B Wilmer 39, Florence Wilmer 31, William B Wilmer 2
1930; Census Place: Chestertown, Kent, Maryland; Roll: 876; Page: 22A; Enumeration District: 0007; Image: 525.0; FHL microfilm: 2340611

CENSUS: 1940 Baltimore City, MD
William Wilmer 49, Florence Wilmer 41, Page Wilmer 12, William Wilmer 7, Henrietta Bissell 67
1940; Census Place: Baltimore, Baltimore City, Maryland; Roll: T627 1541; Page: 9B; Enumeration District: 4-846

William Blackiston Wilmer VI Birth Date: 12 Mar 1928 Birth Place: Baltimore, Baltimore County, Maryland, USA Death Date: 28 Mar 2011 Death Place: Georgia, USA Cemetery: Saint Pauls Kent Churchyard Burial Place: Chestertown, Kent County, Maryland, USA

OBITUARY: William Blackiston Wilmer VI Mr. Wilmer, of Georgia, formerly of Charlotte, died on March 28, 2011, at Park Springs in Stone Mountain. He was born on March 12, 1928 in Baltimore Maryland and grew up in Chestertown, Maryland. During the war years he lived with his Aunt and Uncle, Dr. and Mrs. Donald Stam. Bill graduated from the McDonogh School in Baltimore. He enlisted in the Navy and was sent to Duke University in the NROTC. He graduated with a degree in electrical engineering and was commissioned in 1951. While at Duke, Bill was president of his fraternity, ATO, and was a member of ODK and Red Friars. Also, while at Duke, Bill met his future wife, Lena McArthur Smith, of Clover, SC. They were married after graduation. Having served three years active duty on a destroyer, and 22 years in the Naval Reserve, Bill retired from the Navy as a Commander. Bill worked in engineering management for the DuPont Company in Aiken, SC and at Seaford, DE. In Aiken, Bill was an Explorer Scout Leader, member of the Board of Directors, Executive Committee, and Building Committee of the Crippled Children's Society, Vice President of the PTA, Chairman of the Savannah River Section of the Instrument Society of America, and Chairman of the Joint Council of Scientific and Engineering Societies. In the Naval Reserve, Bill was Commanding Officer of a Surface Unit in Wilmington, DE, and later, Commanding Officer of a Research Unit in Philadelphia, PA. After 30 years with DuPont and the Navy, Bill and Mackie returned to her home state of SC. They lived at Keowee Key near Salem, SC, where Bill worked in real estate sales for the Re/Max Company. He took great pleasure in helping retired couples find their 'dream homes'. Bill was very active in the Duke University Alumna Association. He served for many years as a class agent and in 2000 was awarded the Distinguished Service Award by the Duke University School of Engineering. Bill was a member of Kiwanis International, serving as president of both the Seaford and Walhalla Clubs. He was a Distinguished Lieutenant Governor of the Carolinas District. He was devoted to the 'Terrific Kids' Program of Kiwanis and distributed awards at the Tamassee School for many years. Bill loved his church. He was an Elder of the Seaford, DE, Presbyterian Church and served as a Trustee of the Seneca, SC Presbyterian Church. Bill's hobbies were wood-carving and sailing. He was devoted to his family. Mackie and Bill have three children, Frances W. Richardson of Atlanta, married to Clinton Richardson, and twin sons, William B. Wilmer VII married to the former Kathy Coyle, and Dr. Herbert S. Wilmer who is married to the former Laura Veasey. Bill and Kathy live in Charlotte, Bert and Laura in Denver, NC. Bill and Mackie have five grandchildren and four great grandchildren. Bill's sister, Page W. Flint, was deceased two years ago. Interment will be at St. Paul's Parish-Kent, Chestertown, MD. In lieu of flowers, memorials may be sent to St. Paul's Parish-Kent, 7579 Sandy Bottom Road, Chestertown, MD 21620; or to the Park Springs Employee Appreciation Fund, 500 Springhouse Rd., Stone Mountain, GA 30087. Tom M. Wages Funeral Service, LLC, Snellville Chapel 770-979-3200, 'A Family Company'. Published in Charlotte Observer on March 30, 2011

William Blackiston Wilmer VI was married.

William Blackiston Wilmer had the following child:

+619   i. **William Blackiston Wilmer VII**, born 15 Feb 1955, Mecklenburg County, North Carolina; married Coyle.

Twelfth Generation

612. **Judge Martha Frisby Rasin** (Alexander Parks-11, Alexander Parks-10, Medford Macall-9, Dulany-8, Philip Reed-7, William Blackiston-6, Rosamond Blackiston-5, William-4, Ebenezer-3, George-2, Marmaduke-1) was born on 25 Jun 1947 in Chestertown, Maryland. Chief Judge of the District Court of Maryland. Martha F. Rasin, Chief Judge, District Court of Maryland, September 17, 1996 to September 17, 2001. Resigned as Chief Judge, September 17, 2001. Chair, Administrative Judges Committee, District Court of Maryland, 1996-2001. Member, Executive Committee (legislative subcommittee), Maryland Judicial Conference, 1996-2000; Committee on Criminal and Motor Vehicle Matters, District Court of Maryland, 1996-2001; Maryland Alternative Dispute Resolution Commission, 1998-2001; Judicial Cabinet, 2000-01; Judicial Council, Maryland Judicial Conference, 2000-01. Past member, Board of Directors, Judicial Institute of Maryland. Associate Judge, District Court of Maryland, District 7, Anne Arundel County, 1989-95, and September 17, 2001 to August 8, 2005 (District Administrative Judge, 1995-96). Retired August 8, 2005. Chair, Judicial Education Committee, District Court of Maryland, 1992. Chair, Mental Health, Alcoholism and Addiction Committee, Maryland Judicial Conference, 1992. Member, Committee to Implement Domestic Violence Law, 1992. Member, Judicial Compensation Committee, 1996-2001, Maryland Judicial Conference; Technology Oversight Board, 1999-2005; Public Trust and Confidence Implementation Committee, 2000-05; Advisory Board, Maryland Mediation and Conflict Resolution Office, 2001-05. Chair, Alternative Dispute

Resolution Committee, District Court of Maryland, 2003-05. Member, Administrative Judges Committee, District Court of Maryland, 2003-05. Member, Family Violence Council, 1996-2005. Board of Directors, The Maryland Legal Services Corporation, 2016- Born in Chestertown, Maryland, June 25, 1947. Attended St. Margaret's School, Tappahannock, Virginia; Mary Baldwin College, B.A. (political science), 1969; University of Baltimore School of Law, J.D., 1981. Admitted to Maryland Bar, 1981. Associate Attorney, Bereano and Resnick, P.A., 1981-87. Sole practitioner, 1987-89. Member, Maryland State Bar Association (special committee on anti-discrimination matters, 2004-05); Anne Arundel County Bar Association (board of trustees, 1991-93); Women's Bar Association of Maryland. Member, Women's Law Center of Maryland; American Inns of Court; National Association of Women Judges; Heuisler Honor Society. Board of Governors, St. Margaret's School, Tappahannock, Virginia. Maryland's Top 100 Women, Daily Record, 1998. Special Achievement Award, Family Violence Council, 1998.

Judge Martha Frisby Rasin and Edward Blay Bryan were married. **Edward Blay Bryan** was born on 3 Jan 1944 in Wilmington, Delaware. He died on 29 Aug 2003 at the age of 59 in Maryland. He was buried in Shrewsbury Cem., Kent, Maryland. Son of Robert Leon and Elizabeth Westcott Bryan U.S. Army veteran of the Vietnam War from 1971-72, and was awarded the Bronze Star Medal.

OBITUARY: Edward Bryan Obituary Edward Blay Bryan, age 59, of Kennedyville, Maryland, died on Friday, August 29, 2003 as the result of an automobile accident on Shallcross Wharf Road near Kennedyville. He was the son of Robert Leon and Elizabeth Westcott Bryan of Kennedyville, Maryland. Blay is survived by two daughters, Julia Benfield Bryan of Chicago, Illinois and Rachel Blay Bryan of Montpelier, Virginia; and he is also survived by a brother, Robert L. Bryan Jr. of Kennedyville, Maryland; a sister, Elizabeth Scott Bryan of Chapel Hill, North Carolina. He was the husband of Martha Ras of Annapolis, Maryland. Blay was born in Wilmington, Delaware and reared in Seaford, Delaware and Kinston, North Carolina. He was a graduate of Randolph-Macon Military Academy in Front Royal, Virginia; Hampden-Sydney College in Hampden-Sydney, Virginia; and T.C. Williams Law School of the University of Richmond in Richmond, Virginia. As a U.S. Army veteran of the Vietnam War (1971 to 72), he was a awarded the Bronze Star Medal. Mr. Bryan practiced law in the Richmond, Virginia area from 1971 to 1999. After his retirement, he moved to Marsh Point Farm near Kennedyville, which has been in his family since 1678. He was an active member of Shrewsbury Parish Church and volunteered with local organizations including KART. An avid hunter, fisherman and golfer, he enjoyed the Sassafras River with his Chesapeake Bay retriever, Nick. In lieu of flowers, contributions to Shrewsbury Parish Church Building Fund, P.O. Box 187, Kennedyville, Maryland 21645 or Kent Association Riding Therapy, P.O. Box 126, Worton, Maryland 21678 would be appreciated. Published by Richmond Times-Dispatch on Sep. 10, 2003.

615. **Mary Esther Louise Coleman** (Madison Rasin-11, Mary Emmaline Apsley-10, Philip Rasin-9, Sarah Matilda Rasin-8, Philip Reed-7, William Blackiston-6, Rosamond

Blackiston-5, William-4, Ebenezer-3, George-2, Marmaduke-1) was born on 3 Oct 1922. She died on 14 Jun 2001 at the age of 78.

Mary Esther Louise Coleman and Frederick Leroy Crouch were married on 11 Sep 1940. They were divorced. **Frederick Leroy Crouch**, son of Walter Pierce Crouch and Elsie Mae Frampton, was born in 1919. He died on 17 Apr 2001 at the age of 82. He lives in Portland.

Frederick Leroy Crouch and Mary Esther Louise Coleman had the following child:

+620   i. **Jenny Lee Crouch**, born 27 Jan 1944; died 23 Nov 2009.

Mary Esther Louise Coleman and William Easton were married. **William Easton** died on 28 Mar 2001.

616. **Bernard Alfred Barnhouser Jr.** (Lula Grace States-11, Susie Bernice Crouch-10, Charles Wesley-9, Willamina Rasin-8, Philip Reed-7, William Blackiston-6, Rosamond Blackiston-5, William-4, Ebenezer-3, George-2, Marmaduke-1) was born on 10 Feb 1949 in Univ. Hosp., Baltimore City, Maryland. He died on 26 Mar 2010 at the age of 61 in Nashville, Davidson, Tennessee. Bernard often went by Bernie or sometimes Barnie (a name he picked up from dressing up as Barnie the purple dinosaur character.) Bernard and Charmaine divorced in 1981. He then moved to Tennessee from 1981 to 1995 at 11320 Lebanon Rd Mt. Juliet TN 37122. He lived in Baltimore until his father died and then returned to TN in 1998 and eventually died there. He was picked up by a news reporter there and she wrote several news articles about his nomadic life. He and Charmaine had three children.

BIRTH: Bernard Alfred Barnhouser Jr. born Feb 10 1949 4:00 AM address of mother 1928 Eastern Ave. mother has been in Baltimore 5 years, born at University Hosp. father Bernard Alfred Barnhouser 20y machinist, mother Lula Grace States 17y. recorded Mar 1 1949. Dr. Cathecole. Birth Cert #49-04028

MARRIAGE: Bernard A. Barnhouser Jr. age 24 born Maryland single m. Charmine M. Guy age 20 born Maryland single on Jul 16 1973 by Charles L. Hall, Deputy clerk of Court of Common Pleas. license date Jul 12 1973. Marriage Cert. #029762 (Charmaine spelled wrong)

DIVORCE: Docket 121B p. 313 #B122875 Year 1981

OBITUARY: Bernard Alfred Barnhouser Jr., son of the late Bernard A. Barnhouser Sr and "Dottie" Lula G. (States) Barnhouser passed away March 26, 2010, in Nashville, TN. Bernie as he was known to his friends moved to TN some years ago however still has family in Maryland. He was born Feb. 10, 1949 in Baltimore City. His maternal family moved to Baltimore in the 1940s from a very old family called Blackistons who left

England in 1668 to escape persecution by King Charles II, whose father was executed. His father King Charles I's death warrant was signed by Judge John Blackiston and thus his family were persecuted when his son returned to the throne and ouster of Cromwell. The Blackiston family have lived in Kent Co, MD since that time over 300 years. His paternal family were of a mix of English, German, and Polish ancestry. His grandfather Joseph Sidney F. Barnhouser met and knew Babe Ruth during his time at the St. Mary's Industrial Orphanage. His earliest immigrant Barnhouser ancestor was Capt. Richard Barnehouse who arrived in America in 1640 from Bristol England where his ancestors had been long-time mariners of the open seas. Richard settled in America to escape the despotic reign of Oliver Cromwell. In his youth, Richard Barnehouse had been a captive in Algiers and recounted his story in the English High Court of Admiralty after his release, thus the Barnhouser family has been in America for over 300 years as well. Bernie was predeceased by his parents and only brother David A. Barnhouser, Sr. He leaves behind his ex-wife Charmaine M. (Guy) Barnhouser, his 3 children Laura M. Almony, John A. Barnhouser Sr., and Dorothy G. Sanders. He is also survived by 8 grandchildren - Kayla M. McDonald, Guy E. Almony Jr., Constance M. Cummings, John A. Barnhouser Jr., Samantha R. Barnhouser, Sarah N. Barnhouser, Merrick R. Sanders, and Brayden M. Sanders. The Avenue News Apr 1, 2010 P. 13

OBITUARY: Bernard Alfred Barnhouser Jr., age 61, died Mar. 26, 2010 in Nashville, TN. He was a former resident of Baltimore. He was born Feb. 10, 1949 in Baltimore City to the late Bernard A. Barnhouser Sr and "Dottie" Lula G. (States) Barnhouser. Bernie was formerly married to Charmaine May (Guy). He was predeceased by his only sibling David A. Barnhouser Sr. and his parents. His paternal grandfather Joseph Sidney F. Barnhouser was orphaned in 1902 when his mother died and was raised in the St. Mary's Industrial School at the same time as Babe Ruth. Joseph and Babe became friends through that association. Through his mother's ancestry Bernie was descended from the prominent Blackiston family of Durham England which included a Judge John Blackiston who was one of the judges who signed the execution warrant of King Charles I. When King Charles II came to the throne the family were ostracized in England and decided to move to America and settled in Kent Co, Maryland in 1668/1669 where they continued to live until his mother moved to Baltimore

April 1, 2010 • THE AVENUE NEWS • PAGE 13

OBITUARIES

Bernard Alfred Barnhouser, Jr.

Bernard Alfred Barnhouser, Jr., son of the late Bernard A. Barnhouser Sr and "Dottie" Lula G. (States) Barnhouser, passed away March 26, 2010, in Nashville, Tenn. Bernie, as he was known to his friends, moved to Tennessee some years ago, however, he still has family in Maryland. He was born Feb. 10, 1949 in Baltimore City.

His maternal family moved to Baltimore in the 1940s from a very old family called the Blackistons who left England in 1668 to escape persecution by King Charles II, whose father was executed. His father King Charles I's death warrant was signed by Judge John Blackiston and thus his family were persecuted when his son returned to the throne and ouster of Cromwell. The Blackiston family have lived in Kent County, Md. since that time over 300 years.

His paternal family were of a mix of English, German, and Polish ancestry. His grandfather Joseph Sidney F. Barnhouser met and knew Babe Ruth during his time at the St. Mary's Industrial Orphanage. His earliest immigrant Barnhouser ancestor was Capt. Richard Barnehouse who arrived in America in 1640 from Bristol, England where his ancestors had been long-time mariners of the open seas. Richard settled in America to escape the despotic reign of Oliver Cromwell. In his youth, Richard Barnehouse had been a captive in Algiers and recounted his story in the English High Court of Admiralty after his release, thus the Barnhouser family has been in America for over 300 years as well.

Bernie was predeceased by his parents and only brother David A. Barnhouser, Sr. He leaves behind his ex-wife Charmaine M. (Guy) Barnhouser, his three children Laura M. Almony, John A. Barnhouser, Sr., and Dorothy G. Sanders. He is also survived by eight grandchildren - Kayla M. McDonald, Guy E. Almony, Jr., Constance M. Cummings, John A. Barnhouser, Jr., Samantha R. Barnhouser, Sarah N. Barnhouser, Merrick R. Sanders, and Brayden M. Sanders.

in the 1940s. He is the father of Laura M. Almony, John A. Barnhouser Sr., Dorothy G. Sanders and 8 grandchildren - Kayla McDonald, Guy E. Almony Jr., Constance M. Cummings, John A. Barnhouser Jr., Samantha R. Barnhouser, Sarah N. Barnhouser, Merrick R. Sanders, and Brayden M. Sanders. East County Times April 1, 2010 p. 14

Bernard Alfred Barnhouser Jr. and Charmaine May Guy were married on 16 Jul 1973 in Baltimore City, Maryland.

They were divorced. **Charmaine May Guy**, daughter of Lawrence Frederick Guy and Marie Elizabeth Stinebaugh, was born on 11 Nov 1952 at Sinai Hospital in Baltimore City, Maryland. She died on 11 Jan 2021 at the age of 68 in Laurel, Prince Georges Co, MD. Charmaine was buried in Oak Lawn Cem, Baltimore County, Maryland. Charmaine attended Patterson High School and was active in her community. She had lots of friends and was devoted to her children and grandchildren, often having a lively houseful of people. Charmaine was born on Veterans Day in 1952 at 8:25am at Sinai Hosp. to Lawrence and Marie (Stinebaugh) Guy. She had hardships in her life but maintained a positive attitude and kindness to all who knew her. She was a Baltimore girl her whole life. Her father Lawrence worked for the City Sanitation. His mother Helen died when Charmaine was just 16y. her grandfather's grandfather was Capt. Samuel Guy who commanded boats up and down the Chesapeake. Her Mother Marie was raised in an orphanage during the depression years when her father George, a chauffeur, died of TB when she was 5y old. Edith could not take care of all 7 kids and this would have a strong impact on her. Her grandmother Edith died when Charmaine was 3. Both her parents died relatively young at the age of 60y. In 1972 she married a man Bernard Barnhouser whose mother went by the name Dorothy Grace Barnhouser whose family had lived for 300 years on the Eastern Shore and had royal blood as she was descended from Kings of England. However the marriage did not turn into the fairytale of marrying prince charming and within 7 years they were divorced. She had her first child Laura Marie named after grandmothers Lula and Marie but changed to make it more agreeable to Laura Marie. In 1977 her husband's brother drowned accidentally at age 22y and her husband was there and unable to save him. This had a negative impact on him the rest of his life. They named their son John Anthony after his great uncle John Walker and his brother David Anthony. Their 3rd child was born and also named Dorothy Grace after her mother in law who had died on her birth in 1978. After the divorce, she raised these 3 beautiful children on her own - strong willed, independent and loving. Her traits carried on in them too. She was always helpful to all around her. When she was 16 she volunteered with the Red Cross. She volunteered for years with the Moose Lodge and served as the President of its Lady's Auxiliary. Her home welcomed all to it and none remained a stranger. Fun times were had on the picnic bench in her backyard and when she bought her first home, it was always full of family and friends and laughter. She was a religious lady who baptized all her children and her grandchildren and instilled her beliefs in them. She made lifelong friends. Her 1970 Patterson High School Yearbook said she "Plans to marry and have a family". She succeeded. She led an ordinary life but had an extraordinary impact on us all. Charmaine passed away on January 11th at 8:25am. She was the devoted mother of 3 children Laura,

John, and Dottie. She was the devoted grandmother to 8 grandchildren and 4 great grandchildren. Her smile, her laughs, and her kind heart will be forever missed. She was strong of mind and spirit and her untimely loss has left us heartbroken.

BIRTH: Charmaine May Guy born Nov 11 1952 8:25am at Sinai Hosp., mother's residence 1935 E. Fayette St. 21231, mother's whole life in Baltimore. father Lawrence Frederick Guy 35y born Baltimore laborer Bureau of Sanitation and mother Marie Elizabeth Stinbaugh (Stinebaugh) age 28y born Baltimore. mother had 2 other children living. recorded Nov 17 1952. Dr. David Solomon attending physician. Birth Cert. #52-27357.

DEED: She lived for many years in O'Donnell Heights but bought her first home at 6130 Bessemer Ave. on April 28, 2000. Her daughter Laura and granddaughter Constance lived with her.

DEATH: Charmaine Barnhouser died Jan 11 2021 0828 at Laurel Regional Medical Center in Laurel, Prince George's Co. SSN 212-60-3897 Female 68 y born 11/11/1952 MD, usual residence Dundalk, Baltimore Co, at 6904 Morning Rd Apt B 21222. Divorce not remarried. not in armed forces, white, HS or GED edu. Bus Attendant, Baltimore Co Schools, Father Lawrence Frederick Guy Sr (first name misspelled), mother maiden name Marie Elizabeth Stinebaugh. Info. John Barnhouser, son. 8254 Long Point Rd, Dundalk. Funeral Serv. Michael P. Marzullo of Marzullo Funeral Chapel, 6009 Harford Rd, Baltimore MD 21214. died of Ischemic Encephalopathy 2 days, several hypoglycemia 2 days, diabetes mellitus type 2 20 years. Covid-19, End Stage Kidney disease. natural death inpatient. Jason Vourlekis, MD, Death Cert 32021MD002598

OBIT: Barnhouser, Charmaine May. On Monday January 11, 2021 Charmaine May Barnhouser (nee Guy) Passed away. She is survived by son John A. Barnhouser and wife Kimberly, daughter Laura M. McClellan and husband Garrion, daughter Dorothy G. Sanders and husband Carl. Also survived by brothers Lawrence Guy, Jr and the late Joseph Guy and sisters Mary Keener, Late Jean Clark, late Catherine H. Wardwell, and Beverly Guy also survived by eight grandchildren (John, Samantha, Sarah, Kayla, Guy, Constance, Merrick, and Brayden) and four great grandchildren (Guy Almony III, Maylynn Burke, Rocco and Aliza Medri). Family and Friends may call at the family owned Marzullo Funeral Chapel 6009 Harford Road 21214 on Friday January 15th from 4 to 8 PM for visiting. Service will be held January 16th at 10 AM followed by interment at Oak Lawn Cemetery. To send flowers to the family or plant a tree in memory of Charmaine May Barnhouser, please visit our floral store.

OBITUARY: Morzullo Funeral Chapel Barnhouser, Charmaine May. On Monday January 11, 2021 Charmaine May Barnhouser (nee Guy) Passed away. She is survived by son John A. Barnhouser and wife Kimberly, daughter Laura M. McClellan and husband Garrion. Also Dorothy G. Sanders and husband Carl. Also survived by brothers Lawrence Guy, Jr and late Joseph Guy and sisters Mary Keener, Late Jean Clark, late Catherine H. Wardwell, and Beverly Guy also survived by eight grandchildren and two great grandchildren. Family and Friends may call at the family owned Marzullo Funeral Chapel 6009 Harford Road 21214 on Friday January 15th from 4 to 8 PM for visiting. Service will be held January 16th at 10 AM followed by interment at Oak Lawn Cemetery.

Bernard Alfred Barnhouser and Charmaine May Guy had the following children:

+621 i. **Laura Marie Barnhouser**, born 10 Mar 1974, Md General Hospital, Baltimore City, Md; married Bernard McDonald; married Guy Edward Almony Sr., 4 Jun 1998, Reno, Washoe County, Nevada; married Charles Edward Cummings III; died 25 Dec 2021, Baltimore, Maryland.

+622 ii. **John Anthony Barnhouser Sr.**, born 10 Dec 1977, Towson, Baltimore, Maryland; married Kimberly Ruth Lindsey, 1 Sep 2002, Catonsville, Baltimore County, Maryland.

+623 iii. **Dorothy Grace Barnhouser**, born 6 Apr 1979, Md General Hospital, Baltimore City, Md; married Carl Michael Sanders, 21 Aug 2005, Anne Arundel County, Maryland.

617. **David Anthony Barnhouser Sr.** (Lula Grace States-11, Susie Bernice Crouch-10, Charles Wesley-9, Willamina Rasin-8, Philip Reed-7, William Blackiston-6, Rosamond Blackiston-5, William-4, Ebenezer-3, George-2, Marmaduke-1) was born on 12 Aug 1955 in Baltimore City, Maryland. He died on 20 Aug 1977 at the age of 22 in Washington County, Maryland. He was buried in Glen Haven Cemetery, Glen Burnie, Anne Arundel, Maryland. He accidentally drowned in the Potomac while swimming with his brother. This affected his brother the rest of his life.

NEWS: Kite Weather - Raymond Freeman 13, clear gusty weekend weather ideal for kite (left) and David Barnhouser, 11, found the flying yesterday, Clear skies expected today. The Sun March 19 1967 p 26 Photo of the boys flying kite with caption.

NEWS: Search to resume in likely drowning. Harpers Ferry, WV (Special) - State Police plan to resume their search this morning for the body of a Baltimore man believed drowned in the Potomac River last night while fishing. Police said David Anthony Barnhouser, 22, of the 2000 block Sparks Court, disappeared as he and his brother, Bernard, 27, swam to shore from rocks where they were fishing about 200 feet off Sandy Hook, Md. Baltimore Sun August 21, 1977

DEATH: David A. Barnhouser died known August 20 1977 6:40 pm male white born Aug 12 1955 age 22yrs pronounced dead Aug 21 1977 2pm. born Maryland married died Washington County. Hagerstown, Washington Co Hosp. laborer for Airco Co MD Baltimore. Lived 2008 Sparks Ct. Father Bernard A. Barnhouser, mother Dottie Barnhouser, Informant Deborah Barnhouser 2008 Sparks Ct. died accidental drowning sudden, time of injury 6:40 pm Aug 20 1977 drowned while swimming in Potomac River near Sandy Hook. Accident. Examiner H.N. Weeks burial Aug 25 1977 Glen Haven Cem.

Baltimore MD Fun. Dir. John M. Weber and Sons Inc 401 S. Chester #77-20678 Death Cert. index says Baltimore City but actual says Washington County MD.

OBITUARY: August 22 - A 22-year-old Baltimore man, David Anthony Barnhouser, drowned in the Potomac River Saturday, bringing the river's death toll for the year to five people. The Frederick New, Dec. 31, 1977

David Anthony Barnhouser Sr. and Deborah Kerr were married about 1975. **Deborah Kerr** born about 1955 in Maryland. She died about 1998 at the age of 43 in Baltimore, Maryland. She remarried to a Mr. Hatfield. Murdered in Druid Hill Park.

David Anthony Barnhouser and Deborah Kerr had the following child:

+624   i. **David Anthoney Barnhouser Jr.**, born 26 Apr 1976, Baltimore City, Maryland; married Rachel Nicole Budnichuk, 30 Oct 2005.

618. Elizabeth Lena Willis (Anna Cook Coleman-11, Ann Elizabeth Ivens-10, Sarah Ann Elliott-9, Ann Elizabeth Rasin-8, Philip Reed-7, William Blackiston-6, Rosamond Blackiston-5, William-4, Ebenezer-3, George-2, Marmaduke-1) was born on 13 Nov 1930 in Chestertown, Kent County, Maryland. She was also known as Betty Willis. Accepted in the Order of the Crown of Charlemagne #2091 Accepted into the DAR in Oct. 2002 #812224 Accepted into Daughters of 1812.

Elizabeth Lena Willis and Jack Donald Waterfield were married on 19 Oct 1951 in College Park, Prince Georges County, Maryland. **Jack Donald Waterfield**, son of Amos U Waterfield and Ruby C Williams, was born on 19 Jul 1928 in Eastern Neck, Kent County, Maryland. He died on 10 Mar 2022 at the age of 93 in Great Falls, Cascade County, Montana.

Jack Donald Waterfield and Elizabeth Lena Willis had the following children:

+625   i. **Anna Christine Waterfield**, born 14 Jul 1953, Adams, CO; married Randy Craig Orley, 10 Feb 1979, Cascade, MT; married George Donald Copeland, 8 Jan 1986, Key West, Monroe Co, Florida.
626   ii. **Debra Lynn Waterfield** was born on 24 Aug 1954.
627   iii. **Shelena Rachel Waterfield** was born on 19 Jun 1956.
628   iv. **Ruby Cathleen Waterfield** was born on 2 Mar 1958.
629   v. **Rachel Elizabeth Waterfield** was born on 1 Jan 1960.

619. William Blackiston Wilmer VII (William Blackiston-11, William Blackiston-10, William Blackiston-9, William Blackiston-8, William Blackiston-7, Blackiston-6, Rosamond Blackiston-5, Ebenezer-4, Ebenezer-3, George-2, Marmaduke-1) was born on 15 Feb 1955 in Mecklenburg County, North Carolina. William Blackiston Wilmer Gender:

Male Birth Date: 15 Feb 1955 Birth Place: Mecklenburg, North Carolina, Father: Wilmer William Blackiston Mother: Lena McArthur Smith NC Birth Index on Ancestry.com

William Blackiston Wilmer VII and Coyle were married. **Coyle.**

William Blackiston Wilmer and Coyle had the following child:

> 630   i. **William Blackiston Wilmer VIII** was born on 16 Mar 1989 in Mecklenburg County, North Carolina. William Blackiston Wilmer VIII Gender: Male Birth Date:16 Mar 1989 Birth Place: Mecklenburg, North Carolina, Father: Wilmer, William Blackiston Mother: Coyle

Thirteenth Generation

620. **Jenny Lee Crouch** (Mary Esther Louise Coleman-12, Madison Rasin-11, Mary Emmaline Apsley-10, Philip Rasin-9, Sarah Matilda Rasin-8, Philip Reed-7, William Blackiston-6, Rosamond Blackiston-5, William-4, Ebenezer-3, George-2, Marmaduke-1) was born on 27 Jan 1944. She died on 23 Nov 2009 at the age of 65.

Jenny Lee Crouch had the following child:

> 631   i. **Beatrice Raye Taylor**. She is a researcher of the family history.

621. **Laura Marie Barnhouser** (Bernard Alfred-12, Lula Grace States-11, Susie Bernice Crouch-10, Charles Wesley-9, Willamina Rasin-8, Philip Reed-7, William Blackiston-6, Rosamond Blackiston-5, William-4, Ebenezer-3, George-2, Marmaduke-1) was born on 10 Mar 1974 in Md General Hospital, Baltimore City, Md. She was christened on 21 Apr 1974 in Saint Patrick's Ch, Baltimore City, Md. She died on 25 Dec 2021 at the age of 47 in Baltimore, Maryland. She was named after her grandmothers Lula Barnhouser and Marie Guy. (They did not like the name Lula so they settled on Laura). Laura was a beautiful young lady and had lots of friends and was well respected in her neighborhood. She was very accepting of all and people sought out her company. She received her GED on April 28, 2000. She has 3 children - one daughter by Bernard McDonald, one son by Guy Almony and one daughter by Charles "Chris" Cummings.

BIRTH: Laura Marie Barnhouser female born Mar. 10, 1974 Baltimore City maiden name of mother Charmaine May Guy age 20, father Bernard Alfred Barnhouser age 25 Baltimore City Birth Cert. #74-07975. She was 8 lbs 7 oz. 19" long.

BAPTISM: Laura Marie Barnhouser, child of Bernard A. Barnhouser and Charmaine May Guy born in Baltimore, MD on 10 Mar 1974 was baptized 21 Apr 1974 by Rev. Michael J. Orchik, the sponsors being David A. Barnhouser and Patricia A. Kardech.

MARRIAGE: She first married Guy Almony in 1998 in NV. They were on their way to California for employment and to start a new life but she returned to Baltimore after the wedding.

MARRIAGE: Laura Barnhouser m. Garrion "Manny" McClellan on Sep 22 2003 Baltimore City, MD. witnesses Charmaine Barnhouser and Dorothy Barnhouser.

DEATH: Laura died on December 25, 2021 in Baltimore City. Her mother died the same year due to complications from COVID.

Laura Marie Barnhouser and Bernard McDonald were married. **Bernard McDonald** was born on 26 Feb 1973 in Baltimore, Maryland.

Bernard McDonald and Laura Marie Barnhouser had the following child:

+632 i. **Kayla Marie McDonald**, born 5 Nov 1993, Franklin Sq Hosp, Baltimore, Maryland; married Tony Medri.

Laura Marie Barnhouser and Guy Edward Almony Sr. were married on 4 Jun 1998 in Reno, Washoe County, Nevada. **Guy Edward Almony Sr.**, son of Emory Edward Almony and Virginia Lee Almony, was born on 9 Feb 1972 in Baltimore City, Maryland. Guy has 2 children - one daughter by Lisa Erskine and one son by Laura Barnhouser. He was raised by his grandmother Myrtle Almony. He loves his family immensely and would give his life for them. He is extremely smart despite not being able to complete his formal education due to the troubled home life. Despite all his difficulties at home, he is a hard worker and has many skills. He learned to knit and cook.

As a child he was raised by his grandmother Myrtle. He often got into trouble with the law and it led to his leaving the state with his longtime girlfriend Laura Barnhouser. They took a train ride across America to California, stopping along the way in various cities and taking photos and sending home. They stopped off in Reno NV and ran out of money and robbed a Kinkos and was caught. He received a heavy sentence and remained incarcerated, but still tries to communicate with his family often.

BIRTH: Guy Edward Almony born Feb. 9, 1972 Baltimore City, at 4:13am, mother Virginia Lee Almony age 18 born MD, father Emory Edward Miller age 22 born MD, filed March 2, 1972. Baltimore City Cert. #72-02852

MARRIAGE: Guy Almony Sr. of Baltimore m. Laura Barnhouser of Baltimore, mailing address 6111 Toone St., Baltimore, MD 21224 on June 4, 1998 at the Heart of Reno Chapel, Reno, Nevada, License #MA98-9351. (Guy proposed to Laura in Omaha, Nebraska and they got married in Reno, NV. They had taken a train to travel to California for work.)

MARRIAGE: Wedding Announcement. Guy Edward Almony Sr., son of the late Emory Edward Miller Jr. and Virginia Lee Almony, married Laura Marie Barnhouser, daughter of Bernard Alfred Barnhouser, Jr. and Charmaine Mae (Guy) Barnhouser, on June 4 in a small but beautiful wedding. Guy is the grandson of Emory Edward Miller, Sr., Stanley Clinton Almony Sr. and Myrtle Marie Almony. He is the great grandson of Rev. Elmer Cleveland Clouser, Sr. Guy is planning to become a real estate agent. He and his wife will be making a new home for themselves and their son Guy Jr. Koumbari is Christos Christou, Jr. The Avenue News June 18, 1998 p. 16A

Guy Edward Almony and Laura Marie Barnhouser had the following child:

+633   i.   **Guy Edward Almony Jr.**, born 5 Jul 1997, Bayview Hospital, Baltimore City, Md.

Charles Edward Cummings III, son of William Osborne Bowen and Charlene Edith Cummings, was born on 5 Oct 1973. He died on 13 May 2009 at the age of 35 in Baltimore, Maryland. He was buried in Cremated. He was named after an uncle who was named Charles Jr. He uses the nickname Chris. Chris died young due to a contracted disease.

Charles Edward Cummings and Laura Marie Barnhouser had the following child:

+634   i.   **Constance May Cummings**, born 1 Oct 1999, Baltimore City, Maryland.

622. John Anthony Barnhouser Sr. (Bernard Alfred-12, Lula Grace States-11, Susie Bernice Crouch-10, Charles Wesley-9, Willamina Rasin-8, Philip Reed-7, William Blackiston-6, Rosamond Blackiston-5, William-4, Ebenezer-3, George-2, Marmaduke-1) was born on 10 Dec 1977 at Saint Joseph Hospital in Towson, Baltimore, Maryland. He was christened on 19 Feb 1978 in Saint Patrick's Ch, Baltimore City, Md.

John is the adopted son of Christos Christou. John's DNA test states he is 41% UK (English, Scotland, Wales), 34% German, 12.5% Irish, and 12.5% Polish. John was fit and a weightlifter since a teenager. He held various jobs at Goetze's Caramel Factory, as safety instructor at the Rite Aid complex in Aberdeen and in spare time completed his certification and now is HVAC Certified (Lincoln Tech) and Manager in his firm Bowers & Company. He is a graduate of Kenwood High School in Essex. John proposed to his fiancé Kimberly Lindsey on August 11, 1997 in Ocean City and gave her a ring.

BIRTH: Baltimore County. John Anthony Barnhouser born Dec 10, 1977 12:22pm Towson, Baltimore Co; parents Bernard Alfred Barnhouser Jr. 28y and Charmaine May Guy 25y (maiden name). delivered by Physician Danilo Coronel, MD, filed Dec 27, 1977. St. Joseph Hosp. address of mother 1918 Bank St Baltimore MD 21231. John was exactly 8 lbs and 19.5" long. Birth Cert #77-44260

BAPTISM: John was named after his great uncle John Walker and his uncle David Anthony Barnhouser. His great uncle John Walker and his wife Mary Anne are his godparents. He was baptized at St. Patrick's Church. Transcribed St. Patrick's records say "John David Barnhouser child of Bernard Barnhouser and Charmagne Guy born in Baltimore MD on 10 Dec 1977 was baptized 19 Feb 1978 by Rev. Richard D. Novak, the sponsors being John Walker and Mary Ann Walker." Abstract had John's middle name as David and mother's first name spelled as Charlemaine.

DEED: Theresa C. Foley of Baltimore to John A. Barnhouser Sr. Lot No 33 known as 707 Aldworth Road. Sep 10 2000 DB 14757 p. 271 Baltimore Co MD He sold this house and bought a larger house in Waters Edge.

MARRIAGE: John Barnhouser age 24 and Kimberly Lindsey age 23 married at Overhills Mansion in Catonsville, MD on Sep. 1, 2002 at 4pm. by Rev. Christos Christou, Jr. (presiding minister never showed so father of the groom performed the ceremony). Best men Aaron Bryan and Christos Christou, Jr. Cert #16311

John joined many hereditary organizations based on his biological ancestry and is co-author on many genealogical books with his adopted father Christos Christou, Jr. John Sr. has the name of his ancestor Edward Barnhouser on the Immigration Wall at Ellis Island. (A gift from his father Christos). His biological ancestry is given in Prominent Families of Kent Co by Christos Christou, Jr. and John A. Barnhouser, Sr. copyright 1997.

SAR: John Anthony Barnhouser was accepted in the Sons of the American Revolution under the service of Capt. William B. Rasin on May 7, 1997. SAR #148242. MD State #3395.

CAR: John Barnhouser was accepted in the Children of the American Revolution under the service of his ancestor Capt. William B. Rasin on May 2, 1995. CAR #142106. At the time of his joining he was the only father and son members in the Maryland Society history.

OCC: John Barnhouser was accepted as a life member of the Order of the Crown of Charlemagne Member #2051 as of Feb. 23, 2003. through immigrant ancestor George Blackiston back to King Edward III of England then to Charlemagne. John has documented his descent from 17 of the 25 Magna Carta Barons (100% of the known Sureties to have living descendants. The other 8 are not known to have descendants today. Washington's ancestry has been documented to only 9)

John Anthony Barnhouser Sr. was granted a Coat of Arms for himself and his heirs by the DON ALFONSO DE CEBAIIOS-ESCALERA, Cronista de Armas, Junta de Castilla y Leo on April 6 2021. COTEJADA CON SU ORIGINAL, QUE QUEDA REGISTRADA EN MI MINUTARIO CORRESPONDIENTE AL AÑO DE LA FECHA CON EL NÚMERO 19/2021. SEGOVIA, 7 DE ABRIL DE 2021. The Coat of Arms acknowledges his Blackiston descent with the quartering of his arms.

VIRES IN VIRTUTE

John Anthony Barnhouser Sr. and Kimberly Ruth Lindsey were married on 1 Sep 2002 at the Overhills Mansion in Catonsville, Baltimore County, Maryland. **Kimberly Ruth Lindsey**, daughter of Frederick Lindsey and Rosemary Frances Jerome, was born on 31 Dec 1978 in Baltimore City, Maryland.

John Anthony Barnhouser and Kimberly Ruth Lindsey had the following children:

635   i. **John Anthony Barnhouser Jr.** was born on 23 Oct 1997 in Baltimore City, Maryland. He was christened on 22 Feb 1998 at Messiah Lutheran Church in Canton, Baltimore City, Maryland. BIRTH: Cert. #97-52653 John Anthony Barnhouser, Jr. b. Oct. 23, 1977 Baltimore City. weight 7 lbs 4 oz. at 4:46am, maiden name of mother Kimberly Ruth Lindsey age 18 born Maryland, father John Anthony Barnhouser Sr. age 19 born Maryland. recorded Nov. 4, 1977.

He was born at 4:46am, 7 lbs 4.1 oz, 20" at Maryland General Hosp. Rm #207. Kim's mother Rose and John were in the delivery room (which was the same room as her hospital room). Delivered by Dr. Usha Varma.

BAPTISM: He was baptized at Messiah Lutheran Church on Feb. 22, 1998 with a reception afterwards at the Little Tony's store upstairs. Pastor Lee Hudson. Godparents are Aaron M. "Byrd" Bryan and Kimberly McMillan.

NEWS: Congratulations: It's always a pleasure to announce the birth of a new baby. None gives me more pleasure than to announce this one. Congratulations to our member Chris Christou on birth of his new grandson, John Anthony Barnhouser, Jr. born 23 Oct. 1997. This bouncing baby boy weighed in at 7 lbs 4.1 oz and measured 20" long. Parents are John A. Barnhouser, Sr. and Kimberly R. Lindsey. I have never seen Chris so happy. May God's blessings be with the entire family. Baltimore Co. Genealogical Group Newsletter 11/97.

NEWS: Thomas Johnson Society member John Barnhouser Sr has a son born on Oct. 23, 1997. Name is John Anthony Barnhouser, Jr. Weight: 7 lbs 4.1 oz. and 20 inches in length. Mother is Kimberly Ruth Lindsey. THIS IS A FIRST FOR T.J. SOCIETY - Father and son are both C.A.R. members. This we believe is also a first for Maryland. Congratulations to the Family!! T.J.'s Travels Vol. XII issue 3 Dec. 1997. Photos of John and Jr. and grandpop Chris and John Jr.

NEWS: John Anthony Barnhouser, Jr. was born on Oct. 23 at 4:46 am at Maryland General Hospital. He weighed 7 lbs 4 ozs. His proud parents are John A. Barnhouser, Sr. and Kimberly R. Lindsey. His grandparents are Bernard A. Barnhouser, Jr. Charmaine M. Barnhouser, Christos Christou, Jr. Frederick Lindsey, Jr. and Rosemary Lindsey. His great grandparents are Frances A. Jerome, Frederick Lindsey, Sr. and Anna Lindsey. John Jr. will be a member of the Children of the American Revolution, as is his father, under descent from their ancestor, Capt. William B. Rasin, who fought at the Battle of Cowpens during the American Revolution. When he is old enough, he will also be a member of the Sons of the American Revolution, like his father, as well as his grandfather Chris. The Avenue News Nov. 13, 1997. p. 14A.

NEWS: John A. Barnhouser, Jr. born Oct. 23, weighed 7 lbs. 4.1 ozs. Proud parents are John Anthony Barnhouser, Sr. and Kimberly R. Lindsey. Grandparents are Rosemary Lindsey, Charmaine Barnhouser, Great grandmother Francis A. Jerome, Grandfather Christos Christou, Jr. The Essex Times Dec. 11, 1997 p. 20.

NEWS: Two generations in the C.A.R. Thomas Johnson Society, Children of the American Revolution member John Anthony Barnhouser, Sr. holds his son, John Jr. who was born October 23, 1997. Father and son are both members of the C.A.R. This is a first for the Thomas Johnson Society and may be for the State. The Spinning Wheel, MD Society DAR Magazine Vol. 28 no. 2 Feb. 1998.

NEWS: John Anthony Barnhouser Jr., son of John A. Barnhouser Sr. and Kimberly R. Lindsey, turned 3 years old on Oct. 23rd and a big birthday celebration was held at Jeepers in Glen Burnie. There were games, rides, food and even a pinata hitting. John received lots of toys and clothes and of course the toys were more to his liking. Many family members attended including the parents John and Kim; cousins Constance May Cummings age 1 and Guy E. Almony Jr. age 3; sister Samantha R. Barnhouser age 1; grandparents Charmaine Barnhouser, Christos Christou, Jr., and Rosemary Lindsey along with many aunts, uncles, and other relatives and friends. Great grandma Frances Augusta Jerome could not attend but sent gifts. The Avenue News p. 14 Nov. 16, 2000.

NEWS: John Anthony Barnhouser, Jr. celebrated his 3rd birthday on Oct. 23, 2000, with a big party at Jeepers in Glen Burnie. The celebration included rides, games, a pinata, food, and lots of running around by all the young guests. John Jr. is the son of John A. Barnhouser Sr. and Kimberly R. Lindsey, grandson of Charmaine M. Barnhouser, Christos Christou, Jr. and Rosemary F.

Lindsey, and great grandson of Frances A. Jerome. Young guests included sister Samantha R. Barnhouser age 1 and cousins Guy E. Almony Jr. age 3 and Constance M. Cummings age 1. East County Times p. 30 Nov. 22, 2000.

CAR: John Jr. was accepted as a member of Children of the American Revolution #144465 through his ancestor Capt. William B. Rasin on January 6, 1998 his application was accepted. John Jr. is a Member of the Sons of the American Revolution #163294 MD #3693 on. Sep. 14, 2004.

SAR: John Jr. was accepted as a member of the Sons of the American Revolution. The second Junior Member in the Maryland Society history.

OFFM: John Jr. was accepted as a member of the Order of the First Families of Maryland.

636   ii. **Samantha Rose Barnhouser** was born on 26 May 1999 in Baltimore City, Maryland. She was christened on 5 Sep 1999 at Nazareth Lutheran Church in Highlandtown, Baltimore City, Maryland. BIRTH: Samantha Rose Barnhouser female born May 26 1999 7lbs 10oz Baltimore City 7:717 pm, mother Kimberly Ruth Lindsey born MD father John Anthony Barnhouser Sr. born MD. Cert #1999-25540

BIRTH: Born at 7:17pm, weighed 7 lbs. 10 oz. 19 inches long. She was due on June 2 but gave birth a week early. Kim's mom Rose was in the room along with
John Sr. Byrd and Julie visited earlier and Guy Jr. and I waited in the waiting room while she gave birth. She came into the world full of hair, nice complexion and a beautiful little girl with strong lungs. Guy Jr. got to touch her minutes after she was born and was mesmerized by this crying little baby. Delivered by Dr. Usha Varma.

BAPTISM: Nazareth Lutheran Church on Bank St. Godparents are Byrd and Julie Bryan and Kimberly McMillan again (same as John John's, but Julie added as backup godmother) on Sep. 5, 1999. Party afterwards at a friend's house. Pastor Rev. Walter P. Schoenfuhs Sr. (interim pastor)

NEWS: Samantha Rose Barnhouser was born on May 26 at 7:17pm at Maryland General Hospital. She weighed 7 lbs. 9 oz. Her proud parents are John A. Barnhouser, Sr. and Kimberly R. Lindsey. She has an older brother John A. Barnhouser, Jr. age 1 and a little cousin Guy E. Almony Jr. age 2 at home to greet her. Her grandparents are Christos Christou, Jr., Bernard Barnhouser, Jr. Charmaine M. Barnhouser, and Rosemary F. Lindsey. Her great grandparents are Frances A. Jerome and the late Bernard A. Barnhouser, Sr. East County Times
June 24, 1999 p. 28

NEWS: Samantha Rose Barnhouser was born on May 26 at 7:17pm at Maryland General Hosp. She weighed 7 lbs. 10 oz. Her proud parents are John Barnhouser Sr. and Kimberly R. Lindsey. She has an older brother John A. Barnhouser, Jr. age 1, at home. Her grandparents are Christos Christou, Jr., Bernard A. Barnhouser, Jr., Charmaine M. Barnhouser, Frederick Lindsey, Jr. and Rosemary F. Lindsey. Her great grandparents are Frances A. Jerome, Frederick Lindsey, Sr. and Anna Lindsey and Bernard A. Barnhouser, Sr. deceased. The Avenue News June 24, 1999 p. 16.

NEWS: Samantha Rose Barnhouser turned 1 on May 26 and a birthday party was held for her at her grandfather's home with her old brother John Barnhouser Jr. parents John and Kimberly Barnhouser, grandparents Rose Lindsey, Charmaine Barnhouser, Christos Christou, Jr. attending along with many family and friends. Great grandmother Frances Jerome could not be in attendance but sent along gifts. The Avenue News July 13, 2000 p. 14

NEWS: Samantha Rose Barnhouser, dau. of John Barnhouser and Kimberly Lindsey turned one on May 26 and celebrated her birthday at her grandpop's house. East County Times July 6, 2000 p. 26

NEWS: On May 26th, Samantha Rose Barnhouser turned 2 years old and celebrated her birthday with family and friends at her pop-pop Christos Christou, Jr.'s house on Nicholson Road. Her parents are John Barnhouser and Kimberly Lindsey. Young family and friends included brother John Jr. age 3; cousins Guy Jr. age 3 and Constance age 1; friends John age 7, Jada age 6, Catlin age 3, Jason age 2, and Zachary age 1. Her grandfather is Christos Christou, Jr., and grandmothers are Charmaine M. Barnhouser, and Rosemary F. Lindsey. Her great grandmother is Frances Jerome. The Avenue News June 13, 2001 p. 22

CAR: Samantha is a member of the Children of the American Revolution #147969 approved Dec. 17, 2001 through her ancestor Capt. William Blackiston Rasin.
Daughters of 1812: Samantha was accepted as a member of the Daughters of 1812 under the Junior Membership Program.
Children of 1812: Samantha was accepted as a member of the Children of 1812 as a Charter Member of the newly formed Maryland Society.

637   iii.   **Sarah Nicole Barnhouser** was born on 13 Mar 2002 in Md General Hospital, Baltimore City, Md. She was christened on 17 Nov 2002 at Nazareth Lutheran Church in Highlandtown, Baltimore City, Maryland. BIRTH: John called me at 8:43 to say Kim was going into labor and I had to come get the kids while they went to the hospital. I ran out the door with Guy and picked up John and Samantha while John went to the hospital. She was born in room 245 and later moved to 101.

BIRTH: Sarah Nicole Barnhouser born Mar. 13, 2002 Baltimore city, mother's maiden name Kimberly Ruth Lindsey and father John Anthony Barnhouser #2002-13573

Baptism: Nov. 17, 2002 Nazareth Lutheran Church, Baltimore City by Rev. Jacob Gillard

NEWS: Proud grandpop Christos Christou, Jr. announces the birth of his 3rd granddaughter Sarah Nicole Barnhouser who was born on March 13, 2002 at 10:15pm at Maryland General Hosp. She weighed 6 lbs. 14 oz. and 18.5 inches long. Her proud parents are John Anthony Barnhouser Sr. and Kimberly Ruth Lindsey. She has an older brother John A. Barnhouser, Jr. age 4 and older sister Samantha Rose Barnhouser age 2 and cousin Guy E. Almony, Jr. age 4 at home to greet her. Her grandparents are Christos Christou, Jr., Bernard A. Barnhouser, Jr., Charmaine M. Barnhouser, Frederick Lindsey, Jr. and Rosemary F. Lindsey. Her great grandparents are Rosemary Christou, Frances A. Jerome and Anna M. Lindsey.

CAR: Approved member of the Children of the American Revolution through ancestor Capt. William B. Rasin. Approved Nov 2002. CAR#148965.
Daughters of 1812: Sarah was accepted as a member of the Daughters of 1812 under the Junior Membership Program.
Children of 1812: Sarah was accepted as a member of the Children of 1812 as a Charter Member of the newly formed Maryland Society.

623. **Dorothy Grace Barnhouser** (Bernard Alfred-12, Lula Grace States-11, Susie Bernice Crouch-10, Charles Wesley-9, Willamina Rasin-8, Philip Reed-7, William Blackiston-6, Rosamond Blackiston-5, William-4, Ebenezer-3, George-2, Marmaduke-1) was born on 6 Apr 1979 in Md General Hospital, Baltimore City, Md. She was christened in Saint Patrick's Ch, Baltimore City, Md. Dorothy was named after her grandmother Lula Grace Barnhouser who went by the nickname Dottie. Her godfather is her father's cousin Robert Poleski. She was 7lbs 14 oz. 19 inches long. Dottie attended Villa Julie College and joined the U.S. Navy. She graduated with honors from Patterson High School.

Dorothy Grace Barnhouser and Carl Michael Sanders were married on 21 Aug 2005 in Anne Arundel County, Maryland. **Carl Michael Sanders** was born on 28 Apr 1980 in Takoma, Washington. Carl also joined the U.S. Navy like his wife.

Carl Michael Sanders and Dorothy Grace Barnhouser had the following children:

638	i.	**Merrick Richard Sanders** was born on 5 Jul 2004 in Bethesda, Montgomery County, Maryland. BIRTH: Merrick was born at 2pm on July 5, 2004. 19 inches long and 9 lbs. (but 3 days later he was 7 lbs.).
639	ii.	**Brayden Michael Sanders** was born on 3 Feb 2006 in Bethesda, Montgomery County, Maryland. BIRTH: Brayden Michael Sanders born Feb. 3, 2006 2:58am, 6lbs 14.6 oz., 21 inches.

624. **David Anthoney Barnhouser Jr.** (David Anthony-12, Lula Grace States-11, Susie Bernice Crouch-10, Charles Wesley-9, Willamina Rasin-8, Philip Reed-7, William Blackiston-6, Rosamond Blackiston-5, William-4, Ebenezer-3, George-2, Marmaduke-1) was born on 26 Apr 1976 in Baltimore City, Maryland. He was christened on 6 Jun 1976

in Saint Patrick's Ch, Baltimore City, Md. His middle name is spelled Anthoney due to an error on his birth certificate. He spells it that way and likes it because it is unique. He graduated from Villa Julie College where his cousin Dottie Barnhouser also attended. We relocated him in 1997 when his grandfather passed away and introduced him to his Barnhouser family. His mother had not kept in touch with her husband's family and he was being raised by his grandmother until 12 and then by his godmother who had been there his whole life. His father died when he was 2 and his mother did not raise him per David.

BAPTISM: David Anthony Barnhouser, child of David Anthony Barnhouser and Deborah Kerr born in Baltimore on 26th Apr 1976 was baptized on 6 June 1976 by Rev. Michael J. Orchik, the sponsors being Michael Pulaski (Poleski) and Carolyn K. Kramer.

On Oct. 25, 2003 he proposed to his girlfriend at a Good Charlotte Play Concert at the First Mariner Arena and plans to be married Oct. 30, 2005

David Anthoney Barnhouser Jr. and Rachel Nicole Budnichuk were married on 30 Oct 2005. **Rachel Nicole Budnichuk** was born on 28 Aug 1983.

625. **Anna Christine Waterfield** (Elizabeth Lena Willis-12, Anna Cook Coleman-11, Ann Elizabeth Ivens-10, Sarah Ann Elliott-9, Ann Elizabeth Rasin-8, Philip Reed-7, William Blackiston-6, Rosamond Blackiston-5, William-4, Ebenezer-3, George-2, Marmaduke-1) was born on 14 Jul 1953 in Adams, CO.

She is DAR Member #852385, Daughters of 1812 #34568, Order of the First Families of Maryland #00048. She worked as School Counselor at elementary and middle schools while following her husband around the World. Her father retired from the USAF after 23 years and her husband served 20 years in the USMC. She is very active in local MOAA Granbury Chapter. Her husband and her are Life Members of the Military Officers Association of America. She is Vice Regent of the Elizabeth Crockett DAR chapter in Granbury, TX, and Regent May 2025 and a DAR Life Member. She is a Vice President of the National Society Daughters of 1812, will become State President in a year and a Life Member. She is a member First Families of Maryland and the Crown of Charlemagne through her ancestor George Blackiston, the immigrant. She is a member of the National Society Colonial Daughters of the 17th Century, National Society of Colonial Dames of America, National Society Daughters of Colonial Wars and National Society Daughters of American Colonists.

Anna Christine Waterfield and Randy Craig Orley were married on 10 Feb 1979 in Cascade, MT. **Randy Craig Orley** was born on 24 Sep 1953 in NY.

Randy Craig Orley and Anna Christine Waterfield had the following child:

640   i. **Jonathan Cole Waterfield-Orley** was born on 1 Feb 1982 in Gallatin, MT.

Anna Christine Waterfield and George Donald Copeland were married on 8 Jan 1986 in Key West, Monroe Co, Florida. **George Donald Copeland** was born on 25 Jun 1961 in Santa Ana, Orange Co, CA.

George Donald Copeland and Anna Christine Waterfield had the following child:

641   i. **George Devon Waterfield-Copeland** was born on 10 Jan 1987 in Pensacola, Escambia County, Florida.

Fourteenth Generation

632. **Kayla Marie McDonald** (Laura Marie Barnhouser-13, Bernard Alfred-12, Lula Grace States-11, Susie Bernice Crouch-10, Charles Wesley-9, Willamina Rasin-8, Philip Reed-7, William Blackiston-6, Rosamond Blackiston-5, William-4, Ebenezer-3, George-2, Marmaduke-1) was born on 5 Nov 1993 in Franklin Sq Hosp, Baltimore, Maryland. She was christened on 26 Mar 1995 at Saint Leo's Church in Little Italy, Baltimore, Maryland.

BIRTH: Kayla was born 8:10 PM 7 lb. 5 oz Franklin Sq Hosp. 19" long. Laura went to hosp. at 2pm. Her mom Charmaine helped with delivery.

BAPTISM: Kayla was baptized at St. Leo's Church in Little Italy with her family present and a large gathering afterwards in the church to celebrate.

Kayla Marie McDonald and Tony Medri were married. **Tony Medri.**

Tony Medri and Kayla Marie McDonald had the following children:

642   i. **Rocco Arnoldo Medri** was born on 20 Oct 2013 in Baltimore City, Maryland. Rocco Arnoldo Medri. 7 pounds 6 ounces. 18 inches. 10/20/2013 at 12:49am.
643   ii. **Medri** was born on 4 Oct 2019.

633. **Guy Edward Almony Jr.** (Laura Marie Barnhouser-13, Bernard Alfred-12, Lula Grace States-11, Susie Bernice Crouch-10, Charles Wesley-9, Willamina Rasin-8, Philip Reed-7, William Blackiston-6, Rosamond Blackiston-5, William-4, Ebenezer-3, George-2, Marmaduke-1) was born on 5 Jul 1997 in Bayview Hospital, Baltimore City, Md. He was christened on 21 Feb 1999 in Essex Upper M. Ch., Essex, Baltimore County, Maryland. Guy is the godson of Christos Christou and was adopted by him. His biological ancestry is given in Prominent Families of Kent Co copyright 1997 and in the Almony Family of MD and PA copyright 2000 by Christos Christou, Jr. and John A. Barnhouser, Sr.

He is a Foreman at his current company and has worked previously at several construction companies in Baltimore including Iaconi.

BIRTH: Guy Edward Almony Jr. male born July 5, 1997 Baltimore City 2:28am 5lbs 2 oz. father Guy Edward Almony Sr. age 25, maiden name of mother Laura Marie Barnhouser age 23 born MD, Cert. #97-34193. (Born at Johns Hopkins - Bayview Hospital (formerly City Hospital) on July 5th at 2:28am. He was 17 3/4 inches, weighed 5 lbs 2 1/2 oz. Born one month premature. Had small breathing problem and was kept in hosp. for monitoring during first few days, released July 9th. Dr. Alpan was the doctor. Delivered by Dr. Alpan in the emergency room.)

BAPTISM: Guy Edward Almony, Jr. child of Guy Edward Almony Sr. and Laura Marie Almony born at Bayview Center on the 5th of July 1997 received Christian Baptism on the 21st day of February 1999 at Essex United Methodist Church, 524 Maryland Avenue, Baltimore, MD 21221. by Rev. Eddie L. Henry, Pastor. Godfather Christos Christou, Jr. and godmother Dorothy Grace Barnhouser. (Dottie had to fly in from the Navy for the event and Chris held the reception for everyone afterwards in the Fellowship Hall at EUMC.

ADOPTION: Ordered Feb. 7, 2001 by Judge Joseph H.H. Kaplan. Open Adoption. Completed Case #A00355015. Circuit Court of Baltimore City. Godfather Christos Christou granted adoption for Guy Jr. He had been permanently placed in home starting Dec. 16, 1998. Final court decree signed Feb. 5, 2001. Photo taken with Judge on the joyous day.

NEWS: Guy Edward Almony, Jr. born July 5 will celebrate his first birthday with close family and friends. Guy is the son of Guy Edward Almony, Sr. and his wife Laura Marie (Barnhouser) Almony; grandson of Virginia L. Almony, Bernard Alfred Barnhouser Jr. and Charmaine May (Guy) Barnhouser; great grandson of Emory Edward Miller Sr., Stanley Clinton Almony, Sr. and Myrtle Marie Almony; great grandson of Elmer Cleveland Clouser, Sr. Guy has two sisters Kayla Marie McDonald and Na'Tasha Marie Almony. Godparents are Christos Christou, Jr. and Dorothy Grace Barnhouser. The Avenue News July 2, 1998 p. 10A Photo of Chris and Guy Jr.

NEWS: Guy Edward Almony, Jr. born July 5, 1997 will celebrate his first birthday with close family and friends. Guy is the son of Guy Edward Almony, Sr. and his wife Laura Marie (Barnhouser) Almony, grandson of Virginia L. Almony, Bernard Alfred Barnhouser Jr. and Charmaine May (Guy) Barnhouser and the great grandson of Edward Miller Sr. and Stanley Clinton Almony Sr. and Myrtle Marie Almony and great great grandson of Rev. Elmer Cleveland Clouser, Sr. Guy Jr. has two sisters Kayla Marie McDonald and Na'Tasha Marie Almony. Godparents are Christos Christou, Jr. and Dorothy Grace Barnhouser. The Essex Times July 2, 1998 p. 25

NEWS: Guy E. Almony, Jr. turned two on July 5 and celebrated his birthday at home. Four generations of family gathered together including his mother Laura Almony, grandmother Virginia Almony and great grandmother, Myrtle Almony. Twenty-six other family members from the Almony, Barnhouser and Christou families attended, including his sister Na'Tasha Almony and cousins John A. Barnhouser and Samantha Barnhouser. The Avenue News July 29, 1999 p. 14. (picture of Charmaine and Guy)

NEWS: Guy Edward Almony, Jr. turned two on July 5 and to help celebrate his birthday, four generations of family braved the 100 degree weather and attended including his mother Laura M. Almony and father Christos Christou, Jr., grandmothers Virginia L. Almony and Charmaine M. Barnhouser, and great grandmother Myrtle M. Almony. The list of younger members that attended are Na'Tasha M. Almony, John A. Barnhouser Jr., Samantha R. Barnhouser, MacKenzie L. Christou, Sean J. McCauley, Anthony J. Romeo Jr., Eric O. Vidal, and Rana M. Zavalis. Several aunts and uncles attended also. His great-great grandfather Rev. Elmer Clouser Sr. died earlier this year in Florida. East County Times August 5, 1999 p. 26.

NEWS: Four Generations of Almony. Pictured are Guy E. Almony, Jr. age 2 seated on the lap of his great grandmother Myrtle Marie (Clouser) Almony, to their left is his grandmother, Virginia Lee Almony and in the back is his mother Laura Marie (Barnhouser) Almony. Guy Jr. has been accepted in the Children of the American Revolution (CAR) by right of his maternal ancestor Capt. William Blackiston Rasin who fought bravely in the American Revolution during the battle of Cowpens, SC. Guy Jr. will also be applying on a supplemental application in the CAR for a second paternal ancestor Major David Wiley who served in the York Co, PA Militia. The Avenue News Nov. 24, 1999 p. 16

CAR: Guy Edward Almony, Jr. accepted as a member of the Children of the American Revolution through his ancestor Capt. William Blackiston Rasin. CAR #145958, Accepted November 15, 1999.

SAR: Guy Edward Almony, Jr. accepted as a member of the Sons of the American Revolution through his ancestor Major David Wiley. SAR #160713 MD #3664 on July 14, 2003. He holds the record for the most documented Patriots of the American Revolution in the MDSSAR at 50 supplementals including his ancestors Capt. William B. Rasin on Dec. 13, 2004 and John Almony on Dec 14 2006.

WAR of 1812: Guy Edward Almony Jr. accepted as a member of the War of 1812 society through his ancestor Richard Barnhouse. He was granted Honorary Membership by President Clarke Bowers on October 23, 2006 due to attending the Board meetings monthly. He was approved as the first ever Junior Associate Member in the MD society on April 26, 2007. The National Society did not have Jr Membership at the time but registered it on May 12, 2007. Due to a change in the Bylaws at the Triennial, that was presented by Christos Christou Jr., he was approved officially approved as the first Junior National Member on October 10, 2010.

Cub Scouts: Guy was a member of the Boy Scouts of America starting as a Cub Scouts since October 2003 joining Pack 880 of Dulaney District (Warren Elem. School) moving from Tiger to Wolf (May 2004) to Bear (May 2005) to Webelos I (May 2006). He transitioned from Pack 880 by joining dual with Pack 745 in Chesapeake District (Essex United Methodist Church) and officially in August 2006 transferred to Pack 745 as a Webelo I. He became Webelo II in March 2007. On March 1, 2008 at the Blue and Gold Ceremony Court of Honor held at Essex United Methodist Church, Guy graduated into Boy Scout Troop 745 and received his Arrow of Light. In January 2009 he transferred from Troop 745 to Troop 355 (Our Lady of Mt. Carmel) and moved from Scout to Tenderfoot Scout (Aug 5, 2008) to Second Class Scout (Nov 11, 2008) to First Class Scout (Dec 3, 2009).

Baseball: He played baseball for many years with several Essex Baseball Teams of Essex A's (2003), Mariners (2004, 2005), and Devil Rays (2006), skipped (2007), Rockies (2008), Astros (2009), As (2010).

Karate: He studied Tae Kwon Do at Kim's Karate since 2002 going from no Belt to White Belt (Aug. 8, 2003), to Yellow (Mar. 27, 2004), to Green (Dec. 17, 2004), to Blue (Jul 29, 2005) to Purple (July 8, 2007).

Guy has taken several DNA tests and his Ancestral makeup as of 2024 results indicated 100% European ancestry with 79% from United Kingdom (England, Scotland, Ireland), 12% Nordic Countries (Norway, Sweden, Denmark, Finland), and 10% Germany.

Guy Edward Almony Jr. and Mariah Kierra Heaven Bukowski has a son. **Mariah Kierra Heaven Bukowski**, daughter of Joseph Charles Bukowski and Robin Lorraine Lambert, was born on 25 Feb 1999 in Baltimore City, Md. Mariah is a hardworking mother now but attended beautician school, worked in a movie theatre, and a doctors office. She runs a photography business taking professional photos of people for events and special occasions. Her primary work is as devoted mother to her son Guy.

Mariah has taken a DNA test which as of 2024 shows a multicultural ancestry of 72% from United Kingdom (England, Scotland, Ireland, Wales), 13% German/Jewish, 9% African (Cameroon, Congo, Senegal, and Ivory Coast/Ghana), and 6% Norway. Her ancestry includes Lumbee Indians but unfortunately due to limitations in DNA testing comparisons, these traits show up as a mix of European and African. See many online articles on this subject but most scholarship now confirm that the Lumbee are descended from a mix of Siouan, Algonquian, and Iroquoian-speaking peoples. They also intermarried with whites and with free and enslaved blacks. The Lumbee are recognized as an Indian tribe by the State of North Carolina, but the federal government does not fully recognize them and has made it harder for Indians who were not displaced and had negotiated treaties to apply for such status but the Lumbee Nation continue to fight for federal recognition and benefits. The Lumbee are the largest tribe east of the Mississippi.

Guy Edward Almony and Mariah Kierra Heaven Bukowski had the following child:

644   i. **Guy Edward Almony III** was born on 22 Apr 2020 in Baltimore City, Md. Guy Edward Almony III was born April 22, 2020 At 3:56 PM at Mercy Hospital and weighed only 3 lbs. 8 oz. and was 15.5 inches long. He was premature and had a low birth weight so he stayed in the Hospital until May 27th. This was at the start and height of the Corona Virus lock downs and restrictions meant visitation were limited so it was a joyous celebration when he came home finally.

Guy was accepted into the following lineage societies based on his Patriotic ancestry:
War of 1812 Society: Life Member GS #7968 MD#1042 for ancestor 4th Sgt. John Johnson 1789-1875 who fought in the War of 1812 in Virginia in 1813.
Children of 1812 Society: Life Member Natl #105 MD# 41 for Corporal Philip R. Rasin 1793-1841 who fought in War of 1812 in Kent Co MD at battle of Caulk's Field.
Children of the American Revolution: CAR#168500 for ancestor Capt. William Blackiston Rasin 1760-1810 who fought in the American Revolution 1777-1783 in numerous key battles.
Sons of the American Revolution: Jr. Member SAR #216169 MD #4861 for ancestor Major David Wiley 1747-1817 who commanded a Pennsylvania Line in 1779. He holds a record for the youngest Junior member with the most supplementals in the Sons of the American Revolution.
The Hereditary Order of the Families of the Presidents and First Ladies of America: Jr. Member J-37 for his kinship to First Lady Jacqueline Lee (Bouvier) Kennedy Onassis and their mutual ancestor Edward Beck of Kent County, Maryland.

He is the 11th and 12th Generation of Almony in America and descends through three different sons of the Patriot John Almony.

634. Constance May Cummings (Laura Marie Barnhouser-13, Bernard Alfred-12, Lula Grace States-11, Susie Bernice Crouch-10, Charles Wesley-9, Willamina Rasin-8, Philip Reed-7, William Blackiston-6, Rosamond Blackiston-5, William-4, Ebenezer-3, George-2, Marmaduke-1) was born on 1 Oct 1999 in Baltimore City, Maryland. She was christened on 26 Mar 2000 at Saint Elizabeth in Highlandtown, Baltimore City, Maryland. She has one daughter by Jeremiah Burke.

BIRTH: Constance was born at Johns Hopkins Hosp. on Broadway St. in Room #12. Mother and baby were moved to Room #272 on Oct 1,1999 at 7:24 PM. She weighed 6 lbs. 15 oz. and measured 21 inches. Beautiful full color.

BAPTISM: Constance was baptized at St. Elizabeth of Hungary Catholic Church near Patterson Park at 12:30pm on March 26, 2000. John Barnhouser and Kimberly Lindsey are godparents. Rev. Daniel Sinisi baptized. Many members of the family attended the celebration.

NEWS: Congratulations to the parents of Constance May Cummings born October 1, at 7:24pm at Johns Hopkins Hospital. She was 6 lbs. and 15 ozs and 21 inches long. Her parents are Charles Edward "Chris" Cummings III and Laura Marie Barnhouser. Grandparents are William O. Bowen, Charlene Crouch, Bernard A. Barnhouser, Jr. and Charmaine M. Barnhouser. Great grandmother is Marie A. Bowen. Constance was welcomed in to this world by her half-sisters and half-brother Ashley Ann Smith, Kayla Marie McDonald, and Guy Edward Almony, Jr. Baby and parents are home and doing well. The Avenue News Oct. 28, 1999 p. 17

NEWS: Congratulations to the parents of Constance May Cummings, born Oct. 1st 7:24pm at Johns Hopkins Hospital. She is 6 lbs. and 15 oz. She was 21 inches long. Her parents are Charles Edward "Chris" Cummings, III and Laura Marie Almony. Constance has 2 sisters and one brother; Ashley Ann Smith, Kayla Marie McDonald, and Guy Edward Almony, Jr. Grandparents are Bernard A. Barnhouser, Jr., Charmaine M. Barnhouser, William O. Bowen, and Charlene Crouch. Great grandmother is Marie A. Bowen. Baby and parents are home and doing well. East County Times Oct. 28, 1999. p 26

NEWS: Uncle John Barnhouser and Aunt Kimberly Lindsey wish to announce the baptism of their goddaughter Constance May Cummings, daughter of Charles E. Cummings and Laura M. Almony, on Mar. 26 at St. Elizabeth of Hungary Roman Catholic Church. Attending the service were the parents, grandmothers Charmaine Barnhouser and Charlene Crouch, and great grandmother Marie Bowen along with many other family and friends. A celebration was held later in the church hall. East County Times April 13, 2000. p 29

NEWS: On March 26, 2000, Constance May Cummings born Oct. 1, 1999, daughter of Chris E. Cummings and Laura Barnhouser Almony, was baptized at St. Elizabeth of Hungary Roman Catholic Church. God parents were uncle John A. Barnhouser, Sr. and Aunt Kimberly R. Lindsey. Many attended including brother Guy E. Almony, Jr., parents, grandmothers Charmaine Barnhouser and Charlene Crouch, and great grandmother Marie Bowen, as well as numerous cousins, aunts and uncles. A celebration party was held afterwards in the church hall with lots of food and drinks. The Avenue News May 4, 2000

Constance May Cummings and Jeremiah Burke were married. **Jeremiah Burke**.

Jeremiah Burke and Constance May Cummings had the following child:

645   i. **Maylynn Burke** was born on 28 Feb 2020.

Miscellaneous Blackistons

This family appears to be related to one of the many branches of the George Blackiston but unable to link to the specific family.

1. **John Blackiston** was born before 1787. **Sarah** was born before 1787. John Blackiston and Sarah had the following child:

+2   i.   **John Blackiston**, born Jul 1807, Maryland; married Eleanor , abt 1836; married Margaret Coleman, 8 Jul 1880, Queen Anne's County, Maryland; died 20 Oct 1900, Queen Anne County, Maryland, United States.

2. **John Blackiston** (John-1) was born in Jul 1807 in Maryland. He died on 20 Oct 1900 at the age of 93 in Queen Anne County, Maryland, United States. Vouchers Kent Co Bk 6 p 254. I John Blackiston son of Jabez Blackiston late of Kent Co a nephew and one of the heirs at law of Ebenezer decd received $368.25 my distributive share of the estate of Ebenezer.

John Blackiston Born 1811-1820 1840; Census Place: Districts 1 and 2, Queen Anne's, Maryland; Roll: 169; Page: 102;

CENSUS: 1850 Queen Anne's Co, MD
John Blackstone 28 farmer MD, Ellenora Blackstone 26, Solomon Stant 12
John W Stant 10, James M Stant 8, Ann E Stant 7, John T Stant 6, Sarah E Stant 5, Susan J Stant 3, Martha M Stant 0, Mary Reed 50
1850; Census Place: District 2, Queen Anne's, Maryland; Roll: M432 296; Page: 165B; Image: 91

CENSUS: 1860 Queen Anne's Co, MD
John Blackstone 40, Ellender Blackstone 34, John Blackstone 19, Joseph Blackstone 16, Amanda Blackstone 12, Mary Blackstone 8, Francis Blackstone 6, Catherine Blackstone 3
1860; Census Place: District 2, Queen Annes, Maryland; Roll: M653 479; Page: 61; Family History Library Film: 803479

CENSUS: 1870 Queen Anne's Co, MD
John Blackston 60, Ellen Blackston 45, Ann E Blackston 22, Kate Blackston 11
Charles Blackston 2, Isaac Blackston 2/12, Rebecca Blackston 2/12
1870; Census Place: Districts 1 and 2, Queen Annes, Maryland; Roll: M593 593; Page: 324B; Family History Library Film: 552092

CENSUS: 1880 Queen Anne's Co, MD
John Blackston 66, Charles E 12 son

1880; Census Place: Church Hill, Queen Anne's, Maryland; Roll: 514; Page: 332C; Enumeration District: 058

CENSUS: 1900 Queen Anne's Co, MD
John Blackston 92 born Jul 1807 married 19y, Margaret C Blackston 58 born Dec 1841, Cooper Burris 8 grandson born Oct 1891
1900; Census Place: Crumpton, Queen Anne, Maryland; Page: 9; Enumeration District: 0068; FHL microfilm: 1240626

John Blackiston and Eleanor were married about 1836. **Eleanor** died after 1870.

John Blackiston and Eleanor had the following children:

+3   i.   **John Wesley Blackiston**, born 9 Mar 1837, Maryland; married Martha Ann Elburn, 22 Jun 1864, Kent Co, Maryland, United States; married Mary Ann Squires, 14 May 1889, Kent Co, Maryland, United States; died 16 Dec 1924, McGinnis Corner, Queen Anne's, Maryland, United States.

4   ii.   **James W Blackiston** was born in 1842. He died after 1880 at the age of 38. 1850 listed as James M. Stant age 8 in household of John and Eleanor. He married Mary Frances Dill. SERVICE: James Blackston Age: 20 Enlistment Date: 1862 Military Unit: Third Cavalry, O-Y AND Third State Militia, Cavalry AND Third State Militia, Cavalry (2d Organization), A-D. CENSUS: 1870 Queen Anne's Co, MD James Blackston 29, Mary Blackston 18 1870; Census Place: Districts 1 and 2, Queen Annes, Maryland; Roll: M593 593; Page: 325B CENSUS: 1880 Queen Anne's Co MD James Blackston 39 Self (Head), Mary F. Blackston 36 Wife, Magga Blackston 7 Daughter, Carrie Blackston 6 Daughter, James A. Blackston 3 Son, John Blackston 2 Son 1880; Census Place: Church Hill, Queen Anne's, Maryland; Roll: 514; Page: 331B; Enumeration District: 058 SSA: son James Albert Blackiston Gender: Male Race: White Birth Date: 2 Oct 1877 Birth Place: Crumpton, Maryland Father: James W Blackiston Mother: Frances Dill SSN: 216121076 Notes: Sep 1939: Name listed as JAMES ALBERT BLACKISTON

+5   iii.   **Joseph Thomas Blackiston**, born 25 Apr 1845, Queen Anne County, Maryland, United States; married Henrietta Everett, 8 Feb 1865, Queen Annes, Maryland; died 8 Apr 1935, Queen Anne County, Maryland, United States.

6   iv.   **Charles Elsworth Blackiston** was born on 3 Apr 1868 in Queens Annes County Md. He died on 18 May 1940 at the age of 72 in Hempstead, Nassau, New York, United States. CENSUS: 1900 New Castle Co, DE Charles E Blackiston 32, Martha A Blackiston 32,

Bertha G Blackiston 10, Willard T Blackiston 8, Beulah M Blackiston 6, Charles R Blackiston 4 1900; Census Place: Wilmington Ward 5, New Castle, Delaware; Page: 6; Enumeration District: 0017; FHL microfilm: 1240154. CENSUS: 1910 New Castle Co, DE Charles E Blackiston 40, Martha A Blackiston 40, Willard W Blackiston 18, Buella M Blackiston 16, Mable C Blackiston 8, Martha E Blackiston 0 1910; Census Place: Wilmington Ward 4, New Castle, Delaware; Roll: T624 147; Page: 21A; Enumeration District: 0029; FHL microfilm: 1374160 CENSUS: 1930 Queens, NY Charles Blackiston 62,Martha Blackiston 62, Martha Blackiston 20, 1930; Census Place: Queens, Queens, New York; Page: 9A; Enumeration District: 0612; FHL microfilm: 2341345 SSA: Charles Elsworth Blackiston Birth Date: 3 Apr 1868 Birth Place: Queens Anns, Maryland Death Date: 18 May 1940 Claim Date: 14 Jun 1940 SSN: 119056725 Notes: 24 Sep 1976: Name listed as CHARLES ELSWORTH BLACKISTON. Death Index Hempstead NY Cert. #30902

His wife Martha was the daughter of Charles Scone and Mary Swatke. OBITUARY: Mrs. Martha M. Blackiston, 78 years old, widow of Charles E. Blackiston, died Friday at her home, 1915 Seneca road, Canby Park. Funeral services will be at the McCrery funeral home, 2700 Washington street, tomorrow at 2:30 p.m. The Rev. Albert H. Kleffman, D. D., pastor of West Presbyterian church, will officiate. Interment will be in Silverbrook cemetery. Mrs. Blackiston is survived by five children, Mrs. Bertha Lewis, with whom she lived; William T. Blackiston, and Mrs. Beulah Logan, of Wilmington; Mrs. Martha Burke and Mrs. Mabel Quinn, New York, 13 grandchildren, and four great-grandchildren. The Sunday Morning Star (Wilmington, DE), 4 Mar 1945, p. 8

John Blackiston and Margaret Coleman were married on 8 Jul 1880 in Queen Anne's County, Maryland. **Margaret Coleman** was born in Dec 1841. She died on 9 Apr 1924 at the age of 82 in Queen Anne's County, Maryland.

CENSUS: 1860 Queen Anne's Co, MD
Betsey Coleman 34, Thomas Coleman 7, George Coleman 5, James Coleman 2, Nancy Emory 8
1860; Census Place: District 3, Queen Anne's County, Maryland; Roll: M653 479; Page: 68; Family History Library Film: 803479

CENSUS: 1880 Queen Anne's Co, MD
Elizebeth Colemon 63 Self (Head), James R. Colemon 22 Son , Margaret Snitcher 33 Daughter widowed, George Smith 11 Grandson, Lillie Snitcher 8 Granddaughter, Charles Snitcher 2 Grandson, Mary Snitcher 1 Granddaughter

1880; Census Place: Church Hill, Queen Anne's, Maryland; Roll: 514; Page: 332C; Enumeration District: 058

CENSUS: 1920 Queen Anne's Co, MD
Charles Snitcher 42 Head, Margaret Blackiston 78 Mother, Cooper Burris 22 Nephew
1920; Census Place: District 7, Queen Anne's, Maryland; Roll: T625 675; Page: 14B; Enumeration District: 83

SSA: Charles M Snitcher Gender: Male, Race: White Birth Date: 25 Aug 1882 Birth Place: Millington Q, Maryland, Father: Charles Snitcher Mother: Margaret Coleman SSN: 212167641 Notes: Mar 1938: Name listed as CHARLES M SNITCHER

Cooper Burris Gender: Male Race: White Birth Date: 11 Oct 1890
Birth Place: Blanco Kent, Delaware Father: George Burris Mother:
Lillie Snitcher SSN: 219342902 Notes: Aug 1954: Name listed as COOPER BURRIS

John Blackiston and Margaret Coleman had the following child:

> 7   i. **William Gibson Blackiston** was born on 4 Dec 1881 in Queen Anne's County, Maryland. He died on 15 Nov 1939 at the age of 57 in Queen Anne's County, Maryland. He was buried in Crumpton Cemetery, Queen Anne's County, Maryland. CENSUS: 1900 Queen Anne's Co, MD John Blackston 92 Head, Margaret C Blackston 58 Wife, Cooper Burris 8 Grand Son (Grandson) 1900; Census Place: Crumpton, Queen Anne, Maryland; Roll: 626; Page: 9; Enumeration District: 0068; FHL microfilm: 1240626 CENSUS: 1910 Queen Anne's Co, MD William Blackiston 28 Head, Susie Blackiston 25 Wife, Luther G Blackiston 5 Son, Susie Blackiston 67 Mother, Cooper Burris 18 Nephew 1910; Census Place: Crumpton, Queen Anne's, Maryland; Roll: T624 567; Page: 1B; Enumeration District: 0073; FHL microfilm: 1374580 CENSUS: 1920 Queen Anne's Co, MD William G Blackiston 38 Head, Susie M Blackiston 36 Wife, Luther Blackiston 14 Son, Margaret Blackiston 7 Daughter, Harry Burris 31 Nephew 1920; Census Place: District 7, Queen Anne's, Maryland; Roll: T625 675; Page: 12A; Enumeration District: 83

3. **John Wesley Blackiston** (John-2, John-1) was born on 9 Mar 1837 in Maryland. He died on 16 Dec 1924 at the age of 87 in McGinnis Corner, Queen Anne's, Maryland, United States.

CENSUS: 1880 Queen Anne's Co, MD
John Blackston 40, Mary A. Blackston 35, William Blackston 19, John Blackston 15, George E. Blackston 11, Samuel Blackston 6, Kate Blackston 3, Ella Blackston 9m

1880; Census Place: Church Hill, Queen Annes, Maryland; Roll: 514; Family History Film: 1254514; Page: 328C; Enumeration District: 058; Image: 0277.

MARRIAGE: John W. Blackiston m. Mary A. Squires May 14, 1889 Rev. Mr. Smith. Kent Co. MD

CENSUS: 1900 Queen Anne's Co, MD
John Blackston 61 born Mar 1839 MD parents born MD, Mary A Blackston 55 born Nov 1844 m 24y 7 ch 6 lvg born DE, parents DE, John Blackston 16 born Nov 1883 born MD son
1900; Census Place: Crumpton, Queen Anne, Maryland; Roll: 626; Page: 12B; Enumeration District: 68; FHL microfilm: 1240626.

CENSUS: 1910 Queen Anne's Co, MD
John W Blackiston 70 born MD parents born MD married 30y
Martha A Blackiston 65 born DE parents born DE 7 children 6 living
next door is
W John Blackiston 27, Annie Blackiston 24, James Blackiston 3, Clarence Blackiston 2, Florence A Blackiston 1
1910; Census Place: Crumpton, Queen Anne's, Maryland; Roll: T624 567; Page: 12A; Enumeration District: 0073; FHL microfilm: 1374580

CENSUS: 1920 Queen Anne's Co, MD
John W Blackiston 79 born MD parents born MD, Mary Ann Blackiston 65 born DE parents born DE
1920;Census Place: District 7, Queen Anne's, Maryland; Roll: T625 675; Page: 12B; Enumeration District: 83; Image: 985.

John Blackiston 36 born MD, Annie Blackiston 30, Jennings Blackiston 14, Clarence Blackiston 13, Florence Blackiston 10, J Lester Blackiston 7
1920; Census Place: District 7, Queen Anne's, Maryland; Roll: T625 675; Page: 15A; Enumeration District: 83

Samuel Thomas Blackiston born May 12 1873 born Queen Annes Co son of John W. Blackiston and Mary A Squares per SSA record.

PENSION: Served in CW served in C 2 MD Inf. widow applied for pension Jan 26 1925.

John Wesley Blackiston and Martha Ann Elburn were married on 22 Jun 1864 in Kent Co, Maryland, United States. **Martha Ann Elburn**, daughter of James Elburn and Sarah Jones, born about 1845 in De. She died on 19 Dec 1907 at the age of 62 in Kent County, Maryland, United States.

CENSUS: 1880 Queen Anne's Co, MD

Wm. Elburn 50 widowed, Martha A. Elburn 40 sister widowed (divorced 1883), Mary M. Elburn 6, Ella J. Elburn 5, Wm. Elburn 12, Romey Elburn 9, L. Blackston 3 nephew, A. Blackston 6 nephew
1880; Census Place: Ruthsburg, Queen Anne's, Maryland; Roll: 514; Page: 488B; Enumeration District: 006

CENSUS: 1900
James Joiner 60 born MD 1840 married 15y, Martha A Joiner 35 born 1845 MD married 15y 6 children 3 living, William J Downlin 14 grand S born Mar 1886
Joseph L Downey 5 grand D (sic) born Aug 1894
Lewin Blackiston 22 stepson born Apr 1878
1900; Census Place: Edesville, Kent, Maryland; Roll T623 625; Page: 11A; Enumeration District: 52.

Parents are James Elbourn and Sarah Jones per death cert.

John Wesley Blackiston and Martha Ann Elburn had the following children:

+8   i.   **George W. Blackiston**, born 18 Jun 1867, Kent County, Maryland; married Mary Matilda Beck; died 25 Jan 1922, Queen Anne County, Maryland, United States.

9   ii. **William Thomas Blackiston** was born on 11 Apr 1870 in Kent County, Maryland. He was christened on 6 Sep 1873 in Rock Hall, Kent County, Maryland. BAPTISM: Wm Thos. Blackiston born April 11 1870 baptized Sep 6 1873. Parents John W. and Martha Blackiston by Rev. George Leary. Rock Hall.

10   iii. **A Blackiston** born about 1874.

+11   iv. **Lewin Samuel Blackiston Sr**, born 21 Apr 1878, Kent County, Maryland; married Mary Elizabeth Freburger, abt 1901; died 18 Feb 1953, Kent Co, Maryland, United States.

John Wesley Blackiston and Mary Ann Squires were married on 14 May 1889 in Kent Co, Maryland, United States. **Mary Ann Squires** was born in Nov 1844. She died after 1925 at the age of 81. The started having kids after his 1883 divorce from first wife but married in 1889.

John Wesley Blackiston and Mary Ann Squires had the following child:

12   i.   **John Welsey Blackiston Jr.** was born on 10 Dec 1884 in Queen Anne County, Maryland, United States. He died in May 1979 at the age of 94.

5. Joseph Thomas Blackiston (John-2, John-1) was born on 25 Apr 1845 in Queen Anne County, Maryland, United States. He died on 8 Apr 1935 at the age of 89 in Queen Anne County, Maryland, United States. A great grandson Billy Blackiston tried to do his family research but mixed up much of his information and for example said his middle name was Theodore not Thomas.

CENSUS: 1850 Philadelphia PA
John R. Blackiston 38, Martha C. 34, John 12, Joseph 10, Charles 6, Albert 2, Mary 8, John Bowling 6, and others.

CENSUS: 1860 New Castle Co DE
Joseph Blackiston 19 born MD living with Nathaniel Longfellow 33 and family as laborer.

MARRIAGE: Joseph T. Blackiston m. Henrietta Everett on Feb. 8 1865 by Rev. Mr. Barton. Queen Annes Co, MD

CENSUS: 1870

CENSUS: 1880 Queen Anne's Co, MD
Joseph Blackston 36, Heney Blackston 40, John B. Blackston 10, Sarah E. Blackston 8, Anna Blackston 6, Thomas Blackston 1
1880; Census Place: Church Hill, Queen Anne's, Maryland; Roll: 514; Page: 332C; Enumeration District: 058
Next door is John Blackiston 66 and Charles E 12 Also near Lloyds.

CENSUS: 1900 Queen Anne's Co, MD
Joseph Blackston born Apr 1848 52y m 30y born MD, Mary born May 1850 50y m 30y 5 ch 5 lvg born MD
1900; Census Place: Crumpton, Queen Anne, Maryland; Page: 19; Enumeration District: 0068; FHL microfilm: 1240626

CENSUS: 1910 Queen Anne's Co, MD
Joseph Blackiston 64, Henrietta Blackiston 69 wife, Thomas F Blackiston 31 son
Henrietta Blackiston 33 dau in law 8y 3 ch 3 lvg, Johnny Blackiston 7 grandson
Norman Blackiston 5 grandson, Martha E Blackiston 2 granddau.
1910; Census Place: Crumpton, Queen Anne's, Maryland; Roll: T624 567; Page: 2B; Enumeration District: 0073; FHL microfilm: 1374580

1920 Kent Co, MD
Thos F Blackiston 42, Heney Etta Blackiston 43, Norman F Blackiston 11
Martha E Blackiston 12, Woodrow W Blackiston 7, Edna R Blackiston 5, William T Blackiston 0, Jos T Blackiston 75, Henry Etta Blackiston 79
1920; Census Place: Kennedyville, Kent, Maryland; Roll: T625 673; Page: 3A; Enumeration District: 62

CENSUS: 1930 Kent Co, MD
Joseph Everett 62 m. age 25y, Anna R Everett 54 m age 17y, Gladys Everett 20
Joseph Blackiston 84 widower born MD parents born MD, Ben Williams 53
Norman Blackiston 22, Clifton Everett 21 stepson
1930; Census Place: Pomona, Kent, Maryland; Page: 8B; Enumeration District: 0012; FHL microfilm: 2340611

Joseph Thomas Blackiston and Henrietta Everett were married on 8 Feb 1865 in Queen Annes, Maryland. **Henrietta Everett**, daughter of Benjamin Everitt and Sarah , was born on 31 Aug 1840 in Queen Anne County, Maryland, United States. She died on 24 Aug 1922 at the age of 81 in Queen Annes County, Maryland, United States. She was buried in Double Creek Cemetery.

CENSUS: 1850 Queen Anne's Co, MD
Benjamin Everett 35, Sarah Everett 30, Henry Everett 8, Samuel Everett 4, Martha A Everett 0
1850; Census Place: District 1, Queen Anne's, Maryland; Roll: M432 296; Page: 138A; Image: 36

CENSUS: 1860 Queen Anne's Co, MD
Benjamin Everett 40, Sallie Everett 40, Martha Everett 11, John Everett 3
1860; Census Place: District 1, Queen Annes, Maryland; Roll: M653 479; Page: 143; Family History Library Film: 803479

DEATH: Henrietta Blackiston of QA died McGuiness Corner Aug 24 1922 parents Benjamin Everett and Sarah Everett. born Aug 31 1840 married, infor. Joseph Blackiston of Millington RFD buried Double Creek by fun. dir. Charles Dodd.

Joseph Thomas Blackiston and Henrietta Everett had the following children:

13   i.   **Thomas J. Blackiston** was born in 1878 in Maryland.
+14   ii. **Mary M. Blackiston**, born 23 Feb 1883, Maryland; married Walter Hines Everitt; died 29 Dec 1939, Cecil County, Maryland, United States.

8. George W. Blackiston (John Wesley-3, John-2, John-1) was born on 18 Jun 1867 in Kent County, Maryland. He was christened on 13 Aug 1867 in Rock Hall, Kent County, Maryland. He died on 25 Jan 1922 at the age of 54 in Queen Anne County, Maryland, United States. BAPTISM: George W. Blackiston born June 18 1867 baptized Aug 13 1867 parents John W. and M.A. Blackiston by Rev. George Leary. Rock Hall.

CENSUS: 1870

CENSUS: 1880 Kent Co, MD
J. Frank Wheatley 27, Mary E. Wheatley 32, Charles F. Wheatley 5, Flora C. Wheatley 2,
G.W. Blackiston 13 single
1880; Census Place: Piney Neck, Kent, Maryland; Roll: 512; Family History Film:
1254512; Page: 186A; Enumeration District: 055

CENSUS: 1900 Kent Co, MD
George W Blackinstone 35, Mary M Blackinstone 25, George D Blackinstone 5
Daniel W Blackinstone 2
1900; Census Place: Edesville, Kent, Maryland; Page: 10; Enumeration District: 0052;
FHL microfilm: 1240625

CENSUS: 1910 Kent Co, MD
George W Blackiston 47, Mary M Blackiston 35, George D Blackiston 16, Daniel N
Blackiston 13, Fanny M E Blackiston 5, William F Blackiston 2
1910; Census Place: Edesville, Kent, Maryland; Roll: T624 566; Page: 9B; Enumeration
District: 0058; FHL microfilm: 1374579

CENSUS: 1920 Kent Co, MD
Geo W Blackstone 53 Head, Mary M Blackstone 45 Wife, George D Blackstone 24 Son,
Daniel W Blackstone 22 Son, Fanny M Blackstone 14 Daughter, Franklin W Blackstone
11 Son
Year: 1920; Census Place: Edesville, Kent, Maryland; Roll: T625 674; Page: 4A;
Enumeration District: 68

George W. Blackiston and Mary Matilda Beck were married. **Mary Matilda Beck**,
daughter of James Alexander Beck and Martha Elizabeth Kelley, was born on 25 Dec 1881
in Kent County Md. She died on 9 Nov 1952 at the age of 70 in Millington, Queen Anne's,
Maryland, United States. Called Minnie.

George W. Blackiston and Mary Matilda Beck had the following children:

+15   i. **George David Blackiston Sr**, born 20 Mar 1895, Rock Hall, Kent,
Maryland, United States; died 26 Aug 1952, Chestertown, Kent,
Maryland, United States.

16   ii. **Daniel Washington Blackiston** was born on 20 Jun 1897. He died on
5 Feb 1976 at the age of 78 in McGinnis Corner, Queen Anne's,
Maryland, United States. He was buried in Crumpton Cemetery, Queen
Anne's, Maryland, United States. Per nephew Bishop Blackiston,
Uncle Jim was the brother of his father William F. Blackiston Fannie
Blackiston Meekins and George Blackiston (children of George
Washington Blackiston and Mary Beck). He was married to Beatrice

and had the following children: Cecila, Doc, James, Bus, Ralph and Catherine Blackiston. Censuses and the obituary of Beatrice list more children - K. Cecilia Farrow, Charles, George Alfred, James Franklin, Ralph Joseph, and Catherine O. Blackiston (and a Harold in obituary that I did not find in the censuses with the family nor any records. may be a misprint for Charles or George) WWI Draft Card Daniel Wash Blackiston Birth Date 20 Jun 1897 Birth Place Maryland, USA Residence Date 1917-1918 Street Address Chestertown R. R 3 Residence Place Kent County, Maryland, USA Physical Build Medium Height Medium Hair Color Light Brown Eye Color Gray Relative George W. Blackiston CENSUS: 1930 Queen Anne's Co, MD Daniel Blackston 32 Head, Beatrice Blackston 26 Wife, Celia Blackston 10 Daughter, Charles Blackston 6 Son, George A Blackston 4 Son, James Blackston 1 Son Year: 1930; Census Place: Crumpton, Queen Anne's, Maryland; Page: 8B; Enumeration District: 0014; FHL microfilm: 2340613 CENSUS: 1940 Queen Anne's Co, MD Daniel W Blockston 43 Head, Lillian Beatrice Blockston 36 Wife, Charles Blockston 17 Son, George Alferd Blockston 14 Son, James Franklin Blockston 12 Son, Ralph Joseph Blockston 8 Son, Katherine Blockston 5 Daughter Year: 1940; Census Place: Queen Anne's, Maryland; Roll: m-t0627-01559; Page: 1A; Enumeration District: 18-16 WWII Draft Card Daniel Washington Blackiston Race White Age 44 Relationship to Draftee Self (Head) Birth Date 20 Jun 1897 Birth Place Rock Hall, Maryland, USA Residence Place Millington, Q A, Maryland, USA Registration Date 16 Feb 1942 Registration Place Millington, Q A, Maryland, USA Employer Fred Stevens Height 5 8 Weight 155 Complexion Dark Hair Color Brown Eye Color Gray Next of Kin Mrs. Daniel Blackiston. He made his mark and witnessed by Bertha Troutt CENSUS: 1950 Kent Co, MD Daniel W Blackiston 52 Head, Beatrice L Blackiston 46 Wife, George A Blackiston 24 Son, James F Blackiston 21 Son, Ralph J Blackiston 18 Son, Catherine O Blackiston 25 Daughter Census 1950; Group Number: 29; Residence Date: 1950; Home in 1950: Massey, Kent, Maryland; Roll: 2382; Sheet Number: 29; Enumeration District: 15-4 TOMBSTONE has wrong year of birth.

11. **Lewin Samuel Blackiston Sr** (John Wesley-3, John-2, John-1) was born on 21 Apr 1878 in Kent County, Maryland. He was christened on 3 Sep 1879 in Rock Hall, Kent County, Maryland. He died on 18 Feb 1953 at the age of 74 in Kent Co, Maryland, United States. Lewin was buried in Wesley Chapel Cemetery, Kent County, Maryland. BAPTISM: Samuel L. Blackiston born April 21 1878 baptized Sep 3rd 1879 John W and Marthy Ann Blackiston

CENSUS: 1900
James Joiner 60 born MD 1840 married 15y, Martha A Joiner 35 born 1845 MD married 15y 6 children 3 living, William J Downlin 14 grand S born Mar 1886, Joseph L Downey 5 grand D (sic) born Aug 1894, Lewin Blackiston 22 stepson born Apr 1878
1900; Census Place: Edesville, Kent, Maryland; Roll T623 625; Page: 11A; Enumeration District: 52.

CENSIUS: 1910 Kent Co, MD
Levin S Blackiston 32 married 9 years, Mary E Blackiston 36 4 children 3 living born PA father born MD mother born PA, Lewin S Blackiston Jr. 7, Charles C Blackiston 6, Emely Blackiston 1/12
1910; Census Place: Edesville, Kent, Maryland; Roll T624 566; Page: 22A; Enumeration District: 57; Image: 320.

CENSUS: 1920
Lewin S Blackiston 41, Mary Blackiston 44, Lewin S Blackiston 17, Charles C Blackiston 15, Emily B Blackiston 9, Alfred Sheppard 9 grandnephew Homer Sheppard 6 grandnephew, Florence Sheppard 36 niece widow
1920;Census Place: Edesville, Kent, Maryland; Roll T625 674; Page: 3B; Enumeration District: 67; Image: 107.

CENSUS: 1930 Kent Co, MD
Lewin E Blackiston 52, Mary E Blackiston 54, Emily M Blackiston 20
1930; Census Place: Edesville, Kent, Maryland; Roll 876; Page: 6A; Enumeration District: 10; Image: 593.0.

Lewin Samuel Blackiston Sr and Mary Elizabeth Freburger were married about 1901. **Mary Elizabeth Freburger** was born on 21 Jan 1874 in Baltimore, Maryland, United States. She died on 26 Dec 1952 at the age of 78 in Rock Hall, Kent, Maryland, United States. She was buried in Wesley Chapel Cemetery, Kent County, Maryland.

Lewin Samuel Blackiston and Mary Elizabeth Freburger had the following children:

17   i.   **Lewin Samuel Blackiston Jr** was born on 6 Aug 1902. He died on 31 Oct 1983 at the age of 81. He was buried in Wesley Chapel Cemetery, Kent County, Maryland. TOMBSTONE: Captain Lewin Samuel Blackiston Jr. August 6 1902-October 31 1983 "Home is the hunter, Home from the Hill and the Sailor Home from the Sea" In loving Memory Your daughter and son and grandchildren.

18   ii. **David Earnest Blackiston** was born on 20 Aug 1903 in Kent Co, Maryland, United States. He died on 24 Jan 1904 in Rock Hall, Kent, Maryland, United States. DEATH: David Earnest Blackiston died Rock Hall, Kent Co Jan 24 1904 age 5m 4 d male white born Kent co

MD father Lewin Blackiston born MD mother Mary E, Freeburger born MD Info. father Lewin Blackiston. died of membranous croup 8 hours exhaustion 1 hour

14. **Mary M. Blackiston** (Joseph Thomas-3, John-2, John-1) was born on 23 Feb 1883 in Maryland. She died on 29 Dec 1939 at the age of 56 in Cecil County, Maryland, United States. Mary M. Blackiston and Walter Hines Everitt were married. **Walter Hines Everitt** was born on 12 Sep 1880 in Pa.

15. **George David Blackiston Sr** (George W.-4, John Wesley-3, John-2, John-1) was born on 20 Mar 1895 in Rock Hall, Kent, Maryland, United States. He died on 26 Aug 1952 at the age of 57 in Chestertown, Kent, Maryland, United States. He was buried in Wesley Chapel Cem, Kent, Maryland, United States. Georgie David Blackiston of Rock Hall MD born March 20 1895 born Rock Hall MD, employed by James Wood. has father, mother and 1 brother dependent on him. WWI Draft Card.

Margaret Emma Whitlock, daughter of Samuel Whitlock and Margaret Moffett, was born on 19 Oct 1893 in Baltimore, Maryland, United States. She died on 16 Jul 1954 at the age of 60 in Kent County, MD. She was buried in Chester Cem, Chestertown, Kent, Maryland, United States. Tragically, she was killed in an explosion at Kent Manufacturing, a munitions & fireworks manufacturing plant in Chestertown, MD. Unfortunately, her remains, along with those of four other workers, were not able to be identified. These five ladies are all interred in the same burial plot, with a common head stone. The inscription on the stone reads "Working to preserve freedom when suddenly taken"

Margaret Whitlock Batchelor was married to Charles Wilmer Batchelor (1896-1949), son of Charles Henry Batchelor and Emily Cohee Batchelor.

George David Blackiston and Margaret Emma Whitlock had the following child:

19   i. **George David Blackiston Jr.** was born on 18 Aug 1928 in Kent County, Maryland. He died on 2 Jan 2022 at the age of 93 in Chestertown, Kent County, Maryland. He was buried in St. Paul's Kent Churchyard, Chestertown, MD.

Royal Relationship Charts
European Royalty Descent

This chart was commissioned by the author of Ky White to reflect the various descents to George Blackiston from European Royal Houses.

The Royal Ancestry and Descendants of George Blackiston

Egyptian Pharaohs Descent

The Augustan Society was able to link the Royal Houses of Europe to the Ancient Royal Lines of the Pharaohs.

Royal Descent from the Pharaohs of Egypt (over 3,500 years)

1. Pharaoh Ahmose (1590-1525BC) who united all of Egypt (the pyramids were already 1,000 years old by his reign) m Ahmose Nefertari had son
2. Pharaoh Amenhotep I (1525-1504BC) m Ahhotep II had dau.
3. Ahmose m. Pharaoh Tuthmosis I (1504-1492BC) had dau.
4. Pharaoh Hatshepsut I (female Pharaoh 1479-1457BC) m. Pharaoh Tuthmosis II (1492-1479BC) had dau.
5. Hatshepsut II m Pharaoh Tuthmosis III (1479-1425BC) had son
6. Pharaoh Amenhotep II (1427-1399BC) m Tyo had son
7. Pharaoh Tuthmosis IV (1390-1350BC) who unearthed the body of the Sphinx m Mutemwia has son
8. Pharaoh Amenhotep III the Magnificent (1386-1349BC) m. Tiye had son
9. Pharaoh Amenhotep IV (later Akhenaten) 'the heretic' (1350-1340BC) was father of King Tut (1340-1331) whose niece Sitre (granddau of Amenhotep III) inherited the throne
10. Sitre who m Pharaoh Ramesses I (1295-1294BC) had son
11. Pharaoh Sety I (1294-1279BC) m Tuya (great granddau of Amenhotep II) had son
12. Pharaoh Ramesses II 'the Great' (1279-1213BC) was the Pharaoh when Moses led the Jewish people out of Egypt m Isisnofre had son
13. Setnakhte m Titmuretneter had son
14. Pharaoh Ramesses III (1185-1154BC) and had son
15. Pharaoh Ramesses VIII (1127-1126BC) had son
16. Pharaoh Ramesses IX (1125-1137BC) had son and dau
17. Pharaoh Ramesses X (1107-1097BC) m Tyt had son
18. Pharaoh Ramesses XI (1097-1069BC) had dau.
19. Hentawy m. Pharaoh Smenoes (1089-1048BC) had son
20. Pharaoh Psibkhaennu I (1039-991BC) m. Wiay had dau
21. Istemkheb m. High Priest of Amun Monkhopere (1045-992BC) had son
22. High Priest of Amun Pinudjem (980-969BC) had son
23. Pharaoh Psibkhaennu II (959-945BC) had dau.
24. Maatkare m Pharaoh Osorkon I (924-889BC) and son
25. Pharaoh Shoshenk II (890-890BC; m Nesitanebtashru had son
26. Pharaoh Harsiese (c870-c860BC) had son
27. Karomama m. Pharaoh Osorkon II (874-850BC) had son
28. High Priest Shoshenk of Ptah had son
29. High Priest Takelot of Ptah m. Djedbastesankh had dau.
30. Djedbastesankh m. Pharaoh Shoshenk II (825-773BC) had son
31. Pharaoh Pimay (773-767) had son
32. Prince Osorkon of Sais (c773-740BC) had son
33. Pharaoh Tefnakht I (727-718BC) had son
34. Pharaoh Bakenranef (718-712BC) had son
35. Prince Nekauba of Sais (658-672BC; had son
36. Prince Necho I of Sais (672-664BC) had son
37. Pharaoh Psamtek I (664-610BC) had son
38. Pharaoh Necho II (610-595BC) who defeated King Josiah of Judah and defeated King Nebuchadnezzar had son
39. Pharaoh Psamtek II (595-589BC) m Tahhuat had son
40. Pharaoh Haa-bre (589-570BC; who rescued Jerusalem, (named in Bible at Jeremiah 37 4-7, 44-30) had dau
41. Nitetis m. Great King Cyrus II of Persia, Babylon, Sumer and Akkad, had dau
42. Atossa m. Great King Darius I of Persia defeated by the Greeks at the Battle of Marathon (522-486BC) had son
43. Great King Xerxes I of Persia (486-405BC) who was defeated by the Greeks in the battles of Thermopylae and Salamis m. Amestris had son
44. Great King Artaxerxes I Longimanus of Persia (465-424BC) m Kosmartydene
45. Great King Darius II of Persia (423-404BC) m. Parysatis had son
46. King Artaxerxes II of Persia (404-359BC) successor to his dynasty Darius III was defeated by Alexander the Great had son
47. Rodogune m. Satrap Orontes I of Armenia had son
48. Satrap Orontes II of Armenia (c344-331BC) had son
49. King Mithranes I of Armenia had son
50. King Orontes III of Armenia had son
51. King Samos I of Armenia had son
52. King Arsames I of Armenia (c260-c223) had son
53. King Xerxes I of Armenia (c230-212) had son
54. King Zariadres I of Sophene had son
55. King Artaxias I of Armenia (190-159BC) had son
56. King Tigranes I of Armenia (159-123BC) had son
57. King Artavasdes I of Armenia (123-95BC) had son
58. King Artaxias I of Iberia (90-78BC) had son
59. King Artaces I of Iberia (78-63BC) had son
60. King Pharnabazus II of Iberia (63-30BC) had dau
61. NN m Prince Kartam of Kouji do had son
62. King Pharasmanes I of Iberia (1-58AD) during the time of Jesus Christ had son
63. King Mithradates I of Iberia (58-106) had son
64. King Amazaspus I of Iberia (106-116) had son
65. King Pharasmenes II of Iberia (116-132) m. Ghadana had son
66. King Rhadamiste I of Iberia (132-135) had dau
67. King Pharasmenes III of Iberia (135-185) had son
68. NN m Great King Vologeses V of Armenia (180-191) had son
69. King Khusraw I of Armenia (191-216) had son
70. King Tiridat II of Armenia (216-292) had son
71. King Khusraw II of Western Armenia (279-287) had son
72. Great King Tiridates IV of Armenia (298-330) who was the first Christian King of Armenia had son
73. King Chosroes III of Armenia (330-339) had dau.
74. Bambish m. Primate Athenagenes of Armenia had son
75. Primate St. Narses I of Armenia m. Sandukht had son
76. Great Primate St. Isaac I of Armenia had dau.
77. Sahakanoysh m. Prince Hamazasp I of the Mamikonids had son
78. General St. Hmayeak Mamikonian m. Dzoyk had son
79. Patridan Vard Mamikonian of Arrrenia had son
80. Hmayeak had son
81. Mausegh I had son
82. Prince Vahan I Mamikonian of Taraun had son
83. Dawith Mamikonian had son
84. Coropalate Hamazasp II of Armenia (664-658) had son
85. Patridan Hmayeak Mamikonian (703-717) had son
86. Patridan Hmayeak Mamikonian had son
87. Artavasd Mamikonian had son
88. Noble Hmayeak of Adrianople had son
89. Noble Konstantinos of Adrianople had son
90. Eastern Emperor Basil I of Byzantium (867-886) created Macedonian Emp. Dynasty m Eudocia Ingerina (d840-882) had son
91. Eastern Emperor Leo VI of Byzantium (886-912) m Zoe Tzautzina had dau
92. Anna m. Holy Roman Emperor Louis III (901-905) descendant of Emperor Charlemagne had son
93. Count Charles Constantine of Vienne m. Thietberga had dau
94. Constance of Vienne m. Count Boson II of Provence (943-c966) had son
95. Count William II of Provence (979-993; m Adelaide of Anjou had dau
96. Constance of Provence m. King Robert II the Pious of France (996-1031) had son
97. King Henry I of France (1031-1060) m. Anne of Kiev had son
98. King Philip I of France (1060-1108) m Bertha of Holland had son
99. King Louis VI of France (1108-1137) m Adelaide of Savoy had son
100. King Louis VII of France (1137-1180) who led the 2nd Crusade m. Alix of Champagne had son
101. Princess Alice of France (c1180-a1215; m Count William II of Ponthieu (1179-1221) had dau
102. Marie of Ponthieu (1199-1250) m. Count Simon I de Dammartin (c1175-1259) had dau
103. Jeanne de Dammartin (c1215-1279) m King St. Ferdinand III of Castile (1248-1290) had dau
104. Eleanor of Castile (1248-1290) m. King Edward I of England who defeated Scottish hero William Wallace (1259-1307) had son
105. King Edward II of England (1284-1327) m. Isabella of France (1312-1369; had son
106. King Edward III of England (1312-1377) m. Philippa of Hainault (1312-1359) had son
107. Prince Lionel of Antwerp (1338-1368) m. Elizabeth de Burgh (1338-?) had dau
108. Phillipa Plantagenet (1355-?) m. Earl Edmund Mortimer of March (1352-1581) had dau
109. Elizabeth Mortimer (1375-aft 1407; m. Earl Henry "Hotspur" Percy main character in William Shakespeare's Henry IV play (1570-1403) had dau.
110. Elizabeth Percy (1395-1437) m. Lord John Clifford (1390-1422) has son
111. Lord Thomas Clifford (1415-1456) m. Joan Dacre (1415-?) had son
112. Lord John Clifford (1435-1462) m. Margaret Bromfiele (1435-?) had son
113. Lord Henry Clifford (1453-1524) lived during the time of Christopher Columbus' discovery of America m Anne St. John (1453-?) had dau.
114. Elizabeth Clifford (1490-?) m. Knight Ralph Bowes (1485-16?6) had dau
115. Knight George Bowes (1516-1548) m. Muriel Eure (1616-?) had dau.
116. Elizabeth Bowes (1568-?) m John Blackston, Esq. (1537-1567) had dau
117. Rev. Marmaduke Blackiston (1570-1639) m. Margaret James (1575-1636) had son
118. George Blackiston (1611-1660) came with family to America in 1668 m. Barbara Lawson (1620-1668) had son
119. Capt. Ebenezer Blackiston (1650-1709) m. Elizabeth James (1650-bef 1697) had son
120. William Blackiston (1685-1737) m Ann Moore (1708-?) had dau.
121. Rosamond Blackiston (1730-c1772) m. John Rasin (1713-1761) had son
122. Capt. William Blackiston Rasin (1760-1810) Soldier of American Revolution m. Martha Wroth (c1760-a1828) has son
123. Cpl. Philip M. Rasin (1790-1841) m. Sarah Benedict (1792-1856) had dau
124. Wilhelmina Rasin (1830-1907) m. John Wesley Crouch (1823-1897) had son
125. Charles Wesley Crouch (1870-1944) m. Grace F. Blackiston (1875-1945) had dau
126. Susie Bernice Crouch (1915-1965) m Harry Thornton Statos (1910-1965) had dau
127. Lois Grace Statos (1931-1978) m. Bernard Alfred Barnhouser Sr. (1928-1996) had son
128. Bernard Alfred Barnhouser Jr. (1949-living) m. Charmaine May Guy (1952-living) had son
129. John Anthony Barnhouser Sr. (1977-living) and Kimberly Ruth Lindsey (1979-living) and had 3 children John Anthony Barnhouser Jr. (1997-living), Samantha Rose Barnhouser (1999-living), Sarah Nicole Barnhouser (2002-living)
129. Laura Marie Barnhouser (1974-living) m Guy Edward Almony Jr. (1972-living) had son Guy E. Almony, Jr (1997-living)

Prepared by Cerveos Christon, Jr. Updated July 28, 2025

The Royal Ancestry and Descendants of George Blackiston

Royal Descent from the Pharaohs of Egypt (over 3,500 years)

Summary

1.	XVII Dynasty of Egypt (Ruled at Thebes) The Augustan Society Inc. © 1986
2.-10.	XVIII Dynasty of Egypt
11.-12.	XIX Dynasty of Egypt
13.-19.	XX Dynasty of Egypt
20.-23.	XXI Dynasty of Egypt
24.-30.	XXII Dynasty of Egypt
31.-32.	XXIII Dynasty of Egypt
33.-35.	XXIV Dynasty of Egypt
36.-40.	XXVI Dynasty of Egypt
41.	King of Parsa
42.-46.	Kings of Persia
47.-57.	Satraps and Kings of Armenia
58.-67.	Kings of Iberia
68.-73.	Kings of Armenia (also descended of 56.)
74.-76.	Primates of Armenia
77.-87.	Princes of Mamikonids
88.-89.	Nobles of Adrianople
90.-91.	Eastern Emperor of Byzantium
92.	Holy Roman Emperor
93.-94	Counts of Vienne
95.-96.	Counts of Provence
96.-103.	Kings of France
104.-107.	Kings of England
108.-109.	Earl Percy of Northumberland
110.-114.	Lords of Clifford
115.-116.	Knights of Bowe
117.	Knight of Blackiston
118.-120.	Maryland Family of Blackistons
121.-124.	Maryland Family of Rasins
122.-129.	Sons of the American Revolution (#148242) and Children of the American Revolution (#142106)
122.-130.	Children of the American Revolution (#144465, #147969, #148965) and SAR # 163294 and #160713.

References:

1.-105.	Descents of Antiquity, Part I © 1986 Augustan Society Publication
87.-105.	Royalty for Commoners (Known ancestry of John of Gaunt) by Roderick W. Stuart © 1992 Lines 322:42-41, 253.41-38, 25:39-38, 333:36-34, 134:33-29, 133:29-28, 70:29-25, 68:25-24, 1:24-20
89.-111.	Ancestral Roots of Certain American Colonists who came to America before 1700, by Frederick L. Weis. 7th Edition © 1993, Lines 141A:15-21, 101:21-29, 155:29-30, 1:28-30, 5:30-35
92.-111.	Pedigree of Some of Emperor Charlemagne's Descendants Vol. 1-3 by J. Orton Buck and Timothy F. Beard
100.-118.	Plantagenet Ancestry © 2004 by Douglas Richardson p. 1-23, 112-114, 144-145, 190-192, 214-218, 520-526, 574-578
104.-111.	The Magna Charta Sureties 1215, by Frederick L. Weis. 4th Edition © 1991, Lines 161:14-18, 36:9-12, 113:9-10
105.-117.	Royal Descent of 500 Immigrants to the American Colonies by Gary Boyd Roberts
106.-111.	Plantagenet Ancestry of 17th Century Colonists, by David Faris, © 1996 pp. 226-30, 148-9, 179
110.-114.	Complete Peerage Vol III pp. 293-295
114.-119.	Surtees History of Durham Vol 4. pp. 107f. Vol 3. pp. 162-3, Surtees Society Vol 122 pp. 130-1
117.-120.	Maryland Genealogies Vol 1. pp. 48f. Colonial Genealogist Vol. III:2 1970
120.-123	Maryland Genealogical Society Bulletin Vol. 36 No. 2 and 1997 Update at Maryland Historical Society
119.-126.	Descendants of Capt. William Blackiston Rasin undated ca 1996 by Caroline Cooper.
122.-130	Sons of the American Revolution Records (Application #148242 Approved May 1995 and #163294 and #160713) and Children of the American Revolution Records (Applications #142106 Approved May 1997 and #144465 Approved Jan. 1998 and #147969 approved Dec 2001 and #148965 Approved Oct 2002)
103.-130.	Prominent Families of Kent County and Baltimore Maryland by John A. Barnhouser Sr. and Christos Christou, Jr. © 1997

Magna Carta Baron Descent

The Blackiston family has the rare distinction of descending from all of the 17 of the 25 Magna Carta Barons with known descendants.

The Magna Carta Barons

William d'Albini
Belvoir

Hugh Bigod
Framlingham

Roger Bigod
Framlingham

Henry de Bohun
Trowbridge

Gilbert de Clare
Clare

Richard de Clare
Clare

John FitzRobert
Warkworth

Robert FitzWalter
Little Dunmow

William de Fors
Skipton

William Hardel
Mayor of London

William de Huntingfield
Huntingfield

John de Lacy
Pontefract

William de Lanvalei
Walkern

William Malet
Curry Mallet

Geoffrey de Mandeville
Pleshey

William Marshal
Long Crendon

Roger de Montbegon
Hornby

William de Mowbray
Thirsk

Richard de Montfichet
Stansted Mountfichet

Richard de Percy
Topcliffe

Saer de Quincy
Leicester

Robert de Ros
Helmsley

Geoffrey de Say
West Greenwich

Robert de Vere
Castle Hedingham

Eustace de Vesci
Alnwick

MC Sureties' List

There were 25 Barons who signed the Magna Carta as Sureties. Only 17 have known descendants and George Blackiston is descended from 100% of them - quite a unique fact in genealogy. George Washington for example is documented with only 9 Magna Charta ancestors.

William D'Albini/Aubeney, of Belvoir
Hugh Bigod, later Earl of Norfolk
Roger le Bigod, Earl of Norfolk
Henry de Bohun, Earl of Hereford
Gilbert de Clare, Earl of Gloucester and Hertford

Richard de Clare, Earl of Hertford
John FitzRobert, Sheriff of Norfolk and Suffolk
Robert Fitzwalter, Baron of Little Dunmow, Constable of Baynard's Castle, London
William de Forz*
William Hardel, Mayor of London*

William de Huntingfield, Sheriff of Norfolk and Suffolk,
John de Lacy, Constable of Chester
William de Lanvallei, Governor of Colchester Castle, Lord of Walkern
William Malet, Baron of Curry Mellet
Geoffrey de Mandeville*

William Marshal II*
Roger de Montbegon*
Richard de Montfichet*
William de Mowbray, Lord of Thirsk and Mowbray
Richard de Percy*

Saher de Quincy, Earl of Winchester
Robert de Ros, Baron of Topcliffe
Geoffrey de Say, Lord of West Greenwich
Robert de Vere, Earl of Oxford
Eustace de Vesci*

* No known descendants

Magna Carta References

The Barons and some others named in the Magna Charta are among the ancestors of George Blackiston such as King John.

Mormadike Blackiston's descent from 100% of the 17 Known Magna Charta Barons with descendants" by Christos Christou Jr.

Emperor Charlemagne Descent

John Barnhouser is a Life Member of the Order of the Crown of Charlemagne through his documented descent from George Blackiston, the immigrant all the way back to Emperor Charlemagne.

Royal Descent from Emperor Charlemagne
(over 1,200 years of Descent)

43. **Charlemagne, Holy Roman Emperor** (2 Apr 742 – 28 Jan 813/14) King of France (768-814), Emperor of the West (800-814) m. abt 771 to **Hildegarde of Swabia**, Countess of Linzgau (abt 758 – 30 Apr 783). He united most of Europe in one vast state almost all the Christian lands of Western Europe. His coronation as emperor at Rome on Christmas Day 800 AD, after restoring Leo III to the papacy, marks the inception of the Holy Roman Empire. The King of Hearts in a standard deck of playing cards is supposed to represent Charlemagne and many have said that his face is what the medieval artist used for Jesus' likeness. They had son Pepin:

42. **Pepin (Karlmann), King of Italy** (bapt. 15 Apr. 781 – 8 Jul 810) m. to **Chrothais**. They had son Bernard:

41. **Bernard, King of Italy** (abt 797 – 17 Apr 818) m. ca. 814 to **Cunigunde** (abt 800 – after 15 Jun 835). They had son Pepin:

40. **Pepin de Peronne, Seigneur of Peronne** (abt 817 – after 840) m. unknown. They had son Herbert:

39. **Herbert I, Count of Vermandois** (ca 840 – murdered abt 902) He was Seigneur of Senlis, Peronne & St. Quentin and m. to prob. **Liegardis**. They had son Herbert:

38. **Herbert II, Count of Vermandois** (ca. 880 – 23 Feb 942/43) He m. **Adela (Liegardis) of France** (ca 890 – ca. 931). They had son Robert:

37. **Robert of Troyes, Count of Meaux** (ca. 910-915 – 19/29 Aug 967) m. **Adelaide de Burgundy** (abt 920 – after Aug. 967). They had son Geoffrey:

36. **Geoffrey "Grisgonelle" Count of Anjou** (960 – in battle 21 Jul 987) He was Seneschal of France and m. on **Adelaide de Vermandois** (abt 950 – 974-75). They had son Conan:

35. **Conan I "le Tort", Duke of Brittany** (ca. 960 – 27 June 992) killed at Conquereuil. He m. **Ermengarde de Anjou** (ca 965-). They had son Richard:

34. **Richard II "The Good", Duke of Normandy** (ca. 958 – 28 Aug 1027) died at Fecamp. He m. in 1000 **Judith of Brittany** (ca. 982-16 June 1017). They had son Robert:

33. **Robert I° The Devil', Duke of Normandy** (ca. 1000 – 22 Jul 1035) Crusader to the Holy Lands. He had child by **Herleve (Harlette) of Falaise** (ca. 1003-). They had son William:

32. **William I, King of England** (1027/28 – 9 Sept 1087) First Norman King of England. Buried Abbey of St. Stephen, Caen. He m. ca 1051-53 to **Matilda of Flanders** (ca 1032/33 – 3 Nov 1083). Buried Church of the Holy Trinity, Caen. They had son Henry:

31. **Henry I, King of England** (1068/70 – 1 Dec 1135) He m. 11 Nov 1100 to **Matilda of Scotland** (1079 – 1 May 1118). They had dau. Matilda:

30. **Geoffrey V ° Plantagenet, Count of Anjou** (24 Aug 1113 – 7 Sep 1151) He m. 3 Apr 1127 **Princess Matilda of England**, Dowager Empress of Germany, widow of Emperor Henry V of Germany (7 Feb 1102- 10 Sep 1167). They had son Henry:

29. **Henry II, King of England** (5 Mar 1132/3 – 6 Jul 1189) He m. 18 May 1153 **Eleanor of Aquitaine**, former wife of Louis VII, King of France (ca.1122/23 – 31 Mar 1204). They had son John:

28. **John of England, King of England** (24 Dec 1166-18 Oct 1216) He m. 24 Aug 1200 **Isabella Taillefer Of Angouleme** (1188-31 May 1246). She m. secondly, Hugh X de Lusignan, Comte de la Marche. They had son Henry:

27. **Henry III, King of England** (1 Oct 1207-16 Nov 1272) He m. 14 Jan 1237 **Eleanor of Provence** (ca. 1222/23 – 24-25 June1291). They had son Edward:

26. **Edward I, King of England** (17 Jun 1239-7/8 Jul 1307) He went on a Crusade in 1270. He invades Scotland and is known as the Hammer of the Scots having defeated William Wallace. He m. 18 Oct 1254 **Eleanor of Castile** (1246 – 28/29 Nov 1290). They had son Edward:

25. **Edward II, King of England** (25 Apr 1284 – 21 Sep 1327) He m. 25 Jan 1307/08 **Isabella of France** (1292 – 22 Aug 1358). They had son Edward:

24. **Edward III, King of England** (13 Nov 1312 – 21 June 1377) Reigned for 50 years. Started the 100 Year Wars with France which later led to the death of Joan of Arc. He m. **Philippa of Hainault** (24 June 1311 – 15 Aug 1369), dau. of William III d'Avesnes, Count of Holland and Jeanne of Valois. They had son Lionel:

23. **Lionel of Antwerp, Duke of Clarence** (29 Nov. 1338 – 17 Oct. 1368) m. **Elizabeth de Burgh** (6 July 1332 – 10 Dec 1363), dau. of William De Burgh, 4th Earl of Ulster and Maud de Lancaster. They had dau. Phillipa:

22. **Edmund Mortimer 3rd Earl of March** (1 Feb 1352 – 27 Dec. 1381) m. **Phillipa Plantagenet** (16 Aug. 1355 – 1379). Edmund caught a cold crossing a river in Munster and died. They had dau. Elizabeth:

21. **Henry "Hotspur" Percy Knight** (26 May 1364-21 July 1403) He was a famous fighter against the Scottish and earned his nickname Hotspur from his battles. He m. **Elizabeth Mortimer** (12 Feb. 1371 – 20 April 1417). They had dau. Elizabeth:

20. **John Clifford 7th Lord Clifford** (1388 – 13 March 1422) He was also Sheriff of Westmoreland. He took part in a great tournament at Carlisle and he was slain at the siege of Meaux. He m. **Elizabeth Percy** (abt 1390 – 26 Oct 1437). They had son Thomas:

19. **Thomas Clifford 8th Lord Clifford** (25 March 1414 – 22 May 1485) He was also Sheriff of Westmoreland and was slain at battle of St. Albans. He m. **Joan Dacre**, dau. of Thomas Dacre, Lord Dacre and Philippe Nevill. They had son John:

18. **John Clifford 9th Lord Clifford** (8 April 1435 – 28 March 1461) He was killed on the eve of the Battle of Towton by a chance arrow. He m. **Margaret Bromflete** (1435 – 12 April 1493), dau of Henry Bromflete, Lord of Vessy and Eleanor FitzHugh. They had son Henry:

17. **Henry Clifford, 10th Lord Clifford** (1453 – 23 April 1523). He m. **Anne St. John**, dau. of John St. John, Knight of Bletsnesle and Alice Bradshaugh. Anne is also a descendant of Edward III through his son John of Gaunt. They had dau. Elizabeth:

16. **Ralph Bowes Knight of Streatlam and Dalden and South Cowton** (1485 – April 1516) He was High Sheriff of Durham and m. **Elizabeth Clifford**. They had son George:

15. **George Bowes Knight and Lord of Dalden** (1516—1546) He was born posthumously. He m. **Muriel Eure** (1516 – 23 Nov 1557), dau. of William Eure, Baron Eure, Knight and Sheriff of Northumberland and Elizabeth Willoughby. They had dau. Elizabeth:

14. **Elizabeth Bowes** (1538-bef 1582) m. **John Blackiston, Esq.** (1537—abt 1 Feb. 1587) He was a large landowner and Patron of Redmarshall which he assigned in his will to his son Marmaduke. They had son Marmaduke:

13. **Rev. Marmaduke Blackiston** (1570 – abt 1 Sep 1639) of Newton Hall, Newcastle. Vicar of Woodhorne, Rector of Redmarshall, Rector of Sedgefield, Archdeacon of the East Riding of York. He m. **Margaret James** (1575- 8 March 1636). They had son George:

12. **George Blackiston** (abt 1 March 1601—abt Sep. 1669) Alderman and Sheriff of Newcastle. His uncle John Blackiston was a judge who signed the death warrant of King Charles I and so George and his family "suffered much" and emigrated to St. Mary's Co., MD in 1668. He m. **Barbara Lawson** (1620—1660) dau. of Henry Lawson, Sheriff of Newcastle, and Katherine Wormonde. They had son Thomas:

11. **Capt. Ebenezer Blackiston** (1650—abt 24 oct 1709) He came to America with his parents and was Capt of a foot company in Worian and S Sassafras Hundred Cecil Co, MD. He m. **Elizabeth James** (1656—before 1672) They had son William:

10. **William Blackiston, Sr.** (1685 – abt. May 1737) He served in the MD Assembly from Kent Co. He m. **Ann Moore** (19 Aug. 1708 – after 1737), dau. of John Moore and Elizabeth Dowland. They had dau. Rosamond:

9. **John Rasin** (30 July 1713 – abt March 1761) He was a large landowner in Kent Co and a quaker. He m. **Rosamond Blackiston** (1730 – before 1772). They had son William:

8. **Captain William Blackiston Rasin** (1760 – 1810) He served in the light infantry and in the MD Line during the American Revolution. After the Rev., he was made Capt. of the Kent Co. Militia. The MD Gen. Soc. Bulletin Vol. 36 No. 2 1995 has an article about his entire life. He m. **Martha Wroth** (c1760 – after 1828) dau. of Kinvin Wroth Jr. and Frances Beck. They had son Philip:

7. **Corporal Philip R. Rasin** (1790 – 1 April 1841) He served in the 6th Brigade of the Kent Co Militia in the War of 1812. He fought at Caulk's Field. He m. **Sarah Bennett** (1792 – 1856), dau of Samuel and Mary Bennett. They had dau. Wilhelmina:

EDWARD III's COAT OF ARMS

EDWARD III GOLD QUARTER OF CALAIS

BLACKISTON COAT OF ARMS

KING CHARLES I's DEATH WARRANT

Prepared by: Rev. Christos Christou, Jr. July 27, 2025

Byzantium Emperor Descent

One of the many branches of royal lines includes the Emperors of the West – the great Greek Byzantium Empire.

Blackiston Descent from the Greek Emperors of Byzantium

Alexius I Komnenos 1081-1118   John II Komnenos 1118-1143

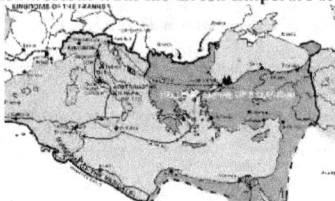

Greek Emperors of the East

1. Emperor Alexius I Komnenos of the East (1048-1118) m. Irene A. Doukaina (c1060-1127) and had son
2. Emperor John II Komnenos of the East (1087-1143) m. Pyriska I of Hungary (c1090-1134) and had son
3. Emperor Manuel Komnenos (1122-1180) m. Marie de Poitiers (c1143-1182) and had dau.
4. Endoxia Komnenos (-a1202) m. William VIII Montpellier (-1218) and had dau.

Kings of Aragon in Spain

5. Marie of Montpelier (1182-1213) m. King Pedro II of Aragon (1176-1213) and had son
6. King James I of Aragon (1208-1276) m. Yolande of Hungary (1213-1251) and had dau.

Kings of France

7. Isabella of Aragon (c1245-1271) m. King Phillip III of France (1245-1283) and had son
8. King Philip IV of France (1268-1314) m. Jeanne of Navarre (1272-1305) and had dau.

Kings of England

9. Isabella of France (1312-1369) m. King Edward II of England (1284-1327) and had son
10. King Edward III of England (1312-1377) m. Philippa of Hainault (1312-1369) and had son
11. Prince Lionel of Antwerp (1338-1368) m. Elizabeth de Burgh (1338-) and had dau.

English Nobility

12. Princess Phillipa Plantagenet (1355-) m. Earl Edmund Mortimer of March (1352-1381) and had dau.
13. Elizabeth Mortimer (1375-aft 1407) m. Earl Henry Percy of Northumberland (1370-1403) and had dau.
14. Elizabeth Percy (1395-1437) m. Lord John Clifford (1390-1422) and had son
15. Lord Thomas Clifford (1415-1453) m. Joan Dacre (1415-) and had son
16. Lord John Clifford (1435-1462) m. Margaret Bromflete (1435-) and had son
17. Lord Henry Clifford (1453-1524) m. Anne St. John (1453-) and had dau.
18. Elizabeth Clifford (1490-) m. Knight Ralph Bowes (1485-1516) and had son
19. Knight George Bowes (1516-1546) m. Muriel Eure (1516-) and had dau.
20. Elizabeth Bowes (1538-) m. John Blackiston, Esq. (1537-1587) and had son
21. Rev. Marmaduke Blackiston (1570-1639) m. Margaret James (1575-1636) and had son

Blackiston Immigration to America 1667

22. George Blackiston (1611-1669) m. Barbara Lawson (1620-1668) and had son
23. Capt. Ebenezer Blackiston (1650-1709) m. Elizabeth James (1650-bef 1697) and had son
24. William Blackiston (1683-1737) m. Ann Moore (1708-) and had dau.
25. Rosamond Blackiston (1730-c1772) m. John Rasin (1713-1761) and had son

American Revolution

26. Capt. William Blackiston Rasin (1760-1810) m. Martha Wroth (c1760-a1828) and had son
27. Crpl. Philip R. Rasin (1790-1841) m. Sarah Bennett (1792-1856) and had dau.
28. Wilhelmina Rasin (1830-1907) m. John Wesley Crouch (1823-1897) and had son
29. Charles Wesley Crouch (1870-1944) m. Grace F. Blackiston (1875-1948) and had dau.
30. Susie Bernice Crouch (1913-1965) m. Harry Thornton States (1910-1985) and had dau.
31. Lula Grace States (1931-1978) m. Bernard Alfred Barnhouser Sr. (1928-1996) and had son
32. Bernard Alfred Barnhouser Jr. (1949-living) m. Charmaine May Guy (1952-living)

GREEK ART

Printed by Christos Christou, Jr. July 27, 2025

King Edward III of England Descent

The most recent King of England documented through several branches of the Blackiston ancestry reach to King Edward III, who created the Order of the Garter and began the 100 Years War with France.

Royal Descent of John Barnhouser and Guy Almony

EDWARD III'S COAT OF ARMS

Edward III King of England (13 Nov. 1312 – 21 June 1377) Became King at age 14 and reigned for 50 years. He started the 100 Year Wars with France which later led to the death of Joan of Arc. Edward founded the Order of the Garter in 1348. They are buried at Westminster Abbey. He m. **Philippa of Hainault** (24 June 1311 – 15 August 1369), dau. of William III d'Avesnes, Count of Holland and Jeanne of Valois. They had son Lionel

Lionel of Antwerp Duke of Clarence (29 November 1338 – 17 October 1368) m. **Elizabeth de Burgh** (6 July 1332 — 10 Dec 1363), dau. of William De Burgh, 4th Earl of Ulster and Maud de Lancaster. They had dau. Phillipa

Edmund Mortimer 3rd Earl of March (1 Feb 1352—27 December 1381) m. **Phillipa Plantagenet** (16 August 1355— 1379). Edmund caught a cold crossing a river in Munster and died. They had dau. Elizabeth

THE ORDER OF THE GARTER

Henry "Hotspur" Percy Knight (26 May 1364-21 July 1403) He was a famous fighter against the Scottish and earned his nickname Hotspur from his battles. He m. **Elizabeth Mortimer** (12 February 1371 – 20 April 1417). They had dau. Elizabeth

John Clifford 7th Lord Clifford (1388 – 13 March 1422) He was also Sheriff of Westmoreland. He took part in a great tournament at Carlisle and he was slain at the siege of Meaux in 1421. He m. **Elizabeth Percy** (abt 1390 – 26 October 1437). They had son Thomas

Thomas Clifford 8th Lord Clifford (25 March 1414— 22 May 1455) He was also Sheriff of Westmoreland and was slain at battle of St. Albans. He m. **Joan Dacre**, dau. of Thomas Dacre, Lord Dacre and Philippe Nevill. They had son John

EDWARD III GOLD QUARTER NOBLE OF CALAIS

John Clifford 9th Lord Clifford (8 April 1435— 28 March 1462) He was killed on the eve of the Battle of Towton by a chance arrow. He m. **Margaret Bromflete** (1435— 12 April 1493), dau. of Henry Bromflete, Lord of Vessy and Eleanor FitzHugh. They had son Henry:

Henry Clifford, 10th Lord Clifford (1452 – 23 April 1523). He m. **Anne St. John**, dau. of John St. John, Knight of Bletsoe and Alice Bradshaugh. Anne is also a descendent of Edward III through his son John of Gaunt. They had dau. Elizabeth:

Ralph Bowes Knight of Streatlam and Dalden and South Cowton (1485 – April 1516) He was High Sheriff of Durham and m. **Elizabeth Clifford**. They had son George

BLACKISTON COAT OF ARMS

George Bowes Knight and Lord of Dalden (1516 – 1546) He was born posthumously. He m. **Muriel Eure** (1516 – 23 November 1557), dau. of William Eure, Baron Eure, Knight and Sheriff of Northumberland and Elizabeth Willoughby. They had dau. Elizabeth

John Blackiston, Esq. (1537—abt 5 February 1587) He was a large landowner and Parson of Redmarshall which he assigned in his will to his son Marmaduke. He m. **Elizabeth Bowes**. They had son Marmaduke:

Rev. Marmaduke Blackiston (1570 – abt 1 September 1639) of Newton Hall, Newcastle, Vicar of Woodhorne, Rector of Redmarshall Rector of Sedgefield, Archdeacon of the East Riding of York. He m. **Margaret James** (1575 - 8 March 1636). They had son George.

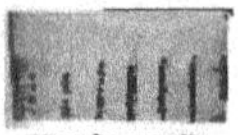
KING CHARLES I'S DEATH WARRANT

George Blackiston (abt 1 March 1611—abt September 1669) alderman and sheriff of Newcastle. His uncle John Blackiston was one of the judges who signed the death warrant of King Charles I and so George and his family "suffered much in public concern" and emigrated to St. Mary's Co., MD in 1668. He m. **Barbara Lawson** (1620—1668) dau. of Henry Lawson sheriff of Newcastle and Katherine Wurmouth. They died shortly after arrival in Maryland. They had son Ebenezer:

Capt. Ebenezer Blackiston (1650 – before 1697) He came to America with his parents. He was commissioned Capt. of a foot company in Worten and South Sassafras Hundred Cecil Co. MD. He was a Justice of the county. He m. **Elizabeth James** (1650 – abt 23 October 1709). They had dau. Hannah:

GEORGE WASHINGTON SIGNING THE DECLARATION OF INDEPENDENCE

Hannah Blackiston (abt 1673- 7 Aug 1740) m. **John Blackiston** (1669-Dec 1732) son of John Blackiston and Sarah Prideaux. They were cousins. John had been raised by his uncle Ebenezer when his parents died shortly after their arrival to this country. They had son Ebenezer

Ebenezer Blackiston (abt 1705-abt Apr 1772) m. **Hannahretta Mahon** (1 Oct 1725 – aft 1794), dau. of Thomas Mahon and Mary Moore. They had son Joseph

Joseph Blackiston (16 Feb 1760 – bef 1830) m. **Mary Stevens** (abt 1760-aft 1810), dau. of Jacob Stephens. They had son Joseph:

Joseph Blackiston (1782 – 20 Jan 1850) m. **Henrietta Eagle** (aft 1784-), probably dau. of James Eagle and Rachel. They had son James:

James Eagle Blackiston, Sr. (1808-30 Mar 1869) m. **Mary Emily Stephens** 21 Jan 1825 – 21 Feb 1902), dau. of John Toppin Stephens and Anna Emily Brown. They had son Joseph:

John Joseph Blackiston (1 Mar 1847 – 1 Feb 1913) m. **Julia Christina Leary** (25 Dec 1845 – 30 Sep 1935), dau. of Rev. George B. Leary and Mary Ann Sims. They had dau. Grace:

Grace Florence Blackiston (27 July 1875—2 February 1948) m. **Charles Wesley Crouch** (21 February 1870— 18 July 1944), son of John Wesley Crouch and Wilhemina Rason. They had dau. Bernice:

Harry Thornton States (8 June 1910 – 27 March 1965) son of George Washington States and Lula Kirby. He m. **Susie Berniky Crouch** (26 July 1913 – 25 October 1965) They had dau. Lula

1928 $20 GOLD COIN

Bernard Alfred Barnhouser Sr. (18 October 1928 – 23 September 1996), son of "Joseph" Sidney Francis Barnhouser and Agnes Catherine Tokodziecki, m. **Lula Grace "Dottie" States** (16 April 1931 – 11 November 1978). They had son Bernard

Bernard Alfred Barnhouser Jr. (born 10 February 1949) m. **Charmaine May Guy** (born 11 November 1952), dau. of Lawrence Frederick Guy and Marie Elizabeth Stinebaugh. They had three children:

Laura Marie Barnhouser (born 10 March 1974), **John Anthony Barnhouser Sr.** (born 10 December 1977), and **Dorothy Grace Barnhouser** (born 6 April 1979)
Laura has 3 children: **Kayla McDonald** b. 5 Nov. 1993, **Guy Almony Jr.** b. 5 Jul. 1997, & **Constance Cummings** b. 1 Oct. 1999. John has 2 children: **John Anthony Barnhouser Jr.** b. 23 Oct. 1997 and **Samantha Rose Barnhouser** b. 26 May 1999.

Prepared by: Christos Christou, Jr., July 27, 2025

The Royal Ancestry and Descendants of George Blackiston

George Washington Relationship

Relationship to President George Washington

Walter de Washington (1212-1264) m. Joan Whitchester (c1220-a1266)

William de Washington (c1240-1289) m. Margaret Morville

Walter de Washington (c1270-a1315)	m.		Robert de Washington (c1275-1324)	m. Joan Strickland (c1275-)
William de Washington (c1295-a1345)	m.	Alice (c1295-)	Robert de Washington (c1305-1347)	m. Agnes Gentyl (c1315-)
Roger Blackiston (1320-a1349)	m	Christina de Washington (c1325-)	John de Washington (c1340-1407)	m. Joan de Croft (c1360-)
William Blackiston (1345-1418)	m.		John de Washington (1385-1423)	m.
William Blackiston Jr. (1370-)	m.	Katherine	Robert Washington (1410-1483)	m. Margaret (c1430-)
Nicholas Blackiston (1398-1460)	m.	Miss Fulthorpe	Robert Washington (1455-1528)	m. Miss Westfield
William Blackiston (1420-1468)	m.	Sibella (1420-a1484)	John Washington (1478-b1528)	m. Margaret Kytson (c1480-)
Thomas Blackiston (1440-1483)	m	Joan Killinghall (1440-a1483)	Lawrence Washington (1500-1584)	m Amy Pargiter (c1520-1564)
William Blackiston (1465-)	m.	Anne Conyers (1465-a1533)	Robert Washington (1544-1620)	m. Elizabeth Light (c1545-1599)
Thomas Blackiston (1495-1557)	m.	Elizabeth Place (1510-1553)	Lawrence Washington (1568-1616)	m. Margaret Butler (c1570-1652)
John Blackiston (1537—1587)	m.	Elizabeth Bowes (1538—)	Lawrence Washington (1602-1653)	m. Amphyllis Twigden (c1610-1655)
Marmaduke Blackiston (1570—1639)	m	Margaret James (1575—1636)	John Washington (1633-1677)	m. Anne Pope (c1635-)
George Blackiston (1611—1669)	m.	Barbara Lawson (1620—1668)	Lawrence Washington (1659-1697)	m. Mildred Warner (c1670-a1700)
Capt. Ebenezer Blackiston (1650—1709)	m.	Elizabeth James (1650—b1697)	Augustine Washington (1694-1743)	m. Mary Ball (1708-1789)
William Blackiston (1685—1737)	m.	Ann Park (1695—)	General George Washington 1st President of the U.S. (1732-1799)	
John Rasin (1713—1761)	m.	Rosamond Blackiston (1730—b1772)		
Capt. William B. Rasin (1760—1810)	m.	Martha Wroth (c1760—a1828)		

Researched by Christos Christou Jr.

Ancestors in Europe

There have been several books that now include the royal ancestor of Marmaduke Blackiston with royal lines and contain many other families and their royal connection. including:

- **Royal Ancestry** by Douglas Richardson Vols. 1-5 copy. 2013 (Vol. 1 p 383 starts the lineage from George back.) This is the best and most well documented publication now in print.
- **Plantagenet Ancestry of 17th Century Colonists** by David Faris second edition 1999 includes ancestry of Marmaduke back to King Edward III.
- **Ancestral Roots** 7th Edition by Frederick L. Weis 1993 includes many of the royal ancestors as well.
- **The Magna Carta Sureties 1215** 4th Edition by Frederick L. Weis 1993 also includes royal ancestors of the Blackiston family.
- **The Royal Descents of 500 Immigrants** by Gary B. Roberts 1993 includes the ancestry of George Blackiston to King Edward III p. 139
- **The Blackiston pedigree** is contained in Robert Surtee's History of Durham Vol. 3 pp159-166, p 402. This record discusses the Blackiston family back to the 1300s but does not mention the royal descent.
- **The Blackistone Family** by Christopher Johnston Maryland Genealogies Vol. 2 pp 48-68 discusses the descendants from Rev. Marmaduke Blackiston down to his descendants in the 1800s and refers to the Surtee's history for earlier generations.
- **Blackiston of Maryland and Delaware** by Mrs. Clarence Cummins 1970 from the Colonial Genealogist III:2 discusses one line of the Blackiston family but has very interesting source material.

First Generation

1. **John Blackiston** was the first of the Blackistons to be born in America in 1669 in Saint Mary's County, Maryland. He died in Dec 1733 at the age of 64 in Kent County, Maryland.

Second Generation

2. **John Blackiston** born about 19 Sep 1639 at Durham in Newcastle, Northumberland, England. He was christened on 19 Sep 1639 in Saint Nicholas, Newcastle, Northumberland, England. He died in 1679 at the age of 40 in Kent, Md, Kent County, Maryland. He came from England with his father in 1669 and other family members. settled in St. Mary's Co then about 1675-1678 moved to Kent Co, MD.
3. **Sarah Prideaux** born about 3 Jun 1647 in Newcastle Upon Tyne, Northumberland, England. She was baptized on 3 Jun 1647 in Newcastle Upon Tyne, Durham, England. She died before Apr 1683 at the age of 35 in Kent, Maryland. Colonial Families of America copied from the Colonial Genealogist III: 2 1970.reprinted by Augustan Society.

Third Generation

4. **George Blackiston** born about Mar 1611 in Crossgate, Durham County, England. He was christened on 1 Mar 1611 or 1 Mar 1612 in Saint Margaret's, Crossgate, Durham County, England. He died about Sep 1669 at the age of 58 in Saint Mary's County,

Maryland. He was a Mercer, Councillor 1644, Alderman 1655, Sheriff of Newcastle in 1656. At the restoration 1660 all property of the two brothers John and George were confiscated, although the Corporation of Newcastle voted 200l to John's widow and 500l to George because "he did many good services for this town." He emigrated to America between May 1668 (marriage of his son in England) and Sept 1669 (admin. of estate) (and possibly pre-May 1669 when Nehemiah was married and supposedly came with George). Burke's American Families lists on p. 2565 the descent of John Blakiston through George the emigrant to Maryland and his son John. John A. Barnhouser was accepted in the prestigious Order of the Crown of Charlemagne based on his descent from George Blackiston the immigrant back to Emperor Charlemagne - 43 generations and 1,200 years proven!! Member #2051 approved February 21, 2003.

5. **Barbara Lawson** born about 1620. She died before 1669 at the age of 49.

6. **Reverend Richard Prideaux** was born before 1625. He died about 17 Mar 1663 at the age of 38 in Newcastle Upon Tyne, Durham, England. Richard Prideaux Entered Cambridge University: 1631 Died: 1663 More Information: Incorp. M.A. 1640. S. of George, of Sutcombe, Devon. Matric. (Exeter College, Oxford) Dec. 2, 1631, age 18; B.A. (Oxford) 1635; M.A. 1638. Fellow of Exeter College, 1635-43. V. of Easton Neston, Northants., 1643. Sequestered to Greens Norton, c. 1645. Lecturer at All Saints, Newcastle-on-Tyne, 1647; probably conformed; still preacher there, 1662. Died 1663, at Newcastle-on-Tyne. (Al. Oxon.; Brand, Newcastle, I. 387.) August 27, 1662 Richard Prideaux of All Saints', of the persuasion called "The Congregational Judgment," seems to have conformed as we now find him settled there, to preach both forenoon and afternoon. Appendix p. 391 of Memoirs of the life of Mr. Ambrose Barnes, late merchant and sometime alderman of Newcastle upon Tyne (accessed FS site) A History of the Newcastle upon Tyne Unitarian Church, through the lives of its ministers, their assistants, and other notable figures from our history By Maurice Large, formerly Chairperson and Acting Secretary July 5th, 1647, Mr. Richard Prideaux was appointed afternoon lecturer, and Mr. William Durant morning lecturer, at All-Saints r. Page 388 March 20th, 1656, by an order of common-council, Mr. Richard Prideaux was appointed morning lecturer, and Mr. William Durant afternoon lecturer of this church s.

WILL: May 17 1661. Will of Richard Prideaux of Newcastle. My eldest son Richard Prideaux 100l and all my estate in Devonshire. Mr. Emmanuel Phaire my bro. in law, Rebecca Prideaux my eldest dau 100l. Sarah my 2nd dau. 100l. George P. my 2nd son 50 l. John my 3rd son 50l. Hannah my 3rd dau 50l. My wife all my goods etc ie. my land at Nortin in the Bishoprick, my houses in Pilgrim St., my tenement at Biker Shore in Northumberland, to pay the above legacies. Mr. Ralph Fell and Mr. Marton overseers. Mr. Kinghtbridge and my bro. Long feoffees. Sir Wm. Morice and Sir Richd. Prideaux to decide disptures. Witness my hand Richd. Prideaux minister in Newcastle proved April 14 1663. p. 129 Durham Probate Records: pre-1858 original wills and inventories (1651-1680) Wills etc proved 1663 Description DPRI/1/1663/P6 Richard PRIDEAUX, minister in Newcastle, clerk, of Newcastle uppon Tine, chapelry of All Saints [Newcastle upon Tyne All Saints, Northumberland] DPRI/1/1663/P6 Richard PRIDEAUX, minister in Newcastle, clerk, of Newcastle uppon Tine, chapelry of All Saints [Newcastle upon Tyne All Saints, Northumberland] DPRI/1/1663/P6/1-2 17 May 1661 will DPRI/1/1663/P6/3 14 April 1663 inventory, actual total £177 14s Burial

Richard Prideaux Death or Burial Date 18 Mar 1662 Death or Burial Place All Saints, Newcastle upon Tyne, Northumberland, England

7. **Phaire** died after 1661. Other references in the Irish Records to the Rev Emanuel PHAIRE are few. We find him mentioned in the Manuscript Depositions in Trinity College under dates 3 May 1642 and 25 May 1642, as having been in debt to Henry KINESTON and Thomas BETTESWORTH, respectively, both of the town of Mallow. It is probable that he, like many other English settlers, left Ireland at this time, and that the Emanuel PHIDIER or PHAYER referred to above as son-in-law of George PRIDEAUX of Sutcombe, Devon, was his son or nephew. This latter Emanuel died in 1670, intestate and childless, and administration of his effects was granted (October 1670) to Thomas PHAYRE of Sutcombe, Samuel PHAYRE of Werrington, and John HOCKING of Frithelstock, all in Devon, his kinsmen. In 1675, lawsuits arose between these persons and one Anstice CRABB, widow of the Rev Nathaniel CRABB, vicar of Sutcombe, regarding the property of the said Emanuel PHAYRE, yeoman, Anstice CRABB claiming that she had become Emanuel's wife 9 days before he died (Chancery Proceedings before 1714, Mitford, bundle 296, No 6, and Keynardson, bundle 63, no 44). There is a regicide connection through brother-in-law Rev. Immanuel Phaire's son.

Fourth Generation

8. **Rev. Marmaduke Blackiston** born about 1563 in England. He died about 1 Sep 1639 at the age of 76 in Durham, England. He was buried in Saint Margarets Catholic Church, Crossgate, Durham, England. He was 16 when he entered Trinity College Oxford in April 1579. Vicar of Woodhorne, Rector of Redmarshall 1585, Rector of 1599, and Prebendary of the 7th Stall, Archdeacon of the East Riding of York, Prebendary of Wistow. He was Prebendary of York and Durham Cathedral. He was Archdeacon of Cleveland (which he resigned to his son-in-law John Cosin). He was a Reverend. Marmaduke of Newton-Hall, County of Palatine and Old Malton, Yorkshire. His family was from Norton Parish, Durham County. Margaret James and Rev. Marmaduke Blackiston were married on 30 Jun 1595 in Saint Mary Le Less, County Durham, England, United Kingdom.

9. **Margaret James** born about 1580. She died about 8 Mar 1636 at the age of 56 in Durham, England. She was buried on 10 Mar 1636 in Saint Margaret's, Crossgate, Durham, England. MARRIAGE: Margareta James Date: 30 Jun 1595 Marriage Place: St. Mary-Le-Bow, Durham, Durham, England Spouse: Marmaducus Blaxton FHL Film Number: 2082460 Reference ID: 39

10. **Henry Lawson** born about 1595 of Newcastle, Newcastle, Northumberland, England. He died after 1636 at the age of 41. A Mercer, Alderman and also Sheriff in 1636 Colonial Genealogist III:2 youngest son He was mentioned in the will of his son-in-law George's brother John's will of 1649. MARRIAGE: Henry Lawson m. Kath. Warmoth on 23 SEP 1622 at Saint Nicholas Parish Reg And Nonconf, Newcastle Upon Tyne, Northumberland, England Katheren Warmouth and Henry Lawson were married on 23 Sep 1622 in Newcastleontyne, Northumberland, England.

11. **Katheren Warmouth** was christened on 10 Mar 1602 in Saint Nicholas Parish, Newcastle Upon T., Durham, England. She was born in Newcastle Upon T., Durham, England. Katherine born 10 MAR 1602 St Nicholas Parish Rec And Nonconf, Newcastle Upon Tyne, Northumberland, England dau of William

12. **George Prideaux** born about 1566. He died about Apr 1651 at the age of 85 in Sutcombe, Devon, England. WILL: In the name of God Amen The ffirst day of May

Anno Dom One Thousand Six hundred fforty nyne I George Prideaux of sutcombe in the County of Devon gent beinge weake in body but (God be praysed) in perfect memory doe make this to bee my Last Will and Testament as ffolloweth ffirst I comand my Soule to God that freely gave it me and my body it beinge chested to be buried in the Church yarde of Sutcomb aforesaid neere and on the west side of the ground of my wife if I dye in Sutcomb. Item I doe give unto my sonne Richard Prideaux my Annuity of Twenty shillings [pa.d] issuing out of Mattacott in Sutcomb my Annuity of sixteene shillings [y.d] issueing out of Jane Tardrewes Tenemts/ in Bradworthy my Annuitie of Sixteen shillings [y.d] yssueing out of worthen in Mylton Damerell and my annuitie of eight shillings [y.d] yssueing out of Hole in Holsworthy with all deeds and Assurances of them and [.ey] of them, And all sumes of Money that are to be paid ffor redeeminge of them and either of them. Item I doe give unto each one of the children of my said sonne that shalle at the day of my death Liveinge [ffoure] pounds in Money to be Payd them by my said sonne out of the said Annuities and money ffor redeeminge of them as each of them shall accomplish the age of One and Twenty years. Item I doe give unto Nattanill Knill and unto Thomas Knill sonnes of my daughter Jane to each of them ffive poundes in Money to be paid them within one yeare after the day of my death. Item I doe give unto every one of the children of my daughter Honor liveing at the day of my death ffive pounds in money to be payd them as each of them shall accomplish the age of one and Twenty Yeares. Item I doe give unto every of the children of my daughter Ffrances liveing at the day of my death ffive poundes in Money to be payd them as each of them shall accomplish the Age of One and Twentye Yeares. Item I doe give unto my Grand sonne Thomas Jeffery ffive poundes in money to be payd him when hee shall be one and Twenty yeares old As also ffive shillings yearely untill that time to be [restre.d] towards his yearly [appare.] [h.ige] Item I doe give unto my Grandchildren Edmund and John [Townsend] three pounds in money to each of them and unto Katherin their sister twenty shillings to be payd to each of them with and yeare of my death. Item I doe will and devise that if any of the children and or of Richard my sonne or of Honer or of Ffrances my daughter doe die before hee or shee bee one and twenty yeares of age that the Legacie to him or her given shall remayne and bee to the rest of them surviving equally to be divided and to be paid to each of them at the [paymente] of their Legacie, if All dye (th God fforbid) their Legacies to remayne to my Executor, Alsoe I doe will that if Emanuell Phaier Henry Lee or Thomas Way doe die and [not ye.] the [.] of their [.], that My Executor doe put their [Band/ in Sute] And pay unto my daughter the wife of him [soe] dyinge [soe much] money [er] as hee shall [reconer] on ye said [Bonds], Alsoe I doe will that my [chattle] [base] and personall goods be sold at the best value and the money theirof to be [imployed] that out of the [handful] their of my Legacies may be the better Payd and some [por.] to the [binding] out of some of my Grandchildren to some [honest Lade] And of this my Will I make and Ordayne Richard Prideaux my sonne to be Executrix And I doe Ordayne Richard Prideaux, Knight and William Morrice Esq to be my Overseers to see that my will faithfully performed. In wittness [I do] hereof I have here unto put my hand [and] seale George Prideaux. Item I doe ffurther Will and devise that if my sonne Richard Prideaux doe either refuse or [fore] [slowe] him to approve this my will that then I doe Ordayne and appoint Emanuell Phayer my sonne in Lawe to be my Executor of this my Will [and] testament hee the said Emanuell Phayer giveing good [and] sufficient securitye unto my overseers hereof or to and of them faithfully to performe the same As alsoe to performe the [wisdom] Subcribed unto a [band] by him given to me for his wifes [p.n] Wittnes to this will one Emanuell Phayer Samuell Phaier [and] Thomas [Payne] Probatum."In Latin regarding the probate of the Will and naming Richard Prideaux as Executor"

13. **Anne** born about 1593. She died.

14. **Emmanuel Phaire** was born in 1579. An Emmanuel PHAYER, is overseer of the will, and son-in-law, of George PRIDEAUX of Sutcombe, Devon (P.C.C., 1021 Grey, 1 May 1649, probate 2 April 1651). Emanuel PHAIR, yeoman of Sutcombe, Devon, was named as a witness (with Samuel PHAIER and Thomas PHAIR or PAYNE?) to the will, signed 1 May 1649, of his father-in-law, George PRIDEAUX of Sutcombe, Devon (proved P.C.C., 2 April 1651), and named as alternate Executor in the event that his son might refuse to so act (the son was named as Executor in the Probate Grant). This Emanuel was probably baptized at Sutcombe, 19 January 1600, son of Miles PHAIER (adm Brasenose Coll, Oxon, 20 July 1578, aged 20, born Lancashire; M.A. 1585; Rector of Sutcombe, 1596). Emanuel died intestate in 1670, and administration of his effects was granted to his kinsmen, Thomas PHAYRE of Sutcombe (his will 1677), Samuel PHAYRE of Werrington (his will 1671) and John HOCKING of Frithelstock (his wife was Ann PHAYRE), all in Devon.

Fifth Generation

16. **John Blackiston Esq.** born about 1535 in Durham, England. He died about 5 Feb 1587 at the age of 52 in Durham, England. He was buried in Norton, Durham, England. son and heir, buried Feb 7 1586/7 will date Jan 5 1586/7 buried at Norton References R. Surtees 1823 The History and Antiquities of the County Palatine of Durham Vols 1-4. The Family of Blackiston of Stappleton-on-Tees by Oxford University Press. In 1578, John Blakiston had to do homage for his manor, and take the oath of Supremacy: "I, John Blakiston, do utterly testify and declare by my conscience, that the Queen's Highness, is the only supreme governor of this realm, as well as in all spiritual, or ecclesiastical things, or causes as temporal, and therefore, I do utterly renounce and forsake all foreign jurisdictions, powers, and authorities." John Blakiston appears to have had enough sense to see that provided he did not offend the authorities he could remain a secret Catholic and keep his land intact. It was one thing for the Government in London to pass legislation, but for it to insure that these laws were vigorously enforced in remote areas, was entirely another. Certainly there is no evidence to suggest that John Blakiston was further troubled by the Government and he died a much respected figure in 1586, his pragmatism having saved his family from a potentially serious crisis. Unfortunately, his son, William did not follow the same and lost part of his estate. "25th April 1570. Pardons for all treason, rebellion and other offences committed between Nov. 1 1569 and 31st Jan. 1570. On report of their penitence for their part in the rebellion in the North, testified before the Queen's Commissioners. Norton Nicholas Blaxton.Roger Netterton, John Blaxton, William Kitchen, Robert Crewe, John Robinson, William Blaxton, Robert Gates, Richard Smyth, Thomas Blaxton.yeomen."

Blakiston of Blakiston.

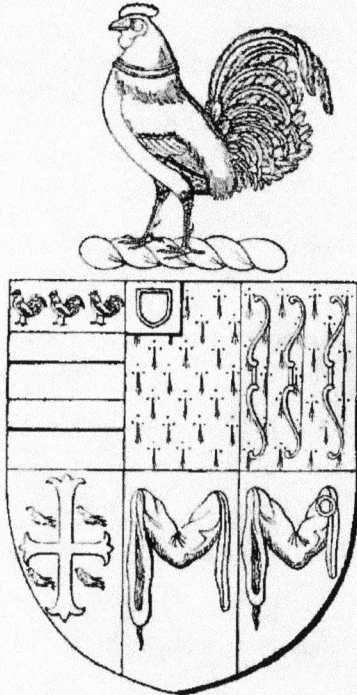

ARMS. 1. Blaykeston—Argent, two bars, in chief three cocks gules.
2. Surtees—Ermine, on a canton gules an orle argent.
3. Bowes—Ermine, three long bows bent in pale gules.
4. Dalden—Argent, a cross patonce between four martlets sable.
5. Conyers—Sable, a maunch or.
6. Conyers—Sable, a maunch or, an annulet for difference
CREST.   A cock or, crested and wattled gules.

17. **Elizabeth Bowes** born about 1538 in Durham, England. She died before 1582 at the age of 44. Surtees History of Durham vol 4 p 107 eldest dau and coheir

18. **Richard James** born about 1544. James, Bishop of Durham. Coat of arms shown does not match the description which is sable a dolphin embowed argent. p 186 James, Bishop of Durham Chart shows John James of Little One in Co. Staffordshire married and had John James of "Little one" Co Staff. m. Ellen, dau of William Bolton of Sandbache in Cheshire by dau of of Venables. He had eldest son William James m Catherine dau of Wm Risby Mayor of Abbington and 2nd Susan no children, and 3rd Isabell, widow of Robert Atkinson, 2nd son Richard m. Margaret dau of Thomas Caldwell of Marston, Co Staff. (they had children 1. John James of Littleone, 2. Edward of London Merchant, 2. William James, one of the prevends of Durham, incumbent of Ryton, married Elizabeth Ewbanck, 3 James James, 4. Francis James, Elizabeth, and

Margaret James), Thomas, Francis, doctor of the Civil Law and Master of Chancery, Judge of Audience and Chancellor of Wells, Edward James 4th son and Merchant of London m. Lidia Masham, 2nd a dau of Pyatt, Alderman of London, and Johanna m. 1st Thomas Wildey, 2nd Thomas Chamberlayne. Pedigrees Recorded at the Visitations of the County Palatine of Durham by William Flower, Richard St. George, William Dugdale edited by Joseph Foster. 1887. Richard and Margaret had John James of Littleone, Edward of London, Merchant; William James, one of the prebends of Durham, incumbent off Ryton, James, Francis, Elizabeth, and Margaret. (James, Bishop of Durham p. 186-187 by Foster) John James of Littleone, in Co Staffordshire, father of John James of Littleone who married Ellen, dau of William Bolt of Sandbache in Cheshire, by a dau of Venables. They had children William, Bishop of Duresemne, Richard James of Littleone who married Margaret dau of Thomas Caldwell of Marston, Co Staffordshire, Thomas, Francis, doctor of the Civil law and Master of Chancery, Judge of Audience and Chancellor of Wells. MARRIAGE: Richard James Record Type: Marriage Date: 8 Dec 1579 Marriage Place: Church Eaton, St Editha, Staffordshire, England Religion: Anglican Spouse: Margerta Cauldwall Page number: 19 Margaret Caldwell and Richard James were married on 8 Dec 1579 in St. Editha, County Staffordshire, England.

19. **Margaret Caldwell** born about 1550.
20. **Robert Lawson Jr.** born about 1560 in Longhirst, Northumberland. Surtees Durham vol 122 p 194 Robert Lawson Jr. was married.
22. **William Warmouth** born about 1570 in Newcastle, Durham, England, England. He died after 1615 at the age of 45. alderman, sheriff and mayor 1598, 1603, and 1615 Colonial Genealogist III:2 Judith Whittingham and William Warmouth were married on 5 Apr 1592.
23. **Judith Whittingham** born about 1570 in Newcastle, Durham, England.
24. **Richard Prideaux of Theuborough** born about 1520. He died in 1603 at the age of 83.
25. **Katherine Arundel** born about 1523. She died about 1578 at the age of 55.

BLAKISTON OF BLAKISTON.

Hugh de Blaykeston━Cecily, dau. of Ralph Fitz-raffe.

Roger Blaykeston of Blaykeston, in the Bishoprick.━ Ralph Blaykeston, priest.

William Blaykeston of Blaykeston, Knight, living temp. E. III. & R. II.━

Sibill.═William Blaykeston made his will in 1467.═Catherine.

Nicholas Blaykeston of Blaykeston, Esq.━ .. dau. of .. Fulthorpe. Thomas Blaykeston. Isabella.

.. Blaykeston, Chap-23 Hen. VII. | William Blaykes-ton of Blaykeston. ═Anne, dau. of Roger Coigniers of Wynyard. | Marmaduke Blaykes-ton, 23 Hen. VIII. ═Elizabeth Fulthorpe, *alias* Place, "licentiatu viro, 1519."

..omas Blaykeston,═Elizabeth, dau. of John Place of ..n & heir, died 1484. | Halnaby, & heir of her mother, the dau. & heir of Thomas Surteys. | Margery wife of John Trollope of Thornely. | William Blakiston of Coxson, *alias* Coxhow, in the Bishop-rick, 2nd son.━ .. dau. of .. Millot.

See p. 21.

..aykes-═Elizabeth, dau. & ..ton, | one of the heirs of George Bowes of Stretlam, Knight. | Dorothy, wife of George Dent of Newcastle, merchant & Esquire. Margaret, wife of Cuthbert Myddleton of Newcastle. | Margery, wife of Francis Bayn-brigg of Whitley Hill. | Marma-duke, 3rd son, attainted. | Humphrey ═Margaret, dau. Blakiston of | of Rich.d Heb-Fulthorpe, | borne of 2nd son. | Hardwicke.

..iam═ .. dau. of .. ..n | Claxton of ..- | Wynyard, co. ..t. | pal. Durham. | Thomas Blakiston═Catherine, dau. of Newton juxta of .. Whitehead Durham, died in a of Tinemouth. 1625 or thereabouts. | Edward Blakiston═ of Great Chilton, Esq., son & heir, living 1615. | Thomasine, dau. of Robert Booth of Old Durham. | Anne, wife to Gerard Salveyn of Croxdale. Barbara, wife to Richard Booth of Old Durham.

..omas B. ..iston,━ | 2. John. 3. Raphe of Newby & co. Yorks. | Eliz. wife of Sir George Tonge of Denton, co. pal. Durham. | William B. of Old ═Anne, dau. and coh. to Malton, Yorks., | Francis Briggs of Old Esq., died in 1628. | Malton, co. Yorks., Esq. | Anne, aged 12, 1615. Thomasine.

.., wife of Sir ..homas Smith of ..oxton, Nott., ..nt. | 2. William Blaki-ton of Old ═Mary, dau. of Malton, co. Yorks., Esq. | Sir William now residing at Pidding Hall, | Bellasses of Garth, in co. pal. Durham, | Murton, co. pal. aged 45, 18 Aug. 16.. | Durham, Knt. | 1. Thomas, d. y. 1. Penelope, d. y. | 2. Eliz. wife of Christopher Copperthwayt of Brignall, co. Yorks. | 3. Mary, wife of Lynley Paget of the city of York. | 4. Cath., wife of George Fenwick of Newcastle upon Tyne.

..tifie't by WILLM. BLAKISTON (1660). Anne, died in her infancy.

This pedigree is verified for true by the subscription hereunto of John Blaykeston of Blaykeston, aforesaid, living at Billingham, on Fryday, 5 August. 1575.

JOHN BLAYKESTON.   HUMPREY BLAYKESTON.

Sixth Generation

32. **Thomas Blackiston Esq.** born about 1495 in Durham, England. He died about Aug 1557 at the age of 62 in Durham, England. died Friday before Holy Trinity in 1557 Great grandfather of William Blackstone of Boston, first settler of Boston. Elizabeth Place and Thomas Blackiston Esq. were married.

33. **Elizabeth Place** born about 1510 in Durham, England. She died after 1 Oct 1553 at the age of 43 in Durham, England.

34. **George Bowes Knight** was born in 1516 of Dalden, Durham, England. He died in 1546 at the age of 30 in England. Surtees History of Durham vol 4 p 107 Lord of Dalden, posthumous son Of Dalden and Streatham, Kent. Bowes, George, knight: Northumb. Chancery: Inquisitions Post Mortem, Series II, and other Inquisitions, Henry VII to Charles I. Bowes, George, knight: Northumb. Held by: The National Archives, Kew - Chancery, the Wardrobe, Royal Household, Exchequer and various commissions Date: 22 April 1546 - 28 January 1547 Subjects: Landed estates Reference: C 142/75/24 Description: Bowes, George, knight: Northumb. Date: 38 Hen. VIII. Held by: The National Archives, Kew Legal status: Public Record(s) Closure status: Open Document, Open Description see also Court of Wards and Liveries: Inquisitions Post Mortem. Reference: WARD 7/2/22 Subjects: Landed estates Held by: The National Archives, Kew Legal status: Muriel Eure and George Bowes Knight were married about 1537 in Witton, Durham, England.

35. **Muriel Eure** born about 1510 in Witton, Durham, England. She died on 23 Nov 1557 at the age of 47 in Durham, England. She was buried in Wycliffe. Surtees History of Durham vol 4 p 107 Visitations of Yorkshire by Glover 1584-1585 has Eure, Lacy, Tyson family descent p. 607-614 Muriel Eure m. George Bowes 2nd William Wycliff who died Aug 5 1584. She died Nov. 23, 1557 both buried at Wycliffe.

36. **John James of Little One** was born before 1524 in Staffordshire, England. John James Burial Date: 1 May 1592 Burial Place: Church Eaton, St Editha, Staffordshire, England Religion: Anglican Phillimore Ecclesiastical Parish Page number: 30 John James Burial Date: 23 Dec 1605 Burial Place: Eccleshall, Staffordshire, England Father: John James

37. **Ellen Bolt** born about 1524.

38. **Thomas Caldwell** was born before 1529 in Staffordshire, England. Thomas Calewaell Record Type: Marriage Marriage Date: 12 Feb 1549 Marriage Place: Burton upon Trent, St Modwen, Staffordshire, England Religion: Anglican Spouse: Margerata Thomas Caldewall Gender: Male Marriage Date: 14 Feb 1549 Marriage Place: St. Modwen'S, Burton Upon Trent, Staffordshire, England Spouse: Margareta Bysshyppe FHL Film Number: 1278931 Reference ID: items 4-10 Margaret Bysshyppe and Thomas Caldwell were married on 12 Feb 1549 in Burton upon Trent, St. Modwen, County Staffordshire, England.

39. **Margaret Bysshyppe** born about 1529.

40. **Robert Lawson Sr.** born about 1530 of Rock, Northumberland. He died on 16 May 1565 at the age of 35. Surtees Durham p 194 inquisition p.m. Surtees Durham p. 47 names sons William, Reginald, Lyonel in 1565. Visitations of Yorkshire by Glover p. 254 Lawson of Brough. Robert Lawson of Usworth co. Durham 2nd husband of Margary sole dau to Ralph Swynnow, sister and heir to John, her 1st husband Edmond Lawson of Newcastle. Margery Swynno and Robert Lawson Sr. were married about 1552.

41. **Margery Swynno** born about 1530 in Rock, Northumberland. widow of Edmond Lawson of Newcastle. Surtees Durham p 194
46. **William Whittingham** was born in 1524 in Chester, Cheshire, England. He was buried on 10 Jun 1579 in Durham Cathedral, Durham, England. Catherine Jaqueman and William Whittingham were married.
47. **Catherine Jaqueman** born about 1529 in Orleans, France. She died in Will Dated 1590.
48. **Humphrey Prideaux** born about 1487. He died on 8 May 1550 at the age of 63 in Theubotough, Cornwall, England. Humphrey m2nd Elizabeth Hatch after 31 Oct 1523
49. **Joane Walrond Fowell** born about 1475. She died about 1523 at the age of 48. Richardson Vol 2 p 404 mentions her and 2nd husband Humphrey. 1st husband was Philip Courtenay.
50. **Sir John "Tilbury Jack" Arundel of Trerice** was born in 1495. He died on 26 Nov 1560 at the age of 65. There is a monumental brass of Sir John IV Arundell (1495–1561) Jack of Tilbury, of Trerice. Stratton Church, Cornwall. Drawing of arms of Sir John IV Arundell (1495–1561) of Trerice, with six quarters, from his brass in Stratton Church:[32] The family's descent is recorded in the Heraldic Visitations of Cornwall. Trerice is an historic manor in the parish of Newlyn East (Newlyn in Pydar), near Newquay, Cornwall, United Kingdom. The surviving Tudor manor house known as Trerice House is located at Kestle Mill, three miles east of Newquay (grid reference SW840584). The house with its surrounding garden has been owned by the National Trust since 1953 and is open to the public. Sir John Arundell (1495–1561), of Trerice, Cornwall, nicknamed "Tilbury Jack" (or Jack of Tilbury), was a commander of the Royal Navy during the reigns of Kings Henry VIII and Edward VI and served twice as Sheriff of Cornwall. Sir John Arundell was the eldest son and heir of Sir John Arundell (1470–1512) of Trerice by his wife Jane Grenville (1474–1551), a daughter of Sir Thomas Grenville (died 1513) KB, lord of the manors of Bideford in Devon and of Stowe in the parish of Kilkhampton in Cornwall, Sheriff of Cornwall in 1481 and in 1486 and an Esquire of the Body to King Henry VII. Arundell was an Esquire of the Body to King Henry VIII, and was knighted at the Battle of the Spurs in 1513. In 1523 he achieved notability by the capture of a notorious pirate. Under King Edward VI he was Vice-Admiral of the West and served twice as Sheriff of Cornwall, in 1542 and in 1553 at the time of the accession of Queen Mary. Sir John Arundell died in 1561 and was buried at Newlyn East.[15] His monumental brass survives in Stratton Church, Cornwall. Drawing of arms of Sir John Arundell, with six-quarters, from his brass in Stratton Church. His monumental brasses survive in St Andrew's Church, Stratton, Cornwall. In 1882 a monument was situated at the east end of the north aisle of the church, formed of a chest tomb on top of which was a slab of stone inlaid with several brasses, of which some were then missing, as revealed by matrices. Today only the slab with brasses survives, The brasses show Sir John flanked by his two wives with two groups of his children below and two individual children between himself and each wife. Other brasses are heraldic escutcheons. The inscription is as follows: "Here lyeth buriede Syr John Arundell Trerise, Knyght, who praysed be God dyed in the Lorde the xxv daye of November in the yeare of Oure Lorde God a MCCCCC lxi and in the iiixx and vii yeare of his age whose soule now resteth wyth the Faythfull Chrystians in our Lorde" The date of death inscribed on his monument (25 November 1561) disagrees with that reported in his Inquisition post mortem, namely 26 November 1560, which

latter appears to be correct as probate of his will was granted to his widow Juliana on 23 January 1560/1.[18] He is shown dressed in full armour with helmet. Of the four original brass escutcheons only two survive. The one above the wife on his right hand side shows the arms of Arundell with six-quarters.

51. **Mary Beville** born about 1495. She died in 1526 at the age of 31.

Seventh Generation

64. **William Blakiston Esq.** was born in 1465 in Durham, England. He died before 1533 at the age of 68. son and heir Anne Conyers and William Blakiston Esq. were married.

65. **Anne Conyers** born about 1465 in Durham, England. She died after 1533 at the age of 68 in Durham, England.

66. **John Place Esq.** born about 1470 in Richmond, England. Catherine Surtees and John Place Esq. were married.

67. **Catherine Surtees** was born in 1485 in Durham, England. She died after 1512 at the age of 27 in Durham, England. heir of the whole blood to Thomas age 26 in 1511. had livery 13 Jul 1512 Co-heiress with her brother Thomas of Dinsdale

68. **Ralph Bowes Sir** born about 1475 of Streatlam. He born about 1494. He died in Apr 1516 at the age of 41. He was also known as Ralph Bowes. Surtees Durham Vol IV p 107 knight app. High Sheriff of Durham 4 Oct 1482. served 30 years, was at Floddenfield 1509, of Streatlam and Dalden Elizabeth Clifford and Ralph Bowes Sir were married.

69. **Elizabeth Clifford** born about 1485. She born about 1490. She died on 8 Oct 1586 at the age of 96 in London, England, United Kingdom. Surtees Durham Vol IV p 107

70. **Baron William Eure 1st Lord Eure** born about 1483 in Witton, Durham, England. He died on 15 Mar 1547 or 15 Mar 1548 at the age of 64. Yorkshire Visitations by Foster p. 612 Sir William Eure Knight, Sheriff of Northumberland 1527, Capta of the town and castle of Berwick upon Tyne 30 Hen. VIII afterwards warden of the East Marches towards Scotland. Created lord Eure of Witton by letters patent date 24 Feb 35 Hen. VIII. He had grant from the crown of the Cell of Jarrow in 1544. He died 15 Mar. 2 Ed. VI 1547/8 Inq p.m. m. Elizabeth dau. of Christopher, Lord Willoughby by D'Eresby. Elizabeth Willoughby and Baron William Eure 1st Lord Eure were married about 1503 in Eresby, Lincolnshire, England.

71. **Elizabeth Willoughby** born about 1483 in Lancaster, England.

72. **John James** born about 1500 in Staffordshire, England.

74. **William Bolt** born about 1500 in Sandbache, Cheshire, England.

75. **Venable** was born before 1505.

80. **William Lawson** born about 1500 in Little Osworth, Durham, England. He was buried in Washington. Surtees Durham p 193 Surtees Durham vol. 2 p. 47

81. **Isabell Hedworth** born about 1500. Surtees Durham p 193 Surtees Durham vol. 2 p. 47 dau of John Hedworth of Harraton.

82. **Ralph Swynno** born about 1500 in Rock, Northumberland. Ralph Swynno was married.

92. **William Whittingham** born about 1498 in <Chester, Cheshire, England William Whittingham was married.

96. **Fulk Prideaux** born about 1471. He died about 1530 at the age of 59. Description: Prideaux, Fulk: Devon Date:22 Hen. VIII.Held by:The National Archives, Kew. Chancery: Inquisitions Post Mortem, Series II, and other Inquisitions, Henry VII to

Charles I. Description available at other catalogue level. Prideaux, Fulk: Devon. Date: 22 April 1530 - 21 April 1531 Reference: C 142/51/12 Subjects: Landed estates

97. **Katherine Poyntz** born about 1467. She died about 1507 at the age of 40.
98. **Sir Richard Fowell** born about 1440. He died about 1507 at the age of 67. Burke's Genealogical and Heraldic History of the Landed Gentry, Volume 1 Pg.347 JOHN DRAKE, Esq. of Ashe, who s. his father in the representation of the family, m. (26 HENRY VIII.,) Amye, dau. of Roger Grenville, Esq. of Stow, co. Cornwall,
99. **Mary Walrond** born about 1450.
100. **Sir John Arundell** was born in 1470. He died in 1512 at the age of 42. Sir John Arundell was the eldest son and heir of Sir John Arundell (1470–1512)[2] of Trerice by his wife Jane Grenville (1474–1551), a daughter of Sir Thomas Grenville (died 1513) KB, lord of the manors of Bideford in Devon and of Stowe in the parish of Kilkhampton in Cornwall, Sheriff of Cornwall in 1481 and in 1486 and an Esquire of the Body to King Henry VII.[3]
101. **Jane Grenville** was born in 1474. She died in 1551 at the age of 77.
102. **John Beville** was of Gwarnick, Cornwall, England.

Eighth Generation

128. **Thomas Blakiston Esq.** was born in 1440 in Durham, England. He died on 30 Sep 1483 at the age of 43 in Durham, England. son and heir age 30 in 1470 had livery inq. pm. 3 Nov 1483 ob. Sept 30 Joan Killinghall and Thomas Blakiston Esq. were married.
129. **Joan Killinghall** born about 1440 in England. She died after 1483 at the age of 43 in Durham, England.
130. **Roger Conyers Knight** born about 1431 of Hornby, York County, England. Sibill Langton and Roger Conyers Knight were married about 1456.
131. **Sibill Langton** born about 1431.
132. **Rowland Place Esq.** born about 1445 in England.
133. **Margery Conyers** born about 1445 in Hornby, England.
134. **Thomas Surteys Esq.** was born in 1456 in Durham, England. He died about 1507 at the age of 51 in Durham, England. had livery 30 August 4 Dudley Elizabeth Conyers and Thomas Surteys Esq. were married about 1475.
135. **Elizabeth Conyers** born about 1456 in Durham, England. She died before 1492 at the age of 36 in Durham, England. enfeoffed of lands by deed 30 May 1465. 5 Edw. IV
136. **Ralph Bowes Knight** born about 1450 of Streatlam. He died about Jul 1482 at the age of 32. Surtees Durham Vol IV p 107 Knight of Steatlam and Dalden Tower. 4th son. Will date 3 July 1482 Margary Conyers and Ralph Bowes Knight were married.
137. **Margary Conyers** born about 1455. She died on 12 Aug 1532 at the age of 77. Surtees Durham Vol IV p 107 dau and coheir of Richard Conyers, will dated 6 Aug 1524
138. **Henry Clifford Lord** was born in 1453 in England. He died on 23 Apr 1523 at the age of 70. Burkes EP Clifford 1st wife Anne St. John 2nd wife Frances Pudsey widow of Thomas Talbot. Complete Peerage vol 3 p 294 10th earl
139. **Anne St. John** born about 1455.
140. **Ralph Eure Knight** born about 1460 in Witton, Durham, England. He died on 22 Oct 1539 at the age of 79. Visitations of Yorkshire 1584-1585 by Glover. Sir Ralph Eure Knight Sheriff of Northumberland in 1504 and Yorkshire in 1506 and 1510 died 22 Apr 31 Henry VIII 1540 Inq. p.m. m. 1st wife Muriel dau of Sir Hugh Hastings Knight of Fenwick Co, York and Ann Gascoigne, license for marriage in the chapel, within the

Manor of Fenwick 18 Jan 1481/2 married 2nd wife Agnes Constable who married first Ralph Bigod. (marriage June 18 1482 was given in Paget Book on Ancestry of Prince Charles) Muriel Hastings and Ralph Eure Knight were married on 18 Jan 1481.

141. **Muriel Hastings** born about 1460 in Fenwick, Yorkshire, England.

142. **Christopher Willoughby Lord** was born in 1453. He died before 13 Jul 1499 at the age of 46 in Campsey, Suffolk, England. AR7 83-12 10th Lord Willoughby Will of Sir Christopher Willoughby Lord of Willoughby and of Erisby PROB 11/11/675 13 July 1499 The National Archives, Kew. Margaret Jenney and Christopher Willoughby Lord were married before 28 Mar 1482.

143. **Margaret Jenney** born about 1455. She died in 1515 or 1516 at the age of 60.

160. **John Lawson** born about 1475 of Washington, Durham, England. Surtees Durham p 193 Surtees Durham vol. 2 p. 47 Hylton and John Lawson were married.

161. **Hylton** born about 1475 of Hylton. Surtees Durham p 193

162. **John Hedworth** born about 1475. Surtees Durham p 193

184. **Seth Whittingham**. Seth Whittingham was married.

192. **William Prideaux** died after 1461.

193. **Alice Gifford of Theuborugh** died after 1511.

194. **Sir Humphrey Poyntz Knight of Elkstone** born about 1434. He died on 10 Oct 1487 at the age of 53 in Devon, England. AR8 p. 212 Humphrey

195. **Elizabeth Pollard** born about 1434. She died after 1486 at the age of 52.

200. **John Arundell** was born circa 1428. He died in 1471 at the age of 43. Sir John Arundell, son, was the Sheriff of Cornwall until his death in 1471. According to the Cornish historian, Richard Carew in his Survey of Cornwall: "Being forewarned that he would be slain on the sands, forsook his house at Efford, as too maritime, and removed to Trerice his more inland habitation in the same county; but he did not escape his fate, for being Sheriff of Cornwall in that year, and the Earl of Oxford surprising Mount Michael for the House of Lancaster, he had the king's commands, by his office, to endeavour the reducing of it, and lost his life in a skirmish on the sands thereabouts". St Michael's Mount had been captured by the earl of Oxford, and as Sheriff it fell to Arundell to obey the king's command. He was buried in the chapel in St Michael's Mount.[9] He married twice: firstly to Margaret Courtenay, daughter of "Sir Hugh Courtenay", whose identity is unclear,[26] by whom he had two sons Robert and Walter, who died young, without children. he married secondly to Anne Moyle, daughter of Sir Walter Moyle of Estwell, by whom he had children four sons, the eldest two of whom, Robert and Sir John III, succeeded to Trerice.

201. **Ann Moyle** born about 1430.

202. **Sir Thomas Grenville** born about 1453. He died about 1513 at the age of 60. Thomas Grenville (died 1513) Detail of Grenville's effigy in St Mary's Church, Bideford Sir Thomas Grenville II, K.B., (c. 1453 – c. 1513), lord of the manors of Stowe in Kilkhampton, Cornwall and Bideford, Devon, Sheriff of Cornwall in 1481 and 1486. During the Wars of the Roses, he was a Lancastrian supporter who had taken part in the conspiracy against Richard III, organised by the Duke of Buckingham. On the accession of King Henry VII (1485–1509) to the throne, Sir Thomas was appointed one of the Esquires of the Body to Henry VII.[4] On 14 November 1501 upon the marriage of Prince Arthur to Katherine of Aragon, he was created a Knight of the Bath.[4] He served on the Commission of the Peace for Devon from 1510 to his death in circa 1513. Grenville's monument in St Mary's Church, Bideford, from the Lady Chapel looking

northwards A monument with recumbent effigy on a chest tomb exists of Sir Thomas Grenville in the Church of St Mary, Bideford. Inscribed on the Tudor arch above is the following Latin text: Hic jacet Thomas Graynfyld miles patron(us) (huius) eccle(siae) q(ui) obiit XVIII die me(n)sis Marcii A(nno) D(omini) MCCCCCXIII cui(us) a(n)i(ma)e p(ro)piciet(ur) D(eus) Amen ("Here lies Thomas Grenville, knight, patron of this church who died on the 18th day of March in the Year of Our Lord 1513, to whose soul may God look on with favour Amen")

203. **Isabel Gilbert** born about 1450.

Ninth Generation

256. **William Blackiston Esq.** was born in 1420 in Durham, England. He died about Aug 1468 at the age of 48 in Durham, England. son and heir, age 40 in 1460 a commissioner of array inq p.m. 1468 Aug 11 Sibella and William Blackiston Esq. were married.

257. **Sibella** born about 1420 in Durham, England. She died after 1484 at the age of 64 in Durham, England.

258. **John Killinghall Esq.** was born in 1412. He died before Aug 1486 at the age of 74. John Killinghall Esq. was married.

260. **Christopher Conyers Knight** born about 1395 of Hornby, York County, England. He died on 6 Aug 1444 at the age of 49. Colonial Gen. Vol. XI 3-4(Augustan Society #219) first wife Ellen Roleston m 2nd Margaret Wadeley Ellyn Ryleston and Christopher Conyers Knight were married before Sep 1415.

261. **Ellyn Ryleston** born about 1399. She died on 6 Aug 1444 at the age of 45. 1st wife of Christopher, one of the heiress of Ryleston

262. **William Langton** born about 1380. He died before 1440 at the age of 60. third son Isabella Elmeden and William Langton were married.

263. **Isabella Elmeden** born about 1400. Surtees Durham: dau of William Elmden. Burke EP: Isabella is wife of Rowland Tempest

264. **Robert Playse Esq.** born about 1410 in England. He died in England. Isabell Pudsey and Robert Playse Esq. were married.

265. **Isabell Pudsey** born about 1420 in Barforth, England. Visitations of Yorkshire p. 294 Elizabeth wife of -- Place, dau of Sir Ralph Pudsey by 2nd wife Margaret Tunstall of Scargill.

266. **John Conyers Knight** born about 1411 of Hornby, York County, England. He died on 14 Mar 1489 or 14 Mar 1490 at the age of 78. Sheriff of Yorkshire, Knight of Hornby EP 1977 says John is son of Sir Christopher Eure and Mariora Eure, Margery Darcy and John Conyers Knight were married before 20 Nov 1431.

267. **Margery Darcy** was born on 1 Sep 1418 in Ravensworth. She died before 20 Apr 1469 at the age of 50.

268. **Thomas Surteys Esq.** was born in 1433 in Durham, England. He died about Jul 1480 at the age of 47 in Durham, England. son and heir age 10 years and upwards 6 Nevill. ob. 1480. Inq. p.m. 4 Jul 4 Dudley. Catherine Ayscough and Thomas Surteys Esq. were married in 1453.

269. **Catherine Ayscough** born about 1435 in Durham, England. She died in Durham, England. apparently married by 1443 young age?

270. **Christopher Conyers Knight** was born in 1421 Of Sockburne. He died on 13 Mar 1487 at the age of 66. of Sockburne Knight. age 9 and upwards in 1431, wardship committed to Richard Bulkeley and Nicholas Hulme Clerk. probate of age 1442, had respite of homage 20 Oct in 21 Hen VI ob 13 Mar 2 Hen. VII 1487. inq p.m. 20 Apr 4

Sherwood 1487. Margery Eure and Christopher Conyers Knight were married on 12 Dec 1432 in Wilton Castle.

271. **Margery Eure** born about 1423. Visitations of Yorkshire by Glover p. 611 Margery married at Witton Castle, 12 Dec. 1432 (dispensation date 10 Jun 1432) To Christopher (later Sir Christopher), son of Robert Conyers, of Sockboburne. He died 13 March, 1487.

272. **William Bowes Knight** born about 1420 of Streatlam. He died on 28 Jul 1466 at the age of 46. Surtees Durham Vol IV p 107 Sheriff of Northumberland. age 30 years and upwards in 1465

On the walls of Streatlam Castle Sr. William Bowes arms and Ralph Lord
Greystock. Sir William d. 1465 and his wife Joan dau. of Ralph fifth lord of
Greystock. Maud Fitz Hugh and William Bowes Knight were married.

273. **Maud Fitz Hugh** born about 1422. She died after 17 Oct 1466 at the age of 44.

274. **Richard Conyers Sir** born about 1432 of South Cowton, York County, England. Surtees Durham Vol IV p 107 EP 1977 says Richard Conyers son of John Conyers by Margaret Darcy, grandson of Sir Christopher who m. Mariora Eure

275. **Alice Wycliffe** born about 1431 in York County, England. HRH Prince Charles Ancestry by Paget, Visitations of Yorkshire by Glover p. 377 Alice wife of Sir Richard Conyers of Cowton, brother to Sir John Conyers dau of John Wycliff and Agnes dau of Sir Thomas Rokeby.

276. **John Clifford Lord** was born on 8 Apr 1435 in Conisborough Castle, England. He died on 28 Mar 1461 at the age of 25 in Towton, England. Complete Peerage vol 3 p 293-4 killed on the eve of the battle of Towton by a chance arrow. buried in a pit there with others who were slain. Margaret Bromflete and John Clifford Lord were married.

277. **Margaret Bromflete** born about 1435. She died on 12 Apr 1493 at the age of 58 in England. Complete Peerage vol 3 p 294 2nd married Lancelot Threlkeld.

278. **John St. John Sir** born about 1430 of Bletso, Beds. He died after 1488 at the age of 58. Complete Peerage vol 3 p 294

Weis 85-36 Alice Bradshaigh and John St. John Sir were married.

279. **Alice Bradshaigh** born about 1430.

280. **William Eure Knight** born about 1440. Visitations of Yorkshire 1584-5 by Glover Sir William Eure, Knight, Sheriff of Yorkshire in 1483 1 Rich. 3 dispensation for 2nd marriage (which already took place) date 3 July 1497 being twice related in 3rd degree. He married 1st to dau. of old Robert Constable of Flambrough, Knight. He is ancestor of President William Howard Taft

281. **Margaret Constable** born about 1440. She died before 1483 at the age of 43. Visitations of Yorkshire by Glover p. 178 Margaret m. Sir William Eure dau of Robert Constable m. Agnes dau of Lord Wentworth of Suffolk. Plan. Anc. says she married Ralph Bigod as his first wife bef 1482.

282. **Hugh Hastings Knight** born about 1435 in Fenwick, Campshall, Yorkshire, England. He died on 7 Jun 1488 at the age of 53. PA1 Elsing 7 Edward Hastings Knight of Elsing, Fenwick, etc. 8th Lord Hastings de jure, was born at Fenwick on 21 May 1382, and was brother and heir of Hugh Hastings. He was married for the first time to Muriel de Dinham, daughter of John de Dinha, Knight of Hartland, Co. Devon by Muriel, daughter of Thomas de Courtenay, Knight of Woodhuish, Co. Devon. He married 2nd to Margary Clifton. Anne Gascoigne and Hugh Hastings Knight were married before 12 Apr 1455.

283. **Anne Gascoigne** born about 1435 in Gawthorpe, Yorkshire, England.
284. **Robert Willoughby** was born in 1427 in Parham, Sussex, England. He died on 30 May 1465 at the age of 38. AR7 83-11 Cecily Welles and Robert Willoughby were married.
285. **Cecily Welles** born about 1430. She died in 1480 at the age of 50. p 335 Royal Ancestry vol 5 by Richardson says dau of Lionel Welles by Joan Waterton
286. **William Jenney Knight** born about 1420 of Knotteshall, Suffolk, England. He died on 23 Dec 1483 at the age of 63. Burkes Commoners Sir William Jenney Knight of Knodishall one of the judges of the King's Bench in 1427 m. Elizabeth dau of Thomas Cawse. Living 1466. Elizabeth Cawse and William Jenney Knight were married.
287. **Elizabeth Cawse** born about 1420. She died about 1470 at the age of 50. Her name given in HRH Prince Charles Ancestry by Paget.
320. **Thomas Lawson** born about 1450. Surtees Durham vol. 2 p. 47 of Usworth in the bishoprick married dau. Of Threlkeld. Threlkeld and Thomas Lawson were married.
321. **Threlkeld** born about 1450.
322. **William Hylton Baron** born about 1450 of Hylton. Surtees Durham p 193 Marie Stapleton and William Hylton Baron were married.
323. **Marie Stapleton** born about 1450. Surtees Durham p 193
384. **Sir John Prideaux Knight of Adeston** died after 1433.
385. **Anne Shapton** born about 1400.
388. **Lord Nicholas Poyntz of Iron Acton** born about 1379. He died after 17 Sep 1450 at the age of 71. AR8 p. 212 Nicholas Poyntz
389. **Elizabeth Mill** born about 1400. She died in 1434 at the age of 34.
390. **Richard Pollard** born about 1410.
391. **Thomasine Cruse** born about 1410.
400. **Nicholas Arundell** born about 1410. Nicholas II Arundell, son, who married Johanna St John (died 1482), daughter of Edward St John of Somerset[16] and heiress of her brother William St John (died 1473). From this marriage the Arundells inherited the manors of Selworthy and Luccombe,[21] on the north coast of Somerset opposite Glamorgan where Fonmon Castle was the family's earliest seat, built by Sir Oliver St. John, one of the Twelve Knights of Glamorgan, followers of Robert FitzHamon (died 1107), the Norman conqueror of Glamorgan. The North Somerset estate of Holnicote was in the parish of Selworthy, and had been inherited on the marriage in 1745 of Sir Thomas Dyke Acland, 7th Baronet (1723–1785) to Elizabeth Dyke, heiress of Holnicote, Tetton and Pixton.[22] The Aclands became heirs to the Arundell estates in 1802 (see below). Fragments of stained glass survive in the east window of the north aisle of Selworthy Church showing the arms of Nicholas I Arundell of Trerys, and of his wife Elizabeth Pellor (alias Pellower) (sable, a chevron or between three bezants), grandparents of Nicholas II Arundell who inherited Selworthy, who clearly inserted the glass in memory of his grandparents as he was the first to have a connection with Selworthy.[23] These Pellor arms are also visible on the monumental brass to Sir John IV Arundell (died 1561) in Stratton Church (see image below).[23]
401. **Johanna St John** born about 1410. She died in 1482 at the age of 72.
402. **Sir Walter Moyle of Estwell** born about 1400.
404. **Sir Thomas Grenville** was born on 21 Jan 1432. He died about 1483 at the age of 51.
405. **Elizabeth Gorges** born about 1425.
406. **Sir Otis Gilbert** born about 1425 of Compton Castle.

407. **Elizabeth Hill** born about 1425.

Tenth Generation

512. **Nicholas Blackiston** was born in 1398 in Durham, England. He died about May 1460 at the age of 62 in Durham, England. heir to his grandfather. age 20 on Aug 18 1418, a commissioner of Array, 1436 and 1455. obit. Inq. p.m. May 3 1460 Fulthorpe and Nicholas Blackiston were married.

513. **Fulthorpe** born about 1400.

516. **John Kelynghall** was born in 1395. He died on 21 Feb 1442 at the age of 47. Beatrix Clarvaux and John Kelynghall were married.

517. **Beatrix Clarvaux** born about 1395.

520. **John Conyers** born about 1370 of Hornby Castle, York County, England. Foster Yorkshire: of Hornby Castle, chief justice Margaret St. Quintin and John Conyers were married.

521. **Margaret St. Quintin** born about 1380. She died after Oct 1426 at the age of 46. There is a question of her mother being Margaret Swynho and having Margaret illegitimately by Anthony St. Quintin per Royal Descents of 600 Immigrants p. 431.

522. **Thomas Rolleston** born about 1370 of Mablethorp, Lincoln County, England. Footnote in MCS4 164-10. Beatrice Hauley and Thomas Rolleston were married.

523. **Beatrice Hauley** born about 1370 of Ingleton, York County, England.

524. **Simon Langton** born about 1340. He died in 1380 at the age of 40. heir of his other brothers. 5th son. order of birth is correct for siblings.Lord of Wynwarde. Avice Carrow and Simon Langton were married.

525. **Avice Carrow** born about 1345. coheir of her nephew John Carrowe the younger

526. **William Elmedon** born about 1380. He died before 28 Oct 1447 at the age of 67. of Elmeden Burke EP: Elizabeth De Umfreyville and William Elmedon were married.

527. **Elizabeth De Umfreyville** was born in 1381. She died on 23 Nov 1424 at the age of 43. Charlemagne Desc/

528. **Robert Playse Esq.** born about 1375 in England. He died in 1429 at the age of 54 in England. Katherine De Halnaby and Robert Playse Esq. were married in 1408.

529. **Katherine De Halnaby** born about 1385 in England. She died in 1461 at the age of 76 in England. dau of Halnath de Halnaby

530. **Ralph Pudsey Knight** born about 1402. He died after 1452 at the age of 50. Lord of Bolton 31 Hen 6 1552. made marriage agreement in 1448 for his son John. Margaret Tunstall and Ralph Pudsey Knight were married.

531. **Margaret Tunstall** born about 1400. 1st wife of Ralph

532. **Christopher Conyers** is the same as person number 260.

533. **Ellyn Ryleston** is the same as person number 261.

534. **Philip Darcy Lord** born about 1398. He died on 2 Aug 1418 at the age of 20. Lord of Darcy and Meignill Eleanor Fitz Hugh and Philip Darcy Lord were married on 28 Oct 1412.

535. **Eleanor Fitz Hugh** born about 1400. She died on 30 Sep 1457 at the age of 57. of Ravensworth will date 21 May 1466 pro 31 Jan. 1468/9. Complete Peerage vol 3 p 294

536. **Thomas Surteys Esq.** was born in 1411 in Durham, England. He died on 25 Dec 1443 at the age of 32 in Durham, England. only son named in his father's will age 24. had livery 17 May 29 Langley. Commissioner of Array for Sadberge 31 Langley, and of the Peace 1 and 2 Nevill. died Christmas day 22 Hen Vi 1443. Inq. p.m. 3 Feb 6

Nevill. and for Northumberland 4 Jun 22 Hen VI. Alice and Thomas Surteys Esq. were married.

537. **Alice** born about 1411 in England.

538. **William Ayscough Esq.** born about 1410. William Ayscough Esq. was married.

540. **Robert Conyers Lord** was born in 1371 of Sockburne. He died on 25 Apr 1433 at the age of 62 in Durham, England. of Sockburne, age 25 in 1396. did homage for the lands of his mother 19 May 1420, died 25 Apr 1433 Inq. p.m. 25 Langley. will dated 18 Apr 1431. proved at Durham Isabel Pert and Robert Conyers Lord were married.

541. **Isabel Pert** born about 1376. She died after 1428 at the age of 52.

542. **William Eure Knight** born about 1396. He died before 12 Feb 1466 at the age of 70. He was buried in Malton Abbey. Visitations of Yorkshire p 611 by Glover Sir William Eure knight age 26, 10 Henry V, 1422, married in 1411, when under age, license date 25 Jan. 1410/11, Sheriff of Yorkshire, 1445. He was at the battle of Agincourt in the retinue of Lord Fitz Hugh, died before 12 Feb. 1466/7 buried in the chancel of Malton Abbey. m. Matilda dau. of Hen. Lord FitzHugh of Ravensworth, co. York. Her will dated 12 Feb 1466/7, and proved at York, 30 May following, to be buried in Malton Abbey near her husband Maud Fitz Hugh and William Eure Knight were married about 25 Jan 1411.

543. **Maud Fitz Hugh** born about 1395. She died about May 1467 at the age of 72. She was buried in Malton Abbey. will dated Feb 12 1466/7 and proved at York May 30. to be buried by husband in Malton Abbey.

544. **William Bowes Knight** born about 1400 of Streatlam. He died about Oct 1465 at the age of 65. Surtees Durham Vol IV p 107 called old Sir Wm Bowes, succeeded his grandfather William Bowes 14 May 1410, heir to his mother Joan Bromflete 1438, Knighted at Vernoyle 1424, served in France 20y, rebuilt Streatlam Castle on a model sent from France. Inq p.m. 11 Oct 1465 widowed for 50 years Jane Greystock and William Bowes Knight were married.

545. **Jane Greystock** born about 1402. She died about 1420 at the age of 18. Surtees Durham Vol 4 p 107 Bowes under 20 years of age at death

546. **William Fitz Hugh Lord** born about 1398 of Ravensworth. He died on 22 Oct 1452 at the age of 54. Surtees Durham Vol IV p 107 says father is Henry Fitzhugh, EP p 207 Fitzhugh. Complete Peerage vol 3 p 294 Margary Willoughby and William Fitz Hugh Lord were married before 18 Nov 1406.

547. **Margary Willoughby** born about 1398. EP p 207

548. **John Conyers** is the same as person number 266.

549. **Margery Darcy** is the same as person number 267.

550. **John Wycliffe** born about 1400. Agnes Rokeby and John Wycliffe were married.

551. **Agnes Rokeby** born about 1400.

552. **Thomas De Clifford Lord** was born on 25 Mar 1414. He died on 22 May 1455 at the age of 41 in Saint Albans. He was buried in Saint Albans Abbey. Complete Peerage vol 3 p 294 Sheriff of Westmoreland, slain at battle of St. Albans. he married aft 1424 (his grandmother's death) Weis AR7 5-35 Joan Dacre and Thomas De Clifford Lord were married after Mar 1424.

553. **Joan Dacre** born about 1415. Complete Peerage vol 3 p 294 AR 5-35

554. **Henry Bromflete Lord** born about 1410 of Vesci. He died about 16 Jan 1468–16 Jan 1469 at the age of 58. Complete Peerage vol 3 p 294 Baron of Vessy. CP Lord Vessy 1st Lord of Vessy. Son of Sir Thomas Bromflete by Margaret dau of Sir Edward

St. John and Anastasia 1st dau of William de Aton, Lord Aton, son of Gilbert de Aton heir of Lord William de Vescy. Eleanor Fitz Hugh and Henry Bromflete Lord were married about 1434.

555. **Eleanor Fitz Hugh** is the same as person number 535.

556. **Oliver St. John Knight** born about 1405 of Penmark, Gloucestershire. He died in 1437 at the age of 32. Weis 85-35 Margaret De Beauchamp and Oliver St. John Knight were married.

557. **Margaret De Beauchamp** born about 1410. She died in 1482 at the age of 72.

558. **Thomas Bradshaigh Sir** born about 1410 of Haigh, Lancaster County, England. Weis 85-36 Complete Peerage vol 3 p 294 Thomas Bradshaigh Sir was married.

560. **Ralph Eure Sir** born about 1420 of Witton. Visitations of Yorkshire by Glover Sir Ralph Eure Knight killed at Towton Field on Palm Sunday 9 Mar 1461 12 Ed. IV. A shield on his arms impaling Greystock was in a window in Lincoln's Inn old Hall. m. Eleanor dau of John, Baron of Greystock living 1468. Eleanor Greystock and Ralph Eure Sir were married.

561. **Eleanor Greystock** born about 1420. She died after 1468 at the age of 48.

562. **Robert Constable** born about 1420. Visitations of Yorkshire p. 197 Agnes Wentworth and Robert Constable were married.

563. **Agnes Wentworth** born about 1420. Visitation of 1612 had the wives Agnes as a first and second wife of the son Robert.

564. **John Hastings Lord** was born in 1411 in Elsing, England. He died on 9 Apr 1477 at the age of 66 in Elsing, England. He was buried in Gressenhall Ch., England. PA1 Elsing 6 John Hastings of Gressenhall, Elsing, Fenwick, etc. 9th Lord Hastings de jure, son and heir by first marriage born about 1412 (aged 26 and more at his father's death). He was married after 21 Apr 1434 to Anne Morley, daughter of Thomas Morley, 5th Lord Morley, by Isabel daughter of Michael de la Pole, Earl of Suffolk. They were mentioned in the will of her mother dated 3 May 1464. She died in 1471. John died at Elsing on 9 Apr 1477. They were buried in Gressenhall Church. Anne Morley and John Hastings Lord were married after 21 Apr 1434.

565. **Anne Morley** was born in 1413. She died in 1471 at the age of 58. She was buried in Gressenhall Ch., England.

566. **William Gascoigne Esq.** born about 1410 in Gawthorpe, Yorkshire, England. He died before 1466 at the age of 56. Margaret Clarell and William Gascoigne Esq. were married before 7 Feb 1425.

567. **Margaret Clarell** born about 1410 in Aldwork, Yorkshire, England. William was her 3rd husband.

568. **Thomas Willoughby** born about 1400. He died before 1 Jul 1439 at the age of 39. CP p. 672 Robert Willoughby son of Thomas Willoughby 2nd son of William Willoughby the 5th Lord. Joan Fitz Alan and Thomas Willoughby were married.

569. **Joan Fitz Alan** born about 1400.

570. **Lionel Welles Lord** was born in 1406. He died on 29 Mar 1461 at the age of 55 in Towton. MCS4 82-10 Joan Waterton and Lionel Welles Lord were married about 1426.

571. **Joan Waterton** born about 1406 in Yorkshire. She died in 1434 or 1447 at the age of 28 in Towton. 1st wife. p 333 Royal Ancestry by Richardson says dau of Robert Waterton by 2nd wife Cecily Fleming.

572. **John Jenney Esq.** born about 1400. Burkes Commoners Jenney of Bradfield John Jenney Esq of Knodishall was a burgess of Norwich in 1452 m. Maud dau and heir of

John Bokill of Friston in Suffolk by Jasyston by Maud dau and heir of William Gerrard. Maud Bokill and John Jenney Esq. were married.

573. **Maud Bokill** born about 1400.

574. **Thomas Cawse** born about 1400. Thomas Cawse was married.

768. **Giles Prideaux of Adeston** died after 1404.

776. **Sir Robert Poyntz Sheriff** born about 15 Jun 1359 in DIrchenfield, Herefordshire, England. He died on 15 Jun 1439 at the age of 80 in Gloucestershire, England. AR8 p. 212 Robert

777. **Catherine Fitz Nichol** born about 1360.

778. **Thomas Mill** born about 1350.

779. **Juliana Le Rous** born about 1350.

800. **Sir John Arundell** born about 1375. Sir John Arundell, son and heir, who married Jane Durant, daughter and heiress of John Durant (or Jane Lupus daughter of Lupus of Crantock by his wife a daughter and heiress of Lupus of Durant).[16] His second son was Richard Arundell of Penbigell, Sheriff of Cornwall in 1408.

801. **Jane Durant** born about 1375.

802. **Edward St John of Somerset** was born in 1394. He died in 1448 at the age of 54.

803. **Joan Le Jewe** born about 1400.

808. **William de Grenville Esq** was born before 1381. He died in 1450 at the age of 69. William de Grenville, Esq. (born by 1381 - died 1450) (younger brother). He married twice, firstly to Thomasine Cole, daughter of John Cole, by whom he had no children. His second marriage was to Philippa Bonville (living 1464), a daughter or sister[27] of William Bonville, 1st Baron Bonville (1392–1461). Lord Bonville was an enemy of the Courtenay Earls of Devon of Tiverton Castle, but an ally of their cousins the Courtenays of Powderham. By his second marriage Grenville had several children: his son and heir was Sir Thomas Grenville.[28]

809. **Philippa Bonville** died after 1464.

810. **Sir Theobald Gorges Knight Baron, Lord of Wraxall** born about 1390. The Royal Descents of 600 Immigrants p 524 has his lineage back to Henry I, King of France.

811. **Jane Hankford** born about 1390.

814. **Robert Hill Esq** born about 1400 of Shilston.

Eleventh Generation

1024. **William Blackiston Jr.** born about 1370 in Durham, England. He died after 1396 at the age of 26 in Durham, England. his father gave him land by charter 28 nov 20 Richard II 1396, died within lifetime of his father. wife living 28 Nov 20 Rich. II. Katherine and William Blackiston Jr. were married.

1025. **Katherine** born about 1375 in Durham, England. She died after 1396 at the age of 21 in Durham, England.

1032. **John Kelynghall** born about 1365. He died on 19 Oct 1417 at the age of 52. Agnes De Herdwyk and John Kelynghall were married.

1033. **Agnes De Herdwyk** born about 1370. widow of Gilbert de Hoton

1034. **John Clarvaux Esq.** born about 1370. of Croft, co York. John Clarvaux Esq. was married.

1040. **Robert Conyers Lord** born about 1350 of Ormesby, Cleveland, Of Hornby Castle. He died in 1392 at the age of 42. Colonial Gen. Vol. XI 3-4(Augustan Society #219) says Robert m. 3 times - first Joan de Melton, mother of John, 2nd Juliana Percy, 3rd Aline dela Hey. He may be Robert de Conyers of Stubhouse about 1340. Durham vol

4 p 107 says Robert and Aline parents of Joan. Foster Yorkshire: of Hornby Castle. Robert, father of John Conyers Joan De Melton and Robert Conyers Lord were married.

1041. **Joan De Melton** born about 1350 of Ormesby. Yorkshire Pedigrees says she married Thomas Conyers.

1042. **Anthony St. Quintin** born about 1360. He died about 1444 at the age of 84. Foster Yorkshire said died 22 Hen 6 1444 Elizabeth Gascoigne and Anthony St. Quintin were married.

1043. **Elizabeth Gascoigne** born about 1360. Foster Yorkshire p. 238 Elizabeth dau of Nicholas married Anthony St. Quinton of Harpham who died 22 Hen Vi.

1048. **Henry Langton** born about 1300. He died after 1342 at the age of 42. Lord of Winyard and Redmarshall 1316 in which estates he had a charter of free warren 1342. Margery Fulthorpe and Henry Langton were married.

1049. **Margery Fulthorpe** born about 1300. She died after 1316 at the age of 16. Given land by Roger and Alice Fulthorpe. (Alice may be second wife and not her mother).

1050. **John Carrow** born about 1325. John Carrow was married.

1054. **Thomas De Umfreyville** born about 1361 in Harbottle Castle. He died about Mar 1390–Mar 1391 at the age of 29. Charlemagne Desc: also Weis AR7 121D-33 Burke EP: says 1364-1391 Agnes Grey and Thomas De Umfreyville were married.

1055. **Agnes Grey** born about 1361. She died on 25 Oct 1420 at the age of 59. Weis AR7 121d-33 possibly dau. of Thomas Grey of Heton.

1058. **Halnath De Halnaby** was born before 1330. He died before 1410 at the age of 80. Joan and Halnath De Halnaby were married.

1059. **Joan** born about 1330. She died after 1410 at the age of 80.

1060. **John Pudsey Knight** born about 1375. He died in 1421 at the age of 46 in Bauge, France. Lord of Bolton killed in battle at Bauge in France 1421
Visitations of Yorkshire p. 294 John Pudsey of Bolton m.Margaret dau of Sir
Williem Evers Knight. Margaret Eure and John Pudsey Knight were married.

1061. **Margaret Eure** born about 1382. She died about Dec 1444 at the age of 62. She was buried in Beverly. Visitations of Yorkshire by Glover p. 611 Margaret de Eure, wife to Sir John Pudsey, knt, lord of Bolton, he was killed at the battle of the Bauge in France, in 1421. Her will dated Dec 25 1444 and proved at York Jan 7 1445. to be buried at Beverley.

1062. **Thomas Tunstall Knight** born about 1380 of Scargill. Pedigree of Pudsey of Bolton says Thomas Tunstall of Scargill. possibly Thomas Tunstall of Thurland Castle. Thomas Tunstall Knight was married.

1068. **John D'Arcy Baron** born about 1377. He died on 9 Dec 1411 at the age of 34. 5th Baron D'arcy of Knath Margaret De Grey and John D'Arcy Baron were married.

1069. **Margaret De Grey** born about 1380. She died on 1 Jun 1454 at the age of 74. Charlemagne Desc.

1070. **Henry Fitz Hugh Lord** born about 1358. He died on 11 Jan 1424 or 11 Jan 1425 at the age of 66 in Ravensworth. Knight of the Garter, 4th Lord Fitz Hugh. Henry FitzHugh, 3rd Baron FitzHugh KG (c.?1363 – 11 January 1425) of Ravensworth Castle in North Yorkshire, was an administrator and diplomat who served under Kings Henry IV and Henry V.

1072. **Thomas Surtees Knight** was born in 1380 in Durham, England. He died on 12 Apr 1435 at the age of 55 in York, England. He was buried in Saint Nicholas, Walmegate, England. son and heir 20 weeks at his father's death, in ward of Bishop Hatfield's nephew John de Popham. had livery of his lands 10 Oct 1392. Sheriff of Northumberland 10 Hen V in Commission of the Peace for the Peace for co Pal. Durham from 3-38 Langley, commissioner of array for Sadberge Wapontake and Stockton Wards. will dated 1 Apr 1435 proved at York. Inq. 22 Apr 29 Langley. buried in the church of St. Nicholas in Walmegate. died at York 12 Apr 1435. Isabella Eure and Thomas Surtees Knight were married about 1398.

1073. **Isabella Eure** born about 1380 in England. History of Durham by Surtees says Thomas Surtees wife was Isabella, dau. of Sir Ralph Eure Knight of Witton Castle, on which marriage divers lands were settled 10 Oct. 3 Skirlaw. Foster History of Yorkshire said wife of Wm Claxton who died 1430 and John Conyers of Ormesby who died 1438.

1080. **John Conyers Knight** was born before 1340 of Sockburne. He died in 1395 at the age of 55. He was buried in Sockburne, England. nephew and heir male of Sir John. living 1134 1393 died 1395 Elizabeth De Aton and John Conyers Knight were married before 1385.

1081. **Elizabeth De Aton** born about 1347. She died in 1419 at the age of 72. married before 1385 had land of her father 1389. inq. pm. 8 May 1419

1082. **William Pert** was born before 1350 in York County, England. Joane Scrope and William Pert were married.

1083. **Joane Scrope** was born before 1350.

1084. **Ralph De Eure Knight** born about 1353. He died on 10 Mar 1422 at the age of 69. History of Yorkshire by Foster: will proved 9 Sep 1422. Sheriff of Northumberland 1389-1397, Governor of the Castle of Newcastle, Constable of York Castle age 36 in the Grosvenor-Scrope controversy. 1386-1389. Visitations of Yorkshire by Glover p. 610 Sir Ralph de Eure, knt, sheriff of Northumberland, 13 and 21 Rich. II, and governor of the Castle of Newcastle upon Tyne, sheriff of Yorksh., and constable of York Castle, 15 and 19 R. II. In 1410 he had licence from Langley, bishop of Durham, to fortify his castle at Witton. In right of his wife, he had most of Malton and Boughton Spittle. He was a witness in the Scrope and Grosvenor controversy (famous case regarding same coat of arms being used by two different families), and then age 36 and upwards. See. Vol. II p. 315-317. He died 10 Mar. 10 Hen. V 1422. Ing p.m. York, will proved 9 Sep. 1422, before the Bishop of Durham, at Stockton. married 1st wife Isabel dau and eventually coheir of Sir Adomar de Athol, Lord of Felton, brother of David de Athol-Argent, three pallets sable, on centre pallet a lion passant or. 2nd wife Catherine and dau. and coheir of William de Aton. Barry of 6 or and azure, on a canton gules a cross patence argent. Catherine De Aton and Ralph De Eure Knight were married bef. 1387.

1085. **Catherine De Aton** born about 1360. 2nd wife of Ralph

1086. **Henry Fitz Hugh** is the same as person number 1070.

1087. **Elizabeth Grey De Marmion** is the same as person number 1071.

1088. **Robert Bowes Knight** born about 1375 of Streatlam. He died in 1421 at the age of 46 in Baugy Bridge. Durham vol 4 p 107 slain with Thomas Duke of Clarence at Baugy Bridge He was created at the siege of Rouen in 1419 and was slain with Thomas, Duke of Clarence son of King Henry IV at Baugy Bridge in France in 1421 per Col. and Rev. Lineages of America co 1944. Joan Conyers and Robert Bowes Knight were married.

1089. **Joan Conyers** born about 1375. She died on 7 Nov 1438 at the age of 63. Durham vol 4 p 107 married second Thomas Bromflete. HRH Prince Charles Ancestry by Paget said she was born c 1395 and died 7 Nov 1438.

1090. **Ralph Greystock Lord** was born on 18 Oct 1353. He died on 6 Apr 1418 at the age of 64. Durham vol 4 p 107. An LDS file says he is 7th Lord Greystock and son of John 6th Lord and Elizabeth Ferrers. Catherine Clifford and Ralph Greystock Lord were married.

1091. **Catherine Clifford** born about 1353. She died on 23 Apr 1413 at the age of 60.

1092. **Henry Fitz Hugh** is the same as person number 1070.

1093. **Elizabeth Grey De Marmion** is the same as person number 1071.

1094. **William Willoughby Lord** born about 1370 in De Eresby, Durham, England. He died on 4 Dec 1409 at the age of 39. EP p 207 4th Baron Willoughby of Erresby died on Wednesday next ensuing the Festival of St. Andrew the Apostle in 1409 called 5th Lord per HRH Prince Charles Ancestry by Paget. CP p. 672 William son by first wife b. c 1370 given seis of his lands 27 Sep 1396 present at the tower 29 Sep 1399 at abdication of Richard II. K.G. 1401, negotiated with Owen Glendower for ransom of Reynold, Lord Grey of Ruthin. He married 1st bef 23 Apr 1383 Lucy dau of Roger Le Strange 5th Lord by Alince dau of Edmund Fitzalan. She was living 28 Apr 1398 m. 2nd bet Aug 1 1402 and 9 Aug 1404 Joan widow of Edmund of Langley Duke of York son of Edward III. He died 4 Dec 1409 at Edgefield buried at Spilsby. M.I. Lucy Le Strange and William Willoughby Lord were married.

1095. **Lucy Le Strange** born about 1370. She died after Apr 1398 at the age of 28.

1100. **William Wycliffe** born about 1375. William Wycliffe was married.

1102. **Thomas Rokeby Sir** born about 1380. Thomas Rokeby Sir was married.

1104. **John Clifford Lord** born about 1388. He died on 13 Mar 1421 or 13 Mar 1422 at the age of 33 in Meaux, France. Complete Peerage vol 3 p 294 Lord Clifford, Sheriff of Westmoreland, 3y at father's death. proved age 1410, in the great tournament at Carlisle also he served in the French War and was killed at the siege of Meaus in Frfance 13 March 1421/2 and is supposed to have been buried at Bolton Priory. AR 5-34, 26-34. 7th Lord Clifford, Sheriff of Westmoreland, a famous soldier Elizabeth Percy and John Clifford Lord were married in 1403 or 1412.

1105. **Elizabeth Percy** born about 1390. She died on 26 Oct 1437 at the age of 47. Complete Peerage vol 3 p 294 married between Aug 1403 and Nov 1412. m2nd Ralph Nevill as his first wife. 2nd Earl of Westmoreland. AR 5-34

1106. **Thomas Dacre Lord** was born on 27 Oct 1387 of Gillesland. He died on 5 Jan 1457 or 5 Jan 1458 at the age of 69. He was buried in Lanercost Priory. Complete Peerage vol 3 p 294 AR 5-35. CP 4 p. 7 Thomas Dacre born at Naworth castle 27 and bapt. at Brampton Cumberland 28 Oct. 1387. He married v.p. Philippe, 3rd dau of Ralph de Neville Earl of Westmoreland by his wife Margaret dau of Hugh de Stafford, Earl of Stafford. She was living 8 July 1433 but died before him. He died 5 Jan 1457/8 and was buried in Lanercost Priory. Visitations of Yorkshire says his father was Thomas who married a FitzHugh and the grandparents were William and Joan. p. 84 Philippe Nevill and Thomas Dacre Lord were married.

1107. **Philippe Nevill** born about 1390. Complete Peerage vol 3 p 294 AR 5-35

1108. **Thomas Bromflete Sir** born about 1385. Margaret St. John and Thomas Bromflete Sir were married.

1109. **Margaret St. John** born about 1385.

1112. **John St. John Sir** died in Faumont, Glamorganshire.

1113. **Elizabeth Umfreyville**.

1114. **John De Beauchamp Knight** born about 1385 of Bletsoe. He died about 1412 at the age of 27. Weis 85-34 2nd wife was Esther Stourton Margaret Holand and John De Beauchamp Knight were married in Jan 1405 or Jan 1406.

1115. **Margaret Holand** born about 1385.

1120. **William Eure** is the same as person number 542.

1121. **Maud Fitz Hugh** is the same as person number 543.

1122. **John Greystoke Baron** was born before 1389. CP VI p. 190-196 m. Elizabeth de Ferrers of Owseley.Yorkshire Visitation Greystoke, Alianora m. Dominio Radulpo Ivers, 4th Lord Greystoke. Elizabeth De Ferrers and John Greystoke Baron were married.

1123. **Elizabeth De Ferrers** born about 1395 of Owseley. She died in 1434 at the age of 39. She was buried in York. AR 62-35

1124. **Robert Constable Sir** born about 1380. Visitations of Yorkshire by Glover p. 178 Robert Constable m. Agnes dau of Sir William Gascoigne chief justice., son of Marmaduke Constable and Katherine Cumberworth. Agnes Gascoigne and Robert Constable Sir were married.

1125. **Agnes Gascoigne** born about 1380.

1126. **Roger Wentworth Sir** born about 1390 of North Elmsall, York County, England. He died after 5 Jun 1452 at the age of 62. Visitations of Yorkshire by Glover p. 378 Roger Wentworth of whom the Lord Wenworth is descended, son of John Wentworth and Beaumont of Whitley Hall, son of John Wentworth m. Agnes dau of William Dransfield of West Bretton, son of John Wentworth m. dau of Bisset, son of John Wentworth of Elmsall 2nd son of William m. Joan, dau of Richard Tyas. Margary Despenser and Roger Wentworth Sir were married before 25 Jun 1423.

1127. **Margary Despenser** born about 1398. MCS4 74-10 Margaret Despenser age 24+ or 26+ at father's death d. 20 Apr 1478 m. 2nd bef June 25 1423 Sir Roger Wenworth Knight d. after 5 June 1452 of North Elmsall, Co, York, and Nettlesteasd, Suffolk CP IV 290.

1128. **Edward Hastings Knight** was born on 21 May 1382 of Elsing, Fenwick, England. He died on 6 Jan 1437 or 6 Jan 1438 at the age of 54. PA1 Elsing 7 Edward Hastings Knight of Elsing, Fenwick, etc. 8th Lord Hastings de jure, was born at Fenwick on 21 May 1382, and was brother and heir of Hugh Hastings. He was married for the first time to Muriel de Dinham, dau of John de Dinham, Knight of Hartland co Devon by Muriel, daughter of Thomas de Courtenay, Knight of Woodhuish, co. Devon. He was married 2nd to Margary Clifton. He was committed to the Tower on 11 July 1403. The right to bear the undifferenced Arms of Hastings was decided against him in the court of Chivalry on 9 May 1410 and in favour of his opponent Reynold Lord Grey of Ruthin heir to the sister of the whole blood, in preference to his own claim as heir of the brother of the half-blood of John Lord Hastings ancestor of the Earls of Pembroke. On refusing to pay the costs of his suit of appeal (lest he should thereby acknowledge its justice), he was imprisoned (about 1417) in the Marshalsea apparently till his death. Edward died age 55 on 6 Jan. 1437/8. His widow married John Wymondham. She died in 1456 and was buried at Austin Friars', Norwich. Muriel De Dinham and Edward Hastings Knight were married.

1129. **Muriel De Dinham** born about 1382. She was said to be daughter of John de Dinham and Muriel but Muriel died in 1369, I believe to be daughter of son John de Dinham Jr.

1130. **Lord Thomas Morley 5th Lord Morley** born about 1393. He died on 6 Dec 1435 at the age of 42. He was buried in Hingham. CP 5th Lord Morley age 23 at grandfather's death, Marshal of Ireland. Isabel De La Pole and Lord Thomas Morley 5th Lord Morley were married.

1131. **Isabel De La Pole** born about 1393. She died on 8 Feb 1466 or 8 Feb 1467 at the age of 73. She was buried in Norwich. PA1 Pole 12 Isabel de la Pole died testate 8 Feb 1466/7 will mentions granddaughter Eleanor and her daughter Ann, wife of John Hastings married on or before 5 Feb 1402/3 Thomas Morley 5th Lord Morley of Morley, Norfolk, born about 1393 (age 23 at grandfather's death) grandson and heir of Thomas Lord Morley, took part in the sieges of Rouen, Melun, and Meaux, and was present at the death of King Hen. V, summoned to Parliament from 15 July 1427 died 6 Dec. 1435, buried Hingham, Co. Norfolk, son and heir of Robert Morley by his wife Isabel. 3 May 1463 pro 27 Feb 1466.

1132. **William Gascoigne Sir** born about 1380 in Harewood, Yorkshire, England. He died on 28 Mar 1422 at the age of 42. Joan Wyman and William Gascoigne Sir were married.

1133. **Joan Wyman** born about 1380 in Yorkshire, England.

1134. **Thomas Clarell** born about 1390 of Aldwark. He died on 1 May 1442 at the age of 52. Matilda Montgomery and Thomas Clarell were married.

1135. **Matilda Montgomery** born about 1390.

1136. **William Willoughby** is the same as person number 1094.

1137. **Lucy Le Strange** is the same as person number 1095.

1138. **Richard Fitz Alan** born about 1375. He died on 3 Jun 1419 at the age of 44.

1139. **Alice** born about 1375. She died on 30 Aug 1436 at the age of 61. widow of Roger Burley

1140. **Eudo Welles** born about 1375 in Gainsby. He died before Aug 1421 at the age of 46. Maud Greystoke and Eudo Welles were married.

1141. **Maud Greystoke** born about 1380.

1142. **Robert De Waterton Esq, of Methley** born about 1362 in York, England. Robert de WATERTON Esq. of Methley, York , died in England. m. Cecily FLEMING died in England Cecily Fleming and Robert De Waterton Esq, of Methley were married.

1143. **Cecily Fleming** was born before 1380.

1144. **William Jenney** born about 1370. Burkes Commoners William of Knoddishall and Theberton by Maud, son of Edmund. Jenneys were Guisnes, near Calais, France. Maud and William Jenney were married.

1145. **Maud** born about 1370.

1146. **John Bokill** born about 1380 of Friston, Suffolk, England. Joan Leyston and John Bokill were married.

1147. **Joan Leyston** born about 1380. Per Burke's Commoners, the grandmother of Sir William Jenney was Maud Gerrard.

1536. **John Prideaux** was born in 1286. He died in 1350 at the age of 64.

1537. **Joan Adeston** died before 1373.

1552. **Sir John Poyntz Lord of Acton, Winston and Elkstone** born about 1310. He died on 24 Feb 1376 at the age of 66.

1553. **Elizabeth de Clanvowe** was born before 1320.

1554. **Thomas Fitz Nichol of Hull and Nympsfield** born about 1358. He died in 1418 at the age of 60. Sir Thomas Fitz-Nichol of Hull and Nympsfield, who was the 8th in descent from Eobert 1st Lord Berkeley, who granted to his son Nicholas for his portion the manors of Hull or Hill, and Nympsfield, which grant was afterwards confirmed by King Henry II. In 12th Henry IV Sir Thomas Fitz-Nichol entailed his manor of Hull al's Hill, where he mostly lived (seldom at Nympsfield) to himself and Agnes his wife and to the heirs male of his body, remainder to Robert Poyntz and Katherine his wife, p. 54 of Pointz Family Book

1600. **Nicholas Arundell** born about 1350.

1601. **Elizabeth Peltor** born about 1350.

1616. **Sir Theobald Grenville** born about 1343. He died in Jul 1381 at the age of 38.

1617. **Margaret Courtenay** was born bef. 1350. She died after Jul 1381 at the age of 31.

Twelfth Generation

2048. **William Blackiston Knight** born about 1345 in Durham, England. He died about Aug 1418 at the age of 73 in Durham, England. Sir William knight Lord of Blackiston, commissioner of Array, Fordham 1385, owned manors of Blackiston and Coxhow and lands in Whitton and Washington. inquisition post mortem. William Blackiston Knight was married.

2066. **John De Herdwyk** born about 1350. John De Herdwyk was married.

2080. **Robert Conyers** born about 1300 of Stubhouse. Colonial Gen. Vol. XI 3-4 (Augustan Society #219) may be Robert de Conyers of Stubhouse about 1340 Robert Conyers was married.

2082. **Henry De Melton** born about 1325 in York, England. Colonial Gen. Vol. XI 3-4 (Augustan Society #219) first Joan de Melton neice of William de Melton, Archbishop of York 1317-1340. Yorkshire Pedigrees says Henry living 1328 m. Joan Joan and Henry De Melton were married.

2083. **Joan** born about 1325.

2084. **John St. Quintin Lord** born about 1340. He died on 17 Jan 1397 at the age of 57. He was buried in Brandsburton. Foster Yorkshire: of Brandsburton, in Holderness, Lord of Newbiggin and lands in Pickering Lyth, in right of second wife abt 1347 served under Earl of Lancaster. 1382 keeper of the castle of Scarborough. in 1316 knight of the shire for co York. Agnes Warren and John St. Quintin Lord were married.

2085. **Agnes Warren** born about 1345. She died in Apr 1404 at the age of 59. She was buried in Sigglesthorne. Foster Yorkshire: Agnes 2nd wife dau and heiress of Robert Warren. will dated 24 Jan 1404 and proved 9 Apr. to be buried at Sigglesthorne. Visitations of Yorkshire by Foster says Agnes Constable dau of John Constable and Margaret Umfraville who married 2nd William Skipwith. Visitations of Yorkshire by Glover says Agnes Constable m 1st to Mr. St. Quintin and 2nd to Sir William Skipwith Knight of Ormesby co Lncoln. p. 56

2086. **Nicholas Gascoigne** born about 1340. Foster Yorkshire Margaret Clitheroe and Nicholas Gascoigne were married.

2087. **Margaret Clitheroe** born about 1340. Visitations by Foster p. 384 says Margaret dau and cohier to John Gras. Visitations by Foster p. 238 Nicholas Gascoigne of Laisingcroft 2nd son living 16 Ric. II. married Mary dau and heir of Sir Hugh or John Clitheroe King of Salebury by Isabel dau of Sir John Gras. (also called Mary dau and Heir to Sir John Gras of STudley). Sir Hugh son of Robert Clitherow m. Sibell, son of Adam Clitherow Knight son of John Clitherwoof Salesbury, co. Lanc.

2096. **Alan Langton** born about 1280. He died about 1316 at the age of 36. He was buried in Saint Peter, Grindon Church, England. Burgess of Newscastle and Berwick, Lord of

Winyarde in right of his wife. Will date 1311 pro. 1316. Catherine Lisle and Alan Langton were married.

2097. **Catherine Lisle** born about 1280.

2098. **Roger Fulthorpe** born about 1275. He died in 1337 at the age of 62. Roger Fulthorpe was married.

2100. **Carrow** born about 1300. Carrow was married.

2108. **Thomas De Umfreyville** born about 1300 of Harbottle. He died on 21 May 1387 at the age of 87. Charlemagne Desc: also Weis AR Burke EP: of Harbottle Castle Joan De Roddam and Thomas De Umfreyville were married.

2109. **Joan De Roddam** born about 1325. also Weis AR

2116. **Halnath De Halnaby** was born before 1280. He died about 1335 at the age of 55. Halnath De Halnaby was married.

2120. **Henry Pudsey** born about 1350. marriage covenant 1352, received land of Barford from wife. Visitations of Yorkshire p. 294 Henry Pudsey 27 E. iii, m. Elizabeth dau and heir of John Layton, dominus de Barford.

2121. **Elizabeth Layton** born about 1350. She died in Nov 1424 at the age of 74. She was buried in East Layton.

2122. **Ralph De Eure** is the same as person number 1084.

2123. **Isabel De Athol** born about 1361. She died before 1387 at the age of 26. first wife said also to be Isabella de Valence

2136. **Philip Darcy Baron** was born on 21 May 1352. He died on 24 Apr 1399 at the age of 46. Weis AR: Baron Darcy of Knayth

2137. **Elizabeth Gray** born about 1352. She died on 11 Aug 1412 at the age of 60.

2138. **Henry De Grey Lord** born about 1335 of Wilton. He died in 1394 or 1396 at the age of 59. Lord Grey of Wilton on Wye Elizabeth De Talbot and Henry De Grey Lord were married.

2139. **Elizabeth De Talbot** born about 1355. She died on 10 Jan 1402 at the age of 47. History of Rutland p 162f. Per MCS4 26-8. She is said to not be a daughter of Gilbert Talbot, however per CP XII (1) p 614.

2140. **Henry Fitz Hugh Baron** born about 1340. He died in 1386 at the age of 46. 3rd Baron Fitz Hugh. summoned to Parliament 4 Aug 1377 to 8 Aug 1385. Engaged in the French Wars of King Edward III from 33rd to 43rd year.

2141. **Joane Le Scrope** born about 1340.

2142. **Robert Marmion De Grey** born about 1340. He died before 30 Nov 1367 at the age of 27. 3rd husband of Lora. took the name of Marmion History of Rutland: dead 41 Ed 3. EP 207 Fitz Hugh Lora St. Quenton and Robert Marmion De Grey were married.

2143. **Lora St. Quenton** born about 1350. Foster Yorkshire: 3rd husband Robert Grey, 4th husband John St. Quintin; 2nd dau of Herbert, married 4 times History of Rutland: 2nd dau of H. de St. Quinton

2144. **Alexander Surteys Knight** was born in 1357 in Durham, England. He died in 1381 at the age of 24 in Durham, England. son and heir age 22, was a Knight. 34 Hatfield. In the same year founded a Chantry in the Church of Dinsdale. 18 Mar 1380 enfeoffed Sir. Robert Conyers and Sir William Skypwith, Knt. and others of all his lands. Inq. on the Eve of St. Math. Apost. 36 hatfield and Inq. apud Corbrig 24 Sep 4 Rich II. Margaret and Alexander Surteys Knight were married.

2145. **Margaret** born about 1360 in England. She died after 1384 at the age of 24 in Durham, England. had dower in Gosford 8 Rich. II.

2146. **Ralph De Eure** is the same as person number 1084.

2147. **Isabel De Athol** is the same as person number 2123.

2160. **Roger Coigniers** born about 1290. He died after 1323 at the age of 33. 2nd son Roger Coigniers was married.

2162. **William De Aton Knight** born about 1300. He died in 1389 at the age of 89. Member of Parliament 1317-1320 , Lord Vesci, Knight, summoned to Parliament Jan 3 1371, 2nd Baron. Isabel De Percy and William De Aton Knight were married before 1347.

2163. **Isabel De Percy** born about 1322.

2166. **Stephen Scrope** born about 1320. He died after 1359 at the age of 39. at the battle of Cressy 1346, held lands in the town of Leybrun in Thornton and other places in Yorkshire. Isabella and Stephen Scrope were married.

2167. **Isabella** born about 1320. She died after 1359 at the age of 39.

2168. **John De Eure Knight** born about 1330. He died on 22 Feb 1393 at the age of 63. Visitations of Yorkshire by Glover p. 610 Sir. John de Eure, knt, among the principal warriors of his time. He died 22 Feb. 1393, being then constable of Dover Castle and lord Steward of the King's House. m. Isabella dau of Robert Lord Clifford married 35 Ed. III 1361. Isabella De Clifford and John De Eure Knight were married in 1361.

2169. **Isabella De Clifford** born about 1330.

2170. **William De Aton** is the same as person number 2162.

2171. **Isabel De Percy** is the same as person number 2163.

2176. **William Bowes Knight** born about 1325 of Streatlam. He died after 1384 at the age of 59. Durham vol 4 p 107. Surtees Vol. 1 Plate 1 has his effigy.

2177. **Maud De Dalden** born about 1350. She died about Apr 1420 at the age of 70. Durham vol 4 p 107 will dated Jan 17 1420 inq p.m. 28 Apr 1420

2178. **Robert Conyers** is the same as person number 1040.

2179. **Aline Of Hamildon** born about 1350. Durham vol 4 p 107 widow of Wm de Dalden see vol 1 p 5,6. Robert Conyers 2nd wife Aline, Lady of Hamildon per HRH Prince Charles Ancestry by Paget.

2180. **William Greystock Lord** born about 1321. He died on 10 Jul 1359 at the age of 38. He was buried in Greystoke Church. 2nd Lord of Greystock. CP 6 p. 193 William de Greystoke son and heir born at Grimthorpe 6 Jan. 1320/1. On 1 May 1342 paid homage. On 24 Jan 1346/7 the king took his fealty and he had livery of the land which Elizabeth late the wife of Robert Fitz Ralph his grandfather who held in dower of his inheritance. He was at the seige of Calais in 1347. He married first Lucy dau of Sir Anthony de Lucy. m. 2nd abt Oct 1351 Joan dau of Sir Henry Fitz Henry of Ravensworth by Joan sister and coheir of William de Fourneuz and younger dau of Sir Richard de Fourneux of Derby. He died 10 July 1359 at Brancepeth age 38 and was buried in Greystoke Church. His widow remarried Sir Anthony de Lucy who died Aug 19 or Sep 1368 in the Holy Land. Then 3rdly Sir Matthew Redman knight to Levens Westmoreland who died about 1390. She died at Clerkenwell 1 Sep 1403 and was buried there. Joan Fitz Henry and William Greystock Lord were married about 1351.

2181. **Joan Fitz Henry** born about 1325. She died on 1 Sep 1403 at the age of 78.

2182. **Roger Clifford Lord** was born on 10 Jul 1333. He died on 13 Jul 1389 at the age of 56. Complete Peerage vol 3 p 292 Lord and Sheriff, gave evidence 12 Oct 1386 in famous Scrope and Grosvenor controversy. 5th Lord Clifford History of Rutland p 15 Sheriff of Westmoreland and Cumberland, served in Parliament and the wars with

Scotland and France. Governor of Carlisle Castle and Warden of the East and West Marches. Maud Beauchamp and Roger Clifford Lord were married.

2183. **Maud Beauchamp** born about 1338. Complete Peerage vol 3 p 292

2188. **Robert Willoughby Baron** born about 1350. He died on 20 Aug 1397 at the age of 47. 3rd Baron of Willoughby in Durham England. Called 4th Lord of Willoughby by HRH Prince Charles Ancestry by Paget. CP Took part in Lancaster's historic but futile march from Calais to Bordeaux Aug-Dec. 1373. Alice Skipwith and Robert Willoughby Baron were married.

2189. **Alice Skipwith** born about 1350. History of Yorkshire by Glover p. 634 add'l pedigrees Alice married Robert domino Willoughby, dau of Willielmus de Skipwith, miles, Capitalis, Justiciarius Angliae m. Alice filia et haer Willielmi de Hiltoft, militis, son of Willielmus, filius Johannis de Skipwith, dominus de Skipwith, inter Ouse et Derwent et de Beekeby, co. Linco. 10 Ed. III m. Margaret filia Raluphia Simonis, de Ormesby in com. Linc. et haeres unice Simonis, filii Radulphie fratris sui.

2190. **Roger Le Strange Baron** born about 1325. He died on 23 Aug 1382 at the age of 57 in Kenewylswode, Wales. 5th Lord le Strange by HRH Prince Charles Ancestry by Paget. CP12 (1) p 354 Roger Lord Strange son and heir aged 22 or 23 at father's death. Summoned to Parl. 20 Sep 1355 to 9 Aug 1382. He served in France in his father's place until 1351. He m. in or bef 1338 Aline dau of Edmund FitzAlan by Alice dau of William Warrenne. He died 23 Aug 1382 at Kenewyleswode in the March of Wales. His wife d. 20 Jan. 1385/6 Aliva Fitz Alan and Roger Le Strange Baron were married.

2191. **Aliva Fitz Alan** born about 1325. She died on 20 Jan 1385 or 20 Jan 1386 at the age of 60.

2208. **Thomas Clifford Lord** was born in 1363. He died on 18 Aug 1391 at the age of 28 in Spruce, Germany. Complete Peerage vol 3 p 293 Lord Clifford, Sheriff of Westmoreland age 26 at father's daeath. Knight of the King's chamber, Gov. of Carlisle for life. Did not die 4 Oct 1393 by some accounts. Sheriff of Westmoreland, Governor of Carlisle Castle Elizabeth Ros and Thomas Clifford Lord were married.

2209. **Elizabeth Ros** born about 1363. She died in 1424 at the age of 61. Complete Peerage vol 3 p 292

2210. **Henry Percy Lord** was born on 20 May 1364. He died on 21 Jul 1403 at the age of 39 in Shrewsbury, England. He was also known as Hotspur Percy. Complete Peerage vol 3 p 294 Henry "Hotspur" Percy, Very famous rebel. He got his nickname for his gallantry in battle and his personality. His biography given in English Biographies. He helped put Henry of Lancaster on the throne. death given as Aug. 14, AR 5-33 Date of death Jul 21 per David Baker which is the same date given by the English Biographies as he died on Saturday morning at Berwick on Tweed which was foretold to him that he would die at Berwick. His battles were notorious. He fought hard and won many victories. The King's own troops often lost while Henry Percy was victorious. He also gave evidence in the famous Scrope and Grosvenor controversy. He was so victorious the King's favorites feared him and sent him to battle the French but he won at Yarmouth and then they sent him to Scotland where he won his most famous Battle at Otterburn. Elizabeth Mortimer and Henry Percy Lord were married on 10 Dec 1379.

2211. **Elizabeth Mortimer** was born on 12 Feb 1371 in Usk, England. She died on 20 Apr 1417 at the age of 46. Complete Peerage vol 3 p 293, AR 5-33 living 8 Oct 1407

2212. **William Dacre Lord** born about 1357. He died on 20 Jul 1399 at the age of 42. CP 4 p 6 William age 26 or more at his father's death. He married Joan Douglas. He died

20 July 1399 and was buried in Lanercost priory. He married Mary. Joan Douglas and William Dacre Lord were married.

2213. **Joan Douglas** born about 1357. CP 4 p 6 He married Joan Douglas. Joan was said to be daughter of James Earl of Douglas but that would make him a grandfather at 29. She is most likely the daughter of the 3rd Earl of Douglas whose wife was Joan, not the dau. of James.

2214. **Ralph De Neville Earl** was born before 1364 of Westmoreland. He died on 21 Oct 1425 at the age of 61 in Raby. AR 5-35, 10-33, 207-34 1st Earl of Westmoreland created 1397 Margaret Stafford and Ralph De Neville Earl were married.

2215. **Margaret Stafford** born about 1370. She died on 9 Jun 1396 at the age of 26. AR 10-33 as his first wife.

2218. **Edward St. John** born about 1358. Anastasia De Aton and Edward St. John were married.

2219. **Anastasia De Aton** born about 1358.

2226. **Henry Umfreyville Sir.** Isabella and Henry Umfreyville Sir were married.

2227. **Isabella.**

2228. **Roger De Beauchamp Baron** was born in 1363. He died on 3 May 1406 at the age of 43. Weis 85-33 2nd Baron of Beauchamp of Bletsoe and Lydiard Tregoze. Joan Clopton and Roger De Beauchamp Baron were married.

2229. **Joan Clopton** born about 1363. Weis 85-33

2230. **John Holand Knight** born about 1360. He died in 1400 at the age of 40. Weis 85-34 AR7 47C-32 K.G. b. after 1350 d. 1400 Duke of Exeter, Earl of Huntingdon, Lieutenant of Ireland, Justic of Chester, Admiral of Fleet m. June 24 1386 Elizabeth d. 1425 dau of John of Gaunt. Elizabeth Of Gaunt and John Holand Knight were married.

2231. **Elizabeth Of Gaunt** born about 1365. AR7 93b-33

2244. **Ralph Greystock** is the same as person number 1090.

2245. **Catherine Clifford** is the same as person number 1091.

2246. **Robert Ferrers** born about 1373. He died before 29 Nov 1396 at the age of 23. AR 62-34 Sir Robert de Ferrers b. 1373 d. bef 29 Nov. 1396 m. Joan de Beaufort d. Howden 13 Nov 1440 dau of John of Gaunt, Duke of Lancaster. He was age 8 in Dec. 1380. Joan De Beaufort and Robert Ferrers were married.

2247. **Joan De Beaufort** born about 1379. She died on 13 Nov 1440 at the age of 61 in Howden. She was buried in Lincoln Cath.

2248. **Marmaduke Constable** born about 1360. Alice Cumberworth and Marmaduke Constable were married.

2249. **Alice Cumberworth** born about 1360.

2250. **William Gascoigne** born about 1350 in Gawthorpe, Yorkshire, England. He died on 17 Dec 1419 at the age of 69 in Harewood, Yorkshire, England. Chief Justice. He was a judge and imprisoned Prince Henry. Appears in Shakespeare. Elizabeth Mowbray and William Gascoigne were married.

2251. **Elizabeth Mowbray** born about 1350 in Kirkington, Yorkshire, England. She died in Harewood, Yorkshire, England. She was 1st wife. Visitations Or Yorkshire by Glover p. 384 says Elizabeth is daughter and heir of Roger Mowbray lord chief justice. 2nd wife of William was Jane Lisle.

2252. **John Wentworth** born about 1360. Beaumont and John Wentworth were married.

2253. **Beaumont** born about 1360.

2254. **Philip De Despenser Knight** was born in 1365 or 1366. He died on 20 Jun 1424 at the age of 59. MCS4 74-9 Elizabeth Tibetot b 1371 d. bef her husband m. 2nd Philip le Despenser Knight of Goxhill, Camoys Manor, Lord le Despenser b. 1365/6 age 36+ on 4 Aug 1401 d. 20 Jun 1424. MCS4 9-9 Elizabeth Tibetot and Philip De Despenser Knight were married.

2255. **Elizabeth Tibetot** was born in 1371. She died before 1424 at the age of 53.

2256. **Hugh Hastings Knight** born about 1350. He died on 6 Jun 1386 at the age of 36. PA1 Elsing 8 Hugh Hastings Knight of Elsing, Norfolk, and Norton, co. York, son of and heir of Hugh Hastings Knight by his wife Margaret. On 16 June 1386 he gave evidence in the Scrope and Grosvenor controversy. Hugh died on an expedition to Spain with the Duke of Lancaster on 6 Nov. 1386. She married second to Thomas Morley 4th Lord. Said to be of Magna Carta Surety descent but not given in MCS4. Anne Despenser and Hugh Hastings Knight were married before 1 Nov 1376.

2257. **Anne Despenser** born about 1360. She died on 30 Oct 1426 at the age of 66. PA1 Elsing 8 Anne Despenser 3rd daughter was married 1st before 1 Nov. 1376 to Hugh Hastings. She married second to Thomas de Morley. Anne Despenser died testate on 30 or 31 Oct. 1426.

2258. **John De Dinham Lord** born about 1359–1360. He died on 25 Dec 1428 at the age of 69. probably father of Muriel, not brother as given in MCS4. Ellen and John De Dinham Lord were married before 3 Feb 1379.

2259. **Ellen** born about 1360. Her name is given in CP 4 p. 375

2260. **Robert Morley** born about 1370. He died in 1399 or 1403 at the age of 29. CP 6:360, 9 218-9 Robert Morley was not lord, died within lifetime of his father and his son became 5th Lord. He was living 8 Jan. 1398/9 died bef 12 Nov. 1403. Isabel Molines and Robert Morley were married.

2261. **Isabel Molines** born about 1370.

2262. **Michael De La Pole Earl** born about 1367 of Suffolk. He died on 18 Sep 1415 at the age of 48 in Harfleur, England. Katherine Stafford and Michael De La Pole Earl were married before 23 Nov 1383.

2263. **Katherine Stafford** born about 1367. She died on 8 Apr 1419 at the age of 52 in England. PA1 Pole 12 Katherine Stafford was married before 23 Nov. 1383 to Michael de la Pole, 2nd Earl of Suffolk, son and heir of Michael de la Pole, 1st Earl by Katherine dau of John Wingfield, Knight of Wingfield Castle, Suffolk. He was born in or before 1367. He was summoned to Parliament from 19 Aug 1399. Michael died testate of the flux at the siege of Harfleur on 18 Sep 1415. His widow died on 8 Apr. 1419. They were buried at Wingfield.

2264. **William Gascoigne** is the same as person number 2250.

2265. **Elizabeth Mowbray** is the same as person number 2251.

2266. **Henry Wyman** born about 1350. He died on 5 Aug 1411 at the age of 61. Agnes Barden and Henry Wyman were married.

2267. **Agnes Barden** born about 1350.

2268. **William Clarell** born about 1350. He died before 1383 at the age of 33. Elizabeth Reygate and William Clarell were married.

2269. **Elizabeth Reygate** born about 1350. She died after 1389 at the age of 39.

2270. **Nicholas Montgomery Sir** born about 1370. Margary Foljambe and Nicholas Montgomery Sir were married.

2271. **Margary Foljambe** born about 1370. She died about 1456 at the age of 86.

2276. **John De Arundel Knight** born about 1342. He died on 15 Dec 1379 at the age of 37. Marshall of England MCS4 121-7 Eleanor Maltravers and John De Arundel Knight were married on 17 Feb 1358 or 17 Feb 1359.

2277. **Eleanor Maltravers** born about 1345. She died in 1405 at the age of 60. age 19 in 1364. MCS4 88-8

2280. **John Welles Sir** was born on 20 Apr 1352 in Coinsholme, Lincolnshire, England. He died in 1422 at the age of 70. Eleanor Mowbray and John Welles Sir were married before May 1384.

2281. **Eleanor Mowbray** was born in 1355.

2282. **Ralph Greystock** is the same as person number 1090.

2283. **Catherine Clifford** is the same as person number 1091.

2286. **Robert Fleming Knight** was born before 1360.

2288. **Edmund Jenney** born about 1350. Edmund Jenney was married.

2294. **John Leyston** born about 1360. Anne Gerrard and John Leyston were married.

2295. **Anne Gerrard** born about 1360.

3072. **Roger Prideaux** was born in 1260.

3073. **Elizabeth Clifford** was born in 1270. She died in 1340 at the age of 70.

3104. **Sir Nicholas Poyntz 2nd Lord Poyntz** born about 1278. He died before 1311 at the age of 33. He was also known as Nicholas Pointz. Historical and Genealogical Memoir of the Family of Poyntz or, eight centuries of an English house by Sir John Maclean (1811-1895) privately printed by William Pollard, North Street, Exeter, 1886; reprinted for the benefit of the Owsley Family Historical Society in 1983. Dwynn p 256 Maud De Acton and Sir Nicholas Poyntz 2nd Lord Poyntz were married.

3105. **Maud De Acton** born about 1275.

3106. **Sir Philip de Clanvowe** was born before 1300.

3107. **Philippa Talbot** was born before 1300.

3108. **Reginald Fitz Nichol** born about 1330. He died about 1375 at the age of 45.

3200. **Ralph Arundell** born about 1325. Ralph Arundell of Kierhaies (or Kenelhelvas) who during the reign of King Edward III (1327–1377) married Jane de Terise, heiress of Trerice.

3201. **Jane de Terise of Trerice** born about 1325.

3202. **Martin Peltor Esq** born about 1325.

3234. **Sir Hugh Courtenay 2nd Baron/10th Earl of Devon** was born on 12 Jul 1303. He died on 2 May 1377 at the age of 73. Hugh de Courtenay, 2nd/10th Earl of Devon, Effigy (restored) of Hugh de Courtenay, 2nd/10th Earl of Devon, south transept, Exeter Cathedral. In 1342 the Earl was with King Edward III's expedition to Brittany.[15] Richardson states that the Earl took part on 9 April 1347 in a tournament at Lichfield.[16] However, in 1347 he was excused on grounds of infirmity from accompanying the King on an expedition beyond the seas, and about that time was also excused from attending Parliament, suggesting the possibility that it was the Earl's eldest son and heir, Hugh Courtenay, who had fought at the Battle of Crecy on 26 August 1346, who took part in the tournament at Lichfield. In 1350 the King granted the Earl permission to travel for a year, and during that year he built the monastery of the White Friars in London. He died at Exeter on 2 May 1377 and was buried in Exeter Cathedral on the same day. His will was dated 28 Jan 13--.[8][26]

3235. **Margaret de Bohun** was born on 3 Apr 1311. She died on 16 Dec 1391 at the age of 80.

Thirteenth Generation

4096. **Roger De Blackiston** born about 1320 in Durham, England. He died after 1349 at the age of 29 in Durham, England. acquired land from Richard del park 1349 Christina De Washington and Roger De Blackiston were married.

4097. **Christina De Washington** was born before 1325. Inquisition post mortem for son includes her. see Colonial Families published
in Colonial Genealogist III:2 1970

4160. **John Conyers** born about 1275 of Stubhouse. He died after 1306 at the age of 31. Colonial Gen. Vol. XI 3-4(Augustan Society #219) probably a younger son of the house of Conyers of Sockburn. John Conyers was married.

4164. **John Melton** born about 1300. He died after 1321 at the age of 21. Yorkshire Pedigrees John Melton living 1321 m. Elizabeth Hilton. Elizabeth Hilton and John Melton were married.

4165. **Elizabeth Hilton** born about 1300.

4168. **William St. Quintin** born about 1320. He died in 1379 at the age of 59. He was buried in Harpham. Foster Yorkshire: tomb of alabaster, under the arch between the chancel and north chancel. Joan Thweng and William St. Quintin were married.

4169. **Joan Thweng** born about 1320. She died in 1380 at the age of 60. She was buried in Harpham. Foster Yorkshire

4170. **Robert Warren**. Robert Warren was married.

4172. **William Gascoigne Sir** born about 1315 in Gawthorpe, Yorkshire, England. He died before 1383 at the age of 68. Visitations of Yorkshire by Glover p. 384 says William Gascoigne m. Margaret, dau and heir of Nicholas Frank. They had children Nicholas Gascoigne, Alice married Robert Constable and William. Agnes Franke and William Gascoigne Sir were married.

4173. **Agnes Franke** born about 1320 in Alwoodly, Yorkshire, England. She was also known as Margaret Franke.

4174. **Hugh Clitheroe King** born about 1310 of Salebury. Isabel De Gras and Hugh Clitheroe King were married.

4175. **Isabel De Gras** born about 1310.

4194. **John Lisle** born about 1260. Surtees Durham John Lisle was married.

4196. **Adam Fulthorpe** born about 1240. He died after 1262 at the age of 22. Adam Fulthorpe was married.

4200. **Walter Carrow** born about 1275. Walter Carrow was married.

4216. **Robert De Umfreyville Earl** was born in 1277 of Angus. He died on 2 Apr 1325 at the age of 48. Charlemagne Desc: Also Weis AR: age 30+ in 1307 2nd wife Eleanore Burke EP: summoned to Parliament 1309-1324. 1st wife Lacy de Kyme Alianore and Robert De Umfreyville Earl were married.

4217. **Alianore** born about 1277. She died on 21 Mar 1368 at the age of 91. also Weis AR: married 2nd Roger Manduit, she was 2nd wife of Robert, Charlemagne Desc: Burke EP

4218. **Adam De Roddam** born about 1300. also Weis AR Adam De Roddam was married.

4232. **Roger De Halnaby** was born before 1245. He died before 1297 at the age of 52. Elizabeth and Roger De Halnaby were married.

4233. **Elizabeth** born about 1245. She died after 1297 at the age of 52.

4240. **John Pudsey** born about 1325. Visitations of Yorkshire. John Pudsey was married.

4242. **John Layton Lord** born about 1325 of Barford. Lord of Barford Christiana Sheffied and John Layton Lord were married.

4243. **Christiana Sheffied** born about 1325.

4246. **Adomar De Athol Lord** born about 1340 of Felton. Lord of Felton Adomar De Athol Lord was married.

4272. **John Darcy Baron** was born in 1317. He died on 5 Mar 1355 or 5 Mar 1356 at the age of 38 in Cresy. Weis AR: 2nd baron Darcy, Baron of Knayth Co, Lincoln, slain at Cresy. His second wife was Elizabeth Meinell Elizabeth De Meinill Baroness and John Darcy Baron were married.

4273. **Elizabeth De Meinill Baroness** was born on 15 Oct 1331 in Whorlton. She died on 9 Jul 1368 at the age of 36. Weis AR: Baroness Meinill of Whorlton

4274. **Thomas Grey** born about 1330 of Heton. Weis AR Margaret De Presfen and Thomas Grey were married.

4275. **Margaret De Presfen** born about 1330.

4276. **Reginald De Grey Baron** was born on 1 Nov 1311 of Wilton. He died on 4 Jun 1370 at the age of 58 in Shirland. of Wilton Maud Boutetourt and Reginald De Grey Baron were married before 10 Jan 1327.

4277. **Maud Boutetourt** born about 1312. She died on 14 Sep 1391 at the age of 79 in Shirland.

4278. **Gilbert Talbot Lord** born about 1332 of Ecclesfield, Hereford County, England. He died on 24 Apr 1387 at the age of 55. Weis AR Lord Talbot of Ecclesfield, Co Hereford, Member of Parliament 1362 Petronilla Butler and Gilbert Talbot Lord were married before 1352.

4279. **Petronilla Butler** born about 1335. She died about 1368 at the age of 33. living 1365 dead 1368

4280. **Henry Fitz Hugh** born about 1320. died in lifetime of his father. Joane Fourneys and Henry Fitz Hugh were married.

4281. **Joane Fourneys** born about 1320.

4282. **Henry Le Scrope Lord** born about 1315. He died on 31 Jul 1391 at the age of 76. Knight Baron. 1st Baron of Scrope of Masham. age 25 in 1341. served in wars of France and Scotland and at the siege of Berwick in 1333. at the battles of Cressy 1346, Durham. governor of Guisnees and Calais 1360, capt of Calais 1369. summoned to Parliament 1350-1391 Joan and Henry Le Scrope Lord were married.

4283. **Joan** born about 1315.

4284. **John De Grey Lord** was born on 9 Oct 1300 in Rotherfield, Oxford County, England. He died on 1 Sep 1359 at the age of 58. Knight of the Garter, of Rotherfield, 1st Baron Grey of Rotherfield, K.G. 23 Apr 1349. History of Rutland: Baron of Rotherfield. proved his age 15 Edw. 2 summoned to Parliament as Baron 25 Aug 12 Ed 3. died 1 Oct 33 Edw 3. first wife Catherine Fitz Alan EP p 207 Fitz Hugh Avice De Marmion and John De Grey Lord were married.

4285. **Avice De Marmion** born about 1320. She died after 1359 at the age of 39. 2nd wife History of Rutland living 33 Ed 3

4286. **Hubert St. Quenton Baron** born about 1315. He died about Jul 1347 at the age of 32. Sir of St. Quenton of Brandesburton in Holderness. Margery D'Insula and Hubert St. Quenton Baron were married.

4287. **Margery D'Insula** born about 1315. She died in 1362 at the age of 47.

4288. **Thomas Surteys Knight** was born before 1323 in Durham, England. He died in 1379 at the age of 56 in Durham, England. son and heir. full of age in 1345. heir to his uncle Goceline 22 Hatfield. Then age 30 and upwards. Sheriff of Northumberland 47 Edw. III 1372 and 2 Rich. II. 1378. Died seised of North Gosford. Inq. p.m. Saturday before St. James the Apostle, 34 Hatfield, 1379. knight by 1366 Alice and Thomas Surteys Knight were married.

4289. **Alice** was born before 1325 in England. She died after 1379 at the age of 54 in Durham, England.Father in law settled lands on her heir male in 1345. in Middleton, Morton, and Sadberge.

4320. **John Coigniers Knight** born about 1265 of Sockbourne. He died after 1299 at the age of 34. Knight of Sockburne, Scolastica De Cotam and John Coigniers Knight were married.

4321. **Scolastica De Cotam** born about 1270. She died after 1298 at the age of 28.

4324. **Gilbert De Aton** born about 1275. He died in Apr 1350 at the age of 75. inherited lands of the Barons of Vesci. He was summoned to Parliament Dec 30 1324 until 1342. will dated at Wintringham 10 apr 1350. Gilbert De Aton was married.

4326. **Henry De Percy Knight** was born in 1299. He died on 26 Feb 1351 or 26 Feb 1352 at the age of 52. Knight of the Garter, 2nd Lord Percy of Alnwick, Member of Parliament 1322-1352, knighted 1323, constable of Scarborough Castle, Warden of the Marches of Scotland. Idoine De Clifford and Henry De Percy Knight were married about 1320.

4327. **Idoine De Clifford** born about 1303. She died on 24 Aug 1365 at the age of 62.

4332. **Geffrey Le Scrope Baron** born about 1290. He died in 1340 at the age of 50. He was buried in Coverham Abbey, York County, England. knight, Chief Justice of the King's Bench 1324 til 1328, made Baron 14 Edward 3. purchased the manor of Masham. justice of the Common Pleas. Ivetta Of Ros and Geffrey Le Scrope Baron were married.

4333. **Ivetta Of Ros** born about 1290.

4336. **John De Eure Knight** born about 1307. He died in 1366 or 1367 at the age of 59. Visitations of Yorkshire by Glover p. 610 Sir John de Eure, age 22, 20 Ed. II 1327, was married 14 Ed. III 1340 and died Sat. 4th week of Lent 1367/8 Inq. p.m. married Margaret (supposed to be of the family of Lumley or Heron). Her will dated Tue. before St. George the Martyr, and proved at Durham, 27 May 1378, to be buried in the church of the preaching friars, as Newcastle upon Tyne. Margaret and John De Eure Knight were married.

4337. **Margaret** born about 1310. She died in May 1378 at the age of 68. will dated tues before St. George the Martyr and proved at Durham May 27 1378, to be buried in the church of the preaching friars at Newcastle upon Tyne.

4338. **Robert De Clifford Lord** was born on 5 Nov 1305. He died on 20 May 1344 at the age of 38. Complete Peerage vol 3 p 291 had seis of his mother's and brother's land 20 Aug 1327. summoned to parliament 10 Dec 1327 to 20 Apr 1344. his great aunt Idoine de Vipont left large estates. served in Scottish wars and repaired castle at Skipton. Served in Parliament, inherited considerable Vipont estates from his great-aunt Idoine, served in the Scottish wars, and repaired Skipton Castle. Isabel Berkeley and Robert De Clifford Lord were married in Jun 1328 in Berkeley Castle.

4339. **Isabel Berkeley** born about 1305. She died on 25 Jul 1362 at the age of 57. Complete Peerage vol 3 p 291 married 2nd Thomas Musgrave History of Rutland p 15

4352. **Robert Bowes Lord** born about 1300 of Streatlam. He died after 1330 at the age of 30. Durham vol 4 p 107 living son and heir 1330 2nd wife Elizabeth Elizabeth Lilburne and Robert Bowes Lord were married.

4353. **Elizabeth Lilburne** born about 1300. She died in 1384 at the age of 84. Durham vol 4 p 107 inq p.m. 1384

4354. **Robert Dalden Lord** born about 1325 of Dalden. Durham vol 4 p 107 Lord of Dalden, Pallion, Hamildon and Clowcroft. sole heir Robert Dalden Lord was married.

4360. **Ralph Greystoke** was born on 15 Aug 1299. He died on 14 Jul 1323 at the age of 23 in Gateshead. He was buried in Westminster. CP 6 p. 190 Ralph de Greystoke son and heir of Robert Fitz Ralph by Elizabeth his wife and grandson and heir of Sir Ralph Fitz William of Grimthrope and Hildreskelk, co. York (lord Fitz William) and was born 15 Aug 1299. On death of his father Apr 1317 he became feudal Lord of Greystoke he fought for the King at the battle of Boroughbridge 16 Mar. 1321/2. He married after 25 Nov. 1317 Alice sister of Hugh Earl of Gloucester and dau of Hugh (Audley) Lord Audley by Iseude widow of Sir Walter de Balum of Much Marcle, co Hereford and dau of Sir Edmund de Mortimer of Wigmore, co Hereford. He died at Gateshead, being poisoned 14 July 1323 near 24 and was buried in Westminster Abbey. His widow had livery of her dower 12 Aug and 27 Sep 1323. She married 2nd 14 Jan. 1326/7 Sir Ralph Nevill of Raby. He died 5 Aug 1367 and was buried in Durham Cathedral Church. She died 13 Jan. 1374/5 and was buried with him. Alice De Audley and Ralph Greystoke were married after 25 Nov 1317.

4361. **Alice De Audley** born about 1300. She died on 12 Jan 1374 or 12 Jan 1375 at the age of 74. She was buried in Durham Chapel. Weis 207-32

4362. **Henry Fitz Hugh Lord** born about 1295 of Ravensworth. He died in 1356 at the age of 61 in Ravensworth. His descendants kept the name Fitz Hugh. Engaged in the Scottish wars. He was also called Henry Fitz Henry of Ravensworth. Joan Fournez and Henry Fitz Hugh Lord were married.

4363. **Joan Fournez** born about 1300.

4364. **Robert De Clifford** is the same as person number 4338.

4365. **Isabel Berkeley** is the same as person number 4339.

4366. **Thomas Beauchamp Earl** was born on 14 Feb 1313 in Warwick Castle. He died on 16 Nov 1369 at the age of 56 in Calais, France. He was buried in Warwick. Complete Peerage vol 3 p 292 Weis 87-31 will made 6 Sep 1369 K.G. 23 Apr 1349 3rd Earl of Warwick, also called 11th Earl of Warwick Catherine De Mortimer and Thomas Beauchamp Earl were married in 1337.

4367. **Catherine De Mortimer** born about 1315. She died about 4 Aug 1369 at the age of 54. She was buried in Warwick. Complete Peerage vol 3 p 292 Weis 87-31 will made 4 Aug 1369 120-34 Daughter of Roger de Mortimer, Earl of March

4376. **John Willoughby Baron** born about 6 Jan 1328–6 Jan 1329 in Eresby Manor, Lincolnshire, England. He died on 29 Mar 1372 at the age of 44. He was buried in Spilsby. CP John Willoughby b. at Eresby Manor bap. 6 Jan. 1328/9 on Church of St. James, Spain m. bef 1349 Cecily sister of William de Ufford 2nd Earl of Suffolk dau of Robert 1st Earl of Suffolk by Margaret dau of Walter de Norwich of Norfolk She d. bef him. Cecily Of Ufford and John Willoughby Baron were married before 1349.

4377. **Cecily Of Ufford** born about 1330. She died before 1372 at the age of 42.

4378. **William Skipwith Baron** born about 1325. Alice Hiltoft and William Skipwith Baron were married.

4379. **Alice Hiltoft** born about 1325 in Lincolnshire, England.

4380. **Roger Le Strange Baron** was born on 15 Aug 1301. He died on 29 Jul 1349 at the age of 47. CP 12 (1) p 353 Roger Lord Strange brother and heir b. 15 Aug 1301. On 20 Jan. 1326/7 he was made a Banneret. In 1335 he was heir to his uncle Ebles Lestrange whose widow Alice granted in 1336/7 a life estate in manor of Ellesmere. He married 1st Maud and 2nd Joan bef 25 Mar 1344 dau and coh. of Oliver de Ingham. He died 29 Jul 1349 in the manor of Sedgebrook. Linc. Joan had no issue m 2nd Miles Stapleton and died bef 12 Dec 1365. Maud and Roger Le Strange Baron were married.

4381. **Maud** born about 1301.

4382. **Edmund Fitz Alan Earl** born about 1290. The Wilkinson Book p. 189 2nd Earl of Arundel Alice De Warenne and Edmund Fitz Alan Earl were married.

4383. **Alice De Warenne** born about 1285.

4416. **Roger Clifford** is the same as person number 2182.

4417. **Maud Beauchamp** is the same as person number 2183.

4418. **Thomas Ros Lord** was born on 13 Jan 1336 or 13 Jan 1337 in Stoke, Albany, Northamptonshire. He died on 8 Jun 1384 at the age of 48 in Uffington, Lincolnshire. Complete Peerage vol 3 p 292 4th Lord Ros of Helmsley Beatrice De Stafford and Thomas Ros Lord were married in 1358.

4419. **Beatrice De Stafford** born about 1340.

4420. **Henry De Percy Knight** was born on 10 Nov 1341 of Northumberlan. He died on 19 Feb 1407 or 19 Feb 1408 at the age of 65 in Bramham Moor. Weis 19-31 Lord marshal of England, Earl Percy 6 Jul 1377 Margaret Neville and Henry De Percy Knight were married on 12 Jul 1358.

4421. **Margaret Neville** born about 1341. She died in May 1372 at the age of 31. Weis 19-31, 186-6 widow of William de Ros of Helmsley

4422. **Edmund Mortimer Earl** was born on 1 Feb 1352 of March, Langonith. He died on 27 Dec 1381 at the age of 29 in Cork. Complete Peerage vol 3 p 293 AR 5-32 3rd Earl of March Philipa Plantagenet and Edmund Mortimer Earl were married in 1368.

4423. **Philipa Plantagenet** was born on 16 Aug 1355. She died in 1379 at the age of 24. History of Rutland p 42 AR 5-32 Duchess of Clarence and Countess of March

4424. **Hugh Dacre Lord** born about 1335. He died on 24 Dec 1383 at the age of 48. He was buried in Lanercost Priory. CP 4 p. 5 Hugh next brother and heir was age 40 or more at brother's death, which he was suspected of having caused. he was released from the Tower on 2 Jul 1376. He married between 8 Oct. 1354 and 1 Jul 1355 Elizabeth widow of Sir William de Douglas, sometime Earl of Athol who died Aug 1353., dau perhaps of Sir John Maxwell of Carlaverock co Dumfries. She died before 1 Jan. 1369/70. He died 24 Dec. 1383 and was buried in Lanercost priory. Elizabeth Maxwell and Hugh Dacre Lord were married about 1354–1355.

4425. **Elizabeth Maxwell** born about 1335. She died before 1 Jan 1369 at the age of 34. perhaps daughter of John Maxwell.

4426. **Earl Archibald Douglas 3rd Earl Douglas** born about 1325. He died on 24 Dec 1400 at the age of 75. He was also known as the Grime Douglas. CP 3rd Earl Archibald Douglas illegitimate b. c. 1325 died Dec 24 1400 m. bef 23 Jul 1362 m. Joan Stratherne. buried at Bothwell. History of Rutland p. 181 says Archibald the 2nd son who was 3rd Earl ob 1400 m. Elizabeth dau of Thomas Murray, Lord of Bothwell in Scotland son of Sir William Douglas 2nd Earl m. Margaret dau of Patrick Earl of Mar. Archibald Douglas, Earl of Douglas and Wigtown, Lord of Galloway, Douglas and Bothwell, called Archibald the Grim or Black Archibald, was a late medieval Scottish nobleman. Archibald was the bastard son of Sir James "the Black" Douglas, Robert I's trusted lieutenant, and an unknown mother. A first cous of William 1st Earl of Douglas, he inherited the earldom of Douglas and its entailed estates as the third earl following the death without legitimate issue of James 2nd Earl of Douglas at the Battle of Otterburn.

4427. **Joan of Moravia** born about 1325. Archibald further increased his power by his marriage to the widow and heiress Joanna de Moravia in 1362. Joanna de Moravia was the daughter of Thomas Murray and granddaughter of Sir Andrew Murray. Archibald is said to have offered to fight five English knights in single combat for her hand. The Lady of Bothwell and heiress to the de Moravia dynasty, Joanna brought with her large estates and lordships throughout Scotland, which Archibald claimed de jure uxoris. This included the semi-ruined Bothwell Castle, which he promptly started to rebuild. The marriage was a device of the king to ensure that the Moray inheritance would be passed into safe (and loyal) hands. Since the death of Joanna's first husband, Sir Thomas de Moravia, the Lord of Bothwell, in 1361, she and her widowed mother had been wards of the court. Joanna was declared to be not only heiress of her father's unentailed lands, but also those of her first husband. The estates stretched from Aberdeenshire, Moray and Ross in the north, to Lanarkshire and Roxburghshire in the south. Although Douglas did not inherit his wife's father's Earldom of Strathearn, Douglas would be able to use his newfound kindred ties to the advantage of the King in the center of the kingdom.

4428. **John De Neville Knight** born about 1327. He died on 17 Oct 1388 at the age of 61 in Newcastle. He was buried in Durham. Weis 207-33, 2-32 Baron Neville of Raby Knight 1360, K.G. 1369 Maud Percy and John De Neville Knight were married.

4429. **Maud Percy** born about 1327. She died before 18 Feb 1378 at the age of 51. Weis 207-33, 2-32 first wife Maud

4430. **Hugh Stafford Earl** born about 1342 of Stafford. He died on 10 Oct 1386 at the age of 44. AR 10-32 3rd Baron Stafford, 2nd Earl of Stafford Philippa De Beauchamp and Hugh Stafford Earl were married before 1 Mar 1350.

4431. **Philippa De Beauchamp** born about 1342. She died before 6 Apr 1386 at the age of 44.

4438. **William De Aton** is the same as person number 2162.

4439. **Isabel De Percy** is the same as person number 2163.

4452. **John Umfreyville Sir** died before 1314.

4453. **Alice De La Hurne.**

4456. **Roger De Beauchamp** born about 1340. He died before 1379 at the age of 39. Weis 85-32 Roger De Beauchamp was married.

4458. **William Clopton** born about 1340. Weis 85-33 William Clopton was married.

4460. **Thomas Holland Knight** was born before 1320. He died on 26 Dec 1360 at the age of 40. He was also known as Thomas Holland 1st Earl of Kent. He assumed the Earldom of Kent j.u. AR7 47-31 Sir Thomas de Holdan K.G. Earl of Kent d. 26 or 28 Dec. 1360 m. as her 2nd husband after annulment of 1st m. William de Montacute m. Joan Plantaganet. Joan Of Kent and Thomas Holland Knight were married.

4461. **Joan Of Kent** was born on 29 Sep 1328. She died on 7 Aug 1385 at the age of 56. AR7 236-12 Joan "Fair Maid of Kent", dau by Edmund of Woodstock and Margaret Wake d. 7 Aug 1385 m. William Montacute first 2nd Sir Thomas de Holand, 3rd Edward the Black Prince by whom mother of Richard II of England.

4462. **John Of Gaunt Duke** was born in 6 Mar 1340 of Lancaster, Ghent. He died 3 Feb 1399 at the age of 58 in Leicester Castle. AR7 1-31 Duke of Lancaster through his wife. His descendants were part of the line of Lancaster (part of the War of the Roses). Blanche Of Lancaster and John Of Gaunt Duke were married on 19 May 1359. He was an English royal prince, military leader and statesman. He was the son of King Edward III of England, and father of King Henry IV. Because of Gaunt's royal origin, advantageous marriages and some generous land grants, he was one of the richest men of his era and an influential figure during the reigns of both his father and his nephew, Richard II. As Duke of Lancaster, he is the founder of the royal House of Lancaster, whose members would ascend the throne after his death. His birthplace, Ghent in Flanders, then known in English as Gaunt, was the origin of his name.

4463. **Blanche Of Lancaster** born about 1340. She died on 30 Sep 1369 at the age of 29. AR7 1-31

4492. **Robert De Ferrers Sir** born about 1350 of Willisham. He died on 31 Dec 1380 at the age of 30. AR 62-33 Elizabeth Le Botiller and Robert De Ferrers Sir were married about 27 Sep 1369.

4493. **Elizabeth Le Botiller** born about 1350 of Oversley. AR 77-34

4494. **John Of Gaunt** is the same as person number 4462.

4495. **Catherine Roet** was born on 25 Nov 1340 in Picardy, Hainaut. She died on 10 May 1403 at the age of 62. She was buried in Lincoln Cath. John had children by his mistress Catherine whom he later married.
She was widow of Sir Hugh Swynford and often called Catherine Roet Swynford.

4496. **Robert Constable** born about 1340. Visitations of Yorkshire by Glover p. 178 Robert Constable m. dau of Sir William Skipwith. Skipwith and Robert Constable were married.

4497. **Skipwith** born about 1340.

4498. **Robert Cumberworth** born about 1330 in Staffordshire, England. Visitations of Yorkshire by Glover p. 178 Robert Cumberworth m. Sibille Argum dau and coheir of William Argum, son of Richard Argum, son of Richard Argum. Sibilla Argum and Robert Cumberworth were married.

4499. **Sibilla Argum** born about 1330.

4500. **William Gascoigne** is the same as person number 4172.

4501. **Agnes Franke** is the same as person number 4173.

4502. **Alexander Mowbray** was born in 1314. Yorkshire Visitation by Foster p. 282 Alexander Mowbray of Kirklington, Knight m. Elizabeth dau and heir of Hy. Monasteriis, father of Elizabeth da and co heir wife of Sir William Gascoigne. Alexander son of John Mowbray of Kirklington, Knight m. Margaret sister of Sir Alexander Percy of Kildale. son of Willielmus de Mowbray m. Agnes. son of Johannes de Mowbray. Elizabeth Musters and Alexander Mowbray were married.

4503. **Elizabeth Musters** was born in 1316.

4504. **John Wentworth** born about 1340.

4505. **Agnes Dransfield** born about 1340.

4508. **Philip De Despenser** was born on 18 Oct 1342 in Gedney. He died on 4 Aug 1401 at the age of 58 in Goxhill. MCS4 9-8 Sir Philip le Despenser b. Gedney 18 Oct 1342 d. Goxhill 4 Aug 1401 m. Elizabeth d. bef 1401.

4509. **Elizabeth** born about 1342. She died before 1401 at the age of 59.

4510. **Robert De Tibetot Lord** born about 1350 of Nettlestead, Suffolk, England. He died on 13 Apr 1372 at the age of 22. MCS4 74-8 Margaret Deincourt d. 2 Apr 1380 m. 1st Sir Robert de Tybetot, Lord Tybetot of Nettlestead, Suffolk d. 13 Apr 1372. Tybetot Pedigree in History of Rutland p.44

4511. **Margaret Deincourt** born about 1350. She died on 2 Apr 1380 at the age of 30. married 2nd John Cheyne

4512. **Hugh Hastings** born about 1328. He died before 1369 at the age of 41. Margaret De Everingham and Hugh Hastings were married.

4513. **Margaret De Everingham** born about 1325. She died about 1375 at the age of 50. will dated 1375

4514. **Edward Le Despenser Knight** was born on 24 Mar 1336 in Essendine, Rutland, England. He died on 11 Nov 1375 at the age of 39 in Llanbethian, Glamorgan County, England. He was buried in Tewkesbury Abbey, England. PA1 Clare 9 Edward le Despenser Knight, K.G. 4th Lord Despenser of Glamorgan and Morgannwg, Wales, son and heir was born at Essendine, Rutland, about 24 Mar. 1335/6 and was nephew and heir of Hugh le Despenser. He was married before 2 Aug. 1354 to Elizabeth de Burghersh, dau and heiress of Bartholomew de Burghersh of Ewyas Lacy, co. Herefore, Stert and Colerne, Co. Wilts. 4th Lord Burghersh by his first wife Cecliy, daughter of Richard de Weyland, Knight. She was born in 1342 (age 27 at her father's death). He accompanied the Prince of Wales to Gascony in Sep. 1355. He was summoned to Parliament from 15 Dec. 1357 by writs directed Edwardo le Despenser, whereby he is held to have become Lord le Despenser. He was with the King in the invasion of France, Oct. 1359 to 1360. Edward le Despenser, lord of Glowmorg died testate age 39 at Llanbethian, Co. Galmborgan on 11 Nov. 1375. Elizabeth de Burghersh, Dame le Despenser died testate about 26 Jul 1409. There were buried at Tewkesbury Abbey. MCS4 14-8 Sir Edward Despenser K.G. b. Essendine 24 Mar. 1335/6 d. Llanbethian 11 Nov 1375 m. bef. Dec. 1364 Elizabeth de Burghersh d. 26 July 1409. Elizabeth De Burghersh and Edward Le Despenser Knight were married before 2 Aug 1354.

4515. **Elizabeth De Burghersh** was born in 1342. She died on 26 Jul 1409 at the age of 67. She was buried in Tewkesbury Abbey, England. MCS4 14-8, 13-9

4516. **John De Dinham Knight** born about 1318. He died on 7 Jan 1382 or 7 Jan 1383 at the age of 64. MCS4 125-6 Muriel Courtenay d. bef 12 Aug 1369 m. Sir John de Dinham Knight age 14+ in 1332, d. 7 Jan. 1382/3 son of Sir John de Dinham and Margaret. CP IV p 373. Muriel Courtenay and John De Dinham Knight were married.

4517. **Muriel Courtenay** born about 1340. She died before 12 Aug 1369 at the age of 29.

4520. **Thomas Morley Lord** born about 1350. He died in 1416 at the age of 66. CP Thomas 4th Lord de jure Lord Marshal after Richard Fitzalan condemned he was made Marshal of England. m1st Joan died bef 2 Dec 1384.She was buried White Friar's in Norwich. m 2nd Anne Depenser widow of Hugh Hastings d. 1386. CP 214-6 Joan and Thomas Morley Lord were married.

4521. **Joan** born about 1350. She died before 2 Dec 1384 at the age of 34. She was buried in White Friars, Norwich, England.

4524. **Michael De La Pole Earl** born about 1340. 1st Earl of Suffolk. History of Rutland p. 65 Michael de la Pole Knight summoned to Parliament as baron 20 Jan 29 Ed. 3 1355/6 appointed chancelor of England 13 Mar 6 Rich 2 1382/3 created Earl of Suffolk 6 Aug 9 Rich. 2 1385 ob 5 Sep 12 Rich 2 1388 K.G. m. Catherine dau and heir of John de Wingfield Knight was wife 1358. Katherine Wingfield and Michael De La Pole Earl were married.

4525. **Katherine Wingfield** born about 1340.

4526. **Hugh Stafford** is the same as person number 4430.

4527. **Philippa De Beauchamp** is the same as person number 4431.

4534. **John Barden** born about 1325. Alice Thirkell and John Barden were married.

4535. **Alice Thirkell** born about 1325.

4536. **Thomas Clarell** born about 1330. He died about 1363 at the age of 33. Isabella St. Philibert and Thomas Clarell were married.

4537. **Isabella St. Philibert** born about 1330.

4538. **William Reygate** born about 1330. Theophania Funtaynes and William Reygate were married.

4539. **Theophania Funtaynes** born about 1330.

4542. **Godfrey Foljambe Knight** born about 1345. He died in 1376 at the age of 31. Margaret Of Paganus and Godfrey Foljambe Knight were married about 1367.

4543. **Margaret Of Paganus** born about 1350.

4552. **Richard Fitz Alan** born about 1313. He died on 24 Jan 1375 or 24 Jan 1376 at the age of 62. AR7 121-6 says he married 1320. not possible if born 1313. Eleanor Plantagenet and Richard Fitz Alan were married.

4553. **Eleanor Plantagenet** born about 1313.

4554. **John Maltravers** born about 1315. He died on 22 Jan 1348 or 22 Jan 1349 at the age of 33. Gwenllian and John Maltravers were married.

4555. **Gwenllian** born about 1320. She died in 1375 at the age of 55.

4560. **John Welles Lord**. 3rd Lord Welles

4561. **Maud Roos**.

4562. **John Mowbray** was born on 25 Jun 1340 in Epworth. He died on 9 Oct 1368 at the age of 28 in Thrace, Constantinople. Crusader to the Holy Land, slain by the Saracens. MCS4 63-6 Ancestry of John Mowbray to Roger de Albini given in History of Rutland p. 114 Elizabeth Seagrave and John Mowbray were married in 1349.

4563. **Elizabeth Seagrave** was born on 25 Oct 1338. She died on 24 Mar 1398 or 24 Mar 1399 at the age of 59.

4590. **William Gerrard** born about 1330 of Darsham, Suffolk, England. William Gerrard was married.

6146. **John de Clifford** was born in 1277. He died in 1323 at the age of 46. Clarice Treverbain and John de Clifford were married about 1304.

6147. **Clarice Treverbain** was born in 1293. She died in 1349 at the age of 56.

6208. **Hugh Pointz 1st Lord** was born on 25 Aug 1252. He died before 4 Jan 1308 at the age of 55. Margaret Paveley and Hugh Pointz 1st Lord were married.

6209. **Margaret Paveley** born about 1252.

6210. **Sir John Acton II** was born before 1250. He died in 1312 at the age of 62.

6211. **Helen**.

6216. **John Fitz Nichol** born about 1300. He died about 1375 at the age of 75.

6468. **Hugh De Courtenay Sir** born about 1272. He died on 23 Dec 1340 at the age of 68. MCS4 125-5 Sir Hugh de Courtenay d. 23 Dec. 1340 9th Earl of Devon m. 1292, Agnes d. 11 June 1345 dau of John de St. John by Alice. Agnes St. John and Hugh De Courtenay Sir were married in 1292.

6469. **Agnes St. John** born about 1272. She died on 11 Jun 1345 at the age of 73.

6470. **Humphrey VIII De Bohun 4th Earl of Hereford and Essex** was born in 1276. He died on 16 Mar 1322 at the age of 46. AR7 6-29, 97-31 Earl of Hereford and Essex. He was a member of a powerful Anglo-Norman family of the Welsh Marches and was one of the Ordainers who opposed Edward II's excesses. Humphrey de Bohun's birth year is uncertain although several contemporary sources indicate that it was 1276. He succeeded his father in 1298 as Earl of Hereford and Earl of Essex, and Constable of England (later called Lord High Constable). Humphrey held the title of Bearer of the Swan Badge, a heraldic device passed down in the Bohun family. Humphrey was one of several earls and barons under Edward I who laid siege to Caerlaverock Castle in Scotland in 1300 and later took part in many campaigns in Scotland. He also loved tourneying and gained a reputation as an "elegant" fop. In one of the campaigns in Scotland Humphrey evidently grew bored and departed for England to take part in a tournament along with Piers Gaveston and other young barons and knights. On return all of them fell under Edward I's wrath for desertion, but were forgiven. It is probable that Gaveston's friend, the future Edward II, had given them permission to depart. Later Humphrey became one of Gaveston's and Edward II's bitterest opponents. Humphrey de Bohun received many of Robert Bruce's forfeited properties. After Bruce's defeats, Humphrey took Lochmaben, and Edward I awarded him Annandale and the castle. Lochmaben was retaken by the Scots in 1312 and remained in Scottish hands until 1333 when it was once more seized by the English. At the Battle of Bannockburn (23–24 June 1314), Humphrey de Bohun should have been given command of the army because that was his responsibility as Constable of England. However, since the execution of Piers Gaveston in 1312 Humphrey had been out of favour with Edward II, who gave the Constableship for the 1314 campaign to the youthful and inexperienced Earl of Gloucester, Gilbert de Clare. Nevertheless, on the first day, de Bohun insisted on being one of the first to lead the cavalry charge. In the melee and cavalry rout between the Bannock Burn and the Scots' camp he was not injured although his rash young cousin Henry de Bohun, who could have been no older than about 22, charged alone at Robert Bruce and was killed by Bruce's axe. On the second day, Gloucester was killed at the start of the battle. Hereford fought throughout the day, leading a large company of Welsh and English knights and archers. Humphrey de Bohun was ransomed by Edward II, his brother-in-law, on the pleading of Edward's wife Isabella. This was one of the most interesting ransoms in English history. The Earl was traded for Bruce's queen, Elizabeth de Burgh and daughter, Marjorie Bruce, two bishops amongst other important Scots captives in England. Isabella MacDuff, Countess of Buchan, who had crowned Robert Bruce in 1306 and for years had been locked in a cage outside Berwick, was not included; presumably, she had died in captivity. Although the details have been called into question by a few historians, his death may have been particularly gory. As recounted by Ian Mortimer:

6471. **Elizabeth Plantagenet** was born on 7 Aug 1282. She died on 5 May 1316 at the age of 33.

Fourteenth Generation

8192. **Hugo De Blackiston** born about 1290 in Durham, England. He died after 1341 at the age of 51 in Durham, England. bought land of Richard del Park 1341. Surtees' History of Durham Vol. iii, pp 162f, 402 Cecilia Fitz-Ralfe and Hugo De Blackiston were married.

8193. Cecilia Fitz-Ralfe born about 1295 in Durham, England. She died in Durham, England.

8194. William De Washington was born before 1295. He died after 1345 at the age of 50. also called Wessington. Alice and William De Washington were married.

8195. Alice born about 1295.

8330. Robert Hilton born about 1275. Was siezed of the manors of Swine and Killome Robert Hilton was married.

8336. Geoffrey St. Quintin born about 1300. Foster Yorkshire Constable and Geoffrey St. Quintin were married.

8337. Constable born about 1290.

8338. Marmaduke Thweng born about 1300 of Over Helmsley. He died after 1369 at the age of 69. Foster Yorkshire: called Sir Agnes Norton and Marmaduke Thweng were married about 1344.

8339. Agnes Norton born about 1300.

8344. William Gascoigne born about 1290 in Harewood, Yorkshire, England. He died in 1330 at the age of 40. Visitation of Yorkshire by Foster p. 238 Elizabeth dau and heir of William Bolton. Elizabeth Bolton and William Gascoigne were married.

8345. Elizabeth Bolton born about 1290.

8346. Nicholas Franke born about 1300. Katherine Ellis and Nicholas Franke were married.

8347. Katherine Ellis born about 1300.

8348. Robert Clitherow born about 1285. Sibell and Robert Clitherow were married.

8349. Sibell born about 1285.

8350. John Gras Knight born about 1285 in Essex, England. Knight during time of King Edward I. Pauline and John Gras Knight were married.

8351. Pauline born about 1285.

8388. John Lisle born about 1230. Surtees Durham John Lisle was married.

8392. Roger Fulthorpe Knight born about 1210. Roger Fulthorpe Knight was married.

8400. Thomas Carrow born about 1250. Thomas Carrow was married.

8432. Gilbert De Umfreyville Earl was born in 1244 of Angus. He died before 13 Oct 1307 at the age of 63. Charlemagne Desc: Also Weis AR, Earl of Angus. Burke EP: attained majority in 43 Hen III 1259, in 20 Edward I he was governor of the castle of Forfar and the whole territory of Angus in Scotland in right of his mother, Earl of Angus, died 1308 Elizabeth Comyn and Gilbert De Umfreyville Earl were married.

8433. Elizabeth Comyn born about 1244.

8464. Halnath De Halnaby was born before 1220. He died after 1286 at the age of 66. Halnath De Halnaby was married.

8480. Simon Pudsey born about 1300. Visitations of Yorkshire p. 284 Symon Pudsey, temp. E II m. Catherine. Catherine Bolton and Simon Pudsey were married.

8481. Catherine Bolton born about 1300.

8486. Christopher Sheffied born about 1300. Christopher Sheffied was married.

8544. John Darcy Baron born about 1290. Weis AR Baron of Knayth, Emmeline Heron and John Darcy Baron were married.

8545. Emmeline Heron born about 1290.

8546. Nicholas De Meinill Baron born about 1307. He died before 20 Nov 1341 at the age of 34. Weis AR 54-35, 88-32: natural son 1st Baron of Meinill of Whorlton Alice De Ros and Nicholas De Meinill Baron were married about 1329.

8547. **Alice De Ros** born about 1307. She died before 4 Jul 1344 at the age of 37. Weis AR:54-35 Under age in 1322.

Not possible for her to be daughter of Margaret due to chronology.

8552. **Henry De Grey Baron** was born on 28 Oct 1282 of Wilton. He died on 16 Dec 1342 at the age of 60. Anne Rockley and Henry De Grey Baron were married.

8553. **Anne Rockley** born about 1282. History of Rutland Baron Grey p 162f

8556. **Richard Talbot Baron** born about 1302. He died on 23 Oct 1356 at the age of 54. Weis AR Ancestor of the Earls of Shrewsbury per EP (Valence) Elizabeth Comyn and Richard Talbot Baron were married in 1325.

8557. **Elizabeth Comyn** was born on 1 Nov 1299. She died on 20 Nov 1372 at age of 73.

8558. **James Butler Earl** was born in 1305 of Carrick, Ireland. He died on 6 Jan 1337 or 6 Jan 1338 at the age of 32. created Earl of Ormond Oct 1328. Collins RA: 1st Earl of Ormonde, Chief Butler of Ireland AR7 7-30, 73-32 Eleanor De Bohun and James Butler Earl were married in 1327.

8559. **Eleanor De Bohun** born about 1310. She died on 7 Oct 1363 at the age of 53.

8560. **Henry Fitz Hugh** is the same as person number 4362.

8561. **Eve Bulmer** born about 1295.

8562. **Richard Fourneys** born about 1300. Richard Fourneys was married.

8564. **Geffrey Le Scrope** is the same as person number 4332.

8565. **Ivetta Of Ros** is the same as person number 4333.

8568. **John De Grey Baron** was born in 1273 of Rotherfield. He died on 17 Oct 1311 at the age of 38. History of Rutland, Baron of Rotherfield. son and heir age 24 23 Ed 1. dead 5 Ed 2. Margaret De Odingsells and John De Grey Baron were married.

8569. **Margaret De Odingsells** born about 1275. History of Rutland: dau and coheir of William

8570. **John De Marmion Lord** born about 1292. He died on 30 Apr 1335 at the age of 43. 2nd baron summon to parliament Dec 3 1326 to Apr 1 1335. engaged in the Scottish wars. History of Rutland: dau Avice m. John de Grey Maud Of Furnival and John De Marmion Lord were married.

8571. **Maud Of Furnival** born about 1295. She died after 1343 at the age of 48.

8572. **Hubert St. Quenton** born about 1295. succeeded his grandfather married by dispensation. Lora Fauconberg and Hubert St. Quenton were married.

8573. **Lora Fauconberg** born about 1295.

8574. **Warren D'Insula Lord** born about 1290. Lord of Lisle Warren D'Insula Lord was married.

8576. **Thomas Surteys Knight** was born in 1294 in Durham, England. He died about Mar 1345 at the age of 51 in Durham, England. son and heir of Dinsale, Knight age 24 12 Edward II, seneschal to Bishop bury 137. died before 13 Mar 1345. 12 Bury. widow Avice living. Avice and Thomas Surteys Knight were married.

8577. **Avice** born about 1295 in Durham, England. She died after 1345 at the age of 50 in Durham, England.

8640. **Humphrey Conyers Knight** born about 1235 of Bishopton. He died after 1270 at the age of 35. styled of Bishopton in grant of Robert son of Roger de Coigniers, of lands in Stainton granted to the Abbey of Rievaulx 1270.

8642. **Ralph De Cotam** born about 1250. Ralph De Cotam was married.

8648. **William De Aton** born about 1250. Isabel De Vere and William De Aton were married.

8649. Isabel De Vere born about 1250.

8652. Henry De Percy Knight born about 25 Mar 1273. He died in Oct 1314 at the age of 41. 9th Baron Percy, Knighted 1296, Member of Parliament 1299-1341, Baron of Alnwick, co. Northumberland 1309. Eleanor Fitz Alan and Henry De Percy Knight were married about 1298.

8653. Eleanor Fitz Alan born about 1284. She died in 1328 at the age of 44.

8654. Robert De Clifford Baron born about 1 Apr 1274. He died on 24 Jun 1314 at the age of 40 in Bannockburn, Scotland. He was buried in Shap Abbey, Westmoreland. Lord of Appleby, Westmoreland, Sheriff of Westmoreland 1291, Member of Parliament 1299-1313. History of Rutland: said Baron summoned to Parliament 29 Dec 28 Ed 1. Complete Peerage vol 3 p 290-291 succeeded grandfather in 1286 and 1291 part of moiety of mother's family. served in Scottish wars. First Lord Clifford, Lord of Appleby, Sheriff of Westmoreland, Justice in Eyre north of the Trent, Governor of Nottingham Castle, served in Parliament, killed at the Battle of Bannockburn. He Owned Skipton Castle. The history of the castle is inseparable from that of the Clifford family who were granted the property by Edward II in 1310, when Robert Clifford was appointed first Lord Clifford of Skipton and Guardian of Craven, the wide tract of countryside to the north and west of Skipton. The Clifford's Norman forebears took the name from Clifford Castle in Herefordshire which they also owned. Robert Clifford began heavily fortifying the castle, but he was killed at the Battle of Bannockburn in 1314 with his new stronghold barely completed. Maud De Clare and Robert De Clifford Baron were married on 13 Nov 1295.

8655. Maud De Clare born about 1275. She died on 1 Feb 1324 or 1 Feb 1325 at the age of 49. Complete Peerage vol 3 p 290-1 m2nd Robert de Welle who died 1320.

8664. William Le Scrope Knight was born before 1260. He died after 1303 at the age of 43. lands in Bolton, co York 1296 Constance Of Gillo and William Le Scrope Knight were married.

8665. Constance Of Gillo born about 1260.

8666. William De Ros born about 1230 of Igmanthorpe. He died about 28 May 1310 at the age of 80. 3rd son, served in Scotland 1257-1258, n Gascony 1294. of Igmanthorpe Eustache Fitz Hugh and William De Ros were married in 1268.

8667. Eustache Fitz Hugh born about 1250. widow of Sir Nicholas de Cauntelo

8672. John De Eure Knight born about 1275. He died in 1326 at the age of 51. Visitations of Yorkshire by Glover p. 610 Sir John de Eure, of Stokesley and Ingoldby, knighted before 1307. In 35 Ed. I he obtained a grant of free warren of his manor of Easby, and was sheriff of Yorkshire, 1309 to 1311. In the wars with the Scots, 8 (1314/5) and 12 (1318/9) Ed. II and died 20 Ed. II, 1326/7. Agnes married 2nd Sir Roger de Burton, knight.

8673. Agnes De Insula born about 1280.

8676. Robert De Clifford is the same as person number 8654.

8677. Maud De Clare is the same as person number 8655.

8678. Maurice Berkeley Lord born about Apr 1281. He died on 31 May 1326 at the age of 45 in Wallingford. Complete Peerage vol 3 p 291 MCS4 88-5 Lord of Berkeley Castle Eve La Zouche and Maurice Berkeley Lord were married in 1289.

8679. Eve La Zouche born about 1280. She died on 5 Dec 1314 at the age of 34.

8704. Adam Bowes Knight born about 1275 of Richmond. He died after 1346 at the age of 71. Durham vol 4 p 107 styled of Richmond, Chief Justice of the Court of Common.

Pleas by patent, 1331, steward of Richmondshire, Lord of Streatlam in right of his wife 28 Mar 1346 Alice Trayne and Adam Bowes Knight were married.

8705. **Alice Trayne** born about 1275 of Streatlam.

8706. **John Lilburne Knight** born about 1275 of Lilburne, Northumberland, England. Durham vol 4 p 107 John Lilburne Knight was married.

8720. **Robert Fitz Ralph** born about 1270. He died in Apr 1317 at the age of 47. Elizabeth and Robert Fitz Ralph were married.

8721. **Elizabeth** born about 1270. She died about 1346 at the age of 76. Livery was given to her grandson for lands belonging to her husband.

8722. **Hugh De Audley Ambassador** born about 1270. Weis 207-31 2nd husband Isolde De Mortimer and Hugh De Audley Ambassador were married.

8723. **Isolde De Mortimer** born about 1283. She died in 1338 at the age of 55. Weis 207-31 2nd husband Hugh, 1st husband Walter de Balun. She is dau. of Edmund Mortimer but her mother would be very young.

8724. **Hugh Fitz Henry** born about 1260. He died on 12 Mar 1304 at the age of 44 in Berwick On Tees. He was buried in Romaldkirk Ch, Richmondshire. 2nd son Aubrey and Hugh Fitz Henry were married.

8725. **Aubrey** born about 1270. She died about 25 Jan 1302–25 Jan 1303 at the age of 32. She was buried in Jervaulx Abbey. called Albreda in Knight of Edward I.

8732. **Guy De Beauchamp Earl** was born in 1278 of Warwick. He died on 10 Aug 1315 at the age of 37 in Warwick Castle. Weis 86-30 knighted 25 Mar 1296, will made Jul 25 1315. 10th Earl of Warwick Alice De Toeni and Guy De Beauchamp Earl were married on 12 Feb 1309.

8733. **Alice De Toeni** born about 1283. She died on 1 Jan 1324 or 1 Jan 1325 at the age of 41. Weis 86-30, 98-31 widow of Thomas Leybourne. 2nd Guy Beauchamp 3rd William Zouche

8734. **Roger De Mortimer Baron** was born on 25 Apr 1287 of Wigmore. He died on 29 Nov 1330 at the age of 43 in Tyburn, England. History of Rutland p 42 Baron of Wigmore, created Earl of March. hanged on the eve of St. Andrew Weis 27-31 created Earl of March Oct 1328. Complete Peerage vol 3 p 292 1st Earl of March Weis 120-33. He was the lover of the Queen Isabella of England and helped depose the King Edward II her husband. A Marcher Lord who supported the Earl of Lancaster's fight against Edward II. After the battle of Boroughbridge and the defeat of Lancaster, Mortimer was arrested and sent to the Tower of London. After the Parliament at York in May 1322 many of the Lancastrian rebels were executed as traitors but some including Mortimer were spared, but remained in prison. In late 1323 Mortimer was able to escape from the Tower by offering his guards large amounts of liquor and climbing down a rope. He fled to France where he joined Queen Isabella's cause against her husband and the Despensers. In 1326, Isabella and Mortimer, now her lover sailed to England. Edward had to flee from London whose inhabitants were against him and who welcomed Isabella. Isabella and Mortimer chased Edward to Bristol. Edward II was forced to abdicate and his son Edward III became king. In 1330 when the new King was old enough to reign in his own right he arrested Mortimer for the crimes against his father and Mortimer was executed. Joan De Geneville and Roger De Mortimer Baron were married before 6 Oct 1306.

8735. **Joan De Geneville** was born on 2 Feb 1285 or 2 Feb 1286. She died on 19 Oct 1356 at the age of 71. History of Rutland p 42, Weis 27-31, 71-32

8752. **John Willoughby Lord** was born on 6 Jan 1303 or 6 Jan 1304 in Eresby Manor, Lincolnshire, England. He died on 13 Jun 1349 at the age of 46. CP John Willoughby Lord b. 6 Jan 1303/4 Knight Banneret 20 Jan 1326/7, m. bef 2 Jul 1323 Joan dau of Peter Roscalyn of Edgefield, Norfolk. he died 13 June 1349 age 45 buried Spilsby, Lincolnshire. His widow m bef 24 June 1351 William de Swinithwaite. She was living 15 Oct 1354. Joan Roscelyn and John Willoughby Lord were married before 2 Jul 1323.

8753. **Joan Roscelyn** born about 1303. She died after Oct 1354 at the age of 51.

8754. **Robert De Ufford Earl** born about 1300. Earl of Suffolk Margaret Norwich and Robert De Ufford Earl were married.

8755. **Margaret Norwich** born about 1300.

8756. **William Skipwith** born about 1300. CP refers to Early York Charters 9 p 138 Margaret Simones and William Skipwith were married.

8757. **Margaret Simones** born about 1300.

8758. **William Hiltoft** born about 1300 in Ingoldwells, Lincolnshire, England. William Hiltoft was married.

8760. **John VI Strange Lord** born about 1282. He died before 6 Feb 1310 at the age of 28. CP 12 p 353 John VI Lord Strange son and heir aged 27 at his father's death. He married Iselt. He died on or before 6 Feb 1310/1. His widow was living 18 May 1324. Iselt and John VI Strange Lord were married.

8761. **Iselt** born about 1282.

8764. **Richard Fitz Alan Earl** was born on 3 Feb 1266 or 3 Feb 1267. He died on 9 Mar 1301 or 9 Mar 1302 at the age of 35. 7th earl of arundel Alasia De Saluzzo and Richard Fitz Alan Earl were married about 1284.

8765. **Alasia De Saluzzo** born about 1266. She died on 25 Sep 1292 at the age of 26.

8766. **William De Plantagenet Warenne** born about 1256. He died in 1286 at the age of 30. Joan De Vere and William De Plantagenet Warenne were married in 1283.

8767. **Joan De Vere** born about 1266.

8836. **William De Ros Baron** born about 1285 of Helmsley. He died on 3 Feb 1342 or 3 Feb 1343 at the age of 57. 2nd Lord Ros of Helmsley, Sheriff of Yorkshire MCS4 1-5 says he died abt Aug 1, 1359. Weis 54-34, 89-31 Margaret De Badlesmere and William De Ros Baron were married before 25 Nov 1326.

8837. **Margaret De Badlesmere** was born on 3 Dec 1314. She died on 18 Oct 1363 at the age of 48. Weis 54-34 Margary de Badlesmere b. 1306 d. 18 Oct 1363 m. bef 25 Nov 1326 William de Ros. MCS4 2-6 John de Tybetot Lord Tybetot b. 20 July 1313 d. 13 Apr 1367 m. first (as her 2nd husband) Margaret de Badlesmere

8838. **Ralph De Stafford Earl** was born on 24 Sep 1301. He died on 31 Aug 1372 at the age of 70 in Tumbridge Castle, Kent, England. He was buried in Tonbridge, Kent. Complete Peerage vol 3 p 292 first Earl of Stafford created on Mar. 5, 1350/1. 2nd Lord Stafford. Baron of Stafford AR 55-32, 9-31 Margaret De Audley and Ralph De Stafford Earl were married before 6 Jul 1336.

8839. **Margaret De Audley** born about 1318. She died on 16 Sep 1348 at the age of 30. She was buried in Tonbridge, Kent. AR 9-31, 55-32 his second wife. She was aged 18 before 1343. She was 12 when Ralph kidnapped and married her.

8840. **Henry De Percy** was born in 1320. He died on 18 May 1368 at the age of 48. Weis 19-30 fought at Crecy 26 Aug 1346 Mary Plantagenet and Henry De Percy were married in Sep 1334.

8841. **Mary Plantagenet** was born in 1320. She died on 1 Sep 1362 at the age of 42. Weis 19-30 14 when married

8842. **Ralph De Neville Baron** born about 1291 of Raby, Durham, England. He died on 5 Aug 1367 at the age of 76. He was buried in Durham Chapel, Durham, England. Weis 207-32, 186-5 Alice De Audley and Ralph De Neville Baron were married about 14 Jan 1326–14 Jan 1327.

8843. **Alice De Audley** is the same as person number 4361.

8844. **Roger De Mortimer Earl** was born on 11 Nov 1328 of March, Ludlow. He died on 26 Feb 1359 at the age of 30. History of Rutland p 42 Philippa Montacute and Roger De Mortimer Earl were married.

8845. **Philippa Montacute** born about 1330. She died on 5 Jan 1381 or 5 Jan 1382 at the age of 51.

8846. **Lionel Plantagenet Duke** was born on 29 Nov 1338 in Antwerp, Of Clarence. He died on 17 Oct 1368 at the age of 29 in Alba, Italy. History of Rutland p 42 AR 5-31 Lionel of Antwerp, Duke of Clarence. It is through him and his brother Edmund's children that the Yorkist line of the War of the Roses was formed. Elizabeth Burgh and Lionel Plantagenet Duke were married in 1352.

8847. **Elizabeth Burgh** was born on 6 Jul 1332. She died on 10 Dec 1363 at the age of 31.

8848. **William Dacre Lord** born about 1319. He died on 18 Jul 1361 at the age of 42. He was buried in Lanercost Priory. CP 4 p. 3 William De Dacre Lord Dacre son and heir age 20 or more at his father's death. He was at the battle of Neville's Cross 17 oct. 1346. Appointed Sheriff of Co. Dumfries 30 Jan. 1346/7. He married Katherine 2nd dau of Sir Ralph de Neville of Raby Co Durham by Alice dau of Sir Hugh d'Audley. He died s.p. 18 July 1361 and was buried in Lancercost Priory. Will date 29 Sep 1359 pr. at Rose 16 Aug 1361. His wife or widow died bef. 1 Sep 1361. Catherine Neville and William Dacre Lord were married.

8849. **Catherine Neville** born about 1319.

8852. **Sir James Douglas 6th Lord Douglas** born about 1290. He died in 1330 at the age of 40. He was also known as Good Sir Douglas. CP He was called the Good Sir James Douglas died 1330 Lord of Douglas. He was not an Earl. He was slain 25 Aug 1330. Signer of the Declaration of Arbroath. Sir James Douglas (also known as Good Sir James and the Black Douglas) He was one of the chief commanders during the Wars of Scottish Independence.

8854. **Thomas Murray**. Thomas Murray was married.

8856. **Ralph De Neville** is the same as person number 8842.

8857. **Alice De Audley** is the same as person number 4361.

8858. **Henry De Percy** is the same as person number 4326.

8859. **Idoine De Clifford** is the same as person number 4327.

8860. **Ralph De Stafford** is the same as person number 8838.

8861. **Margaret De Audley** is the same as person number 8839.

8862. **Thomas Beauchamp** is the same as person number 4366.

8863. **Catherine De Mortimer** is the same as person number 4367.

8904. **Gilbert Umfreyville** Gilbert Umfreyville was married.

8906. **John De La Hurne Sir**. Margaret Fitz John and John De La Hurne Sir were married.

8907. **Margaret Fitz John**

8912. **Roger De Beauchamp Baron** born about 1315. He died on 3 Jan 1379 or 3 Jan 1380 at the age of 64. Sybil De Patshull and Roger De Beauchamp Baron were married before 1336.

8913. **Sybil De Patshull** born about 1316. She died after 26 Oct 1351 at the age of 35. Weis 85-31, CP vol 2 p 45

8920. **Robert De Holand Lord** born about 1283. He died on 7 Oct 1328 at the age of 45. He was buried in Preston, Lancaster County, England. Maud La Zouche and Robert De Holand Lord were married before 1309.

8921. **Maud La Zouche** was born in 1289. She died on 31 May 1349 at the age of 60. AR7 32-30 Maud La Zouche b. 1289 d. 31 May 1349 m. by 1309/10 Sir Robert de Holand of Upholland, co. Lancaster b. ca 1283 d 7 Oct 1328 bureid at Preston, co. Lancaster, first Lord Holland M.P. 1314-1321, son of Sir Robert de Holand and Elizabeth de Samlesbury CP VI 528-531, XII 1 558 footnote c, p. 588, NGSQ 60-25-26).

8922. **Edmund Of Woodstock Earl** was born on 5 Aug 1301 of Kent. He died on 19 Mar 1330 at the age of 28. AR7 155-31 Edmund of Woodstock, Earl of Kent b. 5 Aug 1301, beheaded 19 Mar 1330 m. 1327 Margaret Wake by whom he left a dau Joan Fair Maid of Kent his eventual Heiress. Margaret Wake and Edmund Of Woodstock Earl were married about 25 Dec 1325.

8923. **Margaret Wake** born about 1299. She died on 29 Sep 1349 at the age of 50. AR7 236-11 Margaret Wake b. ca 1299 d. 29 Sep 1349 m. John Comyn of Badenoch d.s.p. 24 Jun 1314 m2nd Edmund of Woodstock.

8924. **Edward III Of England King** was born on 13 Nov 1312 in Windsor, Windsor Castle, London, England. He died on 21 Jun 1377 at the age of 64 at Sheen in Richmond, Surrey, England. He was buried in Westminster. AR 5-30, 1-30 King of England 1327-1377. Edward was made king at age 14. He imprisoned his mother Isabella and had her lover Roger Mortimor executed. He defeated the Scottish army at Halidon Hill in 1333. He started 100 Years War with France in 1337 to claim the French throne which later involved Joan of Arc who was martyred. David II of Scotland invades England but is defeated at Neville's Cross in 1346. He started the Order of the Garter in 1348. Plague of 1349-50. He had 13 children, including his son Edward the Black Prince. It is his descendants that start the War of the Roses by son John Gaunt (Lancastrians) and through Lionel of Clarence and Edmund of York (Yorkist). Philippa Of Hainaut and Edward III Of England King were married on 24 Jan 1328 in York, Westminster, York, England.

8925. **Philippa Of Hainaut** was born on 24 Jun 1311 in Hainault, Belgium. She died on 15 Aug 1369 at the age of 58 in Windsor Castle, Berkshire, England. She was buried in Westminster. AR 1-30, 103-34

8926. **Henry Of Grosmont Duke** born about 1300. He died in 1361 at the age of 61. He was the Duke of Lancaster, Steward of England. AR7 72-33 Isabel De Beaumont and Henry Of Grosmont Duke were married about 1337.

8927. **Isabel De Beaumont** born about 1310. She died after 1361 at the age of 51.

8984. **Robert De Ferrers Sir** was born on 25 Mar 1309. He died on 28 Aug 1350 at the age of 41. AR 61-32 His first wife was Margaret.

8985. **Joan De La Mote** born about 1320. She died on 29 Jun 1375 at the age of 55. She was 2nd wife.

8986. William Le Botiller Lord was born before 1331 of Oversley. He died on 14 Aug 1369 at the age of 38. AR 77-33 Lord of Wem and Oversley Elizabeth Holand and William Le Botiller Lord were married before Jul 1343.

8987. Elizabeth Holand born about 1331.

8990. Paon Roet Sir born about 1325 in Gascony. His dau. Philippe de Roet was the wife of poet Geoffrey Chaucer. Paon Roet Sir was married.

8992. William Constable born about 1300. Visitations Of Yorkshire by Glover p. 178 William Constable m. dau of Lord Fitz Hugh, son of Marmaduke Constable. Visitations by Yorkshire by Glover p 197 William Constable son of Robert Constable 17 Ed. III, son of Robert 13 Ed. II,

8993. Fitz Hugh born about 1310.

8994. William Skipwith is the same as person number 8756.

8998. William Argum born about 1310. William Argum was married.

9004. John Mowbray born about 1285. Margaret Percy and John Mowbray were married.

9005. Margaret Percy born about 1285.

9006. Henry Monaster born about 1280. Henry Monaster was married.

9008. John Wentworth born about 1310. Bisset and John Wentworth were married.

9009. Bisset born about 1310.

9010. William Dransfield born about 1310. William Dransfield was married.

9016. Philip Le Despenser was born on 6 Apr 1313 in Lincoln County, England. He died on 22 Aug 1349 at the age of 36. Joan De Cobham and Philip Le Despenser were married.

9017. Joan De Cobham born about 1313. She died about 15 May 1357 at the age of 44.

9020. John De Tybetot Lord was born on 20 Jul 1313. He died on 13 Apr 1367 at the age of 53. MCS4 2-6 John de Tybetot Lord Tybetot b. 20 July 1313 d. 13 Apr 1367 m. first (as her 2nd husband) Margaret de Badlesmere b. 3 Dec 1344 - 4 Dec 1347 dau of Bartholomew de Badlesmere and Margaret de Clare. Margaret De Badlesmere and John De Tybetot Lord were married after 1342.

9021. Margaret De Badlesmere is the same as person number 8837.

9022. William Deincourt Lord born about 1300. He died on 2 Jun 1364 at the age of 64. MCS4 74-6 Milicent la Zouche d. 22 Jun 1379 m. bef 26 Mar. 1326 Sir William Deincourt of Blankney, Co. Lincoln 2nd Lord Deincourt d. June 2 1364. MCS4 149A-6 Sir William Deincourt 2nd Lord deincourt age 26+ in 1326/7 d. 2 June 1364 m. bef 26 Mar 1326 Milicent la Zouche d. 22 June 1379 dau of Sir William by Maud Lovel dau of John Lovel, 1st Lord Lovel of Titchmarsh by his 1st wife Isabel de Bois. Milicent La Zouche and William Deincourt Lord were married before 26 Mar 1326.

9023. Milicent La Zouche born about 1300. She died on 22 Jun 1379 at the age of 79.

9024. Hugh Hastings born about 1308. CP Hastings of Sutton Scotney. 2nd son of John 1st Lord by 2nd wife Isabel m. bef 18 May 1330 Margary sister of Richard Foliot of Gressenhall dau of Sir Richard Foliet by Joan dau of William de Breouse, Lord of Bramber and Gower (Lord Breouse). He died 29 or 30 July 1347. buried Elsing Church Norfolk. Margary Foliet and Hugh Hastings were married.

9025. Margary Foliet born about 1310.

9028. Edward Le Despenser Knight born about 1310. He died on 30 Sep 1342 at the age of 32 in Morlaix. PA1 Clare 10 Edward Le Despenser Knight of Buckland, co Buckingham, Eyworth, Co. Bedford, West Winterslow, Co. Wilts, Essendine, Rutland, etc. 2nd son was married by Groby, Co. Leicester on 20 Apr. 1335 to Anne de Ferrers, dau of William Ferrers, Knight of Groby by Ellen possible dau of John Seagrave. She died on 8 Aug. 1367. Sir Edward was slain at Morlaix on 30 Sep. 1342 v.f. MCS4 14-7 Sir Edward Despenser d. 30 Sep 1342 m. Groby, 20 Apr 1335, Anne de Ferrers d. 8 Aug. 1337 dau of William Ferrers. Anne De Ferrers and Edward Le Despenser Knight were married on 20 Apr 1335.

9029. **Anne De Ferrers** born about 1310. She died on 8 Aug 1367 at the age of 57.

9030. **Bartholomew De Burghersh Knight** born about 1330. He died on 5 Apr 1369 at the age of 39. MCS4 13-8 Bartholomew de Burghersh, K.G. age 26+ at father's death d. 5 Apr 1369, Lord Burghersh, fought at Crecy, an original Knight of the Garter m. 1 act 10 May 1335 Ciceley, living aug. 1354, dau of Richard de Weyland m2nd bef Aug. 1366 Margaret widow of John de Loveyne d. 1 Jul 1393. Ciceley Weyland and Bartholomew De Burghersh Knight were married about 10 May 1335.

9031. **Ciceley Weyland** born about 1310. She died after Aug 1354 at the age of 44.

9032. **John De Dinham** was born on 14 Sep 1295 in Nutwell, Devon, England. He died before 14 Apr 1332 at the age of 36. MCS4 125-6, AR7 214-32 His ancestry in CP 4 p. 372. Margaret De Botreaux and John De Dinham were married.

9033. **Margaret De Botreaux** born about 1300. She died on 28 Nov 1361 at the age of 61.

9034. **Thomas De Courtenay Sir** born about 1300. MCS4 125-5 Muriel Moels and Thomas De Courtenay Sir were married.

9035. **Muriel Moels** born about 1322.

9040. **William Morley Lord** was born on 24 Jun 1319. He died on 30 Apr 1379 at the age of 59 in Hallingbury, Essex, England. He was buried at Austin's Friars in Norwich, England. CP William 3rd Lord b. 24 Jun 1319 Barony of Marshal from mother m. by 6 Mar. 1344/5 Cecily dau of Thomas Bardolph (Lord Bardolph). He died 30 Apr 1379 at Hallingbury Essex and buried Austin's Friars Church at Norwich. will date 26 Apr 1379 pro. 6 Feb 1379/80. widow had dower. She di. 23 or 25 Nov. 1386 and buried with him. will date 20 Sep 1386 pro. 7 Feb 1386/7. Cecily Bardolph and William Morley Lord were married before 6 Mar 1344.

9041. **Cecily Bardolph** born about 1320. She died on 23 Apr 1379 at the age of 59. She was buried at Austin's Friars in Norwich, England.

9050. **John Wingfield Knight** born about 1320 in Wingfield Manor, England. He died in 1361 at the age of 41 in Wingfield Manor, England. History of Rutland p. 65 Sir John Wingfield Knight in Suffolk 1330 and 1358 (In 1358 John Wingfield and his wife Alianore settled the Netherhall Manor in Salingham in Norfolk on themselves in tail, remainder to Catharine wife of Sir Michael de la Pole, Knight remainder to Thomas Wingfield and William Wingfield brothers of Sir John.

9051. **Alianore De Glanville** born about 1320. She died after 1362 at the age of 42. History of Rutland p. 65 Alianore dau of Sir Gilbert de Glanville living 1362.

9068. **Thomas Barden** born about 1300.

9069. **Elizabeth Mauduit** born about 1300.

9070. **Thomas Thirkell** born about 1300. Thomas Thirkell was married.

9072. **William Clarell** born about 1300. He died in 1332 at the age of 32.

9073. **Agnes Waleis** born about 1300.

9074. **John St. Philibert Sir** born about 1300. John St. Philibert Sir was married.

9076. **Robert Reygate** born about 1300. Elizabeth and Robert Reygate were married.

9077. **Elizabeth** born about 1300.

9078. **William De Funtaynes** born about 1300. of Co. Linc.

9084. **Godfrey Foljambe** born about 1316. He died about 1377 at the age of 61.

9085. **Avena Ireland** born about 1316.

9104. **Edmund Fitz Alan** is the same as person number 4382.

9105. **Alice De Warenne** is the same as person number 4383.

9106. **Henry Lancaster Earl** born about 1285. He died on 22 Sep 1345 at the age of 60. Weis 17-29, 19-29, Created Earl of Lancaster Maud De Chaworth and Henry Lancaster Earl were married in 1298.

9107. **Maud De Chaworth** born about 1281. She died after 1345 at the age of 64. Weis 17-29, 72-32

9108. **John Maltravers** born about 1290. He died on 16 Feb 1363 or 16 Feb 1364 at the age of 73. Milicent Berkeley and John Maltravers were married about 1313.

9109. **Milicent Berkeley** born about 1299. She died after 1322 at the age of 23.

9122. **William De Ros** is the same as person number 8836.

9123. **Margary de Baldesmere**.

9124. **John Mowbray Baron** was born on 29 Nov 1310 in Hovringham, Yorkshire, England. He died on 4 Oct 1361 at the age of 50 in York, England. 3rd Baron Mowbray Joan Of Lancaster and John Mowbray Baron were married on 28 Feb 1326 or 28 Feb 1327.

9125. **Joan Of Lancaster** born about 1310. She died on 7 Jul 1349 at the age of 39.

9126. **John Seagrave Lord** born about 1320. He died on 20 Mar 1353 at the age of 33. Margaret Of Norfolk and John Seagrave Lord were married.

9127. **Margaret Of Norfolk** born about 1320. She died on 24 Mar 1398 or 24 Mar 1399 at the age of 78.

12292. **Reginald Clifford** was born in 1248. He died in 1324 at the age of 76.

12416. **Nicholas Pointz**. Elizabeth Dyall and Nicholas Pointz were married.

12417. **Elizabeth Dyall**.

12418. **William Paveley** was born before 1230.

12432. **Nicholas Fitz Randolph** was born on 6 Dec 1261 in Nymphsfield, Gloucestershire, England. He died about 1312 at the age of 51.

12936. **Hugh De Courtenay Sir** was born on 25 Mar 1248 or 25 Mar 1249 of Oakhampton. He died on 28 Feb 1291 or 28 Feb 1292 at the age of 42. MCS4 124-3 Earl of Devon Eleanor Le Despenser and Hugh De Courtenay Sir were married.

12937. **Eleanor Le Despenser** born about 1255. She died on 30 Sep 1328 at the age of 73.

12938. **John De St. John** born about 1250. Alice and John De St. John were married.

12939. **Alice** born about 1250.

12940. **Humphrey VII De Bohun Earl** born about Sep 1248 of Hereford. He died on 31 Dec 1298 at the age of 50 in Pleshey. Weis AR: Earl of Hereford and Essex, Constable of England Maud De Fiennes and Humphrey VII De Bohun Earl were married in 1275.

12941. **Maud De Fiennes** born about 1250.

12942. **Edward I of England King** was born on 17 Jun 1239 in Westminster, London, Westminster, England. He died on 7 Jul 1307 at the age of 68 in Burgh, Burgh On Sands, Cumbria, England. He was also known as Longshanks England. Edward was buried in Westminster. He was nicknamed Longshanks because he was 6 feet tall. He went on a Crusade in 1270-1273. He hears that his father dies and he is made king. He returns to England in 1274. He is crowned Aug 19 1274. Edward invades north Wales to compel Prince Llywelyn to pay homage to him in 1277. He again invades in 1282 and later Llywelyn is killed. He makes Wales part of his kingdom and names his son as Prince of Wales in 1301. He picks John Baliol to be King of Scotland. When Balliol is asked to invade France with Edward, he sides with French and Edward invades Scotland. He defeats the Scots and takes the Stone of Scone to Westminster. In 1297 the Scots rise against English with William Wallace and defeat Edward at the Battle of Stirling Bridge in 1297. Edward invades Scotland again in 1298 and defeats William Wallace at the Battle of Falkirk. Wallace is betrayed and executed in London in 1305. Robert Bruce takes over leadership of Scottish resistance and is crowned King in 1306. Edward invades again in 1307 but dies on way. He expelled all Jews from England in 1290. He was given the nickname "Hammer of the Scots" as he tried to unite the two kingdoms. (A story about his encounters with William Wallace were made into a movie starring Mel Gibson called Braveheart.) AR7 1-28, 6-28 Crusader to the Holy Land. Eleanor Of Castile Princess and Edward I of England King were married on 18 Oct 1254 in Las Huegas, Castile, Burgos, Spain.

12943. **Eleanor Of Castile Princess** was born in 1246 in Castile. She died on 28 Nov 1290 at the age of 44 in Grantham, Lincolnshire, Nottinghamshire, England. She was buried in Westminster Abb., London, England. Edward was very much in love with Eleanor and when she died her body was brought to Westminster Abbey. At 12 places where the cortege stopped, Edward erected a memorial.

Fifteenth Generation

16386. **Ralfe Fitz-Ralfe** born about 1270. Ralfe Fitz-Ralfe was married.

16388. **Walter De Washington** was born before 1270. He died after 1315 at the age of 45.

16672. **Galfrid St. Quintin** born about 1280. Alice Ros and Galfrid St. Quintin were married.

16673. **Alice Ros** born about 1280. Foster Yorkshire

16674. **Robert Constable Knight** born about 1250 of Flamborough. Foster Yorkshire Katherine Mauley and Robert Constable Knight were married.

16675. **Katherine Mauley** born about 1260.

16676. **Edmund De Thwenge Sir** born about 1280. He died on 15 Oct 1344 at the age of 64. Isabel Constable and Edmund De Thwenge Sir were married.

16677. **Isabel Constable** born about 1280. She died in 1346 at the age of 66. She was buried in Flamborough.

16688. **William Gascoigne** born about 1250 in Harewood, Yorkshire, England. He died in 1270 at the age of 20. This is a large gap in the line here, may be a generation missing. Visitation of Yorkshire p. 238 William Gascoigne of Harewood, Co. York m. Maude dau and heir of John Gawthorpe of Gawthorpe. Maud Gawthorpe and William Gascoigne were married in Harewood, Yorkshire, England.

16689. **Maud Gawthorpe** born about 1250.

16690. **William Bolton** born about 1260. William Bolton was married.

16696. **Adam Clitherow** born about 1260. Adam Clitherow was married.

16784. **Alan Fulthorpe Lord** born about 1190. Alan Fulthorpe Lord was married.

16800. **John Carrow** born about 1215. John Carrow was married.

16864. **Gilbert De Umfreyville Baron** born about 1210 of Prudhoe. He died in 1245 at the age of 35. Charlemagne Desc: Also Weis AR: Baron of Prudhoe by 1st wife Burke EP: married 1243 died 1245. son and heir of tender years Maud Of Angus Countess and Gilbert De Umfreyville Baron were married in 1243.

16865. **Maud Of Angus Countess** born about 1210. Weis AR: Countess of Angus. Burke EP: Countess of Angus, son was Earl of Angus in right of his mother Maud.

16866. **Alexander Comyn Earl** born about 1220 of Buchan. He died about Apr 1290 at the age of 70. Weis AR: Earl of Buchan, Constable of Scotland and Justiciar Burke EP: dau Agnes wife of Gilbert Umfraville.

16867. **Elizabeth De Quincy** born about 1220. She died before Nov 1328 at the age of 108. Weis AR: 3rd dau

16928. **Acharis De Halnaby** was born before 1195. Acharis De Halnaby was married.

16962. **John De Bolton** born about 1275. John De Bolton was married.

17090. **Walter Heron** born about 1270 of Hedlestone, Northumberland.

17091. **Alice De Hastings** born about 1270. Weis AR

17092. **Nicholas De Meinill Lord** was born on 6 Dec 1274. Weis AR: 2nd Lord Meinill of Whorlton Lucy De Thwenge and Nicholas De Meinill Lord were married.

17093. **Lucy De Thwenge** was born on 24 Mar 1278 or 24 Mar 1279 in Kilton Castle. She died on 8 Jan 1346 or 8 Jan 1347 at the age of 67. Weis AR: not married to Nicholas, natural dau of Robert

17094. **William De Ros** is the same as person number 8836.

17104. **John Grey Lord** born about 1267 in Wilton. He died in 1323 at the age of 56. of Wilton 2nd Lord Grey History of Rutland age 40 in 1307

17105. **Anne De Ferrers** born about 1267. of Groby History of Rutland 1st wife

17106. **Richard Rockley** born about 1260. History of Rutland Baron Grey p 162f

17107. **Isabella De Clare** born about 1260.

17112. **Gilbert Talbot Lord** was born on 18 Oct 1276. He died on 24 Feb 1345 or 24 Feb 1346 at the age of 68. AR7 84a-30 1st Lord Talbot of Eccleswall, Co. Hereford.

17113. **Anne Boteler** born about 1276. said to be daughter of William Botiler of Wem, Sakop Co.

17114. **John Comyn Lord** born about 1279 of Badenock. He died in 1306 at the age of 27. Weis AR: Lord of Badenock, called the Red Comyn/

17115. **Joan De Valence** born about 1265.

17116. **Edmund Le Boteler Earl** born about 1285 of Carrick, Ireland. He died on 13 Sep 1321 at the age of 36 in London, England. Weis AR: Justiciar and Governor of Ireland, Castle and Manors of Karryk Macgriffyn and Roscnea, Lord of Arklow. Joan Fitz Thomas and Edmund Le Boteler Earl were married in 1302.

17117. **Joan Fitz Thomas** born about 1285.

17118. **Humphrey VIII De Bohun** is the same as person number 6470.

17119. **Elizabeth Plantagenet** is the same as person number 6471.

17122. **John De Bulmer Knight** born about 1260. He died before 4 Dec 1299 at the age of 39. He was buried in Wilton Church. of Wilton in Cleveland and Bulmer, Yorkshire.

17123. **Theophania De Morwick** was born in 1253. She died before 28 Aug 1315 at the age of 62. She was buried in Wilton Church. age 15 in 1268, 61 in 1315

17136. **Robert De Grey Baron** born about 1250 of Rotherfield. He died before 27 May 1295 at the age of 45. of Rotherfield, Somerton, and Hardwick, Co Oxford, Sulcoates and Kettlewell, Co York. History of Rutland: son and heir ob. 23 Ed 1.

17137. **Joan De Valoines** born about 1250. She died before 12 Nov 1312 at the age of 62. History of Rutland: wife said to be Avice dau of William de St. Liz (Lice)

17138. **William De Odingsells** born about 1250. He died in 1294 at the age of 44. of Maxtoke, co Warwick. Ela Fitz Robert and William De Odingsells were married.

17139. **Ela Fitz Robert** born about 1250. History of Rutland: dau and coheir

17140. **John De Marmion Baron** born about 1270. He died before 7 Mar 1322 at the age of 52. Baron de Marmion. M.P. 1313-1322

17141. **Isabel** born about 1270.

17142. **Thomas Furnival Lord** born about 1261. He died in 1332 at the age of 71. Burkes EP p 1056-7 had livery 1281 parliament 1295-1331 First Lord Joan Despenser and Thomas Furnival Lord were married before Jan 1292.

17143. **Joan Despenser** born about 1263. not listed in History of Rutland p 19

17144. **Hubert St. Quenton** born about 1270. He died before 1303 at the age of 33. died in lifetime of father Anastasia Maltravers and Hubert St. Quenton were married.

17145. **Anastasia Maltravers** born about 1270.

17146. **William Fauconberg Lord** born about 1270. Lord of Skelton William Fauconberg Lord was married.

17152. **Nicholas Surteys** was born in 1265 in Durham, England. He died in 1318 at the age of 53 in Durham, England. son and heir age 8y 2 Edward I, died seised of North Gosford and third part of Ryehill in Tindale Ward. Inq. p.m. 12 Edward II 1318.

17153. **Isabella Fishburne** born about 1270 in Durham, England. She died after 1344 at the age of 74 in Durham, England. said to be sister of Sir. Thomas Fishburne but in another record said to be daughter of Sir Thomas who was living 1313.

17280. **John Conyers Lord** born about 1190 of Sockbourne. He died after 1238 at the age of 48. son and heir of Jeffrey. living 23 Hen III had the manor of Sockburne, Bishopton, Stainton, Auckland, etc. confirmed to him by fine from his cousin Roger Conyers of Hoton Conyers John Conyers Lord was married.

17296. **William De Aton Lord** born about 1225. Lord of Aton William De Aton Lord was married.

17298. **Adam De Vere** born about 1225. Burke CP: dau Isabel said to marry Gilbert de Aton. her father said to be Simon de Vere of Goxhill co Lincoln and Sproatley in Holderness and her mother was Ada Bertram coheir of Roger Bertram of Mitford. Simon married 1st and had heir Simon Jr. and Simon Sr. had brother Roger de Vere.

17299. **Ada De Bertram** born about 1225. youngest dau and coheir

17304. **Henry De Percy Knight** born about 1235. He died on 29 Aug 1272 at the age of 37. 7th Baron of Percy, knighted 1257 Eleanor De Warenne and Henry De Percy Knight were married on 8 Sep 1268 in York, England, York, England.

17305. **Eleanor De Warenne** was born in 1251. She died after 1282 at the age of 31.

17306. **Richard Fitz Alan** is the same as person number 8764.

17307. **Alasia De Saluzzo** is the same as person number 8765.

17308. **Roger De Clifford** born about 1240. He died on 6 Nov 1282 at the age of 42 in Menai Straits. drowned, died in lifetime of father History of Rutland: killed in Wales Complete Peerage vol 3 p 290 Isabel Vespont and Roger De Clifford were married in 1269.

17309. **Isabel Vespont** was born in 1254. She died on 14 May 1292 at the age of 38. Lady of Appleby and Broughham. History of Rutland: Lady of Essedine Complete Peerage vol 3 p 290 sister of Richard Fitz John and his heir

17310. **Thomas De Clare Earl** born about 1248 of Incheguin. He died on 29 Aug 1287 at the age of 39 in Ireland. Complete Peerage vol 3 p 291 Collins RA: Governor of London, Lord of Inchequin and Youghae. was killed in battle in Ireland Julian Fitz Maurice and Thomas De Clare Earl were married in 1276.

17311. **Julian Fitz Maurice** born about 1268.

17328. **William Le Scrope** was born before 1230. He was buried in Wensley. buried with ancestors at Wensley.

17330. **Thomas Of Gillo** born about 1240. of Newsam upon Tees Thomas Of Gillo was married.

17332. **William De Roos Sir** was born after 1192. He died about 1264 at the age of 72. Member of Parliament 1235/6 Lucy Fitz Piers and William De Roos Sir were married.

17333. **Lucy Fitz Piers** born about 1200. She died after 1266 at the age of 66.

17334. **Ralph Fitz Hugh** born about 1225.

17335. **Agnes De Greasley** born about 1225.

17344. **Hugh De Eure Knight** was born in 1240. He died in 1295 at the age of 55. He was also known as Fitz Robert Eure. Visitations of Yorkshire by Glover Sir Hugh de Eure, knight seated at Eure Co Bucks. temp Hen III to whom K. Ed I by charter in the 19th year of his reign 1290 confirmed Stokesley and Ingoldby. He died 23 Ed. I 1295. Added, as generally alleged, three escallops to the bend. In Baliol College, Oxford, however exists his seal attached to a deed in which he is part as executor of John de Balliol, who founded the college. married dau of Roger Bertram, baron of Mitford.

17345. **Of Bertram** born about 1250.

17346. **John De Insula Knight** born about 1260. John De Insula Knight was married.

17356. **Thomas Berkeley** born about 1255. He died on 31 Jul 1321 at the age of 66. Taken prisoner at Battle of Bannockburn. They were married in 1267.

17357. **Jane Ferrers** born about 1255. She died on 19 Mar 1309 or 19 Mar 1310 at the age of 54.

17358. **Eudo La Zouche** born about 1253 in Ashby, Leicester. Complete Peerage vol 3 p 291 MCS4 74-4 says Eudes is not son of Alan la Zouche. They are brothers. Age is too great to be brothers. Millicent De Cantalope and Eudo La Zouche were married before 13 Dec 1273.

17359. **Millicent De Cantalope** born about 1255 in Warwick. She died on 7 Jan 1298 at the age of 43 in Haryngworth.

17410. **John Trayne Knight** born about 1250. Durham vol 4 p 107 Agnes De La Hay and John Trayne Knight were married.

17411. **Agnes De La Hay** born about 1250.

17440. **Ralph Fitz William** born about 1250. Ralph Fitz William was married.

17444. **James De Audley** born about 1240. He died on 11 Jun 1276 at the age of 36. Burkes peerage and Baron p 136 Ela Longespee and James De Audley were married in 1244.

17445. **Ela Longespee** born about 1240. She died before 22 Nov 1299 at the age of 59.

17446. **Edmund De Wigmore Mortimer Baron** was born in 1261 of Wigmore. He died on 17 Jul 1304 at the age of 43. History of Rutland p 42 age 21 in 1282. Baron by Writ 23 Jun 23 Ed 1. Weis 27-30 7th Baron Mortimer of Wigmore Margaret De Fiennes and Edmund De Wigmore Mortimer Baron were married about 1285.

17447. **Margaret De Fiennes** born about 1270. She died on 7 Feb 1333 or 7 Feb 1334 at the age of 63. History of Rutland p 42 kinswoman to Queen Eleanor Weis 27-30

17448. **Henry Fitz Randolph** born about 1240. He died in 1262 at the age of 22. He was buried in Jervaulx Abbey. Henry Fitz Randolph was married.

17464. **William De Beauchamp Earl** was born in 1237 of Warwick. He died about 22 Jun 1298 at the age of 61. He was buried on 22 Jun 1298. Weis 86-29 9th Earl of Warwick Maud Fitz John and William De Beauchamp Earl were married before 1270.

17465. **Maud Fitz John** born about 1237. She died about 18 Apr 1301 at the age of 64. She was buried on 7 May 1301. Weis 86-29, 72-30

17466. **Ralph Toeni VII** was born in 1255. He died before 29 Jul 1295 at the age of 40. Mary and Ralph Toeni VII were married before 1276.

17467. **Mary** died after 1283.

17468. **Edmund De Wigmore Mortimer** is the same as person number 17446.

17469. **Margaret De Fiennes** is the same as person number 17447.

17470. **Piers De Geneville Sir** born about 1260. He died before 8 Jun 1292 at the age of 32. Baron de Geneville History of Rutland p 42 Jeanne Lusignan and Piers De Geneville Sir were married before 11 Oct 1283.

17471. **Jeanne Lusignan** born about 1260.

17504. **Robert De Willoughby Lord** born about 1250–1260 in Lincolnshire, England. He died before 25 Mar 1317 at the age of 67. CP Robert de Willoughby b. abt 1250-60 granted manor of Eresby by grandfather John Beke in 1301/2 m. Margaret dau of Edmund Deincourt 1st Lord Deincourt by isabel dua of Reynold de Mohun of Dunsert, Somerset. He died sh. bef 25 Mar. 1317. She died sh. bef 18 Oct. 1333. Margaret Deincourt and Robert De Willoughby Lord were married.

17505. **Margaret Deincourt** born about 1275. She died before 18 Oct 1333 at age of 58.

17506. **Peter Roscelyn** born about 1280. Peter Roscelyn was married.

17510. **Walter De Norwich** born about 1275. Walter De Norwich was married.

17514. **Ralph De Simones** born about 1275 of Ormesby, Lincolnshire, England. Ralph De Simones was married.

17520. **John Le V. Strange Baron** was born in 1253 of Knokyn. He died before 8 Aug 1309 at the age of 56. Royal Descents p 409 Weis AR p 158 CP 12 p 352 John Lestrange V son and heir aged 22 or more at time of his father's death. In 1277 he was going to Wales on the King's service. He married 1st Alienore dau of Joan de Somery and 2nd Maud. He died before 8 Aug 1309. His widow was living 30 Oct. 1309. Joan de Somery was the widow of Stephen de Somery of the Essex family who died about 1240 leaving his 4 sisters heirs. Joan died 1282. She must have remarried or Alienore would have been his heir. her second husband was Godfrey de Crawcumbe. AR 249-32 said 2nd wife Maud de Walton. mother of Elizabeth who mar. Gruffyd ap Madog. Alianore Crawcumbe and John Le V. Strange Baron were married.

17521. **Alianore Crawcumbe** born about 1255. She died after 1309 at the age of 54.

17528. **John Fitz Alan Earl** was born on 14 Sep 1246. He died on 18 Mar 1271 or 18 Mar 1272 at the age of 24. Lord of Clun, 6th Earl of Arundel Isabella De Mortimer and John Fitz Alan Earl were married.

17529. **Isabella De Mortimer** born about 1248.

17530. **Thomas I. Of Saluzzo Marquis** born about 1240. Marquis of Saluzzo Luisa De Cave and Thomas I. Of Saluzzo Marquis were married.

17531. **Luisa De Cave** born about 1240.

17532. **John De Warenne Earl** was born in 1231. He died in 1305 at the age of 74. 7th Earl of Surrey Alice De Lusignan and John De Warenne Earl were married in 1247.

17533. **Alice De Lusignan** born about 1231. She died in 1291 at the age of 60.

17534. **Robert De Vere Lord** born about 1240. Lord Chamberlain Alice De Saunford and Robert De Vere Lord were married.

17535. **Alice De Saunford** born about 1240.

17672. **William Ros Lord** born about 1255. He died about Aug 1316 at the age of 61. 1st Lord Ros of Helmsley, M.P. 1295-1316. Maud Vaux and William Ros Lord were married before 1287.

17673. **Maud Vaux** born about 1255.

17674. **Bartholomew De Badlesmere** born about 1275. He died on 14 Apr 1322 at the age of 47. History of Rutland p 42 He was age 26 in 1301. Weis 54-33 Hanged on Apr 14 1322, Margaret De Clare and Bartholomew De Badlesmere were married on 28 Apr 1317 in Windsor, England.

17675. **Margaret De Clare** born about 1283. She died in 1365 at the age of 82. Weis 54-33 first wife of Gilbert de Umfraville. dead 1303

17676. **Edmund Stafford Baron** was born on 15 Jul 1273. He died before 12 Aug 1308 at the age of 35. Weis 55-31 M.P. 1300 1st Baron Stafford Margaret Basset and Edmund Stafford Baron were married before 1298.

17677. **Margaret Basset** born about 1275. She died on 17 Mar 1336 or 17 Mar 1337 at the age of 61. Weis 55-31

17678. **Hugh Audley Earl** born about 1298. He died on 10 Nov 1347 at the age of 49. He was buried in Tonbridge, Kent. MCS: 8th Earl of Gloucester. Lord Audley, 8th Earl of Gloucester, Ambassador to France Margaret De Clare and Hugh Audley Earl were married on 28 Apr 1317 in Windsor, England.

17679. **Margaret De Clare** was born in Oct 1299. She died on 9 Apr 1342 at the age of 42. age 22 at time of her brother's death would make he born 1292

17680. **Henry De Percy** is the same as person number 4326.

17681. **Idoine De Clifford** is the same as person number 4327.

17682. **Henry Lancaster** is the same as person number 9106.

17683. **Maud De Chaworth** is the same as person number 9107.

17684. **Randolph Neville Earl** was born on 18 Oct 1262 of Raby. He died after 18 Apr 1331 at the age of 68. He was buried in Coverham. MCS: First Lord of Raby 1st Baron Neville of Raby Euphemia De Clavering and Randolph Neville Earl were married.

17685. **Euphemia De Clavering** born about 1267.

17688. **Edmund De Mortimer Earl** born about 1306 of March. He died on 26 Jan 1331 at the age of 25. History of Rutland p 42 knighted at coron. of Edward 3. Elizabeth De Badlesmere and Edmund De Mortimer Earl were married on 27 Jun 1316.

17689. **Elizabeth De Badlesmere** born about 1308. She died in Jun 1356 at the age of 48.

17690. **William Montacute Earl** born about 1300 of Salisbury. He died in 1344 at the age of 44. History of Rutland p 42 Earl of Salisbury Katherine Grandison and William Montacute Earl were married.

17691. **Katherine Grandison** born about 1300. She died in 1349 at the age of 49. Weis 27-31

17692. **Edward III Of England** is the same as person number 8924.

17693. **Philippa Of Hainaut** is the same as person number 8925.

17694. **William De Burgh Earl** was born on 17 Sep 1312 of Ulster. He died on 6 Jun 1333 at the age of 20 in Leford, Belfast. History of Rutland p 42 AR 5-31, 94A-33, 4th Earl of Ulster, he was murdered. Maud De Lancaster and William De Burgh Earl were married on 1 May 1327.

17695. **Maud De Lancaster** born about 1310. She died on 5 May 1377 at the age of 67. AR 94A-33

17696. **Randolf De Dacre** born about 1290. He died before 20 Apr 1339 at the age of 49. He was buried in Lanercost Priory. CP 4 p 1 Sir Randolf de Dacre (son and heir of William de Dacre of Dacre, Cumberland b. 12 Mar 1265/6 d. sh.bef 24 Aug 1318 bur at Prescot. Co Lancaster by Joan da and heir of Benet Gernet of Halton, Fishwick and Eccleston, co. Lancaster.) Aged 28 at father's death. A banneret 14 Mar. 1336/7. Sheriff of Cumberland 1330-35/6. He married in or before 1315 Margaret da and h. of Thomas De Multon of Gilsland Cumberland by a dau of Piers de Mauley of Mulgrave co. York, Lord Mauley. He died sh. bef. 20 Apr 1339 and was buried in Lanercost Priory. His widow who was born at Mulgrave Castle 20, and bapt. at Lythe 24 Jul. 1300 had livery of divers manors which she and her husband held jointly. She died 10 Dec. 1361. Visitations of Yorkshire p. 83 says Randolf is the son of William Dacre and Anne Derwentwater. Margaret De Multon and Randolf De Dacre were married before 1315.

17697. **Margaret De Multon** was born on 20 Jul 1300 in Mulgrave Castle. She died on 10 Dec 1361 at the age of 61. Visitations of Yorkshie says Maud Moulton of Gylsland dau of Moulton and MaudVaux, dau of Vaux of Gylsland who married dau of Hugh Morvley p. 83

17698. **Ralph De Neville** is the same as person number 8842.

17699. **Alice De Audley** is the same as person number 4361.

17704. **Sir William Douglas 4th Lord Douglas** born about 1270. He died in 1298 at the age of 28. Margaret Mar and Sir William Douglas 4th Lord Douglas were married.

17705. **Margaret Mar** born about 1270. the daughter of Patrick Earl of Mar per Rutland p. 181.

17708. **Sir Andrew Murray** was born of Bothwell. Sir Andrew Murray was married.

17808. **Richard Umfreyville**. Sybella Toriton and Richard Umfreyville were married.

17809. **Sybella Toriton**.

17824. **Giles De Beauchamp Sir** born about 1290. He died in Oct 1361 at the age of 71. Catherine De Bures and Giles De Beauchamp Sir were married before 21 May 1329.

17825. **Catherine De Bures** born about 1290. She died after Oct 1355 at the age of 65. Weis 85-30,189-6,84-30

17826. **John De Patshull Sir** born about 1290 of Bletsoe. He died in 1349 at the age of 59. Weis 85-31 Lord of Pateshull, Northampton and Bletsoe, Bedford Mabel De Grandison and John De Patshull Sir were married about 1312.

17827. **Mabel De Grandison** born about 1290.

17840. **Robert De Holand Sir** born about 1260. Elizabeth De Samlesbury and Robert De Holand Sir were married.

17841. **Elizabeth De Samlesbury** born about 1260.

17842. **Alan De Zouche Baron** was born in 1267. He died in 1313 or 1314 at the age of 46. AR7 31-29 Alan La Zouche b. 1267 d. 1313/4, Baron Zouche of Ashby 1299-1314, Governor of Rockingham Castle and Steward of Rockingham Forest m. Eleanor de Segrave dau of Sir Nicholas Segrave d. sh. bef. 12 Nov. 1395 1st Lord Segrave by his wife Maud. Eleanor's maritagium was the manor of Great Dalby, co. Leicester). Eleanor De Seagrave and Alan De Zouche Baron were married.

17843. **Eleanor De Seagrave** born about 1267.

17844. **Edward I of England** is the same as person number 12942.

17845. **Marguerite Of France** born about 1275. She died on 14 Feb 1317 at the age of 42. She was buried in Marlborough, Wiltshire.

17846. **John Wake Lord** born about 1268. He died before 10 Apr 1300 at the age of 32. AR7 236-10 John Wake 1st Lord Wake b. prob. 1268 d. sh. bef 10 Apr 1300 m. bef 24 Sep 1291 Joan.d sh. bef. 26 Oct. 1309 said to be dau of William Fiennes and Blanch de Brienne. Joan De Fiennes and John Wake Lord were married before 24 Sep 1291.

17847. **Joan De Fiennes** born about 1268. She died before 26 Oct 1309 at the age of 41. Possibly dau of William de Fiennes and Blanche de Brienne. MC4 114-4 says perhaps dau. of Sir. John Fitz Barnard of Kindsdown, Kent.

17848. **Edward II Of England King** was born on 25 Apr 1284 in Caernarvon, Wales, Caernarvon, Wales. He died on 21 Sep 1327 at the age of 43 in Berkeley Castle, Near Gloucester, England. He was buried in Gloucester Cath., England. AR 1-29 King of England 1307-1327 He was the only surviving son of Edward I. He was not close to his father and raised by his sisters. He became reliant on his homosexual friend Piers Gaveston who was murdered by his nobles in 1312 and Hugh Despenser and his son Hugh who were put to death in 1326. He was deposed in favor of his 14-year old son Edward and was later murdered by his wife who took to her lover Roger Mortimer. His wife ordered him to be killed in a way that would leave no marks. He was disemboweled by sticking a red hot iron into his rectum (a conventional death for homosexuals at the time). Edward II was routed at the Battle of Bannockburn by Robert Bruce in 1314 which helped establish Scottish independence.

17849. **Isabella Of France Princess** was born in 1292. She died on 22 Aug 1358 at the age of 66 in Roseing. She was buried in Grey Friars, London. AR 101-31, 1-29

17850. **William III D' Avesnes** born about 1285 in Hainault, Belgium. He died on 7 Jun 1337 at the age of 52 in Valenciennes. Count of Holland Jeanne Of Valois and William III D' Avesnes were married on 19 May 1305.

17851. **Jeanne Of Valois** born about 1285 in Valois. She died on 7 Mar 1342 at age of 57.

17852. **Henry Lancaster** is the same as person number 9106.

17853. **Maud De Chaworth** is the same as person number 9107.

17854. **Henry De Beaumont Knight** born about 1250. He died on 10 Mar 1339 or 10 Mar 1340 at the age of 89. He was knighted in 1308, M.P. 1308/9-1332, Lord Beaumont, Earl of Buchan, Justiciar of Scotland 1338. Alice Comyn and Henry De Beaumont Knight were married.

17855. **Alice Comyn** born about 1250. She died before 10 Aug 1349 at the age of 99. AR7 114a-29

17968. **John De Ferrers** was born on 20 Jun 1271 in Cardiff. He died in Aug 1312 at the age of 41 in Gascony. AR 57-31 They are first cousins. Hawise Muscegros and John De Ferrers were married in 1298 or 1300.

17969. **Hawise Muscegros** was born on 21 Dec 1276. She died after 24 Jun 1340 at the age of 63. AR 189-5

17972. **William Botiller** was born on 8 Sep 1296 of Oversley, Warwick County, England. He died in Dec 1361 at the age of 65. AR 77-32 He married first Margaret Fitz Alan and 2nd to Joan de Sudeley. Margaret Fitz Alan and William Botiller were married.

17973. **Margaret Fitz Alan** born about 1295.

17984. **Marmaduke Constable** born about 1270. Visitations of Yorkshire say Marmaduke p. 178 and call him Robert on p. 197 Marmaduke Constable was married.

17996. **Richard Argum** born about 1280. Richard Argum was married.

18008. **William Mowbray** born about 1260. Yorkshire Visitation by Foster p. 282 Alexander Mowbray of Kirklington, Knight m. Elizabeth dau and heir of Hy.

Monasteriis, father of Elizabeth da and co heir wife of Sir William Gascoigne. Alexander son of John Mowbray of Kirklington, Knight m. Margaret sister of Sir Alexander Percy of Kildale. son of Willielmus de Mowbray m. Agnes. son of Johannes de Mowbray. Agnes and William Mowbray were married.

18009. **Agnes** born about 1260.

18010. **Alexander Percy Sir** born about 1260 of Kildale. Alexander Percy Sir was married.

18016. **John Wentworth** born about 1290 of Elmsall, York, England. John Wentworth was married.

18032. **Philip Le Despenser** born about 1290. He died on 24 Sep 1313 at the age of 23. MCS4 9-6 Sir Philip le Despenser d. 24 Sep 1313 m. Margaret b. 12 May 1294 d. 29 Jul 1349 dau of Ralph de Gousille, Lord of Camoys Manor, Essex. Margaret Gousille and Philip Le Despenser were married.

18033. **Margaret Gousille** was born on 12 May 1294. She died on 29 Jul 1349 at the age of 55.

18034. **John De Cobham Lord** born about 1290. John De Cobham Lord was married.

18040. **Pain De Tybetot Lord** was born on 11 Nov 1279. He died in 1314 at the age of 35. MCS4 2-5 Agnes de Ros d. sh. bef 25 Nov 1328 m. ca 25 Apr 1298 Pain de Tybetot, 1st Lord Tybetot b. 11 Nov 1279 or 24 June 1281 slain at battle of Bannockburn 1314, son of Sir Robert de Tybetot and Eva dau of Pain de Chaworth. Agnes De Ros and Pain De Tybetot Lord were married about 25 Apr 1298.

18041. **Agnes De Ros** born about 1278. She died before 25 Nov 1328 at the age of 50.

18044. **John Deincourt** born about 1275. John Deincourt was married.

18046. **William La Zouche** was born in 1276. He died in Mar 1351 or Mar 1352 at the age of 75. MCS4 74-5 Sir William la Zouche, Knight, Lord Zouche of Haryngworth b. 1276 d. Mar 1351/2, M.P. 1308-1348 m. bef 15 Feb 1295/6 Maud dead 1346 dau of John Lovel, Lord Lovel. Maud Lovel and William La Zouche were married before 15 Feb 1295.

18047. **Maud Lovel** born about 1276. She died before 1346 at the age of 70.

18048. **John Hastings Sir** was born on 6 May 1262 in Allesley, Warwick County, England. He died on 10 Feb 1312 or 10 Feb 1313 at the age of 49. CP Sir John Hastings b. May 6 1262 at Allesley Co Warwick d. 10 Feb 1312/3. m1 Isabel dau of William Valence and Joan Munchaney. She died 5 Oct 1305 buried Coventry Parish m2 Isabel dau of Hugh de Despenser and Isabel Beauchamp, Earl of Winchester. She d. 4 or 5 Dec 1334. She m2 Ralph Mounthermer, Earl of Gloucester (He died 5 Apr 1325). Isabel Despenser and John Hastings Sir were married after 1306.

18049. **Isabel Despenser** born about 1280. She died on 4 Dec 1334 at the age of 54.

18050. **Richard Foliet Sir** born about 1285. Joan Breouse and Richard Foliet Sir were married.

18051. **Joan Breouse** born about 1285.

18056. **Hugh Le Despenser Knight** born about 1286. He died on 24 Nov 1326 at the age of 40. He was buried in Tewkesbury Abbey, England. MCS4 14-6 Sir Hugh le Despenser hanged and quartered 24 Nv. 1326 Lord Despenser m. 1306 after 14 Jun Alianore de Clare. He was the lover of King Edward II of England after Piers Gaveston his brother in law was executed. This execution split England. There were many who thought that the Lords Ordainer acted unlawfully. Many followed Hugh DeSpencer who quickly filled Gaveston's spot as the King's advisor and confidante. King

Edward's fortunes continued to plummet as he was defeated by Robert 'the' Bruce at the Battle of Bannockburn. Therefore, Scotland regained its independence. In 1326, King Edward's wife, Isabella and her lover Roger Mortimer led an army against Edward. Edward was captured and held prisoner in Kenilworth Castle. He abdicated the throne on January 25, 1327. Later that year Edward was murdered at Berkeley Castle in Gloucestershire. He was held down while a red-hot poker was pushed into his bowels. Alianor De Clare and Hugh Le Despenser Knight were married in 1306 in Westminster, England.

18057. **Alianor De Clare** born about 1290. She died on 30 Jun 1337 at the age of 47. PA1 Clare 11 Alianor de Clare was sister and coheiress of Gilbert de Clare. She was married at Westminster in 1306, after 14 June to Hugh le Despenser Knight 2nd Lord Despenser, son and heir of Hugh le Despenser, Knight of Loughborough, Co. Leicester, etc by Isabel daughter of William de Beauchamp of Elmley, co. Worcester, 9th Earl of Warwick. He was summoned to Parliament from 29 July 1314 by writs directed Hugoni le Despenser Juniori. he was disinherited and exiled on 19 Aug. 1321. He took refuge in the Cinque Ports, and engaging in piracy, with the King's connivance, did considerable damage. After the battle of Boroughbridge, he received large grants of the lands forfeited by the rebels. He accompanied the King in his flight to Wales in Oct. 1326, and with the King was captured near Llantrisant, co. Glamborgan, on 16 Nov. 1326. Hugh was taken to Hereford, tried, without being allowed to speak in his own defence, condemned to death as a traitor, and hanged on 24 Nov. 1326, buried some years afterwards at Tewkesbury Abbey. His widow was married for the second time, as his second wife, about Jan. 1328/9 to William la Zouche de Mortimer who had abducted her from Hanley Castle. He died 28 Feb. 1336/7. Alianor de Clare died on 30 June 1337.

18058. **William Ferrers** was born on 30 Jan 1271 or 30 Jan 1272 in Yoxale, Stafford County, England. He died on 20 Mar 1324 or 20 Mar 1325 at the age of 53. MCS4 100-5 Sir William de Ferrers of Groby b. Yoxale, co. Stafford, 30 Jan. 1271/2 d. 20 Mar. 1324/5 1st Lrod Ferrers m. Ellen lviing 9 Feb 1316/7 possibly daughter of Sir John de Savage. Ellen Savage and William Ferrers were married.

18059. **Ellen Savage** born about 1290.

18060. **Bartholomew De Burghersh Lord** born about 1300. He died on 3 Aug 1355 at the age of 55. Elizabeth De Verdon and Bartholomew De Burghersh Lord were married before 11 Jun 1320.

18061. **Elizabeth De Verdon** born about 1306. She died on 1 May 1360 at the age of 54. MCS4 13-7 Elizabeth de Verdon dau of first wife b. c. 1306 d. 1 May 1360 m. bef 11 June 1320 Sir Bartholomew de Burghersh. d 3 Aug 1355 Lord Burghersh, son of Robert, Lord Burghersh, and Maud de Badlesmere.

18062. **Richard De Weyland** born about 1290. Richard De Weyland was married.

18064. **Josce De Dinham** born about 1273. He died on 30 Mar 1301 at the age of 28. Margaret De Hydon and Josce De Dinham were married about 1290.

18065. **Margaret De Hydon** died on 13 May 1357. She was buried at Saint Katherine's Chapel in Hemyock, Devon, England.

18068. **Hugh De Courtenay** is the same as person number 6468.

18069. **Agnes St. John** is the same as person number 6469.

18070. **John De Moels Knight**. Joan Lovel and John De Moels Knight were married.

18071. **Joan Lovel**.

18080. **Robert De Morley Lord** born about 1290. CP Robert de Morley 2nd Lord son by 1st wife minor in 1304/5. Lord of Morley, Norfolk. m bef 1316 1st Hawise sister of John Marshal dau of William Marshall Hereditary Marshal of Ireland. m2nd Joan by Sep 1334 possibly dau of Piers de Tyes. Hawise Marshal and Robert De Morley Lord were married before 1316.

18081. **Hawise Marshal** born about 1290. She died before 1327 at the age of 37. sister of John Marshal and Denise. dau of William Marshal Hereditary Marshal of Ireland.

18082. **Thomas Bardolph Lord** was born on 4 Oct 1282. He died on 15 Dec 1328 at the age of 46. AR7 257-32 Thomas Barolf 2nd Lord ancestry. Agnes Grandison and Thomas Bardolph Lord were married.

18083. **Agnes Grandison** born about 1285. She died on 11 Dec 1357 at the age of 72. probably dau of William Grandison per PA "Bardolf" p. 8

18100. **John Wingfield** born about 1300 in Wingfield Manor, England. He died in 1327 at the age of 27 in Wingfield Manor, Suffolk, England. From Book "Wingfiled, its Church, Castle, and College" published i 1925 by S.W.H. Aldwell, Vicar of Weyfield p. 6. Also Burke's Peerage and Baronetage. Elizabeth Honeypot and John Wingfield were married.

18101. **Elizabeth Honeypot** born about 1300. dau. of John Honeypot per Mary Rogers.

18102. **Gilbert Glanville Sir** born about 1300. Gilbert Glanville Sir was married.

18138. **John Mauduit** born about 1275. Johanna Becard and John Mauduit were married.

18139. **Johanna Becard** born about 1275.

18168. **Thomas Foljambe** born about 1290. Alice Furnival and Thomas Foljambe were married.

18169. **Alice Furnival** born about 1290.

18212. **Edmund Of England Earl** was born on 16 Jan 1244 or 16 Jan 1245 in London, England. He died on 5 Jun 1295 at the age of 51 in Bayonne. Weis 17-28 called Crouchback Created Earl of Lancaster and Leicester, and High Steward of England Blanche Of Artois and Edmund Of England Earl were married in 1276.

18213. **Blanche Of Artois** born about 1254. She died on 2 May 1302 at the age of 48 in Paris, France. Weis 17-28 his second wife Blanche

18214. **Patrick Chaworth Sir** was born in 1253. He died on 7 Jul 1283 at the age of 30. Lord of Kidwelley, Wales Isabel De Beauchamp and Patrick Chaworth Sir were married.

18215. **Isabel De Beauchamp** born about 1260. She died on 30 May 1306 at the age of 46. MCS4 4-5 Isabel de Beauchamp d. by 30 May 1306 m. 1st Patrick de Chaworth d. by 7 Jul 1283 Lord of Kempsford, co. Gloucester, and Kidwelley, Wales, married 2nd by 1286 Sir Hugh le Despenser b. 1 Mar. 1260/1 hanged 27 Oct. 1326, Earl of Winchester, son of Hugh le Despenser and Aline Basset.

18216. **John Maltravers** born about 1265. Eleanor De Gorges and John Maltravers were married.

18217. **Eleanor De Gorges** born about 1265.

18218. **Maurice Berkeley** is the same as person number 8678.

18219. **Eve La Zouche** is the same as person number 8679.

18248. **John Mowbray Baron** was born on 4 Sep 1286. He died on 23 Mar 1321 at the age of 34 in York, England. Hanged. Alice Braiose and John Mowbray Baron were married in 1298 in Swansea.

18249. **Alice Braiose** born about 1286 in Wales. She died before 30 Jul 1331 at the age of 45. Called Aline and Alice

18250. **Henry Lancaster** is the same as person number 9106.

18251. **Maud De Chaworth** is the same as person number 9107.

18252. **Stephen De Segrave Lord** died about 1325. Alice and Stephen De Segrave Lord were married.

18253. **Alice.**

18254. **Thomas Of Brotherton** was born on 1 Jun 1300. He died in Aug 1338 at the age of 38. Alice Halys and Thomas Of Brotherton were married.

18255. **Alice Halys** born about 1300.

24584. **Giles Clifford** was born in 1190. He/she died in 1276 at the age of 86. Eve Whitchurch and Giles Clifford were married.

24585. **Eve Whitchurch** was born in 1190. He/she died in 1255 at the age of 65.

24832. **Hugh Pointz Knight.** Hawise Malet and Hugh Pointz Knight were married before 23 Mar 1216.

24833. **Hawise Malet** was born before 1200. She died after May 1287 at the age of 87.

24834. **Timothy Dyall.** Timothy Dyall was married.

24864. **Randolph Fitz Nicholas** was born in 1226. He died in 1290 at the age of 64.

25872. **John De Courtenay** born about 1220. He died on 3 May 1274 at the age of 54. MCS4 124-2 Isabel De Vere and John De Courtenay were married.

25873. **Isabel De Vere** born about 1230. She died on 11 Aug.

25874. **Hugh De Despenser Sir** born about 1225 of Ryhall. He died on 5 Aug 1265 at the age of 40. Aline Basset and Hugh De Despenser Sir were married.

25875. **Aline Basset** born about 1240. She died in 1307 at the age of 67. History of Rutland p 19 second married Roger Bigod Earl of Norfolk.

25880. **Humphrey VI De Bohun Earl** born about 1225 of Hereford. He died on 27 Oct 1265 at the age of 40. Weis AR: Earl of Hereford and Essex Eleanor De Braiose and Humphrey VI De Bohun Earl were married.

25881. **Eleanor De Braiose** born about 1230. Weis AR: first wife of Humphrey

25882. **Ingelram De Fiennes** born about 1220. He died in 1265 at the age of 45. Weis AR 152A-28 not certa of his mother, could be first or second wife. Of Conde and Ingelram De Fiennes were married.

25883. **Of Conde** born about 1220.

25884. **Henry III Of England King** was born on 1 Oct 1207 in Winchester, Hampshire, England. He died on 16 Nov 1272 at the age of 65 in Westminster, London, England. He was buried in Westminster Abb., London, England. Weis AR7 1-27:King of England 1216-1272 He was 9 years old at the time of his accession. William Marshal and Hubert de Burgh are made regents during minority of Henry. They ruled wisely. In 1227 he took over the government. He married Eleanor of Provence and put many foreigners in leading positions. This caused a revolt led by Simon de Montfort which was late defeated. Weis AR:King of England 1216-1272 Eleanor Of Provence Princess and Henry III Of England King were married on 14 Jan 1237 in Canterbury, Kent, England.

25885. **Eleanor Of Provence Princess** was born in 1222 in Aix-En-Provence, France. She died on 24 Jan 1291 at the age of 69 in Amesbury, England.

25886. **Ferdinand III Of Castile King** was born in Aug 1201 in Castile, Spain. He died on 30 May 1252 at the age of 50 in Seville. Saint Ferdinand, canonized by Pope

Clement X on 15 Nov. 1671. King of Castile 1217 and Leon 1230 Jeanne De Dammartin and Ferdinand III Of Castile King were married in 1237 in Burgos, Spain.

25887. **Jeanne De Dammartin** born about 1215. She died on 16 Mar 1279 at the age of 64 in Abbeville. She was buried in Valoires.

Sixteenth Generation

32776. **William De Washington** was born before 1240. He died about 1289 at the age of 49. Margaret De Morville and William De Washington were married.

32777. **Margaret De Morville** born about 1240.

33344. **William St. Quintin** born about 1260. Foster Yorkshire Hesharton and William St. Quintin were married.

33345. **Hesharton** born about 1260.

33346. **William De Ros** is the same as person number 8666.

33347. **Eustache Fitz Hugh** is the same as person number 8667.

33350. **Piers De Mauley** born about 1250. Piers De Mauley was married.

33352. **John De Thwenge Knight** was born in 1261 of Kilton. He died on 2 Dec 1330 at the age of 69. Joan De Mauley and John De Thwenge Knight were married.

33353. **Joan De Mauley** born about 1261. She died on 13 Jul 1347 at the age of 86.

33354. **Robert Constable** is the same as person number 16674.

33355. **Katherine Mauley** is the same as person number 16675.

33376. **William Gascoigne** born about 1200 in Lasingcroft, Yorkshire, England. William Gascoigne was married.

33378. **John Gawthorpe** was born in 1196. John Gawthorpe was married.

33392. **John Clitherow** born about 1240. John Clitherow was married.

33600. **Walter Carrow** born about 1175. He died after 1200 at the age of 25. Walter Carrow was married.

33728. **Richard De Umfreyville Lord** born about 1190 of Prodhue. He died after 1216 at the age of 26. Burke EP: feudal lord appears in 7 Rich I to have pledged lands of Turney to Aaron a jew for a debt. In 5 King John he obtained the right of preventing all persons from grazing hunting and cutting down timber in the forest of Riddesdale. lost his lands when sided with the Barons but in Henry III made peace and restored to castle of Prodhue etc. not trusted by the king and an inquiry was made of certain buildings at the castle of Herbotil to tear down any fortifications. Richard De Umfreyville Lord was married.

33730. **Malcolm Of Angus Earl** born about 1190. Malcolm Of Angus Earl was married.

33732. **William Comyn Count** born about 1160. He died in 1233 at the age of 73. Weis AR:created Earl of Buchan because of wife Marjorie Of Buchan and William Comyn Count were married.

33733. **Marjorie Of Buchan** born about 1175. Weis AR: Countess of Buchan, William Comyn's second wife

33734. **Roger De Quincy Earl** born about 1190 of Winchester. He died on 25 Apr 1264 at the age of 74. 2nd Earl of Winchester and Constable of Scotland, accompanied his father on the 5th Crusade in 1219. Crusader to the Holy Land. Weis 53-28 Helen Of Galloway and Roger De Quincy Earl were married.

33735. **Helen Of Galloway** born about 1200. She died in 1245 at the age of 45. Weis AR: eldest dau and coheir of Alan AR 38-27 by first wife unknown.

elsewhere first wife was dau of Roger de lacy of Pontefract

33856. **Halnath De Halnaby** was born before 1170. He died after 1216 at the age of 46. Halnath De Halnaby was married.

34182. **Nicholas De Hastings** born about 1245 of Allerton, York County. Weis AR: York co and Gissing co Norfolk Nicholas De Hastings was married.

34184. **Nicholas De Meinill** born about 1250. Weis AR Christina and Nicholas De Meinill were married.

34185. **Christina** born about 1250.

34186. **Robert De Thwenge** born about 1250. Weis AR: not married Lucy De Brus and Robert De Thwenge were married.

34187. **Lucy De Brus** born about 1250. Weis AR: de Brus of Skelton and Daneby

34208. **Reginald De Grey Baron** born about 1235 of Ruthin. He died in 1307 at the age of 72. History of Rutland p 162f heir in 1266 Baron of Shirland and Wilton
Weis 55-30 Matilda Fitz Hugh and Reginald De Grey Baron were married.

34209. **Matilda Fitz Hugh** born about 1235.

34210. **William De Ferrers Baron** born about 1240 of Groby, Leicester. He died in 1287 or 1288 at the age of 47. Anne Le Despenser and William De Ferrers Baron were married.

34211. **Anne Le Despenser** born about 1240. of Ryhall-Rutland

34214. **William De Clare** born about 1235. History of Rutland Baron Grey p 162f William De Clare was married.

34224. **Richard Talbot** born about 1250. He died about 3 Sep 1306 at the age of 56. Sarah De Beauchamp and Richard Talbot were married.

34225. **Sarah De Beauchamp** born about 1250. She died after Jul 1317 at the age of 67.

34228. **John Comyn Lord** born about 1245 of Badenock. He died about 1303 at the age of 58. Weis AR: Lord of Badenock, called the Black Comyn Alianora De Baliol and John Comyn Lord were married in 1279 or 1283.

34229. **Alianora De Baliol** born about 1245. Weis AR
Sister of John Baliol, King of Scotland.

34230. **William De Valence Knight** born about 1225 in Valence. He died before 18 May 1296 at the age of 71. Weis AR: Lord of Valence, Montignac, Bellac, Rancon and Champagnac, Knighted 13 Oct 1247, Crusader to the Holy Land 6 Mar 1250 Joan De Munchensi and William De Valence Knight were married on 13 Aug 1247.

34231. **Joan De Munchensi** born about 1225. She died before 30 Sep 1307 at age of 82.

34232. **Theobald Le Boteler** born about 1242. He died on 26 Sep 1285 at the age of 43. Weis AR Joan Fitz John and Theobald Le Boteler were married about 1268.

34233. **Joan Fitz John** born about 1245. She died about 26 May 1303 at the age of 58.

34234. **John Fitz Thomas Fitz Gerald** born about 1260. Weis AR: of Kildare John Fitz Thomas Fitz Gerald was married.

34244. **John De Bulmer II** born about 1230. He died about 1265 at the age of 35. Alice Fitz Ralph and John De Bulmer II were married.

34245. **Alice Fitz Ralph** born about 1230. possible dau of William Fitz Ralph

34272. **Walter De Grey Baron** born about 1215 of Rotherfield. He died before 1268 at the age of 53. Sir. of Rotherfield and Somerton. History of Rutland: dead 52 Hen 3 Isabel De Duston and Walter De Grey Baron were married.

34273. **Isabel De Duston** born about 1215. History of Rutland: called Dunster

34274. **Thomas De Valoines** born about 1225. Thomas De Valoines was married.

34276. **William Odingsells** born about 1225. Joan and William Odingsells were married.

34277. **Joan** born about 1225.

34278. **Walter Fitz Robert** born about 1219. He died before 10 Apr 1258 at the age of 39. of Woodham-Walter, Burnham, Roydon, Dunmow, Henham, Wimbish and Tey, Essex. Ida Longespee and Walter Fitz Robert were married.

34279. **Ida Longespee** born about 1204. She died after 1262 at the age of 58. She was also known as Idonea Longespee.

34280. **William De Marmion Sir** born about 1240. He died on 27 Jul 1275 at the age of 35. Lorette De Dover and William De Marmion Sir were married in 1268.

34281. **Lorette De Dover** born about 1240.

34284. **Thomas De Furnival Lord** born about 1240 of Hallamshire. He died before 1279 at the age of 39. Burkes EP p 1056-7 license to rebuild castle in 1270 of Sheffield Thomas De Furnival Lord was married.

34286. **Hugh De Despenser** is the same as person number 25874.

34287. **Aline Basset** is the same as person number 25875.

34288. **Hubert St. Quenton** born about 1250. He died in 1303 at the age of 53 in Frome, Saint Quintn, Dorset County, England. Mary Fauconberg and Hubert St. Quenton were married.

34289. **Mary Fauconberg** born about 1250.

34290. **John Maltravers Lord** born about 1250. John Maltravers Lord was married.

34304. **Walter Surteyse** was born before 1249 in Durham, England. He died in 1273 at the age of 24 in Durham, England. son and heir, sometime in ward of Sir Adam de Gesemurhe (Gesemond) but of full age on the Vigil of St. John ante Port. Lat. 55 H. III, died seised of North osforth and the manor of Tinsalle. Inq 2 Edw. I 1273/4. Walter Surteyse was married.

34306. **Thomas Fishburne Knight** born about 1250. He died after 1313 at the age of 63. Thomas Fishburne Knight was married.

34560. **Galfrid Conyers Lord** born about 1165 of Bishopton And, Sockbourne. He died before 1238 at the age of 73. Lord of Bishopton in cart. s.d. and Lord of Sockburne. living 14 John. Died bef. 23 Hen. III 1238. Ellinor and Galfrid Conyers Lord were married.

34561. **Ellinor** born about 1165.

34592. **Gilbert De Aton** born about 1200. He died in 1235 at the age of 35. died in the 19 hen III, Margerie De Vesci and Gilbert De Aton were married.

34593. **Margerie De Vesci** born about 1200. She died after 1235 at the age of 35. only dau and heir.

34598. **Roger De Bertram Baron** born about 1200. He died after 1264 at the age of 64. Baron of Mitford Joan and Roger De Bertram Baron were married.

34599. **Joan** born about 1200. She died after 1264 at the age of 64. Burkes EP: she m. 2nd Robert de Nevill

34608. **William De Percy Baron** born about 1193. He died about 28 Jul 1245 at the age of 52. 6th Baron Percy Ellen De Baliol and William De Percy Baron were married about 1233.

34609. **Ellen De Baliol** born about 1200. She died before 22 Nov 1281 at the age of 81.

34610. **John De Warenne** is the same as person number 17532.

34611. **Alice De Lusignan** is the same as person number 17533.

34616. **Roger De Clifford** born about 1220 of Westmoreland. He died in 1285 at the age of 65. Baron of Hereford, Justice of the Forest South of Trent grandson Robert inherited property. Complete Peerage vol 3 p 290 Hawise Bottrell and Roger De Clifford were married.

34617. Hawise Bottrell born about 1220.

34618. Robert De Vespont Lord born about 1238 of Essendine. He died on 7 Jun 1264 at the age of 26. Lord of Westmoreland. History of Rutland: Baron of Appleby, Lord of Essendine. p 15 Isabel Fitz John and Robert De Vespont Lord were married.

34619. Isabel Fitz John born about 1238.

34620. Richard De Clare Earl was born on 4 Aug 1222 of Hertford. He died on 15 Jul 1262 at the age of 39. Collins RA: 8th Earl of Clare, 6th Earl of Hertford, and Earl of Gloucester. Complete Peerage vol 3 p 291 Maud De Lacy Countess and Richard De Clare Earl were married on 25 Jan 1237 or 25 Jan 1238.

34621. Maud De Lacy Countess born about 1221 of Lincoln. She died before Mar 1288 at the age of 67. Collins RA: 2nd wife of Richard

34622. Maurice Fitz Maurice Lord born about 1225. He died in 1286 at the age of 61 in Ross. Lord of Offaly in Ireland, Justiciar. Complete Peerage vol 3 p 291 Lord justice of Ireland Emmeline De Longespee and Maurice Fitz Maurice Lord were married about 1266.

34623. Emmeline De Longespee born about 1250. She died in 1291 at the age of 41.

34656. Henry Le Scrope was born before 1185. He died after 1205 at the age of 20. Wensley Julian Brune and Henry Le Scrope were married.

34657. Julian Brune born about 1185.

34664. Knight Templar Robert I de Roos Knight of Helmsley born about 1170 of Helmsley, Holderness, York County, England. He died before 23 Dec 1226 at the age of 56. He was also known as Magna Carta Surety Roos. of Helmsley in Holderness, co York. Magna Carta Surety 1215, Knight Templar. MAGNA CARTA: signed the Magna Carta as surety in 1215 Isabel Huntingdon of Scotland and Knight Templar Robert I de Roos Knight of Helmsley were married in 1191 in Haddington.

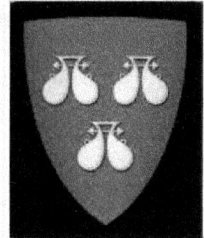

34665. Isabel Huntingdon of Scotland born about 1170. She is the natural dau of William the Lion by Isabel per MCS4 116-1

34666. Piers Fitz Herbert born about 1150. He died after 19 May 1235 at the age of 85. He was buried in Reading. MAGNA CARTA: mentioned in the Magna Carta as advisor to King John 1215 Alice Fitz Roger Wareworth and Piers Fitz Herbert were married on 28 Nov 1203.

34667. Alice Fitz Roger Wareworth born about 1175. She died before 1225 at the age of 50.

34668. Hugh Fitz Ralph born about 1200. Hugh Fitz Ralph was married.

34670. Ralph De Greasley born about 1200. Ralph De Greasley was married.

34688. Baron John Fitz Robert 3rd Lord Warkworth born about 1180. He died in 1240 at the age of 60. He was also known as Magna Carta Surety Fitz Robert. 3rd baron of Warkworth co Northumberland, Magna Carta surety 1215. Sheriff of Northumberland 1224-1227. MCS4 44-1 MAGNA CARTA: signed the Magna Carta as surety in 1215, of Walworth, Northumberland. Visitations of Yorkshire by Glover p. 607-614 John Fitz Robert, 3rd baron of Warkworth. In a Henry III he

obtained a charter for a fair in his (j.u.) manor of Stokesley, to be held yearly on the festival (29th Dec.) of St. Thomas the Martyr (a Beckett). Sheriff of Northumber. 1224 to 1227 Ob 1249. married Ada dau of Hugh, grandson of Bernard de Baliol. She was a sister to John de Baliol, the founder 1263 of Baliol College, Oxford, and aunt to John de Baliol, King of Scotland. By Inq. p.m. 35 Hen. III she enfeoffed her sons Hugh and Robert with the manor of Stokesly, which was given to her by her father. She died on Sat. before St. James; day, July 1251. Ada De Baliol and Baron John Fitz Robert 3rd Lord Warkworth were married on 5 Jun 1215.

34689. **Ada De Baliol** born about 1200. She died on 29 Jul 1251 at the age of 51. enfeoffed her sons Hugh and Robert with the manor of Stokesley from her father died sat. before St. James day Jul 1251 She is said to have married June 5, 1215.

34690. **Roger Of Bertram Baron** born about 1225 of Mitford. Baron of Mitford Roger Of Bertram Baron was married.

34712. **Maurice De Berkeley Lord** born about 1230. He died on 4 Apr 1281 at the age of 51. 6th Lord Berkeley Isabel De Credonia and Maurice De Berkeley Lord were married on 12 Jul 1247.

34713. **Isabel De Credonia** born about 1230. She died on 7 Jul 1276 at the age of 46.

34714. **William De Ferrers Earl** born about 1193 of Derby. He was buried on 30 Mar 1254. He died about 31 May 1254 at the age of 61 in Evington, Leicestershire, England. Weis AR: 5th Earl of Derby said to m1 Sibilla Marshall 2nd Margaret de Quincy History of Rutland Weis AR: 5th Earl of Derby said to m1 Sibilla Marshall 2nd Margaret de Quincy History of Rutland Weis AR: 5th Earl of Derby said to m1 Sibilla Marshall 2nd Margaret de Quincy History of Rutland Margaret De Quincy and William De Ferrers Earl were married.

34715. **Margaret De Quincy** born about 1215. She died about 12 Mar 1280–12 Mar 1281 at the age of 65. Weis AR: second wife Margaret de Quincy, first wife was Sibyl Marshall

34716. **Roger La Zouche** born about 1170. He died before 14 May 1238 at the age of 68. Descendant in the male line of the Counts of Porhoet in Brittany Margaret and Roger La Zouche were married.

34717. **Margaret** was born before 1170. She died after 1220 at the age of 50.

34718. **William Cantilupe** born about 1227. He died on 25 Sep 1254 at the age of 27. Eva Braiose and William Cantilupe were married on 13 Feb 1247.

34719. **Eva Braiose** born about 1227. She died on 28 Jul 1255 at the age of 28 in Calstone, Wilts.

34822. **Ralph De La Hay Lord** born about 1225 of Staynton, In the Street. Durham vol 4 p 107 Lord of Staynton-in the street Ralph De La Hay Lord was married.

34888. **Henry Aldithley** born about 1200. He died after 1223 at the age of 23. Burkes peerage and Baron p 136 founded Hulton Abbey and built the castle of Heleigh. several of his descendants buried in the Abbey Henry Aldithley was married.

34890. **William Longespee Sir** born about 1202. He died on 7 Feb 1249 at the age of 47 in Nile River, Egypt. He died in battle with the Saracens at Mansura on the Nile. Idoine Camville and William Longespee Sir were married in 1226.

34891. **Idoine Camville** born about 1204. She died about 1251 at the age of 47.

34892. **Roger III De Mortimer Baron** born about 1231. He died about 30 Oct 1282 at the age of 51 in Kingsland. 6th Baron of Mortimer of Wigmore. Maud De Braiose and Roger III De Mortimer Baron were married in 1247.

34893. **Maud De Braiose** born about 1231. She died before Mar 1300 at the age of 69.

34894. **William De Fiennes Knight** born about 1240. He died on 11 Jul 1304 at the age of 64. History of Rutland p 42 a Spaniard. Fendles or Fienles Blanche Of Loupeland Brienne and William De Fiennes Knight were married in 1269.

34895. **Blanche Of Loupeland Brienne** born about 1251.

34896. **Randolph Fitz Henry** born about 1210. He died before 13 Jan 1242 at the age of 32. or 1262 Alice Stavely and Randolph Fitz Henry were married.

34897. **Alice Stavely** born about 1210.

34928. **William De Beauchamp Baron** born about 1210 of Elmley Castle. He died in 1270 at the age of 60. weis 86-28 5th Baron Beauchamp of Elmley Castle Isabel Mauduit and William De Beauchamp Baron were married.

34929. **Isabel Mauduit** born about 1217. She died on 7 Jan 1268 or 7 Jan 1269 at the age of 51. She was buried in Cokehill Nunnery. weis 86-28, 84-28

34930. **John Fitz Geoffrey Lord** born about 1200. He died on 23 Nov 1258 at the age of 58. of Shere, Farnbridge, etc. Justiciar of Ireland 1245-1256.
also Weis AR History of Rutland: Justiciar of Ireland Isabel Bigod and John Fitz Geoffrey Lord were married after 1230.

34931. **Isabel Bigod** born about 1208. Weis AR also: 2nd husband was John; widow of Gilbert de Lacy of Ewyas Lacy History of Rutland

34932. **Roger V. Toeni Lord** born about 1235 of Flamstead, Hertford County, England. He died before 12 May 1264 at the age of 29. Weis 98-29, 86-30 Alice De Bohun and Roger V. Toeni Lord were married.

34933. **Alice De Bohun** born about 1230. Royal Descents of 600 Immigrants p. 475 says dau. Alice may be by Isabel de Bohun sister of this Alice.

34940. **Geoffrey Geneville Sir** born about 1235 of Trim, Ireland. He died on 21 Oct 1314 at the age of 79. History of Rutland p 42 Maud Lacy and Geoffrey Geneville Sir were married.

34941. **Maud Lacy** born about 1228. She died on 11 Apr 1304 at the age of 76.

34942. **Hugh Lusignan XII** died in 1270. Count de la Marche and Angouleme Joanne Fougeres and Hugh Lusignan XII were married on 29 Jan 1253 or 29 Jan 1254.

34943. **Joanne Fougeres.**

35008. **William De Willoughby** born about 1225. He died before 29 Mar 1300 at the age of 75. CP Alice Beke and William De Willoughby were married about 1250–1260.

35009. **Alice Beke** born about 1225.

35010. **Edward De Deincourt Lord** born about 1250. He died on 6 Jan 1326 or 6 Jan 1327 at the age of 76. MCS4 149A-4 Isabel de Mohun m. Sir Edward Deincourt 1st Lord Deincourt d. 6 Jan 1326/7 son of Sir John Deincourt by Agnes Neville, Widow and 2nd wife of Richard de Percey who d. bef 18 Aug 1244; Agnes who d. bef 20 July 1293 was the daughter of Sir Geoffrey de Neville of Raby, Co. Durham. Isabel De Mohun and Edward De Deincourt Lord were married.

35011. **Isabel De Mohun** born about 1255.

35040. **John Le IV Strange Lord** born about 1235 of Knokyn. He died before 26 Feb 1275 at the age of 40. Royal Descents p 409 Weis AR p 158 p 165. CP 12 p. 351 John leStrange IV 1st son and heir. In 1256 with Roger and his brother Herbert was taken prisoner. He married Joan dau of Roger de Somery by Nichole dau and coh. of William de Aubigney Earl of Aurndel by Mabel sister and heir of Ranulph Earl of Chester. He died on or before 26 Feb 1275/6 probably by drowning before Feb 2. Joan De Somery and John Le IV Strange Lord were married.

35041. **Joan De Somery** born about 1235. She died in 1282 at the age of 47. Royal Descents p 409, Weis AR p 158

35042. **Godfrey De Crawcumbe** born about 1220. Joan and Godfrey De Crawcumbe were married after 1240.

35043. **Joan** born about 1230. She died in 1282 at the age of 52.

35056. **John Fitz Alan** born about 1220. He died about Nov 1267 at the age of 47. 5th Earl of Arundel 1243, made will Oct 1267 proved 10 Nov 1267. received property of Hugh Albini. Maud Le Boteler and John Fitz Alan were married.

35057. **Maud Le Boteler** born about 1220. She died on 27 Nov 1283 at the age of 63.

35058. **Roger III De Mortimer** is the same as person number 34892.

35059. **Maud De Braiose** is the same as person number 34893.

35062. **George De Cave Marquis** born about 1220.

35064. **Earl William De Warenne 6th Earl of Surrey** born about 1170. He died in 1240 at the age of 70. He was also known as Magna Carta Supporter Warenne. 6th Earl of Surrey. Magna Carta Supporter MAGNA CARTA: named in the Magna Carta as an advisor to King John in 1215 Maud Marshall and Earl William De Warenne 6th Earl of Surrey were married in 1225.

35065. **Maud Marshall** born about 1193. She died on 27 Mar 1248 at the age of 55. 2nd wife of William de Warenne

35066. **Hugh X. De Lusignan** born about 1180. called Hugh le Brun, Comte de la Marche Extinct Peerages (Valence) Isabella Taillefer Of Angouleme and Hugh X. De Lusignan were married in 1217.

35067. **Isabella Taillefer Of Angouleme** was born in 1188 in Angouleme. She died on 31 May 1246 at the age of 58. She was buried in Fontevrault, Maine-Et-Loire.

35068. **Hugh Vere Earl** born about 1200 of Oxford. He died before 23 Dec 1263 at the age of 63. Hugh de Vere 4th Earl of Oxford, K.B. Pedigrees of Charlemagne. Vol 11 p 176 Hawise De Quincy and Hugh Vere Earl were married after 11 Feb 1222.

35069. **Hawise De Quincy** born about 1200.

35344. **Robert Roos Lord** born about 1220. He died on 17 May 1285 at the age of 65. Of Helmsley and Belvoir, Leicester Isabel D'Aubeney and Robert Roos Lord were married before 17 May 1246.

35345. **Isabel D'Aubeney** born about 1220. She died on 15 Jun 1301 at the age of 81.

35346. **John Vaux** born about 1230. John Vaux was married.

35350. **Thomas De Clare** is the same as person number 17310.

35351. **Julian Fitz Maurice** is the same as person number 17311.

35352. **Nicholas Stafford** born about 1240. He died about 1293 at the age of 53 in Droselan Castle.

35354. **Ralph Basset Lord** born about 1260 of Drayton. He died on 21 Dec 1299 at the age of 39 in Drayton, Staffordshire, England. Weis 55-30 M.P. 1295-1299. Weis 55-30 M.P. 1295-1299 Lord Bassett of Drayton. His coat of arms is the oldest still in existence from the Order of the Garter at St. Georges Chapel, Windsor.

35355. **Joan De Grey** born about 1260.

35356. **Hugh De Audley** is the same as person number 8722.

35357. **Isolde De Mortimer** is the same as person number 8723.

35358. **Gilbert De Red Clare Knight** was born on 12 Sep 1243 in Christ Church, Hampshire, England. He died on 7 Dec 1299 at the age of 56 in Monmouth Castle. 3rd Earl of Gloucester, 7th Earl of Hertford, 9th Earl of Clare, AR7 8-29, 63-30 Joanne D'Acre Plantagenet Princess and Gilbert De Red Clare Knight were married about 30 Apr 1290 in Westminster, England.

35359. **Joanne D'Acre Plantagenet Princess** was born in 1272 in Acre, Holy Land. She died on 23 Apr 1307 at the age of 35.

35368. **Robert Neville** born about 1240. He died before 1282 at the age of 42. Mary Fitz Randolph and Robert Neville were married.

35369. **Mary Fitz Randolph.**

35370. **Robert Fitz Roger Lord** was born in 1247 of Clavering. He died in 1310 at the age of 63. MCS: Lord Fitz Roger of Clavering MP 1295-1309 Margery De La Zouche and Robert Fitz Roger Lord were married in 1265.

35371. **Margery De La Zouche** born about 1247.

35376. **Roger De Mortimer** is the same as person number 8734.

35377. **Joan De Geneville** is the same as person number 8735.

35378. **Bartholomew De Badlesmere** is the same as person number 17674.

35379. **Margaret De Clare** is the same as person number 17675.

35380. **William De Montecute** born about 1275. Elizabeth Montfort and William De Montecute were married.

35381. **Elizabeth Montfort** born about 1275.

35382. **William De Grandison** born about 1265. He died in 1335 at the age of 70. Weis 85-31 Sybil De Tregoz and William De Grandison were married.

35383. **Sybil De Tregoz** born about 1265. She died in 1334 at the age of 69.

35388. **John Burgh** born about 1295. He died on 18 Jun 1313 at the age of 18. Not an Earl Elizabeth Clare and John Burgh were married on 30 Sep 1308.

35389. **Elizabeth Clare** was born on 16 Sep 1295. She died on 4 Nov 1360 at the age of 65. AR7 94A-32

35390. **Henry Lancaster** is the same as person number 9106.

35391. **Maud De Chaworth** is the same as person number 9107.

35392. **William De Dacre** was born on 12 Mar 1265 or 12 Mar 1266. He died before 24 Aug 1318 at the age of 53 in Lancaster, England.

35393. **Joan De Gernet** born about 1266 in Lancaster, England. Visitations of Yorkshire says she is Anne Derwentwater.

35394. **Thomas De Multon** born about 1280. Mauley and Thomas De Multon were married.

35395. **Mauley** born about 1280.

35408. **William Douglas Sir** born about 1240. He died in 1274 at the age of 34. William Douglas Sir was married.

35410. **Patrick Of Mar Earl.** Patrick Of Mar Earl was married.

35616. **Henry Umfreyville.** Nest and Henry Umfreyville were married.

35617. **Nest.**

35618. **William Toriton.** William Toriton was married.

35648. **Walter Beauchamp** was born before 1250. He died in 1303 at the age of 53. Steward of the Household of King Edward I AR 84-28

35649. **Alice Toeni** born about 1260. She died in 1306 at the age of 46.

35650. **John Bures Sir** born about 1275. He died on 22 Dec 1350 at the age of 75 in Bodington. Hawise Muscegros and John Bures Sir were married on 21 Dec 1315.

35651. **Hawise Muscegros** is the same as person number 17969.

35652. **Simon Pateshull** born about 1271. He died in 1295 at the age of 24. Isabella Stonegrave and Simon Pateshull were married.

35653. **Isabella Stonegrave** born about 1271. She died about 1324 at the age of 53.

35654. **William De Grandison** is the same as person number 35382.

35655. **Sybil De Tregoz** is the same as person number 35383.

35684. **Roger La Zouche Sir** born about 1245. He died in 1285 at the age of 40. AR7 53-30 Sir Roger la Zouche d. 1285 Baron Zouche of Ashby m. Ela Longespee. Ela Longespee and Roger La Zouche Sir were married.

35685. **Ela Longespee** born about 1245. AR7 31-28

35686. **Nicholas De Seagrave Sir** born about 1240. He died before 12 Nov 1295 at the age of 55. AR7 31-29 says died sh. before 12 Nov 1395 must be 1295.

35687. **Maud** born about 1240.

35690. **Philip III Of France King** was born on 30 Apr 1245 in Poissy, France. He died on 5 Oct 1285 at the age of 40 in Perpignan, France. King Philip III (The Bold) of France Weis 101-29 1st wife Isabella of Aragon 2nd wife Marie of Brabant m 1272 d. 1321 Marie Of Brabant and Philip III Of France King were married on 21 Aug 1274.

35691. **Marie Of Brabant** born about 1254. She died on 12 Jan 1321 at the age of 67.

35692. **Baldwin Wake** was born in 1236. He died before 10 Feb 1281 at the age of 45. married 1st Ela Beauchamp dau of William Beauchamp and Ida Longespee. Hawise De Quincy and Baldwin Wake were married.

35693. **Hawise De Quincy** born about 1250. She died before 27 Mar 1284 at the age of 34. AR7 236-9 Hawise de Quincy b. ca 1250 d. by 27 Mar. 1284/5 heiress of Bidford, Co. Warwick m. as 2nd wife Baldwin Wake b. 1236 d. by 10 Feb 1281/2, son of Hugh Wake by his wife John.

35694. **William De Fiennes** is the same as person number 34894.

35695. **Blanche Of Loupeland Brienne** is the same as person number 34895.

35696. **Edward I of England** is the same as person number 12942.

35697. **Eleanor Of Castile** is the same as person number 12943.

35698. **Philip IV Of France King** was born in 1268 in Fontainbleau, France. He died on 29 Nov 1314 at the age of 46 in Fountainbleau, France. He was buried in Saint Denis. Weis 101-30 King of France 1285-1314 called The Fair, Jeanne Of Navarre and Philip IV Of France King were married on 16 Aug 1284 in Paris.

35699. **Jeanne Of Navarre** was born in Jan 1272. She died on 2 Apr 1305 at the age of 33 in Vincennes. Weis 101-30,45-31

35700. **Jean D'Avesnes II** was born in 1247 in Brabant, Holland. He died on 22 Aug 1304 at the age of 57. Philippa Of Luxembourg and Jean D'Avesnes II were married in 1270.

35701. **Philippa Of Luxembourg.**

35702. **Charles Of Valois Count** was born on 12 Mar 1270 or 12 Mar 1271 in Vincennes, France. He died on 16 Dec 1325 at the age of 55 in Paris, France. He was buried in Saint Jacques, Paris, France. Margaret Of Naples Princess and Charles Of Valois Count were married on 16 Aug 1290 in Corbeil, France.

35703. **Margaret Of Naples Princess** born about 1270. She died on 31 Dec 1299 at the age of 29.

35708. **Louis De Brienne Viscount** born about 1225. Vicount of Beaumont in Maine. Agnes De Beaumont and Louis De Brienne Viscount were married.

35709. **Agnes De Beaumont** born about 1225.

35710. **Alexander Comyn** born about 1250. Joan Latimer and Alexander Comyn were married.

35711. **Joan Latimer** born about 1250.

35936. **Robert De Ferrers Earl** was born in 1239. He died in 1279 at the age of 40. AR 57-30 Earl of Derby Alianore De Bohun and Robert De Ferrers Earl were married.

35937. **Alianore De Bohun** born about 1245. She died on 20 Feb 1313 or 20 Feb 1314 at the age of 68. AR 68-30

35938. **Robert Muscegros Sir** born about 1252. He died on 27 Dec 1280 at the age of 28. Agnes Ferrers and Robert Muscegros Sir were married.

35939. **Agnes Ferrers** born about 1252. She died after 9 May 1281 at the age of 29.

35944. **William De Botiller** born about 1270 of Oversley, Warwick County, England. Beatrice and William De Botiller were married.

35945. **Beatrice** born about 1270. First wife.

35946. **Richard Fitz Alan** is the same as person number 8764.

35947. **Alasia De Saluzzo** is the same as person number 8765.

35968. **Robert Constable** born about 1245. Visitations of Yorkshire say Marmaduke p. 178 and call him Robert on p. 197 Robert Constable was married.

35992. **Richard Argum** born about 1250. Richard Argum was married.

36016. **Johannes Mowbray** born about 1240. He is possibly John the son of Roger and Matilda named in History of Rutland p. 114.

36032. **William Wentworth** born about 1275.

36033. **Joan Tyas** born about 1275.

36064. **Hugh Le Despenser Knight** was born on 1 Mar 1260 or 1 Mar 1261. He died on 27 Oct 1326 at the age of 66. Isabel De Beauchamp and Hugh Le Despenser Knight were married before 1286.

36065. **Isabel De Beauchamp** is the same as person number 18215.

36066. **Ralph De Gousille Lord** born about 1270. Ralph De Gousille Lord was married.

36080. **Robert De Tybetot** born about 1250.

36081. **Eve Chaworth** born about 1250.

36082. **William Ros** is the same as person number 17672.

36083. **Maud Vaux** is the same as person number 17673.

36088. **Edward De Deincourt** is the same as person number 35010.

36089. **Isabel De Mohun** is the same as person number 35011.

36092. **Eudo La Zouche** is the same as person number 17358.

36093. **Millicent De Cantalope** is the same as person number 17359.

36094. **John Lovel Lord** born about 1275.

36095. **Isabel De Bois** born about 1275.

36098. **Hugh Le Despenser** is the same as person number 36064.

36099. **Isabel De Beauchamp** is the same as person number 18215.

36102. **William De Breouse Lord** born about 1260.

36112. **Hugh Le Despenser** is the same as person number 36064.

36113. **Isabel De Beauchamp** is the same as person number 18215.

36114. **Gilbert De Red Clare** is the same as person number 35358.

36115. **Joanne D'Acre Plantagenet** is the same as person number 35359.

36116. **William De Ferrers** is the same as person number 34210.

36117. **Anne Le Despenser** is the same as person number 34211.

36118. **John Savage** born about 1270. John Savage was married.

36120. **Robert Burghersh** born about 1275.

36121. **Maud De Badlesmere** born about 1275.

36122. **Theobald De Verdon Knight** was born on 8 Sep 1278. He died on 27 Jul 1316 at the age of 37 in Alton. MCS4 13-6 Sir Theobald de Verdon, Knight b. 8 Sep 1278 d. Alton, 27 Jul 1316, 2nd Lord Verdon, M.P. 1299-1314 m. 1st Wigmore 29 Jul 1302 Maud de Mortimer d. 17 or 18 Sep 1312 dau of Sir Edmund de Mortimer and Margaret de Fiennes m2nd Elizabeth de Clae dau of Sir Gilbert de Clare and Joan Plantagenet. They were married on 29 Jul 1302 in Wigmore.

36123. **Maud De Mortimer** born about 1285. She died on 17 Sep 1312 at the age of 27.

36124. **John de Weyland**. Mary de Braose and John de Weyland were married.

36125. **Mary de Braose**. She is said to be daughter of Richard de Braose and Alice Rus per Burke's Dormant and Extinct Peerages. London: 1866 but Roberts, Richardson, etc. do not have a daughter Mary listed for this couple.

36128. **Oliver De Dinham** born about 1234. He died on 26 Feb 1298 at the age of 64 in Devon, England. Isabel De Vere and Oliver De Dinham were married before 1276.

36129. **Isabel De Vere** is the same as person number 25873.

36140. **John De Moels**. Maud De Grey and John De Moels were married.

36141. **Maud De Grey**.

36160. **William Morley Lord** born about 1265. He died before 1302 at the age of 37. CP William 1st Lord expedition to Cascony with Roger de Mohaut m1 Isabel sister of Robert de Mohaut Lord Mohaut d. 1324 m2 Cicely. He dead 1302. buried in Reydon Church. Isabel De Mohaut and William Morley Lord were married.

36161. **Isabel De Mohaut** born about 1265. sister of Robert de Mohaut Lord Mohaut d. 1324. brother of Roger.

36162. **Lord William le Marshal Marshal of Ireland** born about 1265. He died in 1320 at the age of 55. EP Christian de Burgh and Lord William le Marshal Marshal of Ireland were married.

36163. **Christian de Burgh**.

36164. **Hugh Bardolf Lord** born about 29 Sep 1259. He died in Sep 1304 at the age of 45. AR7 257-31 Isabel Aguillon and Hugh Bardolf Lord were married before 1282.

36165. **Isabel Aguillon** born about 1258. She died after 1316 at the age of 58.

36166. **William De Grandison** is the same as person number 35382.

36167. **Sybil De Tregoz** is the same as person number 35383.

36200. **John Wingfield** born about 1280 in Wingfield Manor, Suffolk, England. Ann Peche and John Wingfield were married.

36201. **Ann Peche** born about 1280.

36202. **John Honeypot** born about 1280 in Wingfield Manor, Suffolk, England.

36278. **John Becard** born about 1250.

36279. **Alicia Greystock** born about 1250.

36336. **Thomas Foljambe** born about 1270. Catherine Eure and Thomas Foljambe were married.

36337. **Catherine Eure** born about 1270.

36338. **Gerard Furnival** born about 1270. Gerard Furnival was married.

36424. **Henry III Of England** is the same as person number 25884.

36425. **Eleanor Of Provence** is the same as person number 25885.

36426. **Robert I Of France King** was born in Sep 1216. He died on 9 Feb 1250 at the age of 33 in Mansoure, Egypt. Matilda Of Brabant and Robert I Of France King were married on 14 Jun 1237 in Campiegne.

36427. **Matilda Of Brabant** born about 1217. She died on 29 Sep 1288 at the age of 71. She was buried in Chercamp, Artois.

36428. **Patrick Chaworth** was born before 1200. He died in 1258 at the age of 58. Hawise London and Patrick Chaworth were married.

36429. **Hawise London** died in 1273.

36430. **William De Beauchamp** is the same as person number 17464.

36431. **Maud Fitz John** is the same as person number 17465.

36496. **Roger Mowbray Baron** born about 1250. He died in Nov 1297 at the age of 47 in Ghent, Flanders. He was buried in Fountains Abbey. Roesse Clare and Roger Mowbray Baron were married in 1270.

36497. **Roesse Clare** born about 1250.

36498. **William Braiose Lord** born about 1250. He died before May 1326 at the age of 76. Left Bramber and Gower to his son in law Sir John de Mowbray William Braiose Lord was married.

36508. **Edward I of England** is the same as person number 12942.

36509. **Marguerite Of France** is the same as person number 17845.

36510. **Roger Halys Sir** born about 1275. Roger Halys Sir was married.

49168. **Walter De Clifford** born about 1165. He died in 1225 at the age of 60. Sheriff of Herefordshire. died 7th Hen III. Agnes De Cundi and Walter De Clifford were married.

49169. **Agnes De Cundi** born about 1165.

49664. **Hugh Pointz** died after 1218.

49665. **Juliana Bardolf** was born before 1170.

49666. **Sir William II Malet High Sheriff of Somerset** born about 1176. He died about 1216 at the age of 40. He was also known as Magna Carta Surety Malet. Magna Carta Surety, Sheriff of Somerset and Dorset. He accompanied King Richard the Lionheart on the third crusade and took part in the Siege of Acre. MCS4 57-1 MAGNA CARTA: signed the Magna Carta as surety in 1215 Alice Basset and Sir William II Malet High Sheriff of Somerset were married.

49667. **Alice Basset** born about 1176.

49728. **Nicholas Fitz Roger** was born in 1194. He died in 1261 at the age of 67 in Nymphsfield, Gloucestershire, England.

51744. **Robert De Courtenay Baron** born about 1183 of Oakhampton. He died about 27 Jul 1242–27 Jul 1243 at the age of 59. He was buried in Ford Abbey, Devon County, England. Mary De Vernon and Robert De Courtenay Baron were married.

51745. **Mary De Vernon** born about 1185.

51746. **Hugh Vere** is the same as person number 35068.

51747. **Hawise De Quincy** is the same as person number 35069.

51748. **Hugh Le Despenser** born about 1200. He died after 1237 at the age of 37. History of Rutland p 19 Hugh Le Despenser was married.

51750. **Philip Basset Baron** born about 1215 of Wicombe, Bucks. History of Rutland p 19 Hawise De Louvain and Philip Basset Baron were married.

51751. Hawise De Louvain born about 1220.

51760. Humphrey V. De Bohun Earl was born in 1208 of Hereford. He died on 24 Sep 1275 at the age of 67. Weis AR: 2nd Earl of Hereford and Earl of Essex, Constable of England, Sheriff of Kent. first wife Maud Maud Lusignan and Humphrey V. De Bohun Earl were married.

51761. Maud Lusignan was born before 1200. She died on 14 Aug 1241 at the age of 41. Weis AR: or d. Aug 24

51762. William De Braiose Baron was born in 1195. He died on 2 May 1230 at the age of 35. 6th Baron de Braiose, 14th Lord of Abergavenny Eva Marshall and William De Braiose Baron were married.

51763. Eva Marshall born about 1195. She died before 1246 at the age of 51.

51764. William De Fiennes Lord born about 1190. He died in 1241 at the age of 51. Agnes De Dammartin and William De Fiennes Lord were married.

51765. Agnes De Dammartin born about 1190.

51766. Jacques Conde born about 1200. Roeux and Jacques Conde were married.

51767. Roeux born about 1200.

51768. John Of England King was born on 24 Dec 1166 in Beaumont Palace, Oxfordshire, England. He died on 18 Oct 1216 at the age of 49 in Newark Castle, Nottingham, Lincolnshire, England. He was buried in Worcester Cath., London, England. King of England 1199-1216 forced to sign the great Magna Carta 1215. He was the youngest son of Henry II and inherited the throne from his brother Richard (the lion-hearted). He ruled England while his brother was often on crusades. The legend of Robin Hood is written about this time period. Because of his failure to claim Plantagenent dominions in France, and his dispute with the Pope over the Archbishop of Canterbury and high taxation, the nobility rebelled against him forcing him to sign the great Magna Carta in 1215. John also had the first stone bridge over the Thames completed which was started by his father (now known as London Bridge). He received the nickname Lackland. MAGNA CARTA: signed as the King on the Magna Carta in 1215 Isabella Taillefer Of Angouleme and John Of England King were married on 24 Aug 1200 in Bordeaux, Gironde, France.

51769. Isabella Taillefer Of Angouleme is the same as person number 35067.

51770. Raymond V. Berenger Count was born in 1198 in France. He died on 19 Aug 1245 at the age of 47 in Aix, France. Weis AR: Count of Provence and Forcalquier. 101-28, 111-29 Beatrice Of Savoy and Raymond V. Berenger Count were married in Dec 1220 in Dez.

51771. Beatrice Of Savoy was born in 1198 in Savoie. She died in Dec 1266 at age of 68.

51772. Alfonso IX Of Leon King was born on 15 Aug 1171 in Zamora, Leon, Spain. He died on 24 Sep 1230 at the age of 59 in Villanueva, De Sarria, Spain. Weis AR: King of Leon 1188-1229, 2nd wife Berengaria. Berengaria Of Castille and Alfonso IX Of Leon King were married in Dec 1197 in Valladolid.

51773. Berengaria Of Castille was born in 1180 in Burgos, Spain. She died on 8 Nov 1246 at the age of 66 in Las Huelgas. Weis AR 2nd husband Alfonso IX

51774. Simon II De Dammartin Count born about 1175 of Aumale. He died on 21 Sep 1239 at the age of 64 in Abbeville, France. He was buried in Valoires. Weis, AR. line 109 Count of Aumale. 2nd son. Called Simon II by Stuart. Marie Of Ponthieu and Simon II De Dammartin Count were married before 1211.

51775. Marie Of Ponthieu was born on 17 Apr 1199. She died in Sep 1250 at the age of 51. Countess of Ponthieu

Seventeenth Generation

65552. Walter De Washington born about 1212. He died about May 1264 at the age of 52. had lands in Northumberland, probably killed at the Battle May 14, wife was widow in 1266. fought at Lewes 1264.

65553. Joan Of Whitchester born about 1212.

66688. William St. Quintin Knight born about 1240. Foster Yorkshire Routh and William St. Quintin Knight were married.

66689. Routh born about 1247.

66690. John Hesharton Knight born about 1240. Foster Yorkshire John Hesharton Knight was married.

66704. Marmaduke De Thwenge Knight was born in 1225 of Kilton Castle, Yorkshire, England. He died in Dec 1279 at the age of 54. Weis AR: Lord of Kilton Castle in Cleveland and Daneby, Yorkshire

66705. Lucia De Brus was born in 1225. She died in 1272 at the age of 47.

66752. William Gascoigne born about 1175 in Lasingcroft, Yorkshire, England. William Gascoigne was married.

67200. Peter Carrow Lord born about 1140. He died after 1189 at the age of 49. Lord of Seton-Carrow

67456. Robert De Umfreyville Knight born about 1165 of Tours. Burke EP: Robert with the Beard. Lord of Tours and Vian. Robert De Umfreyville Knight was married.

67464. Richard Comyn born about 1110 of Badenoch. He died in 1176 or 1182 at the age of 66. Weis AR: son of William , son of John, son of Robert Hextilda and Richard Comyn were married about 1145.

67465. Hextilda born about 1110.

67468. Saher IV de Quincy 1st Earl of Winchester was born in 1155. He died on 3 Nov 1219 at the age of 64 in Near Damietta, Egypt, Egypt. He was also known as Magna Carta Surety Quincy. Saher was buried in Acre, Holy Land. Created Earl of Winchester by King John, 1207, Magna Carta Surety 1215, Crusader to the Holy Land during the 5th Crusade in 1219. MAGNA CARTA: signed the Magna Carta as surety in 1215 AR7 53-27 quotes The Ancestry of Saher de Quincy Earl of Winchester NEHGR 112:61 et seq. Margaret De Beaumont and Saher IV de Quincy 1st Earl of Winchester were married before 1173.

67469. Margaret De Beaumont born about 1165. She died on 12 Jan 1235 or 12 Jan 1236 at the age of 70.

67470. Alan Macdonald Of Galloway Lord born about 1170. He died in 1234 at the age of 64. Weis AR: Constable of Scotland, Lord of Galloway named in Magna Carta 1215. MAGNA CARTA: mentioned in the Magna Carta as advisor to the King John Ragnhild De Lacy and Alan Macdonald Of Galloway Lord were married.

67471. Ragnhild De Lacy born about 1185. She died before 1208 at the age of 23. dau of Roger de Lacy of Pontefract. The Wilkinson book says she is Regnhild (Hilda of the Isles)

67712. Acharis De Halnaby was born before 1150.

68372. Marmaduke De Thwenge is the same as person number 66704.

68373. Lucia De Brus is the same as person number 66705.

68416. **John De Grey Lord** born about 1210 of Shirland, Derbyshire, England. He died before 1266 at the age of 56. History of Rutland p 162f Lord of Shirland in Derbyshire living 1241, 1248,
dead 1266 Emma Glanville and John De Grey Lord were married.

68417. **Emma Glanville** born about 1210. History of Rutland p 162f first wife , 2nd wife died 1256

68418. **William Fitz Hugh** born about 1210 of Torporley, Cheshire, England. History of Rutland p 162f

68419. **Matilda Longchamp** born about 1210.

68420. **William De Ferrers** is the same as person number 34714.

68421. **Margaret De Quincy** is the same as person number 34715.

68428. **Richard De Clare Earl** born about 1210. History of Rutland Baron Grey p 162f Richard De Clare Earl was married.

68448. **Gilbert Talbot** born about 1225. He died in 1274 at the age of 49.

68449. **Gwenthlian Mechyll** born about 1225.

68456. **John Comyn Lord** born about 1225 of Badenoch. He died after 1273 at the age of 48. Weis AR: seen 1243 died aft 1273, called the Red Comyn #1

68457. **Alicia** born about 1225. She died after 1273 at the age of 48.

68458. **John de Balliol King of Scotland** was born before 1208. He died on 25 Oct 1268 at the age of 60 in Barnard Castle, Gainford, County Durham, England. Weis AR: founders of Baliol College. Devorgilla Of Galloway and John de Balliol King of Scotland were married in 1233.

68459. **Devorgilla Of Galloway** born about 1215. She died on 28 Jan 1289 or 28 Jan 1290 at the age of 74.

68460. **Hugh X. De Lusignan** is the same as person number 35066.

68461. **Isabella Taillefer Of Angouleme** is the same as person number 35067.

68462. **Warin De Munchensi Lord** born about 1195 of Swanscomb. Weis AR

68463. **Joan Marshall** born about 1198.

68464. **Theobald Le Boteler** born about 1220. He died in 1248 at the age of 28. Weis AR Collins RA Margery De Burgh and Theobald Le Boteler were married about 1242.

68465. **Margery De Burgh** born about 1220.

68466. **John Fitz Geoffrey** is the same as person number 34930.

68467. **Isabel Bigod** is the same as person number 34931.

68488. **John De Bulmer** born about 1200. Alice and John De Bulmer were married.

68489. **Alice** born about 1200. She died after 1219 at the age of 19.

68544. **Robert De Grey** born about 1190 of Rotherfield, Oxford County. He died before 1245 at the age of 55. History of Rutland: dead 29 Hen 3 Beatrix and Robert De Grey were married.

68545. **Beatrix** born about 1190.

68546. **William De Duston** born about 1190. of Duston, Co Northhampton History of Rutland: dau Isabel m. Walter de Grey William De Duston was married.

68556. **Baron Robert Fitz Walter of Dunmow Castle** born about 1180. He died on 9 Dec 1235 at the age of 55. He was also known as Magna Carta Surety Fitz Walter. of Dunmow and of Woodham. Leader of Barons who fought against King John. Magna Carta Surety 1215. MAGNA CARTA: signed the Magna Carta as surety in 1215 Rohese and Baron Robert Fitz Walter of Dunmow Castle were married after 1207.

68557. **Rohese** born about 1185.

68558. **William Longespee Earl** was born in 1176. He died on 7 Mar 1225 or 7 Mar 1226 at the age of 49. Earl of Salisbury. MAGNA CARTA: mentioned in the Magna Carta as an advisory to King John in 1215. William de Longespée, 3rd Earl of Salisbury or William Longsword (ca. 1176 - March 7, 1226) was an English noble, primarily remembered for his command of the English forces at the Battle of Damme and for remaining loyal to King John. He was an illegitimate son of Henry II of England. His mother was unknown for many years, until the discovery of a charter of William mentioning "Comitissa Ida, mater mea" (see Cartulary of Bradenstoke Priory, 1979). This Ida was further identified as the wife of Roger Bigod, 2nd Earl of Norfolk. His father acknowledged him, and gave him the honor of Appleby, Lincolnshire in 1188. Ten years later his half-brother King Richard I married him to a great heiress, Ela, countess of Salisbury in her own right, and daughter of William of Salisbury, 2nd Earl of Salisbury. Ela Of Salisbury and William Longespee Earl were married in 1198.

68559. **Ela Of Salisbury** was born in 1178 in Amesbury, Amesbury, Wiltshire. She died on 24 Aug 1261 at the age of 83. Countess of Salisbury

68560. **Robert De Marmion** born about 1210. called the Younger. Surtees and Burkes' Extinct Peerage Amice Fitz Hugh and Robert De Marmion were married.

68561. **Amice Fitz Hugh** born about 1210. husband received Budington and Northampton by her rights. Burke said above land came from Lora de Dover. Surtees said that wife was Avice de Tanfield.

68562. **Richard Fitz Roy** born about 1200. natural son of King John, by dau of Earl of Warenne or dau of Hamelin. Plantagenet. Rohese Of Dover and Richard Fitz Roy were married.

68563. **Rohese Of Dover** born about 1200. She died in 1264 or 1265 at the age of 64.

68568. **Thomas De Furnival Lord** born about 1205 of Hallamshire. He died before 1249 at the age of 44. EP p 1057 Bertha and Thomas De Furnival Lord were married.

68569. **Bertha** born about 1205. She died after 1249 at the age of 44. EP married second Ralph Bigod 3rd son of 3rd Earl of Norfolk. supposed to be of the family of Ferrers, Earls of Derby

68576. **William St. Quintin Baron** born about 1225. He died after 1241 at the age of 16. Foster Yorkshire 4th son Beatrix De Sutton and William St. Quintin Baron were married.

68577. **Beatrix De Sutton** born about 1225.

68578. **Walter Fauconberg** born about 1225. of Skelton Walter Fauconberg was married.

68608. **William Surteyse** was born in 1233 in Durham, England. He died about Oct 1270 at the age of 37 in Durham, England. next of kin to Ralph Surteyse 41 Hen III. age 24 died before 18 Oct seised of North Gosford. son of Walter. William Surteyse was married.

69120. **Roger Conyers Lord** born about 1125 of Bishopton And, Sockbourne. He died after 1174 at the age of 49. a baron of the Bishoprick of Durham and Lord of Bishopton; living 1143 and 1174. joined with his son and heir Robert Conyers, in the gift of the Churches of Bishopton and Sockburne to Sherburne House. Matilda and Roger Conyers Lord were married.

69121. **Matilda** born about 1125. She died after 1174 at the age of 49. named in her husbands grant of lands in Bishopton to St. Mary of Nesham.

69184. **Gilbert De Aton** born about 1175. assumed the surname de Aton. Gilbert De Aton was married.

69186. **Warine De Vesci Lord** born about 1170. by gift of his brother, Lord of Knapton Matilda Of Wellom and Warine De Vesci Lord were married.

69187. **Matilda Of Wellom** born about 1170.

69196. **Roger Bertram** born about 1180. He died in 1241 at the age of 61. Burke EP: feudal lord involved in the proceedings of the barons in 1216, that castle and lands of Mitford were seized and conferred upon hilip de Ulecotes but afterwards making his peace and Philip de Ulecotes not seeming willing to obey King John's order he was threatened with the immediate confiscation of his own territory. After this period Roger appears to have enjoyed the royal favour and in 13 Hen III he went to meet with Alexander of Scotland at York with the king and other great barons.

69216. **Henry Percy Knight** born about 1160. He died in 1198 at the age of 38. Isabel De Brus and Henry Percy Knight were married.

69217. **Isabel De Brus** born about 1160. She died after 1230 at the age of 70. Uncertain as to her mother, could be either wife. married 2nd Sir Roger Maudit

69218. **Sir Enguerrand de Balliol of Urr and Redcastle** born about 1180. De Berkeley and Sir Enguerrand de Balliol of Urr and Redcastle were married.

69219. **De Berkeley** born about 1170.

69232. **Roger De Clifford** born about 1185. He died in 1251 at the age of 66. Sibyl De Ewyas and Roger De Clifford were married.

69233. **Sibyl De Ewyas** born about 1180. She died in 1236 at the age of 56. widow of Robert I de Tregoz. d 1213

69234. **John Bottrell** born about 1200. John Bottrell was married.

69236. **John De Vipont Baron** born about 1200 of Essedine. He died in 1241 at the age of 41. History of Rutland: Lord of Essendine, Baron of Appleby p 15 Sibilla Ferrars and John De Vipont Baron were married.

69237. **Sibilla Ferrars** born about 1220. History of Rutland p 15 married 2nd Franco de Bohun of Midhurst.

69238. **John Fitz Geoffrey** is the same as person number 34930.

69239. **Isabel Bigod** is the same as person number 34931.

69240. **Gilbert De Clare Earl** born about 1180. He died on 25 Oct 1230 at the age of 50 in Penros, Brittany. He was also known as Magna Carta Surety Clare. 7th Earl of Clare, Earl of Hertford and Gloucester. Magna Carta surety 1215 MAGNA CARTA: signed the Magna Carta as surety in 1215 Isabel Marshall and Gilbert De Clare Earl were married on 9 Oct 1217.

69241. **Isabel Marshall** born about 1196. She died on 17 Jan 1239 or 17 Jan 1240 at the age of 43 in Berkhampstead, England.

69242. **Earl John De Lacy of Lincoln** was born in 1192 of Lincoln. He died on 22 Jul 1240 at the age of 48. He was also known as Magna Carta Surety Lacy. Magna Carta Surety 1215 created Earl of Lincoln 1232, Constable of Chester. Lord of Pontefract Castle. 7th Baron of Halton Castle. direct descendant of King Alfred the Great. MAGNA CARTA: signed the Magna Carta as surety in 1215 Margaret De Quincy and Earl John De Lacy of Lincoln were married before 21 Jun 1221.

69243. **Margaret De Quincy** born about 1198. She died before 30 Mar 1266 at age of 68.

69244. **Maurice Fitz Gerald Knight** was born in 1190. He died on 8 May 1257 at the age of 67 in Youghal. 2nd Baron of Offaly, Knighted Jul 1217, Lord of Lea, Justiciar of Ireland Sep 1232-1245, Commissioner of the Treasury and Councillor 1250.

69245. **Juliane Cogan** born about 1190.

69246. **Stephen Longespee** born about 1220 in Sutton, Northampton. He died in 1260 at the age of 40. Lord Justice of Ireland 1256, of Sutton, Northampton Emmeline De Ridelisford and Stephen Longespee were married about 1243–1244.

69247. **Emmeline De Ridelisford** born about 1225. She died in 1276 at the age of 51. widow of Hugh de Lacy

69312. **Simon Le Scrope** was born before 1165. He died after 1205 at the age of 40. He was buried in Wensley, York County, England. 2nd son Ingoliana and Simon Le Scrope were married.

69313. **Ingoliana** born about 1165.

69314. **Roger Brune** born about 1160. of Thornton, co York

69315. **Isabel** born about 1160.

69328. **Everard Of Ros** born about 1150. He died in 1183 at the age of 33. Roese Trusbutt and Everard Of Ros were married.

69329. **Roese Trusbutt** born about 1150.

69330. **William I. Of Scotland King** was born in 1143. He died on 4 Dec 1214 at the age of 71 in Stirling, Scotland. called William the Lion Isabel Avenal and William I. Of Scotland King were married.

69331. **Isabel Avenal** born about 1145.

69332. **Herbert Fitz Herbert** born about 1120. He died before 18 Jul 1204 at the age of 84. Lucy Of Hereford Blaen Llyfni Lady and Herbert Fitz Herbert were married.

69333. **Lucy Of Hereford Blaen Llyfni Lady** born about 1130. She died after 1219 at the age of 89. of Blaen Llyfni and Bwlch y Dinas

69334. **Robert Fitz Roger Baron** born about 1150. He died about 1215 at the age of 65. 2nd Baron of Warkworth, Lord of Clavering, Sheriff of Northumberland in Co Essex by Henry II. Richard I granted him the manor of Eure co Bucks, Ambassador to Scotland 1209, he founded the priory of Langley co Norfolk 1215. Margaret Fitz Walter and Robert Fitz Roger Baron were married.

69335. **Margaret Fitz Walter** born about 1155. She died after 1215 at the age of 60.

69376. **Robert Fitz Roger** is the same as person number 69334.

69377. **Margaret Fitz Walter** is the same as person number 69335.

69378. **Hugh Balliol Lord of Bywell, Barnard Castle and Gainford** born about 1181. He died about 2 May 1229 at the age of 48 in Barnard Castle, Gainford, County Durham, England, United Kingdom. He was also known as Hugh De Balliol. Cecily de Fontaines and Hugh Balliol Lord of Bywell, Barnard Castle and Gainford were married.

69379. **Cecily de Fontaines** born about 1182. She died on 2 Feb 1228 at the age of 46 in Barnard Castle, Gainford, County Durham, England, United Kingdom. She was also known as Cicely De Fontaines.

69424. **Thomas De Berkeley** born about 1210. He died on 29 Nov 1245 at the age of 35. Joan De Someri and Thomas De Berkeley were married.

69425. **Joan De Someri** born about 1210. She died after 1273 at the age of 63.

69426. **Richard Fitz Roy** is the same as person number 68562.

69427. **Rohese Of Dover** is the same as person number 68563.

69428. **William De Ferrers Earl** born about 1165 of Derby. He died on 22 Sep 1247 at the age of 82. Weis AR: 4th Earl of Derby Agnes Of Chester and William De Ferrers Earl were married in 1192.

69429. **Agnes Of Chester** born about 1172. She died on 2 Nov 1247 at the age of 75. Collins RA: Lady of Chartley

69430. **Roger De Quincy** is the same as person number 33734.

69431. **Helen Of Galloway** is the same as person number 33735.

69432. **Alan La Zouche** was born before 1140. He died in 1190 at the age of 50. He was also known as Ceoche Zouche. Of North Moulton Devon

69433. **Alice Belmeis** was born before 1140. She died after 1190 at the age of 50.

69436. **William Cantelou II** born about 1201. He died in 1251 at the age of 50. Milicent Gournay and William Cantelou II were married.

69437. **Milicent Gournay** born about 1201. She died in 1260 at the age of 59.

69438. **William De Braiose** is the same as person number 51762.

69439. **Eva Marshall** is the same as person number 51763.

69780. **William Longespee** is the same as person number 68558.

69781. **Ela Of Salisbury** is the same as person number 68559.

69782. **Richard De Camville** born about 1150.

69783. **Eustacia Basset** born about 1150.

69784. **Ralph De Mortimer** born about 1205. He died on 6 Aug 1246 at the age of 41. He was buried in Wigmore, Hereford, England. Lord Mortimer of Wigmore Gladys Dhu Of Wales and Ralph De Mortimer were married in 1230.

69785. **Gladys Dhu Of Wales** born about 1205. She died in 1251 at the age of 46. widow of Reynold de Braiose

69786. **William De Braiose** is the same as person number 51762.

69787. **Eva Marshall** is the same as person number 51763.

69788. **Ingelram De Fiennes** is the same as person number 25882.

69789. **Of Conde** is the same as person number 25883.

69790. **Jean De Brienne** born about 1231. He died in 1296 at the age of 65. Grand Butler of France Jeanne Dame De Chateaudun and Jean De Brienne were married in 1251.

69791. **Jeanne Dame De Chateaudun** born about 1231.

69792. **Henry Fitz Harvey** born about 1180. He died in 1201 at the age of 21. said to be living 16 May 1212 per Charlemagnes Desc. Alice Fitz Walter and Henry Fitz Harvey were married.

69793. **Alice Fitz Walter** born about 1180.

69794. **Adam De Staveley Lord** born about 1190. Alice De Percy and Adam De Staveley Lord were married.

69795. **Alice De Percy** born about 1190.

69856. Wacheline De Beauchamp born about 1190. Joane De Mortimer and Wacheline De Beauchamp were married.

69857. Joane De Mortimer born about 1190.

69858. William Maudit born about 1190. He died in Apr 1257 at the age of 67. Alice Newburgh and William Maudit were married.

69859. Alice Newburgh born about 1197.

69860. Geoffrey Fitz Piers Earl born about 1160 of Essex. He died on 14 Oct 1213 at the age of 53. He was buried in Shouldham Priory. Weis AR: 4th Earl of Essex married Beatrice de Say Aveline De Clare and Geoffrey Fitz Piers Earl were married.

69861. Aveline De Clare born about 1162. Collins RA: her second husband was Geoffrey Fitz Pier (his second wife). Her first husband William de Munches, Collins RA: her second husband was Geoffrey Fitz Pier (his second wife). Her first husband William de Munches

69862. Hugh le Bigod Earl born about 1180 of Norfolk. He died in Feb 1224 or Feb 1225 at the age of 44. He was also known as Magna Carta Surety Bigod. Magna Carta Surety 1215, 3rd Earl of Norfolk Feb 1221. MAGNA CARTA: signed the Magna Carta as surety in 1215 Maud Marshall and Hugh le Bigod Earl were married in 1207.

69863. Maud Marshall is the same as person number 35065.

69864. Ralph VI Toeni Lord was born in 1189 of Flamstead, Hertford County, England. He died in 1239 at the age of 50. Petronilla Lacy and Ralph VI Toeni Lord were married in 1232 or 1233.

69865. Petronilla Lacy born about 1190. She died after 1288 at the age of 98.

69866. Humphrey V. De Bohun is the same as person number 51760.

69867. Maud Lusignan is the same as person number 51761.

69880. Simon Joinville born about 1210. Senechal of Champagne, Seigneur de Vaucouleurs Beatrix D'Auxonne and Simon Joinville were married.

69881. Beatrix D'Auxonne born about 1210.

69882. Gilbert Lacy born about 1200. He died in 1230 at the age of 30. Isabel Bigod and Gilbert Lacy were married.

69883. Isabel Bigod is the same as person number 34931.

69884. Hugh Lusignan XI was born in 1220. He died in 1260 at the age of 40. Yolande Dreux and Hugh Lusignan XI were married in Jan 1235 or Jan 1236.

69885. Yolande Dreux was born in 1218. She died in Oct 1272 at the age of 54.

69886. Raoul Fougeres. Raoul Fougeres was married.

70016. Robert De Willoughby Lord born about 1210. He died in Feb 1257 or Feb 1258 at the age of 47. CP Robert de Willoughby tenant of Gilbert de Gaunt m. a lady of Orreby, Lords of Oresby and Ingoldmells, Linc. died bet. 3 Feb 1256/7 and 21 Feb 1257/8

70017. Orreby born about 1225.

70018. John Beke Lord born about 1200. He died about 1303–1304 at the age of 103. CP Lord Beke John Beke Lord was married.

70020. John Deincourt Sir born about 1210. John D'Eincourt Baron of Blankney, son and heir of Oliver 30 Henry 3 m. Agnes de Percey, sister of Robert and Geoffrey Nevill widow of Richard de Percey who was living 7 Hen 3. Collins Peerage. History of Rutland p. 150 Agnes Neville and John Deincourt Sir were married after 1245.

70021. Agnes Neville born about 1210. She died before 20 Jul 1293 at the age of 83.

70022. **Reynold De Mohun Justice** born about 1225. He died on 20 Jan 1257 or 20 Jan 1258 at the age of 32. MCS4 149a-3 Isabel de Ferrers d. by 26 Nov 1260 m. as his 2nd wife Sir Reynold de Mohun of Dunser, Somerset, a minor 1228, d. 20 Jan. 1257/8 Justice of Common Pleas, Chief Justice. Isabel De Ferrers and Reynold De Mohun Justice were married.

70023. **Isabel De Ferrers** born about 1225. She died before 26 Nov 1260 at the age of 35.

70080. **John III Strange Lord** born about 1190 of Knockyn. He died on 26 Mar 1269 at the age of 79. CP 12 (1) p. 350 John Lestrange III son and heir. In 1213 he attended upon the King to pay a debt on behalf of his father. In 1235 he was Constable of Montgomery and on 24 Oct 1236 was app. sheriff of Salop and Staffs. In 1240 or 1241 he was app. Justice of Chester. He is said to have married Lucy dau of Robert Tregoz. He died before 26 Mar. 1269. Weis AR p 165 Lucy Tregoz and John III Strange Lord were married.

70081. **Lucy Tregoz** born about 1218. Weis AR p 165

70082. **Roger De Somery Lord** born about 1210 of Dudley, Warwick County. He died before 26 Aug 1273 at the age of 63. Weis 55-28 1st wife Nichole 2nd wife Amabil Chaucombe, widow of Gilbert de Segrave Nichole D'Aubigny and Roger De Somery Lord were married before 1254.

70083. **Nichole D'Aubigny** born about 1210. She died before 1254 at the age of 44. Weis 55-28, 126-30, Royal Descents p 409, Weis AR p 158, Weis 55-28, 126-30

70112. **John Fitz Alan** born about 1172. He died in 1239 at the age of 67. took up arms with the other barons against King John. took up arms with the other barons against King John in 1215 Isabel D'Aubigny and John Fitz Alan were married.

70113. **Isabel D'Aubigny** born about 1195.

70114. **Theobald Le Boteler** born about 1200 of Ireland. Rohese De Verdon and Theobald Le Boteler were married.

70115. **Rohese De Verdon** born about 1200.

70128. **Hamelin Plantagenet Earl** born about 1145. He died on 7 May 1202 at the age of 57. Earl of Surrey, natural son of Geoffrey V Isabelle De Warenne Countess and Hamelin Plantagenet Earl were married in 1163.

70129. **Isabelle De Warenne Countess** born about 1145. She died on 13 Jul 1199 at the age of 54. 2nd husband Hamelin Plantagenet

70130. **Knight Templar William Marshal 1st Earl of Pembroke** born about 1146. He died on 14 May 1219 at the age of 73 in Caversham. He was buried in Knights Templar, London, England. 3rd Earl of Pembroke, Marshall of England, Protector, Regent of the Kingdom 1216-1219. He was made regent during the minority of Henry III. He was considered a wise ruler and he helped defeat the French forces in 1217 who tried to take the English crown. A biography was written about his life shortly after his death. He was considered the greatest Knight of the Templar at the time of his death. He was captured in 1167 but was ransomed by the Queen. History of Rutland: Earls of Pembroke. Weis 66-27 MAGNA CARTA: mentioned in the Magna Carta, advisor to King John in 1215. William Marshal (also called William the Marshal), 1st Earl of Pembroke, is one of the most important figures in the history of medieval England. He was a knight and nobleman who lived between the 12th and 13th centuries AD, during which he served five English monarchs – Henry the Young King, Henry II, Richard I, John, and Henry III. Due to William's efforts, the House of Plantagenet was saved during this period of time, and survived for around 250 years after. William Marshal died in 1219, and was interred in the Temple Church, London. Apparently, whilst in the Holy Land, William had promised the Templars that he would die as one of them. Thus, he was allowed burial in their church. His tomb, and its effigy, can still be seen there today. Tomb effigy of William Marshal in Temple Church, London.

70131. **Isabel De Clare** born about 1173. She died in 1220 at the age of 47. She was buried in Tintern Abbey.

70134. **Aymer De Valence Count** born about 1160 in Angouleme. He died on 16 Jun 1202 at the age of 42 in Limoges. Count of Angouleme Alice De Courtenay and Aymer De Valence Count were married in Apr 1186.

70135. **Alice De Courtenay** born about 1168 in Courtenay, Loriet. She died after 14 Sep 1205 at the age of 37.

70136. **Earl Robert De Vere 3rd Earl of Oxford** born about 1160 of Oxford. He died after 1215 at the age of 55. He was also known as Magna Carta Surety Vere. Magna Carta Surety 1215 Earl of Oxford. MAGNA CARTA: signed the Magna Carta as surety in 1215 Isabel De Bolbec and Earl Robert De Vere 3rd Earl of Oxford were married.

70137. **Isabel De Bolbec** born about 1180.

70138. **Saher IV de Quincy** is the same as person number 67468.

70139. **Margaret De Beaumont** is the same as person number 67469.

70688. **William De Roos** is the same as person number 17332.

70689. **Lucy Fitz Piers** is the same as person number 17333.

70690. **William D'Aubeney Lord** born about 1200 of Belvoir. He died in 1242 at the age of 42. Lord of Belvoir. Isabel and William D'Aubeney Lord were married.

70691. **Isabel** born about 1200. second wife.

70692. **Oliver Vaux Sir** born about 1200. Oliver Vaux Sir was married.

70704. **Robert Stafford** born about 1215. He died in 1282 at the age of 67. Alice Corbet and Robert Stafford were married.

70705. **Alice Corbet** born about 1215.

70708. **Ralph Basset Baron** born about 1235. He died on 4 Aug 1265 at the age of 30 in Evesham. Weis 55-29 Baron Basset of Drayton, slain at Evesham.

70709. **Margaret De Somery** born about 1235. She died after 18 Jun 1293 at the age of 58. Weis 55-29 first husband Ralph Basset, 2nd Ralph de Cromwell who died bef 1289

70710. **Reginald De Grey** is the same as person number 34208.

70711. **Matilda Fitz Hugh** is the same as person number 34209.

70716. **Richard De Clare** is the same as person number 34620.

70717. **Maud De Lacy** is the same as person number 34621.

70718. **Edward I of England** is the same as person number 12942.

70719. **Eleanor Of Castile** is the same as person number 12943.

70736. **Robert Neville** born about 1215. He died in 1282 at the age of 67. Ida Bertram and Robert Neville were married.

70737. **Ida Bertram** born about 1215.

70738. **Ralph Fitz Randolph Lord**. Lord of Middleham Ralph Fitz Randolph Lord was married.

70740. **Roger Fitz John Lord** born about 1215 of Clavering. He died about 1249 at the age of 34 in Normandy. MCS: Lord of Warkworth and of Clavering He cannot be son of Ada as they were married in 1250. Isabel and Roger Fitz John Lord were married.

70741. **Isabel** born about 1215.

70742. **Alan La Zouche Sir** born about 1222. He died on 10 Aug 1270 at the age of 48. Constable of the Tower of London Helen Quincy and Alan La Zouche Sir were married in 1242.

70743. **Helen Quincy** born about 1222. She died on 20 Aug 1296 at the age of 74. She was also known as Elena Quincy.

70762. **Peter Montfort** born about 1250. Peter Montfort was married.

70766. **John Tregoz Sir** born about 1240. He died in Sep 1300 at the age of 60. Mabel Fitz Warin and John Tregoz Sir were married.

70767. **Mabel Fitz Warin** born about 1250.

70776. **Richard Burgh Earl** born about 1270. He died on 29 Jul 1326 at the age of 56 in Athassel. 3rd Earl of Ulster Margaret Of Guines and Richard Burgh Earl were married before 27 Feb 1281.

70777. **Margaret Of Guines** born about 1270. She died in 1304 at the age of 34.

70778. **Gilbert De Red Clare** is the same as person number 35358.

70779. **Joanne D'Acre Plantagenet** is the same as person number 35359.

70784. **Randulf De Dacre** born about 1240. Roose and Randulf De Dacre were married.

70785. **Roose** born about 1240 of Kendall.

70786. **Benet Gernet** born about 1240 in Lancaster, England. Benet Gernet was married.

70790. **Piers De Mauley** is the same as person number 33350.

70816. **Archibald Douglas** was born in 1213. He died in 1240 at the age of 27.

71232. **Gilbert Umfreyville Sir** died before 1189. Gilbert Umfreyville Sir was married.

71296. **William De Beauchamp** is the same as person number 34928.

71297. **Isabel Mauduit** is the same as person number 34929.

71298. **Roger V. Toeni** is the same as person number 34932.

71299. **Alice De Bohun** is the same as person number 34933.

71304. **John Pateshull Sir** born about 1250. He died in 1290 at the age of 40. Hawise and John Pateshull Sir were married.

71305. **Hawise** born about 1250.

71306. **John Stonegrave Sir** born about 1230. He died in 1295 at the age of 65. Lord of Stonegrave and Nunnington, co. York Ida Wake and John Stonegrave Sir were married before 1273.

71307. **Ida Wake** born about 1240.

71368. **Alan La Zouche** is the same as person number 70742.

71369. **Helen Quincy** is the same as person number 70743.

71370. **Stephen Longespee** is the same as person number 69246.

71371. **Emmeline De Ridelisford** is the same as person number 69247.

71380. **Louis IX Of France King** was born on 25 Apr 1214 in Poissy, France. He died on 25 Aug 1270 at the age of 56 in Near Tunis. He was buried in Saint Denis. Weis 101-28 Crusader to the Holy Land, King of France 1226-1270. He was made a Saint. Margaret Of Provence and Louis IX Of France King were married on 27 May 1234 in Saint Etienne, Sens, France.

71381. **Margaret Of Provence** was born in 1221 in Saint Maime. She died on 20 Dec 1295 at the age of 74 in Paris. She was buried in Saint Denis. Weis 101-28

71382. **Henry III Of Brabant Duke** died on 21 Feb 1291. Alix Of Champagne and Henry III Of Brabant Duke were married.

71383. **Alix Of Champagne** died on 23 Oct 1273. She was also known as Adelaide Champagne.

71384. **Hugh Wake** born about 1200. He died before 18 Dec 1241 at the age of 41 in Holy Land. Joan Stuteville and Hugh Wake were married before 29 Mar 1229.

71385. **Joan Stuteville** born about 1200. She died before 6 Apr 1276 at the age of 76.

71386. **Robert Quincy** born about 1218. He was the second son named Robert, the other died 1217 per AR7. Helen Of Wales Princess and Robert Quincy were married.

71387. **Helen Of Wales Princess** born about 1218. She died in 1253 at the age of 35. AR7 236-8 Ellen or Helen d. 1253 received manors of Bidford, co. Warwick and Suckley co. Worcester as maritagium m. 1st John Le Scot, Earl of Hungtingdon m. 2nd Robert de Quincy d. 1257

71396. **Philip III Of France** is the same as person number 35690.

71397. **Isabella Of Aragon** born about 1245. She died on 28 Jan 1271 at the age of 26 in Clermont, Auvergne, France. Weis 101-29, 105-30 1st wife Isabella of Aragon

71398. **Henry I. Of Navarre King** born about 1244. He died on 22 Jul 1274 at the age of 30. Count of Champagne, then Henry III, then Henry I of Navarre. Weis 101-30 Blanche Of Artois and Henry I. Of Navarre King were married in 1269.

71399. **Blanche Of Artois** is the same as person number 18213.

71400. **Jean I. D'Avesnes** was born on 1 May 1218 in Etraeungt Nord, France. He died on 24 Dec 1257 at the age of 39. He was buried in Valenciennes. Adelaide Of Holland and Jean I. D'Avesnes were married on 9 Oct 1246.

71401. **Adelaide Of Holland** born about 1225. She died in 1284 at the age of 59.

71402. **Henry III Of Luxembourg Count** was born in 1217. He died on 24 Nov 1281 at the age of 64. Count of Luxembourg Mathilde De Bar and Henry III Of Luxembourg Count were married on 4 Jun 1240.

71403. **Mathilde De Bar** died on 23 Nov 1275.

71404. **Philip III Of France** is the same as person number 35690.

71405. **Isabella Of Aragon** is the same as person number 71397.

71406. **Charles II Of Naples King** was born in 1254. He died on 5 Jun 1309 at the age of 55 in Caranova. Marie Of Hungary and Charles II Of Naples King married in 1270.

71407. **Marie Of Hungary** born about 1254. She died on 25 Mar 1323 at the age of 69. Assassinated

71416. **Jean De Brienne King** born about 1168. He died on 21 Mar 1237 at the age of 69. Berengaria was his 3rd wife. King of Jerusalem, 1210-1215 (which had been recaptured from the Moslims during the Crusades, Emperor of Constantinople, Crusader to the Holy Land during the 3rd Crusade. His ancestry in AR7 114-28, Also called Aumary I Berenguela Of Leon and Jean De Brienne King were married in 1223.

71417. **Berenguela Of Leon** born about 1198. She died on 12 Apr 1237 at the age of 39.

71418. **Raoul VI De Beaumont** born about 1150. He died in 1235 at the age of 85. Agnes and Raoul VI De Beaumont were married.

71419. **Agnes** born about 1170.

71420. **Alexander Comyn** is the same as person number 16866.

71421. **Elizabeth De Quincy** is the same as person number 16867.

71872. **William De Ferrers** is the same as person number 34714.

71873. **Margaret De Quincy** is the same as person number 34715.

71874. **Humphrey VI De Bohun** is the same as person number 25880.

71875. **Eleanor De Braiose** is the same as person number 25881.

71876. **John Muscegros Sir** was born on 10 Aug 1232. He died on 8 May 1275 at the age of 42. Of Charlton Cecily Avenal and John Muscegros Sir were married.

71877. **Cecily Avenal** born about 1235. She died about 10 Aug 1301 at the age of 66.

71878. **William De Ferrers** is the same as person number 34714.

71879. **Margaret De Quincy** is the same as person number 34715.

71888. **William Boteler** born about 1250.

71889. **Ankaret Ap Griffith.**

71936. **William Constable Sir** born about 1220. Visitations Of Yorkshire by Glover p. 178 William Constable and Julianna, son of Robert. Juliana and William Constable Sir were married.

71937. **Juliana** born about 1220.

72032. **Roger Mowbray Baron** born about 1216. He died in 1266 at the age of 50. Maud Beauchamp and Roger Mowbray Baron were married.

72033. **Maud Beauchamp** born about 1216. She died before Apr 1273 at the age of 57.

72066. **Richard Tyas** born about 1250. Richard Tyas was married.

72128. **Hugh De Despenser** is the same as person number 25874.

72129. **Aline Basset** is the same as person number 25875.

72162. **Patrick De Chaworth** born about 1225. Patrick De Chaworth was married.

72244. **Theobald De Verdon** born about 1248. He died on 24 Aug 1309 at the age of 61 in Alton, Stafford County, England. MCS4 13-5 Theobald de Verdon b. c 1248 d. Alton, Co. Stafford, 24 Aug 1309, Lord Verdun, m. bef 6 Nov 1276 Margery. Margery and Theobald De Verdon were married before 6 Nov 1276.

72245. **Margery** born about 1248.

72246. **Edmund De Wigmore Mortimer** is the same as person number 17446.

72247. **Margaret De Fiennes** is the same as person number 17447.

72249. **Anne de Coleville.** Anne de Coleville was married.

72250. **Richard de Braose.** Alice le Rus and Richard de Braose were married.

72251. **Alice le Rus.**

72320. **Robert Morley** born about 1240. He was buried in Prussia. He died buried in Prussia. His heart was brought back to Reydon. Robert Morley was married.

72324. **John Marshal Baron** born about 1240. He died in 1284 at the age of 44. Hawise de Say and John Marshal Baron were married.

72325. **Hawise de Say.**

72327. **Devorguilla de Burgh Lady Fitz Walter.** Devorguilla de Burgh Lady Fitz Walter was married.

72328. **William Bardolf** born about 1230. He died in 1289 at the age of 59.

72329. **Juliana De Gournay** born about 1230. She died in 1295 at the age of 65.

72330. **Robert Aguillon** born about 1225. He died after 1267 at the age of 42. AR7 257-30 Joan Ferrers and Robert Aguillon were married before Aug 1256.

72331. **Joan Ferrers** born about 1235. She died before Oct 1267 at the age of 32.

72400. **Thomas Wingfield** born about 1260.

72401. **Alice Weyland** born about 1260.

72402. **John Peche Sir** born about 1260. John Peche Sir was married.

72558. **Thomas Greystock** born about 1225. Thomas Greystock was married.

72672. **Thomas Foljambe** born about 1250. Landed Gentry p. 798

72673. **Margaret De Gernon** born about 1250.

72674. **William Eure** born about 1250 of Hope.

72852. **Louis VIII Of France King** was born on 5 Sep 1187 in Paris, France. He died on 8 Nov 1226 at the age of 39 in Montpensier, Auvergne, France. He was buried in Saint Denis. He was called The Lion-Heart Blanche Of Castile and Louis VIII Of France King were married on 23 May 1200 in Bapaume, Normandy, France.

72853. **Blanche Of Castile** was born on 4 Mar 1188 in Palencia, Spain. She died on 27 Nov 1252 at the age of 64 in Paris. She was buried in Montbuisson.

72854. **Henry II Of Brabant Duke** was born in 1207. He died on 1 Feb 1247 or 1 Feb 1248 at the age of 40 in Louvain. Duke of Brabant Marie Of Swabia and Henry II Of Brabant Duke were married before 22 Feb 1215.

72855. **Marie Of Swabia** was born in 1201. She died in 1235 at the age of 34 in Louvain.

72858. **Thomas London** died before 1222. Thomas London was married.

72992. **Roger Mowbray** is the same as person number 72032.

72993. **Maud Beauchamp** is the same as person number 72033.

72994. **Richard De Clare** is the same as person number 34620.

72995. **Maud De Lacy** is the same as person number 34621.

72996. **William De Braose Lord** born about 1220. He died before Jan 1290 at the age of 70. Aline De Mulford and William De Braose Lord were married.

72997. **Aline De Mulford**.

98336. **Walter De Clifford** was born before 1116. He died in 1190 at the age of 74. Took his surname from his residence, Clifford Castle Margaret De Toney and Walter De Clifford were married.

98337. **Margaret De Toney** born about 1130. She died before 1185 at the age of 55.

98338. **Roger De Cundi Lord** born about 1140. He died before 1194 at the age of 54. Lord of the manors of Covenby and Glentham, co Lincoln.Seneschal to the Bishop of Lincoln of whom he held 8 knight's fees Alice de Cheney Lady of Horncastle and Roger De Cundi Lord were married.

98339. **Alice de Cheney Lady of Horncastle** born about 1140.

99328. **Nicholas Fitz Pons** was born before 1170. He died after 1218 at the age of 48.

99329. **Johanna de Traily** was born before 1170. She died after 1218 at the age of 48.

99332. **Gilbert Malet Baron** born about 1150. Baron of Curry Malet, Somerset and Steward in reign of Henry II Alice Picot and Gilbert Malet Baron were married.

99333. **Alice Picot** born about 1150.

99334. **Thomas Basset Lord** born about 1150. He died in 1220 at the age of 70. Lord of Headington, Oxford and Colynton and Whitford, Devon Philippa Malbank and Thomas Basset Lord were married.

99335. **Philippa Malbank**.

99456. **Roger Fitz Nicholas** born about 1165. He died in 1230 at the age of 65.

103488. **Reginald De Courtenay** born about 1150. He died on 27 Sep 1194 at the age of 44. He was buried in Ford Abbey, Devon County, England. Hawise De Courcy and Reginald De Courtenay were married.

103489. **Hawise De Courcy** born about 1150. She died on 31 Jul 1219 at the age of 69.

103490. **William De Vernon Earl** born about 1155 of Devon. He died in Sep 1217 at the age of 62. 5th Earl of Devon Maud De Beaumont and William De Vernon Earl were married.

103491. **Maud De Beaumont** born about 1166. She died after 1 May 1204 at the age of 38.

103496. Almaric Le Despenser born about 1170. He died after 1193 at the age of 23. History of Rutland p 19 Amabil De Chesnei and Almaric Le Despenser were married.

103497. Amabil De Chesnei born about 1175.

103502. Matthew De Louvain born about 1200. He died before Jun 1258 at the age of 58. Ancestry in 155a-27, 155-25 Muriel and Matthew De Louvain were married.

103503. Muriel born about 1200.

103520. Henry de Bohun Earl was born in 1176. He died on 1 Jun 1220 at the age of 44. He was also known as Magna Carta Surety Bohun. Weis AR: Magna Carta Surety 1215. died on pilgrimage to Holy Land, Sheriff of Kent. 5th Earl of Hereford, 1200 Hereditary Constable of England. MAGNA CARTA: signed the Magna Carta as surety in 1215 Maud Fitz Geoffrey and Henry de Bohun Earl were married.

103521. Maud Fitz Geoffrey born about 1180 of Mandeville. She died on 27 Aug 1236 at the age of 56. Weis AR: Countess of Essex

103522. Raoul I. De Lusignan Count born about 1181. He died on 1 May 1219 at the age of 38. Weis AR Count D'eu Alice D'Eu Countess and Raoul I. De Lusignan Count were married.

103523. Alice D'Eu Countess born about 1181. She died on 15 May 1246 at the age of 65. Weis AR: Countess of Eu, Lady of Hastings

103524. Reginald De Braiose born about 1170. He died in 1227 or 1228 at the age of 57. Gracia De Briwere and Reginald De Braiose were married.

103525. Gracia De Briwere was born before 1170. She died before 1215 at the age of 45.

103526. William Marshal is the same as person number 70130.

103527. Isabel De Clare is the same as person number 70131.

103528. Ingelram De Fiennes born about 1150. He died in 1189 at the age of 39. Sibyl De Boulougne and Ingelram De Fiennes were married.

103529. Sibyl De Boulougne born about 1150. She died after 1207 at the age of 57.

103530. Alberic II Of Dammartin Count born about 1150. He died on 19 Sep 1200 at the age of 50 in London, London, England. He was also known as Aubrey Dammartin. Alberic was buried in Jumieges. Count of Dammartin Weis AR Maud Of Ponthieu and Alberic II Of Dammartin Count were married.

103531. Maud Of Ponthieu born about 1150. She died after Oct 1200 at the age of 50. She was also known as Mathilda Ponthieu.

103532. Nicholas Conde born about 1180. He died in 1250 at the age of 70. Isabel Moreaumes and Nicholas Conde were married.

103533. Isabel Moreaumes born about 1180.

103534. Eustache Roeux III. Mortaigne and Eustache Roeux III were married.

103535. Mortaigne.

103536. Henry II Of England King was born on 5 Mar 1132 or 5 Mar 1133 in Le Mans, Sarthe, France. He died on 6 Jul 1189 at the age of 57 in Chinon, Indre-Et-Loire, France. He was buried in Fontevrault. King of England called Curt Mantel. He was the King that had Thomas A'Becket killed when he would not agree with his reforms of the English Church in 1170. He and his wife did not get along and she constantly put her children up to overthrow their father. Known as the Greatest of the Plantagenet Kings of England King of England called Curt Mantel. Eleanor Of Aquitaine and Henry II Of England King were married on 18 May 1153 in Bordeaux, Gironde, France.

103537. **Eleanor Of Aquitaine** was born in 1123 in Bordeaux. She died on 31 Mar 1204 at the age of 81 in Fontevrault, France. She was buried in Fontevrault Abb., France.

103540. **Alfonso Of Provence Count** born about 1175 in Barcelona. He died in Feb 1209 at the age of 34 in Palermo, Sicily. Weis AR Alfonso of Aragon Gersenda II Of Sabran and Alfonso Of Provence Count were married in 1193.

103541. **Gersenda II Of Sabran** born about 1175 in Sabran. She died after 1222 at the age of 47 in Le Celle.

103542. **Thomas I. Savoy** was born on 20 May 1177 at Carbonierres in Savoie, France. He died on 1 Mar 1233 at the age of 55 in Provincia di Aosta, Italy. He was buried in Saint Michael, Aosta. Margaret Of Geneva and Thomas I. Savoy were married in May 1195.

103543. **Margaret Of Geneva** born about 1175. She died on 13 Apr 1236 at the age of 61 in Pierre Chatel, Hautecombe.

103544. **Ferdinand II Of Leon King** was born in 1137. He died on 22 Jan 1188 at the age of 51 in Benavente, Italy. Weis AR: King of Leon 1157-1188 Urraca Of Portugal and Ferdinand II Of Leon King were married in 1165. They were divorced.

103545. **Urraca Of Portugal** born about 1145. She died on 16 Oct 1188 at the age of 43 in Bamba, Spain. Weis AR

103546. **Alfonso VIII Of Castile King** was born on 11 Nov 1155 in Soria. He died on 5 Oct 1214 at the age of 58 in Avevalo. He was buried in Burgos. Weis AR Eleanor Of England Princess and Alfonso VIII Of Castile King were married in 1179.

103547. **Eleanor Of England Princess** was born on 13 Oct 1162 in Falais, Calvados, France. She died on 25 Oct 1214 at the age of 52 in Burgos, Spain.

103548. **Alberic II Of Dammartin** is the same as person number 103530.

103549. **Maud Of Ponthieu** is the same as person number 103531.

103550. **William III Of Ponthieu Count** was born in 1179. He died on 6 Oct 1221 at the age of 42. Weis AR: 109 Crusader to the Holy Land. Count of Ponthieu commanded the French right wing at Bouvines on the Albigensian Crusade. Alice Of France Princess and William III Of Ponthieu Count were married on 20 Aug 1195 in Meudon.

103551. **Alice Of France Princess** born c1180. She died after 18 Jul 1218 at age of 38.

Eighteenth Generation

131104. **William De Washington** was born before 1187. He died about 1239 at the age of 52. Alice De Lexington and William De Washington were married in 1211.

131105. **Alice De Lexington** born about 1187.

133376. **Alexander St. Quintin** born about 1220. Foster Yorkshire: 5th son Margery Albino and Alexander St. Quintin were married.

133377. **Margery Albino** born about 1227.

133378. **John Routh Knight** born about 1225. Foster Yorkshire John Routh Knight was married.

133408. **Robert De Thwenge Knight** was born in 1202. He died in 1247 at the age of 45. Matilda De Kilton and Robert De Thwenge Knight were married in 1224.

133409. **Matilda De Kilton** was born in 1202. She died in Jun 1279 at the age of 77.

133410. **Peter II De Brus Baron** born about 1200 of Skelton. He died before 1247 at the age of 47. Weis AR: Crusader to the Holy Land, Lord of Skelton Helwise De Lancaster and Peter II De Brus Baron were married.

133411. **Helwise De Lancaster** born about 1200. Weis AR 88-28

133504. **William Gascoigne** born about 1150 in Lasingcroft, Yorkshire, England. William Gascoigne was married.

134930. **Huctred Of Tyndale** born about 1080. Weis AR Bethoc and Huctred Of Tyndale were married.

134931. **Bethoc** born about 1075. Weis AR

134936. **Robert De Quincy Lord** born about 1135 of Buckley. He died about 1198 at the age of 63. Weis 53-27 Lord of Buckley and Fawside, Crusader to the Holy Land during the 3rd Crusade (1189-92).

134937. **Orabella Of Leuchars** born about 1135.

134938. **Robert III De Beaumont Earl** was born before 1135 of Leicester. He died in 1190 at the age of 55 in Durazzo, Greece. Weis 53-26 Crusader to the Holy Land during the 3rd Crusade (1189-92), 3rd Earl of Leicester, Lord Steward of England Pernell Grantmesnil and Robert III De Beaumont Earl were married about 1155.

134939. **Pernell Grantmesnil** born about 1135. She died on 1 Apr 1212 at the age of 77. Weis 53-26

134940. **Roland Of Galloway Lord** was born before 1150. He died in Dec 1200 at the age of 50. Weis 38-25 Lord of Galloway, Constable of Scotland Elena De Morville and Roland Of Galloway Lord were married.

134941. **Elena De Morville** born about 1165. She died on 11 Jun 1217 at the age of 52.

134942. **Roger De Lacy** born about 1165. He died in 1211 at the age of 46. Visitations of Yorkshire p. 609 Roger de Lacy constable of Chester, Lord of Halton and Pontefract, who gave to his brother Robert the lordship of Flamborough, participated in the achievements of the lion-hearted Richard at Acre, 1192. m. Matilda dau of Richard Clare, Earl of Gloucester, 3rd Earl of Clare. She died 1213. called Roger de Lacy of Pontefract Maud De Clare and Roger De Lacy were married before 1192.

134943. **Maud De Clare** born about 1167. She died in 1213 at the age of 46.

136832. **Henry De Grey Baron** born about 1175 of Codnoure, Derbyshire, England. He died before 1219 at the age of 44. History of Rutland p 162f living 1199 Extinct Peerages says he was the father of Robert of Rotherfield, but History of Rutland shows different. Isolda Bardolf Baroness and Henry De Grey Baron were married.

136833. **Isolda Bardolf Baroness** born about 1175 of Codnoure. She died in 1246 at the age of 71. History of Rutland p 162f married 2nd Reginald de Mondr. both living 1239 niece of Robert Bardolf Baron of Codnoure.

136834. **Geoffrey De Glanville** born about 1185. History of Rutland p 162f Emma dau and coheir of Geoffrey Geoffrey De Glanville was married.

136838. **Henry Longchamp Lord** born about 1175 of Wilton, Upon Wye, Herefordshire, England. History of Rutland p 162f Henry Longchamp Lord was married.

136898. **Rhys Mechyll Ap Rhys Lord** born about 1170 of Dinefwr. He died in 1244 at the age of 74. WFP p 68 says wife was of Croft of Croft Castle. Burkes Guide to the Royal Family p 325 wife was Matilda. AR7 84a-29. Matilda De Breos and Rhys Mechyll Ap Rhys Lord were married.

136899. **Matilda De Breos** born about 1170 in England. WFP p 68 says wife was of Croft Castle. Burkes Guide to the Royal Family p 324-325 received his wife for the rescue of her father by his father Rhys.

136912. **Richard Comyn Lord** born about 1200 of Badenoch. He died in 1244 or 1249 at the age of 44. Weis AR: unknown wife Richard Comyn Lord was married.

136916. **Hugh Balliol** is the same as person number 69378.

136917. **Cecily de Fontaines** is the same as person number 69379.

136918. **Alan Macdonald Of Galloway** is the same as person number 67470.

136926. **William Marshal** is the same as person number 70130.

136927. **Isabel De Clare** is the same as person number 70131.

136928. **Theobald Le Boteler** was born in 1200. He died on 19 Jul 1230 at the age of 30. Collins RA: Lord Justice Joan De Marais and Theobald Le Boteler were married.

136929. **Joan De Marais** born about 1200.

136930. **Richard De Burgh Lord** born about 1195 of Connaught. He died in 1243 at the age of 48. Weis AR, Collins RA: Lord of Connaught, Governor of Ireland Hodierna De Gernon and Richard De Burgh Lord were married.

136931. **Hodierna De Gernon** born about 1195.

136976. **Stephen De Bulmer** born about 1180. Stephen De Bulmer was married.

137088. **John De Grey** born about 1170. He died after 1199 at the age of 29. History of Rutland: living 22 Hen 2 and 1 John Hawise and John De Grey were married.

137089. **Hawise** born about 1170. History of Rutland: mother of Walter and Robert. son Walter was Archbishop of York.

137112. **Walter Fitz Robert Lord** born about 1120. He died in 1198 at the age of 78. Lord of Dunmow Castle Maud De Lucy Lady and Walter Fitz Robert Lord were married.

137113. **Maud De Lucy Lady** born about 1145. Lady of Dis, Norfolk.

137116. **Henry II Of England** is the same as person number 103536.

137117. **Ida de Toeni** born about 1160. Later wife of Roger Bigod, 2nd Earl of Norfolk. per Gary Roberts she was the mother of William Longespee.

137118. **William Fitz Patrick Of Salisbury Earl** born about 1150. He died on 17 Apr 1196 at the age of 46. Earl of Salisbury Alianore De Vitrie and William Fitz Patrick Of Salisbury Earl were married about 1178.

137119. **Alianore De Vitrie** born about 1150.

137122. **Jerneygan Fitz Hugh** born about 1175. Jerneygan Fitz Hugh was married.

137124. **John Of England** is the same as person number 51768.

137125. **Suzanne De Warenne** was born in 1180.

137126. **Robert Of Dover Lord** born about 1190. Lord of Chilham, said to be Fulbert of Dover in Burke

137127. **Isabel De Briwere** born about 1190. 2nd dau

137136. **Gerard De Furnival Lord** born about 1180 of Hallamshire. He died in 1219 at the age of 39 in Jerusalem. Maud Luvetot and Gerard De Furnival Lord were married before 1204.

137137. **Maud Luvetot** born about 1180 of Hallamshire. She died after 1249.

137152. **Herbert St. Quintin Baron** born about 1195. succeeded brother as feudal baron of St. Quintin and lord of Brandsburton.

137153. **Anne De Estouteville** born about 1195.

137154. **Saier De Sutton Lord** born about 1200. Lord of Sutton in Holderness Saier De Sutton Lord was married.

137216. **Walter Surteyse** born about 1210 in Durham, England. He died after 1236 at the age of 26 in Durham, England. Walter Surteyse was married.

138240. **Roger De Coisners Jr.** born about 1080 of Rungeton, Yorkshire, England. He died about 1128 at the age of 48. to whom Bishop Ranulph have the manor of Rungeton, in Yorkshire between 1099 and 1128 Roger De Coisners Jr. was married.

138368. **Laci** born about 1150. Burkes' Extinct Peerage Laci was married.

138372. **William De Vesci Lord** born about 1125. He died in 1180 or 1184 at the age of 55. heir of his mother, sheriff of Northumberland 3 to 15 Henry II, Lord of Alnwick, co Northumberland. taken prisoner at the battle of Alnwick in 1174 and died 1180/4. Burga De Knaresborough and William De Vesci Lord were married.

138373. **Burga De Knaresborough** born about 1135. she received the town of Langton upon her marriage. sister of Robert de Estosteville or Stuteville, Lord of Knaresborough.

138374. **Waldran De Wellom** born about 1150. Waldran De Wellom was married.

138392. **William Bertram** born about 1160. He died in 1206 at the age of 46. Burkes EP: obtained a grant from the crown in 5 John 1204 of the manor of Felton in Northumberland. in the 7 John 1206 King John awarded the wardship of his lordships son and heir Roger upon Peter de Brus during his minority.

138393. **Alice Umfreyville** born about 1160.

138432. **Jocel of Louvain** born about 1110. He died before 1180 at the age of 70. Agnes De Percy and Jocel of Louvain were married after 1154.

138433. **Agnes De Percy** was born in 1134. She died before 13 Oct 1204 at the age of 70. She was buried in Whitby.

138434. **Adam II De Brus** born about 1125. He died in 1200 at the age of 75. Of Skelton in Cleveland Agnes Of Aumale and Adam II De Brus were married.

138435. **Agnes Of Aumale** born about 1125.

138436. **Eustace de Balliol of Bywell and Barnard Castle** was born before 1155. He died in 1209 at the age of 54 in Barnard Castle, Gainford, County Durham, England, United Kingdom.

138437. **Ada de Fontaines**.

138438. **Walter De Berkeley** born about 1150. Walter De Berkeley was married.

138464. **Walter De Clifford** is the same as person number 49168.

138465. **Agnes De Cundi** is the same as person number 49169.

138466. **Robert II De Ewyas Lord** born about 1140. He died in 1198 at the age of 58. Lord of Ewyas Harold, baron of Herefordshire.
Great baron of Hereford Pernel and Robert II De Ewyas Lord were married.

138467. **Pernel** born about 1150. She died after 1204 at the age of 54.

138472. **Robert De Vipont Baron** born about 1170. He died in 1227 or 1228 at the age of 57. History of Rutland. Baron of Appleby, in Westmoreland. 12 Hen 3 Idonea Builly and Robert De Vipont Baron were married.

138473. **Idonea Builly** born about 1170 of Esendine. She died in 1240 or 1241 at the age of 70. History of Rutland: Lady of Essendine. 25 Hen 3

138474. **William De Ferrers** is the same as person number 34714.

138475. **Sibilla Marshall** born about 1195. History of Rutland, first wife of William Ferrers p. 15

138480. **Richard De Clare Earl** born about 1150. He died about 28 Nov 1217 at the age of 67. He was also known as Magna Carta Surety Clare. Collins RA: 6th Earl of Clare, 4th Earl of Hertford and Gloucester, Magna Carta Surety 1215. MAGNA CARTA: signed the Magna Carta as surety in 1215

138481. **Amice Of Gloucester Countess** born about 1150. She died on 1 Jan 1224 or 1 Jan 1225 at the age of 74. Countess of Gloucester

138482. **William Marshal** is the same as person number 70130.

138483. **Isabel De Clare** is the same as person number 70131.

138484. **Roger De Lacy** is the same as person number 134942.

138485. **Maud De Clare** is the same as person number 134943.

138486. **Robert De Quincy Earl** born about 1175. He died in 1217 at the age of 42 in London, England. Crusader to the Holy Land during the 4th Crusade (1202-04), 1st Earl of Winchester.

138487. **Hawise Of Chester Countess** was born in 1177. She died in 1242 or 1243 at the age of 65. Countess of Lincoln

138488. **Gerald Fitz Maurice Baron** born about 1150. He died before 15 Jan 1203 at the age of 53 in Sligo, Ireland. 1st Baron of Offaly. was at the siege of Dublin 1171. Eve De Bermingham Bermingham and Gerald Fitz Maurice Baron were married.

138489. **Eve De Bermingham Bermingham** born about 1170. She died before Dec 1226 at the age of 56.

138492. **William Longespee** is the same as person number 68558.

138493. **Ela Of Salisbury** is the same as person number 68559.

138494. **Walter Ridelisford** born about 1200. He died before 12 Dec 1244 at the age of 44. Annora Vitre and Walter Ridelisford were married.

138495. **Annora Vitre** born about 1200.

138624. **Robert Le Scrope** was born before 1140. He died after 1198 at the age of 58. Robert Le Scrope was married.

138656. **Robert De Ros** born about 1150. Sibyl De Valognes and Robert De Ros were married.

138657. **Sibyl De Valognes** born about 1150.

138658. **William Trussebut Lord** born about 1130. Audrey De Harcourt and William Trussebut Lord were married.

138659. **Audrey De Harcourt** born about 1130.

138660. **Henry Of Huntingdon Earl** was born in 1114 in Scotland. He died on 12 Jun 1152 at the age of 38. He was buried in Kelso, Roxburgh, Scotland. Earl of Northumberland and Huntingdon. Ada De Warenne and Henry Of Huntingdon Earl were married in 1139.

138661. **Ada De Warenne** born about 1120 in County of Surrey. She died in 1178 at the age of 58.

138662. **Richard Avenal** born about 1120. Sibyl and Richard Avenal were married.

138663. **Sibyl** born about 1120.

138664. **Herbert Fitz Herbert** born about 1100. He died before 1155 at the age of 55. Chamberlain to Henry I.

138665. **Sibyl Corbet** born about 1070. Collins RA: mistress of Henry I

138666. **Miles Fitz Walter Earl** born about 1090 of Hereford. He died on 24 Dec 1143 at the age of 53. Earl of Hereford 1141, of Gloucester. Created Earl of Hereford 1143 Sibyl De Neufmarche and Miles Fitz Walter Earl were married in 1121.

138667. **Sibyl De Neufmarche** born about 1090.

138668. **Roger Fitz Richard Baron** born about 1130. He died before 1178 at the age of 48. 1st Baron of Warkworth of co Northumberland, Visitations of Yorkshire by Foster p. 608. Roger FitzRichard, Baron of Warkworth Co. Northumb. by gift of Henry II, added a bend sable to his arms. Adeliza De Essex and Roger Fitz Richard Baron were married.

138669. **Adeliza De Essex** born about 1130. She died after 1185 at the age of 55. Visitations of Yorkshire p. 608 Adeliza dau and coheir of Henry de Essex by Adeliza de Vere, sister of Aubrey 1st Earl of Oxford.

138670. **William Fitz Robert** born about 1120.

138671. **Sibilla Cheney** born about 1120.

138756. **Eustace de Balliol** is the same as person number 138436.

138757. **Ada de Fontaines** is the same as person number 138437.

138848. **Maurice De Robert Berkeley** born about 1165. He died on 16 Jun 1190 at the age of 25. Alice De Berkeley and Maurice De Robert Berkeley were married.

138849. **Alice De Berkeley** born about 1180.

138850. **Ralph Somery Lord** born about 1190. He died in 1211 at the age of 21. Weis 81-28 says he died 1211,he was probably born 1211. Margaret Marshall and Ralph Somery Lord were married.

138851. **Margaret Marshall** born about 1190.

138856. **William De Ferrers Earl** born about 1140 of Derby. He died about Oct 1190 at the age of 50 in Acre, Palestine. Weis AR: Crusader to the Holy Land during the 3rd Crusade (1189-92) in which he died, 3rd Earl of Derby.

138857. **Sibyl De Braiose** born about 1148. She died after 1227 at the age of 79. Weis AR: probably living aft Feb 5 1227/8

138858. **Hugh Of Kevelioc Earl** was born in 1147 of Chester, Monmouth, England. He died in 1181 at the age of 34. Collins RA: Earl of Chester, Vicomte d'Avranches. Bertrade D'Evreux Montfort and Hugh Of Kevelioc Earl were married in 1169.

138859. **Bertrade D'Evreux Montfort** born about 1150. She died in 1227 at the age of 77 in Fontevrault. Later mistress of Philip I of France

138864. **Geoffrey De Porhoet** was born before 1100. He died in 1141 at the age of 41. Hawise Of Brittany and Geoffrey De Porhoet were married.

138865. **Hawise Of Brittany**.

138866. **Philip Belmeis** was born before 1100. Maud La Meschine and Philip Belmeis were married before 1139.

138867. **Maud La Meschine** born about 1130. She was also known as Matilda La Meschine.

138874. **Hughes V. Gournay** born about 1175 in France. He died in 1214 at the age of 39. descent to Hugh Bardolf given in AR7 257-31 Juliane De Dammartin and Hughes V. Gournay were married.

138875. **Juliane De Dammartin** born about 1175.

139564. **Richard Camville**. Richard Camville was married.

139566. **Gilbert Basset** born about 1100. He died after 1165 at the age of 65. Of Wellingford, Oxford Edith D'Oilly and Gilbert Basset were married.

139567. **Edith D'Oilly**.

139568. **Roger II De Mortimer Baron** born about 1150. He died before 19 Aug 1214 at the age of 64. He was buried in Wigmore Abbey. Lord Mortimer of Wigmore Baron of Wigmore Isabel De Ferrieres and Roger II De Mortimer Baron were married.

139569. **Isabel De Ferrieres** born about 1160. She died before 29 Aug 1252 at age of 92.

139570. **King Llewellyn Ap Iorworth of Gwynedd** was born in 1173 in Dolwyddelan. He died on 11 Apr 1240 at the age of 67 in Aberconway. He was also known as The Great Iorworth. Llewellyn was buried in Aberconwy Abbey. Prince of North Wales. called Llywelyn Fawr (the Great). He was a great warrior and knew how to attack castles. He encouraged Welsh poets. He gave new buildings to the Monks and encouraged them to teach Latin, history and religion. After the Magna Carta signing, Llewellyn used this time to secure his territory in Wales from John. Llewellyn established the principle of one man succession. He named his second son and required his council to swear allegiance. His eldest son disagreed with the alliance with England and so he worried about a continued war. Weis AR p 164 Burke RL p 322 Joan Of England Princess and King Llewellyn Ap Iorworth of Gwynedd were married in 1204.

139571. **Joan Of England Princess** born about 1184. She died on 2 Feb 1237 at the age of 53 in Aber. She was buried in Llanfaes. natural daughter of King John, legitimated. Weis AR p 164, Burke RL p 322

139580. **Jean De Brienne** is the same as person number 71416.

139581. **Berenguela Of Leon** is the same as person number 71417.

139582. **Geoffrey IV De Chateaudun** born about 1200. Descendant of Charlemagne per David Faris Clemence Roches and Geoffrey IV De Chateaudun were married.

139583. **Clemence Roches**. AR7 120:30

139584. **Harvey Fitz Azaris Knight** born about 1150. He died about 1182 at the age of 32. noble and good knight

139586. **Randolph Fitz Walter** born about 1160. ancestor of Barons of Greystoke

139590. **William De Percy** born about 1110. of Kildale, of Riddel

139712. **William De Beauchamp** born about 1130. He died in 1167 at the age of 37.

139713. **Bertha De Brewes** born about 1155.

139714. **Roger II De Mortimer** is the same as person number 139568.

139715. **Isabel De Ferrieres** is the same as person number 139569.

139716. **Robert Maudit** born about 1170. Isabel Basset and Robert Maudit were married.

139717. **Isabel Basset** born about 1170.

139718. **Waleran Newburgh** was born before 1153. He died on 12 Dec 1204 at the age of 51. Alice Harcourt and Waleran Newburgh were married about 1196.

139719. **Alice Harcourt** born about 1180.

139720. **Piers Of Essex Earl** born about 1140. He died before 1198 at the age of 58. Maud Mandeville and Piers Of Essex Earl were married.

139721. **Maud Mandeville** born about 1140.

139722. **Roger De Clare Earl** was born in 1116 of Hertford. He died in 1173 at the age of 57. Collins RA: 2nd Earl of Hertford, Earl of Clare. called the Good, History of Rutland p 162f Maud De St. Hilary and Roger De Clare Earl were married.

139723. **Maud De St. Hilary** born about 1140. She died in 1173 at the age of 33. widow of Roger de Clare Earl of Hertford

139724. **Roger le Bigod Earl** born about 1150 of Norfolk. He died before Aug 1221 at the age of 71. He was also known as Magna Carta Surety Bigod. 2nd Earl of Norfolk 1189, Baron le Bigod, Lord High Stewart of England. Magna Carta Surety 1215. MAGNA CARTA: signed as a surety on the Magna Carta in 1215 Ida de Toeni and Roger le Bigod Earl were married.

139725. **Ida de Toeni** is the same as person number 137117.

139728. **Roger IV De Conches Toeni Lord** born about 1150 of Flamstead, Hertford County, England. He died in Jan 1209 at the age of 59. Constance Beaumont and Roger IV De Conches Toeni Lord were married before 1190.

139729. **Constance Beaumont** born about 1150. She died after 1226 at the age of 76. AR7 98-27

139730. **Walter Lacy** born about 1170. He died in 1241 at the age of 71. Margery Braiose and Walter Lacy were married in Nov 1200.

139731. **Margery Braiose** born about 1170. She died on 19 Nov 1200 at the age of 30. She was also known as Margaret Braiose.

139762. **Stephen III** born about 1190. Beatrice De Chalons and Stephen III were married.

139763. **Beatrice De Chalons** born about 1190.

139764. **Walter Lacy** is the same as person number 139730.

139765. **Margery Braiose** is the same as person number 139731.

139770. **Pierre Dreux** died in May 1250. Alix Thouars and Pierre Dreux were married in 1212.

139771. **Alix Thouars** born about 1182. She died in 1221 at the age of 39. Duchess of Brittany

140032. **William De Willoughby** born about 1175. He died about 1225–1227 at the age of 50. CP William de Willoughby in lawsuit 1200-1202 jury 1209, 1205 Knight's fee in the Marsh of Gilbert de Gaunt 1212 m. Maud dau and heir of William de Fullet. He was living 1225 but died 1227. Maud Fullet and William De Willoughby were married.

140033. **Maud Fullet** born about 1190.

140040. **Oliver Deincourt Baron** born about 1180. He died before 1246 at the age of 66. Oliver D'Eincourt Baron of Blankney, son and heir of Oliver 3 Jo. dead 30 Hen 3. m. 2nd wife Matilda Peeche, m1st (mother of John) Nichola grandau of Nichola de la Hay. Nichola was dau of unknown who married dau of Nichola de la Hay.

140041. **Nichola** born about 1180.

140042. **Geoffrey De Neville** born about 1190. He died after 1248 at the age of 58. Geoffrey De Neville was married.

140046. **William De Ferrers** is the same as person number 34714.

140047. **Sibilla Marshall** is the same as person number 138475.

140160. **John II Strange Lord** born about 1170. He died before Jan 1233 at the age of 63. CP 12 p. 349 In 1196/7 he acquired right in land at Knockin, Salop, from his cousins, daus of his uncle Guy. In 1204 the king asked Llewelin Prince of North Wales to grant John a safe conduct to go to and return to him. On 29 Aug. 1226 John Lestrange Sr. was granted a pardon on his debts. He married Amice. He was dead by 20 Jan. 1233/4.

140161. **Amice** born about 1170.

140162. **Robert II De Tregoz** was born in 1200 of Ewyas Harold. He died in 1265 at the age of 65 in Evesham. Weis AR p 165 Juliane De Cauntelo and Robert II De Tregoz were married before 1245.

140163. **Juliane De Cauntelo** born about 1200. She died after 1285 at the age of 85. Weis AR p 165 does not seem like she could be mother of Lucy

140164. **Ralph Somery** is the same as person number 138850.

140165. **Margaret Marshall** is the same as person number 138851.

140166. **William D'Aubigny Earl** born about 1173 of Arundel. He died on 1 Feb 1220 or 1 Feb 1221 at the age of 47 in Cainell, Provincia di Roma, Italy. He was also known as Magna Carta Supporter D'Aubigny. William was buried in Wymondham Abbey, Norfolk. MAGNA CARTA: mentioned in the Magna Carta as advisor to King John. Different from William D'Aubeney Lord of Belvoir who signed as surety. Earl of

Arundel, named in the Magna Carta 1215, Crusader to the Holy Land during 4th crusade (1202-1204). Mabel Of Chester and William D'Aubigny Earl were married.

140167. **Mabel Of Chester** born about 1175. She died before 1232 at the age of 57. said to have died before her brother Ranulph

140224. **William Fitz Alan** born about 1150. He died about 1172 at the age of 22. Mary De Erington and William Fitz Alan were married.

140225. **Mary De Erington** born about 1150.

140226. **William D'Aubigny** is the same as person number 140166.

140227. **Mabel Of Chester** is the same as person number 140167.

140230. **Nicholas De Verdon** born about 1180. He died in 1231 at the age of 51.

140231. **Joan** born about 1180.

140256. **Geoffrey V. Plantagenet Duke** was born on 24 Aug 1113 in Anjou, France. He died on 7 Sep 1151 at the age of 38 in Eure-Et-Loire, France. Count of Anjou, Duke of Normandy Born Nov. or Aug. Geoffrey V. Plantagenet Duke was married.

140258. **William De Warenne Earl** was born in 1118. He died in 1148 at the age of 30. 3rd Earl of Surrey Ela Talvas and William De Warenne Earl were married.

140259. **Ela Talvas** born about 1125. She died in 1178 at the age of 53.

140260. **John Fitz Gilbert Marshall** born about 1120. He died in 1164 at the age of 44. Sibyl Devereux and John Fitz Gilbert Marshall were married.

140261. **Sibyl Devereux** born about 1120.

140262. **Richard Strongbow De Clare Earl** born about 1130. He died about 20 Apr 1176 at the age of 46. He was buried in Cathedral Church, Dublin, Ireland. 2nd Earl of Pembroke 1150, Justiciar of Ireland. called the Richard the Strongbow. He d. 1176, English nobleman, also known as Richard Strongbow. He went as an adventurer (1170) to Ireland at the request of the hard-pressed Dermot McMurrough, king of Leinster. Strongbow subdued much of E Ireland, including Dublin, in victories over Rory O'Connor, king of Connacht, and married Dermot's daughter. Henry II of England, although he had given permission for the earl's expedition, visited him in 1171 to claim the rich coastal cities and to receive Strongbow's homage for the fief of the interior of Leinster. Pembroke fought for Henry in Normandy and was rewarded by a grant of additional territory in Ireland. He then returned to Ireland as the king's governor. Badly defeated (1174) at Thurles, he was engaged in almost continuous fighting against the Irish until his death. Eva Of Leinster and Richard Strongbow De Clare Earl were married about 26 Aug 1171.

140263. **Eva Of Leinster** born about 1130. She died in 1177 at the age of 47. She was buried in Cathedral Church, Dublin, Ireland. of ancient Irish lineage

140268. **William IV Of Angouleme Count** born about 1120. He died on 7 Aug 1179 at the age of 59 in Messina, Sicily. He was also known as Taillefer Angouleme. Count of Angouleme Marguerite De Turenne and William IV Of Angouleme Count were married in 1147.

140269. **Marguerite De Turenne** born about 1120.

140270. **Peter Of France** born about 1125. He died on 10 Apr 1183 at the age of 58. Crusader to the Holy Land during the 2nd Crusade (1147-48), was in England in 1178. Elizabeth De Courtenay and Peter Of France were married after 1150.

140271. **Elizabeth De Courtenay** was born in 1127 in Courtenay. She died after 1205 at the age of 78.

140272. **Aubrey De Vere Earl** born about 1120 of Oxford. He died on 26 Dec 1194 at the age of 74. 1st Earl of Oxford MCS4 154-2 Agnes Of Essex and Aubrey De Vere Earl were married.

140273. **Agnes Of Essex** born about 1125. His 3rd wife.

140274. **Hugh De Bolbec** born about 1160. Hugh De Bolbec was married.

141380. **William D'Aubeney Lord of Belvoir** was born after 1160 of Belvoir, Leicester, England. He died on 1 May 1236 at the age of 76. He was also known as Magna Carta Surety D'Aubeney. Lord of Belvoir Castle, Leicester, Magna Carta Surety. MAGNA CARTA: signed the Magna Carta as surety in 1215 Margary Umfreyville and William D'Aubeney Lord of Belvoir were married.

141381. **Margary Umfreyville** was born after 1160.

141408. **Hervey Stafford** born about 1180. He died in 1237 at the age of 57. Petronill Ferrers and Hervey Stafford were married.

141409. **Petronill Ferrers** born about 1180.

141410. **Thomas Corbet** born about 1190. Of Caus, Salop Thomas Corbet was married.

141416. **Ralph Of Drayton Basset** born about 1210. Ralph Of Drayton Basset was married.

141418. **Roger De Somery** is the same as person number 70082.

141419. **Nichole D'Aubigny** is the same as person number 70083.

141472. **Geoffrey De Neville** is the same as person number 140042.

141473. **Margaret.**

141474. **Robert Bertram** born about 1190. Robert Bertram was married.

141480. **John Fitz Robert** is the same as person number 34688.

141481. **Ada De Baliol** is the same as person number 34689.

141484. **Roger La Zouche** is the same as person number 34716.

141485. **Margaret** is the same as person number 34717.

141486. **Roger De Quincy** is the same as person number 33734.

141487. **Helen Of Galloway** is the same as person number 33735.

141532. **Robert II De Tregoz** is the same as person number 140162.

141533. **Juliane De Cauntelo** is the same as person number 140163.

141534. **Fulk Fitz Warin Sir** born about 1220 of Salop. Fulk Fitz Warin Sir was married.

141552. **Walter Burgh Earl** born about 1240. He died on 28 Jul 1271 at the age of 31. 2nd Earl of Ulster Avelina Fitz John and Walter Burgh Earl were married.

141553. **Avelina Fitz John** born about 1240. She died on 20 May 1274 at the age of 34.

141554. **Arnoul Guines III** born about 1235. He died in 1283 at the age of 48.

141555. **Alice De Couci** born about 1240.

141568. **Thomas Dacre** born about 1220.

141569. **Morley** born about 1220.

141632. **William Douglas** was born in 1174. He died in 1213 at the age of 39. CP Has descent of James Douglas from William CP 4 p 432

142464. **Robert Umfreyville Sir.**

142612. **Simon Stonegrave** born about 1200.

142613. **Beatrice Foliot** born about 1200.

142614. **Baldwin Wake** is the same as person number 35692.

142615. **Ela Beauchamp** born about 1220. She died before 1265 at the age of 45.

142760. **Louis VIII Of France** is the same as person number 72852.

142761. **Blanche Of Castile** is the same as person number 72853.

142762. **Raymond V. Berenger** is the same as person number 51770.

142763. **Beatrice Of Savoy** is the same as person number 51771.

142764. **Henry II Of Brabant** is the same as person number 72854.

142765. **Marie Of Swabia** is the same as person number 72855.

142766. **Hugh Champagne IV** was born in 1212. He died on 27 Oct 1272 at the age of 60. He was buried in Citeaux. Yolande De Dreux and Hugh Champagne IV were married in 1229.

142767. **Yolande De Dreux** died on 30 Oct 1248. She was buried in Citeaux.

142768. **Baldwin Wake** born about 1180. He died in 1213 at the age of 33. Isabel Briwere and Baldwin Wake were married.

142769. **Isabel Briwere** born about 1180. She died in 1233 at the age of 53.

142770. **Nicholas De Stuteville Lord** died in 1233. Lord of baronies of Cottingham, York and Liddell Strength, Cumberland

142771. **Devorgilla Of Galloway.**

142772. **Saher IV de Quincy** is the same as person number 67468.

142773. **Margaret De Beaumont** is the same as person number 67469.

142774. **Llewellyn Ap Iorworth** is the same as person number 139570.

142775. **Joan Of England** is the same as person number 139571.

142794. **James I. Of Aragon King** was born on 2 Feb 1208 in Montpellier. He died on 25 Jul 1276 at the age of 68 in Valencia. He was buried in Cabret. Yolande Of Hungary and James I. Of Aragon King were married on 8 Sep 1235 in Barcelona.

142795. **Yolande Of Hungary** was born in 1213. She died on 12 Oct 1251 at the age of 38 in Huesca, Spain.

142796. **Theobald I. Of Navarre King** was born on 3 May 1201 in Navarre, Spain. He died on 8 Jul 1253 at the age of 52 in Pamplona. Margaret Of Foix and Theobald I. Of Navarre King were married on 12 Sep 1232.

142797. **Margaret Of Foix** born about 1210. She died on 12 Apr 1256 at the age of 46 in Provins, Brie, France.

142800. **Bouchard D'Avesnes** was born in 1180. He died in 1244 at the age of 64 in Etraeungt Nord, France. He was buried in Clairefontaine. Archdeacon of Laon, Canon of St. Pierre de Lille Margaret Of Hainaut and Bouchard D'Avesnes were married in Jul 1212.

142801. **Margaret Of Hainaut** was born on 2 Jun 1202 in Constantinople, Turkey. She died on 10 Feb 1280 at the age of 77.

142802. **Florent IV Of Holland** was born on 24 Jun 1210. He died on 19 Jul 1234 at the age of 24. Mechtild Of Brabant and Florent IV Of Holland were married before 1224.

142803. **Mechtild Of Brabant** died on 21 Dec 1267. She was also known as Matilda Brabant. She was buried in Loosdunen.

142804. **Waleran IV Of Monschou Duke** born about 1195. He died on 2 Jul 1226 at the age of 31. He was buried in Rolduc. Ermesinde Of Namur and Waleran IV Of Monschou Duke were married in May 1214.

142805. **Ermesinde Of Namur** was born in Jul 1186. She died on 12 Feb 1247 at the age of 60.

142806. **Henry II Of Bar Count** was born in 1190. He died on 13 Nov 1239 at the age of 49 in Gaza, Palestine. Philippa De Dreux and Henry II Of Bar Count were married in 1219.

142807. **Philippa De Dreux** was born in 1192. She died on 17 Mar 1242 at the age of 50.

142812. **Charles I. Of Naples King** was born in Mar 1226. He died on 7 Jan 1285 at the age of 58 in Provincia di Foggia, Italy. He was buried in Provincia di Napoli. King of Naples, Sicily, and Jerusalem. Beatrix Of Provence and Charles I. Of Naples King were married on 31 Jan 1246.

142813. **Beatrix Of Provence** was born in 1234. She died on 23 Sep 1267 at the age of 33 in Nocera Inferiore. She was buried in Roque-Pymont.

142814. **Stephen V. Of Magyars King** was born in Dec 1239. He died on 1 Aug 1272 at the age of 32. Elizabeth Of Bosnia and Stephen V. Of Magyars King were married in 1253.

142815. **Elizabeth Of Bosnia** born about 1240. She died after 1290 at the age of 50.

142832. **Erard II Of Brienne Count** born about 1140. He died on 8 Feb 1191 at the age of 51 in Acre, Holy Land, Acre. Crusader to the Holy Land during the 3rd Crusade (1189-92) in which he was killed Agnes De Montfaucon and Erard II Of Brienne Count were married in 1166.

142833. **Agnes De Montfaucon** born about 1140.

142834. **Alfonso IX Of Leon** is the same as person number 51772.

142835. **Berengaria Of Castille** is the same as person number 51773.

142836. **Richard I. De Beaumont** born about 1120. He died after 1194 at the age of 74. Viscount of Maine, Seigneur of Beaumont le Vicomte, Fresnay and Ste. Suzanne. AR7 98-26 De L'Aigle and Richard I. De Beaumont were married.

142837. **De L'Aigle** born about 1120.

143752. **Robert Muscegros Sir** born about 1210. He died before 29 Jan 1254 at the age of 44. Of Charlton, Somerset Hawise Malet and Robert Muscegros Sir were married before 11 Feb 1220.

143753. **Hawise Malet** is the same as person number 24833.

143754. **William Avenal Sir** William Avenal Sir was married.

143778. **Griffith Ap Madog** born about 1225. Griffith Ap Madog was married.

143872. **Robert Constable Lord** born about 1175 of Flamborough. Visitations by Yorkshire by Glover p. 178 Constable of Flamborough by gift of his brother Roger Earl of Lincoln. Robert Lord of Flamborough m. Agnes, son of Dominus Robertus, son of Johannes Lacy, son of Richard Fitz Eustace and Albreda Lisours., son of Eustace Fitz John and Agnes de Cestria uxor 2nd, son of Ivon Vesy, Lord of Alnwich, John dau of Sir William Tyson. Albreda is dau of Robert De Lisours and Albreda de Lacy sister of Ilbert de Lacy.

143873. **Agnes** born about 1190.

144064. **Baron William Mowbray 1st Lord Mowbray** born about 1172 of Axholme. He died in 1222 at the age of 50 in Axholme. He was also known as Magna Carta Surety Mowbray. Baron of Axholme, Magna Carta Surety 1215 MCS4 63-1. MAGNA CARTA: signed as Magna Carta surety in 1215.

144065. **Avice** born about 1172. She was called Agnes dau of Earl of Arundel in History of Rutland p. 114 but the Earl of Arundel part is questioned by same author.

144066. **William Beauchamp**. William Beauchamp was married.

144488. **John De Verdun** born about 1226. He died on 21 Oct 1274 at the age of 48. Margaret De Lacy and John De Verdun were married on 14 May 1244.

144489. Margaret De Lacy born about 1226. She died in 1256 at the age of 30. MCS4 13-4 Margaret de Lacy d. 1256 Lady of Dulek m. as 1st wife 14 May 1244. John de Verdun b. c 1226 d. 21 Oct. 1274 son of Theobald le Boteler and Rohese de Verdun.

144498. Roger de Coleville. Beatrix de Stuteville and Roger de Coleville were married.

144499. Beatrix de Stuteville.

144500. John Braose Lord of Bramber. Margaret Verch Llewellyn and John Braose Lord of Bramber were married.

144501. Margaret Verch Llewellyn.

144502. William le Rus of Stinton. Agatha de Clare and William le Rus of Stinton were married. William is the son of Henry Le Rus d 1230 who married Alice Huntingfield, dau of **William de Huntingfield,** Knight who died c1225. He was Sheriff of Norfolk and Suffolk and one of the Sureties of the Magna Carta. MAGNA CARTA 1215. He participated in the fifth Crusade.

144503. Agatha de Clare.

144640. Matthew Morley born about 1215. He died after 1250 at the age of 35. Matthew Morley was married.

144650. William III de Say, Gov. of Rochester Castle. William III de Say Gov. of Rochester Castle was married. William was the son of Baron **Geoffrey de Say** d 1230 who married Margarey Brieerre. Geoffrey claimed the Mandeville inheritance of his grandmother Beatrice de Mandeville. Geoffrey was a Surety of the Magna Charta 1215 and Lord of West Greenwich.

144654. John II de Burgh Lord Lanvallei. Cecilia de Balliol Lady Lanvallei and John II de Burgh Lord Lanvallei were married. John is the son of John de Burgh 1210-1725 who married Hawise de Lanvallei d 1249, dau. of **William III de Lanvallie** who died 1217. Magna Charta Surety 1215. He succeeded his father as a minor. He secured a grant of custody of Colchester Castle. His effigy is on the tomb in the Church of St. Mary the Virgin, Walkern.

144655. Cecilia de Balliol Lady Lanvallei.

144658. Hugh De Gournay born about 1210. He died in 1239 at the age of 29.

144659. Maud born about 1210.

144660. William Aguillon born about 1190. Joan De Fitz Peter and William Aguillon were married in 1212.

144661. Joan De Fitz Peter born about 1190.

144662. William De Ferrers is the same as person number 34714.

144663. Sibilla Marshall is the same as person number 138475.

144800. Robert Wingfield born about 1230.

144801. Joanna Falstaf born about 1230.

144802. Nicholas Weyland born about 1230. Nicholas Weyland was married.

145344. John Foljambe born about 1225. John Foljambe was married.

145704. Philip II Augustus Of France King was born on 21 Aug 1165 in Gonesse, France, Gonesse, France. He died on 14 Jul 1223 at the age of 57 in Nantes, France, Mantes. He was buried in Saint Denis. AR7 101-26 Crusader to the Holy Land during the 3rd Crusade (1189-92) as one of its Leaders with Richard I of England and Frederick I of Germany. Philip tried to restore France to its greatness as it had under

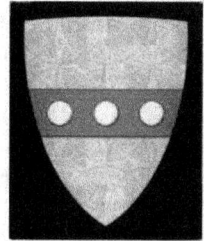

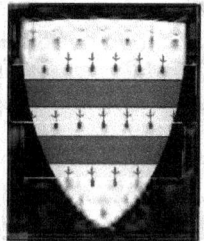

Charlemagne. He seized some of the Angevin domains in 1193 when Richard I of England was imprisoned in Germany, only to lose them again when Richard was released. However during John's reign he regained all the land completely defeating John and his claim. He defeated the Chateau-Gaillard castle which was thought impregnable. Isabella Of Hainaut Count and Philip II Augustus Of France King were married on 28 Apr 1180 in Bapaume, France, Bapaume.

145705. **Isabella Of Hainaut Count** was born in Apr 1170 in Valenciennes, France. She died on 15 Mar 1190 at the age of 19 in Paris, France. She was buried in Notre-Dame. Countess of Artois. AR7 163-28

145706. **Alfonso VIII Of Castile** is the same as person number 103546.

145707. **Eleanor Of England** is the same as person number 103547.

145708. **Henry I. Of Brabant Duke** was born in 1165. He died on 5 Sep 1235 at the age of 70 in Cologne. He was buried in Saint Peter's, Louvain. Maud Of Flanders and Henry I. Of Brabant Duke were married in 1179.

145709. **Maud Of Flanders** died in 1211 in Louvain.

145710. **Philip II Von Hohenstauffen** was born in 1176. He died on 21 Jun 1208 at the age of 32 in Bamberg, Germany. He was buried in Speyer. Emperor of Germany, murdered by Otto of Wittelsbach Irene Angelica and Philip II Von Hohenstauffen were married in 1196.

145711. **Irene Angelica** was born in 1181. She died on 27 Aug 1208 at the age of 27 in Hohenstauphen. She was buried in Lorsch. Murdered

145994. **Thomas De Mulford**. Maud De Vaux and Thomas De Mulford were married.

145995. **Maud De Vaux**.

196672. **Richard Fitz Pons** died about 1130. Maud Of Gloucester and Richard Fitz Pons were married about 1105.

196673. **Maud Of Gloucester**.

196674. **Ralph De Toney** born about 1080. He died about 1126 at the age of 46. He was buried in Conches, France. descendant of William Fitz Osborn, Earl of Hereford per Burke. Alice Of Northumberland and Ralph De Toney were married in 1103.

196675. **Alice Of Northumberland** born about 1090. She died after 1126 at the age of 36.

196676. **Robert de Condet Baron of Thorngate** born about 1120. Adelaide Cheney and Robert de Condet Baron of Thorngate were married.

196677. **Adelaide Cheney** born about 1120.

196678. **William De Cheney** born about 1100. Lord of the maors of Covenby and Glentham. of Cheney in co Norfolk. Sheriff of Norfolk and Suffolk

198664. **William Malet** born about 1125. He died in 1169 at the age of 44. Steward and favorite of Henry II

198666. **Ralph Picot** born about 1125.

198912. **Nicholas Fitz Robert** born about 1145. He died in 1189 at the age of 44.

206976. **Renaud De Courtenay** born about 1120 in Courtenay, Loiret. He died about Dec 1190 at the age of 70. Of Sutton, Berks, Sire de Courtenay exiled 1150 Maud De Fitz Edith and Renaud De Courtenay were married after 1172.

206977. **Maud De Fitz Edith** born about 1125.

206978. **William De Courcy** born about 1110. Maud D'Avranches and William De Courcy were married before 1150.

206979. **Maud D'Avranches** born about 1100.

206980. **Baldwin De Reviers** born about 1130..

206981. Adelise born about 1130.

206982. Robert De Beaumont Count born about 1130 in De Meulan. He died in 1207 at the age of 77. Maud De Fitz Roy and Robert De Beaumont Count were married in 1166.

206983. Maud De Fitz Roy born about 1130.

206992. Tourstan Despenser born about 1150. History of Rutland p 19 Tourstan Despenser was married.

206994. Walter De Chesnei born about 1150. History of Rutland p 19

207004. Godfrey De Lovaine born about 1175. He died about 26 Apr 1226 at the age of 51. Alice De Hastings and Godfrey De Lovaine were married about 1199.

207005. Alice De Hastings born about 1175.

207040. Humphrey IV De Bohun Earl born about 1150 of Hereford. He died in 1182 at the age of 32. Weis AR: Lord of Hereford, Constable of England

Baron de Bohun, Lord of Hereford, Constable of England Margaret Of Huntingdon and Humphrey IV De Bohun Earl were married after 1171.

207041. Margaret Of Huntingdon born about 1147. Weis AR: First husband was Conan IV Duke of Brittany, 2nd husband was Humphrey IV Per the Family Charts p. 188 of Trigg Manor, Cornwall, she is dau of Henry Hastings of Huntington and other records show Henry of Huntindon (son of King David I of Scotland) and Ade De Warrene.

207042. Geoffrey Fitz Piers is the same as person number 69860.

207043. Beatrice De Say born about 1160.

207044. Hugh VIII De Lusignan Sire born about 1160. Weis AR: Sire de Lusignan Bourgogne De Fonenay Dame and Hugh VIII De Lusignan Sire were married.

207045. Bourgogne De Fonenay Dame born about 1160. Weis AR: Dame de Fonenay,

207046. Henry D'Eu Count born about 1160. He died on 11 Mar 1183 at the age of 23. Weis AR: Count of Eu, Lord of Hastings, History of Rutland: Earl of Ewe 6 R 1. Maud De Warenne and Henry D'Eu Count were married.

207047. Maud De Warenne born about 1170. She died about 1212 at the age of 42. Weis AR: first husband Henry

207048. William De Braiose Baron born about 1151. He died on 9 Aug 1211 at the age of 60 in Corbeil. 5th Baron de Braiose Matilda De St. Valerie and William De Braiose Baron were married.

207049. Matilda De St. Valerie born about 1150. She died in 1210 at the age of 60. de Haia. Murdered by King John who had her walled up alive in her castle walls with her young son William

207050. William De Briwere Sir born about 1150. He died in 1226 at the age of 76. Beatrice De Vaux and William De Briwere Sir were married.

207051. Beatrice De Vaux born about 1150. She is called Beatrice de Valle by David Baker.

207056. Eustace II De Fiennes Baron born about 1125.

207057. Margaret Of Guines born about 1125. She died in 1187 at the age of 62.

207058. Faramus De Boulogne born about 1110. He died about 1183–1184 at age of 73.

207059. Matilda born about 1110.

207060. Alberic I. Of Dammartin Count was born in 1125. He died in 1183 at the age of 58. He was also known as Aubrey Dammartin. Count of Dammartin

207061. Joan Basset born about 1125.

207062. Renaud II Of Clermont born about 1090. He died in 1162 at the age of 72. Clemence Of Bar-Le-Duc and Renaud II Of Clermont were married in 1140.

207063. **Clemence Of Bar-Le-Duc** born about 1125. She died after 20 Jan 1183 at the age of 58. Weis AR

207064. **Roger Conde** born about 1160. They were married about 1200.

207065. **Alice Mons** born about 1160.

207066. **Arnoul Moreaumes** born about 1160. Arnoul Moreaumes was married.

207072. **Geoffrey V. Plantagenet** is the same as person number 140256.

207073. **Matilda Of England Princess** was born in Feb 1104. She died on 10 Sep 1167 at the age of 63 in Le Mans, France. widow of Henry V, Emperor of Germany AR7 1-24

207074. **William VIII Of Poitou Count** was born in 1099. He died on 9 Apr 1137 at the age of 38 in Galicia. Count of Poitou 1126-1137 and Duke of Aquitaine. Eleanor De Chastellerault and William VIII Of Poitou Count were married in 1121.

207075. **Eleanor De Chastellerault** born about 1099. She died after Mar 1130.

207080. **Alfonso II Of Aragon King** was born in Mar 1157. He died on 25 Apr 1196 at the age of 39 in Perpignan. He was buried in Poblet. Weis AR: King of Aragon 1163-1196 Sancha Of Castile and Alfonso II Of Aragon King were married in 1175 in Zaragoza, Spain.

207081. **Sancha Of Castile** was born on 21 Sep 1154. She died on 9 Nov 1208 at the age of 54 in Sijena. She was buried in Sijena. Weis AR: 2nd wife

207082. **Rainou Of Forcalquier** born about 1150. He died in 1224 at the age of 74. Gersinde Of Provence and Rainou Of Forcalquier were married.

207083. **Gersinde Of Provence** born about 1150. She died after 1193 at the age of 43.

207084. **Saint Humbert III Savoy** was born on 4 Aug 1136 in Aveillave, Savoie. He died on 4 Mar 1189 at the age of 52 in Cyprus. He was made a Saint. Beatrix Of Macon and Saint Humbert III Savoy were married in 1175.

207085. **Beatrix Of Macon** born about 1160. She died on 8 Apr 1230 at the age of 70.

207086. **William I. Of Geneva Count** was born in 1130. He died on 27 Jul 1195 at the age of 65.

207087. **Beatrix De Faucigny**.

207088. **Alfonso VII Of Castile King** was born on 1 Mar 1105 in Castile. He died on 21 Aug 1157 at the age of 52 in Grenada, Spain. He was buried in Toledo. Weis AR: King of Castile and Leon., then Emperor of Spain.

207089. **Berenguela Of Barcelona** born about 1114. She died on 3 Feb 1148 at the age of 34 in Palencia. Weis AR: said to be 2nd wife but chronology makes her 1st wife.

207090. **Alfonso I. Henriques Of Portugal King** was born on 25 Jul 1110 in Guinaraes, Portugal. He died on 6 Dec 1185 at the age of 75 in Coimbra. He was buried in Coimbra. Weis AR: King of Portugal 1128-1185 Mathilda Of Savoy and Alfonso I. Henriques Of Portugal King were married in 1146.

207091. **Mathilda Of Savoy** born about 1125. She died on 4 Dec 1157 at the age of 32 in Coimbra. David Faris said she died Nov. 4, 1157.

207092. **Sancho II Of Castile King** born about 1130. He died on 31 Aug 1158 at the age of 28 in Toledo, Spain. Weis AR Blanche Of Navarre and Sancho II Of Castile King were married on 30 Jan 1151 in Spain.

207093. **Blanche Of Navarre** born about 1130. She died on 12 Aug 1156 at the age of 26.

207094. **Henry II Of England** is the same as person number 103536.

207095. **Eleanor Of Aquitaine** is the same as person number 103537.

207100. **John I. Of Ponthieu Count** born about 1159. He died on 30 Jun 1191 at the age of 32 in Acre, Palestine. Weis AR line 109

Count of Ponthieu Beatrice Of St. Pol and John I. Of Ponthieu Count were married before 1177.

207101. **Beatrice Of St. Pol** born about 1159. She died after 1204 at the age of 45. Weis AR third wife also called Candavaine

207102. **Louis VII Of France King** was born in 1120. He died on 18 Sep 1180 at the age of 60 in Paris, France. He was buried in Fontainebleau. Weis AR: King of France Dec 25 1137-1180, his third wife Alix. He was called Louis VII (The Young) Alix De Champagne and Louis VII Of France King were married on 13 Nov 1160.

207103. **Alix De Champagne** born about 1126. She died on 24 Jun 1206 at the age of 80 in Paris. She was buried in Fontigny. Her name may have been Alice

Index

About the Authors

Christos Christou, Jr. is an author, historian, genealogist and analyst. Christos is an expert genealogist and has published many genealogical works and helped hundreds of people join various hereditary societies. He is a proud father and grandfather.

He was President of the Maryland Society Sons of the American Revolution 2006-7, War of 1812 in the State of Maryland 2012-2015 and Sr. President of the Thomas Johnson Society of the Children of the American Revolution. He served as its youngest MDSSAR President in over its 125+ year history and the only Greek-American President.

Guy Edward Almony Jr. is his amazing son. He is a young entrepreneur, became the youngest foreman at his company, and now is a proud father.

He was President of the Thomas Johnson Society Children of the American Revolution and elected and served in various officer roles in the Maryland State Board CAR as well as a founding member and officer of the Children of 1812 Society in Maryland. He is a member of the Sons of the American Revolution and broke the record for the most approved American Revolution Ancestors in the MDSSA at 50+ Patriots and still going.

www.ingramcontent.com/pod-product-compliance
Lightning Source LLC
Chambersburg PA
CBHW060128280326
41932CB00012B/1459